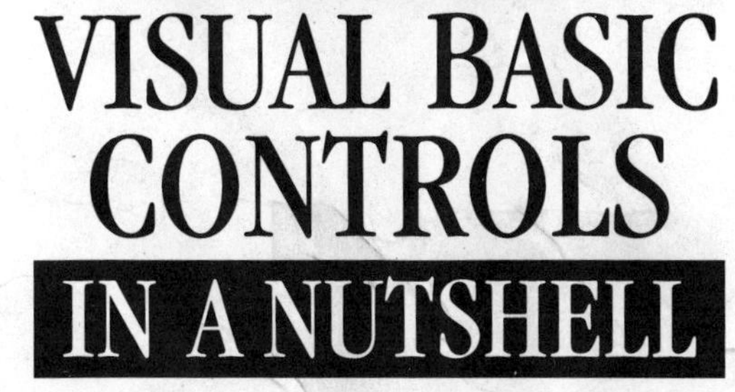

VISUAL BASIC CONTROLS IN A NUTSHELL

The Controls of the Professional and Enterprise Editions

VISUAL BASIC CONTROLS IN A NUTSHELL

The Controls of the Professional and Enterprise Editions

Evan S. Dictor

O'REILLY®

Beijing · Cambridge · Farnham · Köln · Paris · Sebastopol · Taipei · Tokyo

Visual Basic Controls in a Nutshell: The Controls of the Professional and Enterprise Editions

by Evan S. Dictor

Published by O'Reilly & Associates, Inc., 101 Morris Street, Sebastopol, CA 95472.

Editor: Ron Petrusha

Production Editor: Sarah Jane Shangraw

Printing History:

July 1999: First Edition.

This book is printed on acid-free paper with 85% recycled content, 15% post-consumer waste. O'Reilly & Associates is committed to using paper with the highest recycled content available consistent with high quality.

ISBN: 1-56592-294-8

Table of Contents

Part II: Reference

Part III: Appendixes

Preface

I can remember my first bad experience with Visual Basic controls. I was developing a small data entry form for a larger application and started to write the data validation logic. Being pretty logical myself, I put my code into the LostFocus events of the text boxes on the form. After all, my code would execute when the control "lost focus," right? Actually, in my limited testing, it worked fine. Then Quality Assurance got their hands on it. "If we type bad data and hit the Escape key, the program crashes!" they said. They continued, "If we use the ALT key combination for the Save button, bad data gets saved!" What had I done?

Actually, this isn't an uncommon tale. The same thing happens to many programmers who are starting out. In fact, I began asking questions about validation and the LostFocus event in technical interviews to divine who was an experienced Visual Basic developer and who was less experienced. What I found was that even many advanced VB developers weren't quite clear on the interactions between TextBox controls and CommandButton controls on a form.

What This Book Is About

In part, this is a reference work that attempts to fully document Visual Basic controls. It does that, though, with a particular slant; while providing relatively complete documentation of the controls included with the Professional and Enterprise editions of Visual Basic 5.0 and 6.0, it's really a book that focuses on problems that developers encounter when using Visual Basic's controls.

I started this book by concentrating on all of the problems I've had with Visual Basic controls and detailing how I got around them. All of the undocumented interactions between controls. All of the tricks to get controls to do what I really wanted in the first place. Then I moved on to try to learn more about this undocumented and underdocumented aspect of VB controls. I wrote dozens of programs just to test how the controls would react to different situations.

In doing this, I learned quite a few things. The first thing was that the documentation that comes with Visual Basic for the controls is quite incomplete and sometimes inaccurate. I learned that conventions used in some parts of the documentation were eliminated for other parts. And I learned that Visual Basic controls were more complex than I had ever imagined.

After I had documented the controls that I used on a daily basis, I moved on to the controls that I had used rarely or hadn't yet used at all. Some of these controls, of course, can be of surprising complexity, like the Internet Transfer control, the Winsock control, and the MSChart control, with its extensive object model. While writing this book, Visual Basic 6.0 was released along with a few controls I had never seen, like the MonthView control and the Hierarchical FlexGrid control. With these controls, I had to start from scratch writing programs to use them in ways their creators had probably never expected. I loaded up all events with `Debug.Print` statements to nail down the order of events and interactions between events and properties. I executed methods. I put thousands of values into thousands of properties.

This book is the result of two things. It is the result of all of my experience with Visual Basic. It is also the result of about 15 months of work that went into writing it. That's about four times the amount of time I figured it would take when I started the project. So much for my scheduling skills. However, I think that the book accomplishes what I set out to do: it details the intricacies of most of the controls that come with Visual Basic.

What This Book Covers

This is a book that documents most of the controls included with the Professional and Enterprise editions of Microsoft Visual Basic 5.0 and 6.0.

You may have noticed the qualifier. So, what doesn't this book cover? It covers all of the controls displayed in the Visual Basic toolbox when you select the VB Enterprise (or Professional) Edition Controls option in the New Project dialog, except for the following:

- Controls that come only with the Enterprise Edition of Visual Basic. That's why you won't find the RDO Data Control documented here.
- Controls that I felt were on the decline and that (at least in my opinion) are best replaced by some more robust, more flexible, or more user-friendly control. The MAPI controls (MAPISession and MAPIMessages) didn't make it because MAPI has taken a backseat to SMTP. Similarly, controls like the Drive, Directory, and File controls are not documented because the CommonDialog control offers the same functionality, typically requires less programming, and presents users with a familiar and, in many ways, elegant interface.

Who This Book Is For

The primary aim of this book is to assist developers of all levels in using Visual Basic controls. While Chapters 6 through 8 briefly describe all properties, methods, and events, each control's entry in Chapter 5 serves to go beyond the control elements to give the in-depth data necessary for application development.

Alone, this book will not teach Visual Basic programming. In fact, it teaches very little about programming itself. Instead, it concentrates exclusively on programming in respect to using the controls. Therefore, a novice programmer could not simply buy this book and write an application. However, what a novice programmer will get from this book is complete coverage of how to use the controls, how to avoid problems with controls, and how controls interact with other controls.

For the intermediate developer, this book goes beyond the information contained in the manuals to show how a control fits into an application. For example, a simple alarm clock application based on the Timer control works just fine until an innocent message box displayed for just a moment causes the alarm to be missed. There are only two ways of learning about this problem. The first is to have fallen victim to it once, as I had and as I'm sure thousands of other Visual Basic developers have. The second is for someone to have explained the problem in advance. Now, with this book, there is a third way: you can read about it under Timer Control, in Chapter 5, *Controls*.

For the advanced developer, these features that appeal to novice and intermediate programmers are not as important. After all, the advanced developer has probably already found all the pitfalls in the Timer control. However, what happens the first time you need to use the MSChart control, with its 40-plus objects and 250-plus properties? Perhaps, instead, you find that you must suddenly use one of the newer controls, like the MonthView control. After a time, advanced programmers will certainly understand these as well as they do the Timer control. With this book, a quick read of the control's section in Chapter 5 should give all the knowledge necessary to get up to speed with these controls very, very quickly and painlessly.

How This Book Is Organized

Part I, *Introducing VB Controls*, offers an overview of VB controls and covers the elements that all controls share. Properties like Tag and Left, methods like ZOrder, events like KeyDown, and concepts like OLE Drag and Drop are all covered in this section. It also deals with the Form and MDIForm objects, since all controls are ultimately contained by one of them.

Part II, *Reference*, forms the basic reference to Visual Basic controls. Chapter 5 covers each control in detail. Useful properties, methods, and events are explained, many with examples. Each control's section includes information on the order in which events are fired, and "Interaction" tables showing unexpected interactions that occur between properties and methods. When you want to start working with a control, this is the place to look.

Chapters 6 through 8 detail the controls' properties, methods, and events, respectively. If you have a question about a control element that isn't covered in that control's section in Chapter 5, it should certainly be covered here. For each property, the book indicates its design-time and runtime status, accurate datatype, and a description of what the property contains. For each method, the book lists the method's syntax, along with the datatypes of all parameters. The section on events contains descriptions of how the events are fired and lists their parameters.

Part III, *Appendixes*, contains the appendixes. Appendix A contains information about using colors in Visual Basic, along with a list of color constants. Appendix B contains the list of keyboard code constants used by the KeyDown event.

My hope is that we've designed this book—both its content and its organization—in a way that helps you find the information you need, both when you're trying to learn how to work with a control for the first time and when you encounter one of those "gotchas" that are so common with Visual Basic controls.

Conventions in This Book

Throughout this book, we've used the following typographic conventions:

`Constant width`
: Constant width in body text indicates a language construct such as a VBA statement (like `For` or `Set`), an intrinsic or user-defined constant, a user-defined type, or an expression (like `dElapTime = Timer() - dStartTime`). Code fragments and code examples appear exclusively in constant width text. In syntax statements and prototypes, text in constant width indicates such language elements as the function's or procedure's name and any invariable elements required by the syntax.

`Constant width italic`
: Constant width italic in body text indicates parameter and variable names. In syntax statements or prototypes, constant width italic indicates replaceable parameters.

Italic
: Italicized words in the text indicate intrinsic or user-defined functions and procedure names. Many system elements like paths and filenames are also italicized as are new terms.

This symbol indicates a tip.

This symbol indicates a warning.

VB6
: This book documents the controls in both Visual Basic 5.0 and Visual Basic 6.0. This symbol indicates that the discussion applies to Visual Basic 6.0 only.

DT **RT**
: Some property values can be viewed and set at design time using the Properties window in the Visual Basic integrated development environment (IDE);

almost all of these properties are available at runtime as well. Others do not appear in the Properties window and are available only in the runtime environment. We've used **DT** to indicate the first set of properties and **RT** to denote the second.

RO **RW**

At runtime, most properties are either read-only or read/write. We've indicated the former with **RO** and the latter with **RW**.

How to Contact Us

We have tested and verified all the information in this book to the best of our ability, but you may find that features have changed (or even that we have made mistakes). Please let us know about any errors you find, as well as your suggestions for future editions, by writing to:

O'Reilly & Associates, Inc.
101 Morris Street
Sebastopol, CA 95472
1-800-998-9938 (in the U.S. or Canada)
1-707-829-0515 (international/local)
1-707-829-0104 (fax)

You can also send messages electronically. To be put on our mailing list or to request a catalog, send email to:

nuts@oreilly.com

To ask technical questions or comment on the book, send email to:

bookquestions@oreilly.com

Call for Additions and Amendments

It is our hope that, as the Visual Basic language continues to evolve, so too will *VB Controls in a Nutshell,* and that the book will come to be seen by VB developers as the official (so to speak) unofficial documentation on Visual Basic controls. To do that, we need your help. If you're looking for information on the controls that are documented in this book and you can't find it here, we'd like to hear about it. If you would like to contribute your favorite control-related programming tip or gotcha, we'll do our best to include it in the next edition of this book. You can request these additions and amendments to the book at the discussion forum on our web site, *vb.oreilly.com.*

Acknowledgments

During the time it took me to write this book (about 15 months), my wife, Alison, dealt with a husband who came home each day from work only to continue writing late into the night. If it weren't for her love and understanding, I never would have been able to write this book.

When I was 13, my parents thought that I might have a knack for computers and bought me an Apple II. I never looked back. Without their keen insight, I probably wouldn't have been qualified to write this book. However, because of them, here I am (no pun intended).

My editor, Ron Petrusha, is most likely responsible for more of this book's content than I am. This being my first book, I didn't know what to expect from an editor, but I'm quite sure that what Ron contributed was much more than I should have expected. Ron has a deeper knowledge of Visual Basic than any developer I have worked with, and without his enormous contribution, this book would not exist.

I would like to thank Tara McGoldrick and Katie Gardner from O'Reilly for all their help in getting this book finished and released. This book took longer than anyone ever expected, but they both were able to keep me focused on the project until its completion.

My agent, Claire Horne, put me together with this project. She certainly had many potential authors to choose from, and I thank her for choosing to submit me to O'Reilly.

My technical reviewers, Josh Holcomb and Andres Rodriguez, are both top Visual Basic developers who provided sound advice as well as pointed out errors that had snuck by. Josh and Marvin Dean were two people I could always call to get answers on "all things VB" when I needed them.

Other people who contributed technically were Jose Mojica, Bill Wheelock, Gary Adler, Richard Pavlicek, Anthony Marino, Santiago Perez, Henry Timmes, Aviel Alkon, Randon Loeb, and Stuart Henry. People who contributed to my sanity were Kelly Grasso, Mike and Lori Massa, Josh and Felicia Holcomb, Serge and Susan Small, Dan and Diane Chiafair, Ed Day, Wayne Dictor, George Martin, everyone from Thursday-night poker, Jeff and Steve from the store, the entire BYFL crew, Erik, Craig, Peter, Obe, Harold, Murray, Mike, Sean, Art, Barry, and my other friends from the club, and most of all, Paul Foster.

I would also like to thank the following people for getting me to this point technically. For the most part they probably don't remember me, and if they do, for some it may not be fondly, but their influence helped to put me where I am. They are Richard Candido, Jr., Richard Candido, Sr., Mike Feibish, Brad Freisz, Jeff Fiddleman, Ken Jomsky, Eric Weisman, Mitchell Pierce, Don Smith, Bill Hunt, and Gary Adler (for the second time). It has been a long journey, and your help and guidance are still appreciated.

I would finally like to mention two people who passed away before this book was finished. My father, Paul Dictor, certainly the most influential person in my life, died just as I started work on this book. I'm sure he would have been very happy and proud of my achievement. While back in my hometown for his funeral, I learned that a very good friend of mine since high school, Paul Jordan, had died two days earlier. I miss them both very much.

PART I

Introducing VB Controls

This part aims at providing a general overview of Visual Basic controls and discussing common control-related topics.

Specifically, Chapter 1, *Introduction*, examines the appeal of Visual Basic's controls, discusses ways to add controls to your project, and looks at some of the difficulties developers encounter when working with controls. Although this is the book's introductory chapter, it is not intended as an introduction to programming with Visual Basic; it assumes that you have some familiarity with either Visual Basic or another programming language.

Chapter 2, *Common Control Features*, covers the properties that are common to most or all controls and that you should be aware of whenever you use a control in your application. It also discusses two of the tasks—OLE Drag and Drop and data binding—that you might want to implement with any of a number of controls.

Chapter 3, *The Form*, and Chapter 4, *The MDI Form*, discuss Visual Basic forms and MDI forms (known to Windows C/C++ programmers as windows, SDI windows, and MDI windows), since these necessarily serve as the containers for all controls.

CHAPTER 1

Introduction

Microsoft's release of the initial version of its Visual Basic development environment for Windows in 1991 was immediately hailed as a major breakthrough in software development. Visual Basic's novelty, from the viewpoint of its early proponents, was that it featured an interface design package (its critics described it as a "drawing program") that supported drag-and-drop creation of interface controls. To create an application, the programmer could begin by dragging common Windows interface elements, like text boxes and command buttons, from a toolbox onto a form (also known as an application window). To finish the application, the programmer needed only to attach code snippets to these interface elements.

Until the release of Visual Basic, developing Windows applications required a sound knowledge of C or C++ programming as well as extensive familiarity with the Windows application programming interface (or API), the core set of system services provided to applications by Windows itself. To illustrate how different Visual Basic is from the traditional C/C++ style of programming, Example 1-1 shows a very simple "Hello World" application written in C for the 32-bit Windows platforms.

Example 1-1: A C Language Version of "Hello World"

```
#include <windows.h>

LRESULT CALLBACK WndProc (HWND, UINT, WPARAM, LPARAM);

int WINAPI WinMain (HINSTANCE hInstance, HINSTANCE hPrevInstance,
                    PSTR szCmdLine, int iCmdShow)
   {
   static char szAppName[] = "SayHello" ;
   HWND hwnd ;
   MSG msg ;
   WNDCLASSEX wndclass ;
```

Example 1-1: A C Language Version of "Hello World" (continued)

```
    wndclass.cbSize        = sizeof (wndclass) ;
    wndclass.style         = CS_HREDRAW | CS_VREDRAW ;
    wndclass.lpfnWndProc   = WndProc ;
    wndclass.cbClsExtra    = 0 ;
    wndclass.cbWndExtra    = 0 ;
    wndclass.hInstance     = hInstance ;
    wndclass.hIcon         = LoadIcon(NULL, IDI_APPLICATION) ;
    wndclass.hCursor       = LoadCursor(NULL, IDC_ARROW) ;
    wndclass.hbrBackground = (HBRUSH) GetStockObject(WHITE_BRUSH) ;
    wndclass.lpszMenuName  = NULL ;
    wndclass.lpszClassName = szAppName ;
    wndclass.hIconSm       = LoadIcon(NULL, IDI_APPLICATION) ;

    RegisterClassEx(&wndclass) ;

    hwnd = CreateWindow(szAppName, "Hello World",
                        WS_OVERLAPPEDWINDOW,
                        CW_USEDEFAULT, CW_USEDEFAULT,
                        CW_USEDEFAULT, CW_USEDEFAULT,
                        NULL, NULL, hInstance, NULL) ;

    ShowWindow(hwnd, iCmdShow) ;
    UpdateWindow(hwnd) ;

    while (GetMessage(&msg, NULL, 0, 0))
       {
       TranslateMessage(&msg) ;
       DispatchMessage(&msg) ;
       }
    return msg.wParam ;
    }

LRESULT CALLBACK WndProc(HWND hwnd, UINT iMsg, WPARAM wParam,
                         LPARAM lParam)
    {
    int wNotifyCode ;
    HWND hwndCtl ;
    static HWND  hwndButton ;
    static RECT  rect ;
    static int   cxChar, cyChar ;
    HDC          hdc ;
    PAINTSTRUCT  ps ;
    TEXTMETRIC   tm ;

    switch (iMsg)
       {
       case WM_CREATE :
          hdc = GetDC(hwnd) ;
          SelectObject(hdc, GetStockObject (SYSTEM_FIXED_FONT)) ;
          GetTextMetrics(hdc, &tm) ;
          cxChar = tm.tmAveCharWidth ;
          cyChar = tm.tmHeight + tm.tmExternalLeading ;
```

Example 1-1: A C Language Version of "Hello World" (continued)

```
        ReleaseDC(hwnd, hdc) ;
        GetClientRect( hwnd, &rect ) ;

        hwndButton = CreateWindow("BUTTON", "&Say Hello",
                     WS_CHILD | WS_VISIBLE | BS_PUSHBUTTON,
                     (rect.right-rect.left)/20*9,
                     (rect.bottom-rect.top)/10*4,
                     14 * cxChar, 3 * cyChar,
                     (HWND) hwnd, 1,
                     ((LPCREATESTRUCT) lParam)-> hInstance, NULL);

        return 0 ;

     case WM_SIZE :
        rect.left   = 24 * cxChar ;
        rect.top    =  2 * cyChar ;
        rect.right  = LOWORD (lParam) ;
        rect.bottom = HIWORD (lParam) ;
        return 0 ;

     case WM_PAINT :
        InvalidateRect(hwnd, &rect, TRUE) ;

         hdc = BeginPaint(hwnd, &ps) ;
         EndPaint(hwnd, &ps) ;
         return 0 ;

     case WM_DRAWITEM :
     case WM_COMMAND :
        wNotifyCode = HIWORD(wParam) ;
        hwndCtl = (HWND) lParam ;

         if ((hwndCtl == hwndButton) &&
            (wNotifyCode == BN_CLICKED))
            MessageBox(hwnd, "Hello, World!",
                       "Greetings", MB_OK) ;

         ValidateRect(hwnd, &rect) ;

         break ;

     case WM_DESTROY :
        PostQuitMessage (0) ;
        return 0 ;
     }
  return DefWindowProc (hwnd, iMsg, wParam, lParam) ;
  }
```

Our simple Windows program requires a number of steps:

- Defining the main window's class and its class attributes.
- Creating and displaying an instance of the window class.

- Defining and implementing a message loop to handle event notification.
- Creating the CommandButton control.
- Handling the `BN_CLICKED` notification to display the message dialog.

For the most part, to identify those steps and to read the program, you have to be fairly well versed in C and extremely knowledgeable about the Win32 API and the operation of Windows.

In contrast, the Visual Basic version of this "Hello World" program, the source code for which is shown in Example 1-2, contains only a few lines of code and is extremely easy to read and understand. Much of the work of creating the application was handled in the design-time environment without any coding at all. For example:

- When a new Standard Executable project is started, Visual Basic by default adds a form to the project and makes it the project's startup object so that it loads automatically when the program is run.
- A CommandButton control was positioned on the form.
- The form's caption was changed.

Example 1-2: A Visual Basic Version of "Hello World"

```
Private Sub Command1_Click()

MsgBox "Hello, World", vbOKOnly Or vbExclamation, "Hi!"

End Sub
```

Of course, "Hello World" is hardly an example of a real-world program, but it nevertheless does illustrate how much easier developing programs can be with Visual Basic than with C or C++. Visual Basic's ease of development, in fact, made it the first major package in a new software category, the rapid application development (or RAD) tools.

How was Visual Basic able to simplify software development so dramatically? The answer lies in part in its controls, the basic interface objects that are included with Visual Basic. First of all, the programmer can create instances of controls simply and easily, just by selecting them from a toolbox and dropping them onto a form. We'll examine this, as well as other ways of creating controls, in the following section. But the programmer can do more than simply drop controls onto a form; he or she can control them programmatically. Visual Basic provides three ways of doing this: by assigning and retrieving values from control properties, by calling control methods, and by responding to control events.

Creating Instances of Controls

While the hallmark of Visual Basic is its drag-and-drop creation of controls, VB offers a number of ways in which you can create instances of controls. We'll examine those before looking at the kinds of problems that arise in working with controls.

Drag and Drop

The easiest way to create an instance of a control is simply to select it at design time from the Visual Basic toolbox, which is shown in Figure 1-1, move the mouse pointer to a form, and use the mouse to position the control.

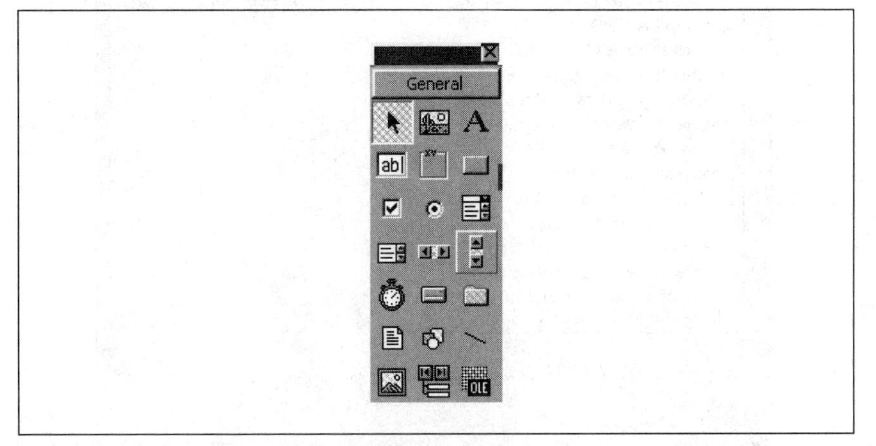

Figure 1-1: The standard Visual Basic toolbox

You can, incidentally, add additional controls to the toolbox by selecting the Components option from the Project menu. Visual Basic opens the Controls tab of the Components dialog, as shown in Figure 1-2. Just check the box beside the control to add it to the toolbox and make it available to your VB project. To remove it from the toolbox, open the dialog and uncheck the box; this requires, though, that there not be any instances of the control on the project's forms.

Control Arrays

A slight variation on the drag-and-drop creation of controls at design time is the creation of a control array. A control array is, quite simply, an array of controls that share the same name and are distinguished from one another by an index number. (In the event that you dislike working with multidimensional arrays, the index value can be one-dimensional only.) The only restriction on the creation of control arrays is that the controls all be of the same type. You cannot have a control array that includes four command buttons and one checkbox control, for example.

There are two methods to create a control array at design time—the first manual and labor intensive, the second more or less automatic.

To create a control array manually:

1. Place the first control on the form and assign it a name (using the Name property in the Properties window) that you plan to assign to the other elements of the array as well.
2. Select the second control, position it on the form, and change its Name property to the name you want to assign to the control array. Visual Basic will

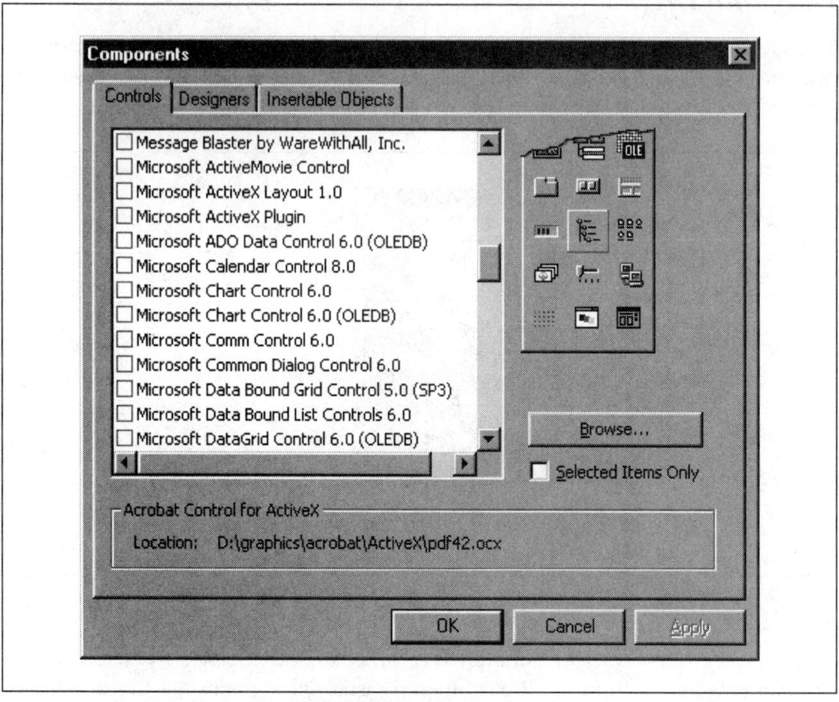

Figure 1-2: The Controls tab of the Components dialog

automatically assign a value of 1, which is the next available index value, to its Index property.

3. Repeat the previous step for each control you'd like to include in the array.
4. If you prefer working with one-based rather than zero-based arrays, you may want to modify the value of each control's Index property when you're finished adding controls to the control array.

The automatic method is considerably easier:

1. Place the first control on the form and assign it a name (using the Name property in the Properties window) that you plan to assign to the other elements of the array as well.
2. Copy the control to the Clipboard. (You can either select the Copy option from the Edit menu or click the Copy button on the VB Toolbar.)
3. Paste the control onto the form from the Clipboard. Visual Basic will prompt with the dialog shown in Figure 1-3, which asks whether you want to create a control array. Click the Yes button. Visual Basic will place the control on the form, assign it the same name as the first control, and assign it an Index value one greater than the previous control's.
4. Repeat the previous step for each control you'd like to add to the array. Visual Basic, however, will simply assume that you want to add elements to the control array and will no longer display the dialog in Figure 1-3.

Microsoft Visual Basic

You already have a control named 'cmdArray'. Do you want to create a control array?

Yes | No | Help

Figure 1-3: The prompt to create a control array

Dynamic Control Arrays

You may not always know precisely how many controls you want to include in a control array at design time. In that case, you can create a control array dynamically at runtime. This requires that you define a control array consisting of at least a single control at design time and that you use the `Load` statement to create the remaining controls at runtime. The following code fragment, for instance, dynamically adds two option buttons to a control array named `optPaymentType`:

```
Dim intCtr As Integer

For intCtr = 1 To 2
   Load optPaymentType(intCtr)
   If intCtr = 1 Then
      optPaymentType(intCtr).Caption = "Check"
   Else
      optPaymentType(intCtr).Caption = "Credit Card"
   End If
   optPaymentType(intCtr).Top = _
                  optPaymentType(intCtr - 1).Top + 300
   optPaymentType(intCtr).TabIndex = _
                  optPaymentType(intCtr - 1).TabIndex + 1
   optPaymentType(intCtr).Visible = True
Next
```

You can remove an element from a control array by using the `Unload` statement. The following statement removes the third element from the `optPaymentType` control array:

```
Unload optPaymentType(2)
```

If you need to know the upper and lower limits of a control array, you can call their UBound and LBound methods, respectively. UBound returns a value representing the highest index value in the array, while LBound returns the lowest index value. If you want to know how many controls are in the array, you can call the control array's Count method.

VB6 *Dynamic Control Creation*

Although you can still create control arrays dynamically, VB6 also allows you to create controls dynamically at runtime without requiring that you create a control array. You do this by calling the Controls collection's Add method. Its syntax is:

```
object.Add(ProgID, Name, [Container])
```

where the parameters are as follows:

ProgID
: The programmatic identifier of the control as it is defined in the system registry. Some common programmatic identifiers are shown in Table 1-1.

Name
: A string containing the name to assign to the control.

Container
: An optional object reference indicating the new control's container. If not specified, it defaults to *object*.

The method returns a reference to the newly created control. For example, the following code dynamically creates and displays a command button named `cmdOK`:

```
Option Explicit

Dim WithEvents cmdOK As CommandButton

Private Sub Form_Load()

Set cmdOK = Me.Controls.Add("VB.CommandButton", "cmdOK", Me)
cmdOK.Visible = True

End Sub
```

As the sample shows, creating a control dynamically requires that you do the following:

1. Declare the control variable using the `WithEvents` keyword (so that it receives event notification from the VB runtime engine) in the declarations section of the form's code module. Actually, although the declaration is always necessary, use of the `WithEvents` keyword is required only if you want to respond to the events raised by the control you're creating.
2. Add the control to the Controls collection.
3. If you want the control to be visible, set its Visible property to `True`. The default value of a dynamically created control is `False`. Note that the `cmdOK` object reference is not prefaced with the `Me` keyword; this generates a syntax error. If you want to include the `Me` keyword when referencing the control, it has to take the following form:

   ```
   Me.Controls("cmdOK").Visible = True
   ```
4. Size the control. This is best handled in the form's Resize event procedure.
5. Add any event code required by the control. (Events are discussed in the next section.)

Table 1-1: ProgIDs of VB's Intrinsic Controls

Control	*ProgID*
CheckBox	`VB.CheckBox`
ComboBox	`VB.ComboBox`

Table 1-1: ProgIDs of VB's Intrinsic Controls (continued)

Control	*ProgID*
CommandButton	VB.CommandButton
Frame	VB.Frame
HScrollBar	VB.HScrollbar
Image	VB.Image
Label	VB.Label
Line	VB.Line
ListBox	VB.ListBox
Option Button	VB.OptionButton
PictureBox	VB.PictureBox
Shape	VB.Shape
TextBox	VB.TextBox
Timer	VB.Timer
VScrollBar	VB.VScrollBar

Although Table 1-1 lists VB intrinsic controls, you can in fact instantiate any control. The general format of the ProgID is:

```
Library_Name.Control_Name
```

The Object Browser (which appears when you press F2 or select the Object Browser option from the View menu) can be used to provide both the control name and the library name. The latter appears in the bottom of the dialog ("Member of...") when the control is selected in the Classes list box. In Figure 1-4, for example, the Object Browser shows that the library name for the CommonDialog control is **MSComDlg**. Hence, the call to the Add method would appear as follows:

```
Set cdlgOpen = Me.Controls.Add("MSComDlg.CommonDialog", _
               "cdlgOpen", Me)
```

Successfully instantiating a nonintrinsic custom control dynamically requires that a reference to the control be added to the project and also that the "Remove information about unused ActiveX controls" option for the project be disabled (it appears on the Make tab of the Project Properties dialog) unless another instance of the control has been added to one of the project's forms at design time.

Properties, Methods, and Events

We've discussed creating a control. The next step in using them is to control them programmatically by using their properties, methods, and events. If you're accustomed to programming in Visual Basic or in virtually any object-oriented language, or if you're familiar with callback procedures or the Windows event loop, you're already familiar with properties, methods, and events. Visual Basic's implementation of properties, though, is somewhat different; it's visual.

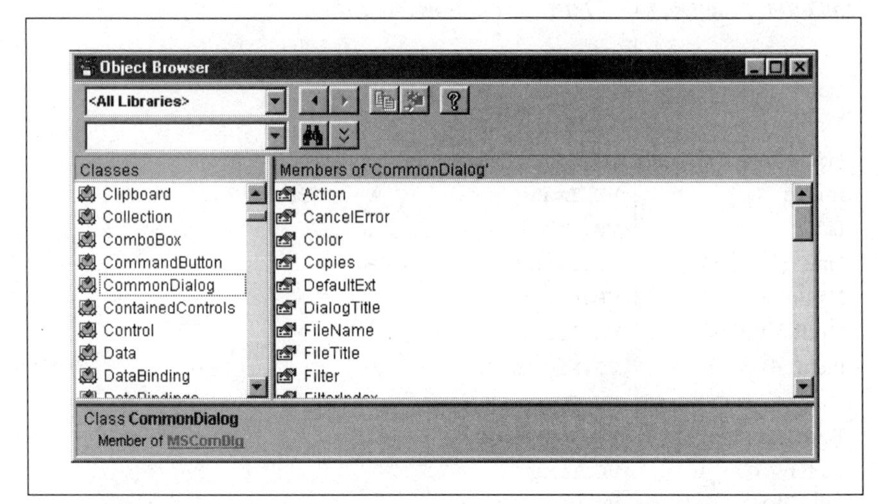

Figure 1-4: Using the Object Browser to find a control's library name

Control Properties

Each control exposes properties, or basic attributes, that can be retrieved and/or set. To express it in nonobject terms, properties are variables that belong to a particular object or control. For example, by retrieving the Text property of a TextBox control, a program can get text entered by the user and assign it to a variable. For example:

```
strName = txtName.Text
```

stores the string found in the Text property of a text box named *txtName* to a string variable named *strName*. Similarly, by assigning a new value to a CommandButton control's Caption property, a program can modify the text displayed on the button. For example:

```
cmdToggle.Caption = IIf(cmdToggle.Enabled, "&Disable", _
                    "&Enable")
```

changes the caption of a command button named `cmdToggle` depending on whether the button is enabled (its Enabled property is `True`) or disabled (its Enabled property is `False`).

In each of these example code fragments, property values are retrieved and set through code, at runtime. But Visual Basic offers an additional alternative: many properties can also be set at design time, within the Visual Basic environment. In keeping with its visual character, Visual Basic makes this very easy: assuming that the Properties window is open, it will display the properties of the form or the control that's selected in the Visual Basic IDE. Figure 1-5, for example, shows the Properties window when a CommandButton control named `cmdOK` is selected.

Using the Properties window, setting the value of a property at design time (which then becomes the initial value of that property at runtime) is extremely easy. In cases in which the property can assume virtually any value (such as the Caption

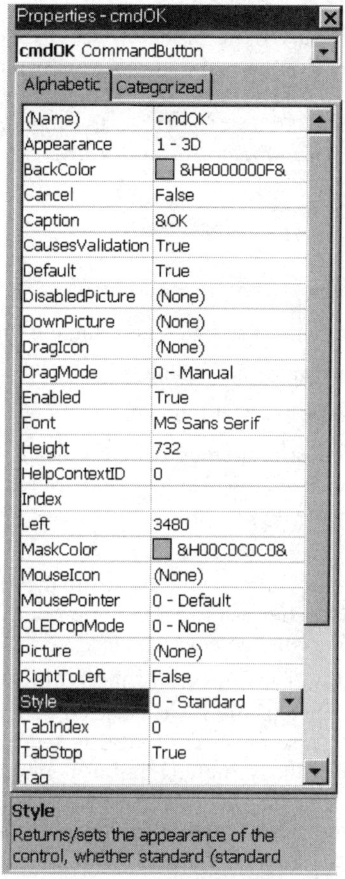

Figure 1-5: The Properties window

property in Figure 1-5, which can be assigned any combination of alphanumeric characters), the user can simply type the value in the field to the right of the property name. In other cases, the choices are more circumscribed, and as a result the probability of error is significantly reduced or eliminated. For example, Cancel in Figure 1-5 is a Boolean property; it is assigned a default value of `False`, but the programmer can change this simply by selecting `True` from a drop-down list. Similarly, the value of the Style property is an enumerated datatype. While 0–Standard is the default value, the programmer can change it to its alternate value, 1–Graphical, simply by selecting it from a drop-down list.

Aside from the convenience that it offers in setting a form or control's startup property values, Visual Basic also displays changes to visual properties immediately. For instance, if you change a form or control's Caption property, that caption is immediately modified. If you change a form's Icon property, the icon displayed in the form's menu control box changes immediately.

To put it another way, Visual Basic makes it easy to modify property values at design time, makes it difficult to make errors in assigning property values, and does its best to indicate to you whether the changes you're making are really the changes that you want to make. In comparison to programming in languages such as C or C++, this marks a major step forward in the ease of use of development tools.

Property availability

As we've seen, when working with properties, you can:

- Set and inspect their value at design time using the Properties window.
- Retrieve the property's value at runtime.
- Assign a value to the property at runtime.

But while this is true of most properties, it by no means is true of all. In addition to properties that are available at design time and are read/write at runtime, properties also fall into the following categories:

Runtime-only

Some control properties are not available in the design-time environment. Most commonly, this is the case because the property value makes sense only within the context of a runtime environment.

For example, the ListIndex property of the ListBox and ComboBox controls indicates which member of the list is selected; if no member is selected, its value is -1. It makes sense to speak of the selected member of a list, however, only if a program is actually running and a member of the list is capable of being selected. As a result, you cannot view or assign the value of the ListIndex property in the design-time environment; the property's value can be retrieved or assigned at runtime only.

Read-only

While you can usually both assign values to properties and retrieve their current value in the runtime environment, a number of properties must have their values assigned in the design-time environment. Most commonly, this is done because it is either not practical or simply not possible to allow a property value to change once a program is running.

The Name property of any control furnishes an excellent example of this. The Name property is important because it represents a control's identifier, the name by which it is referred to in code. If you've ever begun writing code and only later changed the name of a control at design time, you know how inconvenient changes to the Name property can be. All of your references to the control produce either design-time compiler errors ("Variable not defined") if you've configured VB to require variable declaration or runtime errors ("Object required") if you haven't. And any of the original event handlers you've created for the control (like a command button's Click event) just don't work.

If changing the name of a control at design time can be fraught with peril, permitting it to change at runtime makes no sense at all. To be practical, it would seem to require the ability to generate code dynamically from within a running application, something that Visual Basic does not allow.* Consequently, Name is a read-only property at runtime: although you can retrieve the value of the Name property, you cannot set it.

Write-only

There are a very few instances of properties in the runtime environment that are write-only. That is, although you can set their value from your code, you cannot read it. Often, this may be the case because of security considerations. For example, the ADO Data Control's Password property, which sets the user's password for a connection request, is write-only. While your code can set the Password property, it cannot retrieve its value.

Property types

We have been speaking of properties as if they are all scalar values—that is, as if each property has a single value. And in fact, that is true of most properties. Some properties, however, contain arrays of values.

Property arrays. A *property array* is simply an ordered group of values stored by their property that are accessible by their index value. Note that property arrays are different from properties that return Collection objects, which are discussed in the following section. Property arrays allow you to retrieve a particular element of the array by its *index* only—that is, by its ordinal position in the array.

For example, the ListBox control's List and Selected properties are implemented as arrays. (The List property contains the items in the ListBox; the Selected property indicates whether the list item at a particular ordinal position is selected.) The following code fragment retrieves the fifth item from its List property array and determines whether it is selected:

```
strItem = lstProducts.ListItem(4)
blnSelected = lstProducts.Selected(4)
```

Although property arrays are decidedly arrays, most of VBA's facilities for handling arrays don't work with them. The `OPTION BASE` statement, for example, allows you to define the lower bound of all arrays. However, the statement has no effect on property arrays, whose first value always has an index of zero. Similarly, attempting to pass a property array as an argument to the *LBound* function, which returns the index of an array's lower bound, or the *UBound* function, which returns the index of an array's upper bound, generates a compile-time error. Because of this, many controls have a corresponding property that indicates how many elements are stored in a property array. For example, in the case of the

* Interestingly, you could develop an add-in that uses the VB extensibility object model to generate code dynamically at design time. For details, see *Developing Visual Basic Add-ins*, written by Steven Roman and published by O'Reilly & Associates. However, add-ins are not available to running applications.

ListBox control, the ListCount property indicates the number of elements contained in both the List, Selected, and ItemData property arrays.

Frequently, rather than retrieving a particular value from an array, you need to iterate it. You do this using the "traditional" Visual Basic `For` loop with an index counter, as the following code fragment shows:

```
Dim intCtr as Integer
For intCtr = 0 To List1.ListCount - 1
   If List1.Selected(intCtr) Then
      ' Do something
   End If
Next
```

The `For. . .Next` statement, which automatically iterates every member of an array or collection, does not work with property arrays.

Properties returning collections. While some properties return scalar values and others hold arrays, still other properties return Collection objects. A Collection object is simply an object that serves as a container for one or more objects or values and that has a number of special properties to help it manage the collection's members. (To put it another way, a collection is an array in the age of object-oriented programming.)

For example, the StatusBar control has a Panels property that contains (not surprisingly) Panel objects. But whereas you can access only a single element at a time from a property array, you can retrieve the entire collection with a single statement:

```
Dim objCollection As Panels
objCollection = sbrMain.Panels
```

When this code finishes executing, what `objCollection` actually holds, though, is not a copy of a structure containing a number of Panel objects, but rather a reference (that is, a four-byte pointer) to the Panels collection, the same reference, in fact, that is returned by the Panels property itself.

A Collection object usually supports a number of properties and methods that allow you to work with the collection. To retrieve a particular element from a property that returns a collection, you use its Item property (although sometimes you'll see Item referred to as a method). The Item property allows you to retrieve a member of a collection based on its ordinal position in the collection. In addition, many collections allow you to retrieve a member based on its *key value*, a unique string that usually is assigned to the member when it is added to the collection. For example, the statement:

```
objPanel = sbrMain.Panels.Item(1)
```

retrieves the first Panel object in the Panels collection, while the statement:

```
objPanel = sbrMain.Panels.Item("TXT")
```

retrieves the Panel object whose key is `TXT`.

Whereas property arrays are zero-based, properties that return collections are usually (although not necessarily) one-based. It is difficult to tell whether any particular collection is zero-based or one-based, though, since the VBA *LBound* and *UBound* functions do not work with arrays. To determine whether the collection is zero-based or one-based, you'll have to either consult the control's documentation or rely on experimentation. What is easy is determining the total number of members of the collection; every collection has a Count property for that purpose.

To iterate the collection, you can use either the traditional `For` loop or the `For...Next` statement. For example, to iterate the Panels collection, you'd use code like the following:

```
Dim objPanel as Panel
For Each objPanel in sbrMain.Panels
   Debug.Print objPanel.Index
Next
```

Incidentally, if you are trying to find out whether a collection is zero-based or one-based and the members of that collection have an Index property, you can use a `For...Next` statement like the previous one to retrieve the value of the Index property of each collection member.

Although there is considerable variation in the properties and methods that Collection objects support, the following are fairly common:

Add method
: Adds a member to the collection. The syntax of each Add method depends on the objects being added to the collection, although most variations of the Add method include an *`Index`* parameter or an *`Insert`* parameter for defining the member's position in the collection, as well as a *`Key`* parameter to assign the member a unique string identifier.

  Not all collections support the Add method. Read-only collections don't, while members are added to some other collections by method calls that do not belong to the Collection object.

Clear method
: Removes all members from the collection. Not all collections have a Clear method.

Count property
: Returns the total number of members in the collection.

Item property
: Provides access to individual members of the collection by an index value or in some cases by a key value.

Remove method
: Removes a member from the collection based on its index value or sometimes on its key value. Not all collections have a Remove method.

The default member

Each control has a default member (which usually—although not always—happens to be a property) that is referenced whenever there is an unresolved reference to the control.

For example, the TextBox control's default member is its Text property. Hence, whenever the name of a TextBox control is encountered and that reference is ambiguous, the Text property is assumed. In the code:

```
Set objCtrl = txtName
```

the reference to the `txtName` TextBox control isn't ambiguous (the statement assigns a reference to the control to another object variable, ***objCtrl***), so the value of the Text property isn't assigned to ***objCtrl***. On the other hand, in the statement:

```
frmQuery.Caption = txtQueryName
```

the reference to the `txtQueryName` text box is ambiguous (it makes no sense to assign an instance of a control to a form's Caption property), so the statement is resolved as follows:

```
frmQuery.Caption = txtQueryName.Text
```

A number of Visual Basic developers have recommended that the use of default members in code be avoided, since it tends to make code less readable while providing minimal benefit. Although this is true, the problem of relying on the default member when programming goes well beyond that; it also encourages sloppy thinking and careless coding and tends to obscure the relationship between collections, their members, and the latter's properties and elements.

The clearest case of this is the Item property, which is the default member of any Collection object. Hence, in the case of the Panels collection, you can retrieve a reference to a Panel object with the statement:

```
Set objPanel = Panels.Item("NUMLOCK")
```

or

```
Set objPanel = Panels("NUMLOCK")
```

But the members of a collection (if the collection is a container for other objects) also have a default member, which frequently is the Name property. Because of this, the statement:

```
strName = objCollection(3)
```

will work because it's merely shorthand for this:

```
strName = objCollection.Item(3).Name
```

The first statement, though, makes it appear that the members of the collection are strings or that you can retrieve string values directly from the collection. It also tends to make a statement like:

```
Set objMember = objCollection.Item(3)
```

(which retrieves an object reference from the collection) seem nonsensical. After all, if you can retrieve the string value you want "directly" from a collection, why bother working with more troublesome and more indirect object references?

Control Methods

Whereas properties are attributes of an object, methods are its verbs. Actually, methods are simply functions, except that the methods of a control apply to and operate on that control exclusively. Each control supports methods or allows its own code to be called from outside to perform some operation, provide some service, or define the behavior of the control.

For example, calling a control's SetFocus method moves the focus to the control whose SetFocus method is called.

Most (although not all) methods accept parameters or data passed to the function when it is called that affect its precise operation. For example, calling the Move method of any control with a visual interface positions that control on the form or moves it from its current position to a new position. Its syntax is:

```
Move(Left, [Top], [Width], [Height])
```

The method takes four parameters, all of them values of type single and all of them optional except the first. The parameters are:

Left
: The coordinate at which the control's left edge should be positioned. It is relative to the top edge of the control's container.

Top
: The coordinate at which the control's top edge should be positioned. It is relative to the left edge of the control's container.

Width
: The total width of the control.

Height
: The total height of the control.

Move is a very common class of method; it allows you to perform in a single operation what you can do a little more slowly and with a little more code by assigning new values to the corresponding properties. In the case of the Move method, the code:

```
Me.cmdOK.Move Me.Width / 10, Me.Height / 10 * 6, 1200, 725
```

is equivalent to the following four property assignment statements:

```
cmdOK.Width = Me.Width / 10
cmdOK.Height = Me.Height / 10 * 6
cmdOK.Width = 1200
cmdOK.Height = 725
```

Like their non-object-oriented counterparts, methods can be grouped into two categories: procedures and functions. Procedures typically perform some operation but don't return a value; most methods fall into this category. Functions, on the other hand, do return a value. For example, the ListView control has a ListItems property that returns a ListItems collection. The collection has an Add method whose syntax is:

```
ListItems.Add [Index], [Key], [Text], [Icon], [SmallIcon])
```

where the parameters allow you to specify the item's position (the *Index* parameter), a unique string that identifies the item and can be used to retrieve it (*Key*), the item's text or caption (*Text*), and the icons stored in an ImageList control that are displayed along with the item's text (*Icon* and *SmallIcon*). If it's successful, the method returns a reference to the ListItem object that was added to the collection. For example:

```
Set objLItem = ListItems.Add(,"ORANGES", "Oranges", _
                "ORANGEL", "ORANGESM")
```

The ability to retrieve an object reference in this way is particularly useful, since the Add method itself allows you to set only a few properties of the new ListItem object. By referencing the new item, it becomes easy to set the values of the object's other properties. For example:

```
objLItem.Selected = True
objLItem.Bold = True
```

As Visual Basic has matured, and as Visual Basic controls have become more complex, the importance of methods has increased. Until Visual Basic 4.0, the major methods were ones shared by a number of controls that provided some utility function, such as Move, ZOrder (which moves a control to the front or back in relation to overlapping controls), and Show (which displays a form). In fact, many Visual Basic programmers could get by quite nicely without calling any control methods at all with a few exceptions (such as Show)—while these methods were in some cases useful or convenient, they were rarely essential.

From Visual Basic 4.0 onward, however, these methods have been supplemented by another set of methods that are not so much useful as they are essential. The ListItems collection's Add method is a good example of this type of method. It provides the only means available of populating a ListView control with data. Without it, the ListView control becomes unusable. In short, ListItems.Add is an essential method: it is one that must be used if its associated ListView control is to work at all.

Control Events

Events are actually methods of a particular kind. Ordinarily, your program invokes an object's methods by calling them directly. (And in fact, you can evoke event procedures in this way as well, although it isn't recommended.) Events, however, are also known as *callback methods* or *callback procedures*. While you can call event procedures directly, most commonly they are executed by the Visual Basic runtime engine in response to some event.

For example, the most common of events is probably the Click event, which is fired whenever the user clicks on a form, MDI form, control, or menu item. By attaching code to that object's Click event, you create an *event procedure* or an *event handler* that determines how the object responds when it is clicked. Without an event handler, such operations as clicking a command button or selecting a menu item would have no effect. With the event handler, when the user clicks on the command button or selects the menu item, the event handler that you've written for it is automatically executed by the Visual Basic runtime engine.

For example, the following code shows the Click event procedure for a command button named *cmdBrowse*:

```
Private Sub cmdBrowse_Click()

Dim strFilename As String
Dim tstrFileToView As TextStream
Dim objFileSys As New FileSystemObject

cdlgBrowse.ShowOpen
If Not cdlgBrowse.FileName = "" Then
   strFilename = cdlgBrowse.FileName
   Set tstrFileToView = objFileSys.OpenTextFile(strFilename)
   txtFile.Text = tstrFileToView.ReadAll
End If

End Sub
```

When the user clicks the button, the VB runtime engine automatically checks to see if an event handler named `cmdBrowse_Click` exists. If it doesn't, the click goes unhandled. If it does, the event handler is automatically invoked. In this case, the File Open common dialog is displayed to allow the user to select a filename. If the user selects a file, the FileSystemObject object's OpenTextFile method is called to open the file and return a reference to a TextStream object. Finally, the TextStream object's ReadAll method is called to display the file's contents in a text box. (The FileSystemObject and TextStream objects are both parts of the File System object model that's included in the Microsoft Scripting Runtime that ships with VB6.)

Unlike a "normal" method, an event handler cannot return a value; that is, all event handlers are procedures, and none are functions. (There is a way around this restriction, as you'll see in the "ByRef and ByVal" section, which follows shortly.)

Events and control arrays

If you've defined a *control array*—that is, an array of controls that share the same name but that can be differentiated from one another by the values of their Index property—Visual Basic supports only a single event handler for the entire control array. However, you can determine which control fired the event by examining the *Index* parameter, which Visual Basic passes to the event procedure when it is fired.

ByRef and ByVal

In addition to the *Index* parameter, which is used only in the case of control arrays and allows you to determine which individual control was responsible for firing the event, many events have parameters that provide additional information about the event. Note that the Visual Basic runtime engine is responsible for assigning the values to those parameters. This is, of course, the reverse of a "regular" method call, in which you are responsible for providing arguments to the method that in turn are passed on to the VB runtime engine.

The MouseDown event, which is fired when the user depresses a mouse button, provides a good example of an event with parameters whose values are supplied when the event is fired. Its syntax is:

```
object_MouseDown(Button As Integer, Shift As Integer, _
X As Single, Y As Single)
```

The *Button* parameter is a constant whose value allows you to determine which mouse button was pressed, in the event that that's important to your program. *Shift* indicates whether any of the "special" keys (Shift, CTRL, or ALT) were depressed when the mouse button was pressed. And the *X* and *Y* parameters indicate the position of the mouse pointer when the event was fired.

Visual Basic provides two methods of passing parameters: by reference (indicated using the `ByRef` keyword or, because it is the default method, no keyword at all) and by value (indicated using the `ByVal` keyword). Passing a parameter by reference indicates that what the event procedure is actually receiving is a pointer to the data; therefore, any modifications to the data that the event handler might make are reflected in the variable's value in the calling program. On the other hand, passing a parameter by value indicates that the event procedure receives a *copy* of the data. Therefore, any changes made to the value of the parameter within the event handler are not passed back to the calling routine; these changes affect only the local copy, which goes out of scope when the event handler terminates.

The issue of how parameters are passed to event handlers is considerably complicated by the fact that Visual Basic's default method is by reference. Consequently, you can modify the values of the parameters passed to the program, and presumably the new values will be returned to the calling routine in the VB runtime engine. To be meaningful, the variables receiving those values must then be used. In most cases, however, they are not. For example, in the case of the MouseDown event, we can change the values of *X* and *Y* in our event handler, and presumably these values are returned to the calling program. However, you won't notice a resulting change in the position of the mouse pointer, since these variables are never used again.

Some variables passed by reference, however, are used by the VB runtime engine when the event handler returns. By modifying their value, our event handler can more precisely control the event. The Form object's QueryUnload event is a good example of this type of event. The event procedure has the syntax:

```
Form_QueryUnload(Cancel As Integer, UnloadMode As Integer)
```

Both parameters are passed to the event handler by reference. *UnloadMode*, which indicates the source of the request to unload the form, is passed by reference but is subsequently unused by the calling program; it could have been passed to the event procedure by value instead. *Cancel*, however, is subsequently used by the VB runtime engine. When the event handler is called, Cancel always has its default value of `False`, indicating that the request to unload the form should not be cancelled. Setting it to `True`, however, notifies the runtime engine that the request to unload the form should be denied and that the form should not be unloaded.

Working with Controls

It's important to recognize that although Visual Basic has enormously simplified the process of application development by hiding the complexity of the Windows API and replacing it with drag-and-drop user interface design, simplification is not the same thing as simplistic. Although Visual Basic has enabled developers to speed the application development process in general, it has also introduced a new set of problems of its own. In this section, we'll discuss some of the issues that arise when working with controls and that the reference portion of *VB Controls in a Nutshell* is intended to address.

A Wealth of Controls

Visual Basic's controls have always been one of the product's most important and most appealing features. Visual Basic has spawned a lively market for add-on controls, and the announcement that Version 5.0 of Visual Basic would allow VB programmers to create their own custom controls was met with an enormously enthusiastic reception in the VB community.

As a result, there is no shortage of controls for Visual Basic. Visual Basic itself includes 20 intrinsic controls—controls that are part of the Visual Basic library—along with a vast array of custom controls that are bundled with the Professional and Enterprise editions of Visual Basic.* If you select the VB Enterprise Edition Controls option when creating a new project with the Enterprise Edition, you'll end up with a toolbox containing 63 different controls.

Many controls, like most of the intrinsic controls that come with Visual Basic, are extremely easy to use. In contrast, many custom controls are extremely full featured and complex. Some, like the MSChart control, even expose a complex and rich programmable object model. (And it seems to be a secular trend for the newer controls to be both more powerful and more complex.) But each control seems to have its own *gestalt*, a mindset that it requires you to adopt if you're going to use the control to the greatest effect. *Visual Basic Controls in a Nutshell* in part aims at providing the context behind the control, along with the basic information you need to put the controls of the Professional and Enterprise editions to the best use in the least amount of time.

An Abundance of Members

In our previous discussion, we've presented using controls as a relatively simple matter: you set a few properties, call a few methods, and write an event handler or two. But in fact, for most controls, there are a bewildering array of properties, a surprising number of methods, and an excess of events.

Visual Basic offers several facilities to make online information on control properties, methods, and events as accessible as possible. Using the Object Browser, shown earlier in Figure 1-4, you can see the members of each control at a glance,

* Some of these controls, in fact, are completely undocumented. A list of controls, "Controls Shipped in Visual Basic 6.0," is available from Microsoft in the Visual Basic Knowledgebase.

along with method and event syntax, datatypes, and a brief description. By checking the Auto Quick Info box on the Editor tab of the Options dialog, you can see a prototype, like the one shown in Figure 1-6, for each function or method as you type it. Finally, when you check the Auto List Members box on the Editor tab of the Options dialog, VB displays lists of available constants or datatypes that allow you to complete some statements, as Figure 1-7 shows.

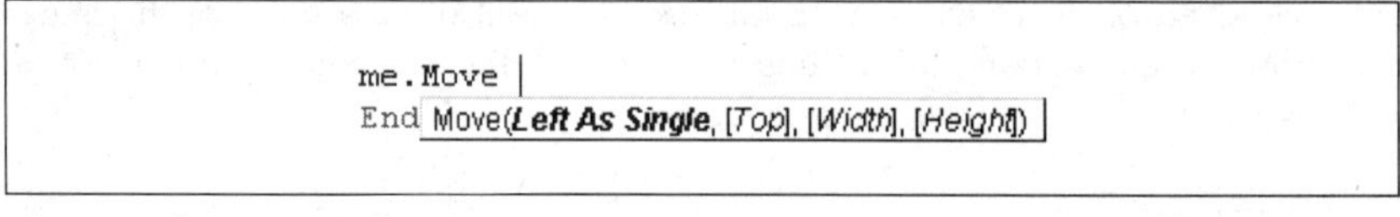

Figure 1-6: Auto Quick Info

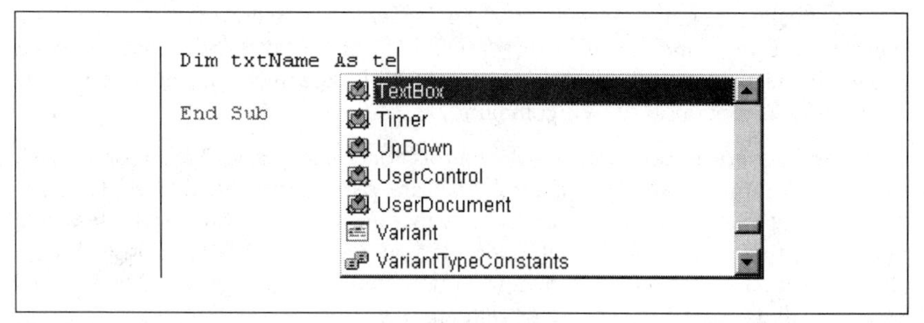

Figure 1-7: Auto List Members

In addition, Visual Basic comes with extensive online help, which for Version 6.0 consists of the HTML Help engine (an innovation that has not exactly been greeted warmly by developers) and a special edition of the MSDN Library, a CD-ROM that includes core documentation, the Visual Basic KnowledgeBase, and selected articles and papers. Instead of this special edition CD-ROM, Visual Basic will take advantage of the quarterly MSDN CD-ROM releases, which ensures that help information will be as current as possible.

Certainly, these features are extremely helpful and make coding much faster and less painful. But although they ease the problem of having to familiarize yourself with large numbers of properties, methods, and events, they don't solve it. Just remembering which properties you should set, which event handlers you must code, and which methods you should call can be daunting. Frequently, you still have to know which property, method, or event you want to use in order to get further information about it. And of course, once you've written your code, some features of VB controls just don't work as advertised, and you lose valuable time diagnosing and fixing the problem.

Timing Is Everything

One of the related problems that you'll frequently encounter in writing VB code is that the order in which you write code is important.

For example, have you ever created a form, written most of its code, realized that you'd forgotten to name your command button control using your standard naming conventions, and renamed it? Your program, which you just tested moments before, no longer works. If you assign a nondefault name to a control's Name property (and you always should), it must always be the first thing that you change.

In other cases, it is much less important to set properties in a particular order. At least, failing to set property values in the proper order will not break working code. But when you have a number of properties to set, methods to call, and event handlers to write, approaching them in a random manner ensures that something will be overlooked. And the result, of course, almost invariably, is that you have to spend time doing additional testing and debugging when you find that your program doesn't work as you intended it to (because, of course, you've forgotten to set the property that you're absolutely, 100% certain that you set at design time).

It is precisely to address these issues that *Visual Basic Controls in a Nutshell* was written. In Chapter 5, *Controls*, each entry attempts to provide a step-by-step guide to working with the control. If you're unfamiliar with a particular control, this helps you to master that control as quickly as possible. If you're experienced in working with the control, it provides you with a checklist of what you have to do to make a control "application ready" and ensures you won't forget anything.

Interactions

With events firing, properties being set, and methods being called, it's not surprising that sometimes controls get in the way of one another (or a control gets in the way of itself). To put it another way, controls—or the properties, events, and methods of a single control—often interact in ways that are surprising and undesirable.

A good example is the option button's Click event. In some cases, you attach code to the event to perform some operation as soon as the user changes the selected button. You may have some code like the following in your Form_Load event procedure to select one of the buttons:

```
optSelection(1).Value = True
```

If you had set the value of *`optSelection(1)`* to `True` at design time, the Click event would not be fired at startup. But because your code does it at runtime, the Click event is fired, even though in this case you almost certainly don't want it to be.

Interactions of this type are surprisingly common. Typically, they're also either not well documented or totally undocumented. As a result, tracking them down can be a real nightmare. *Visual Basic Controls in a Nutshell* aims at documenting as many of them as possible.

CHAPTER 2

Common Control Features

Many Visual Basic controls share common properties, methods, and events. Instead of covering these in the individual chapters, I will cover them here. In cases in which an individual control differs from the description here or special considerations apply, the distinctions will be covered in the specific control's chapter.

Control Tasks

The following sections describe the tasks that are executed when creating various VB controls.

Set Properties

1. Define the form or control's name.

   Except for the Form object, which can be referenced in code contained within the form by using the `Me` keyword, all forms and controls must be referred to by name in code. This name is determined by the Name property, which must be set at design time (and is read-only at runtime). In addition, a control's event handlers all take the general form *`controlname_event`*. (A form's event handlers all use the `Form` keyword, as in `Form_Load`.) Since Visual Basic's default naming convention (which simply increments the number attached to the control's type, as in Command1, Command2, etc.) makes the function of individual controls unclear, it's important to assign your own name.

   This should *always* be the first step in using any control or form. There are two very practical reasons for this:

- While you can rename a form or control at any time in the design-time environment, the Visual Basic editor will never rename its event handlers. They continue to use the old name of the form or control, so you must rename them manually; they can be found at the beginning of the containing form's declarations section.
- If you refer to a form by its original name in code, these references remain unchanged when the form is renamed.

The following table lists some common controls and the three-letter code that is commonly used at the beginning of its name to identify the control type in code:

Control	*Abbreviation*
ADO Data Control	ado
Animation	ani
CheckBox	chk
ComboBox	cbo
CommandButton	cmd
CommonDialog	dlg
CoolBar	cbr
Data	dat
DataCombo	dtc
DataGrid	dtg
DataList	dtl
DTPicker	dtp
DBCombo	dbc
DBGrid	dbg
DBList	dbl
FlatScrollbar	fsb
Form	frm
Frame	fra
HScrollbar	hsz
Image	img
ImageCombo	icb
ImageList	iml
Internet Transfer	itc
Label	lbl
Line	lin
ListBox	lst
ListView	lvw
MaskedEditBox	meb
Menu	mnu

Control	*Abbreviation*
MonthView	mvw
MSChart	cht
MSFlexGrid	flx
MSHFlexGrid	hfl
Multimedia	mci
OLE	ole
Option Button	opt
PictureBox	pic
ProgressBar	pbr
RichTextBox	rtf
Shape	sha
StatusBar	sta
SysInfo	sin
TabStrip	tab
TextBox	txt
Timer	tmr
Toolbar	tlb
TreeView	tre
UpDown	upd
VScrollbar	vsb
Winsock	sck

2. Specify the control's position in the tab order (optional).

   Visual Basic forms have a *tab order*. This is the order in which the contained controls are accessed once their form gains the focus. As the user tabs through the controls on the form, each control is accessed in the order determined by the tab order.

   TabStop
   : When TabStop is set to `True` (its default value), the control is accessed as normal in the tab order. When set to `False`, the control is skipped. This is desirable when you want a control to be accessed only by mouse or keyboard events, as opposed to by tabbing through a form.

   TabIndex
   : With zero (0) being first and the highest numbered TabIndex being last, this is the order in which the controls are accessed in the tab order.

     When a control that cannot have the focus (such as a Label or Frame control) receives focus through the tab order, it is passed to the next control (that is, the control whose Index value is one greater). By using mnemonic access keys on these controls, you can give access to controls that do not have access keys (such as TextBox controls).

When the TabIndex property is changed for one control on a form, the TabIndex values for other controls are updated, as the entire tab order is renumbered to allow for the change.

3. Set caption and tool tip (optional).

Caption

Controls with the Caption property allow for descriptive text to be entered programmatically onto the control. In most cases, this text can contain mnemonic access keys that highlight a character in the caption. This allows the user to press the ALT key plus the highlighted key to set the focus to that control. Generally, this is done by putting an ampersand (&) in front of the desired letter in the caption. For example, to highlight the "r" in Price, the caption would contain the string "P&rice". The user would then see "Price" as the caption. When you need to include an ampersand in a caption, use two ampersands in a row.

ToolTipText

When the mouse pointer hovers over a control whose ToolTipText property is set to a string, that string appears in a box over the control until the mouse moves from over that control. This is useful to give the user more detailed information about the control.

4. Adjust control location (optional).

Left, Top, Width, Height

These properties control the location and size of the control on its container. Each of these properties is measured in units based on the control's container's SizeMode property. While these properties are useful for determining a control's size and location, the Move method is preferable for changing the size and location.

5. Set control's general appearance (optional).

Enabled

A control with its Enabled property set to `False` cannot get the focus, does not respond to user actions, and usually appears grayed. Controls contained by a control that has its Enabled property set to `False` are also disabled but usually do not appear grayed.

Visible

A control with its Visible property set to `False` does not appear visibly on its container.

BackColor

A control's background color is determined by its BackColor property. This is a long integer that represents either the RGB color (in which case it takes the form &H00BBGGRR) or an index to the system color palette (in which case it takes the form &H800000II). (See Appendix A for more information.) At design time, colors can be selected from the Properties window by using the color picker on the Palette tab or the drop-down list on the System tab. Frequently, a control's background color is expected to match that of the form or other control that contains it. This is easily done with the following code fragment (assuming a label control named Label1):

```
Label1.BackColor = Label1.Container.BackColor
```

6. Define other properties (optional).

CausesValidation VB6

The CausesValidation property, along with the Validate event, provides developers with a way to easily validate data. When set to `True`, the Validate event fires when the control is about to lose the focus. When set to `False`, the Validate event does not fire, providing the same functionality as previous versions of Visual Basic.

Tag

All intrinsic controls, most custom controls, and many objects have a Tag property. The Tag property does absolutely nothing by itself. It is merely an area for the developer to store information. For example, you might use the text box's GotFocus event procedure to store the current value of the Text property to the Tag property, in the event that the user modifies it. Then the original value can be easily obtained if it's needed. The only caveat is that the Tag property is particularly slow to use, so try not to use it during tight execution loops.

Useful Methods

ZOrder

The ZOrder method has one parameter, an integer (or constant) named *`position`*. When this method of a control is called with a *`position`* parameter of 0–vbBringToFront, the control is placed in front of any other controls in the same container. When called with a *`position`* parameter equal to 1–vbSendToBack, the control is placed behind other controls in the same container. This is useful for "popping" a control in front of another control.

Drag

The Drag method has one parameter, an integer (or constant) named *`action`*. When the Drag method of a control is called with an *`action`* equal to `vbBeginDrag`, that control begins to be dragged. When an *`action`* equal to `vbEndDrag` is passed, a dragged control is dropped. To cancel a current drag operation without dropping, pass an *`action`* value of `vbCancel`.

Move

The Move method requires a parameter for the new Left position of the control. However, new Top, Width, and Height values can also be specified. Using the Move method to relocate a control on a form is faster than setting the control's individual Left, Top, Width, and Height properties.

SetFocus

This method makes the control the current ActiveControl (the control that currently has the application focus) on the form. It allows for the program to override the form's Tab Order. When the SetFocus method is called for a control that cannot accept the focus (for example, a control with its Enabled or Visible properties set to `False`), runtime error 5 ("Invalid procedure call or argument") occurs.

Write Event Handlers

Click, DblClick, MouseDown, MouseUp, and MouseMove

The mouse events are provided to respond to actions taken with the mouse. The most useful of these, Click, is generally the best way to determine if a user has clicked on a control. However, if it is important to know exactly where the user has clicked, along with any buttons pressed or modifier keys held, the MouseDown and MouseUp events provide that information to the program. The MouseMove event is useful when tracking mouse movement in an application, such as when changing the mouse pointer when the mouse enters a certain area of the screen.

Change, KeyPress, KeyDown, and KeyUp

While the Change event is present in most controls, its usefulness is limited in most nondata entry controls. However, in controls such as the TextBox, where the text is generally edited by the user, the Change event is useful to intercept these changes. Other controls can better rely on the KeyDown and KeyPress events to check for keyboard interaction.

LostFocus and GotFocus

As the user proceeds through the tab order, each control generally gets a GotFocus event as it receives the focus and a LostFocus event as the focus is passed to the next control. Where this interaction is changed, such as with the command button, the differences will be noted.

Validate

Fires when the control is about to lose the focus and the CausesValidation property is set to `True`. The event handler is passed one parameter, *`Cancel`*. If *`Cancel`* is set to `True` when the event is finished executing, the control will retain the focus. Otherwise, the focus changes normally. The main advantage to using the Validate event over other events such as LostFocus is that the Validate event always fires before the control loses the focus. In some cases (see, for example, the "Order of Events" section in the CommandButton entry in Chapter 5, *Controls*), the order in which events are fired can change based on the user's actions.

OLE Drag and Drop Tasks

The following sections describe the tasks that are executed when giving a control OLE Drag and Drop capabilities.

Set OLE Drag and Drop Properties

1. Control properties

   OLEDragMode

   Controls that have an OLEDragMode property can be dragged using OLE Drag and Drop. Setting the OLEDragMode property to 0–vbOLEDrag-Manual allows the control to be dragged using the OLEDrag method only. When set to 1–vbOLEDragAutomatic, the user initiates OLE Drag and Drop by dragging the control with the mouse.

OLEDropMode

The OLEDropMode property controls how the control reacts to dragged OLE objects being dropped on it. Possible values are 0–vbOLEDrop-None, when the control does not accept dropped OLE objects; 1–vbOLEDropManual, when the OLEDragDrop event is fired so that the program can determine how to proceed; and 2–vbOLEDropAutomatic, when the drop action is successful if the OLE object and control have compatible formats.

2. DataObject Properties

The DataObject object is passed as a parameter to many of the OLE Drag and Drop events. It includes a number of methods (described under DataObject methods, later in this section) and the following property:

Files

The Files property contains a reference to a DataObjectFiles collection. This is the case only when the GetFormat method for `VbCFFiles` returns `True`, denoting that the OLE object contains files. Each element of the DataObjectFiles collection contains a string that is the name of a file associated with the DataObject.

OLE Drag and Drop Methods

1. Control methods

OLEDrag

When the OLEDrag method is called, the control is used as the OLE object being dragged by the user. When the control's OLEDragMode property is set to `vbOLEDragManual`, this is the only way to begin dragging the control.

2. DataObject methods

Clear

The Clear method clears all object data from the DataObject object.

GetData

The GetData method returns data from the DataObject object in the format defined by the *`Format`* parameter. Possible values for the *`Format`* parameter include 1–vbCFText for text data, 2–vbCFBitmap for Windows bitmap files, 3–vbCFMetafile for Windows metafile files, 8–vbCFDIB for device independent bitmap files, 9–vbCFPalette for color palette data, 14–vbCFEMetafile for an enhanced metafile file, 15–vbCFFiles for a collection of filenames, and -16639–vbCFRTF for a Rich Text file. The data is returned in a variant.

GetFormat

If the drop target is expected to access data provided by the drop source, the former must make sure that the latter can provide the data in a suitable format. This is done by the GetFormat method. When the GetFormat method is called with its *`Format`* parameter matching a format for the

DataObject object, the value `True` is returned. Otherwise, `False` is returned. Possible values for the *`Format`* parameter are the same as in the GetData method.

SetData

The SetData method puts data into the DataObject object. Parameters are supplied for the data itself (*`Data`*) as well as the type of format being sent (*`Format`*). Possible values for the *`Format`* parameter are the same as in the GetData method.

Control Features

OLE Drag and Drop Events

OLECompleteDrag, OLEDragDrop

When a dragged OLE object is dropped onto a control, the source control's OLECompleteDrag event is fired. If the OLECompleteDrag event accepts the drop and the OLEDropMode property of the target is set to vbOLEDrop-Manual, the OLEDragDrop event is then fired for the target control. The OLECompleteDrag event includes *`Effect`*, a parameter for the drop effect. Values for *`Effect`* are 0–vbDropEffectNone for no dropping allowed, 1–vbDropEffectCopy when a copy can be dropped, and 2–vbDropEffectMove when the OLE object is moved. The OLEDragDrop event supplies parameters for the DataObject object (*`Data`*), the drop effect (*`Effect`*), the state of the mouse buttons (*`Button`*) and modifier keys (*`Shift`*), and the X (*`X`*) and Y (*`Y`*) coordinates of the mouse. Possible values for the *`Effect`* parameter are 0–vbDropEffectNone for no dropping allowed, 1–vbDropEffectCopy when a copy can be dropped, 2–vbDropEffectMove when the OLE object is moved, and -2147483648–vbDropEffectScroll to provide information when you are performing scrolling based on the event.

OLEDragOver, OLEGiveFeedback

When an OLE object is dragged over a control, the OLEDragOver event is fired for the control being dragged over, followed by the OLEGiveFeedback event being fired for the source control. The OLEDragOver event supplies parameters for the DataObject object (*`Data`*), the drop effect (*`Effect`*), the state of the mouse buttons (*`Button`*) and modifier keys (*`Shift`*), X (*`X`*) and Y (*`Y`*) coordinates, and the current state of the mouse (*`State`*). Possible values for *`Effect`* are 0–vbDropEffectNone for no dropping allowed, 1–vbDropEffectCopy when a copy can be dropped, 2–vbDropEffectMove when the OLE object is moved, and -2147483648–vbDropEffectScroll to provide information when you are performing scrolling based on the event. Possible values for *`State`* are 0–vbEnter when the dragged object enters the control's area, 1–vbLeave when the dragged object leaves the control's area, and 2–vbOver when the dragged object moves within the control's area. Parameters for the OLEGiveFeedback event include the drop effect (*`Effect`*) and whether the default mouse cursor should be used (*`DefaultCursors`*). Possible values for the *`Effect`* parameter are the same as for the OLEDragOver event covered earlier in this paragraph.

OLESetData

If the DataObject associated with an OLE Drag and Drop action has not yet had its data populated when the GetData method is called, the OLESetData event is fired. Parameters are supplied for the DataObject object (`Data`) and the type of format for the data (`Format`). Possible values for the `Format` parameter are the same as in the GetData and SetData methods.

OLEStartDrag

The OLEStartDrag event is fired when the user begins dragging a control with its OLEDragMode property set to Automatic or when its OLEDrag method is called. A DataObject object is provided (`Data`) as a parameter, as is the type of dropping that is allowed (`AllowedEffects`). Possible values for `AllowedEffects` are 0–vbDropEffectNone for no dropping allowed, 1–vbDropEffectCopy when a copy can be dropped, and 2–vbDropEffectMove when the OLE object is moved. The vbDropEffectCopy and vbDropEffect-Move values can be combined using the OR operator.

Example

The following example shows how to use OLE Drag and Drop to allow the user to drag selected text from a TextBox control to a ListBox control. Feel free to drag text from the TextBox to WordPad or drag text to the ListBox from other applications such as Visual Basic's code window:

```
Option Explicit

Dim WithEvents txtMain As TextBox
Dim WithEvents lstMain As ListBox

Private Sub Form_Load()
   'Create and set up controls.
      Set txtMain = Me.Controls.Add( _
          "vb.textbox", "txtMain", Me)
      txtMain.Text = ""
      txtMain.Visible = True
   'Setting the OLEDragMode to automatic makes _
      detecting a drag operation much easier than _
      monitoring the mouse position.
      txtMain.OLEDragMode = vbOLEDragAutomatic

      Set lstMain = Me.Controls.Add( _
          "vb.listbox", "lstMain", Me)
      lstMain.Clear
      lstMain.Visible = True
   'We'll handle all the Drop logic.
      lstMain.OLEDropMode = vbOLEDropManual
End Sub

Private Sub Form_Resize()
    If Me.ScaleHeight < 990 Or Me.ScaleWidth < 1095 Then
        Exit Sub
    End If

    txtMain.Move 120, 120, Me.ScaleWidth - 240, 315
    lstMain.Move 120, 555, Me.ScaleWidth - 240, _
        Me.ScaleHeight - 675
```

```
End Sub

Private Sub txtMain_OLEStartDrag(Data As DataObject,  _
    AllowedEffects As Long)
  'We'll clear the DataObject first so we have full _
    control over its contents.
    Data.Clear
  'Now we'll put the selected text into the DataObject.
    Data.SetData txtMain.SelText, vbCFText
End Sub

Private Sub lstMain_OLEDragOver(Data As DataObject, _
    Effect As Long, Button As Integer, _
    Shift As Integer, X As Single, Y As Single, _
    State As Integer)
  'We only want the user to drop text data on the _
    ListBox
    If Data.GetFormat(vbCFText) Then
        Effect = vbDropEffectCopy Or vbDropEffectMove
    Else
        Effect = vbDropEffectNone
    End If
End Sub

Private Sub lstMain_OLEDragDrop(Data As DataObject, _
    Effect As Long, Button As Integer, _
    Shift As Integer, X As Single, Y As Single)
  'Now we'll add the text contents of the DataObject _
    to the ListBox.
    lstMain.AddItem Data.GetData(vbCFText)
End Sub
```


Data-Binding Tasks

Many of VB's intrinsic controls allow you to bind to a data source—that is, to a control that is responsible for connecting to and querying a database and for handling the resulting recordset returned to it. Typically, the data source then automatically provides one or more fields from the current record to the bound control and continues to provide the bound control with updated information whenever the record pointer moves. Similarly, if the bound control is used to modify the data, these changes are passed back to the data source and, if the recordset is updateable, are eventually written back to the database.

The following intrinsic controls can all be bound to a data source:

- CheckBox
- ComboBox
- Image
- Label
- ListBox

- OLE
- PictureBox
- TextBox

Note, though, that the ListBox and ComboBox controls do *not* bind to an entire column of data, as you might expect.

The following categories reflect the tasks that are executed when binding a control to a data source.

Set Data-Binding Properties

DataSource

The DataSource property should contain a reference to the data provider to which the control is bound. For example, the control can be bound to a DAO database using the following syntax:

```
Set txtMain.DataSource _
  = DBEngine.Workspaces(0).OpenDatabase("mydb.mdb")
```

where *mydb.mdb* is the filename of the DAO database, along with an optional path.

If the data source of a control is either the intrinsic VB Data control or the Remote Data control, you must set the DataSource property at design time. Attempting to set it at runtime generates a runtime error.

DataMember

The DataMember property contains the name of one of multiple data sets available from the data provider. Different types of providers can make various data members available based on the type of provider. The property is unused if only one data member is available from the data source.

DataField

The DataField property contains the name of the field within the object referenced by the DataSource property to which the control is bound.

DataFormat **VB6**

The DataFormat property contains a reference to a StdDataFormat object. The StdDataFormat object contains information about how data should be formatted when read from or written to the data provider; for details, see *VB & VBA in a Nutshell*, by Paul Lomax, published by O'Reilly & Associates.

DataChanged

The DataChanged property returns `True` when the contents of the control differ from those contained by the data source. `False` is returned when the values match. You can retrieve the value of the DataChanged property to determine if there's been any change to the local copy of the data before updating the original data source.

CHAPTER 3

The Form

The Visual Basic form is the rough equivalent of a window on other Windows development platforms, like Microsoft Visual C++. In most cases, a form is the heart of a Visual Basic application and a container for the application's individual interface. While the form is not exactly a control, all controls are ultimately contained by a form. The form has many properties that affect the behavior of contained controls.

In addition to the general-purpose, resizable window, a Form object can take on a number of other forms (no play on words intended!), ranging from a nonresizable About box to a captionless toolbox. The exact type of window that a Form object represents is determined by setting properties of the Form object.

Form Tasks

The following sections describe the tasks that are executed when creating a form.

Set Properties

1. Determine form type.

   BorderStyle

   Sets the type of border and therefore the type of form displayed. Possible values are members of the `FormBorderStyleConstants` enumeration and include 0–vbBSNone for no border, caption, or buttons; 1–vbFixedSingle for a form that cannot be resized but that can show a caption and buttons; 2–vbSizable for a standard form that can be resized and can show a caption and buttons; 3–vbFixedDialog for a form that cannot be resized but can show a caption, control box, and Close button but not other buttons; 4–vbFixedToolWindow for a nonresizable form with a reduced-size caption and a Close button; and 5–vbSizableTool-Window for a resizable form with a reduced-size caption and a Close

button. The following table shows the type of form created for each of the `FormBorderStyleConstants` constants:

Constant	*Border*	*Titlebar*	*Control Menu*	*Buttons*
`vbBSNone`	None	None	None	None
`vbFixedDialog`	Single	Yes	Close, Move only	Close only
`vbFixedSingle`	Single	Yes	Close, Move only	Close only
`vbFixedToolWindow`	Single	Small	No	Close only
`vbFixedSizable` (default)	Resizable	Yes	Yes	All
`vbSizableToolWindow`	Resizable	Small	No	Close only

Caption

The Caption property of a form is displayed on its titlebar and appears in the Windows taskbar. In order for it to appear, the BorderStyle property cannot be set to `vbBSNone`.

For forms with border styles other than `vbBSNone`, display of the titlebar can be suppressed by setting the Caption property to a null string and the ControlBox, MaxButton, and MinButton properties to `False`.

ControlBox

Set to `True` to display a control box in the upper-left corner of the form and a Close button in the upper-right corner. Setting the property to `False` causes these elements not to appear. The value of the BorderStyle property can also affect the presence of a control box.

MinButton, MaxButton

These properties determine whether the appropriate button appears in the upper-right corner of the form. The BorderStyle property's value can affect whether these properties have any effect.

ShowInTaskbar

If `True`, causes a form, even one with its Caption property set to `vbNullString`, to display in the Windows taskbar. Setting the property to `False` causes the form not to display in the taskbar. The value of the BorderStyle property can affect the value of this property.

2. Set graphical properties.

AutoRedraw

When set to `True`, the form's Paint event will not be fired if a portion of the form that was obscured (perhaps by another form) is exposed; painting is handled automatically by an image of the form stored in memory. When set to `False`, the form is not automatically redrawn; instead, the Paint event is fired, and your code is responsible for handling repainting the form. Because setting the AutoRedraw property to `True` stores the image of the form in memory at all times, there can sometimes be an adverse effect on both performance and memory. Therefore, set AutoRedraw to `True` only when the form's contents are not easily redrawn through code.

ClipControls

When the Paint event is fired due to an obscured portion of the form becoming exposed with the AutoRedraw property set to `False`, any graphic methods called from the Paint event are clipped to the newly exposed area when the ClipControls property is set to `True`. When set to `False`, graphic methods called from the Paint event affect the entire form.

There is a noticeable performance hit when the ClipControls property is set to `True` on complex forms.

PaletteMode, Palette

The PaletteMode property controls the way color images are displayed on systems displaying only 256 colors. Possible values are 0–vbPaletteModeHalftone (the default), when the Windows system halftone palette is used to display images; 1–vbPaletteModeUseZOrder, when the topmost control's palette is used for all displayed images; 2–vbPaletteModeCustom, when the palette in the image referred to in the Palette property is used as the palette.*

3. Set behavioral properties.

KeyPreview

When set to `False`, controls on a form receive keyboard events (KeyPress, KeyDown, KeyUp) and the form does not. When set to `True`, the form receives the keyboard events before the control does. This is useful when trapping certain keyboard events (such as application hot keys) in a form.

MDIChild

When set to `True`, the form becomes an MDI child form to be used with an MDI form. This allows the form to respond to certain MDI-specific functions. When set to `False`, the form is a standard form. See Chapter 4, *The MDI Form*, for more information about MDI forms.

Moveable

When set to `False`, the form cannot be moved by the user. When set to `True` (the default), the form can be dragged to a new location by the user by dragging the form's titlebar.

* The PaletteMode property can take on three other values, though none are valid for Form objects or for the controls documented in this book.

ScaleHeight, ScaleWidth

These properties provide the height and width of the window's usable area. This is useful when resizing or repositioning controls on the form. Setting the ScaleHeight or ScaleWidth properties in any way changes the ScaleMode property to `vbUser`.

ScaleLeft, ScaleTop

These properties represent the origin (0,0) of the form. Changing these properties moves the origin to an area other than the top-left corner of the form. Setting the ScaleLeft or ScaleTop properties in any way changes the ScaleMode property to `vbUser`.

ScaleMode

Controls the units reported by ScaleHeight, ScaleWidth, ScaleLeft, and ScaleTop properties. Possible values are 0–vbUser when the ScaleHeight, ScaleWidth, ScaleLeft, or ScaleTop properties have been changed; 1–vbTwips for twips; 2–vbPoints for points (72 points = 1 inch); 3–vbPixes for pixels; 4–vbCharacters for character size (120 Twips wide by 240 Twips high); 5–vbInches for inches; 6–vbMillimeters for millimeters; or 7–vbCentimeters for centimeters.*

StartUpPosition

Sets the location where a form appears when it is first loaded. Possible values are 0–vbStartUpManual to use the form's Left and Top properties, 1–vbStartUpOwner to center the form on its owner form, 2–vbStartUpScreen to center the form on the screen, or 3–vbStartUpWindowsDefault to allow Windows to position the form. The property is read-only at runtime.

WindowState

Contains the current state of the form. Possible values are 0–vbNormal for a normal, restored form; 1–vbMinimize for a minimized form; and 2–vbMaximize for a maximized form. Setting the WindowState property to one of these values will change the current state of the form to that state.

4. Set or retrieve general properties.

ActiveControl

Available at runtime only; returns a reference to the control that currently has the focus. This can be useful when checking which control is active from another control on the form, as in the following code fragment:

```
If Me.ActiveControl Is Me.txtMain Then
   'The txtMain control has the focus.
End If
```

Controls collection, Control object

Available at runtime only; returns one Control object for each control on the form. This is useful when performing one action on all controls in a form, as in the following example:

* The ScaleMode property can take on three other values, though none are valid for Form objects or for the controls documented in this book.

```
Dim ctlVar As Control

For Each ctlVar in Me.Controls
   'Perform action on all controls
Next ctlVar
```

The Controls collection can also be used to dynamically create controls at runtime by using the Control collection's Add method, as follows:

```
Set txtMain = Me.Controls.Add("vb.textbox", "txtMain", Me)
```

When you are dynamically creating controls at runtime, read-only properties such as Index cannot be set. Instead, they use their default values. Therefore, a control array cannot be created dynamically. However, as always, if there is an existing control array, additional elements can be added by using the `Load` statement.

Useful Methods

Circle, Cls, Line, PaintPicture, Point, PSet
: These graphic methods are covered in Chapter 7, *Methods*.

Hide
: Hides the form until it is unloaded or displayed again with the Show method. Modal forms that are hidden in this way release control to the application. This way, information can be retrieved frm the form.

PopupMenu
: Displays a pop-up menu on the form. Parameters are provided for the name of a menu with submenus to pop up (*MenuName*), flags to control the location and behavior of the pop up (*Flags*), coordinates to place the pop up based on the form's ScaleMode (*X* and *Y*), and the name of a menu item to appear in bold (*BoldCommand*). Possible values for the *Flags* parameter are 0–vbPopupMenuLeftButton to force the menu to react to only the mouse's left button, 2–vbPopupMenuRightButton to allow the menu to respond to either button, 0–vbPopupMenuLeftAlign to left-align the menu on the *X* parameter, 4–vbPopupMenuCenterAlign to center the menu on the *X* parameter, and 6–vbPopupMenuRightAlign to right-align the menu on the *X* parameter.

PrintForm
: Sends the image of the form directly to the default printer.

Show
: Loads and displays a form that has not been loaded, or displays a form that has been loaded or has been hidden using the Hide method. A parameter, *Style*, determines whether the form should be modal or nonmodal; it can be set to 0–vbModeless for a nonmodal form or 1–vbModal for a modal form.

TextHeight, TextWidth
: Both of these methods take a string as a parameter. The TextHeight method returns the height of that string based on the form's current font and ScaleMode property. The TextWidth method returns the width of the text.

Write Event Handlers

Activate

Fired when the form receives the focus from a different form in the application. Therefore, only actions that should be executed every time the user switches forms should be fired from this event.

Initialize

Fired when the form is first referenced. The reference can occur due to loading the form, referencing a property of the form, or showing the form.

Load

Fired when the form is loaded. This is the event handler that's generally used to set up the form for use in the application.

Paint

Fired when the form needs to be repainted if the AutoRedraw property is set to `False`. Generally, graphic methods are called from the Paint event.

QueryUnload

Called when the form is about to be unloaded. A parameter, *`Cancel`*, is supplied to control whether the form should actually be unloaded. If the *`Cancel`* parameter is set to `True`, the form will not unload. A second parameter, *`UnloadMode`*, that indicates how the form is being unloaded. Possible values are 0–vbFormControlMenu if the Close option was selected from the form's Control menu, 1–vbFormCode if the form is being unloaded from code, 2–vbAppWindows if Windows is being exited, 3–vbAppTaskManager if the End Task button was pressed from the Task Manager, 4–vbFormMDIForm if the form is an MDI child form (MDIChild property set to `True`) and the MDI form is being closed, or 5–vbFormOwner if the form's owner is being closed.

Resize

Fired when the form is resized. The Resize event is called once when the form is loaded automatically. Any code that moves or resizes controls based on the form's size should be located in the Resize event.

Terminate

Fired when all references to the form have been set to `Nothing` or otherwise have been lost.

Unload

The Unload event is fired when the form is unloading from memory. In order for the Unload event to fire, the QueryUnload event must have already been fired and the QueryUnload event's *`Cancel`* parameter must have remained set to `False`. Cleanup code is usually stored in the Unload event.

Order of Events

Since event handlers frequently make assumptions about the timing of other events, here is the sequence of events when a form is loaded normally at startup or when it is loaded and displayed by calling its Show method:

1. Initialize event
2. Load event

3. Resize event
4. Activate event
5. GotFocus event
6. Paint event

If the form is referenced without being explicitly loaded (as, for example, when a property value is retrieved) or if it is explicitly loaded by the `Load` statement but not shown, only the first two events are fired. When a form that is already loaded is displayed by a call to the Show method, only the Resize, Activate, GotFocus, and Paint events are fired.

When a form is unloaded, if the application remains open, the order in which events are fired is:

1. QueryUnload event
2. Unload event

The Unload event is fired only if the value of the *`Cancel`* parameter of the QueryUnload event procedure remains `False` when the function returns.

While the Terminate event can be fired by implicitly setting the form to `Nothing`, it is normally fired only once per application—when the application terminates. For example, given the following example in which a simple application whose startup procedure is a subroutine named *Main*:

```
Public Sub Main()
    Load Form1
    Load Form2
    Unload Form2
    Unload Form1
End Sub
```

the unload events are fired in the following order:

1. Form 2's QueryUnload event
2. Form 2's Unload event
3. Form 1's QueryUnload event
4. Form 1's Unload event
5. Form 1's Terminate event
6. Form 2's Terminate event

If the `End` statement is used to terminate an application, none of the events typically fired when a form unloads are invoked, including the Terminate event.

Interactions

Action	*Result*
Call Show method	Visible property set to `True`
Call Hide method	Visible property set to `False`
Call Refresh method	Fires Paint event if AutoRedraw is `False`

The Form

CHAPTER 4

The MDI Form

The MDI form is a special type of form that can contain MDI child forms. (The MDI child forms are Visual Basic forms whose MDIChild property is set to `True` instead of its default value of `False`.) Basically, the MDI form has little function aside from serving as a container for its children. This is typical of MDI applications; in Microsoft Word 97, for instance, the appearance of the MDI window changes in response to which child window is active. Besides child forms, only controls that can be aligned to a side of the MDI form's container (the CoolBar, DataGrid, PictureBox, StatusBar, and Toolbar controls) or that lack an interface (the ADO, CommonDialog, Data, ImageList, Internet, MAPISession, MAPIMessages, MSComm, PictureClip, RemoteData, SysInfo, Timer, and Winsock controls) can be placed onto an MDI form.

MDI Form Tasks

The following sections describe the tasks that are executed when creating an MDI form.

Set Properties

1. Set graphical properties.

   StartUpPosition
   : Sets the location where an MDI form will appear when it is first loaded. Possible values are 0–vbStartUpManual to use the MDI form's Left and Top properties, 2–vbStartUpScreen to center the MDI form on the screen, or 3–vbStartUpWindowsDefault to allow Windows to pick a location for the MDI form.

   ScrollBars
   : Controls whether one or more scrollbars are displayed when an MDI child form is partially outside the MDI form's viewable area. When set to `True`, scrollbars appear based on where the child form is located. When

set to `False`, scrollbars never appear, regardless of the location of child forms.

WindowState
: Defines the current state of the MDI form. Possible values are 0–vbNormal for a normal, restored MDI form; 1–vbMinimize for a minimized MDI form; and 2–vbMaximize for a maximized MDI form. Setting the WindowState property to one of these values will change the current state of the MDI form.

2. Set behavioral properties.

AutoShowChildren
: Controls whether an MDI child form should be automatically shown when it is loaded. When set to `True`, the form is shown when it is loaded. When set to `False`, the form is not shown until shown manually through code.

Moveable
: When the Moveable property is set to `False`, the MDI form cannot be moved by the user. When set to `True`, the MDI form can be dragged to a new location by the user by dragging the MDI form's titlebar.

ScaleHeight, ScaleWidth
: These properties provide the height and width of the window's usable area. This is useful when resizing or repositioning controls or MDI child forms on the MDI form.

3. Determine the active child form.

ActiveForm
: The ActiveForm property, which is available only at runtime, returns a reference to the currently active MDI child form contained by the MDI form.

Useful Methods

Arrange
: Arranges the MDI child forms contained by the MDI form. A parameter, *`Arrangement`*, is supplied to control the type of arrangement. Possible values are 0–vbCascade to cascade the MDI child forms from the upper left down and to the right, 1–vbTileHorizontal to tile the MDI child forms horizontally, 2–vbTileVertical to tile the MDI child forms vertically, and 3–vbArrangeIcons to arrange the icons for any minimized MDI child forms.

Hide
: When the Hide method is called, the MDI form becomes hidden until it is unloaded or displayed with the Show method.

Show
: The Show method displays an MDI form that has not been loaded or has been hidden using the Hide method.

Write Event Handlers

Activate

Fired when the MDI form receives the focus from a different form in the application. Therefore, only actions that should be executed every time the user switches forms should be fired from this event.

Initialize

Fired when the MDI form is first referenced. The reference can occur due to loading the MDI form, referencing a property of the MDI form, or showing the MDI form.

Load

Fired when the MDI form is loaded. This is generally where the MDI form is set up for use in the application.

QueryUnload

Called when the MDI form is about to be unloaded. A parameter, *`Cancel`*, is supplied to control whether the MDI form should actually be unloaded. If *`Cancel`* is set to `True`, the MDI form will not unload. A second parameter, *`UnloadMode`*, lets the application know how the MDI form is being unloaded. Possible values are 0–vbFormControlMenu if the Close option was selected from the MDI form's Control menu, 1–vbFormCode if the MDI form is being unloaded from code, 2–vbAppWindows if Windows is being exited, 3–vbApp-TaskManager if the End Task button was pressed from the Task Manager, or 5–vbFormOwner if the Form's owner is being closed.

Resize

Fired when the MDI form is resized. The Resize event is called once when the MDI form is loaded automatically.

Terminate

Fired when all references to the MDI form have been set to `Nothing` or otherwise have been lost.

Unload

Fired when the MDI form is unloading from memory. In order for the Unload event to fire, the QueryUnload event must have already been fired and the QueryUnload event's *`Cancel`* parameter must have remained set to `False`. Cleanup code is usually stored in the Unload event.

Example

Although this chapter details the properties, methods, and events of the MDIForm object, the major task in working with MDI forms is creating and maintaining their child windows. The following example shows how to do this with multiple MDI child forms.

This code is from the MDI form:

```
Option Explicit

'This MDIForm should be set as the StartUp Object. _
  It should contain a menu named mnuFileTop. _
```

```
    mnuFileTop should contain a submenu named mnuFile _
      with its Index property set to 0. _
    There should be a menu named mnuWindowTop. _
    mnuWindowTop should contain a submenu named _
      mnuWindow with its Index property set to 0. _
    mnuWindowTop should also contain a submenu named _
      mnuWindowList with its WindowList property set _
      to True.

Private iFormCount As Integer

Private Sub MDIForm_Load()
    Me.mnuFileTop.Caption = "&File"

    Me.mnuFile(0).Caption = "&New"
    Load Me.mnuFile(1)
    Me.mnuFile(1).Caption = "Confirm &Text"
    Load Me.mnuFile(2)
    Me.mnuFile(2).Caption = "-"
    Load Me.mnuFile(3)
    Me.mnuFile(3).Caption = "E&xit"

    Me.mnuWindowTop.Caption = "&Window"

    Me.mnuWindow(0).Caption = "Tile &Horizontally"
    Load Me.mnuWindow(1)
    Me.mnuWindow(1).Caption = "Tile &Vertically"
    Load Me.mnuWindow(2)
    Me.mnuWindow(2).Caption = "&Cascade"
    Load Me.mnuWindow(3)
    Me.mnuWindow(3).Caption = "&Arrange Icons"
    Load Me.mnuWindow(4)
    Me.mnuWindow(4).Caption = "-"

    Me.mnuWindowList.Caption = "Open Windows"
End Sub

Private Sub mnuFile_Click(Index As Integer)
    Dim frmVar As Form

    Select Case Index
        Case 0  'New
            Set frmVar = New frmChild
            iFormCount = iFormCount + 1
            frmVar.Caption = _
                "New Form Number " & iFormCount
            frmVar.Show
        Case 1  'Confirm text
  'Here we just want to show the text from _
    the current window.
            MsgBox Me.ActiveForm.txtMain.Text
        Case 2  'Exit
            Unload Me
```

The MDI Form

```
        End Select
    End Sub

    Private Sub mnuWindow_Click(Index As Integer)
        Select Case Index
            Case 0    'Tile horizontally
                Me.Arrange 1
            Case 1    'Tile vertically
                Me.Arrange 2
            Case 2    'Cascade
                Me.Arrange 0
            Case 3    'Arrange icons
                Me.Arrange 3
        End Select
    End Sub
```

This code is from frmChild:

```
Option Explicit

'This form should have its Name property set to _
    frmChild. _
  It should also contain a TextBox named txtMain _
    with its MultiLine property set to True.

Private Sub Form_Load()
    Me.txtMain.Text = ""
End Sub

Private Sub Form_Resize()
    If Me.ScaleWidth < 1335 Or Me.ScaleHeight < 555 Then
        Exit Sub
    End If

    Me.txtMain.Move 120, 120, _
        Me.ScaleWidth - 240, Me.ScaleHeight - 240
End Sub
```

Order of Events

In the case of an MDI application, it's often important to understand the sequence of events not only of the MDI form, but of its child forms as well. The following is the sequence of events when an MDI child form is designated as the startup form:

1. The child form's Initialize event
2. The MDI form's Initialize event
3. The MDI form's Load event
4. The child form's Load event
5. The MDI form's Resize event
6. The child form's Resize event
7. The MDI form's Activate event

8. The child form's Activate event
9. The child form's GotFocus event
10. The child form's Paint event

If the MDI form is the startup form and the first child form is loaded by the MDI_ Load event procedure, the firing sequence is slightly different:

1. The MDI form's Initialize event
2. The MDI form's Load event
3. The child form's Initialize event
4. The child form's Load event
5. The MDI form's Resize event
6. The child form's Resize event
7. The child form's Paint event
8. The MDI form's Activate event
9. The child form's Activate event
10. The child form's GotFocus event

When an MDI form is unloaded, if the application remains open, the order in which events are fired is:

1. The MDI form's QueryUnload event
2. The child form's QueryUnload event
3. The child form's Unload event
4. The MDI form's Unload event

However, the Unload event is fired only if the value of the *`Cancel`* parameter of the QueryUnload event procedure for both the MDI form and all child forms remains 0 when the function returns.

An MDI form's Terminate event is fired only once per application, when the application terminates. The order in which the Terminate events fire is:

1. The child form's Terminate event
2. The MDI form's Terminate event

Interactions

Action	*Result*
Call Show method	Visible property set to `True`
Call Hide method	Visible property set to `False`

PART II

Reference

This reference section to Visual Basic controls composes the bulk of the book, and consists of four chapters:

Chapter 5, *Controls*, documents the controls of the Professional and Enterprise Editions of Visual Basic 5.0 and 6.0. If you are using a control with which you're completely unfamiliar, or if you're encountering difficulties using a particular control, you'll want to look up its entry in this section. In addition, if you tend to write your code for individual controls in a rather haphazard way, you'll benefit from the chapter's step-by-step approach to using each control.

Chapter 6, *Properties*, is an alphabetical reference to the properties of controls discussed in Chapter 5, as well as of Form and MDIForm objects. Many of these properties are also discussed in the entry for their respective controls in Chapter 5, or in Chapter 3, *The Form*, and Chapter 4, *The MDI Form*.

Chapter 7, *Methods*, is an alphabetical reference to the methods of the controls discussed in Chapter 5, as well as of Form and MDIForm objects. Once again, many of these properties are also discussed in the entry for their respective controls in Chapter 5, or in Chapter 3 and Chapter 4.

Chapter 8, *Events*, is an alphabetical reference to the events of the controls discussed in Chapter 5, as well as of Form and MDIForm objects. Many of these properties are also discussed in the entry for their respective controls in Chapter 5, or in Chapter 3 and Chapter 4.

CHAPTER 5

Controls

This chapter offers a step-by-step approach to using each of the basic controls included in the Professional and Enterprise editions of Visual Basic 5.0 and 6.0. (For a discussion of which controls are documented here and which ones are excluded and why, see "What This Book Covers" in the Preface.)

The entries for most of the controls follow a uniform format, which includes the following:

- The steps that you should follow either at design time or at runtime to use the control effectively. For the older and more commonly used Visual Basic intrinsic and custom controls, this is largely a matter of setting the appropriate properties.
- Useful methods that you can or must call when using the control.
- The event handlers that you should code to handle the control's events.
- The order in which events are fired, if the precise timing of multiple events is likely to be a source of confusion.
- Any unexpected interactions between properties, methods, and events.

I've departed from this basic organization, though, in the case of more complex controls, which seemed to require an approach more in keeping with their unique features. For these controls, effectively using the control (or even using the control at all) is not a matter of performing some control tasks—that really amounts to setting some properties. Instead, properties, methods, and events are frequently intertwined. Methods, for example, which are merely convenient for some controls, are essential when using others. In addition, some controls, such as the MSChart control, expose object models of varying complexity. These are also documented in these nonstandard entries.

If you're already familiar with a control, you can use its entry as a kind of rough checklist to make sure that you haven't forgotten to set a property or write some code. If you're not familiar with a control, you can use the entry to bring yourself up to speed as quickly as possible. And if your control doesn't behave as you'd expect, the general discussion of individual properties, methods, and events, as well as the sections on the order of events and unexpected interactions, can be invaluable.

VB6 ADO Data Control

The ADO Data Control (ADO DC), provided with the Professional and Enterprise editions of Visual Basic, aims at making viewing and editing information stored in a wide variety of data sources easier. In particular, the ADO Data Control aims at wrapping Microsoft's ActiveX Data Objects (ADO) technology and providing a consistent, Visual Basic-like interface to ADO. ADO and the ADO Data Control in turn are individual components in Microsoft's broader Universal Data Access strategy, which aims at providing seamless access to heterogeneous data sources using a common technology.

Like the Data control, the ADO Data Control makes it fairly easy to link to a variety of data sources. It also handles navigation between records of the resulting recordset and updating of the data displayed by the ADO DC's bound controls.

Note that the precise operation of the ADO Data Control depends on the precise way in which the OLE DB data provider has implemented the features of OLE DB and ADO.

The Microsoft ADO Data Control (*MSADODC.OCX*) is included with Visual Basic Professional and Enterprise editions.

When you add the ADO DC to a project, you automatically add a reference to the Microsoft ActiveX Data Objects Library as well. In fact, most of the constants used by the ADO Data Control are not defined in the control's own type library; instead, they are defined in the ADO type library.

Opening a Data Source

To define a data source, the Data control requires a series of steps that depend on the character of that data source. In contrast, the ADO DC offers a fairly uniform set of steps that can be performed either at design time or at runtime:

1. Assign a valid connection string to the ConnectionString property.

   The connection string indicates how ADO should connect to the data source. Supplying a valid connection string to data access technologies that require them typically is one of the tasks that developers find the most difficult. The ADO DC, however, has made enormous strides forward in simplifying the process of assembling a valid connection string.

   A valid string can be assigned to the ConnectionString property either at design time or at runtime. At design time, this string can be built interactively by opening the ADO DC's custom property page and clicking the Build button on the General tab, as shown in Figure 5-1. In fact, even if you provide the connection string dynamically at runtime, using the control to build a prototype of the string is a good idea.

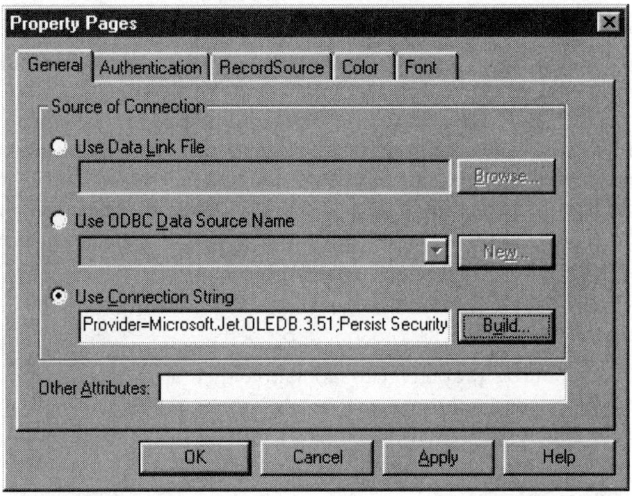

Figure 5-1: The General tab of the ADO DC's custom property page

At runtime, the connection string contains a semicolon-delimited list of name/value pairs that includes the data provider (`Provider=`), the database name (`Data Source=`), and other optional parameters. For example, a ConnectionString property to connect to an Access database named *book.mdb* located in the root directory of the C: drive would look like:

```
Provider=Microsoft.Jet.OLEDB.3.51;Data Source=C:\book.mdb;
UID=Evan;PWD=nutshell
```

2. Optionally, indicate the command type—that is, the resource to be executed or retrieved—by assigning a `CommandTypeEnum` constant to the CommandType property.

   The CommandType property controls the type of Command object used to issue commands to the data source. Possible values are as follows:

Constant	*Value*	*Description*
`adCmdText`	1	An SQL statement.
`adCmdTable`	2	A table name.
`adCmdStoredProc`	4	A stored procedure.
`adCmdUnknown`	8	Unknown; the ADO engine determines the type of Command object to use.

Constant	Value	Description
adExecuteNoRecords	128	An SQL statement or stored procedure that doesn't return rows. It must be added or Ored with either adCmdText or adCmdStoredProc.
adCmdFile	256	The name of a persisted recordset.
adCmdTableDirect	512	A table name whose columns are all returned.

When you use adCmdTable, the ADO engine generates an SQL statement internally. Therefore, using adCmdTable with a RecordSource property of "People" has the same effect as using adCmdText with a RecordSource property of "Select * from People." Because adCmdUnknown must determine the type of command, either of the former choices will generally execute faster.

3. Define the source responsible for returning a recordset to the control by assigning a string to the RecordSource property.

   The RecordSource property can contain either an SQL statement that will return a recordset or the name of a table to be retrieved. The data returned will be available when the next Refresh method is called for the ADO Data Control.

4. Optionally, assign the username to the UserName property and the user's password to the Password property.

   When the data source of the ADO Data Control requires a user to log in, the UserName property should contain the username, and the Password property should contain the password to connect. Note that the Password property is write-only; it cannot be read.

   Note that both the username and the password can be supplied as parameters (the UID and PWD parameters, respectively) within the connection string. If the properties are explicitly assigned and username and password are supplied in the connection string, the connection string's values override the initial property values.

5. If the value of the ConnectionString property was supplied at runtime, call the Refresh method to open the database. (If the values were supplied at design time, the ADO DC will automatically attempt to open the data source when its form loads.)

Defining the Character of the Connection

The ADO Data Control offers a number of properties that allow you to define both the character of the database connection and the precise relationship of the data managed by the control to the database.

Although the properties are all read/write, most changes take effect only after calling the ADO Data Control's Refresh method. The exceptions are CacheSize (takes effect the next time that records are written to the cache) and BOFAction and EOFAction (applies to the recordset immediately).

The fact that you can modify property values without modifying the configuration of the connection to the data source makes retrieving the value of any of these properties problematic; they do not necessarily reflect the state of the underlying database connection. If your program absolutely needs to know the state of a particular setting, see "Working with the Database Directly," under Data Control, later in this chapter.

BOFAction, EOFAction

These properties control what the ADO Data Control does when the record pointer in a recordset is moved before the first record (BOF) or after the last record (EOF). The behavior of the control changes as soon as each property value is modified.

Possible values for BOFAction include the following:

`adDoMoveFirst` *(0)*

Does not allow the record pointer to move before the first record in the recordset. When the user attempts to do so, the WillMove event fires, followed by the EndOfRecordset and the WillMove events.

`adStayBOF` *(1)*

Moves the pointer past the first record and displays an empty record. When the user navigates before the first record, the WillMove event fires, followed by the EndOfRecordset event.

Possible values for EOFAction include the following:

`adDoMoveLast` *(0)*

Does not allow the record pointer to move after the last record in the recordset. When the user attempts to do so, the Willmove event fires, followed by the EndOfRecordset and the WillMove events.

`adStayEOF` *(1)*

Moves the pointer past the last record and displays a blank record. When the user navigates after the last record, the WillMove event fires, followed by the EndOfRecordset event.

`adDoAddNew` *(2)*

Moves the pointer past the last record and then puts the ADO Data Control into AddNew mode. When the user navigates after the last record, these events fire in the following order: WillMove, EndOf-Recordset, WillMove, WillChangeRecord, and RecordChangeComplete.

CacheSize

Controls the number of records cached locally; its default value is 50 records. When the record pointer is moved beyond the number of records indicated by CacheSize, another block of records is retrieved. The value of CacheSize cannot be 0. The cache can be refreshed by calling the Resync method. The default value of CacheSize is 50 records.

CommandTimeout

Indicates the number of seconds to attempt to execute a command on the data source before firing the Error event. Its default value is 30 seconds.

ConnectionTimeout property

Indicates the number of seconds to attempt to connect to the data source before firing the Error event. Its default value is 15 seconds. If set to 0, the control will wait indefinitely until a connection is established.

CursorType, CursorLocation

These properties control how the Recordset contained by the ADO Data Control will be opened. Possible values for the CursorType property include 0–adOpenForwardOnly for a forward-only cursor, 1–adOpenKeyset for a keyset cursor where records added by other users where the cursor was opened are not available, 2–adOpenDynamic for a dynamic cursor where all changes by other users are visible, or 3–adOpenStatic for a copy of the data that will not reflect other users' changes to the data once the cursor is opened. The default value is `adOpenStatic`. Possible values for the Cursor-Location property include 2–adUseServer for a server-side cursor or 3–adUseClient for a client-side cursor. The choice of whether to use client-side or server-side cursors depends on the data source being used.

LockType

Controls the type of locking in effect for the recordset. Possible values include 1–adLockReadOnly, where the control cannot alter the data; 2–adLockPessimistic, so that other users cannot edit records that the current user is editing; 3–adLockOptimistic, so that other users can edit records that the current user is editing and edited records are locked only during the call to the Update method; or 4–adLockBatchOptimistic, the setting required for batch updates. The type of locking that should be used varies based on the application's needs; the default value is `adLockOptimistic`.

MaxRecords

Sets the maximum number of rows that will be returned by the recordset contained by the ADO Data Control. Setting this property to 0, its default value, causes all records to be retrieved.

Mode

Controls how the recordset is opened locally and in relation to other connections to the data source. The property can return or be set to one of the following values from the `ConnectModeEnum` enumeration:

Constant	*Value*	*Description*
`adModeUnknown`	0	The mode is not yet known; this is the default value.
`adModeRead`	1	The data source is read-only.
`adModeWrite`	2	The data source is write-only.
`adModeReadWrite`	3	The data source is opened with standard read/write access.
`adModeShareDenyRead`	4	While this data source is opened, no other process can open the same data source with read access.
`adModeShareDenyWrite`	8	While this data source is opened, no other process can open the same data source with write access.

Constant	*Value*	*Description*
adModeShareExclusive	12	While this data source is opened, no other process can open it.
adModeShareDenyNone	16	While this data source is opened, no other process can open the same data source regardless of access permission.

Defining the ADO DC Interface

The ADO Data Control is typically used as a service component that retrieves a recordset from an OLE DB data provider and provides individual records to its bound data controls. Because of this, the ADO Data Control often remains hidden in an application; that is, its Visible property is set to `False` so that it does not appear on a form. (Note that its Visible property is `True` by default.)

However, the Data control does have an interface, as shown in Figure 5-2. In particular, it allows the user to easily navigate from the current record to the beginning of the recordset, to the end of the recordset, to the previous record, or to the next record. For the most part, this navigation is performed automatically, without the need for you to write any code. By setting its Orientation property to 0–adHorizontal, the control can be displayed horizontally, as it is on the right in Figure 5-2; by setting its Orientation property to 1–adVertical, it can be displayed vertically, as it is on the left in Figure 5-2.

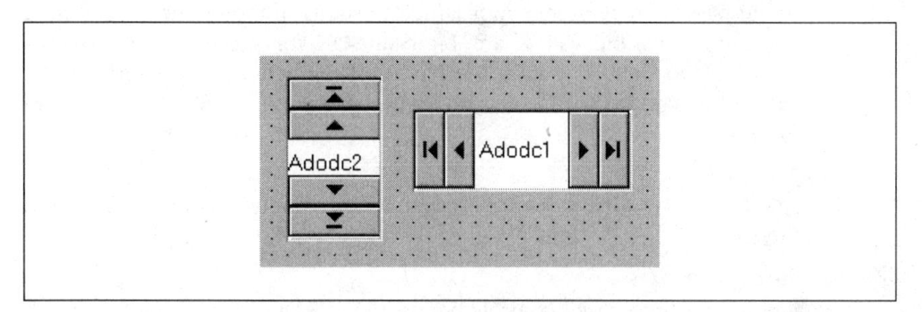

Figure 5-2: ADO Data Controls oriented horizontally and vertically

In addition, the control provides a text box area that can be used in either of two ways:

- It can simply be left blank (this is controlled by its Caption property), and optionally its color can be modified to match that of some other interface component, most likely the scrollbars (this is controlled by its BackColor property). For example:

```
adoMain.Caption = ""
adoMain.BackColor = vbScrollBars
```

- It can display some information about the recordset or the current record, such as a record number, a count of the total number of records in the recordset, or both, as in the following example:

```
Private Sub adoMain_MoveComplete( _
        ByVal adReason As ADODB.EventReasonEnum, _
```

```
        ByVal pError As ADODB.Error, _
        adStatus As ADODB.EventStatusEnum, _
        ByVal pRecordset As ADODB.Recordset)
    Me.datMain.Caption = LTrim(Me.adoMain.Recordset!FirstName _
        & " ") Trim(Me.adoMain.Recordset!LastName)
End Sub
```

Handling Database Operations

The ADO Data Control features one method and a number of events that can aid in performing basic database operations, such as navigating a recordset, performing data validation, handling updates to the database, and synchronizing the data displayed by bound controls with values contained in the database. They are:

EndOfRecordset event

Fired whenever the record pointer is moved past the end of file (EOF). The event is passed the following parameters:

`fMoreData`

A flag passed by reference indicating whether more data has been added to the recordset. Its default value is `True`. By setting it to `False` before the event handler returns, you indicate to the control that you do not intend to add a new record.

`adStatus`

Value passed by reference indicating the status of the operation that fired the event. Possible values are 1–adStatusOK for success or 3–adStatus-CantDeny to not allow the cancellation of the action. The event handler can set this value to 5–adStatusUnwantedEvent to stop this event from firing again.

`pRecordset`

A reference to the Recordset object whose EndOfRecordset event has fired.

UpdateControls method

Updates the contents of all controls bound to the ADO Data Control to match the recordset.

WillChangeField, FieldChangeComplete events

Called before one or more fields in a recordset is about to be changed (Will-ChangeField) and after they have been changed (FieldChangeComplete). The events are passed the following parameters:

`cFields`

Number of fields being changed.

`Fields`

A variant string array containing the field value before the change (in the case of WillChangeField) and after the change (in the case of FieldChangeComplete).

`pError` *(FieldChangeComplete only)*

If `adStatus` is `adStatusErrorsOccurred`, the ADO Error object; otherwise, an object variable whose value is `Nothing`.

adStatus

A value passed by reference indicating the status of the change.

For the WillChangeField event, possible values are 1–adStatusOK if the operation that raised the event is successful or 3–adStatusCantDeny if the change cannot be cancelled. You can set ***adStatus*** to 4–adStatusCancel to cancel the change if ***adStatus*** did not equal `adStatusCantDeny` or to 5–adStatusUnwantedEvent to stop this event from firing.

For the FieldChangeComplete event, possible values are 1–adStatusOK if the change completed successfully or 2–adStatusErrorsOccurred if errors have occurred; in the latter case, ***pError*** contains a reference to the Error object with information about the error. You can set ***adStatus*** to 5–adStatusUnwantedEvent to stop future notification of this event.

pRecordset

A reference to the Recordset object whose field is being changed.

WillChangeRecord, RecordChangeComplete events

Called before one or more records in a recordset are about to be changed (WillChangeRecord) and after they have been changed (RecordChangeComplete). The events are passed the following parameters:

adReason

A member of the `EventReasonEnum` enumeration indicating the reason for the change. Its value can be 1–adRsnAddNew for new records, 2–adRsnDelete for deletions, 3–adRsnUpdate for modifications to existing records, 4–adRsnUndoUpdate to undo updates, 5–adRsnUndoAddNew to undo the addition of new records, 6–adRsnUndoDelete to undo deletions, or 11–adRsnFirstChange to modify an existing record for the first time.

cRecords

Number of records being changed.

pError (RecordChangeComplete only)

If ***adStatus*** is `adStatusErrorsOccurred`, the ADO Error object; otherwise, an object variable whose value is `Nothing`.

adStatus

A value passed by reference indicating the status of the change.

For the WillChangeRecord event, possible values are 1–adStatusOK if the operation that raised the event is successful or 3–adStatusCantDeny if the change cannot be cancelled. Set ***adStatus*** to 4–adStatusCancel to cancel the change if the initial value of ***adStatus*** is not `adStatusCantDeny` or to 5–adStatusUnwantedEvent to stop this event from firing.

For the RecordChangeComplete event, possible values are 1–adStatusOK if the change completed successfully or 2–adStatusErrorsOccurred if errors have occurred; in the latter case, ***pError*** contains a reference to the Error object with information about the error. You can set ***adStatus*** to 5–adStatusUnwantedEvent to stop future notification of this event.

pRecordset

A reference to the Recordset object whose records are being changed.

WillChangeRecordset, RecordsetChangeComplete events

Called when the recordset as a whole is about to be updated in some way (WillChangeRecordset) and after it has been updated (RecordsetChangeComplete). The events are supplied the following parameters:

`adReason`

A member of the `EventReasonEnum` enumeration indicating the reason for the change. Its value can be 7–adRsnReQuery when the data source is requeried, 8–adRsnReSynch when the cache and the data source are resynchronized, or 9–adRsnClose when the data source is closed. The documentation also lists `adRsnOpen`, though this is not a valid constant.

`pError` (RecordsetChangeComplete only)

If *`adStatus`* is `adStatusErrorsOccurred`, the ADO Error object; otherwise, an object variable whose value is `Nothing`.

`adStatus`

A value passed by reference indicating the status of the change.

For the WillChangeRecordset event, possible values are 1–adStatusOK if the raising operation is successful or 3–adStatusCantDeny if the change cannot be cancelled. You can set *`adStatus`* to 4–adStatusCancel to cancel the change if the initial value of *`adStatus`* is not `adStatusCantDeny` or to 5–adStatusUnwantedEvent to stop this event from firing.

For the RecordsetChangeComplete event, possible values are 1–adStatusOK if the change completed successfully or 2–adStatusErrorsOccurred if errors have occurred; in the latter case, *`pError`* contains a reference to the Error object with information about the error. You can set *`adStatus`* to 5–adStatusUnwantedEvent to stop future notification of this event.

`pRecordset`

A reference to the Recordset object that is being changed.

WillMove, MoveComplete events

Called when the record pointer is about to be moved (WillMove) and after it has moved (MoveComplete). The event is passed the following parameters:

`adReason`

The reason for the move. Possible values are 7–adRsnRequery when the data source is requeried, 10–adRsnMove for an unspecified move, 12–adRsnMoveFirst when the pointer is moved to the beginning of the recordset, 13–adRsnMoveNext when the pointer is moved to the next record, 14–adRsnMovePrevious when the pointer is moved to the prior record, and 15–adRsnMoveLast when the pointer is moved to the end of the recordset.

`pError` (MoveComplete only)

If *`adStatus`* is `adStatusErrorsOccurred`, a reference to an ADO Error object; otherwise, an object variable whose value is `Nothing`.

`adStatus`

A value passed by reference indicating the status of the move.

For the WillMove event, possible values are 1–adStatusOK if the operation that raised the event is successful or 3–adStatusCantDeny if the move cannot be cancelled. You can set *adStatus* to 4–adStatusCancel to cancel the move if the initial value of *adStatus* is not adStatus-CantDeny or to 5–adStatusUnwantedEvent to stop this event from firing.

For the MoveComplete event, possible values are 1–adStatusOK if the move completed successfully or 2–adStatusErrorsOccurred if errors have occurred; in the latter case, *pError* contains a reference to the Error object with information about the error. You can set *adStatus* to 5–adStatusUnwantedEvent to stop future notification of this event.

Handling Errors

Most data access errors that occur as a result of the operation of the ADO Data Control are not part of Visual Basic's error-handling system. That is, they cannot be handled by the standard VBA `ON ERROR` statement. This makes a good deal of sense: while most Visual Basic runtime errors are "bad" and more often than not indicate an error in program design or execution, data access errors are often routine and need not interrupt program execution.

The ADO Data Control signals the presence of a data access error in its own operation or that of its bound controls by firing the Error event. The event is passed the following parameters:

ErrorNumber
: An integer indicating the error number. This is an ADO error code, rather than a VBA error code.

Description
: A string containing the text of the error message.

SCode
: A long containing the error code returned by the OLE DB data provider.

Source
: The name of the control.

HelpFile
: The location of a standard help file with additional information about the error.

HelpContext
: The help context for the error information within *HelpFile*.

fCancelDisplay
: A Boolean passed by reference that should be set to `False` to stop the error message from being displayed to the user. Its default value is `True`.

Accessing the ADO Recordset Directly

The ADO Data Control handles the details of basic navigation through the user interface and of updating the contents of bound controls. Although these features are very convenient, the functionality of the ADO DC often fails to meet the requirements of most database applications. However, the control allows you to take advantage of the functionality of ADO through its Recordset property.

The Recordset property returns a reference to the ADO Recordset object contained by the ADO Data Control. This Recordset object can then be used in code to perform additional operations not available through the ADO Data Control. In addition, this property can be set to any valid existing ADO Recordset object.

Once you have a valid reference to the Recordset object, you can access its properties and methods. Some of the more useful of these include the following:

AbsolutePage, PageCount, PageSize properties
: These properties aid in dividing a recordset into logical pages, which can then be accessed individually. The PageSize property defines the number of records that reside on each page. This automatically sets the PageCount property, which indicates the total number of pages, according to the number of records in the recordset. Retrieving the value of the AbsolutePage property indicates the page on which the current record resides; setting it moves the record pointer to the first record of a page.

AbsolutePosition property
: Returns the number of the current record within the recordset. If the number cannot be derived, the AbsolutePosition property returns -1–adPosUnknown if the position is unknown, -2–adPosBOF if the pointer is at the beginning of file, or -3–adPosEOF if the pointer is at the end of file.

ActiveConnection property
: Returns the connection string (see the ConnectionString property under ADO Data Control).

AddNew method
: Begins to edit a new record in the recordset. This affects the Recordset object's EditMode property. No changes are saved until the Update method is called. Changes can be cancelled by calling the CancelUpdate method.

BOF, EOF properties
: These read-only properties report whether the record pointer is at the beginning of the recordset (BOF) or the end of the recordset (EOF). When this is the case, the appropriate property returns `True`; otherwise, it returns `False`.

Bookmark property
: Contains an identifier that can be used to store, and later to return to, a record within a recordset.

CacheSize property
: Controls the number of records cached by the data source. When the record pointer is moved beyond the extent of the cache, another block of up to ***`CacheSize`*** records is retrieved. The value of CacheSize cannot be 0.

: The CacheSize property of a Recordset object is the same as the CacheSize property of the ADO Data Control from which the recordset was derived.

Cancel method
: Causes a pending recordset command to be cancelled.

CancelBatch method
: Causes a pending batch update to be cancelled. Its syntax is:

```
rsVar.CancelBatch AffectRecords
```

where *AffectRecords* specifies the records to be affected by the cancellation and can be one of the following constants: 1–adAffectCurrent to cancel only the current record, 2–adAffectGroup to cancel all records valid for the current setting of the Filter property, or 3–adAffectAll to cancel all records.

CancelUpdate method

Causes a current AddNew or editing action to be cancelled.

Clone method

Returns an identical recordset to the current Recordset object. Its syntax is:

```
rsVar.Clone(LockType)
```

where *LockType* specifies the type of locking to use on the new recordset. *LockType* can be set to 0–adLockUnspecified to use the same locking as the original recordset or 1–adLockReadOnly to set the new recordset to be read-only.

Delete method

Deletes the current record from the recordset. Its syntax is:

```
rsVar.Delete AffectRecords
```

where *AffectRecords* optionally deletes more than one record. Possible values for *AffectRecords* are 1–adAffectCurrent to delete only the current record (the default) or 2–adAffectGroup to delete all records valid for the current setting of the Filter property.

EditMode property

Indicates what action is currently taking place in the control. Possible values are 0–dbEditNone when no edit is in progress, 1–dbEditInProgress when an edit is taking place, or 2–dbEditAdd when a new record is being added.

Filter property

Causes certain records to be ignored when displaying the recordset. Possible values for the Filter property include a valid SQL `Where` clause, an array of bookmarks (see the Bookmark property), 0–adFilterNone for no records filtered, 1–adFilterPendingRecords to show only changed records waiting to be sent to the server, 2–adFilterAffectedRecords to show only records affected by the last command, 3–adFilterFetchedRecords to show only records retrieved by the last cache, or 5–adFilterConflictingRecords to show only records that were unsuccessful in the last batch update.

LockType property

Indicates the types of locks placed on the recordset; it is the same as the LockType property of the ADO Data Control from which the recordset was derived.

MarshalOptions property

Controls which records are sent back to the server. Possible values are 0–adMarshalAll to send all rows or 1–adMarshalModifiedOnly to send only rows that have been modified.

MaxRecords property

Indicates the maximum number of records to return from a query; it is the same as the MaxRecords property of the ADO Data Control from which the recordset was derived.

Move method

Moves the record pointer. Its syntax is:

```
rsVar.Move NumRecords, Start
```

where ***NumRecords*** specifies the number of records to move, and ***Start*** indicates the point of origin from which ***NumRecords*** is counted. Possible values for ***Start*** are 0–adBookmarkCurrent to offset from the current record, 1–adBookmarkFirst to offset from the first record in the recordset, or 2–adBookmarkLast to offset from the last record in the recordset.

MoveNext, MovePrevious, MoveFirst, MoveLast methods

These navigational methods reposition the record pointer to the next record, previous record, first record, or last record within the recordset, respectively.

RecordCount property

Returns either the number of rows in the recordset or -1, indicating that the number of rows cannot be determined. Issuing a MoveLast method followed by a MoveFirst method generally forces the RecordCount property to be populated with the correct value but can cause a serious performance hit.

Requery method

Causes the command that created the recordset to be executed again on the data source.

Resync method

Causes the data in the recordset to be refreshed from the data source.

Sort property

A comma-delimited string of field names to sort on, each followed by a space and the keyword `ASCENDING` or `DESCENDING` (or `ASC` and `DESC`), depending on the sort order desired.

Source property

The Source property of a recordset is the same as the RecordSource property of the ADO Data Control from which the recordset was derived; it indicates the source of the recordset's data and can be an SQL statement, a table name, or a stored procedure.

State property

Returns the current state of an asynchronous command while it is running. Possible values include 0–adStateClose when the recordset is closed, 1–adStateOpen when the recordset is open, 2–adStateConnecting when the recordset is connecting, 4–adStateExecuting when a command is executing, or 8–adStateFetching when data is being retrieved from the data source.

Status property

Indicates the status of the current record as it relates to the last batch update. Possible values for the Status property are:

Constant	*Value*	*Description*
`adRecOK`	0	The record was updated.
`adRecNew`	1	The record was added.
`adRecModified`	2	The record was modified.

Constant	Value	Description
adRecDeleted	4	The record was deleted.
adRecUnmodified	8	The record was not modified.
adRecInvalid	16	Unsuccessful: invalid bookmark.
adRecMultipleChanges	64	Unsuccessful: update affected multiple records.
adRecPendingChanges	128	Unsuccessful: record still pending was inserted into the data source.
adRecCancelled	256	Unsuccessful: cancelled.
adRecCantRelease	1,024	Unsuccessful: record locking.
adRecConcurrencyViolation	2,048	Unsuccessful: concurrency issue with optimistic record locking.
adRecIntegrityViolation	4,096	Unsuccessful: integrity errors.
adRecMaxChangesExceeded	8,192	Unsuccessful: pending change limit exceeded.
adRecObjectOpen	16,384	Unsuccessful: object was opened elsewhere.
adRecOutOfMemory	32,768	Unsuccessful: memory error.
adRecPermissionDenied	65,536	Unsuccessful: insufficient rights.
adRecSchemaViolation	131,072	Unsuccessful: violation of a data source schema element.
adRecDBDeleted	262,144	Unsuccessful: record no longer exists.

Update method

Causes the pending editing or AddNew action to be saved. Its syntax is:

```
Recordset.Update Fields, Values
```

where ***Fields*** is the name of a field, an array containing the names of fields, or an array containing the ordinal positions of fields whose values are to be modified and ***Values*** is a single value or an array of values that are to be used to update ***Fields***.

UpdateBatch method

Causes all batch updates to be sent to the data source. Its syntax is:

```
rsVar.UpdateBatch AffectRecords
```

where ***AffectRecords*** defines the records affected by the update; possible values are 1–adAffectCurrent to update only the current record, 2–adAffectGroup to update all records valid for the current setting of the Filter property, or 3–adAffectAll to update all records.

Order of Events

In general, events in the ADO DC are paired into Will(*event*) and (*event*)Complete events. Although other events may occur in between, unless cancelled, the second event will fire.

When a recordset is returned to the control, the following events are fired:

1. The WillMove event with an *adReason* parameter of `adRsnMove` and an *adStatus* parameter of `adStatusCantDeny`.
2. The MoveComplete event with an *adReason* parameter of `adRsnMove`.
3. The WillMove event with an *adReason* parameter of `adRsnMove` and an *adStatus* parameter of `adStatusOK`.
4. The MoveComplete event with an *adReason* parameter of `adRsnMove`.

When a field is changed, and the record pointer is moved to another record, the following events are fired:

1. The WillChangeRecord event
2. The WillChangeField event
3. The FieldChangeComplete event
4. The RecordChangeComplete event
5. The WillMove event
6. The WillChangeRecord event
7. The RecordChangeComplete event
8. The MoveComplete event

The ADO DC's Recordset property is set to a valid ADO Recordset object when the following events are fired:

1. The WillChangeRecordset event
2. The RecordsetChanged event
3. The WillMove event
4. The MoveComplete event

The *adStatus* parameter of a Will(action) event is set to `adStatusCancel` by firing the Error event.

Animation Control

The Animation control is useful for playing certain *.AVI* files in an application. These *.AVI* files cannot contain sound and must be uncompressed or RLE compressed. In other words, the Animation control is not intended as a multimedia viewer; instead, it aims at adding simple animated effects to forms and dialogs. A common example of an Animation control playing an *.AVI* file is the animated recycle bin in the Emptying the Recycle Bin dialog. (See Figure 5-3.) A selection of these *.AVI* files are on the Visual Studio CD in the *\Common\Graphics\AVIS* folder.

The Animation control is contained in the Windows Common Controls 2 (*COMCT232.OCX*) that comes with Visual Basic Professional and Enterprise editions.

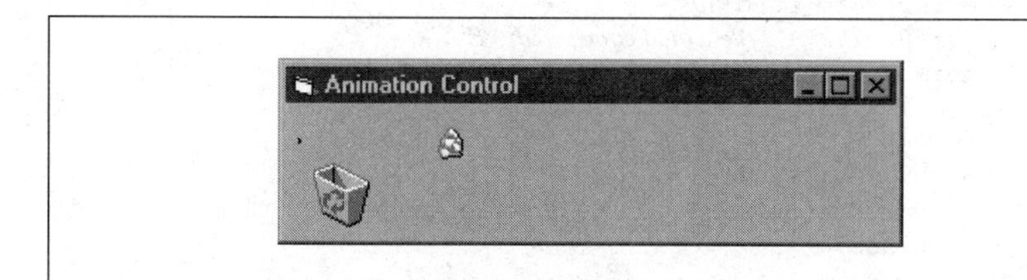

Figure 5-3: The Animation control playing the FILENUKE.AVI animation

Control Tasks

The following categories reflect the tasks that are executed when creating an Animation control.

Set Properties

1. Set behavior.

    AutoPlay

    When set to `True`, an *.AVI* file begins playing as soon as it is loaded into the Animation control. The only ways to stop it from playing are to set the AutoPlay property to `False` or use the Close method to unload it.

    Center

    When set to `True`, the *.AVI* file is centered within the Animation control. When set to `False` (the default), the *.AVI* is aligned to the upper-left corner of the control. However, if the control is not large enough to display the entire animation, the picture will be clipped. Center is a design-time-only property.

    BackStyle

    When set to 0–cc2BackstyleTransparent (its default value), the Animation control's BackColor will show through transparent portions of the *.AVI* file. When set to 1–cc2BackstyleOpaque, the *.AVI* file's background color will be used. BackStyle is a design-time-only property.

Useful Methods

Open, Close

The Open method loads an *.AVI* file into the Animation control. The Close method unloads the *.AVI* file.

Play, Stop

These methods control whether the *.AVI* file loaded into the Animation control is being played. The following example shows how an Animation control can be loaded with an *.AVI* file and played.

Example

```
Option Explicit
'For this example, create the following controls: _
  an Animation control named aniMain with the Center _
  property set to True, and the BackStyle property _
  set to 0-cc2BackstyleTransparent.
```

```
Private Sub Form_Load()
  'I used the FILENUKE.AVI file which comes with VB.
   Me.aniMain.Open "FILENUKE.AVI"
End Sub

Private Sub Form_Resize()
  If Me.ScaleHeight < 555 Or Me.ScaleWidth < 1095 Then _
      Exit Sub

   Me.aniMain.Move 120, 120, Me.ScaleWidth - 240, _
                     Me.ScaleHeight - 240
End Sub

Private Sub Form_Activate()
   Me.aniMain.Play
End Sub
```

Interactions

Action	*Result*
Load an *.AVI* file is loaded into an Animation control with the AutoPlay property set to `True`.	The *.AVI* begins playing immediately.
Call the Stop method on an Animation control that has its AutoPlay Property set to `True` and has an *.AVI* loaded.	An error occurs.
Call the Play method on an Animation control that does not have an *.AVI* loaded.	An error occurs.

CheckBox Control

A checkbox consists of a caption and a square graphic that can appear checked, empty (unchecked), or grayed to reflect the yes (or `True` or on), no (or `False` or off), and unavailable (or inapplicable) states, respectively, as Figure 5-4 illustrates. Ordinarily, when a checkbox is grayed, it appears both checked and grayed. For instance, in a word processing application, a checkbox labeled Bold, when checked, indicates that the selected text is bold; when unchecked, that the selected text is not bold; and when grayed, that the selection consists of text that is bolded as well as unbolded. While checkboxes are very similar to option buttons, multiple checkboxes in one container can be selected at once.

Figure 5-4: The CheckBox control in its three states

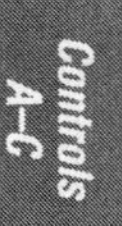

A lightweight version of the CheckBox control is also available; see Windowless Controls, later in this chapter.

Control Tasks

The following categories reflect the tasks that are executed when creating checkboxes.

Set Properties

1. Set value (optional).

   The three states of a checkbox are represented by the following constants:

Constant	*Value*	*Description*
`vbUnchecked`	0	Unchecked or unselected.
`vbChecked`	1	Checked or selected.
`vbGrayed`	2	Grayed; the Value property can be set to `vbGrayed` only at design time or by code at runtime, and not through the user interface at runtime.

   Use these values to show the user when the data is `True`, `False`, or `Unavailable`.

2. Specify graphical label (optional).

   Style
   Set to the default, 0 or `vbButtonStandard`, to display the standard, square graphic. Set to 1 or `vbButtonGraphical` to display an alternate graphic for the box specified by the Picture, DisabledPicture, and DownPicture properties.

   Picture
   Pictures can be set at design time to a graphic file on the disk or at runtime to any picture object. The picture will be invisible unless the Style property is set to 1–Graphical.

   DisabledPicture
   The image to be used when the Enabled property is `False`.

   DownPicture
   The image to be used when the button is pressed. If no image file is supplied, the image will be the one specified in the Picture property. Although the selected option will appear different from unselected options, using a specific picture for this is usually desirable.

When using graphical labels with checkboxes, grayed (unavailable) options will appear identical to unchecked options.

Write Event Handlers

Click

Takes place when the user clicks a checkbox with the mouse or presses a keyboard alternative to select the checkbox.

Example

The following example illustrates the changes in the state of the CheckBox control, which depend on items selected in a list box (illustrated in Figure 5-5):

```
Option Explicit

'For this example, createa ListBox called _
  lstNumbers with the MultiSelect property _
  set to 1–Simple.

Dim chkEven As CheckBox
Dim chkOdd As CheckBox

Private Sub Form_Load()
  'Create and/or set up controls.
   Me.Caption = "CheckBox Example"

   Me.lstNumbers.TabIndex = 0
   Me.lstNumbers.AddItem 1
   Me.lstNumbers.AddItem 2
   Me.lstNumbers.AddItem 3
   Me.lstNumbers.AddItem 4
   Me.lstNumbers.AddItem 5
   Me.lstNumbers.AddItem 6
   Me.lstNumbers.AddItem 7
   Me.lstNumbers.AddItem 8
   Me.lstNumbers.AddItem 9
   Me.lstNumbers.AddItem 10

   Set chkEven = Me.Controls.Add("vb.checkbox", "chkEven", Me)
   chkEven.Visible = True
   chkEven.Caption = "Even Numbers Selected"

   Set chkOdd = Me.Controls.Add("vb.checkbox", "chkOdd", Me)
   chkOdd.Visible = True
   chkOdd.Caption = "Odd Numbers Selected"
End Sub
```

```
Private Sub Form_Resize()
   If Me.ScaleHeight < 1425 Or Me.ScaleWidth < 1335 Then _
      Exit Sub

   Me.lstNumbers.Move 120, 120, Me.ScaleWidth - 240, _
                      Me.ScaleHeight - 1110
   chkEven.Move 120, Me.ScaleHeight - 870, _
                Me.ScaleWidth - 240, 315
   chkOdd.Move 120, Me.ScaleHeight - 435, _
                Me.ScaleWidth - 240, 315
End Sub

Private Sub lstNumbers_Click()
   'This will fire every time the selection changes.
    UpdateCheckBoxes
End Sub

Private Sub UpdateCheckBoxes()
   Dim iCtr As Integer
   Dim iEven As Integer
   Dim iOdd As Integer

  'First, we'll get a count of odd and even numbers selected.
   For iCtr = 0 To Me.lstNumbers.ListCount - 1
      If Me.lstNumbers.Selected(iCtr) Then
         If Val(Me.lstNumbers.List(iCtr)) Mod 2 = 0 Then
            iEven = iEven + 1
         Else
            iOdd = iOdd + 1
         End If
      End If
   Next iCtr

  'Then we'll update the state of the CheckBoxes based on those counts.
   If iEven = 0 Then
      If iOdd = 0 Then
         chkEven.Value = vbUnchecked
         chkOdd.Value = vbUnchecked
      Else
         chkEven.Value = vbUnchecked
         chkOdd.Value = vbChecked
      End If
   Else
      If iOdd = 0 Then
         chkEven.Value = vbChecked
         chkOdd.Value = vbUnchecked
      Else
         chkEven.Value = vbGrayed
         chkOdd.Value = vbGrayed
      End If
   End If
End Sub
```

Figure 5-5: A CheckBox responding to other form elements

Interactions

Action	*Result*
Change a checkbox's Value property.	Fires the checkbox's Click event.
Click event fires.	Changes the checkbox's Value property to `vbChecked` if it is `vbUnChecked` and to `vbUnchecked` if it is either `vbChecked` or `vbGrayed`.
Checkbox's Click event procedure invoked from code.	None; the checkbox's Value property remains unchanged. (You might expect that invoking the Click event handler is equivalent to the user clicking on the checkbox; it is not.)

ComboBox Control

The combo box allows the user to select an item from a scrollable list. This list can be made invisible or can be "dropped down" from the combo box.

The combo box can be populated at design time by entering data into the List property. Multiple items can be added by pressing CTRL-Enter after each item. More commonly, though, data is assigned to a combo box at runtime by calling the AddItem method, usually in the Form_Initialize or Form_Load event procedure.

A lightweight version of the ComboBox control is also available; see Windowless Controls, later in this chapter.

Control Tasks

The following categories reflect the tasks that are executed when creating and working with a combo box.

Set Properties

1. Specify style (optional).

   Style

   When set to 0–DropDown Combo, the user can type directly into the text portion of the combo box and enter an item not present in the list. When set to 1–Simple Combo, the combo box acts the same as a drop-down combo, except that the list portion is always visible. When set to 2–DropDown List, only items in the list can be selected. Figure 5-6 shows the combo boxes created by the various values of the Style property.

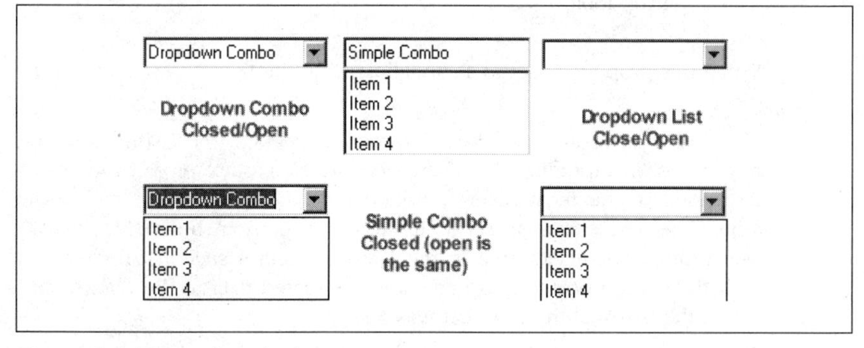

Figure 5-6: Types of combo boxes

2. Set the list.

   List( )

   The contents of a list box are contained in this array, which is read-only at runtime. Items are added to this list interactively at design time or by using the AddItem method at runtime. Because some types of combo boxes allow for the user to enter an item not in the list, the Text property should be used to determine the current value.

   ListIndex

   This read/write property contains the currently selected item in a combo box. If no item is selected, this property will contain -1. Otherwise, it will contain the zero-based element number of the List array; in this case, the value of ListIndex ranges from 0 to `ListCount - 1`.

   ListCount

   This read-only property contains the total number of items in a combo box. The items of the list can then be iterated with a `For...Next` loop like the following:

```
For counter = 0 to lstVar.ListCount - 1
   < statements >
Next
```

Note that the `For Each...Next` construct cannot be used to iterate the items in a list box.

Text

Provides the contents of the currently selected item in the list if an item is selected. When the Style property is set to 0–DropDown Combo or 1–Simple Combo, the Text property can also display a value entered by the user that is not present in the list.

ItemData( )

Each item in the list has an additional, hidden value associated with it. This long value is contained in the ItemData array, each element of which corresponds to an element of the List array. Generally, this array is used to associate the descriptive, visible items in the list with additional data, such as a database key.

3. Specify sorting (optional).

Sorted

When this property is set to `True`, all items in the list are alphabetized.

NewIndex

When new items are added to a sorted combo box, the ListIndex of the new items is unpredictable. Therefore, the NewIndex property contains the index of the most recently added item. Using this, you will know where the new item is to set its ItemData property. A function similar to the AddItemToList example in the ListBox Control section can be used with the combo box to add items and associated data to the control and return the index of the row that was added.

4. Set sizing mode (optional).

IntegralHeight

This property can be set to `True` only when the style of the combo box is set to 1–Simple Combo. When it is set to `True`, the simple combo will resize its height only to complete visible rows. If a height is set that allows for half a row to be visible, that row will not be shown at all and the combo box will resize to one less row. When set to `False`, the combo box will resize like all other controls.

5. Determine visible items (optional).

TopIndex

This property contains the index of the top visible item on the list. The value of this property will change as the user scrolls through the list and can also be placed under program control.

Useful Methods

AddItem

When adding items to a combo box, the AddItem method accepts parameters for both the text of the item to be added as well as the index to use for that item. When the *`Index`* parameter is supplied with a sorted combo box, the item will still be added in the position set by the Index. This can cause items to be added out of the sort order. This can be easily avoided by not passing the *`Index`* parameter.

RemoveItem

To remove items from a combo box, pass the Index of the item to remove to the RemoveItem method.

Clear

This method removes all items from the combo box.

Write Event Handlers

Change

In the case of simple and drop-down combo boxes, indicates that the text in the text box portion of the control has changed.

Click

Anytime the user scrolls through the list selecting items, whether by mouse, keyboard, or code, the Click event is fired. When used with the ListIndex property, you can react to various items being selected.

Scroll

The Scroll event is called each time the combo box is scrolled, either by a Mouse or Keyboard event. When used with the TopIndex property, this will help to ascertain which items of the list are currently being displayed.

Example

A common need in applications is to add items to the list when they are entered in a drop-down or simple combo. This can be achieved as follows:

```
Private Sub cboMain_LostFocus()
    Dim bFound As Boolean
    Dim iCtr As Integer

    If cboMain.ListIndex = -1 Then
    'Item is not on the list
        If IsEmpty(cboMain.Text) Then
        'Nothing entered
            Exit Sub
        End If
        For iCtr = 0 To cboMain.ListCount - 1
        'See if entered item is in the list
            If StrComp( _
                Trim(cboMain.List(iCtr)), _
                Trim(cboMain.Text), _
                vbTextCompare) = 0 Then
                    'Disregard case
                bFound = True
                    'It is in the list
                Exit For
            End If
        Next iCtr
        If bFound Then
            cboMain.ListIndex = iCtr
            'Go to entered item
        Else
            cboMain.AddItem cboMain.Text
            'Add entered item
```

```
            cboMain.ListIndex = cboMain.NewIndex
            'Go to new item
        End If
    End If
End Sub
```

Interactions

Action	*Result*
Move through the list using the keyboard, mouse, or code.	Fires Click event. Changes values of ListIndex and Text properties. If the list is scrolled, then after the previous action, the Scroll event is fired and the TopIndex property is updated.
Select an item in a list.	Fires Click event.
Assign a value to the Text property.	For simple and drop-down combo boxes, fires the Change event.
Change the ListIndex property in code.	Fires the Click event.
Resize the control, or the Height property is modified in code, if IntegralHeight is `True`.	Further adjusts the Height property to display only complete items.

CommandButton Control

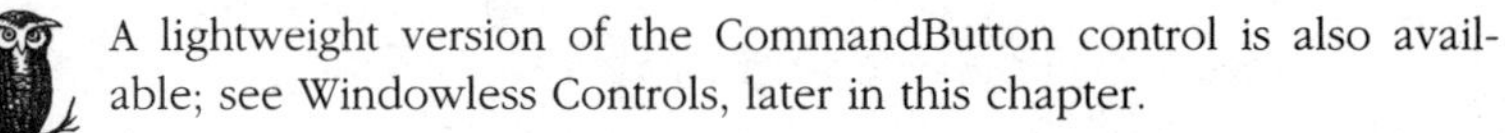

A lightweight version of the CommandButton control is also available; see Windowless Controls, later in this chapter.

A command button is a one-click control for confirming a set of selections, for initiating a new action, or for ending the current process. The surface of a button can display a text caption, a graphic image, or both. The information on the button should concisely indicate the effect of a click. Visually, a click produces a push-button effect on the screen; the button is released into its normal position when the mouse button is released.

When using a command button to interrupt or end a process, be sure that the running process contains *DoEvents* commands to allow it to respond to the command button.

Control Tasks

The following categories reflect the tasks that are executed when creating a command button.

Set Properties

1. Specify graphical label (optional).

Style

When set to the default, 0 or `vbButtonStandard`, a text caption appears on the command button. When set to 1 or `vbButtonGraphical`, the Picture property is used to display a graphic on the command button.

Picture

Pictures can be set at design time to a graphic file on the disk or at runtime to any picture object. The picture will be invisible unless the Style property is set to 1–Graphical.

DisabledPicture

The image to be used when the Enabled property is `False`. If no image is specified in this property, a grayed version of the Picture property image will be displayed when the command button is disabled. (See Figure 5-7.)

DownPicture

The image to be used when the button is pressed. If no image file is supplied, the image will be the one specified in the Picture property. This is sufficient for most applications. (See Figure 5-7.)

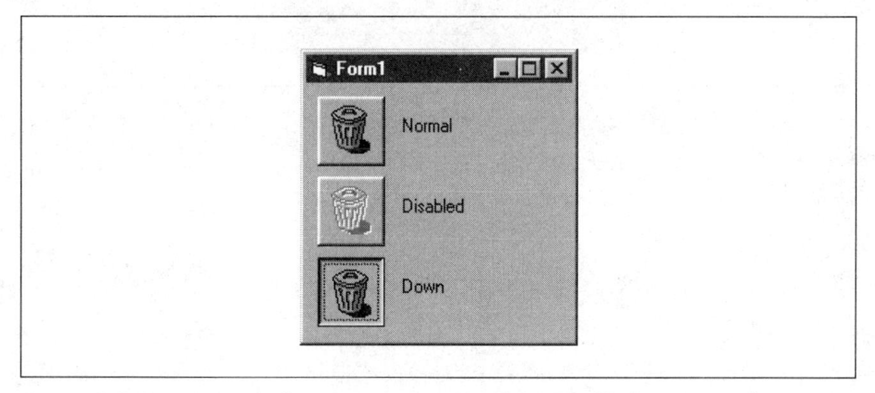

Figure 5-7: Images used when none are assigned for DisabledPicture and DownPicture

2. Set keyboard associations (optional).

Cancel

The Cancel property is initially `False`. Set it to `True` to invoke the button's Click event when the user presses the Escape key anywhere in the current form.

Default

The Default property is set initially to `False`. Set to it `True` to invoke the button's Click event when the user presses the Enter key anywhere in the current form.

Write Event Handlers

Click

Takes place when the user clicks the command button with the mouse or presses a keyboard alternative to select the button. In code, setting the Value property to `True` triggers the Click event.

MouseDown

The MouseDown event is useful when you need to intercept a command button click before other events take place.

Example

The following example is a simple data validation form with OK and Cancel buttons, as shown in Figure 5-8, that illustrates the order in which the command button fires its events (see the "Order of Events" section after this example). Both buttons are created dynamically, and the OK button's Default property and the Cancel button's Cancel property are set to `True` at runtime.

Figure 5-8: A simple data validation example

This example prompts for a quantity, which must be numeric and closes the form by accepting or cancelling the user's input:

```
Option Explicit

Dim WithEvents lblQty As Label
Dim WithEvents txtQty As TextBox
Dim WithEvents cmdOK As CommandButton
Dim WithEvents cmdCancel As CommandButton

'Set to True only when the Cancel button is pressed.
Dim bmFormCancel As Boolean

Private Sub Form_Load()
  'Create and set up controls.
    Set lblQty = Me.Controls.Add("vb.label", "lblQty", _
                 Me)
    lblQty.Visible = True
    lblQty.Caption = "&Quantity:"
    lblQty.TabIndex = 0

    Set txtQty = Me.Controls.Add("vb.textbox", _
                 "txtQty", Me)
    txtQty.Visible = True
    txtQty.Text = "0"
```

```
    txtQty.TabIndex = 1

    Set cmdOK = Me.Controls.Add("vb.commandbutton", _
                "cmdOK", Me)
    cmdOK.Visible = True
    cmdOK.Caption = "Ok"
    cmdOK.Default = True
    cmdOK.TabIndex = 2

    Set cmdCancel = Me.Controls.Add("vb.commandbutton", _
                    "cmdCancel", Me)
    cmdCancel.Visible = True
    cmdCancel.Caption = "Cancel"
    cmdCancel.Cancel = True
    cmdCancel.TabIndex = 3

  'Set up screen.
    Me.Caption = "Enter Quantity"
    Me.Move Me.Left, Me.Top, 3750, 1455
End Sub

Private Sub Form_Resize()
    If Me.ScaleWidth < 2550 Or Me.ScaleHeight < 1050 Then
        Exit Sub
    End If
    lblQty.Move 120, 180, 945, 255
    txtQty.Move 1185, 120, Me.ScaleWidth - 1305, 315
    cmdOK.Move Me.ScaleWidth - 2430, 555, 1095, 375
    cmdCancel.Move Me.ScaleWidth - 1215, 555, 1095, 375
End Sub

Private Sub cmdCancel_Click()
  'If the user uses the shortcut or escape to press _
  the Cancel button, this is set just in case _
  the LostFocus gets called.
    bmFormCancel = True

  'Any cleanup code here


    Unload Me
End Sub

Private Sub cmdCancel_MouseDown( _
      Button As Integer, Shift As Integer, X As Single, _
      Y As Single)
  'If the user uses the mouse to press the Cancel _
  button, this is set to cancel the last control's _
  LostFocus.
    bmFormCancel = True
End Sub

Private Sub CmdOk_Click()
```

Controls A–C

```
    'These commands force the last control's LostFocus _
    before continuing.
      cmdOK.SetFocus
      DoEvents

    'When validation fails in a control's LostFocus, _
    we set focus back to that control. So, if _
    this control doesn't have the focus now, we should _
    exit.
      If Me.ActiveControl <> cmdOK Then
         Exit Sub
      End If

    'Save data here.

      MsgBox "Data saved.", vbInformation + vbOKOnly
      Unload Me
   End Sub

   Private Sub txtQty_LostFocus()
    'If this is set to True, that means the Cancel _
    button was pressed.
      If bmFormCancel Then
         Exit Sub
      End If

      If Not IsNumeric(txtQty.Text) Then
         MsgBox "Quantity must be numeric", _
                vbExclamation + vbOKOnly
         txtQty.SelStart = 0
         txtQty.SelLength = Len(txtQty.Text)
         txtQty.SetFocus
      End If
   End Sub
```

Order of Events

Here is the sequence of events in response to a mouse click on a command button named Command1 when a text box named Text1 has the initial focus. In all cases, the CausesValidation property in VB6 is set to `False`. Setting the CausesValidation property to `True` forces the Validate event to fire first in all of the following cases and greatly simplifies the process of validating data:

1. Command1_MouseDown
2. Text1_LostFocus
3. Command1_GotFocus
4. Command1_Click

If Command1's shortcut key is used instead of clicking, the sequence changes:

1. Text1_KeyDown
2. Command1_Click

3. Text1_LostFocus
4. Command1_GotFocus

If Command1 is using the Default or Cancel properties, the sequence changes again:

1. Command1_Click (Only!)

Because of the differences in the sequence, you must be careful when a user clicks a button that confirms or cancels a process. If each control on a form does its own validation, an OK button needs to let that validation take place. Conversely, a Cancel button should skip the validation.

Interactions

Action	*Result*
Call SetFocus method.	Fires ActiveControl's LostFocus event and button's GotFocus event.
Set Value property to `True`.	Fires Click event.

CommonDialog Control

Both Windows and Visual Basic provide dialog boxes for many standard operations through the CommonDialog control. This control can activate the standard Open, Save, Font, Color, and Printer dialogs and control the Windows Help engine and its Help window. Note that, except when used with help files, the CommonDialog control provides information needed for a particular process but does not handle the process itself. For example, the File Open common dialog allows you to identify the file to be opened, but it does not actually open the file.

The CommonDialog control is contained in the Microsoft Common Dialog control (*COMDLG32.OCX*) that comes with Visual Basic Professional and Enterprise editions.

Control Tasks

Typically, opening one of the common dialogs requires setting some properties that control the dialog and then calling the specific method to open that particular kind of dialog (e.g., the ShowOpen method opens the File Open dialog). The user selection is then retrieved from one of the control's properties (e.g., the Color property in the case of the Color dialog). The following categories reflect the tasks that are executed when creating a CommonDialog.

Set Properties

1. Set flags.

The Flag property is the heart of the CommonDialog control. Adding additional flag values to the property can control nearly every aspect of the applicable dialog box. These multiple flags can be combined by using addition or the `Or` operator.

Flags (Color Dialog)

The following flags control the operation and appearance of the Color common dialog box (shown in Figure 5-9):

The 1–cdlCCRGBInit flag causes the value of the Color property to be used as the initial selected color in the dialog box. For example, the code fragment:

```
CommonDialog1.Color = vbRed
CommonDialog1.Flags = cdlCCRGBInit
CommonDialog1.ShowColor
```

causes the Color dialog to open showing red as its selected color.

When set, the 2–cdlCCFullOpen flag causes the custom colors section of the dialog box to be initially opened.

The 4–cdlCCPreventFullOpen flag prevents the user from accessing the custom colors section by disabling the Define Custom Colors button.

The 8–cdlCCHelpButton causes a Help button to appear along with the OK and Cancel buttons. Although the documentation indicates that you are responsible for providing the help file, it indicates neither how to detect that the Help button was clicked nor how to call the help file in response to a Help button click.

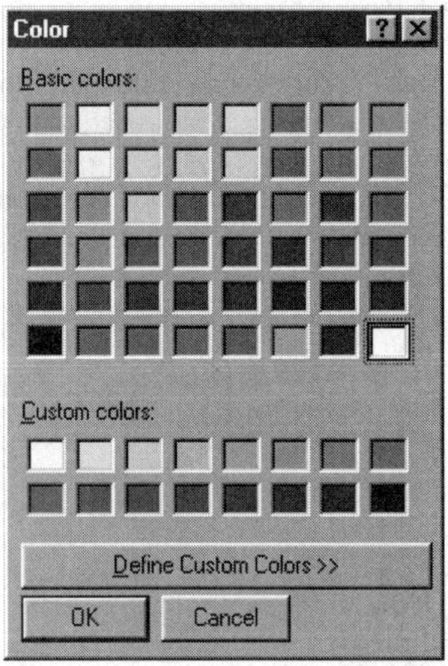

Figure 5-9: The Color dialog

Flags (Font Dialog)

The following flags control the operation and appearance of the Font common dialog box (shown in Figure 5-10):

The 1–cdlCFScreenFonts, 2–cdlCFPrinterFonts, and 3–cdlCFBoth flags control which types of fonts appear in the dialog. One of these three flags should be selected prior to activating the dialog box, or a runtime error is generated.

The 4–cdlCFHelpButton flag causes a Help button to appear along with the OK and Cancel buttons. Although the documentation indicates that you are responsible for providing the help file, it indicates neither how to detect that the Help button was clicked nor how to call the help file in response to a Help button click.

By default, the strikethrough, underline, and color selections do not appear on the Font dialog box. By setting the 256–cdlCFEffects flag, these options will appear.

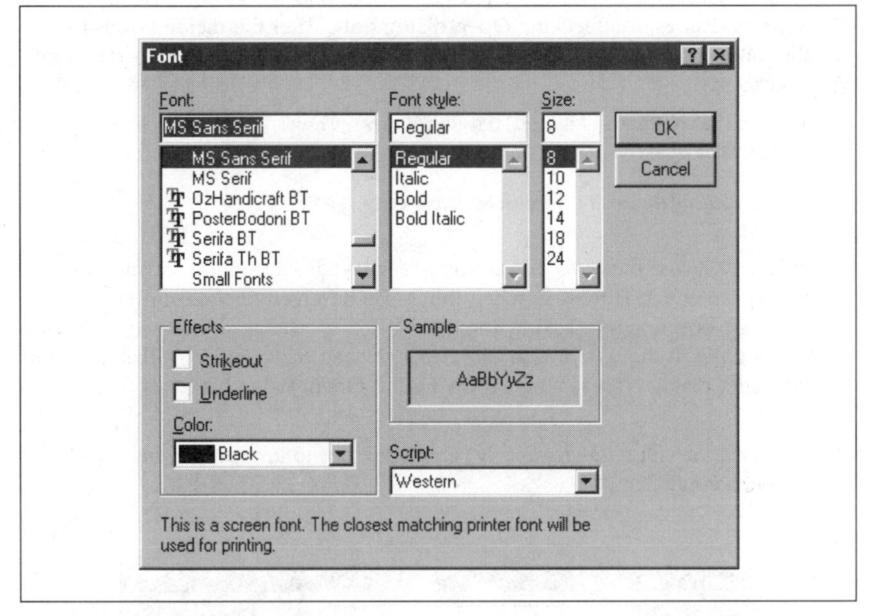

Figure 5-10: The Font dialog

The 516–cdlCFApply is meant to display an Apply button. However, at this time, this flag has no effect.

The 1,024–cdlCFANSIOnly causes symbol (noncharacter) fonts not to appear on the dialog.

The 2,048–cdlCFNoVectorFonts causes vector fonts not to appear on the dialog box.

When the 8,192–cdlCFLimitSize is not set, there is no limit to font size. When the flag is set, the upper and lower font sizes are limited to the values of the Max and Min properties, respectively.

The 16,384–cdlCFFixedPitchOnly, 32,768–cdlCFWYSIWYG, 131,072–cdlCFScalableOnly, and 262,144–cdlCFTTOnly flags limit the font types displayed to the appropriate type.

The 65,536–cdlCFForceFontExist flag causes a message box to appear if a font that does not exist on the system is entered into the dialog box.

The 524,288–cdlCFNoFaceSel, 1,048,576–cdlCFNoStyleSel, and 2,097,152–cdl CFNoSizeSel flags cause each of the font attributes named to initially appear empty when the dialog box appears, even if values have been assigned to the FontName, FontBold, FontItalic, and FontSize properties.

Flags (Open/Save As Dialogs)

The following flags control the operation and appearance of the Save and Open common dialog boxes (the latter is shown in Figure 5-11):

If 1–cdlOFNReadOnly is set before activating the dialog box, the "Open as read-only" checkbox will be checked; though shown on both the Open and Save As dialogs, it affects the Open dialog only. After the dialog box is exited, the following code can be used to check the status of the "Open as read-only" checkbox:

```
If (cdlMain.Flags And cdlOFNReadOnly) Then:
   'The Value of the Read Only checkbox was True.
Else
   'The Value of the Read Only checkbox was False.
End If
```

Normally, when the Save dialog box is displayed, selecting an existing file has no special effect. However, when the 2–cdlOFNOverwritePrompt flag is set, a message box appears asking the user if he or she wants to overwrite the existing file. If the user selects No, he or she returns to the Save dialog; otherwise, the dialog closes. When showing the Open dialog box, this flag has no effect.

To cause the "Open as read-only" checkbox not to appear, set the 4–cdlOFN-HideReadOnly flag.

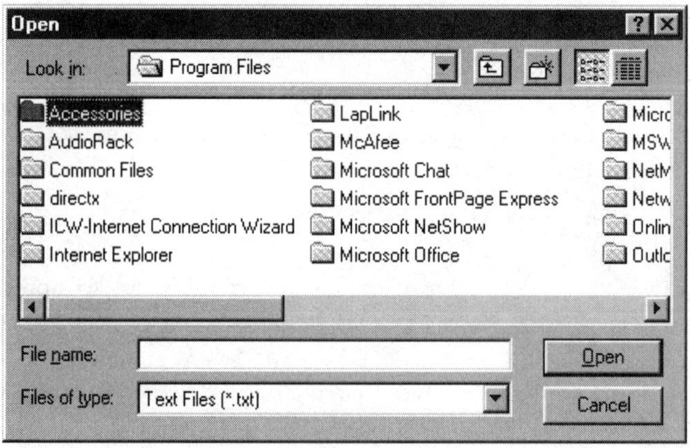

Figure 5-11: The Open dialog

The 8–cdlOFNNoChangeDir flag is supposed to prevent the user from changing directories. However, at this time, the flag has no effect.

The 16–cdlOFNHelpButton flag causes a Help button to appear along with the OK and Cancel buttons. Although the documentation indicates that you are responsible for providing the help file, it indicates neither how to detect that the Help button was clicked nor how to call the help file in response to a Help button click.

When the 256–cdlOFNNoValidate flag is set, filenames entered in the dialog can contain any characters, including invalid ones.

The 512–cdlOFNAllowMultiselect flag allows the user to select more than one file from the Open dialog box. When set, the 262,144–cdlOFNNoLongNames flag is set as well. This flag causes the 16-bit Windows File Open dialog box to appear. When the dialog closes, the FileName property contains a space-delimited string with the directory name followed by the name of each file selected. To allow multiple selections and show the standard 32-bit File Open dialog box, both the 512–cdlOFNAllowMultiselect and the 524,288–cdlOFNExplorer flags must be set. When the dialog closes, the FileName property contains a *Chr(0)*-delimited string with the directory name followed by the name of each file selected. The following code fragment extracts the filenames into a string array named ***strFiles***, with element 0 containing the path:

```
StrFiles = Split(dlgMain.FileName, Chr(0))
```

The 2,048–cdlOFNPathMustExist and 4,096–cdlOFNFileMustExist flags force the user to choose an existing directory or file, respectively. If the user enters the name of a directory or file that does not exist, a message box is displayed that informs the user of that fact. `cdlOFNPathMustExist` can apply to both the File Open and Save operations, while `cdlOFNFileMustExist` applies only to File Open.

When displaying the Open dialog box with the 8,192–cdlOFNCreatePrompt flag set, if the user chooses a file that doesn't exist, a message box is displayed that asks if he or she wants to create that file. This flag overrides the `cdlOFNFileMustExist` flag.

When set, the 16,384–cdlOFNShareAware flag should cause sharing violations for the file to be ignored. Normally, these violations should be reported with a message box. However, this flag currently has no effect.

If the 32,768–cdlOFNNoReadOnlyReturn flag is set, the user cannot select a read-only file. If the user attempts to select a read-only file with either the Open or Save dialog, a message box informs the user that he or she cannot.

Normally, when a shortcut (*.lnk*) file is selected using the Open dialog box, the filename returned is not the shortcut file but the file that the shortcut references. When the 1,048,576–cdlOFNNoDereferenceLinks flag is set, the name of the shortcut file is returned.

After the dialog box is closed, the 1,024–cdlOFNExtensionDifferent flag can be checked to see if the user used a different extension from the default extension as follows:

```
If (cdlMain.Flags And cdlOFNExtensionDifferent) Then
    The extension is different from the default.
Else
    The extension is the default extension.
End If
```

This flag is set whenever either a file with a file extension other than the default extension is opened or saved or if a file is opened using a filter other than the default.

Flags (Print Dialog)

The following flags control the operation and appearance of the Print common dialog box (shown in Figure 5-12):

The 0–cdlPDAllPages, 1–cdlPDSelection, and 2–cdlPDPageNums flags determine which option button in the Print Range frame is activated. After the dialog is exited, the value of these flags can be checked to ascertain which option was selected.

The 4–cdlPDNoSelection and 8–cdlPDNoPageNums flags disable option buttons in the Print Range frame.

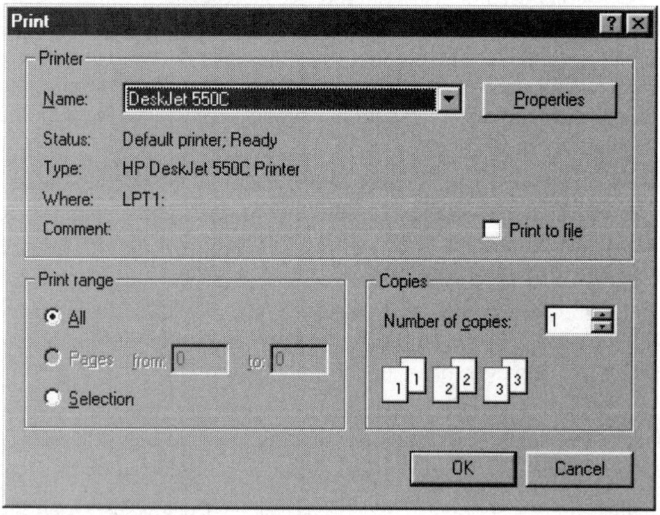

Figure 5-12: The Print dialog

When the 16–cdlPDCollate flag is set, the Collate checkbox is turned on. (The Collate checkbox, though, may not be present on all systems, since it depends on the printer driver's support for collating. In this case, the `cdlPDCollate` flag has no effect.) This flag can be checked after the dialog is exited to see the state of the Collate checkbox with a code fragment like the following:

```
If cdlMain.Flags And cdlPDCollate Then
  'Collating selected
Else
  'Collating disabled
End If
```

The Print To File checkbox can be disabled using 524,288–cdlPDDisablePrintToFile, or hidden using 1,048,576–cdlPDHidePrintToFile, or its value can be set and checked using the 32–cdlPDPrintToFile flag.

When the 64–cdlPDPrintSetup flag is set, the Print Setup dialog (see Figure 5-13) is shown instead of the Print dialog.

Normally, when there is no default printer set up in Windows, a message box alerts the user to this fact when the Print dialog is shown. By setting the 128–cdlPDNoWarning flag, that warning is not given.

Optionally, the Print dialog can return a Device Context or an Information Context in the hDC property after a printer has been selected by setting the 256–cdlPDReturnDC or 512–cdlPDReturnIC flags, respectively.

When the 1,024–cdlPDReturnDefault flag is set, the Print dialog is not displayed at all. Instead, the name of the default printer is returned as if it had been selected from the Print dialog.

The 2,048–cdlPDHelpButton flag should cause a Help button to appear along with the OK and Cancel buttons. However, it currently has no effect.

Some printer device drivers do not support multiple copies automatically. In these cases, setting 262,144–cdlPDUseDevModeCopies causes the Number of Copies text box to be disabled if it is not supported by the printer driver.

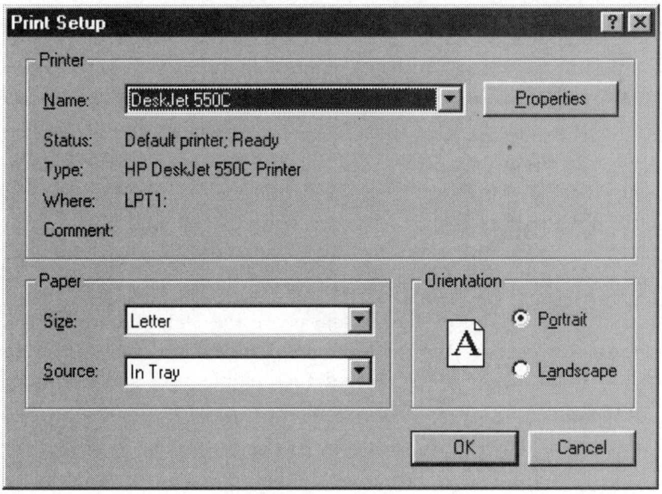

Figure 5-13: The Print Setup dialog

HelpCommand (Help Dialog)

The following flags, when assigned to the HelpCommand property, control the operation and appearance of the Help window, which is launched as a separate process in addition to the VB application:

When the 1–cdlHelpContext flag is set, along with the HelpFile and HelpContext properties, the context-sensitive help for the topic whose context ID is stored to the HelpContext property is displayed.

The 2–cdlHelpQuit flag closes the open Help window. If multiple files are open, it closes the one displaying help information from the help file defined by the FileName property. The following code fragment shows how this flag might be used to implement a delay before closing the open Help window:

```
dlgHelp.ShowHelp

' Timing loop
Dim lngctr As Long
For lngctr = 0 To 100000
   DoEvents
Next

dlgHelp.HelpCommand = cdlHelpQuit
dlgHelp.ShowHelp
```

When the 3–cdlHelpContents flag is set, the Help engine loads the contents page of the file designated by the FileName property. Note that this is the same value as the 3–cdlHelpIndex flag, which supposedly displays the help file's index; however, we found that it behaves identically to the `cdlHelpContents` constant.

When the 4–cdlHelpHelpOnHelp flag is set, help for the Windows Help application is launched. No other HelpCommand flags should be set, and no other properties need to be set before calling ShowHelp to open the Windows Help dialog.

The undocumented 11 (`HELP_FINDER`) flag—although the intrinsic constant is not defined in the common dialog control's type library—opens the help file specified by the FileName property with its most recent active tab selected.

If the 261–cdlHelpPartialKey flag is set but no value is assigned to the Key property, the Help engine's Index tab is displayed. Note that this is the behavior that is supposed to result from the 3–cdlHelpIndex flag. If the 261–cdlHelpPartialKey flag is set and a string is assigned to the Key property, the Help engine's Index tab is displayed, and the first index entry that matches that string is highlighted.

When the 257–cdlHelpKey flag is set, as are the HelpFile and HelpKey properties, help for that keyword or the help index for that partial keyword is displayed. If the keyword is related to multiple topics rather than a single topic, a dialog listing these is displayed.

When the 258–cdlHelpCommandHelp flag is set, a help macro whose name is stored to the HelpKey property is executed.

2. Set color-related properties.

Color

If the Color property is set prior to activating the Color dialog box, that color is selected only if the `cdlCCRGBInit` flag is set. Once the dialog is exited, the Color property contains the color selected by the user.

3. Set font-related properties.

FontName, FontSize, FontBold, FontItalic

All of these Boolean properties can be set before activating the Font dialog box and then retrieved afterward to see what font attributes have been selected.

FontStrikethru, FontUnderline, Color

When the `cdlCFEffects` flag is set, these Boolean properties can be set and checked.

Min, Max

When the `cdlCFLimitSize` flag is set, these properties define the minimum and maximum font size, respectively, that can be chosen by the user. Since both values default to 0, a range must be supplied, or the user will be unable to make a selection.

4. Set File Open/Save-related properties.

FileName, FileTitle

The FileName property can be set to a fully qualified path and filename prior to activating the Open or Save dialog box and will determine the initial directory as well as the file selected. When the dialog is exited, the FileName will contain the path and filename of the selected file. The FileTitle property will contain the filename without the path information of the selected file. However, if the `cdlOFNNoValidate` flag is set, the filename can contain invalid characters, and therefore the FileTitle property is not set. Note that the FileTitle property is a reliable source of a filename only immediately after the ShowOpen or ShowSave method has returned; it is not necessarily accurate before the method call or after a value has been assigned to the FileName property.

Filter, FilterIndex

The Filter property is a string that contains the descriptions and file masks that can be selected from the "Files of Type" combo box in the Open/Save dialog box. For each filter, the string should contain the description for the filter, a pipe (|) character, and the file mask(s) for that filter. If there are multiple masks for one filter, they should be separated by a semicolon (;). A pipe character should separate multiple filters. For example:

```
strFilter = "Doc Files (*.doc,*.dot)|*.doc;*.dot|" & _
            "Document Templates (*.dot)|*.dot|" & _
            "Rich Text Format (*.rtf)|*.rtf"
cdlMain.Filter = strFilter
```

The FilterIndex property is used to set the numeric index of the default filter or to ascertain which filter was selected after the dialog box is exited. The number for filters begins with 1.

DefaultExt

The DefaultExt property contains the extension to be added to filenames to which no extension has been added. Note that you can also determine whether the user has changed the default file extension by checking the state of the `cdlOFNExtensionDifferent` flag.

InitDir

The InitDir property is used to set the initial directory for the Open/Save dialog box.

MaxFileSize

This property determines the maximum amount of space in bytes allocated for filenames. Its default of 256 is usually sufficient in single-selection File Open dialogs, but may be inadequate in multiselection dialogs. In that case its value can be increased. Its effective range is 1–32K.

5. Set print-related properties.

Copies, FromPage, ToPage

All of these properties can be set before activating the Print dialog box and then afterward to see what values have been selected.

hDC

When the `cdlPDReturnDC` or `cdlPDReturnIC` flag has been set, the hDC property will contain the selected Printer's Device Context or Information Context. Otherwise, it is unused. The property is read-only.

6. Set help-related properties.

HelpFile

The filename of a WinHelp (*.HLP*) or HTML Help (*.CHM*) file. This property must always be set unless the ShowHelp method is called with the `cdlHelpHelpOnHelp` flag set.

HelpContext

An integer representing the context ID of a topic in a help file.

HelpKey

A string representing an index keyword in the help file designated by the FileName property. Its value must be set when calling the ShowHelp method with either the `cdlHelpPartialKey` or `cdlHelpKey` flags. Note that keywords are not case sensitive.

7. Set generic properties.

CancelError

When the Cancel button is pressed on a common dialog box, if the CancelError property is set to `True`, runtime error 32755 is generated. Then, in an error-handling routine, that error can be trapped and appropriate actions can be taken.

Without setting the CancelError Property to `True`, it can be very difficult to tell whether the user pressed the Cancel button.

DialogTitle
The default caption of the Color dialog is Color; of the Font dialog, Font; of the Open dialog, Open; of the Save dialog, Save As; of the Print dialog, Print. By assigning a value to the DialogTitle property before displaying the dialog, you can change the caption of the Open and SaveAs dialogs.

Useful Methods

ShowColor, ShowFont, ShowOpen, ShowPrint, ShowSave, ShowHelp
Each of these methods activates the appropriate dialog box using the properties set. Because the dialog boxes are all modal, the program does not get control until after the dialog box is exited.

Example

The following example shows how much of the functionality of a CommonDialog control can be used in an application:

```
Option Explicit
'For this example, create the following controls: _
  a menu named mnuFileTop _
        with 1 child named mnuFile(0), _
  a CommandButton called cmdMain(0), _
  a TextBox named txtMain with MultiLine set to True and _
  a CommonDialog called cdlMain.

Private Sub Form_Load()
  'Set up form.
    Me.Caption = "CommonDialog Sample"

  'Set up CommandButtons.
    Load cmdMain(1)
    Me.cmdMain(1).Visible = True

    Me.cmdMain(0).Caption = "Fon&t"
    Me.cmdMain(0).TabIndex = 1
    Me.cmdMain(1).Caption = "&Color"
    Me.cmdMain(0).TabIndex = 2

  'Set up menu.
    Load mnuFile(1)
    Load mnuFile(2)
    Load mnuFile(3)
    Load mnuFile(4)
    Load mnuFile(5)
    Load mnuFile(6)
```

```
    Load mnuFile(7)
    Load mnuFile(8)

    Me.mnuFileTop.Caption = "&File"
    Me.mnuFile(0).Caption = "&New"
    Me.mnuFile(1).Caption = "&Open..."
    Me.mnuFile(2).Caption = "&Save"
    Me.mnuFile(3).Caption = "Save &As..."
    Me.mnuFile(4).Caption = "-"
    Me.mnuFile(5).Caption = "&Print..."
    Me.mnuFile(6).Caption = "Print Set&up..."
    Me.mnuFile(7).Caption = "-"
    Me.mnuFile(8).Caption = "E&xit"

  'Set up TextBox.
    Me.txtMain.Text = ""
    Me.txtMain.TabIndex = 0

  'Set up CommonDialog.
    Me.cdlMain.CancelError = True

  'Change form size.
    Me.Height = 3465
    Me.Width = 4710
End Sub

Private Sub Form_Resize()
  'We want to make sure there is room for the TextBox _
     and CommandButtons before we resize.
    If Me.ScaleHeight < 1060 Or Me.ScaleWidth < 2550 Then
         Exit Sub
    End If
  'We will put a 120-twip border around all controls.
    Me.txtMain.Move 120, 120, _
         Me.ScaleWidth - 240, Me.ScaleHeight - 735
     Me.cmdMain(0).Move Me.ScaleWidth - 2430, _
         Me.ScaleHeight - 495, 1095, 375
     Me.cmdMain(1).Move Me.ScaleWidth - 1215, _
         Me.ScaleHeight - 495, 1095, 375
End Sub

Private Sub mnuFile_Click(Index As Integer)
  'We need an error handler because the CommonDialog _
  CancelError property is set to True.
    On Error GoTo mnuFile_Click_Error

    Select Case Index
       Case 0
     'New—we just want to clear the TextBox and _
     adjust the CommonDialog and Form caption _
     since there is no current file.
          Me.txtMain.Text = ""
          Me.cdlMain.FileName = ""
```

```
        Me.Caption = "CommonDialog Sample"
    Case 1
'Open
        Me.cdlMain.DefaultExt = "txt"
        Me.cdlMain.Filter = "Text Files (*.txt)|*.txt"
        Me.cdlMain.Flags = cdlOFNHideReadOnly + _
             cdlOFNFileMustExist + cdlOFNPathMustExist
        Me.cdlMain.ShowOpen
'Open the file.
'The actual logic to get the file contents _
into the TextBox does not apply to _
the CommonDialog control.
        MsgBox Me.cdlMain.FileTitle & " opened"
        Me.Caption = "CommonDialog - " & _
                     Me.cdlMain.FileTitle
    Case 2
'Save. If there is no value in the FileName _
property, we need to show the dialog; _
otherwise, we can just save.
        If Me.cdlMain.FileName = "" Then
            Me.cdlMain.DefaultExt = "txt"
            Me.cdlMain.Filter = _
                    "Text Files (*.txt)|*.txt"
            Me.cdlMain.Flags = _
                   cdlOFNHideReadOnly + _
                   cdlOFNFileMustExist + _
                   cdlOFNPathMustExist
            Me.cdlMain.ShowSave
        End If
'Save the file.
'The actual logic to save the text box _
contents into the file does not apply to _
the CommonDialog control.
        MsgBox Me.cdlMain.FileTitle & " saved"
        Me.Caption = "CommonDialog - " & _
                     Me.cdlMain.FileTitle
    Case 3
'Save As—we prompt regardless.
        Me.cdlMain.DefaultExt = "txt"
        Me.cdlMain.Filter = "Text Files (*.txt)|*.txt"
        Me.cdlMain.Flags = _
               cdlOFNHideReadOnly + _
               cdlOFNFileMustExist + _
               cdlOFNPathMustExist
        Me.cdlMain.ShowSave
'Save the file. The actual logic to save the _
text box contents into the file does not _
apply to the CommonDialog control.
        MsgBox Me.cdlMain.FileTitle & " saved"
        Me.Caption = "CommonDialog - " & _
                     Me.cdlMain.FileTitle
    Case 5
'Print
```

```
            Me.cdlMain.Flags = cdlPDAllPages
            Me.cdlMain.ShowPrinter
            MsgBox "Printer Selected"
         Case 6
       'Print Setup
            Me.cdlMain.Flags = cdlPDPrintSetup
            Me.cdlMain.ShowPrinter
            MsgBox "Printer Setup"
         Case 8
            Unload Me
         Case 4, 7
       'Separators—do nothing.
      End Select
      Exit Sub

mnuFile_Click_Error:
   'For normal error handling, pressing the Cancel _
   button generates the 32755-cdlCancel error.
      MsgBox "Operation Cancelled"
      Exit Sub
End Sub

Private Sub cmdMain_Click(Index As Integer)
   On Error GoTo cmdMain_Click_Error

   Select Case Index
      Case 0
      'Font—Get all the font properties from the _
      TextBox into the CommonDialog's defaults.
         Me.cdlMain.FontName = Me.txtMain.FontName
         Me.cdlMain.FontSize = Me.txtMain.FontSize
         Me.cdlMain.FontBold = Me.txtMain.FontBold
         Me.cdlMain.FontItalic = Me.txtMain.FontItalic
         Me.cdlMain.FontStrikethru = _
                  Me.txtMain.FontStrikethru
         Me.cdlMain.FontUnderline = _
                  Me.txtMain.FontUnderline
         Me.cdlMain.Color = Me.txtMain.ForeColor
         Me.cdlMain.Flags = cdlCFBoth + _
                  cdlCFANSIOnly + cdlCFEffects
         Me.cdlMain.ShowFont
      'OK selected—set the properties from the _
      CommonDialog to the TextBox.
         Me.txtMain.FontName = Me.cdlMain.FontName
         Me.txtMain.FontSize = Me.cdlMain.FontSize
         Me.txtMain.FontBold = Me.cdlMain.FontBold
         Me.txtMain.FontItalic = Me.cdlMain.FontItalic
         Me.txtMain.FontStrikethru = _
                    Me.cdlMain.FontStrikethru
         Me.txtMain.FontUnderline = _
                    Me.cdlMain.FontUnderline
         Me.txtMain.ForeColor = Me.cdlMain.Color
         MsgBox "Font changed"
```

```
            Case 1
        'Color—get the BackColor of the TextBox _
        into the default Color in the CommonDialog.
                Me.cdlMain.Color = Me.txtMain.BackColor
                Me.cdlMain.Flags = cdlCCRGBInit
                Me.cdlMain.ShowColor
        'OK selected. Set the BackColor of the _
        TextBox as defined by the CommonDialog _
        selection.
               Me.txtMain.BackColor = Me.cdlMain.Color
               MsgBox "Color Changed"
        End Select
        Exit Sub

    cmdMain_Click_Error:
      'For normal error handling, pressing the Cancel _
      button generates the 32755-cdlCancel error.
        MsgBox "Operation Cancelled"
        Exit Sub
    End Sub
```

VB6 CoolBar Control

To give your applications that Microsoft Office look, VB6 ships with the new CoolBar control, along with the Toolbar control. The CoolBar control provides a series of Band objects, which can be arranged within an alignable control. Each band can be sized and moved using the mouse. By default, when you drop a CoolBar onto your form, the CoolBar control will have three bands.

Each band of the CoolBar control serves as a container for any control that has a window handle. (In other words, the windowless controls, as well as the Image control, cannot be placed in the CoolBar control.) The CoolBar's most common use is to be placed on a form or MDI form so that multiple Toolbar controls can be contained within it, one in each Band object. This is the appearance of the toolbar area of the Visual Basic IDE as well as that of the Microsoft Office applications, as Figure 5-14 shows.

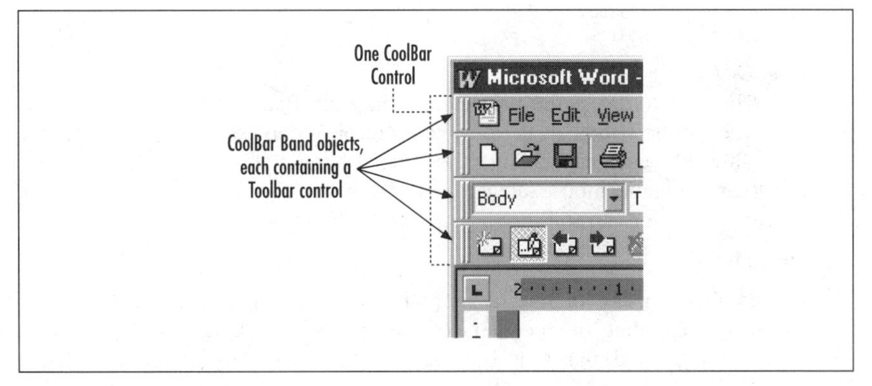

Figure 5-14: The coolbar and toolbar in Microsoft Word

The CoolBar control is contained in the Microsoft Windows Common Controls-3 (*COMCT332.OCX*) that comes with Visual Basic 6.0 Professional and Enterprise editions.

CoolBar Control Tasks

The following categories reflect the tasks executed when creating a CoolBar.

Set Properties

1. Set graphical properties.

   BandBorders

   When set to `False`, no lines appear between Band objects in the CoolBar control. When `True`, the default value, a line appears after each Band object. Setting this property to `False` can appear confusing when the coolbar is used with Toolbar controls contained by the Band objects.

   ImageList

   The name of an ImageList control on the same form as the CoolBar control. Each band placed in the coolbar can choose which image to use from the image list referenced by this property.

   Picture, EmbossPicture, EmbossHighlight, EmbossShadow

   The Picture property can contain an image to be displayed on the CoolBar control. When the EmbossPicture property is set to `True`, that image appears with only two colors, which are defined by the EmbossHighlight and EmbossShadow properties. Dark areas of the image are shown as the EmbossShadow property's color, and light areas are shown as the EmbossHighlight property's color.

Since Toolbar controls are not transparent, any image defined by the Picture property will not be visible through the toolbar when the CoolBar control is used as a container for Toolbar controls.

2. Set general properties.

   FixedOrder

   When set to `True`, the user cannot drag the Band objects to change the order of the bands on the CoolBar control. When set to `False`, its default value, the user can change the order of the Band objects by dragging them with the mouse. Regardless of the value of the FixedOrder property, the user can still resize each band.

3. Create bands.

   The coolbar consists of one or more Band objects (by default, the coolbar contains three) that are members of the Bands collection. You can add or remove bands at design time by selecting the Insert Band or Remove Band button on the Bands tab of the CoolBar control's Property Pages dialog. At runtime, the Bands collection supports the following properties:

Add method

Allows you to add a Band object to the Bands collection (thereby adding a band to the CoolBar control). Its syntax is:

```
objBands.Add(index, key, caption, image, newrow, child, visible)
```

The first parameter, *index*, defines the position of the band in the collection. The second, *key*, is a unique string that can serve to identify the band. The last five parameters are described later in step 5.

Clear method

Removes all bands from the CoolBar control.

Count property

Returns the number of Band objects in the Bands collection.

Item property

Retrieves a particular Band object from the Bands collection based on its index (i.e., its ordinal position) or its key.

Remove method

Removes a Band object from the collection. Its syntax is:

```
objBands.Remove(index)
```

where *index* is the Band object's index or key value.

Note that, although you can specify the ordinal position of a Band object within the Bands collection, that doesn't necessarily correspond to the band's position on the coolbar. For example, the user can move bands without affecting their ordinal position in the Bands collection.

4. Assign controls to the bands.

You can assign controls to the bands at design time by dropping the control onto the CoolBar control and using the CoolBar control's Property Pages dialog, which is shown in Figure 5-15. You can also instantiate the control dynamically at runtime and assign it to a band, as the following code fragment (which requires that the "Remove information about unused ActiveX Controls" box on the Make tab of the Project Properties dialog be unchecked) shows:

```
Set tbrMain = Me.Controls.Add("MSComctlLib.Toolbar", _
              "tbrMain", Me)
'
' Add toolbar buttons here
'
Set tbrMain.Container = cbrMain
Set cbrMain.Bands(1).Child = tbrMain
```

5. Set band properties.

The Band object has a number of properties that you can manipulate individually, as well as assign in a single call to the Add method when the band is created. These properties (which correspond to identically named parameters to the Add method) are:

Caption
Defines the caption at the left end of the Band object.

Image
The index or key of the ListImage within the ImageList control referenced by the CoolBar control's ImageList property.

NewRow
Flag indicating whether the band should start a new row in the CoolBar control. As a parameter to the Band collection's Add method, its default value is `False`.

Child
A reference to the control that should be displayed in the band. For example:

```
Set cbrMain.Bands("Editing").Child = tbrEditing
```

assigns the Editing toolbar to the Editing band of the CoolBar control.

Visible
Flag indicating whether the band is visible. As a parameter to the Add method, its default value is `True`.

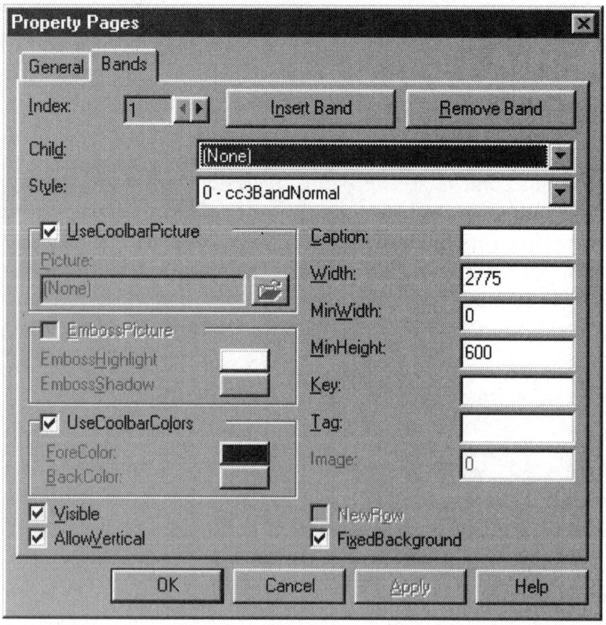

Figure 5-15: The Bands tab of the CoolBar control's Property Pages dialog

Write Event Handlers

HeightChanged

Fired when the height of the coolbar is changed, usually due to the user rearranging the contained Band objects. When the event is fired, it is passed by value a single parameter, ***NewHeight***, which indicates the total height of the control.

Example

The following example shows how Toolbar controls and a CoolBar control can be used together in an application:

```
Option Explicit

'For this example, create the following controls: _
  a CoolBar control named cbrMain, _
  a Toolbar control named tbrMain, _
     with its Index property set to 0, and _
  an ImageList control named imlMain _
     with its Index property set to 0.

Private Sub Form_Load()
    Dim btnVar As Button
    Dim lsiVar As ListImage

    Load Me.tbrMain(1)

    Set lsiVar = Me.imlMain(0).ListImages.Add _
        (1, , LoadPicture("New.bmp"))
    Set lsiVar = Me.imlMain(0).ListImages.Add _
        (2, , LoadPicture("Open.bmp"))
    Set lsiVar = Me.imlMain(0).ListImages.Add _
        (3, , LoadPicture("Save.bmp"))
    Set lsiVar = Me.imlMain(0).ListImages.Add _
        (4, , LoadPicture("Print.bmp"))
    Set lsiVar = Me.imlMain(0).ListImages.Add _
        (5, , LoadPicture("Cut.bmp"))
    Set lsiVar = Me.imlMain(0).ListImages.Add _
        (6, , LoadPicture("Copy.bmp"))
    Set lsiVar = Me.imlMain(0).ListImages.Add _
        (7, , LoadPicture("Paste.bmp"))
    Set lsiVar = Me.imlMain(0).ListImages.Add _
        (8, , LoadPicture("Delete.bmp"))

    Me.tbrMain(0).Align = vbAlignTop
    Me.tbrMain(0).Appearance = ccFlat
    Me.tbrMain(0).BorderStyle = ccNone
    Me.tbrMain(0).Style = tbrFlat

    Set Me.tbrMain(0).ImageList = Me.imlMain(0)

    Set btnVar = Me.tbrMain(0).Buttons.Add(1, , , , 1)
    btnVar.ToolTipText = "New"
```

```
    Set btnVar = Me.tbrMain(0).Buttons.Add(2, , , , 2)
    btnVar.ToolTipText = "Open"
    Set btnVar = Me.tbrMain(0).Buttons.Add(3, , , , 3)
    btnVar.ToolTipText = "Save"
    Set btnVar = Me.tbrMain(0).Buttons.Add(4, , , , 4)
    btnVar.ToolTipText = "Print"

    Me.tbrMain(1).Align = vbAlignTop
    Me.tbrMain(1).Appearance = ccFlat
    Me.tbrMain(1).BorderStyle = ccNone
    Me.tbrMain(1).Style = tbrFlat

    Set Me.tbrMain(1).ImageList = Me.imlMain(0)

    Set btnVar = Me.tbrMain(1).Buttons.Add(1, , , , 5)
    btnVar.ToolTipText = "Cut"
    Set btnVar = Me.tbrMain(1).Buttons.Add(2, , , , 6)
    btnVar.ToolTipText = "Copy"
    Set btnVar = Me.tbrMain(1).Buttons.Add(3, , , , 7)
    btnVar.ToolTipText = "Paste"
    Set btnVar = Me.tbrMain(1).Buttons.Add(4, , , , 8)
    btnVar.ToolTipText = "Delete"

  'The following DoEvents command allows the preceding _
  changes to take place before moving on to the _
  upcoming changes.
    DoEvents

    Do While Me.cbrMain.Bands.Count > 2
        Me.cbrMain.Bands.Remove Me.cbrMain.Bands.Count
    Loop

    Me.cbrMain.Align = vbAlignTop
    Me.cbrMain.Bands(1).Caption = "File"
    Me.cbrMain.Bands(2).Caption = "Edit"

    Set Me.tbrMain(0).Container = Me.cbrMain
    Set Me.tbrMain(1).Container = Me.cbrMain
    Set Me.cbrMain.Bands(1).Child = Me.tbrMain(0)
    Set Me.cbrMain.Bands(2).Child = Me.tbrMain(1)
End Sub
```

Data Control

The Data control is an intrinsic Visual Basic control that aims at making viewing and editing information stored in database tables easier. In particular, the Data control wraps Microsoft's Data Access Objects (DAO) technology and hides much of the detail required to program DAO directly. The Data control makes it fairly easy to link to a data source (to an Access database using the Jet engine, to a variety of other data sources using the Jet engine and special ISAM drivers, and to any ODBC database using ODBC Direct) and handles navigation between records of the resulting recordset and updating the data displayed by bound controls.

Adding the Data control to a project automatically adds a reference to Microsoft Data Access Objects as well.

Opening a Data Source

The first step in using the Data control is to define the data source to which it is bound and therefore the data access technology (Jet or ODBC Direct) used to access that data. This can be done either at design time or at runtime.

Database Access Using the Jet Engine

To access a data source, such as a table in a Microsoft Access database, using Jet, do the following:

1. Optionally, set the DefaultType property (which defines the data access technology used by the control) to `dbUseJet` (2). Since this is the default value, you must do this only if you're changing the value of DefaultType from `dbUseODBC` (1) to `dbUseJet` (2).
2. Supply the name of the database to the DatabaseName property. If the string assigned to DatabaseName does not include a drive and path, Jet will look for the database in the current directory of the current drive. If the file cannot be found, error 3024, "Couldn't find file," is passed to the control's Error event.
3. Indicate the data source by assigning the name of a table, a stored procedure (such as an Access query), or an SQL statement to the RecordSource property. If an SQL statement or a stored procedure is assigned to the RecordSource property, the RecordsetType property cannot be `vbRSTypeTable`.
4. Assign any special attributes to the connection or the data source; see "Defining the Character of the Connection," later in this section.
5. If the value of either the DatabaseName or the RecordSource property was supplied at runtime, call the Refresh method to open the database. (If the values were supplied at design time, the data source is opened automatically when its form loads.)

Database Access Using ODBC Direct

To access a data source using ODBC Direct, do the following:

1. Set the DefaultType property (which defines the data acesss technology used by the control) to `dbUseODBC` (1).
2. Assign the connection string to the Connect property. A minimal connection string consists of the database type (e.g., ODBC) and the data set name, as defined in the ODBC Administrator. For example:

   ```
   datMain.Connect = "ODBC;DSN=NrthWnd"
   ```

   Database name, username, and password are also frequently included in connection strings. Individual fields are delimited with a semicolon.
3. Indicate the data source by assigning the name of a table, a stored procedure (such as an Access query), or an SQL statement to the RecordSource property.

4. Assign any special attributes to the connection or the data source; see "Defining the Character of the Connection," later in this section.
5. If the value of either the Connect or the RecordSource property was supplied at runtime, call the Refresh method to open the database. (If the values were supplied at design time, the data source is opened automatically when the application starts.)

Access to Non-Jet, Non-ODBC Data Sources

The Data control allows your application to connect to a diverse array of data sources—in addition to Access and ODBC databases—for which installable drivers are available. You can connect to these data sources as follows:

1. Set the DefaultType property to `dbUseJet`.
2. Store the name of the data type to the Connect property. (Valid types include Access; dBASE III; dBASE IV; dBASE 5.0; Excel 3.0; Excel 4.0; Excel 5.0; Excel 8.0; FoxPro 2.0; FoxPro 2.5; FoxPro 2.6; FoxPro 3.0; Lotus WK1; Lotus WK3; Lotus WK4; Paradox 3.x; Paradox 4.x; Paradox 5.x; and Text.) Note that each data type name is followed by a semicolon.
3. Various data sources require that various values be assigned to the DatabaseName and Recordset properties. For instance, in the case of a Lotus 4.0 worksheet, the workbook's path and filename must be assigned to the DatabaseName property, and the worksheet name must be assigned to the RecordSource property. In the case of a text file, the path must be assigned to the DatabaseName property, and the filename (without an extension) must be assigned to the RecordSource property.

   To determine the precise requirements, use the DatabaseName property's Browse button and the RecordSource property's drop-down list in the design-time environment to connect to a data source.
4. Assign any special attributes to the connection or the data source; see "Defining the Character of the Connection," in the next section.
5. If the value of either the Connect or the RecordSource property was supplied at runtime, call the Refresh method to open the database. (If the values were supplied at design time, the data source is opened automatically when the application starts.)

Defining the Character of the Connection

The Data control offers a number of properties that allow you to define both the character of the database connection and the precise relationship of the data managed by the control to the database.

Although the properties are all read/write, only changes to the BOFAction and EOFAction properties are immediately applied to the recordset. Instead, the remaining properties are applied the next time that a database is opened or a call is made to the Data control's Refresh method. Note that this makes retrieving the value of any of these properties problematic; they do not necessarily reflect the state of the underlying database connection. If your program absolutely needs to know the state of a particular setting, see "Working with the Database Directly," later in this section.

Cursor type

The property that defines the cursor type depends on whether the Jet engine or ODBC Direct is used to manage the database connection.

For Jet, the cursor is defined by the RecordsetType property and can assume the following values from the `RecordsetTypeConstants` enumeration:

Constant	*Value*	*Description*
`vbRSTypeTable`	0	A table-type recordset. If the recordset contains fields from more than a single table, a runtime error is generated.
`vbRSTypeDynaset`	1	A dynaset-type recordset.
`vbRSTypeSnapshot`	2	A snapshot-type recordset.

The default value is `vbRSTypeDynaset`. Since this is the most "expensive" type of cursor, performance can typically be improved by using either a table-type recordset or a static, snapshot-type recordset.

For ODBC, the cursor is defined by the DefaultCursorType property and can assume one of the following values from the `DefaultCursorTypeConstants` enumeration:

Constant	*Value*	*Description*
`vbUseDefaultCursor`	0	Cursor type is determined by the ODBC driver.
`vbUseODBCCursor`	1	The ODBC cursor library, which is optimized for small result sets.
`vbUseServerSideCursor`	2	A server-side cursor, which is optimized for large result sets but also increases network traffic.

Exclusive use

The Exclusive property determines whether the data source is opened exclusively. When set to `True` and the Data control attempts to open a data source that another process (or another user on a multiuser system) has already opened, runtime error 3356 is generated. When set to `True`, if the database is successfully opened, no other process can open that database. The default value is `False`; multiple processes and users can open the same data source.

Read-only or read/write

The ReadOnly property controls whether the Data control can edit any data within the next data source that is opened. When set to `True`, no data can be added, changed, or deleted. By default, its value is `False`; the data source managed by the data control is updateable. The read/write state of the data source is related to the cursor type; it makes little sense, for instance, to open a read-only dynaset.

A recordset can also be made read-only by setting the `dbReadOnly` flag of the Options property. However, the two settings are independent of each other;

that is, the setting of the ReadOnly property does not affect the `vbReadOnly` flag and vice versa.

Miscellaneous options

The Options property defines additional characteristics of the recordset. It consists of a number of flags (constants of the `RecordsetOptionEnum` enumeration) that can be summed or logically `Ored` together. To determine if a particular flag is set, use the bitwise AND statement, as in:

```
If datMain.Options And flag Then
```

The flags are:

Constant	*Value*	*Description*
`dbDenyWrite`	1	Prevents other users from making changes to data in the recordset.
`dbDenyRead`	2	Prevents other users from reading a `vbRSTypeTable` recordset.
`dbReadOnly`	4	Prevents records from being edited or deleted.
`dbAppendOnly`	8	Prevents records from being read but allows new records to be added.
`dbInconsistent`	16	Allows updates to fields in a multitable join even if they violate a join condition. This flag does not override any rules enforced by the database itself.
`dbConsistent`	32	Allows updates to fields in a multitable join only if they don't violate the join condition.
`dbSQLPassThrough`	64	Sends an SQL statement in the RecordSource property to an ODBC database.
`dbForwardOnly`	256	Supports forward-only movement only.
`dbSeeChanges`	512	Fires an error event if data being edited is changed by another user.

The behavior of the record pointer

The BOFAction and EOFAction properties control the behavior of the record pointer when it is moved before the first record (BOF) or after the last record (EOF) of a recordset, respectively. Setting or modifying the value of either of these properties takes effect immediately; you do not have to call the Refresh first.

Possible values for BOFAction include:

`vbBOFActionMoveFirst` *(0)*

Does not allow the record pointer to move before the first record in the recordset; this is the default value.

`vbBOFActionBOF` *(1)*

Moves the pointer past the first record, thereby forcing the Validate event to fire and disables the Data control's MovePrevious button. Bound controls continue to display data from the first record, even though the current position of the record pointer is at the beginning of the file and before the first record.

Possible values for EOFAction include:

`vbEOFActionMoveLast` *(0)*
: Does not allow the record pointer to move after the last record in the recordset.

`vbEOFActionEOF` *(1)*
: Moves the pointer past the last record, thereby forcing the Validate event to fire and disables the Data control's MoveNext button. Bound controls continue to display data from the last record, even though the current position of the record pointer is at the end of the file and after the last record.

`vbEOFActionAddNew` *(2)*
: Moves the pointer past the last record (triggering the Validate event) and putting the Data control into AddNew mode.

If BOFAction is set to `vbBOFActionBOF` or EOFAction is set to `vbEOFActionEOF`, the record pointer is positioned before the first record in the recordset (in the case of BOFAction) or after the last record (in the case of EOFAction), and the user edits the "phantom" record, error code 3021, "No current record," is passed to the Error event. This can result in an endless loop, since the data control will not permit navigation away from the record. This can be prevented with code like the following in the Data control's Validate event handler:

```
Private Sub datMain_Validate(Action As Integer, _
                             Save As Integer)

If datMain.Recordset.BOF Then
   Action = vbDataActionCancel
   datMain.Recordset.MoveNext
End If
If datMain.Recordset.EOF Then
   Action = vbDataActionCancel
   datMain.Recordset.MovePrevious
End If

End Sub
```

Defining the Data Control's Interface

The Data control forms an intermediate layer between a database and the user interface components and controls that are bound to it, as illustrated in Figure 5-16. Because of this, the Data control itself is often merely a service component in an application; that is, its Visible property is set to `False` so that it does not appear on the form. (The Data control's Visible property is `True` by default.)

However, the Data control does have an interface, as shown in Figure 5-17. In particular, it allows the user to easily navigate to the beginning of the recordset, to

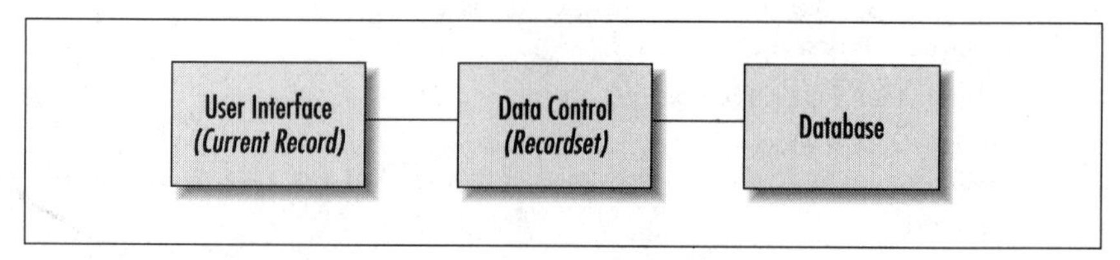

Figure 5-16: The role of the Data control in an application

the end of the recordset, to the previous record, or to the next record. For the most part, this navigation is performed automatically, without the need for you to write any code. In addition, the control provides a text box area that can be used in either of two ways: it can simply be left blank (this is controlled by its Caption property), and optionally its color can be modified to match that of some other interface component, most likely the scrollbars (this is controlled by its BackColor property). For example:

```
datMain.Caption = ""
datMain.BackColor = vbScrollBars
```

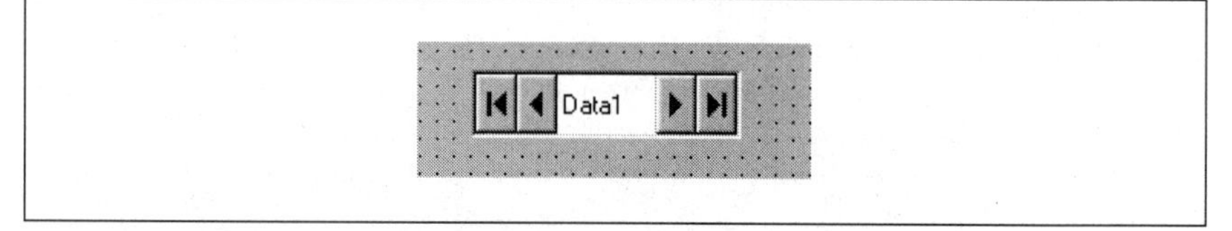

Figure 5-17: The Data control's user interface.

It can display some information about the recordset or the current record, such as a record number, a count of the total number of records in the recordset, or both. The following example shows how the caption can be populated with data from the Data control's recordset:

```
Private Sub datMain_Reposition()
   Me.datMain.Caption = LTrim(Me.datMain.Recordset!FirstName _
         & "  ") _
         & Trim(Me.datMain.Recordset!LastName)
End Sub
```

Handling Database Operations

The Data control features one property, several methods, and a number of events that can aid in performing basic database operations, such as navigating a recordset, performing data validation, handling updates to the database, and synchronizing the data displayed by bound controls with values contained in the database. They are:

EditMode property
: Indicates what action is currently taking place in the Data control. Possible values are 0–dbEditNone when no edit is in progress, 1–dbEditInProgress when an edit is taking place, or 2–dbEditAdd when a new record is being added.

Reposition event

Every time the record pointer is moved to a new record in a recordset contained by the Data control, the Reposition event is fired.

UpdateControls method

Updates all controls bound to the Data control with data from the recordset's current record.

UpdateRecord method

Updates the recordset's current record based on the values of bound controls.

Validate event

Whenever the record pointer is moved to a new record in the Data control's recordset, the Validate event is fired. Two parameters are passed to the event:

Action

A constant of the `VbDataValidateConstants` enumeration passed by reference that indicates how the pointer was moved. Navigation can be cancelled by setting its value to `vbActionCancel`, or the event handler can programmatically change the position to which the record pointer is moved. Possible values are shown in the following table:

Constant	*Value*	*Description*
`vbDataActionCancel`	0	When the Validate event finishes, the move is cancelled.
`vbDataActionMoveFirst`	1	The MoveFirst method was called.
`vbDataActionMovePrevious`	2	The MovePrevious method was called.
`vbDataActionMoveNext`	3	The MoveNext method was called.
`vbDataActionMoveLast`	4	The MoveLast method was called.
`vbDataActionAddNew`	5	The AddNew method was called.
`vbDataActionUpdate`	6	The Update method was called.
`vbDataActionDelete`	7	The Delete method was called.
`vbDataActionFind`	8	The Find method was called.
`vbDataActionBookmark`	9	The Bookmark property was set.
`vbDataActionClose`	10	The Recordset was closed.
`vbDataActionUnload`	11	The form containing the Data control is being closed.

Save

Boolean that indicates if the data has changed and therefore should be saved (a `True` value) or not (`False`).

Handling Errors

Data access errors that occur as a result of the operation of the Data control are not part of Visual Basic's error-handling system. That is, they cannot be handled by the standard VBA `On Error` statement. This makes a good deal of sense: while most Visual Basic runtime errors are "bad" and more often than not indicate an error in program design or execution, data access errors are routine.

The Data control signals the presence of a data access error in its own operation or that of its bound controls by firing the Error event. The event is passed the following parameters:

DataErr
: An integer indicating the error number. This is a DAO error code, rather than a VBA error code.

Response
: An integer passed by reference to the event handler that indicates how to respond to the error. Possible values are 0–vbDataErrContinue to continue executing the application and 1–vbDataErrDisplay to display the normal error message. The default value is `vbDataErrDisplay`.

Working with the Database Directly

The Data control handles the details of basic navigation through the user interface and of updating the contents of bound controls. Although these features are very convenient, the functionality of the Data control is extremely limited from the viewpoint of the requirements of most database applications. However, the Data control allows you to take advantage of the functionality of the Jet engine or of ODBC Direct through two of its properties: Database and Recordset. These return the Jet or ODBC Direct Database and Recordset objects, respectively, and in turn give you access to the properties and methods of these two objects.

The Database Object

A reference to the DAO Database object is returned by the Data control's Database property:

Database property
: Returns a reference to the Database object contained by the Data control. This Database object can then be used in code directly to perform additional operations, as in the following example:

```
Private Sub cmdDeleteAll_Click()
    Dim dbVar As Database
  'The DAO library must be referenced for this to work.

    Set dbVar = datMain.Database
    dbVar.Execute "DELETE FROM PEOPLE"
    datMain.Refresh
End Sub
```

Once you've retrieved a reference to the Database object, you can access its properties and methods. Some of the more useful of these include the following:

Connect property
: The Connect property of a Database object is the same as the Connect property of the Data control from which the database was derived.

Execute method
: Executes a query or SQL statement. Its syntax is:

```
objDB.Execute(Source, Options)
```

where *Source* contains a command that is understood by the data source and does not return any information and *Options* can be any sensible combination of constants from the following list. When the command is complete, the RecordsAffected property of the Recordset object is updated.

`DbDenyWrite`
: Records affected cannot be edited by other users.

`DbInconsistent`
: Fields involved in any joins can be edited by the command.

`DbConsistent`
: Fields involved in any joins cannot be edited by the command.

`DbSQLPassThrough`
: The command is passed as written to the data source.

`DbFailOnError`
: If the command is unsuccessful, any changes are automatically rolled back.

`DbSeeChanges`
: An error is generated if the command attempts to edit a record that is already being edited by another user.

`DbRunAsync`
: Allows a command to be run asynchronously.

QueryTimeout property

When the Database object is connected to an ODBC data source, the QueryTimeout property controls the number of seconds to wait after issuing a query before an error is fired. The QueryTimeout property of a Database object is used as the default QueryTimeout value for all child objects.

RecordsAffected property

After an Execute method is called, the RecordsAffected property contains the number of records that were affected by the command. For example, the following example deletes records from a data source and then reports how many were deleted:

```
Dim dbVar As Database

Set dbVar = Me.datMain.Database
dbVar.Execute "DELETE FROM PEOPLE"
MsgBox dbVar.RecordsAffected & "Records Deleted"
```

Updatable property

When set to `True`, data in the Database object can be changed. When `False`, no data in the database can be changed.

The Recordset Object

A reference to the DAO Recordset object is returned by the Data control's Recordset property:

Recordset property

Returns a reference to the Recordset object contained by the Data control. This Recordset object can then be accessed in code to perform additional operations not available through the Data control. In addition, a reference to any existing, valid Recordset object can be assigned to this property.

Once you have a valid reference to the Recordset object, you can access its properties and methods. Some of the more useful of these include the following:

AbsolutePosition, PercentPosition, RecordCount properties
: Each of these properties returns information about the number of records in the Recordset object or the position of the record pointer within the Recordset. The AbsolutePosition property returns the current location of the record pointer as a zero-based value. PercentPosition and RecordCount depend on an accurate count of the records returned in the Recordset. Normally, this is not available until the last record in the Recordset is read. Therefore, if accurate values for either of these properties are needed, call the MoveLast method at some time before using either of these properties. This will have a cost in performance, but it will then provide accurate information.

AddNew method
: Begins to edit a new record in the Recordset. This affects the Recordset object's EditMode property. No changes are saved until the Update method is called.

BOF, EOF properties
: These properties report whether the record pointer has gone past the extent of the data. The BOF property returns `True` if the pointer has gone before the first record of the Recordset object. The EOF property returns `True` if the pointer has gone after the last record.

Bookmark property
: Contains an identifier used to store, and later return to, a recordset's record.

Bookmarkable property
: If the Recordset object supports bookmarks, the Bookmarkable property returns `True`; otherwise, it returns `False`.

CacheSize property
: Controls the number of records cached by the data source. When the record pointer is moved beyond the extent of the CacheSize, another block of records is retrieved. The value of CacheSize cannot be 0.

CacheStart property
: The CacheStart property is a pointer to the first cached record in the same format as the Bookmark property. The CacheStart property can be set to cache records starting with the record assigned to it. The application can force records to be cached as follows:

```
Me.datMain.Recordset.CacheStart = _
      Me.datMain.Recordset.Bookmark
```

Delete method
: Deletes the recordset's current record.

Edit method
: Allows the Recordset object's currently selected record to be edited. This affects the Recordset object's EditMode property. No changes are saved until the Update method is called.

EditMode property

The EditMode property of a Recordset object is the same as the EditMode property of the Data control from which the recordset was derived.

GetRows method

Copies records from the recordset into a two-dimensional array. Its syntax is:

```
rsVar.GetRows(NumRows)
```

where ***NumRows*** is the number of rows to copy. The first dimension of the returned array iterates through the fields in a record. The second dimension iterates through the records.

LastModified property

Returns the most recently edited record in the recordset in the same format as the Bookmark property.

LockEdits property

Controls the type of locking in effect for the recordset. When set to `True`, other users cannot edit records that the current user is editing; this is usually called *pessimistic locking*. When set to `False`, other users can edit records that the current user is editing; this is usually called *optimistic locking*. The type of locking that should be used depends on the application's needs.

MoveNext, MovePrevious, MoveFirst, MoveLast methods

These navigational methods reposition the record pointer to the next record, previous record, first record, or last record of the recordset, respectively.

Name property

The Name property contains the text of the query used to create the recordset. If that text is more than 255 characters, only the first 255 characters are returned.

NoMatch property

After the Seek method or Find method is called, the NoMatch property is set based on the results of the method. When no records are found by the method, it is set to `True`. When the method is successful, it is set to `False`.

Requery method

Repeats the execution of the command that created the recordset.

Restartable property

Returns `True` if the Recordset supports the Requery method. Otherwise, the property returns `False`.

Type property

Indicates the type of recordset that is currently open. Possible values include 1–vbOpenTable for a table-type recordset, 2–vbOpenDynaset for a dynaset-type recordset, 4–vbOpenSnapshot for a shapshot-type recordset, 8–dbForwardOnly for a recordset that allows only the MoveNext navigational method, or 16–dbOpenDynamic for an ODBC dynamic recordset.

Updatable property

When set to `True`, data in the Recordset object can be changed. When `False`, no data in the recordset can be changed.

Update, CancelUpdate methods

The Update method saves a record that is currently being added or edited. The CancelUpdate method cancels a current edit or new record being added.

DataCombo, DBCombo, DataList, and DBList Controls

The DataCombo, DBCombo, DataList, and DBList controls themselves are not data access controls; that is, they are not responsible for retrieving information from a database or other data source. Instead, they bind to and access data through a Data control (for the DBList and DBCombo controls) or an ADO Data Control (for the DataList and DataCombo controls).

These controls are enhanced versions of the intrinsic ComboBox and ListBox controls that provide additional features when bound to a data source. More specifically, each control:

- Can be bound to a particular field of a recordset, so that the list box or combo box is automatically filled with the entire *column* of data, with one field value for each row of the recordset. In contrast, accomplishing the same thing with the standard ListBox or ComboBox controls requires that you iterate the data set, retrieve the field value for each row, and add it to the list box or combo box.
- Can be bound to another row in a second recordset (represented by a second data control) by means of a common field. When used with two data controls, it can allow the user to select a meaningful value (such as a customer name) while writing its corresponding key value (such as a customer code or some other unique identifier) to a database when a record is added or modified. Figure 5-18 illustrates this relationship.

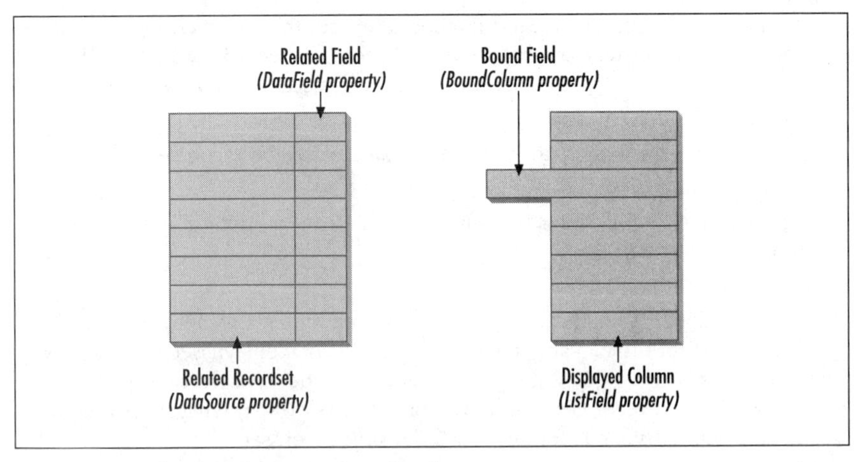

Figure 5-18: The data list controls and a data source

For the most part, the DBList, DBCombo, DataList, and DataCombo controls automatically provide this functionality, with little or no code.

The DataCombo and DataList controls are included with the Microsoft DataList Controls (*MSDATLST.OCX*). The DBCombo and DBList controls are included with the Microsoft Data Bound List Controls (*DBLIST32.OCX*). All four controls are bundled with Visual Basic Professional and Enterprise editions.

Setting the Data Properties

Since these controls are data-aware, the most important aspect of their use necessarily involves populating them with data and defining the necessary relationships so that they can work as effective tools for managing the application's data. The steps involved in doing this depend on the precise way in which the control is used in an application. The first step—filling the control's list box—is mandatory in all applications, while the second—displaying a field that is related to a second recordset based on a hidden, common field—is not. The steps involved in preparing these controls to handle data are:

1. Populating the list.

   Populating the control's list requires that you indicate the data control that is responsible for providing the recordset that contains the data and that you indicate the field to be used to populate the list box. This requires that you supply values to two properties (and sometimes to three properties) either at design time or at runtime:

   RowSource property
   : Defines the data control that contains the recordset used to fill the list. If a control is assigned to the RowSource property through code at runtime, it requires the use of the `Set` keyword. For example:

   ```
   Set Me.dtcMain.RowSource = Me.adcMain
   ```

   RowMember property (DataList and DataCombo only)
   : Defines the specific recordset used to fill the DataCombo or DataList control's list if the data control defined by the RowSource property supports more than one recordset.

   ListField property
   : Names the field of the recordset whose values will fill the control's list component, with one value for each row of the recordset.

   In many cases, setting these two properties is virtually all that's involved in working with the control. You can also select a particular member of the list by assigning its value to the control's Text property. The complete code to populate a DataCombo control that lists the states of the United States and initially selects New York, for example, is:

   ```
   'Fill list of combo.
   Set Me.dtcStates.RowSource = Me.adcStates
   Me.dtcStates.ListField = "State"
   Me.dtcStates.Text = "New York"
   ```

2. Binding to a field in another recordset.

   These controls can be used as lookup tables that update a second recordset based on the value of a hidden key or identifier. To take a concrete example, imagine a title maintenance utility for a publisher/title database. For each title published, the user should be able to use a drop-down combo box to choose from among existing publishers. While the combo box (which is a DataCombo or DBCombo control) displays the names of publishers, however, a unique publisher identifier, rather than a publisher name, is used to relate the publisher and the title tables. It is the value of this common field—and not the value of the publisher name field displayed by the control—that must be added to the title table to correctly relate it to the publisher table. It is this process that the controls handle automatically.

   Using the controls in this way involves a two-way relationship. When a record in the secondary recordset (in the case of our example, the title table) is selected, the control is automatically responsible for selecting the related record (that is, the record for the book's publisher). When a record is added or updated and the user selects a value from the control, the value of its associated identifier is written to the secondary recordset.

   Binding the displayed field and its selected row to a related field in another recordset is accomplished by setting four properties:

   BoundColumn property

   The name of the (typically hidden) field in the RowSource recordset (the recordset containing the ListField field) that is linked to a corresponding field in a second recordset. In the case of our publisher/title example, this field is the publisher identifier in the publisher table.

   DataSource property

   A reference to the data control containing the external recordset to which the field specified by the BoundField property is bound. In the case of our example, this is the data control that manages the title table.

   If the DataSource property is assigned at runtime, note that you must use the `Set` keyword to establish an object reference. For example:

   ```
   Set dtcLookup.DataSource = "adcMain"
   ```

   DataMember property

   Identifies the specific recordset to which the field specified by the BoundField property is bound if the data control defined by the DataSource property supports more than one recordset.

   DataField property

   The name of the field in the external recordset to which the field specified by the BoundField property is bound. In the case of our example, this is the publisher identifier field in the title table.

Defining the Control's Behavior

Like their ComboBox equivalent, the DataCombo and DBCombo controls support a number of available styles, largely depending on whether or not the user is able to enter text into the combo box. In addition, the combo type and list type controls support two different methods of responding to user attempts to search their lists. The properties that control these behaviors are:

Style property (DataCombo only)
: Like the standard ComboBox control, the Style property for the DBCombo and DataCombo control controls the type of combo that the user will be presented with. Possible values include 0–dbcDropDownCombo for a drop-down combo into which the user can enter data, 1–dbcSimpleCombo for a combo that is always dropped down, or 2–dbcDropdownList for a combo that drops down, but in which the user can choose only an item in the list.

MatchEntry property
: Controls how the user searches through the list portion of one of the controls. When set to 0–dblBasicMatching, each letter typed by the user searches for the first record in the RowSource recordset that matches that letter. Subsequent identical letters scroll through records beginning with that letter. When set to 1–dblExtendedMatching, letters typed until a significant pause are combined for a substring search for the record.

IntegralHeight property
: Determines whether partial items can be displayed in the list (a `False` value) or whether the control will resize itself to display only complete items (`True`, the default value).

DataFormat property
: Assigns or retrieves an StdDataFormat object that controls the formatting of list items. (For details on the StdDataFormat object, see *VB & VBA in a Nutshell: The Language* by Paul Lomax, published by O'Reilly & Associates.) In the case of the DBCombo and DataCombo controls, however, the formatting affects only the text displayed in the text box portion of the control, and not in its list portion. Since users find this behavior extremely confusing and disconcerting, you should avoid using the DataFormat property with these controls.

Working with the Control's Data

Although these controls handle most of the details of adding and updating records and synchronizing the lookup table with its bound recordset, sometimes you may need to know which item is selected in the control or whether a particular record has changed. The controls support a number of kinds of properties that you can use to control them directly.

Handling User Input

Several properties allow you to handle and respond to user input:

DataChanged property
: Indicates whether data in the bound control has changed by some process other than the movement of the record pointer. It returns `True` if data has been modified either programmatically or through user input.

MatchedWithList property

If the text entered into a DBCombo or DataCombo control whose Style property is set to either `dbcDropDownCombo` or `dbcSimpleCombo` does not match any records in its list, the MatchedWithList property returns `False`; otherwise, it returns `True`. Note that the property value does not reflect the results of partial matches; it returns `False` until the string entered by the user in the text box portion of the combo box exactly matches an item in the list.

The MatchedWithList property is also implemented for the DBList and DataList control. However, since the control allows the user to select only from predetermined items in the list, the property always returns `True`.

SelLength, SelStart, SelText properties (DataCombo only)

Set or return the total length of selected text, the starting character position of selected text, and the selected text itself.

Determining the Selected Item

Along with the more-or-less standard Text property, several properties allow you to determine which item is selected and to return to it subsequently:

BoundText property

Contains the text of the selected item in the list or the text contained in the text box portion of the combo box. In other words, aside from being read-only, it is identical to the Text property. This differs from the property's documented value, which is the value of the field defined by the BoundColumn property for the selected record.

SelectedItem property

Returns a bookmark that references the currently selected record in the recordset defined by the RowSource property. Subsequently, you can return to and retrieve information about this record by assigning this bookmark to the Recordset object's Bookmark property.

Working with List Items

A number of methods allow you to access individual items in either control's list:

ReFill method

Repopulates the control from the recordset defined by the RowSource property and repaints the control. The method takes no parameters.

VisibleCount property

The number of elements in the VisibleItems property array (and therefore the number of items that are visible in a DBList or DataList control or are visible in a DBCombo or DataCombo control when it is dropped down).

VisibleItems Property array

A zero-based array that contains one element for each item visible in the list. Each element of the array returns a bookmark that, when assigned to the recordset's Bookmark property, can make that record the current record.

Example

The following example shows how to populate a state field with a two-digit state code, but to show a list of full state names (illustrated in Figure 5-19):

```
'For this example, create the following controls: _
   a DataCombo named dtcStates, _
   an ADO Data Control named adcPeople, and _
   an ADO Data Control named adcStates.

Option Explicit

Dim lblName As Label
Dim lblCompany As Label
Dim lblState As Label

Dim txtLastName As TextBox
Dim txtFirstName As TextBox
Dim txtCompany As TextBox

Private Sub Form_Load()
  'Create controls.
   Set lblName = Me.Controls.Add("vb.label", _
                 "lblName", Me)
   lblName.Caption = "&Name:"
   lblName.TabIndex = 0
   lblName.Visible = True

   'These TextBox controls are bound to an ADO Data _
     Control at runtime.
   Set txtFirstName = Me.Controls.Add("vb.textbox", _
                      "txtFirstName", Me)
   Set txtFirstName.DataSource = Me.adcPeople
   txtFirstName.DataField = "FIRSTNAME"
   txtFirstName.TabIndex = 1
   txtFirstName.Visible = True

   Set txtLastName = Me.Controls.Add("vb.textbox", _
                     "txtLastName", Me)
   Set txtLastName.DataSource = Me.adcPeople
   txtLastName.DataField = "LASTNAME"
   txtLastName.TabIndex = 2
   txtLastName.Visible = True

   Set lblCompany = Me.Controls.Add("vb.label", _
                    "lblCompany", Me)
   lblCompany.Caption = "Company:"
   lblCompany.TabIndex = 3
   lblCompany.Visible = True

   Set txtCompany = Me.Controls.Add("vb.textbox", _
                    "txtCompany", Me)
   Set txtCompany.DataSource = Me.adcPeople
   txtCompany.DataField = "COMPANY"
   txtCompany.TabIndex = 4
   txtCompany.Visible = True

   Set lblState = Me.Controls.Add("vb.label", _
                  "lblState", Me)
```

```
    lblState.Caption = "State:"
    lblState.TabIndex = 5
    lblState.Visible = True

'adcPeople is the main ADO Data Control for the _
form. The DataCombo is bound to the StateCode _
column. The rows will be populated from the _
adcStates StateName field, but the StateCode field _
from the adcStates control will be used to set the _
StateCode field in the adcPeople control.
    Set Me.dtcStates.DataSource = Me.adcPeople
    Set Me.dtcStates.RowSource = Me.adcStates
    Me.dtcStates.DataField = "StateCode"
    Me.dtcStates.ListField = "StateName"
    Me.dtcStates.BoundColumn = "StateCode"
    Me.dtcStates.TabIndex = 6

'Here we'll connect to the data provider.
    Me.adcPeople.ConnectionString = _
         "Provider=Microsoft.Jet.OLEDB.3.51; " & _
         "Persist Security Info=False; " & _
         "Data Source=book.mdb"

    Me.adcPeople.RecordSource = _
     "Select FirstName, LastName, Company, StateCode " & _
     "From People " & _
     "Order By LastName, FirstName"

    Me.adcPeople.Caption = ""
    Me.adcPeople.Visible = True
    Me.adcPeople.Align = vbAlignBottom

    Me.adcPeople.Refresh

    Me.adcStates.ConnectionString = _
         "Provider=Microsoft.Jet.OLEDB.3.51;" & _
         "Persist Security Info=False;" & _
         "Data Source=C:\My Documents\Book\book.mdb"

    Me.adcStates.RecordSource = _
         "Select StateCode, StateName " & _
         "From States " & _
         "Order By StateCode"

    Me.adcStates.Visible = False
    Me.adcStates.Refresh

    Me.adcPeople.Recordset.MoveFirst
End Sub

Private Sub Form_Resize()
    If Me.ScaleHeight < 1785 Or Me.ScaleWidth < 3750 Then _
        Exit Sub
```

```
    lblName.Move 120, 180, 1095, 255
    lblCompany.Move 120, 615, 1095, 255
    lblState.Move 120, 1050, 1095, 255
    txtFirstName.Move 1335, 120, 1095, 315
    txtLastName.Move 2550, 120, Me.ScaleWidth - 2670, 315
    txtCompany.Move 1335, 555, Me.ScaleWidth - 1455, 315
    Me.dtcStates.Move 1335, 1035, Me.ScaleWidth - 1455
End Sub
```

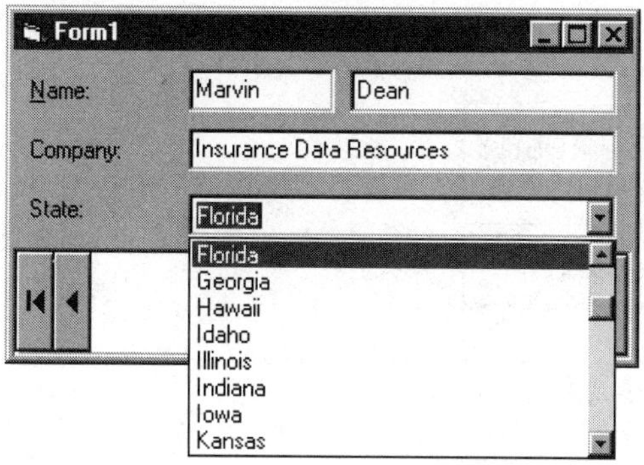

Figure 5-19: Some controls, including a DataCombo, bound to an ADO Data Control

DataGrid Control

The DataGrid control is one the components that Visual Basic provides to make viewing and editing information stored in a database easier and to support data access with little or no coding. Like a number of the other database controls, the DataGrid control binds to and accesses data through an ADO Data Control. Like a spreadsheet, the DataGrid control consists of rows and columns arranged in a grid; these rows correspond to the records of a recordset, while the columns correspond to its fields. In addition, the control automatically supplies the column headers containing the name of each field. The DataGrid, in other words, is an ideal tool for allowing the user to view or edit records while working with an entire recordset at a time. Moreover, if configured at design time rather than at runtime, the DataGrid control can accomplish almost all of its work without requiring any programming.

Despite this apparent simplicity, though, the DataGrid, when controlled programmatically, can be a very flexible and powerful tool for presenting recordsets. In particular, the control exposes an object model that gives you programmatic control over the data grid itself, as well as over its columns and splits. The DataGrid object model is shown in Figure 5-20.

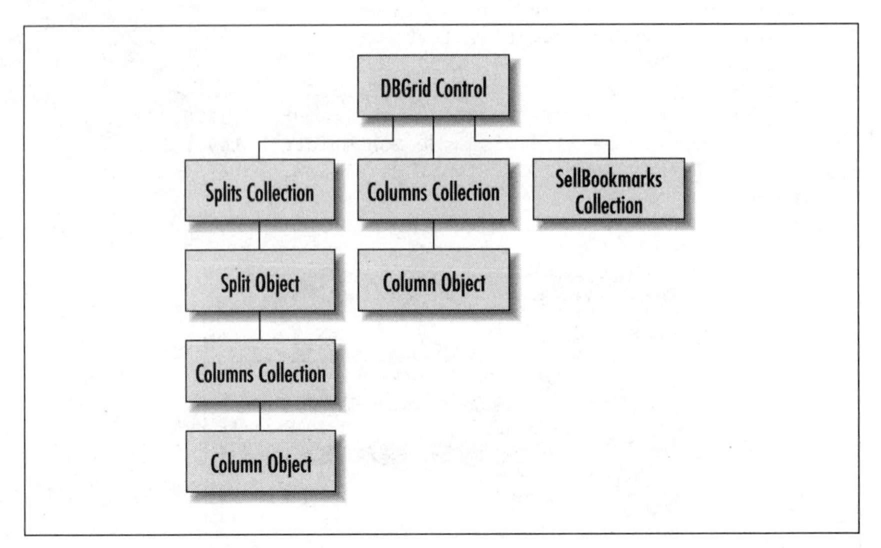

Figure 5-20: The DataGrid control's object model

The DataGrid control is shipped with the Professional and Enterprise editions of Visual Basic. It is listed as the Microsoft DataGrid control in the Components dialog and is found in the file *MSDATGRD.OCX*.

Binding to a Data Source

Binding to a data source is extremely easy—in most cases, a one-step process. (And, if you're a real minimalist, or you're developing a very simple, quick-and-dirty application, it can be the only thing that you need do with the control to complete your "application.") It simply requires that you set the control's DataSource property to an existing ADO Data Control. This can be done either at design time or at runtime. If it's done at runtime, note that you must assign the ADO DC's *object reference*, rather than a string, to the DataSource property, as the following line of code shows:

```
Set dtgEmployees.Datasource = adcEmployees
```

If an ADO Data Control manages more than one recordset, you can use the DataGrid control's DataMember property to indicate which recordset you'd like to use. Again, this property value can be selected either at design time or through code at runtime.

The DataGrid Control

DataGrid's properties control the grid's general appearance and behavior. Default properties have been chosen that reflect a "most common case" scenario in an attempt to reduce the need for programming. Nevertheless, there is substantial flexibility for the programmer to modify and configure its behavior and appearance.

Configuring the Grid's Appearance

The properties that allow you to control the DataGrid's general appearance can be set either at design time or at runtime. Changes to the properties at runtime take effect immediately. The most important properties include:

DefColWidth
: Defines the default column width for all columns in the DataGrid control in units measured by the current ScaleMode of the DataGrid control's container. If the DefColWidth property is set to 0 (its default value), each column is sized according to the data source for that column.

RecordSelectors
: Controls whether there will be an area to the left of the leftmost visible column that can be clicked to select the entire row. When set to `True`, its default value, that selector is shown on each row in the DataGrid control. When the property is `False`, no selectors are displayed.

RowDividerStyle
: Controls the type of line drawn between rows in the DataGrid control. Possible values are shown in the following table:

DividerStyleConstants	*Value*	*Description*
`dbgNoDividers`	0	No dividers are drawn.
`dbgBlackLine`	1	The divider appears as a black line.
`dbgDarkGrayLine`	2	The divider appears as a dark gray line; this is the default.
`dbgRaised`	3	The divider appears as a raised (3-D) line.
`dbgInset`	4	The divider appears as an inset (3-D) line.
`dbgUserForeColor`	5	The divider appears as a line drawn in a color specified by the DataGrid control's ForeColor property.
`dbgLightGrayLine`	6	The divider appears as a light gray line.

RowHeight
: Defines the height of all rows in the DataGrid control in the current ScaleMode of the DataGrid control's container. Setting the RowHeight property to a new value resizes all rows in the DataGrid control.

MarqueeStyle
: Determines whether only the current cell or the entire row is highlighted and defines the appearance of the highlight. The following are valid values for the MarqueeStyle property:

MarqueeStyleConstants	*Value*	*Description*
`dbgDottedCellBorder`	0	A dotted border is drawn around the current cell.
`dbgSolidCellBorder`	1	A solid border is drawn around the current cell.

MarqueeStyleConstants	*Value*	*Description*
`dbgHighlightCell`	2	The colors of the contents of the current cell are inverted.
`dbgHighlightRow`	3	The colors of the contents of the current row are inverted.
`dbgHighlightRowRaiseCell`	4	The colors of the contents of the current row are inverted and the current cell appears raised.
`dbgNoMarquee`	5	The current cell and row are not highlighted.
`dbgFloatingEditor`	6	The current cell will contain a blinking insert caret cursor. This is the default value.

ColumnHeaders
: Determines whether headers are displayed at the top of each column. Setting the ColumnHeaders property to `True`, its default setting, causes headings to be displayed. Setting the property to `False` causes the headings not to appear.

HeadFont
: Contains a reference to a standard Font object used in the headings at the top of each column.

HeadLines
: Defines the number of lines used in the column headings. The default value is 1. Setting the HeadLines property to 0 causes no headings to be displayed.

Defining the Grid's Behavior

A number of the DataGrid control's properties allow you to define how the user navigates the data grid (and the form containing the data grid) and determine whether the data grid can be used for browsing a recordset only or whether it can also be used for adding, editing, and deleting records. All of the following properties can be set either at design time or at runtime and take effect immediately at runtime:

AllowArrows
: Controls whether the arrow keys move between cells in a DataGrid control or between controls on the form. If set to `True`, the arrow keys move from cell to cell when the DataGrid has the focus. If `False`, the arrow keys move the focus to another control on the form.

AllowAddNew
: Setting the AllowAddNew property to `True` displays the Add New row at the bottom of the DataGrid control. Entering data on this row appends a new record to the data source. Setting the property to `False`, its default value, does not display the AddNew row and does not allow the user to add new records to the data source. This setting overrides the ADO Data Control's EOFAction property. However, it does not override the ADO Data Control's Mode property.

AllowDelete

When the AllowDelete property is set to `True`, the user can delete rows from the data source by selecting a row and pressing the Delete key. When the AllowDelete property is set to `False`, the user cannot delete records. Its default is `False`. However, it does not override the ADO Data Control's Mode property.

AllowRowSizing

Controls whether the user can resize rows on the DataGrid control. When `True`, its default value, the user can resize rows. When `False`, the user cannot resize rows.

AllowUpdate

When the AllowUpdate property is set to `False`, no data can be edited in the DataGrid control. When set to `True`, its default value, data can be edited by the user. However, the ADO Data Control must also allow the user to update the record.

TabAcrossSplits

When the TabAcrossSplits property is set to `True`, pressing the Tab key when the last column in the split has the focus (or pressing Shift-Tab when the first column has the focus) moves the focus to the next or previous Split object. When set to `False`, the Tab key acts according to the TabAction and WrapCellPointer properties.

TabAction

Determines the effect of pressing the Tab key while a DataGrid control has the focus. When set to 0–dbgControlNavigation, the Tab key (or Shift-Tab key) navigates to another control on the form based on the form's tab order. When set to 1–dbgColumnNavigation, the Tab key (or Shift-Tab key) navigates between cells on the current row. If the first or last cell in the current row is passed, the next (or previous) control on the form will get the focus. When set to 2–dbgGridNavigation, the Tab key acts the same as dbgColumnNavigation, except that when the first or last cell is passed, the WrapCellPointer property determines which cell will next receive the focus.

WrapCellPointer

When set to `True`, pressing the Right Arrow key while the last column of a row has the focus gives the focus to the first cell in the next row; the Left Arrow key does the opposite. When `False`, the default value, pressing the Left or Right Arrow key doesn't move the focus past the last column (or first column) of the current row.

Working with the DataGrid

A number of the DataGrid control's properties, methods, and events allow you to perform such useful operations as getting or setting the coordinates of the current cell, selecting multicolumn ranges, determining whether a particular column is visible, detecting the current state of the control, or restoring a cell to its previous state. These members include the following:

AddNewMode property

Indicates whether the DataGrid control is currently adding a new record. Possible values include 0–dbgNoAddNew when no record is being added,

1–dbgAddNewCurrent when no record is being added but the current row is the AddNew row, or 2–dbgAddNewPending when a new record is being added.

ApproxCount property

Queries the data source to determine the approximate number of rows in the DataGrid control. When the DataGrid control is bound to a large data source, retrieving the value of this property can go slowly.

BeforeColEdit, ColEdit, AfterColEdit events

The BeforeColEdit event is fired by the user or code performing an action that puts the cell into Edit mode. Its parameters are:

ColIndex

The ordinal position in the Columns collection of the Column object being edited.

KeyAscii

An integer representing the key pressed to begin editing. Its value is 0 if the user began editing by clicking the mouse.

Cancel

A flag passed by reference that, when set to `True`, indicates that the edit operation should be cancelled. Its default value is `False`.

If the edit operation is not cancelled, the ColEdit event is fired; it is passed the *ColIndex* parameter as well. Finally, the AfterColEdit event is fired when the cell is finished being edited; it is also passed the *ColIndex* parameter, indicating the column position of the cell being edited.

BeforeColUpdate, AfterColUpdate events

The BeforeColUpdate event is fired after the AfterColEdit event is finished but before the data entered is stored in the data source. Parameters passed to the BeforeColUpdate event are:

ColIndex

The index of the Column object whose cell is being edited.

OldValue

The original value of the cell before editing began.

Cancel

A flag passed by reference that can be set to `True` to cancel the update operation; its default value is `False`.

If the edit is not cancelled, the data is moved to the data source and the AfterColUpdate event is fired. The event is passed one parameter, *ColIndex*, which represents the index of the Column object that was edited.

BeforeDelete, AfterDelete events

When the user attempts to delete a record from the DataGrid control, the BeforeDelete event is fired. It is passed a single parameter:

Cancel

Flag passed by reference that, when set to `True`, indicates that the deletion should be cancelled; its default value is `False`. If the deletion is successful, the AfterDelete event is fired after the record is deleted.

BeforeInsert, AfterInsert, OnAddNew events

When the user attempts to add a new record to the DataGrid control, the BeforeInsert event is fired as soon as the AddNew row receives the focus. (This is in contradiction to the documentation, which claims that the event is fired only after the user begins to input text into a field.) A single parameter is passed to the event handler:

`Cancel`

Flag passed by reference that, when set to `True`, cancels the record insertion; its default value is `False`.

If the insertion is not cancelled, the AfterInsert event is then fired, followed by the OnAddNew event.

BeforeUpdate, AfterUpdate events

When data that has been edited is about to be moved to the data source, the BeforeUpdate event is fired. It is passed one parameter:

`Cancel`

Flag passed by reference that, when set to `True`, indicates the update operation should be cancelled; its default value is `False`.

If the update is successful, the AfterUpdate event is fired.

Bookmark property

Returns a value that references the current row of the DataGrid control. Setting the Bookmark property to a previously stored value sets the row referenced by the value as the current row. Note that it does not set the current column.

ButtonClick event

Fired when the button within a column is clicked by the user. The following parameter is passed to the event handler:

`ColIndex`

The zero-based index of the Column object containing the button.

CaptureImage method

Returns a reference to a metafile object representing the graphical image of the DataGrid control. This static image of the DataGrid at a particular point in time can then be assigned to the Picture property of a graphical control.

ClearSelCols method

Deselects all columns in the DataGrid control.

Col, Row properties

These properties contain the index of the currently selected column and row in the DataGrid control. The coordinates of the top-left cell are 0,0. Setting these properties to a valid column and row will make that cell the current cell. Note that if no column or row is selected, the Col property returns -1.

ColResize, RowResize events

When the user attempts to resize a row or column, one of these events is fired. The following parameters are passed to these events:

`ColIndex` *(ColResize event only)*

Ordinal position in the Columns collection of the column being resized.

`Cancel`

Flag passed by reference that, if set to `True`, cancels the resize operation. Its default value is `False`.

CurrentCellModified property

Returns `True` when the contents of the current cell differ from the corresponding value in its data source. When those values are the same, the CurrentCellModified property returns `False`. Setting the CurrentCellModified property to `False` cancels any editing and reverts the contents of the cell to those of the data source.

CurrentCellVisible property

Returns `True` if the current cell is visible within the DataGrid control and returns `False` otherwise. Setting the CurrentCellVisible property to `True` when it is `False` causes the DataGrid control to scroll so that the current cell is visible.

DataChanged property

Returns `True` if any data in the DataGrid control is different from the data retrieved from the data source. If no data has been changed, the DataChanged property returns `False`.

EditActive property

Returns `True` when the current cell is in Edit mode; otherwise, it returns `False`. Setting the EditActive property to `True` puts the current cell into Edit mode. Setting the EditActive property to `False` exits Edit mode, but edit-related events still fire. To cancel Edit mode without firing these events, set the CurrentCellModified property to `False`.

FirstRow, LeftCol properties

The FirstRow property returns a bookmark that references the first visible row in the DataGrid control. The LeftCol property contains the index of the left-most visible column in the DataGrid control. Setting the FirstRow property to a previously stored bookmark moves the corresponding row to the top of the DataGrid control. Setting the LeftCol property moves the corresponding column to the left of the DataGrid control.

GetBookmark method

Returns a bookmark for a row relative to the current row. Its syntax is:

```
objDataGrid.GetBookmark value
```

where *`value`* is an integer offset from the current row. For example, specifying a value of -3 returns the bookmark of the row three rows above the current row.

HeadClick event

Fired when the user clicks on the heading at the top of a Column object. A single parameter is passed to the event handler:

`ColIndex`

The ordinal position of the column whose heading was clicked in the Columns collection

hWndEditor property

When the current cell is in Edit mode (the EditActive property returns `True`), the hWndEditor property returns the handle to the DataGrid's editing window. This can then be used with various API calls. When EditActive returns `False`, the hWndEditor property returns 0.

Since the same handle is not necessarily used each time that the editor window opens, this value should not be stored to a variable that persists beyond the life of the particular instance of the editor window for which it was created.

Rebind, ClearFields, HoldFields methods

The Rebind method recreates all links to the data source as if the DataSource property were being set for the first time. The ClearFields method removes all bindings in the DataGrid control, leaving the DataGrid control with two columns with no data. The HoldFields method sets the current layout of the DataGrid control so that the next Rebind method will use that layout instead of overriding it.

RowBookmark method

Returns a bookmark of a visible row. Its syntax is:

```
objDataGrid.RowBookmark value
```

where *`value`* is the zero-based value of the visible row desired. Therefore, passing a parameter of 5 returns the bookmark for the sixth row.

RowColChange event

Fired whenever the current cell changes. The parameters passed to the event handler are:

`LastRow`
: The zero-based position of the row that previously had the focus

`LastCol`
: The zero-based position of the column that previously had the focus

RowTop method

Returns the coordinate of the top border of a particular row. Its syntax is:

```
objDataGrid.RowTop value
```

where *`value`* is the ordinal number of the visible row and can range from 0 to one less than the value of the VisibleRows property. When attempting to determine the boundaries of a cell in the DataGrid control, the RowTop method returns the top of the row, the DataGrid control's RowHeight property returns the height, and the Column object's Left and Width properties return the rest of the boundary. This can be useful when placing other controls directly over a cell, as in this example, which uses a ListBox control to simulate a drop-down value in the DataGrid:

```
Private Sub dtgMain_ButtonClick(ByVal ColIndex As Integer)
    Me.lstStates.Visible = True
    With Me.dtgMain
        Me.lstStates.Move _
            100 + .Left +.Columns(ColIndex).Left, _
            .Top +.RowTop(Me.dtgMain.Row) +.RowHeight,  _
```

```
            .Columns(ColIndex).Width - 100
    End With
    Me.lstStates.SetFocus
End Sub
```

Scroll event

Fired repeatedly whenever the user scrolls through the data grid. The event handler is passed a single parameter:

`Cancel`

Flag passed by reference that, when set to `True`, cancels the scrolling. Its default value is `False`.

Scroll method

Scrolls the DataGrid control. Its syntax is:

`objDataGrid.Scroll colvalue, rowvalue`

where ***`colvalue`*** is the number of columns to scroll horizontally and ***`rowvalue`*** is the number of rows to scroll vertically.

SelBookmarks property

Returns the SelBookmarks collection, which contains one bookmark for each row selected in the DataGrid control. The SelBookmarks collection object has the following members:

Add method

Adds an existing bookmark to the SelBookmarks collection. Its syntax is:

`SelBookmarks.Add bookmark`

where ***`bookmark`*** is the bookmark to be added. This has the effect of extending the selection to include the row that the bookmark references.

Count property

Returns the number of items in the SelBookmarks collection.

Item property

Retrieves a particular bookmark from the collection. Bookmarks can be retrieved by index only. Item is the collection's default property.

Remove method

Removes a bookmark from the collection. Its syntax is:

`SelBookmarks.Remove index`

where ***`index`*** is the ordinal position of the bookmark to be removed. This has the effect of unselecting that row.

SelChange event

Fired whenever the current cell (or range of cells) changes to a new cell (or cells). The event is passed a single parameter:

`Cancel`

Flag passed by reference that, when set to `True`, cancels the change of selection. Its default value is `False`.

SelStartCol, SelEndCol properties

When one or more columns are selected in a DataGrid control, the SelStartCol property indicates the starting left column, while the SelEndCol property indicates the right column. Setting these properties in code changes the selected range on the DataGrid control. If a range consisting of one or more columns is not selected, the two properties return -1.

The documentation also refers to the SelStartRow and SelEndRow properties, but these are not implemented.

Split property

Returns or sets the index of the current split.

SplitChange event

Fired when the current cell changes from a cell in one Split object to a cell in another Split object.

SplitContaining, ColContaining, RowContaining methods

These properties help to return the Split, Column, and Row objects that exist at a particular coordinate. The syntax of ColContaining is:

```
objDataGrid.ColContaining X
```

where *X* is a horizontal coordinate based on the container's coordinate system. The syntax of RowContaining is:

```
objDataGrid.RowContaining Y
```

where *Y* is a vertical coordinate based on the container's coordinate system. Finally, the syntax of SplitContaining is:

```
objDataGrid.SplitContaining X, Y
```

where *X* and *Y* are the horizontal and vertical coordinates based on the container's coordinate system. Each method returns the index of the object (that is, the column, row, and split, respectively) at that coordinate in its respective collection. This is illustrated in the following example:

```
Private Sub dtgMain_MouseMove(Button As Integer, _
            Shift As Integer, X As Single, Y As Single)
   Dim iSplit As Integer
   Dim iRow As Integer
   Dim iCol As Integer

   iSplit = Me.dtgMain.SplitContaining(X, Y)
   iRow = Me.dtgMain.RowContaining(Y)
   iCol = Me.dtgMain.ColContaining(X)

   If iSplit >= 0 And _
      iSplit < Me.dtgMain.Splits.Count Then _
       Me.dtgMain.Split = iSplit

   If iRow >= 0 And _
      iRow < Me.dtgMain.ApproxCount Then _
       Me.dtgMain.Row = iRow

   If iCol >= 0 And _
      iCol < Me.dtgMain.Columns.Count Then _
       Me.dtgMain.Col = iCol
End Sub
```

VisibleCols, VisibleRows properties

These properties return the number of columns visible (VisibleCols) or the number of rows visible (VisibleRows) on the DataGrid control.

Handling Errors

Like the other database controls, the DataGrid control provides an error-handling system separate and independent of the standard Visual Basic error-handling system. It consists of one event and one property:

Error event

Fired when an error occurs in a DataGrid control. It is passed the following parameters:

`DataError`

The error number.

`Response`

An integer passed by reference that indicates whether the standard error message should be displayed in response to the error. Set it to 0 to suppress the display of the error message or 1 (the default) to show the standard error message.

ErrorText property

Returns the text of any error returned by the data source to the DataGrid property. This can be different from the error returned by the Error event. The ErrorText property is in scope only within the DataGrid control's Error event handler.

The Column Object

The columns in a Data Grid control are accessible programmatically through the Columns collection, which is returned by the DataGrid control's Columns property.

The Columns Collection

This collection object contains one column for each column in the data grid. The collection object's members are:

Add method

Adds a column. Its syntax is:

```
objColumn = Columns.Add(index)
```

where *`index`* is the position at which the column is to be added and can range from 0 (to add a column in front of the first column) to the current value of the Count property (to add a column after the last column). The method returns a reference to the newly added Column object.

Count property

Indicates the total number of Column objects in the collection.

Item property

Returns a reference to an individual Column object based on its ordinal position in the collection.

Remove method

Removes a Column object from the collection and deletes the column that it represents from the data grid. Its syntax is:

```
Columns.Remove index
```

where *index* is the ordinal position of the column to remove; it ranges from 0 to one less than the value of the Count property.

Configuring Individual Columns

You can access individual columns within the Columns collection to control their physical appearance and the way that they interface with the user. The properties that allow you to do this are:

AllowSizing

Controls whether the user can resize the column by moving its right border. When `True`, its default value, the user can resize the column; when `False`, the user cannot.

Button

If `True`, causes a drop-down button to appear on the right edge of a selected cell within that column, as shown in Figure 5-21. When the user clicks this button, the ButtonClicked event of the DataGrid control is fired. The property's default value is `False`; no button appears, and the ButtonClicked event is not fired.

Konbu	6	8
Tofu	6	7
Genen Shouyu	6	2
Pavlova	7	3

Figure 5-21: The Button property and the Button drop-down

DefaultValue

The default value that new records will contain for that field (or column) until the user changes it.

DividerStyle

Controls the type of line drawn on the column's right edge. Possible values are shown in the following table:

DividerStyleConstant	*Value*	*Description*
`dbgNoDividers`	0	No dividers are drawn.
`dbgBlackLine`	1	The divider appears as a black line.
`dbgDarkGrayLine`	2	The divider appears as a dark gray line; this is the default value.
`dbgRaised`	3	The divider appears as a raised (3-D) line.
`dbgInset`	4	The divider appears as an inset (3-D) line.

DividerStyleConstant	*Value*	*Description*
`dbgUserForeColor`	5	The divider appears as a line drawn in a color specified by the DataGrid control's ForeColor property.
`dbgLightGrayLine`	6	The divider appears as a light gray line.

NumberFormat

Can contain a valid format string that will be used to format numerical data in that column. The syntax of the format string is identical to that of the VBA *Format* function. The Column object's Text property returns the formatted data from the column's current row; its Value property returns the unformatted data in the column's current row.

WrapText

Determines whether words that would be partially hidden (because the cell is not wide enough to display them in their entirety) are wrapped to a subsequent line. When set to `True`, a new line is created. When set to `False`, its default value, the text is clipped.

In order to see extra lines of text in a cell, the RowHeight property of the DataGrid control must be adjusted manually.

The Split Object

The DataGrid allows the grid to be divided into vertical panes called *splits* that allow the DataGrid control to present different views of the same recordset. Each split can be scrolled independently of the other splits or can be synchronized to scroll with any other split or set of splits.

Each split is represented by a Split object, which in turn is a member of the Splits collection. The Splits collection is returned by the DataGrid's Splits property. Each Split object in turn has its own Columns collection, which contains one Column object for each column in the recordset.

By default, the DataGrid control contains a single split, although additional ones can be created either without code by the user or programmatically through code. The ability to add splits through the user interface can be disabled by setting the default Split object's AllowSizing property to `False` before any splits have been created.

The Splits Collection

The Splits collection object, which is returned by the DataGrid's Splits property, has the following members:

Add method

Adds a Split object to the Splits collection (and a split to the DataGrid control). Its syntax is:

```
objDataGrid.Splits.Add index
```

where *index* is the ordinal position of the new Split object in the collection. Typically, new splits are added to the end of the Splits collection, so that *index* is set equal to `Splits.Count`. The method returns a reference to the newly added Split object.

Count property

Returns the total number of Split objects in the collection.

Item property

Allows you to retrieve a reference to an individual Split object by its ordinal position in the collection.

Remove method

Removes a split from the Splits collection (and deletes that split from the DataGrid control). Its syntax is:

```
objDataGrid.Splits.Remove index
```

where *index* is the ordinal position of the Split object to be removed from the collection.

Configuring Individual Splits

You can access individual splits within the Splits collection to control their physical appearance and the way that they interface with the user. The properties that allow you to do this are:

AllowFocus property

Determines whether cells within the Split object can be selected by the user. When set to `True`, its default value, the cells can receive the focus; when set to `False`, they cannot.

ScrollGroup property

All Split objects with the same zero or positive integer value in the ScrollGroup property scroll vertically together. Split objects with different values for the ScrollGroup property scroll independently. By default, all splits are assigned the same value for the ScrollGroup property.

SizeMode, Size property

The SizeMode property determines the Size property's unit of measure. The Size property sets the size of the Split object. Possible values for the SizeMode property include 0–dbgScalable to size splits relative to the Size values of each split, 1–dbgExact to specify the Size property value in the units defined by the DataGrid control's container, or 2–dbgNumberOfColumns to specify the number of columns that the Split object will contain. When using dbgScalable, setting one Split object's Size property to 1 and the other Split object's Size property to 4 causes the first Split object to be sized to one-fifth of the width of the DataGrid control and the other Split object to four-fifths.

CurrentCellVisible, MarqueeStyle, AllowSizing, AllowRowSizing, Columns, Columns Collection, Column object, FirstRow, LeftCol, RecordSelectors, ScrollBars, SelStartCol, SelEndCol, SelStartRow, SelEndRow properties

Each of these properties acts like the corresponding property of the DataGrid control, except that it applies only to the individual Split object.

Order of Events

The following is the order in which events are fired when deleting a record:

1. BeforeDelete event
2. AfterDelete event
3. BeforeUpdate event
4. AfterUpdate event
5. RowColChange event

The following is the order in which events are fired when adding a record:

1. BeforeInsert event
2. AfterInsert event
3. OnAddNew event

Following OnAddNew, the following events are fired for each field added to the record:

1. RowColChange event
2. BeforeColEdit event
3. ColEdit event
4. ColUpdate event
5. AfterColUpdate event
6. AfterColEdit
7. BeforeUpdate
8. AfterUpdate

Interactions

Action	*Result*
DataGrid loads a recordset	SplitChange event fires

VB6 *DTPicker Control*

The DTPicker (Date/Time Picker) control appears as a TextBox control displaying a date with either a drop-down button or up/down buttons to change the date or time. In the case of dates, the drop-down button displays a calendar that appears similar to the MonthView control; however, the MonthView control cannot be accessed programmatically from the DTPicker control. The DTPicker control handles each element of the date or time as a separate input field (and allows custom fields as well). Along with being able to modify the field value, the user can increment or decrement a field by pressing the Plus or Minus key, respectively. The DTPicker control is shown in Figure 5-22.

The DTPicker control is included with Version 6.0 or later of Microsoft Windows Common Controls-2 (*MSCOMCT2.OCX*).

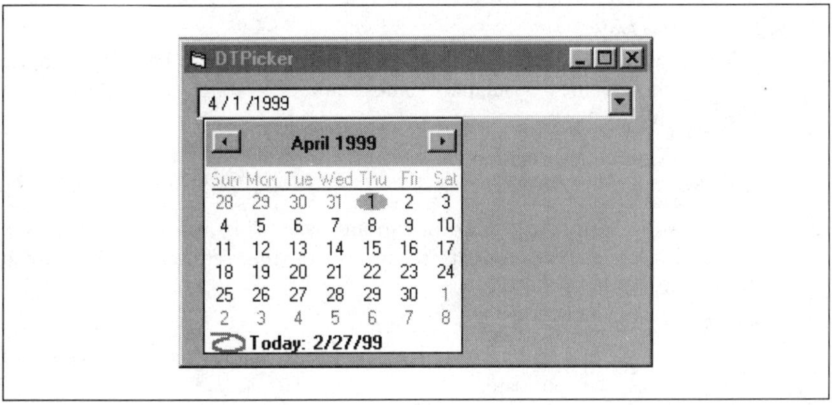

Figure 5-22: The DTPicker control

Control Tasks

The following categories reflect the tasks that are executed when creating a DTPicker control.

Set Properties

1. Set appearance.

Format

Controls the general appearance of the DTPicker control. By setting the Format property to 0–dtpLongDate, the date is shown in the system-defined long date format. When set to 1–dtpShortDate, the date is shown in the Windows short date format. Setting it to 2–dtpTime displays the time in the Windows time format. Finally, setting the Format property to 3–dtpCustom uses the format string in the CustomFormat property.

UpDown

When set to `False`, its default value, a drop-down button can be used to open the MonthView control, which allows a particular date to be selected. When set to `True`, up and down buttons can be used to increment or decrement the selected date or time element.

Figure 5-23 shows two instances of the DTPicker control when the UpDown property is set to `True` and `False`, respectively. Note that in the control on the right, the day can be increased or decreased by clicking on the up or the down button.

When the Format property is set to `dtpTime`, this property has no effect. The control will always display up and down buttons beside the text box.

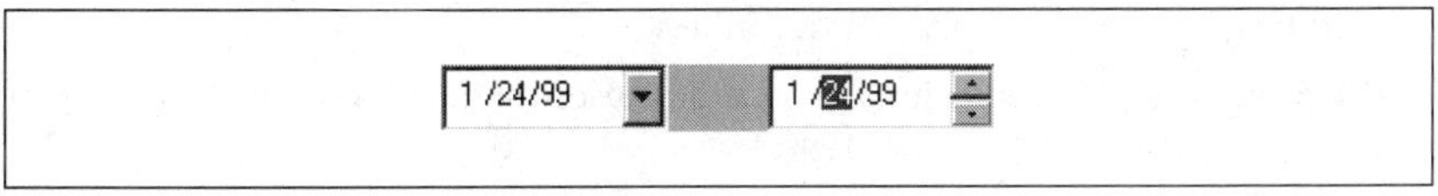

Figure 5-23: The UpDown property

2. Set constraints.

   MinDate, MaxDate

   These properties set the earliest and latest date that can be entered in the DTPicker control. Default values are 1/1/1601 and 12/31/9999, respectively.

3. Set or retrieve date information.

   Value

   Returns or sets the control's current date. This is expressed in the system's short date format, regardless of the setting of the Format property.

   Day, Month, Year, Hour, Minute, Second

   These properties return or set the applicable date or time component of the control's current date.

   DayOfWeek

   Returns or sets the number of the weekday for the currently selected date. The value returned is 1–mvwSunday, 2–mvwMonday, 3–mvwTuesday, 4–mvwWednesday, 5–mvwThursday, 6–mvwFriday, or 7–mvwSaturday. Setting the DayOfWeek property changes the date to the indicated day of the same week as the original date.

Write Event Handlers

DropDown, CloseUp

If the UpDown property is `False` (that is, when the drop-down button is visible and the user presses it to open the MonthView control), the DropDown event is fired prior to the calendar being displayed. When the calendar is closed, the CloseUp event is fired. If the UpDown property is `True`, the DropDown and CloseUp events are not fired.

Define and Handle Custom Formats (optional)

Although the DTPicker control allows you to choose between the long date, short date, and time formats, you aren't limited to these choices. You can define a custom format for displaying the date or time by setting the control's Format property to 3–dtpCustom. The following steps then define and handle the custom format:

1. Define the custom format using the CustomFormat property.

   The CustomFormat property can contain a format string similar to those used with VBA's *Format* function. When the Format property is set to `dtpCustom`, this string is used to control the input and display of the control's value. In addition, one or more groups of one or more capital Xs can be used in the format string as placeholders for callback fields. These callback fields are then passed by reference to the Format event and by value to the FormatSize event so that they can be replaced with values.

   For example, the following assignment causes the DTPicker control to display a date in the format Jan 1st, 1999:

```
Me.DTPicker1.Format = dtpCustom
Me.DTPicker1.CustomFormat = "MMM ddXX, yyyy"
```

In this case, XX is a two-letter string indicating the number's ordinal value (e. g., st, nd, rd, th), depending on the value of dd.

If you don't include one or more callback fields in a custom format, you don't need to do anything else; the control will automatically apply the custom format. However, you must write custom event handlers if you include callback fields.

2. Define the length of the text.

   The FormatSize event is fired whenever the string assigned to the CustomFormat property includes a callback. In other words, it is fired when the program starts (if the CustomFormat property is assigned at design time and includes a callback field) or whenever an assignment to the CustomFormat property includes a callback field. Its syntax is:

```
DTPicker1_FormatSize(ByVal CallbackField As String, _
                     Size As Integer)
```

   where ***CallbackField*** contains the string of Xs for that callback field, and ***Size*** is passed by reference and should be set to the maximum size needed for the callback field.

The actual number of Xs in a callback field has no bearing on the size of the field in the control. The FormatSize event's ***Size*** parameter is used to set the maximum size of the field. By using different numbers of Xs for each callback field in a single custom format, they can be easily distinguished from one another.

To continue the example of displaying a date in the format Jan 1st, 1999, ORthe DTPicker control's FormatSize event might consist of the following:

```
Private Sub DTPicker1_FormatSize( _
            ByVal CallbackField As String, _
            Size As Integer)
Size = 2

End Sub
```

3. Define the text to be placed in the callback field.

   The Format event is fired anytime there is a change to the value of the DTPicker control's contents when its custom format includes a callback field. The event handler's syntax is:

```
Private Sub DTPicker1_Format( _
        ByVal CallbackField As String, _
        FormattedString As String)
```

   where ***CallbackField*** contains the string of Xs for the callback field to be populated and ***FormattedString*** is a parameter that, when the procedure returns, should contain the value to be placed into the callback field.

   To continue the example of displaying a date in the format Jan 1st, 1999, the DTPicker control's Format event might consist of the following:

```
Private Sub DTPicker1_Format( _
        ByVal CallbackField As String, _
        FormattedString As String)

Select Case Day(Me.DTPicker1.Value)
   Case 1
      FormattedString = "st"
   Case 2
      FormattedString = "nd"
   Case 3
      FormattedString = "rd"
   Case Else
      FormattedString = "th"
End Select

End Sub
```

4. Define how the callback field handles user input.

   In some cases, you may want the callback field to be wholly or partially controlled by user interaction. You can do this by writing code for the CallbackKeyDown event, which is fired whenever the user presses a key when the format string reserved for the callback field has the focus. The CallbackKeyDown event handler's syntax is:

   ```
   Private Sub DTPicker1_CallbackKeyDown( _
        ByVal KeyCode As Integer, _
        ByVal Shift As Integer, _
        ByVal CallbackField As String, _
        CallbackDate As Date)
   ```

   where *KeyCode* and *Shift* represent the code of the key pressed and a flag indicating whether the Shift key is depressed (these two parameters are identical to those of the standard KeyDown event procedure), *CallbackField* contains the string of Xs for the callback field, and *CallbackDate* is identical to the control's Value property. Since *CallbackDate* is passed by reference to the event handler, it can be used to modify the date or time.

Example

This example shows how a callback field could be used to show a holiday for a date entered:

```
Option Explicit

'For this example, create the following controls: _
  a DTPicker control named dtpMain.

Private vmHolidays() As Variant

Private Sub Form_Load()
  'We need to load the Holiday array.
   GetHolidays

   Me.Caption = "DTPicker Demo"
```

```
  'We'll use the X as a callback field for the Holiday.
    Me.dtpMain.CustomFormat = "M/d/yyyy X"
    Me.dtpMain.Format = dtpCustom
End Sub

Private Sub Form_Resize()
  If Me.ScaleHeight < 555 Or Me.ScaleWidth < 1335 Then _
      Exit Sub

    Me.dtpMain.Move 120, 120, Me.ScaleWidth - 240, 315
End Sub

Private Sub dtpMain_Format( _
            ByVal CallbackField As String, _
            FormattedString As String)
    Dim iCtr As Integer

  'We actually don't need this here since we have _
  only one callback field.
    If CallbackField <> "X" Then _
        Exit Sub

  'If the Month and Day match the array, populate _
  the callback field.
    For iCtr = 0 To UBound(vmHolidays)
        If vmHolidays(iCtr, 0) = Me.dtpMain.Month _
          And vmHolidays(iCtr, 1) = Me.dtpMain.Day Then
            FormattedString = vmHolidays(iCtr, 2)
            Exit For
        End If
    Next iCtr
End Sub

Private Sub dtpMain_FormatSize( _
            ByVal CallbackField As String, _
            Size As Integer)
    Dim iCtr As Integer
    Dim iSize As Integer

  'We actually don't need this here since we have _
  only one callback field.
    If CallbackField <> "X" Then _
        Exit Sub

  'We'll just set the size to the length of _
  the longest holiday name in the array.
    For iCtr = 0 To UBound(vmHolidays)
        If Len(vmHolidays(iCtr, 2)) > iSize Then _
            iSize = Len(vmHolidays(iCtr, 2))
    Next iCtr

    Size = iSize
End Sub
```

```
Private Sub GetHolidays()
   'In this demo we'll only use simple holidays. _
   We would need much more logic to handle complex _
   holidays, but that would be beyond the DTPicker _
   control.
    ReDim vmHolidays(5, 2)

    vmHolidays(0, 0) = 1
    vmHolidays(0, 1) = 1
    vmHolidays(0, 2) = "New Year's Day"

    vmHolidays(1, 0) = 2
    vmHolidays(1, 1) = 15
    vmHolidays(1, 2) = "Valentine's Day"

    vmHolidays(2, 0) = 4
    vmHolidays(2, 1) = 15
    vmHolidays(2, 2) = "Tax Day"

    vmHolidays(3, 0) = 7
    vmHolidays(3, 1) = 4
    vmHolidays(3, 2) = "Independence Day"

    vmHolidays(4, 0) = 10
    vmHolidays(4, 1) = 31
    vmHolidays(4, 2) = "Halloween"

    vmHolidays(5, 0) = 12
    vmHolidays(5, 1) = 25
    vmHolidays(5, 2) = "Christmas"
End Sub
```

FlatScrollBar Control

See: Scrollbar Controls

Frame Control

Frame is a display-only control for providing information to the user. The most important use of Frame controls is to serve as containers for other controls and in this way to help organize an application's user interface. Typically, a Frame control is used to hold a group of related controls. In Figure 5-24, for example, a Frame control contains three Label controls, two drop-down combo controls, and one TextBox control, all of which are used to present font information.

A lightweight version of the Frame control is also available; see the entry for Windowless Controls, in this chapter.

Figure 5-24: The Frame control

Control Tasks

The following categories reflect the tasks that are executed when creating a frame.

Set Properties

1. Display properties (optional).

   Enabled

   The Enabled property is present in every Visual Basic control. However, the Frame control's Enabled property affects the Enabled property of its contained controls in a somewhat unusual way that makes it worthy of special mention.

   As with other container controls, when a frame is disabled, all contained controls are treated as if they were disabled as well, and each control's Enabled property is set to `False`. However, visually, these controls do not appear to be disabled (or grayed) to the user. Therefore, it is important to disable controls in a frame to give the standard appearance of a disabled control. This can be automated, as in the following code example:

```
Public Sub EnableDisableFrame(frmVar As Form, _
            fraVar As Frame, Enable As Boolean)
  'Pass the Form, Frame, and whether to Enable (True) _
    or Disable (False) the frame.
    Dim ctlVar As Control

  'Loop through all the controls on the form.
    For Each ctlVar In frmVar.Controls
        If ctlVar.Container Is fraVar Then
      'Only Enable/Disable controls on the frame.
            ctlVar.Enabled = Enable
        End If
    Next ctlVar

  'Enable/Disable the frame itself. Don't forget _
    to re-enable a disabled frame!
    fraVar.Enabled = Enable
End Sub
```

At other times, frames can be "juggled" to show different content based on the current operation being performed. This can be done using the Frame control's Visible property or the ZOrder method. However, if you were using the ZOrder method alone, hidden controls would still be present in the tab order and give confusing results to the user.

Interactions

Action	*Result*
Gets the focus through the form's tab order.	Passes the focus to the contained control with the lowest TabIndex.
Enabled property changes.	The Enabled property of all contained controls changes to match the value of the frame's Enabled property, unless the control's Enabled property has been set to `False` independently of its frame.

Hierarchical FlexGrid (MSHFlexGrid) Control

The MSHFlexGrid is very similar to the MSFlexGrid control. It too can be bound to a data source and provides a grid for displaying record (row) and field (column) information from recordsets. In comparison with the FlexGrid control, however, it offers some additional features and some advanced capabilities. These are:

- Support for OLE DB. Whereas the MSFlexGrid control supports only non-OLE DB data sources, the MSHFlexGrid supports only OLE DB data sources, like the ADO Data Control. From this point of view, the MSHFlexGrid is identical to the MSFlexGrid control, except that it is ADO-enabled, whereas the MSFlexGrid is not.
- Ability to bind to a hierarchy of recordsets. As shown in Figure 5-25, which used the Hierarchical FlexGrid control to display the mobile and home phone numbers of contacts by region, its real strength lies in handling relationships in which the child recordset has a many-to-one relationship to its parent.

The MSHFlexGrid control is a superset of the MSFlexGrid control; all properties, methods, and events of the MSFlexGrid control apply as well to the MSHFlexGrid control. Consequently, only the differences will be covered here.

The easiest way to create an MSHFlexGrid control is by using the right mouse button to drag a hierarchical query (a command) from a DataEnvironment onto a form in the same project and choosing the Hierarchical Flex Grid option. This creates a bound MSHFlexGrid on that form. Moreover, most of the power and flexibility of the MSHFlexGrid control is available at design time through the Data Environment Designer simply by selecting a hierarchy of recordsets; in most cases, little or no programming is required.

Phone List

StateName	Last	First	Company	Location	Area	Phone
California	Pacey	Larry	SegaSoft	Home	650	555-7989
				Work	650	555-2845
	Pavlicek	Rich	Pinnacle Technologies	Home	650	555-0456
Florida	Adler	Gary	PSDI	Home	954	555-9861
				Work	954	555-3845
	Dean	Marvin	Insurance Data Resources	Home	954	555-9110
				Work	561	555-2269
	Dictor	Evan	O'Reilly and Associates	Home	954	555-6478
				Work	954	555-2638
				Mobile	954	555-2793
	Henry	Stuart	Insurance Data Resources	Home	954	555-1001
				Work	561	555-1030
	Holcomb	Josh	Insurance Data Resources	Home	954	555-8298
				Work	561	555-8246
				Mobile	954	555-5892
	Loeb	Randon	DAS Enterprises	Home	954	555-9994
				Work	954	555-6762
	Marino	Anthony	Insurance Data Resources	Home	954	555-5339
				Work	561	555-1064
	Mojica	Jose	Maxim	Home	954	555-2439
				Work	561	555-2837
	Perez	Santiago	Insurance Data Resources	Home	561	555-0157
				Work	561	555-5752
	Rodriguez	Andres	Insurance Data Resources	Home	305	555-6951
				Work	561	555-9800
	Timmes	Henry	Insurance Data Resources	Home	954	555-3911
				Work	561	555-3240
Georgia	Fittipaldi	Kristen	Tucker Federal Bank	Work	770	555-4397
				Home	770	555-7878
Illinois	Ulmer	Karen	ABN-AMRO	Work	312	555-3477
				Home	312	555-9711
Michigan	Wheelock	William	CCI	Home	248	555-1243
				Work	248	555-3957
New York	Carvalho	Donna	North Fork Bank	Work	516	555-4387
				Home	516	555-8373
	Korbel	Bill	News 12	Work	516	555-2424
				Home	516	555-8234

Figure 5-25: A populated MSHFlexGrid control

The Microsoft Hierarchical FlexGrid control is shipped with the Professional and Enterprise editions of Visual Basic and is found in the file *MSHFLXGD.OCX*.

1. Set data source.

   DataSource

   The DataSource property is used to link the MSHFlexGrid with an ADO Data Control on the same Form object or a DataEnvironment within the same VB project. If this property is set to an ADO Data Control, the MSHFlexGrid becomes read-only and will contain only one band. If set to a DataEnvironment, you can take advantage of the control's ability to handle hierarchies of records by defining one or more child commands in the DataEnvironment.

The MSHFlexGrid control can be bound to the ADO Data Control but not to the intrinsic Data control. Conversely, the MSFlexGrid can be bound to an intrinsic Data control but to not an ADO Data Control.

It is also possible to handle the entire process programmatically at runtime, as the following Form_Load procedure shows:

```
Private Sub Form_Load()

Dim strConn As String

strConn = "Provider=MSDataShape.1;" & _
   "Data Source=MyBiblio;"

Dim strSh As String

strSh = "SHAPE {SELECT Name, PubID " & _
   "FROM Publishers} AS " & _
   "Publishers APPEND ({SELECT " & _
   "Title, PubID FROM Titles} AS " & _
   "Titles RELATE PubID TO PubID) " & _
   "AS Titles"

With Adodc1
   .ConnectionString = strConn
   .RecordSource = strSh
End With

Set MSHFlexGrid1.DataSource = Adodc1

End Sub
```

Note that it makes use of the `SHAPE` command supported by the MSDataShape OLE DB provider.

2. Set control appearance.

ForeColorBand, ForeColorFixed, ForeColorHeader, ForeColorSel
: These properties set the foreground color for bands (ForeColorBand), the fixed columns and rows (ForeColorFixed), the header (ForeColor-Header), and any selected cells (ForeColorSel). If these are not set, the control's ForeColor property is used.

BackColorBand, BackColorFixed, BackColorHeader, BackColorSel

These properties set the background color for bands (BackColorBand), the fixed columns and rows (BackColorFixed), the header (BackColorHeader), and any selected cells (BackColorSel). If these are not set, the control's BackColor property is used.

GridLines, GridLinesBand, GridLinesFixed, GridLinesHeader, GridLinesIndent, GridLinesUnpopulated

These properties control whether the control (GridLines), bands (GridLinesBand), the fixed columns and rows (GridLinesFixed), the header (GridLinesHeader), the indented area before a band (GridLinesIndent), or cells that are not populated (GridLinesUnpopulated) will have gridlines drawn. When any of these properties is set to `True`, gridlines will appear in the appropriate areas. When set to `False`, no gridlines will appear in those areas.

Controls H–L

GridColor, GridColorBand, GridColorFixed, GridColorHeader, GridColorIndent, GridColorUnpopulated

These properties set the color of the gridlines for the entire control (GridColor), bands (GridColorBand), the fixed rows and columns (GridColorFixed), the header (GridColorHeader), the indented area before a band (GirdColorIndent), or cells that aren't populated (GridColorUnpopulated).

GridLineWidth, GridLineWidthBand, GridLineWidthFixed, GridLineWidthHeader, GridLineWidthIndent, GridLineWidthUnpopulated

The GridLineWidth property sets the width in pixels of gridlines in the MSFlexGrid control (GridLineWidth), in bands (GridLineWidthBand), in the fixed rows and columns (GridLineWidthFixed), in the header (GridLineWidthHeader), in the indented area before a band (GridLineWidthIndent).

FontWidth, FontWidthBand, FontWidthFixed, FontWidthHeader

The FontWidth property sets the width of the font (as opposed to its height, the normal measurement of font size) in points to be used throughout the MSHFlexGrid control (FontWidth), in bands (FontWidthBand), in the fixed rows and columns (FontWidthFixed), or in the header (FontWidthHeader).

CellAlignment, CellPictureAlignment, ColAlignment property array, ColAlignmentBand property array, ColAlignmentFixed property array, ColAlignmentHeader property array

The CellAlignment property controls how the contents of a cell are aligned both vertically and horizontally. The CellPictureAlignment controls how an image within a cell is aligned. Each element of the ColAlignment property array contains the alignment for all cells in the corresponding column. Each element of the ColAlignmentBand property array contains the alignment for all cells within the corresponding band. Each element of the ColAlignmentHeader property array contains the alignment for all cells within the corresponding header. The following table contains values for the CellAlignment, CellPictureAlignment, and ColAlignment properties:

Constant	*Value*	*Description*
`flexAlignLeftTop`	0	The contents of the cell are aligned to the upper-left corner of the cell.
`flexAlignLeftCenter`	1	The contents of the cell are aligned to the left edge of the cell—centered from top to bottom.
`flexAlignLeftBottom`	2	The contents of the cell are aligned to the lower-left corner of the cell.
`flexAlignCenterTop`	3	The contents of the cell are centered at the top of the cell.
`flexAlignCenterCenter`	4	The contents of the cell are centered within the cell.
`flexAlignCenterBottom`	5	The contents of the cell are centered at the bottom of the cell.
`flexAlignRightTop`	6	The contents of the cell are aligned to the upper-right corner of the cell.
`flexAlignRightCenter`	7	The contents of the cell are aligned to the right edge of the cell—centered from top to bottom.
`flexAlignRightBottom`	8	The contents of the cell are aligned to the lower-right corner of the cell.
`flexAlignGeneral`	9	Strings are aligned as per flexAlignLeft-Center, and numbers are aligned as per flexAlignRightCenter. This value is not available for the CellPictureAlignment property.

ColWordWrapOption, ColWordWrapOptionBand, ColWordWrapOptionFixed, ColWordWrapOptionHeader property arrays

These property arrays determine how text is wrapped in a specific column (ColWordWrapOption property array), in a particular band (ColWordWrapOptionBand), in a particular fixed column (ColwordWrap-OptionFixed), or in a particular header (ColWordWrapOptionHeader).

The syntax of ColWordWrapOption is:

```
ColWordWrapOption(Index) = WordWrapSettings
```

where *`Index`* is the zero-based ordinal position of the column. In addition, -1 indicates all columns. The **`WordWrapSettings`** enumeration is shown in a table later in this section.

The syntax of ColWordWrapOptionBand is:

```
ColWordWrapOptionBand(BandNumber, BandColIndex) = _
                            WordWrapSettings
```

where *`BandNumber`* is the zero-based ordinal position of the band and *`BandColIndex`* is the zero-based ordinal position of the column in the band. The **WordWrapSettings** enumeration is shown later in this section. The syntax of ColWordWrapOptionFixed is:

```
ColWordWrapOptionFixed(Index) = WordWrapSettings
```

where ***Index*** is the zero-based ordinal position of the fixed column. In addition, -1 indicates all columns. The **WordWrapSettings** enumeration is shown later in this section.

The syntax of ColWordWrapOptionHeader is:

```
ColWordWrapOptionHeader(BandNumber, BandColIndex) = _
                                WordWrapSettings
```

where ***BandNumber*** is the zero-based ordinal position of the band and ***BandColIndex*** is the zero-based ordinal position of the column header in the band.

The **WordWrapSettings** enumeration can take any of the following four values:

Constant	*Value*	*Description*
flexSingleLine	0	Displays text on a single line only. This is the default value.
flexWordBreak	1	Lines break automatically between words.
flexWordEllipsis	2	Text that doesn't fit in the rectangle is truncated and ellipses added.
flexWordBreakEllipsis	3	Breaks words between lines and adds ellipses if text doesn't fit in the rectangle.

Font, FontBand, FontFixed, FontHeader

These properties can be set to a Font object in order to set the font used by the entire MSHFlexGrid control (Font), bands (FontBand), fixed rows and columns (FontFixed), and the header (FontHeader).

FontWidth, FontWidthBand, FontWidthFixed, FontWidthHeader

These properties set the width of the font (as opposed to the height—the normal measurement of font size) in points to be used throughout the MSFlexGrid control (FontWidth), in bands (FontWidthBand), in fixed rows and columns (FontWidthFixed), and in the header (FontWidthHeader).

3. Set control behavior.

RowSizingMode

When a row within the MSHFlexGrid control is resized, whether by the user or through code, the RowSizingMode property controls whether other rows are resized as well. When set to 0–flexRowSizeIndividual, only the resized row is affected. When set to 1–flexRowSizeAll, all rows in the control are resized.

4. Maintain bands.

   BandDisplay

   Bands within an MSHFlexGrid control can be displayed horizontally or vertically. When the BandDisplay property is set to 0–flexBandDisplay-Horizontal, the bands are displayed horizontally. When it is set to 1–flexBandDisplayVertical, the bands are displayed vertically.

   BandIndent

   When bands are indented, they are indented a number of columns based on the BandIndent property. Setting the BandIndent property causes all bands in the MSHFlexGrid to be indented by that many columns.

   Bands

   Returns the number of bands in the MSHFlexGrid control.

   BandExpandable property array

   Elements of the BandExpandable property array determine whether the user can expand the corresponding band. When set to `True`, the band can be expanded, and the corresponding icon for expanding/collapsing the band is shown. When set to `False`, the band cannot be expanded, and the icons are not shown.

   BandLevel

   Indicates the index of the band that contains the current cell.

5. Maintain hierarchy.

   RowExpandable

   Indicates whether the current row can be expanded. When it is `True`, the row can be expanded; when `False`, the row cannot be expanded.

   RowExpanded

   The RowExpanded property indicates whether the current row is expanded. When the RowExpanded property is `True`, the row has been expanded. When the value is `False`, the row is collapsed.

Useful Methods

BandColIndex

Returns the index of the current cell as it relates to the first cell in the band.

ClearStructure

Clears all band mapping information in the MSHFlexGrid control without clearing the actual data.

CollapseAll, ExpandAll

The CollapseAll method collapses all bands in the MSHFlexGrid control. The ExpandAll method expands all bands in the control.

Write Event Handlers

Collapse

The Collapse event is fired when the user presses the icon to collapse a row in the MSHFlexGrid control. It has one parameter:

Cancel

Flag passed by reference indicating whether the collapse operation should be cancelled. Setting it to `True` cancels the collapsing of the row.

Expand

The Expand event is fired when the user presses the icon to Expand a row in the MSHFlexGrid control. It has one parameter:

Cancel

Flag passed by reference indicating whether the expand operation should be cancelled. Setting it to `True` cancels expansion of the row.

HScrollBar Control

See: ScrollBar Controls

Controls H–L

VB6

ImageCombo Control

New to Visual Basic 6.0, the ImageCombo control acts like a combo box that can display an image on each row of the list. In addition, the contents of the list are treated as a collection of ComboItem objects, which makes the list easier to work with than the standard ComboBox control. An ImageCombo control is shown in Figure 5-26.

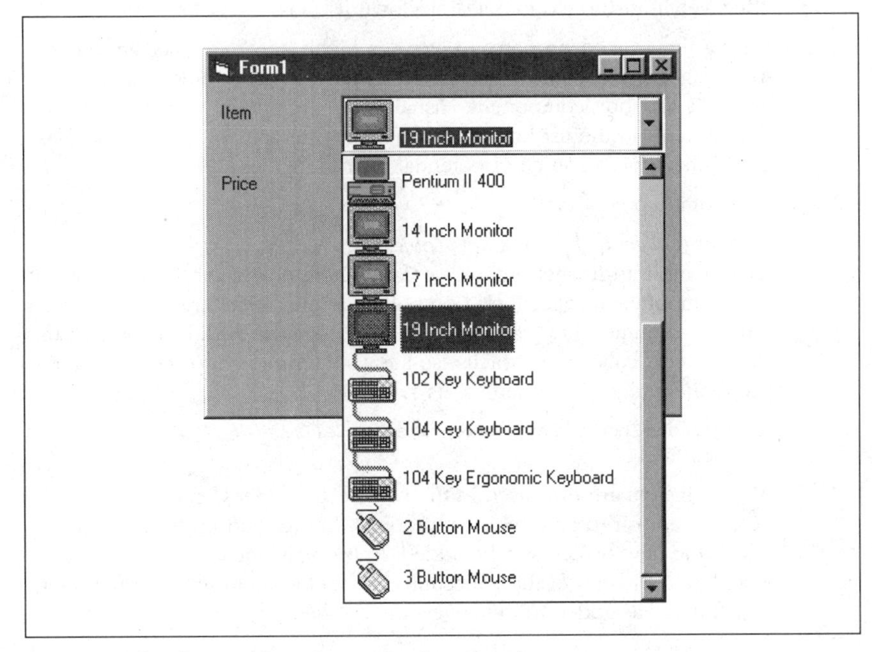

Figure 5-26: A form with an ImageCombo control

The ImageCombo control is included with the Windows Common Controls (*COMCTL32.OCX*) that come with Visual Basic 6.0 Professional and Enterprise editions.

Control Tasks

The following categories reflect the tasks that are executed when creating an ImageCombo control.

Set Properties

1. Set general appearance and behavior.

   ImageList

   Contains a reference to an ImageList control on the same form. The individual ComboItem objects in the ImageCombo control can then use the ListImage objects in this ImageList control. When this property is set, the ImageCombo control's height will be set according to the ImageHeight property of the ImageList control.

   Locked

   By default, the Locked property is `False`, and the user can enter text into the text box portion of the combo box. When you set the Locked property to `True`, the ImageCombo control becomes read-only and is effectively transformed into a drop-down list box.

   Setting the Locked property to `True` is highly recommended in view of the ImageCombo control's behavior. When the user enters text into the control's text box component, Visual Basic attempts to match it with the text of items in the list box only if the user attempts to open the list box. This behavior is a source of potential confusion.

2. Populate combo box.

   ComboItems (collection), ComboItem (object)

   Each item in an ImageCombo is a ComboItem object and is a member of the ComboItems collection. ComboItems cannot be created at design time. At runtime, they can be created by using the Add method of the ComboItems collection, which also allows the program to set some of the ComboItem object's properties. Its syntax is:

```
object.Add(Index, Key, Text, Image, SelImage, _
Indentation)
```

   All parameters are discussed in the next section, "Set ComboItem properties," except for *Index*, which represents the position in the collection at which the new object is to be added. If *Index* is not specified, the object is added to the end of the collection. The method returns the ComboItem object that was added to the collection.

3. Set ComboItem properties.

Text, Image, SelImage, Indentation

The caption of the ComboItem, the index or key of the ListImage to use for unselected and selected ComboItems, respectively, and the amount to indent the ComboItem can be set either as parameters of the ComboItems collection's Add method or by using these properties. The Indentation property is expressed in units of 10 pixels; for instance, a value of 2 indicates that the ComboItem object should be indented in the drop-down list by 20 pixels.

Selected

Fired when set to `True` for a particular ComboItem, that ComboItem becomes the selected ComboItem in the ImageCombo control. When a ComboItem becomes selected through some other method (such as by the user), the Selected property for that ComboItem is set to `True`.

Controls H–L

Tag

Each ComboItem object has its own Tag property that can be used to store internal information about that ComboItem. For example, the Tag property can contain the key of the object represented by the Text property for retrieval from a database.

4. Determine currently selected item.

SelectedItem

The SelectedItem property contains a reference to the currently selected item in the ImageCombo. If there is currently no item selected, the SelectedItem property returns `Nothing`. The property returns a reference to a ComboItem object, rather than the object's text or key.

By assigning a reference to an ImageCombo object to the SelectedItem property, you can also change the selected item programmatically, as shown in the following code fragment, where *`strKey`* is the key of the object to select:

```
Set oComboItem = frmCombo.icoMain.ComboItems(strKey)
If Not oComboItem Is Nothing Then _
   frmCombo.icoMain.SelectedItem = oComboItem
```

You can also determine which item is selected in the ImageCombo control by iterating the ComboItems collection and retrieving the Selected property of each ComboItem object. Similarly, you can set the selected item by iterating the collection and setting the Selected property of the desired ComboItem object to `True` or by using the item's key to retrieve its object reference and setting its Selected property to `True`, as the following code fragment shows:

```
frmMain.icoMain.ComboItems(strKey).Selected = True
```

Text

Contains the text from the text box portion of the ImageCombo control. If an item is selected, its value corresponds to the Text property of the selected ComboItem object. However, this property doesn't invariably indicate which item is selected, since it either is null (if no item is selected) or contains the text entered by the user.

Useful Methods

GetFirstVisible

This method provides the programmer with the ability to retrieve the topmost visible object in the ImageCombo.

When the ImageCombo is collapsed, the GetFirstVisible method will always return the currently selected ComboItem. However, when the list is dropped down, the GetFirstVisible method accurately returns the top visible ComboItem, regardless of which ComboItem is currently selected. The syntax is simply:

```
objImagecombo.GetFirstVisible()
```

The method returns a reference to the top visible ComboItem object.

Write Event Handlers

DropDown

Fired when the user clicks the down-arrow icon on the ImageCombo to view the list.

Change

Fired whenever the ImageCombo control's Text property is changed, whether by the user or programmatically. In the first case, if Locked is set to `False`, it is fired once for each character entered by the user. In the latter case, it is fired once when the control is first initialized and subsequently whenever a value is *explicitly* assigned to the Text property. Changing the selected item programmatically or clicking on an item in the drop-down list box does not fire the Change event.

Click

Fired after the DropDown event whenever the user selects an item by clicking on it, rather than by entering its text in the text box portion of the Image-Combo control. Only if Locked is `True` is the Click event always fired when the selected item is changed.

Example

The following example uses the Tag property to hold the price of an item in the ImageCombo and uses many of the other elements found in this section:

```
Option Explicit

'For this example, create the following controls: _
  an ImageCombo control named icbMain and _
  an ImageList control named imlImages. _
  You'll also need the icons pc03.ico, monitr01.ico, _
    keybrd02.ico, and mouse02.ico, found on the VB CD.

Dim lblItem As Label
Dim lblPrice As Label
Dim WithEvents txtPrice As TextBox

Private Sub Form_Load()
    Dim cbiVar As ComboItem
```

```
'Create Labels and TextBox.
   Set lblItem = Me.Controls.Add("vb.label", _
               "lblItem", Me)
   Set lblPrice = Me.Controls.Add("vb.label", _
                "lblPrice", Me)
   Set txtPrice = Me.Controls.Add("vb.textbox", _
                "txtPrice", Me)

   lblItem.Caption = "Item"
   lblItem.Visible = True
   lblItem.TabIndex = 0

   lblPrice.Caption = "Price"
   lblPrice.Visible = True
   lblPrice.TabIndex = 2

   txtPrice.Text = ""
   txtPrice.Visible = True
   txtPrice.TabIndex = 3
   txtPrice.Locked = True

'Load Images into ImageList.
   Me.imlImages.ListImages.Add , "CPU", _
                        LoadPicture("pc03.ico")
   Me.imlImages.ListImages.Add , "MONITOR", _
                        LoadPicture("monitr01.ico")
   Me.imlImages.ListImages.Add , "KEYBOARD", _
                        LoadPicture("keybrd02.ico")
   Me.imlImages.ListImages.Add , "MOUSE", _
                        LoadPicture("mouse02.ico")

'Set up ImageCombo.
   Me.icbMain.Text = ""
   Set Me.icbMain.ImageList = Me.imlImages

   'Load ComboItems into icbMain. Put the price into _
   the Tag property
   Set cbiVar = Me.icbMain.ComboItems.Add _
       (, "P200", "Pentium 200 MMX", "CPU")
   cbiVar.Tag = 1200
   Set cbiVar = Me.icbMain.ComboItems.Add _
       (, "P233", "Pentium 233 MMX", "CPU")
   cbiVar.Tag = 1400
   Set cbiVar = Me.icbMain.ComboItems.Add _
       (, "P300", "Pentium II 300", "CPU")
   cbiVar.Tag = 1600
   Set cbiVar = Me.icbMain.ComboItems.Add _
       (, "P333", "Pentium II 333", "CPU")
   cbiVar.Tag = 1800
   Set cbiVar = Me.icbMain.ComboItems.Add _
       (, "P360", "Pentium II 360", "CPU")
   cbiVar.Tag = 2000
```

```
    Set cbiVar = Me.icbMain.ComboItems.Add _
        (, "P400", "Pentium II 400", "CPU")
    cbiVar.Tag = 2200
    Set cbiVar = Me.icbMain.ComboItems.Add _
        (, "M14", "14 Inch Monitor", "MONITOR")
    cbiVar.Tag = 250
    Set cbiVar = Me.icbMain.ComboItems.Add _
        (, "M17", "17 Inch Monitor", "MONITOR")
    cbiVar.Tag = 400
    Set cbiVar = Me.icbMain.ComboItems.Add _
        (, "M19", "19 Inch Monitor", "MONITOR")
    cbiVar.Tag = 800
    Set cbiVar = Me.icbMain.ComboItems.Add _
        (, "K102", "102 Key Keyboard", "KEYBOARD")
    cbiVar.Tag = 29.95
    Set cbiVar = Me.icbMain.ComboItems.Add _
        (, "K104", "104 Key Keyboard", "KEYBOARD")
    cbiVar.Tag = 39.95
    Set cbiVar = Me.icbMain.ComboItems.Add _
        (, "K104E", "104 Key Ergonomic Keyboard", _
        "KEYBOARD")
    cbiVar.Tag = 69
    Set cbiVar = Me.icbMain.ComboItems.Add _
        (, "M2", "2 Button Mouse", "MOUSE")
    cbiVar.Tag = 60
    Set cbiVar = Me.icbMain.ComboItems.Add _
        (, "M3", "3 Button Mouse", "MOUSE")
    cbiVar.Tag = 75
End Sub

Private Sub Form_Resize()
   'Resize the items on the form.
     lblItem.Move 120, 180, 1095, 255
     lblPrice.Move 120, 300 + Me.icbMain.Height, 1095, _
                   255
     Me.icbMain.Move 1335, 120, Me.ScaleWidth - 1455
     txtPrice.Move 1335, 240 + Me.icbMain.Height, _
                   Me.ScaleWidth - 1455, 315
End Sub

Private Sub icbMain_Click()
   'The price is formatted as currency.
     txtPrice = Format$(Me.icbMain.SelectedItem.Tag, _
                        "Currency")
End Sub
```

Order of Events

When the user selects an item by opening the drop-down combo box, events are fired in the following order:

1. DropDown event
2. Click event

Image Control

The Image control, like the PictureBox control, can have an image placed within it. However, unlike the PictureBox control, the Image control does not provide graphic methods and is not a container. In addition, the Image control lacks an hWnd property; consequently, it cannot be accessed by Win32 API calls that require a window handle. However, the Image control has a much smaller memory footprint than the PictureBox control.

Set Properties

Using an Image control is a simple matter of setting two properties either at design time or at runtime.

1. Set Picture.

   Picture, Stretch

   The picture shown in an Image control is set by the Picture property. This property can be set in the same ways as the PictureBox control. If the control is smaller or larger than the image and the Stretch property is set to the default value of `False`, the picture shown is clipped to the size of the control. If the Stretch property is set to `True`, the picture shown is stretched to the size of the control.

ImageList Control

The ImageList control stores a series of graphic images for use in an application. Each ImageList can contain only one size of image, so it is often necessary to have multiple ImageList controls in the application. The ImageList control itself does not have an interface; it is merely a storage container for images that makes them readily available to your application. These images are available from the ImageList control in both Picture and Icon format, which should be sufficient for most needs. The ListView, TreeView, and Toolbar controls can all bind to one or more ImageList controls to assist in providing graphics to those controls.

The ImageList control is included with the Windows Common Controls (*COMCTL32.OCX*) that come with Visual Basic Professional and Enterprise editions.

Control Tasks

The following categories reflect the tasks that are executed when creating an ImageList.

Set Properties

1. Set image attributes (optional).

   ImageHeight and ImageWidth

   All images in an ImageList are restricted in size to the dimensions contained in the ImageHeight and ImageWidth properties. If these are not set beforehand, they will be automatically set to match the size of the first image added to the ImageList.

   MaskColor and UseMaskColor

   In an ImageList, you can choose one color that will appear transparent when an image with this color is placed over an existing image or background color. This is illustrated in the code example later in this section, where white is defined as a mask color and an image has a white background with the text "Sold Out" in red. When this image overlays the picture of a product, the image's white background becomes transparent, and the text "Sold Out" appears to be superimposed on the original image. When UseMaskColor is set to the default, `True`, the MaskColor appears transparent. When set to `False`, the MaskColor is ignored.

2. Maintain images.

   ListImages (collection)

   All of the images are contained in the ListImages collection. As with all collections, the ListImages collection has a Count property and an Item property, as well as an Add method, a Remove method, and a Clear method.

   ListImage (object).

   Each image in an ImageList is represented in code by a ListImage object. The properties of the ListImage object control its contents, and its methods help control how it works with the rest of the application.

3. Create ListImages.

   ListImages (collection), ListImage (object)

   Each item in an ImageList is a ListImage that is part of the ListImages collection. ListImage objects can be created at design time through the Custom Property sheet of the ImageList control. At runtime, create them by using the Add method of the ListImages collection. Its syntax is:

   ```
   ImgMain.ListImages.Add(index, key, picture)
   ```

   Images loaded into the ImageList control at design time are included in its containing form's *.FRX* file; they do not need to be distributed along with the application. On the other hand, images defined at runtime using the ListImages collection's Add method are not included in the *.FRX* file or the executable file and therefore must be included in the final application.

4. Set ListImage properties.

   Picture

   Returns a copy of the object's picture and can be used anytime you need to assign a picture to another object. For example, the Picture property of a PictureBox could be set to ListImage number 1 in an application with the following syntax:

```
picMain.Picture = imlMain.ListImages(1).Picture
```

Since the Picture property returns an image, you do not have to use the *LoadPicture* function to assign the picture to another control or object.

Key

Allows the image to be accessed by the key (i.e., a unique string) assigned to it as well as by its index in the ListImages collection. For example:

```
picMain.Picture = _
          imlMain.ListImages("LARGEFILE").Picture
```

Useful Methods

Overlay

The Overlay method of an ImageList is used to combine the images from two different ListImage objects. Overlay returns a picture resulting from taking the first image and then adding the second image—using the ImageList Mask-Color to allow the first image to show through. The image returned by the Overlay method can be treated like any other picture.

Draw

In some cases, an application might need to place an image on a control somewhere other than the upper-left corner. In other cases, it may be necessary to draw an image to be drawn in a control without destroying an existing image. The Draw method can be used in both of these cases. Its syntax is:

```
Sub Draw(hDC As Long, [x], [y], [Style])
```

The Draw method can be used to place an image on any control with a Device Context (usually an hDC property). There are *X* and *Y* parameters to locate the image on the device wherever necessary. The *Style* parameter can be the default of 0–imlNormal, which draws the image on the Device Context, overwriting anything underneath the new image. When set to 1–imlTransparent, the MaskColor is used to combine the image being drawn with the existing image. When set to 2–imlSelected, the image is drawn dithered with the system highlight color, giving the appearance of a "selected" item. When set to 3–imlFocus, the image is again drawn dithered with the system highlight color but this time is also combined with a hatching pattern in the system highlight color giving the image the appearance of having the application focus.

ExtractIcon

Returns an icon, as opposed to a picture. It can be used in situations in which an icon is required, such as a Form object's Icon property.

Example

The following example illustrates the ImageList control and particularly its Overlay method, which is used to combine graphical "signs" with product graphics in an order entry screen (shown in Figures 5-27 and 5-28):

```
Option Explicit

'For this example, create an ImageList control named imlProducts.
Private WithEvents cmdPurchase As CommandButton
Private WithEvents lstProducts As ListBox
Private picProduct As PictureBox

Dim maCounts(1 To 2) As Integer

Private Sub Form_Load()
   'Create and/or set up controls.
    imlProducts.ImageHeight = 128
    imlProducts.ImageWidth = 128
    imlProducts.MaskColor = &HFFFFFF
    imlProducts.UseMaskColor = True
    imlProducts.ListImages.Add _
        1, "A1", LoadPicture(App.Path & "\Product1.bmp")
    imlProducts.ListImages.Add _
        2, "A2", LoadPicture(App.Path & "\Product2.bmp")
    imlProducts.ListImages.Add _
        3, "SOLDOUT", LoadPicture(App.Path & "\SoldOut.bmp")

    Set lstProducts = Me.Controls.Add( _
        "vb.listbox", "lstProducts", Me)
    lstProducts.Visible = True
    lstProducts.TabIndex = 0
    lstProducts.AddItem "Product1"
    lstProducts.ItemData(lstProducts.NewIndex) = 1
    maCounts(1) = 3
   'There are three of this item in stock.
    lstProducts.AddItem "Product2"
    lstProducts.ItemData(lstProducts.NewIndex) = 2
    maCounts(2) = 1
   'There is one of this item in stock.

    Set picProduct = Me.Controls.Add( _
        "vb.picturebox", "picProducts", Me)
    picProduct.Visible = True

    Set cmdPurchase = Me.Controls.Add( _
        "vb.commandbutton", "cmdPurchase", Me)
    cmdPurchase.Visible = True
    cmdPurchase.TabIndex = 1
    cmdPurchase.Caption = "&Purchase"
End Sub

Private Sub Form_Resize()
    Dim lBorderHeight As Long
    Dim lBorderWidth As Long
    Dim lPicHeight As Long
    Dim lPicWidth As Long

   'Determine the size for the PictureBox.
    lBorderHeight = picProduct.Height - picProduct.ScaleHeight
```

```
    lBorderWidth = picProduct.Width - picProduct.ScaleWidth
    lPicHeight = _
        (Me.imlProducts.ImageHeight * Screen.TwipsPerPixelY) _
        + lBorderHeight
    lPicWidth = _
        (Me.imlProducts.ImageWidth * Screen.TwipsPerPixelX) _
        + lBorderWidth

    If Me.ScaleHeight < lPicHeight + 735 Or _
            Me.ScaleWidth < lPicWidth + 1455 Then _
        Exit Sub

    lstProducts.Move _
        120, 120, Me.ScaleWidth - (lPicWidth + 360), _
        Me.ScaleHeight - 735
        picProduct.Move _
        Me.ScaleWidth - (lPicWidth + 120), 120, _
        lPicWidth, lPicHeight
    cmdPurchase.Move _
        Me.ScaleWidth - 1225, Me.ScaleHeight - 495, 1095, 375
End Sub

Private Sub cmdPurchase_Click()
    Dim iImage As Integer

    iImage = lstProducts.ItemData(lstProducts.ListIndex)

    maCounts(iImage) = maCounts(iImage) - 1
   'Reduce the number of that item in stock.

    UpdatePicture
End Sub

Private Sub lstProducts_Click()
    UpdatePicture
End Sub

Private Sub UpdatePicture()
    Dim iImage As Integer

    iImage = lstProducts.ItemData(lstProducts.ListIndex)

    If maCounts(iImage) <= 0 Then
        picProduct.Picture = _
            imlProducts.Overlay(imlProducts.ListImages( _
            iImage ).Key, _
            "SOLDOUT")
        cmdPurchase.Enabled = False
    Else
        picProduct.Picture = _
                    imlProducts.ListImages(iImage).Picture
        cmdPurchase.Enabled = True
    End If
End Sub
```

Controls H–L

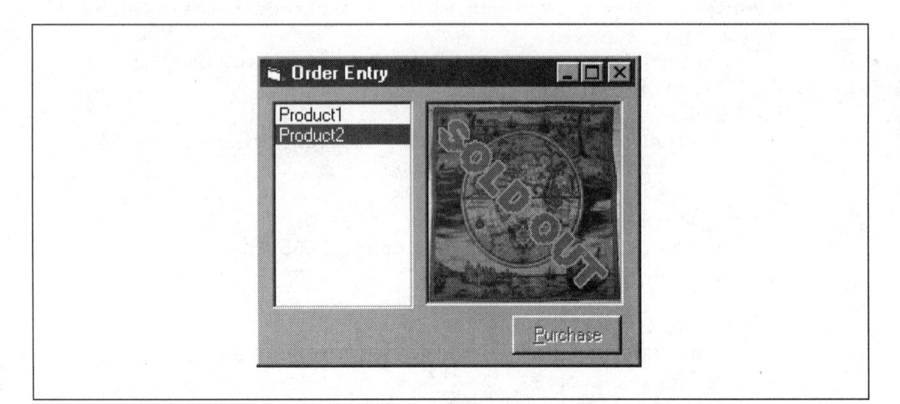

Figure 5-27: The Overlay method at work

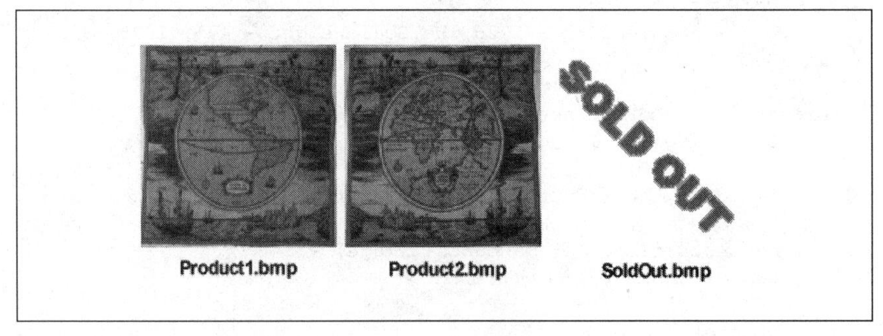

Figure 5-28: Images used in the previous example

Internet Transfer Control

The Internet Transfer control (*MSINET.DLL*), or Inet control, is a *client* control used to transfer information from the Internet using either the HTTP or FTP protocols; that is, it assumes that the control is transferring data either to or from an HTTP or an FTP server. The Internet Transfer control is a service control whose functionality is confined to uploading and downloading bytes from the Internet using either of these two protocols and lacks a visible interface. This means that it is not a particularly appropriate component to use in a web-browsing application (although it could be used as a low-level component in a web browser), since your application would have to retrieve the HTTP data stream from the Internet Transfer control in order to display it. In contrast, both functions—that of transmitting and receiving data as well as displaying it—can be handled by the Microsoft Internet Controls (*SHDOCVW.DLL*), one of the core components of Microsoft's Internet Explorer web browser.

Since it makes developing a web-browsing application more cumbersome than the other available alternatives, why would you want to use the Internet Transfer control? The answer, of course, is that it's suitable for any Internet application where the transfer of data or files via HTTP or FTP is of paramount importance. These include:

- Applications that regularly transfer the same or different sets of files via FTP
- Applications that display FTP directories without a web browser interface
- Applications that parse, analyze, or extract some portion of the content from web pages

Regardless of which protocol it uses to transfer files or data via FTP or HTTP, the basic steps involved in using the Inet control are the same: you define how you'll access the Internet, indicate the resource to which you want to connect, and retrieve the resource. This section examines each of those steps in turn.

This section explains the use of the Internet Transfer control. It is not meant to explain the Internet, Internet protocols, or any other concepts relating to the Internet itself. For this type of information, see *Internet in a Nutshell*, *Webmaster in a Nutshell, Second Edition*, and *The World Wide Web Journal*, vol. 1, issue 2: *Key Specifications of the World Wide Web*, all published by O'Reilly & Associates.

Defining Internet Access

Since the way in which a system connects to the Internet is typically handled by Windows rather than by individual applications, this step is an optional one that can frequently be skipped. In that case, the Internet Transfer control uses Windows default settings. Defining how the application will access the Internet is most important when using a proxy server whose IP address has not been supplied to Control Panel's Internet applet.

Two properties define the way in which the Internet Transfer control connects to the Internet:

AccessType
: Normally, this property can be left set to the default value of 0–icUseDefault. In this case, the type of access is set according to Windows defaults. However, this can be overridden with either 1–icDirect for a direct Internet connection (such as a modem connection or LAN connection), or 2–icNamedProxy for an indirect connection using a proxy server.

Proxy
: When the AccessType property is set to `icNamedProxy`, the Proxy property must contain the name of the proxy server to use for Internet access. The general format of the Proxy property value is:

```
[protocol=]server[:port]
```

where ***protocol*** is either "HTTP" or "FTP," ***server*** is the name of the proxy server in the local network, and ***port*** is the port used by either the FTP or HTTP service. If ***protocol*** is omitted, ***server*** is used for both protocols. If *port* is omitted, the default port for that service is used. To identify separate proxy servers for the FTP and HTTP protocols, separate them with a space. For example:

```
INet1.Proxy = "http=OurWebProxy ftp=OurFTPProxy"
```

Handle Miscellaneous Configuration

The Internet Transfer control requires almost no general configuration other than possibly setting its time-out value with the following property:

RequestTimeout
When an OpenURL or Execute method is processed, the RequestTimeout property specifies the number of seconds to wait before generating an error. The default value is 60 seconds. At the end of the RequestTimeout period, the control raises error 35761, "Request timed out."

Specify an Internet Resource

After defining how your application will connect to the Internet, you next define the particular resource that the Internet Transfer control will handle. Whether you must specify the Internet resource as a distinct step, though, depends on what resource you want to access and how you want to access it; in particular, if you call the OpenURL method, the URL, Protocol, RemoteHost, Document, and RemotePort properties can all be passed as parameters to the method call. In that case, the following properties are optional; otherwise, they should be set in advance:

URL, Protocol, RemoteHost, Document properties
The URL property identifies the resource to be accessed; for example, *http://www.oreilly.com/vb* is a complete URL that might be assigned to the URL property. The property is used with the OpenURL and Execute methods to communicate with an Internet server.

The Protocol property represents the Internet service (HTTP, FTP, etc.) used to access the resource. Possible values are 0–icUnknown, 1–icDefault, 2–icFTP, 3–icReserved, 4–icHTTP, 5–icHTTPS, or 6–icFile.

The RemoteHost property identifies the remote server from which the resource is available. It should contain a fully qualified domain name (such as *www.ora.com*) or an IP address (such as `xxx.xxx.xxx.xxx`).

The Document property specifies the complete path to the resource on the remote host that the control is being used to access (e.g., *homepage.htm* or */webdir/winbooks.html*).

These four properties are interdependent: when any one of them changes, the values of the related properties typically change as well. For example, if the URL property is modified, the Protocol, RemoteHost, and Document properties are all updated to reflect the new information.

UserName, Password properties
If the service being connected requires a login, the UserName and Password properties should be set. Setting the URL property clears these properties, so

be sure to set them after setting the URL property. In addition, setting the UserName property clears the Password property, so be sure to set the username before assigning the password.

Typically, whether you're accessing an FTP server anonymously or as a registered user, you must supply a password. However, if your application attempts to access a resource via FTP and doesn't provide a username or password, the Internet Transfer control automatically supplies "anonymous" as the username and your email address as the password.

RemotePort property
: In some cases, when a particular resource is available on a nonstandard port, a port number needs to be explicitly specified by assigning its value to the RemotePort property. Otherwise, the Internet Transfer control assumes the default port number (80 in the case of HTTP, 21 in the case of FTP).

Retrieve the Resource

The Internet Transfer control allows you to retrieve an Internet resource via FTP either synchronously or asynchronously. In the former case, the method call does not return until the transfer has been completed. In the latter, program execution continues as soon as the Internet Transfer control's method has been called.

Synchronous Downloads: OpenURL

Retrieving an Internet resource synchronously, so that the code immediately following the call to the transfer method executes only when the transfer has been completed, requires only a single method call:

OpenURL
: The OpenURL method returns the resource designated by a URL. Its syntax is:

```
objInet.OpenURL(url, datatype)
```

where the parameters are as follows:

`objInet`
: A reference to an Internet Transfer control.

`url`
: The complete URL of the resource to be retrieved; if the parameter is not supplied, the URL assigned to the URL property is used instead.

`datatype`
: Determines how transferred data is handled by the function. Possible values are 0–icString or 1–icByteArray. Note that this controls the mode in which the transfer occurs. A value of `icString` is suitable for ASCII files and data, while `icByteArray` should be used to download all binary files and data. Typically, the failure to use the proper transfer mode results in an error or in corrupted data.

If the method succeeds, it returns a variant containing the contents of the downloaded resource. OpenURL can be used only to download a resource from a remote computer; it cannot be used to upload a resource. Consequently, a call to OpenURL is equivalent to calling the Execute method (discussed next, in "Asynchronous Transfers: Execute") for a GET operation.

While the OpenURL method executes synchronously, it is important to remember that it is *not* modal; that is, even though the method does not return until the transfer operation has ended, program flow does not stop until the method returns. This means that it is important to prevent multiple calls to the OpenURL method from executing, as well as to prevent code that assumes the completion of the method from executing. The StillExecuting function, which is discussed in the next section, "Asynchronous Transfers: Execute," can be used for this purpose (and is illustrated in the OpenURL code example).

Asynchronous Transfers: Execute

Whereas the OpenURL method operates synchronously and returns the byte stream of the requested resource, asynchronous transfers are somewhat more complicated, since it is necessary to handle any data transmitted by the HTTP or FTP server. The steps are as follows:

1. Call the Execute method, which initiates a command using a particular URL. Unlike OpenURL, it is a more flexible command that allows you to perform a wider variety of operations than simply downloading a file. The method operates asynchronously: control returns immediately to the routine in which the Execute method was called. Its syntax is:

   object.Execute *url*, *operation*, *data*, *requestHeaders*

   Each of the following parameters is optional:

   url
   : The URL on which the transfer operation is to be performed. If no URL is specified, the URL property is used instead.

   operation
   : A string indicating the operation to be performed. Valid values for *operation* are shown later and vary depending on whether the HTTP or the FTP protocol is being used.

   data
   : A parameter used with the HTTP POST and PUT operations that contains the data or resource to be sent to a web server.

   requestHeaders
   : Specifies additional HTTP headers to be sent with the request. The format of a custom header is:

     header_name: *header_value* vbcrlf

     For custom headers to be meaningful, the HTTP server must be prepared to handle them.

   Valid values of *operation* for a transfer using HTTP are shown in the following list:

   GET
   : Submits an HTTP request using the GET method. This is similar to the OpenURL method.

HEAD

Requests that the server return only the HTTP response headers but not the response body or document content of the specified URL.

POST

Submits an HTTP request using the POST method. Data to be submitted with the POST request is included in the *data* parameter. This data consists of one or more name/value pairs in the following format:

name1=value1,name2=value2,name3=value3...

PUT

Writes the file indicated by the *data* parameter to the specified URL. To succeed, it must be supported by the web server, *and* the user must have write permission to the virtual directory designated by the URL.

When used with FTP, the *data* and *requestHeaders* parameters are unused. Instead, any required parameters follow the command that appears at the beginning of the *operation* string. These commands include:

CD

Changes the current directory on the remote system. Its syntax is:

`CD path`

CDUP

Changes to the current directory's parent.

CLOSE

Closes the connection to the host; see the `QUIT` command.

DELETE

Deletes a file. Its syntax is:

`DELETE file1`

where *file1* is the path and filename of the file to be deleted.

DIR

Returns the names of the filesystem objects matching a particular file specification. Its syntax is:

`DIR file1`

If a file specification is absent, the names of all the files in the current directory are returned.

GET

Copies a file from the host to the local system. Its syntax is:

`GET file1 file2`

where *file1* is the file to be copied from the host and *file2* is the path and filename of the copy to be made on the local system. The copy of the file is made automatically; you don't have to call the GetChunk method to retrieve the contents of the file in order to save it.

MKDIR

Creates a directory. Its syntax is:

`MKDIR path`

PUT

Copies a file or files to the host system. Its syntax is:

`PUT file1 file2`

where *file1* is the path and filename of the local file to be copied and *file2* is the path and filename of the copy to be made on the remote system. *file2* must not exist on the local system, or an error occurs.

PWD

Indicates the current directory. Its name can be retrieved using the GetChunk method when the StateChanged event has fired with *state* equal to `icResponseCompleted`.

QUIT

Terminates the connection with the host. When the connection is terminated, the StateChanged event is fired with *state* set equal to `icDisconnected`.

RECV

The same as GET.

RENAME

Renames a file. Its syntax is:

`RENAME file1 file2`

where *file1* is the path and filename of the file on the remote system and *file2* is its new filename.

RMDIR

Removes a directory. Its syntax is:

`RMDIR path`

SEND

The same as PUT.

SIZE

Retrieves the size of a file. Its syntax is:

`SIZE file1`

where *file1* is the path and filename of the file whose size is to be reported.

Note that *operation* is sent to the FTP server as is; the Internet Transfer control does not attempt to modify any portion of the string (such as path separator characters that are contained in a path, for instance) to make them acceptable to the remote system. Also note that file specifications must conform to the conventions of the host system. The names of filesystem objects in Unix systems, for instance, are case sensitive; that means that path and filenames in command strings must match those found on the remote system.

2. Prevent synchronization errors.

It is important that your code not make any assumptions about the timing of Internet Transfer control operations (like retrieving the contents of a file before it's been downloaded), attempt a second operation while the first is still in progress, or otherwise interfere with the operation of the control. The control has one property and one method that are useful for preventing such errors:

StillExecuting property
: Returns `True` if there is currently a request pending for the control; returns `False` if the control is idle.

Cancel method
: Cancels any pending request. Its syntax is simply:

```
objInet.Cancel
```

When a request is processing asynchronously, a forced synchronous event (something which does not allow other code to run), such as a modal window or message box, can cause StateChanged to "miss" events. Therefore, it is important not to allow any of these types of actions to take place while the StillExecuting property is `True`.

3. Handle the StateChanged event.

   In the course of a transfer, the StateChanged event is fired each time there is a change in the status of the connection. The event is passed a single parameter named *state* that can take any of the following values:

Value	*Constant*
0	`icNone`
1	`icResolvingHost`[a]
2	`icHostResolved`
3	`icConnecting`
4	`icConnected`
5	`icRequesting`
6	`icRequestSent`
7	`icReceivingResponse`
8	`icResponseReceived`
9	`icDisconnecting`
10	`icDisconnected`
11	`icError`
12	`icResponseCompleted`

[a] This constant is incorrectly listed in the documentation as `icHostResolvingHost`.

In cases in which the Execute method does not retrieve data (such as the `MKDIR` command, which creates a directory on the remote system, or the `GET` and `RECV` commands, which copy a file from the remote system and save it automatically), the `icResponseCompleted` event signals that the method has completed successfully. Otherwise, you typically use the StateChanged event procedure to handle data downloaded by the call to the Execute method.

4. Retrieve the desired data.

   The Execute method writes data to a buffer that can be retrieved using either the GetChunk method (for FTP and HTTP requests) or the GetHeader method (for HTTP requests only), or generates error information:

   GetChunk method

   For HTTP transfers, the GetChunk method is used to retrieve the HTTP response body received in response to the Execute method; for FTP transfers, it retrieves all information returned by the FTP server other than status information and data transferred as a result of the `GET` and `RECV` commands. Its syntax is:

   ```
   objInet.GetChunk(size, datatype)
   ```

   where ***`size`*** determines the maximum number of bytes to be retrieved from the buffer and ***`datatype`*** indicates the format of the data. Valid values for ***`datatype`*** are 0–icString for ASCII transfers or 1–icByteArray for binary transfers. The ***`datatype`*** parameter determines how data retrieved from the buffer is interpreted but is unrelated to whether you choose to store the data to a string variable or to a binary array.

   Typically, GetChunk is called in response to a StateChanged event whose *`state`* parameter equals `icResponseCompleted`, indicating that the operation is complete and all data has been written to a buffer and is available to be retrieved. However, for large transfers, you may want to call the GetChunk method in response to a *`state`* value of `icResponseReceived` to conserve system resources.

   When using the GetChunk method, you should continue getting the data until none is left to retrieve—i.e., when the string returned has a length of zero, or the byte array returned has no elements.

   GetHeader method

   Retrieves the header (rather than the body) sent in an HTTP response. Conversely, the GetChunk method retrieves only the HTTP response body but not the HTTP response header. The syntax of the GetHeader method is:

   ```
   GetHeader(hdrname)
   ```

   where ***`hdrname`*** is an optional string containing the name of the header to retrieve. If no header is supplied, all headers are retrieved. Typically, header information is retrieved in response to the StateChanged event having a *`state`* value of `icResponseCompleted`.

   ResponseCode, ResponseInfo properties

   When an error occurs in a transfer operation, the StateChanged event is fired with a *`state`* value of `icError`. In that case, the ResponseCode property contains a numeric error code, and the ResponseInfo property contains a textual description of the error. This does not raise an error in your application.

Example

The following example shows how data can be retrieved using the OpenURL method:

```
Option Explicit

'For this example, create the following controls: _
  a RichTextBox control named rtbHTML with the _
  ScrollBars Property set to rtfBoth, _
  a PictureBox control named picGIF, and _
  an Internet Transfer control named itcMain.

Dim WithEvents cmdHTML As CommandButton
Dim WithEvents cmdGIF As CommandButton

Private Sub Form_Load()
   Dim ctlVar As Control

   Me.Caption = "Internet Transfer Control (Synchronous)"

  'Create the CommandButtons and set properties.
   Set cmdHTML = Me.Controls.Add("VB.CommandButton", _
                                  "cmdHTML", Me)
   cmdHTML.Caption = "Get &HTML"
   cmdHTML.TabIndex = 0
   cmdHTML.Visible = True

   Set cmdGIF = Me.Controls.Add("vb.commandbutton", _
                                 "cmdGIF", Me)
   cmdGIF.Caption = "Get &GIF"
   cmdGIF.TabIndex = 1
   cmdGIF.Visible = True

   picGIF.TabIndex = 2
   picGIF.Visible = False

   Me.rtbHTML.TextRTF = ""
   Me.rtbHTML.TabIndex = 3
   Me.rtbHTML.Visible = False

End Sub

Private Sub Form_Resize()
   If Me.ScaleHeight < 1050 Or Me.ScaleWidth < 1050 Then
      Exit Sub
   End If

   cmdHTML.Move Me.ScaleWidth - 2430, _
                Me.ScaleHeight - 495, 1095, 375
   cmdGIF.Move Me.ScaleWidth - 1215, _
                Me.ScaleHeight - 495, 1095, 375
   Me.rtbHTML.Move 120, 120, Me.ScaleWidth - 240, _
                Me.ScaleHeight - 735
```

```
    Me.picGIF.Move 120, 120, Me.ScaleWidth - 240, _
                Me.ScaleHeight - 735
End Sub

Private Sub cmdHTML_Click()
    Dim sHTML As String

    If Me.itcMain.StillExecuting Then
        MsgBox "A request is still processing.", _
                vbExclamation
        Exit Sub
    End If

    If Me.picGIF.Visible Then _
        Me.picGIF.Visible = False

    Me.rtbHTML.Visible = True
    Me.itcMain.Protocol = icHTTP
    Me.itcMain.RemoteHost = _
            "www.oreilly.com/catalog/vbcnut"

    Screen.MousePointer = vbHourglass
    Me.rtbHTML.Text = Me.itcMain.OpenURL()
    Screen.MousePointer = vbDefault
End Sub

Private Sub cmdGIF_Click()
    Dim lHBorder As Long
    Dim lVBorder As Long
    Dim lPicWidth As Long
    Dim lPicHeight As Long
    Dim bytGIF() As Byte

    If Me.itcMain.StillExecuting Then
        MsgBox "A request is still processing.", _
                vbExclamation
        Exit Sub
    End If

    If Me.rtbHTML.Visible Then _
        Me.rtbHTML.Visible = False

    Me.picGIF.Visible = True
    Me.itcMain.Protocol = icHTTP
    Me.itcMain.RemoteHost = _
        "www.oreilly.com/catalog/covers/vbcnut.s.gif"

    Screen.MousePointer = vbHourglass

    bytGIF() = Me.itcMain.OpenURL(DataType:=icByteArray)

   'Store the size of the form's border.
    lHBorder = Me.Width - Me.ScaleWidth
    lVBorder = Me.Height - Me.ScaleHeight
```

```
    'The Width and Height of a GIF file are stored in _
      the 7th and 9th Bytes. Since the bytGIF array is _
      zero based, we will use elements 6 and 8 to find _
      out the size.
      lPicWidth = bytGIF(6)
      lPicHeight = bytGIF(8)

      If Dir("C:\Temp\VBCNut.gif") <> "" Then
         Kill "C:\Temp\VBCNut.gif"
      End If

      Open "C:\Temp\VBCNut.gif" For Binary Access Write _
           As #1
      Put #1, , bytGIF()
      Close #1

      Me.Move Me.Left, Me.Top, _
        lPicWidth * Screen.TwipsPerPixelX + lHBorder + 240, _
        lPicHeight * Screen.TwipsPerPixelY + lVBorder + 735

      Me.picGIF.Picture = LoadPicture("C:\Temp\VBCNut.gif")

      Screen.MousePointer = vbDefault
   End Sub
```

The following code shows how a URL can be returned asynchronously using the Execute and GetChunk methods:

```
Option Explicit

'For this example, create the following controls: _
  a RichTextBox control named rtbHTML with the _
  ScrollBars property set to rtfBoth, _
  an Internet Transfer control named itcMain, and _
  a ProgressBar control named pbrStatus.

Dim WithEvents cmdHTML As CommandButton

Private Sub Form_Load()
   Dim ctlVar As Control

   Me.Caption = "Internet Transfer Control (Asynchronous)"

  'Create the CommandButtons and set properties.
   Set cmdHTML = Me.Controls.Add("VB.CommandButton", _
                 "cmdHTML", Me)
   cmdHTML.Caption = "Get &HTML"
   cmdHTML.TabIndex = 0
   cmdHTML.Visible = True

   Me.rtbHTML.TextRTF = ""
   Me.rtbHTML.TabIndex = 3
   Me.rtbHTML.Visible = True
```

Controls H–L

```
    Me.pbrStatus.Height = 255
    Me.pbrStatus.Align = vbAlignBottom
    Me.pbrStatus.Min = 0
    Me.pbrStatus.Max = 7
End Sub

Private Sub Form_Resize()
    If Me.ScaleHeight < 1050 Or Me.ScaleWidth < 1050 Then
        Exit Sub
    End If

    cmdHTML.Move Me.ScaleWidth - 1215, _
                 Me.ScaleHeight - 750, 1095, 375
    Me.rtbHTML.Move 120, 120, Me.ScaleWidth - 240, _
                 Me.ScaleHeight - 990
End Sub

Private Sub cmdHTML_Click()
    Dim sHTML As String

    If Me.itcMain.StillExecuting Then
        MsgBox "A request is still processing.", _
               vbExclamation
        Exit Sub
    End If

    Me.rtbHTML.Text = ""

    Me.rtbHTML.Visible = True
    Me.itcMain.Protocol = icHTTP
    Me.itcMain.RemoteHost = "www.oreilly.com/catalog/vbcnut"

    Screen.MousePointer = vbHourglass

    Me.itcMain.Execute operation:="GET"
End Sub

Private Sub itcMain_StateChanged(ByVal State As Integer)
    Dim sChunk As String
    Dim sComplete As String

    Select Case State
        Case icResolvingHost, icHostResolved, _
             icConnecting, icConnected, icRequesting, _
             icRequestSent
      'Because these are sequential, we'll use them _
      for the ProgressBar.
            Me.pbrStatus.Value = State
        Case icResponseCompleted
            sComplete = ""
            Do
                sChunk = Me.itcMain.GetChunk(1024, icString)
```

```
            If Len(sChunk) = 0 Then _
               Exit Do
            sComplete = sComplete & sChunk
         Loop

         Me.rtbHTML.Text = sComplete

         Screen.MousePointer = vbDefault
      Case icError
         Me.pbrStatus.Value = 0
         MsgBox "Error " & Me.itcMain.ResponseCode & _
                " has occurred:" & vbCrLf & _
                Me.itcMain.ResponseInfo, vbExclamation
         Screen.MousePointer = vbDefault
      Case icDisconnected
         Me.pbrStatus.Value = 0
   End Select
End Sub
```


The following example shows how some simple FTP operations can be performed with the Execute method:

```
Option Explicit

'For this example, create the following controls: _
a ListBox control named lstDir and _
an INet (Internet Transfer) control named itcMain.

Private sCurrentDir As String

Private Sub Form_Activate()
   Static bDoneAlready As Boolean

  'We only want this to run once. If the user _
  switches to another application while this one _
  is running, and then back to this one, the Activate _
  event will fire again.
   If bDoneAlready Then _
      Exit Sub

   DoEvents

   Me.itcMain.Protocol = icFTP
   Me.itcMain.RemoteHost = "ftp.ora.com"
   Screen.MousePointer = vbHourglass
   Me.itcMain.Execute , "DIR"

   bDoneAlready = True
End Sub

Private Sub Form_Load()
   Me.Caption = "Internet Transfer FTP"
End Sub
```

```
Private Sub Form_Resize()
   If Me.ScaleWidth < 360 Or Me.ScaleHeight < 360 Then _
      Exit Sub
   Me.lstDir.Move 120, 120, Me.ScaleWidth - 240, _
                  Me.ScaleHeight - 240
End Sub

Private Sub itcMain_StateChanged(ByVal State As Integer)
   Dim sChunk As String
   Dim sText As String

   Select Case State
      Case icResponseCompleted
         sText = ""
         Do
            sChunk = Me.itcMain.GetChunk(1024, icString)
            If Len(sChunk) = 0 Then _
               Exit Do
            sText = sText & sChunk
         Loop
         LoadList sText
    End Select
End Sub

Private Sub lstDir_DblClick()
   Dim bDir As Boolean
   Dim sFileName As String

   If Me.itcMain.StillExecuting Then
      MsgBox "A request is still processing.", _
             vbExclamation
      Exit Sub
   End If

   Select Case Me.lstDir.Text
      Case "./"
         'Current Directory - Do nothing
         bDir = True
      Case "../"
         'Previous directory
         If Trim$(sCurrentDir) <> "" Then
           If InStr(Left(sCurrentDir, Len(sCurrentDir) _
                    - 1), "/") = 0 Then
               sCurrentDir = ""
            Else
               sCurrentDir = Left$(sCurrentDir, _
                             InStrRev(Left(sCurrentDir, _
                             Len(sCurrentDir) - 1), "/"))
            End If
         End If
         bDir = True
      Case Else
```

```
        If Mid$(Me.lstDir.Text, Len(Me.lstDir.Text), _
                  1) = "/" Then
           'Directory
           sCurrentDir = sCurrentDir & Me.lstDir.Text
           bDir = True
        Else
          'File
        End If
   End Select

   Screen.MousePointer = vbHourglass

   If bDir Then
      Me.lstDir.Clear
      Me.itcMain.Execute , "DIR " & sCurrentDir
   Else
      sFileName = "C:\Temp\" & Me.lstDir.Text
      If Dir(sFileName) <> "" Then _
         Kill sFileName
      Me.itcMain.Execute , "GET " & sCurrentDir & _
                Me.lstDir.Text & " " & sFileName

      Screen.MousePointer = vbDefault
      MsgBox sFileName & " Saved"
   End If
End Sub

Private Sub LoadList(sDir As String)
   Dim lCtr As Long
   Dim sContents() As String

   sContents() = Split(sDir, vbCrLf)

   For lCtr = 0 To UBound(sContents) - 1
      If sContents(lCtr) <> "" Then
         Me.lstDir.AddItem sContents(lCtr), lCtr
      End If
   Next lCtr

   If Me.lstDir.ListCount = 0 Then
      Me.lstDir.AddItem "../"
   End If

   Screen.MousePointer = vbDefault
   If sCurrentDir = "" Then
      MsgBox "Changed to Root directory"
   Else
      MsgBox "Changed to directory: " & sCurrentDir
   End If
End Sub
```

Interactions

Action	*Result*
Username changes	Password property becomes blank (a null string).

Label Control

A label is a low-resource, display-only control for providing textual information to the user. The control provides properties for formatting the information but provides few useful methods or events. Its most common use is to provide a caption for controls, like the TextBox control, that lack a Caption property. It also can be used as a convenient means of displaying read-only text, particularly text that should blend in well with the form.

Control Tasks

The following categories reflect the tasks that are executed when creating a label.

Set Properties

1. Display properties (optional).

   BackStyle

   By default, the label will be 1–Opaque, and its BackColor property will show as a solid color behind the text. When other elements need to be seen through the text, use the 0–Transparent setting. This actually eliminates the BackColor entirely.

   UseMnemonic

   As described in the overview, normally an ampersand (&) in a caption makes the following character into the access key for the control. When UseMnemonic is set to its default of `True`, this is the case with labels. (But since a Label control cannot receive the input focus—it has no TabStop property—this means that pressing the access key moves the focus to the control whose TabIndex value is one greater than that of the Label control.) However, when set to `False`, ampersands display normally in the caption.

   Caption

   The property that's almost always set when a Label control is used, and in fact the property that accounts for its use in most applications, is the Caption property. The property can be set either at design time or at runtime and defines the text that the label displays.

Write Event Handlers

Click and MouseMove

Although event handlers are rarely assigned to them, labels receive standard mouse events. The MouseMove event is triggered when the user moves the mouse cursor over the label. The Click event is triggered when the user clicks the label with the mouse.

Example

If you want a "hot" area of a form without using a command button, a transparent label with no caption can give the functionality of an invisible button on a form. For example, a form may have an elaborate graphic on the background, and a command button would detract from the form's appearance. The following example uses a form with a control array consisting of five label controls (see Figure 5-29):

```
Option Explicit

'For this example, create a Label named _
   lblHotSpot with the Index Property set to 0. _
   There should also be a bitmap called "backgrnd.bmp" in the_
   current directory.

Private Enum WhichButton
    hsNone = -1
    hsTop = 0
    hsMiddle = 1
    hsOne = 2
    hsTwo = 3
    hsThree = 4
End Enum

Private bmLoaded As Boolean
Private imOverButton As WhichButton

Private Sub Form_Initialize()
   'Initially set the tracking variable.
    imOverButton = hsNone
End Sub

Private Sub Form_Load()
    Dim iCtr As Integer

   'Set up form.
    Me.Picture = LoadPicture("backgrnd.bmp")
    Me.Move Me.Left, Me.Top, 2640, 2925

   'Create labels.
    For iCtr = 0 To 4
        If iCtr > 0 Then _
            Load Me.lblHotSpot(iCtr)

        Me.lblHotSpot(iCtr).Visible = True
        Me.lblHotSpot(iCtr).BackStyle = 0
        Me.lblHotSpot(iCtr).Caption = ""
    Next iCtr

    bmLoaded = True
End Sub

Private Sub Form_MouseMove( _
        Button As Integer, Shift As Integer, _
```

Controls H–L

```
        X As Single, Y As Single)
    'If a button is already highlighted we need to turn it off.
    If imOverButton <> hsNone Then
        lblHotSpot(imOverButton).BorderStyle = vbBSNone
    End If

    'Reset the tracking variable.
    imOverButton = hsNone
End Sub

Private Sub Form_Resize()
    'If the labels have not been created yet, get out.
    If Not bmLoaded Then _
        Exit Sub

    'If the form has been resized, resize it back.
    If Me.Width <> 2640 Or Me.Height <> 2925 Then
        Me.Move Me.Left, Me.Top, 2640, 2925
        Exit Sub
    End If

    'These locations work with the picture I am using. _
    Yours may be different.
    Me.lblHotSpot(0).Move 180, 180, 2175, 435
    Me.lblHotSpot(1).Move 180, 1020, 2175, 435
    Me.lblHotSpot(2).Move 180, 1860, 495, 435
    Me.lblHotSpot(3).Move 1020, 1860, 495, 435
    Me.lblHotSpot(4).Move 1860, 1860, 495, 435
End Sub

Private Sub lblHotSpot_Click(Index As Integer)
    'Stop the highlighting button.
    lblHotSpot(imOverButton).BorderStyle = vbBSNone

    'Reset the tracking variable.
    imOverButton = hsNone

    Select Case Index
        Case hsTop
            MsgBox "Top Button Hit"
        Case hsMiddle
            MsgBox "Middle Button Hit"
        Case hsOne
            MsgBox "Button 1 Hit"
        Case hsTwo
            MsgBox "Button 2 Hit"
        Case hsThree
            MsgBox "Button 3 Hit"
    End Select
End Sub

Private Sub lblHotSpot_MouseMove( Index As Integer, _
        Button As Integer, Shift As Integer, _
        X As Single, Y As Single)
```

```
    'If this button is already highlighted, get out.
     If imOverButton = Index Then
         Exit Sub
     End If

    'If another button is highlighted, turn it off.
     If imOverButton <> hsNone Then
         lblHotSpot(imOverButton).BorderStyle = vbBSNone
     End If

    'Highlight the current button.
     lblHotSpot(Index).BorderStyle = vbBSSolid

    'Set the tracking variable.
     imOverButton = Index
End Sub
```


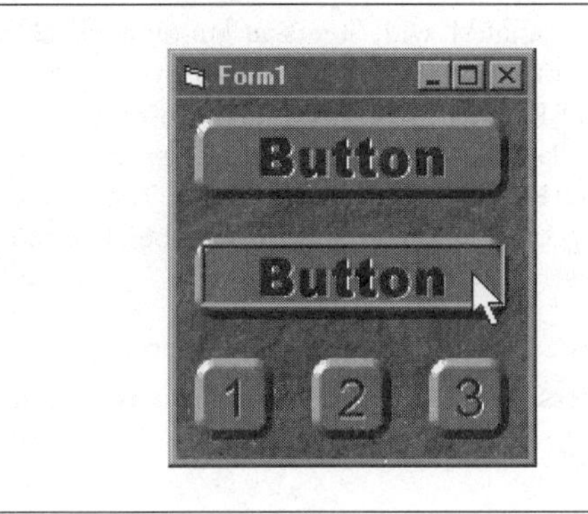

Figure 5-29: A form with a five-label control array

Interactions

Action	*Result*
Gets the focus through the form's tab order	Passes the focus to the next control in the form's tab order

Line Control

The Line control is used to draw a line on a container control.

Set Properties

1. Set location.

   X1, Y1, X2, Y2

   These properties define the endpoints of the Line control. The X1 and Y1 properties denote the location of the first endpoint (in twips), while the X2 and Y2 properties denote the other endpoint of the Line control.

2. Set appearance.

   BorderColor, BorderStyle, BorderWidth, DrawMode
   These properties control the appearance of the Line control. The Border-Color sets the color of the stroked line. The BorderStyle can be set to 0–vbTransparent, 1–vbBSSolid, 2–vbBSDash, 3–vbBSDot, 4–vbBDashDot, 5–vbBSDashDotDot, or 6–vbBSInsideSolid and appear the same as the PictureBox control's DrawStyle property. The BorderWidth acts the same as the PictureBox control's DrawWidth property.

ListBox Control

ListBox allows the user to select items from a scrollable list. The control can be set so that only one item or multiple items can be selected. Optionally, these items can appear with a checkbox next to each selection.

Typically, a list box is populated with items at runtime by calling the AddItem method, usually in the Form_Initialize or Form_Load event procedure. However, if the members of the list are known in advance, this can be done in the design-time environment by entering data into the list box's List property. Multiple items can be added by pressing CTRL-Enter after each item. The list box can then be controlled by setting its properties and its state can be determined by retrieving the values of its properties.

A lightweight version of the ListBox control is also available; see Windowless Controls, later in this chapter.

Control Tasks

The following categories reflect the tasks that are executed when creating and working with a list box.

Set Properties

1. Create the list.

   List( )
   The contents of a list box are contained in this array, which is read-only at runtime. Items are added to this list interactively at design time or by using the AddItem method at runtime. Once the list is filled, a currently selected item can be addressed by the Text property or by using the following syntax:

   ```
   strItem = lstVar.List(lstVar.ListIndex)
   ```

   In order to loop through all items in a list box named `lstVar`, the following should be used:

   ```
   For iCtr = 0 to lstVar.ListCount - 1
      'Perform actions with lstVar.List(iCtr).
   Next iCtr
   ```

ListCount

This read-only property contains the total number of items in a list box. The items of the list can then be iterated with a `For...Next` loop like the following:

```
For counter = 0 to lstVar.ListCount - 1
   < statements >
Next
```

Note that the `For Each...Next` construct cannot be used to iterate the items in a list box.

ListIndex

This read/write property contains the currently selected item in a list box. If no item is selected, this property will contain -1. Otherwise, it will contain the zero-based element number of the List array. Setting the List-Index property to the index of an item within the list selects that item. In a multiselection or a graphical list box, its behavior is somewhat different: it contains the value of the last item to be selected or unselected. If no item has been selected or unselected, it indicates the item that is highlighted when the control has the input focus, even if that item has not been selected. This makes the ListIndex property problematic for use with graphical or multiselection list boxes.

Text

Provides the contents of the currently selected item in the list of a single-selection list box; if no item is selected, its value is a null string (""). For multiple-selection and graphical list boxes, it contains the value indicated by the ListIndex property. The property is read-only. However, it is possible to "assign" a value to the Text property of a single-selection list box; this is actually the equivalent of invoking a Seek method, which the ListBox control otherwise does not support. For example, the statement:

```
List1.Text = "MyString"
```

changes the selected item to `MyString` if it is present in the list box or to a null string if it cannot be found.

ItemData()

Each item in the list has an additional, hidden value associated with it. This long value is contained in the ItemData array, each element of which corresponds to an element of the List array. Generally, this array is used to associate the descriptive, visible items in the list with additional data, such as a database key.

SelCount

Indicates the total number of selected items in the list box. In a single-selection list box, its value can be either 0 (no items selected) or 1; otherwise, its value can range from 0 to ListCount.

Selected()

An array of Boolean values that indicate whether the element at the corresponding position in the List array has been selected. This is useful only for multiselection or graphical controls; for single-selection controls, it's most efficient to work with the ListIndex and Text properties.

2. Specify selection mode (optional).

MultiSelect

Can be set at design time to 0–None for single-select only, 1–Simple to allow the user to click on each item in the list to select it, or 2–Extended, which allows the user to Shift-Click to select consecutive items or CTRL-Click to select multiple nonconsecutive items.

Style

When set at design to 1–CheckBox, each item in the list appears with a checkbox to the left of the item as shown in the right list box in Figure 5-30. The user can select items from the list box by clicking on each checkbox. The MultiSelect property is ignored when this option is chosen; the user can always select multiple items. When Style is set to 0–Normal, the MultiSelect property is used as normal, as shown in the left list box in Figure 5-30.

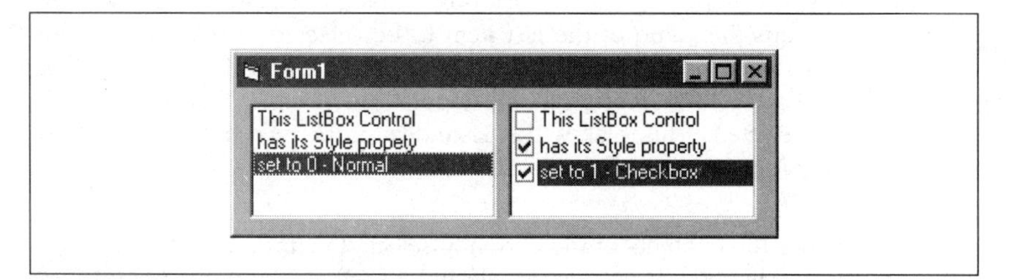

Figure 5-30: The effects of the Style property

3. Specify sorting (optional).

Sorted

When this property is set to `True`, all items in the list are alphabetized.

NewIndex

When new items are added to a sorted list box, the ListIndex of the new items is unpredictable. Therefore, the NewIndex property contains the index of the most recently added item. It is important when you need to know the position of the new list box element so that you can set its ItemData property. The following function automates this process:

```
Public Function AddItemToList( _
        lstVar As ListBox, _
        sItem As String, _
        lData As Long) _
    As Long

    'Adds an Item and corresponding ItemData to a _
    ListBox. Returns the ListIndex for the new item. _
    This is particularly valuable for sorted lists.

    Dim bAdded As Boolean
    Dim lIndex As Long

    On Error GoTo AddItemToList_Error
```

```
        lstVar.AddItem sItem
        bAdded = True
        lIndex = lstVar.NewIndex
        lstVar.ItemData(lIndex) = lData
        AddItemToList = lIndex

        Exit Function

    AddItemToList_Error:
        'Error occurred—item not added
        If Not bAdded Then
            AddItemToList = -1
        Else             'Error Occurred—item added.
            AddItemToList = -2
        End If
        Exit Function
    End Function
```

4. Set sizing mode (optional).

   IntegralHeight

   When set to `True`, the list box will resize its height only to complete visible rows. If a height is set that allows for half a row to be visible, that row will not be shown at all and the list box will resize to one less row. When set to `False`, the list box will resize like all other controls.

5. Determine visible items (optional).

   TopIndex

   This property contains the index of the top visible item on the list. The value of this property changes as the user scrolls through the list and can also be set in code.

Useful Methods

AddItem

When adding items to a list box, the AddItem method accepts parameters for both the text of the item to be added as well as the index to use for that item. When the `Index` parameter is supplied with a sorted list box, the item will still be added in the position set by the Index. This can cause items to be added out of the sort order. This can be easily avoided by not passing the *`Index`* parameter.

RemoveItem

To remove items from a list box, pass the Index of the item to be removed to the RemoveItem method.

Clear

This method removes all items from the list box.

Write Event Handlers

Click

Anytime the user scrolls through the list selecting items, whether by mouse, keyboard, or code, the Click event is fired. When it is used with the ListIndex property, you can react to various items being selected.

ItemCheck

When an item of a checkbox (Style = 1) list box is checked or unchecked, the ItemCheck event is fired. The index of the selected item is passed as a parameter to the event.

Scroll

Called each time the list box is scrolled either by a Mouse or Keyboard event. When used with the TopIndex property, this will help to ascertain which items of the list are currently being displayed.

Interactions

Action	*Result*
Move through the list using the keyboard, mouse, or code.	Fires Click event. Changes values of ListIndex and Text properties. If the list is scrolled, then after the preceding, the Scroll event is fired and the TopIndex property is updated.
Select an item in a list.	Fires Click event. Updates value of SelCount property and Selected array. If the style is CheckBox, fires the ItemCheck event as well.
Assign a value to the Text property.	Fires the Click event. Changes ListIndex to the index that matches the string assigned to Text or to -1 if there is no match. Changes the Text property to the assigned value if there is a match or to a null string if there is none.
Change the ListIndex property in code.	Fires the Click event.
User resizes the control or the Height property is modified in code, if IntegralHeight is `True`.	Further adjusts the Height property to display only complete items.
Set the ListTop property in code.	Fires the Scroll event.

ListView Control

The ListView control provides Visual Basic developers with another way to provide a list of items to the user. However, this information can be provided in multiple formats. Large and small icons can be shown for each item, or the items can be presented in a list with one or more columns. An example of a ListView control used in an application is the Windows Explorer program, where the ListView occupies the right side of the Explorer window.

The ListView control displays one or more ListItem objects, which are added to the list at runtime. ListItem objects are roughly equivalent to records. Each ListItem object itself contains an array of SubItems, which are similar to fields. The first element of the array, `ListItem.SubItems(0)`, is the name of the ListItem, and there is one element in the array for each column header in the ListView. These SubItems can also be accessed through the ListSubItems collection.

The ListView control is contained in the Windows Common Controls (*COMCTL32.OCX*) that come with Visual Basic Professional and Enterprise editions.

Control Tasks

The following categories reflect the tasks that are executed when creating and using a ListView.

Set Properties

1. Set general appearance.

View

There are four ways that the information in the ListView control can be viewed, as Figure 5-31 illustrates. These are controlled by the View property. The contents can be viewed as regular-size icons with a text caption (0–lvwIcon), small icons with text captions that are aligned left to right in rows (1–lvwSmallIcon), small icons with text captions that are aligned top to bottom in columns (2–lvwList), or a multicolumn list with small icons on the left and column headers at the top (3–lvwReport). When set to `lvwIcon` or `lvwSmallIcon`, the user can move these icons within the control. Typically, the user is able to switch between views at runtime by selecting a menu item.

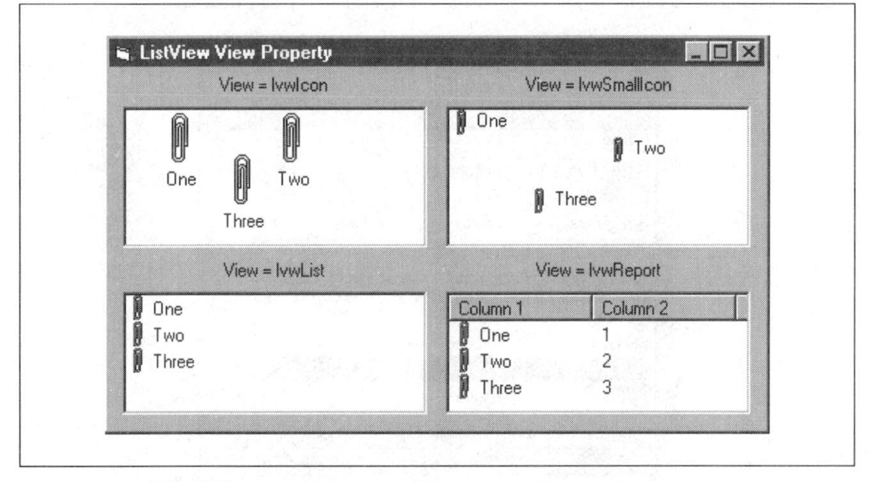

Figure 5-31: The different views of a ListView control

Icons, SmallIcons, ColumnHeaderIcons **VB6**

The Icons, SmallIcons, and ColumnHeaderIcons properties all contain the name of an ImageList control on the same form as the ListView. The Icons ImageList should contain 32×32-pixel icons, while the SmallIcons ImageList should contain smaller, 16×16-pixel or less, icons. The Column-

Controls H–L

HeaderIcons property can contain any size icons to be displayed only when the View property is set to `lvwReport`. (Note that because all of the images stored in a single ImageList control must have the same dimensions, you must use separate ImageList controls to store each set of icons.) Each ListItem object placed in the ListView can choose which icon and small icon to use from the Icons and SmallIcons ImageLists. Each column in the ListView can choose which ColumnHeaderIcon to use from that ImageList.

CheckBoxes **VB6**

Normally, when the CheckBoxes property is set to `False`, each ListItem object in a ListView appears with the appropriate icon for the current view. When CheckBoxes is set to `True`, a checkbox appears next to each ListItem object, along with any icon in all views (see Figure 5-32). The user can then check multiple list items by clicking on the box. Each ListItem has a Checked property that indicates whether it's been checked.

FullRowSelect **VB6**

When View is set to `lvwReport`, normally with FullRowSelect set to `False`, only the first column of a selected row is highlighted. When FullRowSelect is set to `True`, the entire row is highlighted (see Figure 5-32).

GridLines **VB6**

When GridLines is set to `True`, faint lines appear around each cell when View is set to `lvwReport` (see Figure 5-32). This gives the ListView more of a gridlike appearance.

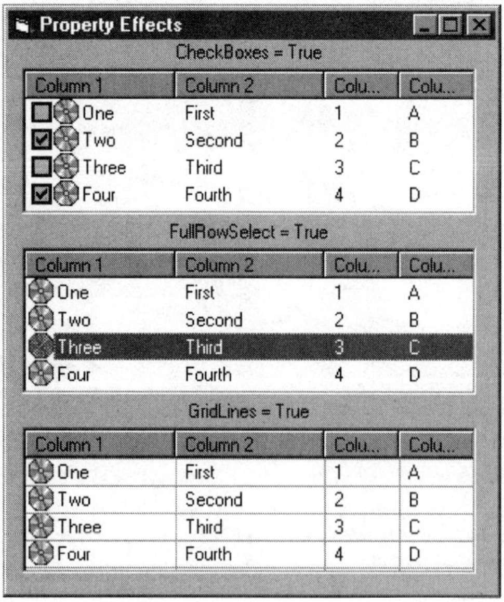

Figure 5-32: The effects of CheckBoxes, FullRowSelect, and GridLines

LabelWrap

Determines whether the text of a ListItem wraps when in icon or small icon view. Its default value is `True`.

FlatScrollBar **VB6**

When FlatScrollBar is set to `True` and a scrollbar is displayed because of the amount of data in the ListView, that scrollbar (or scrollbars) will appear flat instead of taking on the standard raised appearance.

Arrange

Determines the alignment of list items in icon and small icon view. The default value is 0–lvwNone, which aligns list items along the top of the control but allows them to be manually repositioned through drag-and-drop operations. When set to 1–lvwAutoLeft, list items are also aligned along the left side of the control, but they snap back into alignment when dragged and dropped by the user. When set to 2–lvwTop, list items are aligned along the top of the control and snap back into alignment when dragged and dropped.

2. Set ListView behavior.

LabelEdit

By default, the contents of the Text property of each ListItem can be edited by the user simply by clicking on the caption of a selected ListItem. In this case, the LabelEdit property is set to 0–lvwAutomatic. When set to 1–lvwManual, the caption can be edited by the user only after the StartLabelEdit method is called.

AllowColumnReorder **VB6**

When AllowColumnReorder is set to `True`, the user can drag the column headers to change the order in which they appear in the ListView. The Position property of each ColumnHeader object can be used to retrieve the new order of the ColumnHeaders.

Although the user can change the order of the columns to make a different column first, only the column displaying the Text property can be edited by the user.

HotTracking **VB6**

When HotTracking is set to `True`, ListItems are highlighted as the mouse passes over them.

HoverSelection **VB6**

When HoverSelection is set to `True`, a ListItem is selected if the mouse pauses over it.

3. Sort the ListView.

Sorted, SortKey, SortOrder

The list can be sorted in all four views based on the values in any column. To sort the list based on a particular column, that column does not have to be visible. The order of an unsorted list is undefined.

The contents of the ListView can be sorted using these three properties. The Sorted property is a simple Boolean expression that indicates whether the ListView should be sorted or not; its default value is `False`. The column to sort by is contained in the SortKey property. To sort by the Text property, set the SortKey to 0. Otherwise, set the SortKey to the index of the SubItem to sort on. (This corresponds to a column's position in the SubItem array.) Finally, the SortOrder property can be set to 0–lvwAscending or 1–lvwDescending, to denote the direction of the sort.

4. Create columns.

ColumnHeaders (Collection), ColumnHeader (Object)

When displayed in Report mode (View = `lvwReport`), the ListView shows multiple columns. Adding a ColumnHeader object to the ColumnHeaders collection creates each column in the ListView. At design time, these columns can be created through the ListView's custom properties. However, at runtime they must be created using the Add method of the ListView's ColumnHeaders collection. Its syntax is:

```
obColHdr.Add(index, key, text, width, alignment)
```

as shown in the following code fragment:

```
lvwList.ColumnHeaders.Add , "Name", " Name", _
       lvwList.Width / 4, lvwColumnLeft
```

5. Set ColumnHeader properties.

Text, Width, Alignment

The caption at the top of the column, its width, and the alignment of the column should be set when creating the column. When using the ColumnHeaders.Add method, these are all parameters to the Add method. However, every ColumnHeader object also has corresponding properties (Text, Width, and Alignment, respectively) that can be set directly in code.

SubItemIndex

Each ColumnHeader object represents a column in the ListView. The first column contains the ListItem object's Text property. The rest of the columns contain one element of the SubItem property array. At runtime, the column bound to a ColumnHeader can be determined by retrieving that ColumnHeader object's SubItemIndex property. When it is equal to zero, the value of the Text property is returned. Otherwise, the SubItemIndex property contains the index of the SubItem object that's assigned to that column. The most common need for this information is when the user clicks on the column header and the ColumnClick event fires to cause an action to be performed, such as sorting the ListView on that column. The sample ColumnClick event handler later in this section shows how this can be achieved easily.

6. Create ListItems.

ListItems (collection), ListItem (object)

Each item in a ListView is a ListItem object that is part of the ListItems collection. ListItems cannot be created at design time. At runtime, they can be created by using the Add method of the ListItems collection. Its syntax is:

```
objLstItem.Add(index, key, text, icon, smallIcon)
```

7. Set ListItem properties.

Text, Icon, SmallIcon

The caption of the ListItem and the index of the ListImage to use for both large and small icon views can be set either as parameters of the ListItems collection's Add Method or by assigning values to these properties.

SubItem()

After you create a ListItem, a SubItem array is created with as many elements as there are ColumnHeaders in the ListView. Each of these must be set separately and will become the data shown in the column. For example, the following code fragment creates a complete ListItem containing file information:

```
const cSIZE = 1
const cDATE = 2
const cATTRIB = 3

Set objItem = lvwFiles.ListItems.Add(, , strFN, _
    "F1", "F1")

objItem.SubItems(cSIZE) = lngFileSize
objItem.SubItems(cDATE) = datFile
objItem.SubItems(cATTRIB) = strAttrib
```

8. Determine ListItem status.

SelectedItem property, Selected property (ListItem object)

For a single-selection ListView control (i.e., its MultiSelect property is `False`), you can determine which ListItem is selected at the time the selection occurs by handling the ItemClick event, which passes a reference to the selected ListItem object to the event handler. You can also determine which ListItems are selected during processing by examining the SelectedItem property for a single-selection control (it returns a reference to the selected ListItem object) or by iterating the Selected property of each ListItem object. This is illustrated in the following code fragment:

```
If Not ListView.MultiSelect Then
   ' ListView.SelectedItem.Text = name of list item
Else
   Dim objItem As ListItem
   For Each objItem In ListView.ListItems
      If objItem.Selected Then
         ' objItem.Text = name of list item
      End If
   Next
End If
```

Checked (ListItem object) **VB6**

When the CheckBoxes property is set to `True`, checked ListItems have their Checked property set to `True`. Items can be checked by the program by setting the Checked property of a ListItem programmatically.

Controls H–L

Ghosted (ListItem object)

At times it is useful to dim a ListItem in a ListView control, such as when the item has been cut but not yet pasted. The Boolean Ghosted property is provided for each ListItem for this purpose.

Useful Methods

HitTest

When provided with coordinates, the HitTest method will return a ListItem if there is one at those coordinates. Otherwise, the method returns `Nothing`.

StartLabelEdit

When the StartLabelEdit method is called, the caption of the ListItem becomes both selected and editable by the user. This is unnecessary when the LabelEdit property is set to `lvwAutomatic`.

Write Event Handlers

ColumnClick

When the user clicks on a column header when the ListView control is in Report view, the ColumnClick event is fired. The ColumnHeader object on which the user has clicked is passed as a parameter to the event handler. Typically, the event handler is responsible for changing the sort order as well as for determining whether ListItems are displayed in ascending or descending order. The following event handler accomplishes this:

```
Private Sub lvwStyles_ColumnClick( _
       ByVal ColumnHeader As ComctlLib.ColumnHeader)

Dim intCtr As Integer

'Make sure Sorted property is True
If lvwStyles.Sorted = False Then _
   lvwStyles.Sorted = True

'Change sort order if column already is sort key
If ColumnHeader.SubItemIndex = lvwStyles.SortKey Then
   If lvwStyles.SortOrder = lvwAscending Then
      lvwStyles.SortOrder = lvwDescending
   Else
      lvwStyles.SortOrder = lvwAscending
   End If
'Otherwise change sort key to clicked column
Else
   lvwStyles.SortKey = ColumnHeader.SubItemIndex
   lvwStyles.SortOrder = lvwAscending
End If

End Sub
```

ItemClick

When a ListItem is clicked by the user, the ItemClick event is fired. This event also passes the clicked ListItem object as a parameter to the application.

MouseDown

While the ItemClick event is fired only when the user clicks a ListItem, the MouseDown event fires regardless of where it is clicked. When used in conjunction with the HitTest method, the application could react differently based on whether a ListItem was clicked or the background area was clicked.

Example

The following example uses many of the conventions mentioned earlier in this section (the result is shown in Figure 5-33):

```
Option Explicit

'For this example, create the following controls: _
 a ListView control named lvwMain, _
 an ImageList control named imlIcons, _
 an ImageList control named imlSmallIcons, and _
 an ImageList control named imlColumnHeaderIcons.

'Create the following menus: _
  A Menu named mnuListViewTop with the Visible _
     property set to False, _
  a Menu under mnuListViewTop named mnuListView _
     with the Index property set to 0, _
  a Menu named mnuListItemTop with the Visible _
     property set to False, and _
  a Menu under mnuListItemTop named mnuListItem _
     with the Index property set to 0.

Private Sub Form_Load()
    Dim imlItem As ListImage

  'Set up form.
    Me.Caption = "Manage Media"
    Me.Icon = LoadPicture("cd-big.ico")

  'Set up menu.
    Me.mnuListView(0).Caption = "&Icon View"
    Load mnuListView(1)
    Me.mnuListView(1).Caption = "&Small Icon View"
    Load mnuListView(2)
    Me.mnuListView(2).Caption = "&List View"
    Load mnuListView(3)
    Me.mnuListView(3).Caption = "&Report View"

    Me.mnuListItem(0).Caption = "&View Details"
    Load mnuListItem(1)
    Me.mnuListItem(1).Caption = "&Edit Media"

  'Set up ImageList for Icons.
    Me.imlIcons.ImageHeight = 32
    Me.imlIcons.ImageWidth = 32
    Set imlItem = Me.imlIcons.ListImages.Add(, , _
        LoadPicture("cd-big.ico"))
```

```
    Set imlItem = Me.imlIcons.ListImages.Add(, , _
        LoadPicture("lp-big.ico"))
    Set imlItem = Me.imlIcons.ListImages.Add(, , _
        LoadPicture("cass-big.ico"))
    Set imlItem = Me.imlIcons.ListImages.Add(, , _
        LoadPicture("tape-big.ico"))

  'Set up ImageList for Small Icons.
    Me.imlSmallIcons.ImageHeight = 16
    Me.imlSmallIcons.ImageWidth = 16
    Set imlItem = Me.imlSmallIcons.ListImages.Add(, , _
        LoadPicture("cd-sm.ico"))
    Set imlItem = Me.imlSmallIcons.ListImages.Add(, , _
        LoadPicture("lp-sm.ico"))
    Set imlItem = Me.imlSmallIcons.ListImages.Add(, , _
        LoadPicture("cass-sm.ico"))
    Set imlItem = Me.imlSmallIcons.ListImages.Add(, , _
        LoadPicture("tape-sm.ico"))

  'Set up ImageList for ColumnHeaders.
    Me.imlColumnHeaderIcons.ImageHeight = 16
    Me.imlColumnHeaderIcons.ImageWidth = 16
    Set imlItem = _
        Me.imlColumnHeaderIcons.ListImages.Add(, , _
        LoadPicture("uparrow.bmp"))
    Set imlItem = _
        Me.imlColumnHeaderIcons.ListImages.Add(, , _
        LoadPicture("dnarrow.bmp"))

  'Set up ListView.
    Me.lvwMain.View = lvwIcon
    Me.lvwMain.Icons = Me.imlIcons
    Me.lvwMain.SmallIcons = Me.imlSmallIcons
    Me.lvwMain.ColumnHeaderIcons = _
            Me.imlColumnHeaderIcons
    Me.lvwMain.ColumnHeaders.Add , , "Title", 2000, _
            lvwColumnLeft
    Me.lvwMain.ColumnHeaders.Add _
        , , "Performer/Actor", 1500, lvwColumnLeft
    Me.lvwMain.ColumnHeaders.Add , , "Catalog #", _
        1000, lvwColumnLeft
    Me.lvwMain.ColumnHeaders.Add , , "Media", 1000, _
        lvwColumnLeft
    Me.lvwMain.Arrange = lvwAutoTop
    Me.lvwMain.LabelEdit = lvwManual

    GetMediaRecords
End Sub

Private Sub Form_Resize()

   If Me.ScaleWidth < 1335 Or Me.ScaleHeight < 555 _
      Then Exit Sub
```

```
   Me.lvwMain.Move 120, 120, Me.ScaleWidth - 240, _
                    Me.ScaleHeight - 240
End Sub

Private Sub lvwMain_ColumnClick( _
        ByVal ColumnHeader As MSComctlLib.ColumnHeader)
   Dim colVar As ColumnHeader

   'If the ListView is already sorted by the clicked _
   column, just reverse the order. Otherwise, sort the _
   ListView by the column clicked ascending.
   If Me.lvwMain.Sorted = True And _
     ColumnHeader.SubItemIndex = Me.lvwMain.SortKey Then
      If Me.lvwMain.SortOrder = lvwAscending Then
         Me.lvwMain.SortOrder = lvwDescending
      Else
         Me.lvwMain.SortOrder = lvwAscending
      End If
   Else
      Me.lvwMain.Sorted = True
      Me.lvwMain.SortKey = ColumnHeader.SubItemIndex
      Me.lvwMain.SortOrder = lvwAscending
   End If

   'Now, use the sort information to update the up _
   or down arrows on the ColumnHeader.
   For Each colVar In Me.lvwMain.ColumnHeaders
      If colVar.SubItemIndex = Me.lvwMain.SortKey Then
         If Me.lvwMain.SortOrder = lvwDescending Then
            colVar.Icon = 1
         Else
            colVar.Icon = 2
         End If
      Else
         colVar.Icon = 0
      End If
   Next colVar
End Sub

Private Sub lvwMain_DblClick()
   ViewMedia Me.lvwMain.SelectedItem
End Sub

Private Sub lvwMain_MouseDown( _
        Button As Integer, _
        Shift As Integer, _
        x As Single, _
        y As Single)
   'If the mouse was clicked over an Icon, pop up the _
   ListItem menu. Otherwise, pop up the ListView menu.
   If Me.lvwMain.HitTest(x, y) Is Nothing Then
      If Button = vbRightButton Then
         Me.PopupMenu mnuListViewTop
      End If
```

```
   Else
      Set Me.lvwMain.SelectedItem = _
              Me.lvwMain.HitTest(x, y)
      If Button = vbRightButton Then
         Me.PopupMenu mnuListItemTop, , , , _
                      mnuListItem(0)
      End If
   End If
End Sub

Private Sub mnuListItem_Click(Index As Integer)
   Select Case Index
      Case 0
         ViewMedia Me.lvwMain.SelectedItem
      Case 1
         EditMedia Me.lvwMain.SelectedItem
   End Select
End Sub

Private Sub mnuListView_Click(Index As Integer)
   Select Case Index
      Case 0
         Me.lvwMain.View = lvwIcon
      Case 1
         Me.lvwMain.View = lvwSmallIcon
      Case 2
         Me.lvwMain.View = lvwList
      Case 3
         Me.lvwMain.View = lvwReport
   End Select
End Sub

Private Sub GetMediaRecords()
   Dim itmVar As ListItem

  'Normally, I'd get these from a database, but for _
  this sample I'll just put these in by hand.
   Set itmVar = Me.lvwMain.ListItems.Add(, , _
               "Blizzard of Ozz", 1, 1)
   itmVar.SubItems(1) = "Ozzy Osbourne"
   itmVar.SubItems(2) = "7464-36812-2"
   itmVar.SubItems(3) = "CD"

    Set itmVar = Me.lvwMain.ListItems.Add(, , _
               "Jurrasic Park", 4, 4)
    itmVar.SubItems(1) = _
           "Sam Neil, Laura Dern, Jeff Goldblum"
    itmVar.SubItems(2) = ""
    itmVar.SubItems(3) = "Videotape"

    Set itmVar = Me.lvwMain.ListItems.Add(, , _
               "Evan's Classical Favorites", 3, 3)
    itmVar.SubItems(1) = "Assorted"
    itmVar.SubItems(2) = "N/A"
```

```
    itmVar.SubItems(3) = "Cassette"

    Set itmVar = Me.lvwMain.ListItems.Add(, , "Tommy", _
                2, 2)
    itmVar.SubItems(1) = "The Who"
    itmVar.SubItems(2) = ""
    itmVar.SubItems(3) = "LP"

    Set itmVar = Me.lvwMain.ListItems.Add(, , _
                "Men in Black", 4, 4)
    itmVar.SubItems(1) = "Will Smith"
    itmVar.SubItems(2) = ""
    itmVar.SubItems(3) = "Videotape"
End Sub

Private Sub EditMedia(ritmVar As ListItem)
  'Normally, there would be logic to edit the media.
    MsgBox "Editing Media: " & ritmVar.Text
End Sub

Private Sub ViewMedia(ritmVar As ListItem)
  'Normally, there would be logic to view the _
  details about the media.
    MsgBox "Viewing Media: " & ritmVar.Text
End Sub
```

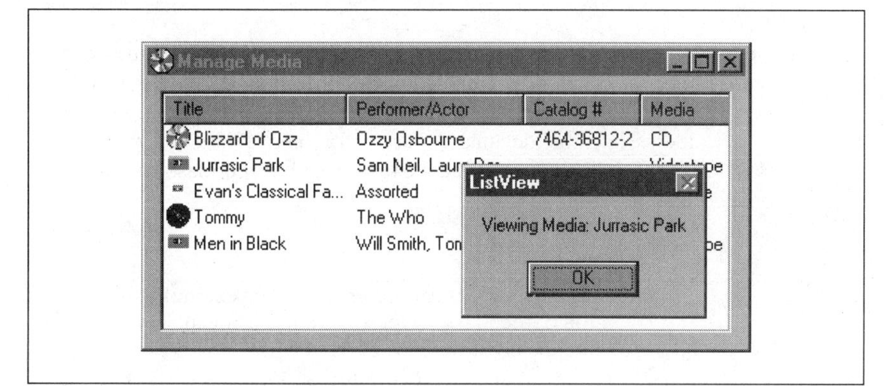

Figure 5-33: The Manage Media example

Order of Events

The following sequence of events are fired when the user clicks on a ListItem:

1. ItemClick
2. Click
3. BeforeLabelEdit, if the LabelEdit property is `True` and the user clicks on a ListItem's text
4. AfterLabelEdit, if the BeforeLabelEdit event fires and the user changes the text of the ListItem

Interactions

Action	*Result*
StartLabelEdit method is called.	BeforeLabelEdit event is fired.

MaskedEditBox Control

The MaskedEditBox control provides the developer with an easy method to accept validated data from the user and provide formatted output through a TextBox-like control. In fact, if its special properties are not used, the MaskedEditBox control is virtually identical to the standard TextBox control. When an input mask is defined, the control displays a customized data entry field. If the user attempts to enter invalid characters, they are rejected, and a ValidateError event is generated. When a format string is supplied, the control can display user input that's formatted in particular ways.

Control Tasks

The following categories reflect the tasks that are executed when using a MaskedEditBox.

Set Properties

1. Define a template for input data.

   Mask

   Defines the exact character map used for entering data into the control. At runtime, an optional prompt character indicates each character position at which user input is expected based on the input mask. Placeholders (like the decimal separator or literals) are not valid input positions. The following characters can be used in the mask to obtain the desired effect:

Character	*Result*
#	Only digits (0–9) can be entered. For example, the value of the Mask property to enter a Social Security Number might be `###-##-####`.
. (Period)	The decimal separator; although a period is used to represent the symbol in the input mask, the actual character used at runtime depends on the system's International Settings.
, (Comma)	The thousands separator; although a comma is used to represent the symbol in the input mask, the actual character used depends on the system's International Settings.
: (Colon)	The time separator; although a colon is used to represent the symbol in the input mask, the actual character used depends on the system's International Settings.

Character	*Result*
/ (Slash)	The date separator; although a slash is used to represent the symbol, the actual character used depends on the system's International Settings.
\ (Backslash)	When the backslash is encountered in the mask, the next character is treated as a literal, even if it is contained in this list. For example, the mask `\T\E\M\P####` allows the user to choose a temporary eight-character filename beginning with the string "TEMP".
& (Ampersand)	Any printable ANSI character can be entered.
> (Greater Than symbol)	Subsequent characters will be uppercase. This does not require that the user input uppercase characters; it converts any lowercase characters input by the user to uppercase.
< (Less Than symbol)	Subsequent characters will be lowercase. This does not require that the user input lowercase characters; it converts any uppercase characters input by the user to lowercase.
A	Alphabetic characters (uppercase or lowercase) or digits (0–9) can be entered.
a	Alphabetic characters (uppercase or lowercase) or digits (0–9) can be entered but are not required.
9	Only digits (0–9) can be entered but are not required.
C	Same as ampersand in this list.
?	Alphabetic characters (uppercase or lowercase) can be entered.
Others	Are unchanged.

AllowPrompt

When set to `False`, its default value, the character denoted by the PromptChar property is considered an invalid character for the control. When set to `True`, this character can be entered if it is valid for the Mask property.

2. Determine the appearance of formatted output.

Format

Defines how text stored to the control is displayed when the control loses the focus or when it is retrieved using the FormattedText property. The Format property should be populated with a format string similar to those used in VB's *Format* function.[*]

* For detailed documentation on the *Format* function, see *VB & VBA in a Nutshell: The Language* by Paul Lomax, also published by O'Reilly & Associates.

3. Retrieve the control's output.

   Text

   Contains the unformatted text stored to the control. This includes characters entered by the user as well literal characters in the Mask property (if one was defined) and prompt characters in positions where the user has not input a character (if the PromptInclude property is `True`).

   The Text property is not read-only, as you might expect. This is because you must be able to clear the control's input data in order to allow the entry of the next record in a multirecord data entry application. Typically, this will generate an error if the string you try to assign to the Text property conflicts with the input mask. Consequently, to clear the current input data, you must first clear the mask and then assign the text property, as the following code fragment shows:

```
mskControl.Mask = ""
mskControl.Text = ""
```

   FormattedText

   A read-only property that returns a string containing the formatted version of the Text property as defined by the Format property.

   ClipText

   A read-only property that returns the text stored to the control without the prompt characters or the literals defined by the Mask property. For example, given a mask of `###-##-####` and user input of `123-12-1234`, the ClipText property returns `123121234`.

   SelText

   Returns the selected text stored to the control. If the value of the ClipText property is 0–mskIncludeLiterals, the default, literal characters in the Mask property are included; if its value is 1–mskExclude literals, literal characters in the Mask property are excluded.

   SelText is a read/write property. Text stored to the control's SelText property behaves as if it were pasted into the control from the Clipboard. This makes it more reliable and less error prone than assigning a string directly to the control's Text property.

   ClipMode

   Determines whether literals defined in the control's Mask property are included (if its value is 0–mskIncludeLiterals, the default) or excluded (1–mskExclude literals) from the string output by the SelText method. Note that this property does not affect the behavior of the ClipText method.

4. Control behavior.

   AutoTab

   When set to `True`, after the final character allowed by the Mask property is entered, the focus advances automatically to the next control in the tab order.

PromptInclude

Determines if prompt characters are included in the control's Text property value after user input. If `True`, its default value, the prompt defined by the PromptChar property is included in the Text property at each character position where the user doesn't input a character. This creates a string that requires parsing. If `False`, the PromptChar character is not included.

PromptChar

Before data is placed into the MaskedEditBox, the areas reserved for user entry are populated with the contents of the PromptChar property. While this property defaults to an underscore character (_), it can be changed to any other printable character. If you try to set its value to a space, the control will restore the default underscore character (_) at runtime.

Write Event Handlers

ValidationError

Whenever a character not allowed by the Mask property is entered into a MaskedEditBox control, the ValidationError event is fired. The following parameters are passed to the event handler:

`InvalidText`

The current contents of the control.

`StartPosition`

The position in *`InvalidText`* where the invalid character was entered. In some cases, the value of *`StartPosition`* may be 0, making it unreliable for identifying the source of input errors.

Controls M–N

Example

```
Option Explicit

'For this example, create a MaskedEditBox _
   named mebMain with the Index _
   property set to 0.

Dim lblName As Label
Dim lblSSN As Label
Dim lblPhone As Label

Private Sub Form_Load()
   'Create/set up controls.
    Set lblName = _
        Me.Controls.Add("vb.label", "lblName", Me)
    lblName.Caption = "&Name:"
    lblName.Visible = True

    Set lblSSN = _
        Me.Controls.Add("vb.label", "lblSSN", Me)
    lblSSN.Caption = "&SSN:"
    lblSSN.Visible = True
```

```
        Set lblPhone = _
            Me.Controls.Add("vb.label", "lblPhone", Me)
        lblPhone.Caption = "&Phone:"
        lblPhone.Visible = True

        Me.mebMain(0).Mask = _
            ">&&&&&&&&&&&&&&&&&&&&&&&&&&&&&&"
        Me.mebMain(0).Format = ""

        Load Me.mebMain(1)
        Me.mebMain(1).Mask = "#########"
        Me.mebMain(1).Format = "###-##-####"
        Me.mebMain(1).Visible = True

        Load Me.mebMain(2)
        Me.mebMain(2).Mask = "###-###-####"
        Me.mebMain(2).Format = "(###) ###-####"
        Me.mebMain(2).Visible = True
    End Sub

    Private Sub Form_Resize()
        If Me.ScaleWidth < 2550 Then _
            Exit Sub

        lblName.Move 120, 150, 1095, 255
        Me.mebMain(0).Move _
            1335, 120, Me.ScaleWidth - 1455, 315
        lblSSN.Move 120, 585, 1095, 255
        Me.mebMain(1).Move _
            1335, 555, Me.ScaleWidth - 1455, 315
        lblPhone.Move 120, 1020, 1095, 255
        Me.mebMain(2).Move _
            1335, 990, Me.ScaleWidth - 1455, 315
    End Sub

    Private Sub mebMain_ValidationError(Index As Integer, _
            InvalidText As String, StartPosition As Integer)
    'Beep when an incorrect character is pressed.
        Beep
    End Sub
```

Interactions

Action	Result
A string is assigned to the Mask property.	The MaxLength property is modified to reflect the maximum number of input characters defined in the mask string.
Text that is invalid based on the Mask property is entered into the control either through code or by the user.	The ValidateError event is fired. The Change event is *not* fired.

Menu Control

Each form in a Visual Basic application is capable of containing a menu. The menu appears at the top of the window, under the titlebar. The menu contains Menu controls that can then contain other menu items, making submenus up to six levels deep. Menu controls can also be displayed in other locations using Visual Basic's *PopupMenu* function.

Generally, the Menu controls that comprise a menu are built through Visual Basic's Menu Editor (see Figure 5-34). This allows the developer to create Menu controls in a hierarchical fashion. Menu controls cannot be created through dynamic control creation, but additional Menu controls can be created in a control array like any other control, as long as one element is assigned to the control array at design time. However, elements in a Menu control array must have the same parent Menu control (or the menu bar itself) and must be contiguous to one another.

A menu and its submenus can be displayed on another control when needed by using the form or MDI form's PopupMenu method. This allows even an invisible menu to be displayed for context-sensitive actions. Chapter 3, *The Form*, and Chapter 4, *The MDI Form*, discuss the PopupMenu method. In addition, the sections on the RichTextBox control and the ListView control in this chapter, contain examples that show how to use the PopupMenu method for context-sensitive actions.

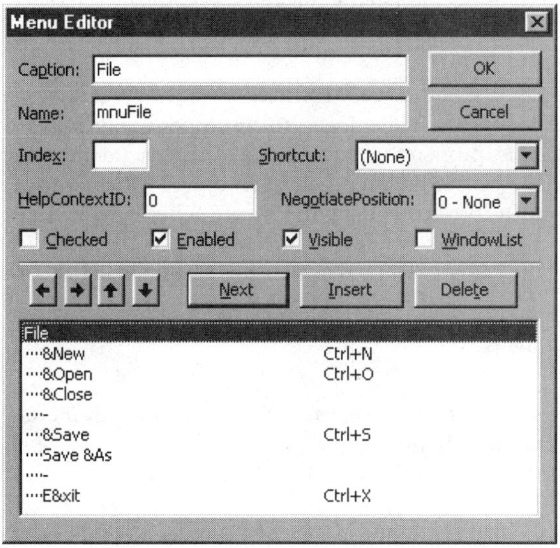

Figure 5-34: The Visual Basic Menu Editor

Control Tasks

The following categories reflect the tasks that are executed when creating or using a menu.

Set Properties

1. Determine visible appearance.

   Caption

   The Caption property contains the text displayed on the Menu control and supports mnemonic access keys, as described in Chapter 2, *Common Control Features*. However, the mnemonic code is available only when the Menu control is currently displayed.

   Shortcut

   The Shortcut property contains a keyboard shortcut to fire the Menu control's Click event. The Shortcut property is available only through the Menu Editor. It cannot be set or viewed through code.

   Checked

   The Checked property allows a check mark to be displayed next to a Menu control's caption. When the Checked property is set to `True`, the check mark is displayed. When set to `False`, the check mark is not shown.

   Visible

   When the Visible property of a Menu control is set to `False`, that Menu control, along with any submenus it might contain, is not displayed. However, the PopupMenu method displays an invisible Menu control and its submenus.

   WindowList

   Generally, a menu for an MDI form includes a Window menu that allows the user to switch the focus to any open child windows. Setting the WindowList property to `True` indicates that the Menu object is a Window menu and causes the menu to list all open MDI child windows belonging to the MDI form containing the menu. When any of the windows in the list is chosen, that window automatically gets the focus in the MDI form. When the parent object is a standard form, setting this property has no effect.

Write Event Handlers

Click

Takes place when the user selects a Menu control with the mouse or presses the Menu control's shortcut key.

Example

Many applications that allow the user to work with a variety of files feature an MRU (most recently used) list on the File menu. The example shows how the

Form_Initialize event can be used to do this. The File menu can be created using the Menu Editor as follows:

Name	*Indent*	*Caption*	*Index*	*Properties*
mnuFile	0	&File		Enabled, Visible
mnuFileNew	1	&New		Enabled, Visible
mnuFileOpen	1	&Open		Enabled, Visible
mnuFileSep1	1	-		Enabled, Visible
mnuFileMRU	1		0	Enabled
mnuFileSep2	1	-		Enabled
mnuFileExit	1	E&xit		Enabled, Visible

The example uses the registry to store MRU information, which it retrieves using the VBA *GetSetting* function. The first named value, `MRUList`, is a string, each letter of which represents the name of the key in which a most recently used filename is stored. The first character represents the most recently used file, the second character the file used second-most recently, and so on. Once the registry information is retrieved, a Menu control array is created dynamically to display the names of the most recently used files:

```
Private strMRUFile() As String

Private Sub Form_Initialize()

Dim intCtr As Integer, intMaxMRU As Integer
Dim strMRUList As String, strMRUName As String
Dim strFileName As String

' Get MRU list
intMaxMRU = GetSetting("OReilly", "VBControls", _
                       "MaxMRU")
strMRUList = GetSetting("OReilly", "VBControls", _
                        "MRUList")

If Len(strMRUList) = 0 Then
   Exit Sub
ElseIf Len(strMRUList) < intMaxMRU Then
   intMaxMRU = Len(strMRUList)
   ReDim strMRUFile(intMaxMRU - 1)
End If

For intCtr = 1 To Len(strMRUList)
   strMRUName = Mid(strMRUList, intCtr, 1)
   strFileName = GetSetting("OREilly", "VBControls", _
                 strMRUName)
   If Not strFileName = "" Then
      If intCtr = 1 Then
         Me.mnuFileSep2.Visible = True
      Else
         Load Me.mnuFileMRU(intCtr - 1)
      End If
```

```
        Me.mnuFileMRU(intCtr - 1).Caption = "&" & intCtr _
                    & " " & strFileName
        Me.mnuFileMRU(intCtr - 1).Visible = True
        strMRUFile(intCtr - 1) = strFileName
    End If
Next

End Sub
```

MM (Multimedia MCI) Control

The MM control gives the application access to Windows' MCI devices, such as the CD-ROM drive, *.AVI* files, *.WAV* files, and other multimedia devices and objects. The control can be used in two ways:

- As the user interface to an MCI (media control interface) device. When you set its Visible and Enabled properties to `True` (their default values), the control displays a series of cassette recorder-like buttons that allow the user to control the operation of the device.
- As an interface to MCI devices that do not have a user interface. When you set the Visible property to `False`, the control does not display its interface and instead exclusively supports programmatic access to the MCI device.

The MM control is listed as the Microsoft Multimedia control in the Components dialog. Its filename is *Mci32.OCX.*

Control Tasks

The following categories reflect the tasks executed when creating an MM control.

Set Properties

1. Set and play MCI device.

   DeviceType

   The DeviceType property should be set to a string based on the type of MCI device you want to use with the MM control; the string is case insensitive. Possible values are shown in the following table:

DeviceType Value	*Description*
Animation	Animation device
AVIVideo	*.AVI* files
CDAudio	Audio CD player/CD-ROM drive
DAT	Digital audio tape player
DigitalVideo	Non-GDI digital video
MMMovie	Multimedia movie (*.MMM* files)
Overlay	Overlay device

DeviceType Value	*Description*
Scanner	Image scanner
Sequencer	MIDI sequencer (*.MID* files)
VCR	Videotape recorder
Videodisc	Videodisc player
WaveAudio	*.WAV* files

FileName

To open a file-based device with the MM control, you must first set the FileName property to the file to be opened. For example, when the DeviceType is set to WaveAudio, the FileName property should be set to the filename of the *.WAV* file.

Command

The Command property issues a command to the MCI device set with the DeviceType property and, if necessary, the FileName property. Different types of devices support different commands. The following table shows different values for the Command property:

Command	*Result*
Open	The MCI device opens.
Close	The MCI device closes.
Play	The MCI device begins to play.
Stop	The MCI device stops playing and the current position is reset to the beginning.
Pause	The MCI device stops playing, but the current position is not reset.
Step	The current position of the MCI device is advanced forward the number of frames in the Frames property.
Back	The current position of the MCI device is moved back the number of frames in the Frames property.
Prev	If the MCI device supports tracks, the current position is set to the beginning of the current track. If the position is already at the beginning of a track, the position is set to the beginning of the previous track.
Next	If the MCI device supports tracks, the current position is set to the beginning of the next track.
Seek	The current position of the MCI device is set to the contents of the To property.
Record	If the MCI device supports recording, it is put into Record mode.
Save	If the MCI device is file-based, its contents are saved to the file specified in the FileName property.
Eject	If the MCI device is a physical device that can be ejected (such as a CD-ROM drive), it is ejected.
Sound	WaveAudio-type MCI devices are played without presenting the control's visual interface. This is preferable when playing a sound from a VB program without giving any control to the user.

2. Set visual behavior.

Visible

When set to `True`, its default value, the MM control displays a cassette recorder-like series of buttons that allow the user to control the operation of a multimedia device. If set to `False`, the control displays no interface; instead, it allows only programmatic control of the device.

AutoEnable

When the AutoEnable property is set to `True`, buttons displayed by the MM control are enabled or disabled based on the actions that can be performed at that time. When AutoEnable is set to `False`, you should use the ButtonEnabled and ButtonVisible properties to control which buttons can be used.

BackEnabled, EjectEnabled, NextEnabled, PauseEnabled, PlayEnabled, PrevEnabled, RecordEnabled, StepEnabled, StopEnabled

Each of these properties can be set to `True` to enable the corresponding button on the MM control. When set to `False`, the button is disabled. When the AutoEnable property is set to `True`, these properties have no effect.

BackVisible, EjectVisible, NextVisible, PauseVisible, PlayVisible, PrevVisible, RecordVisible, StepVisible, StopVisible

Each of these properties can be set to `False` to hide the corresponding button on the MM control. When set to the default value of `True`, the button is shown.

CanEject, CanPlay, CanRecord, CanStep

These read-only properties can be accessed to determine if the corresponding action can be performed on the current MCI device. Generally, these properties are used when using the MM control without its buttons (`Visible = False`). In this case, other controls, such as CommandButtons, are hidden or disabled based on these properties.

Orientation

When the Orientation property is set to 0–mciOrientHoriz, any visible buttons on the MM control are aligned horizontally. When set to 1–mciOrientVert, the buttons are aligned vertically.

3. Manipulate device time.

TimeFormat

The TimeFormat property sets the time basis that other MM control properties use to set or report on the MCI device based on time; these include the From, Length, Position, Start, To, TrackLength, and TrackPosition properties.

The TimeFormat property can be set to 0–mciFormatMilliseconds (milliseconds), 1–mciFormatHms (hours, minutes, and seconds), 2–mciFormatMsf (minutes, seconds, and frames), 3–mciFormatFrames (frames), 4–mciFormatSmpte24 (hours, minutes, seconds, and 24/second frames), 5–mciFormatSmpte25 (hours, minutes, seconds, and 25/second frames), 6–mciFormatSmpte30 (hours, minutes, seconds, and 30/second frames), 7–mciFormatSmpte30Drop (hours, minutes, seconds, and 30/second drop-frames), 8–mciFormatBytes (bytes), 9–mciFormatSamples (samples), or 10–mciFormatTmsf (tracks, minutes, seconds, and frames). The TimeFormats that contain multiple items store them as four-byte numbers ordered from least to most significant byte. If there are less than four elements, the most significant byte(s) are unused. The individual bytes can be obtained as follows:

```
'This example uses the TimeFormat 10–mciFormatTmsf.
iTrack = me.mciMain.Position And 255
iMinutes = (me.mciMain.Position And 65280) \ 256
iSeconds = (me.mciMain.Position And 16711680) \ 65536
iFrames = (me.mciMain.Position And 2130706432) _
        \ 16777216
'Occasionally, the sign bit can be "eaten" by the last _
calculation, so we need to put it back if it did.
If (me.mciMain.Position And -2147483648) <> 0 Then _
      iFrames = iFrames + 128
```

Currently, Visual Basic has a bug in the value for the Length property when a TimeFormat of `mciFormatTmsf` is used. While the Position property contains the correct value based on the TimeFormat, the Length property is reported using the `mciFormatTmsf`. In other words, the Track is left out of the value.

Length

Contains the total length of the MCI device.

Position

Ceturns the current position within the MCI device.

From, To

These properties set the start and end times to be used when the Command property is set to Play or Record.

Tracks, Track, TrackLength, TrackPosition

The Tracks property returns the number of tracks in the current MCI device. The Track property specifies the track to which the TrackLength and TrackPosition properties apply. The TrackLength property returns the length of that track, while the TrackPosition property returns the position in that track.

Frames

The Frames property is used to specify the number of frames to advance or back up when the Command property is set to Step or Back.

4. Set device communication.

UpdateInterval

The StatusUpdate event fires on an interval based on the UpdateInterval property. This interval is in milliseconds. This allows you to specify how often to provide feedback while an MCI device is active.

Wait

When the Wait property is set to `True`, each command issued to the MM control does not give control back to the program until the command is finished. When set to `False` (its default value), the program gets control immediately after the command is issued. The Done event is still fired as normal to report that the command has finished.

Notify, NotifyMessage, NotifyValue

When the Notify property is set to `True`, each command issued to the MM control thereafter fires the Done event when it has finished, and the NotifyValue and NotifyMessage properties are populated with the result of the last command. NotifyValue can be set to 1–mciNotifySuccessful, 2–mciNotifySuperseded, 4–mciNotifyAborted, or 8–mciNotifyFailure. When the Notify property is set to `False`, the Done event is not fired, and the NotifyMessage and NotifyValue properties are not populated. Note that, by default, the Notify property is set to `False`.

Error, ErrorMessage

The Error property contains the error returned from the last command issued to the MM control. If there was no error returned, the Error property will contain 0. The ErrorMessage property contains the message associated with the error in the Error property.

5. Set other important properties.

Shareable

When the Shareable property is set to `True`, other applications can access the same MCI device as the MM control. When set to `False`, only the MM control can access the MCI device.

RecordMode

When the Record command is issued to an MCI device, the RecordMode property determines how the recorded information interacts with the existing information in the device. The RecordMode property can be set to 0–mciRecordInsert or 1–mciRecordOverwrite.

Write Event Handlers

BackClick, EjectClick, NextClick, PauseClick, PlayClick, PrevClick, RecordClick, StepClick, StopClick

When a button on the MM control is clicked, its corresponding event is fired. In each case, a single parameter, *`Cancel`*, is passed to the event handler. When you set it to `True`, the default execution of the action controlled by the event can be cancelled.

BackGotFocus, EjectGotFocus, NextGotFocus, PauseGotFocus, PlayGotFocus, PrevGotFocus, RecordGotFocus, StepGotFocus, StopGotFocus, BackLostFocus, EjectLostFocus, NextLostFocus, PauseLostFocus, PlayLostFocus, PrevLostFocus, RecordLostFocus, StepLostFocus, StopLostFocus

These events act as individual GotFocus and LostFocus events for their respective buttons on the MM control.

BackCompleted, EjectCompleted, NextCompleted, PauseCompleted, PlayCompleted, PrevCompleted, RecordCompleted, StepCompleted, StopCompleted

When one of the buttons on the MM control is pressed to issue a command to the MCI device and that command is completed, the corresponding event is fired. In each case, a single parameter, *`ErrorCode`*, is passed to the event handler. A value of 0 indicates that the command completed successfully; any other value indicates that it did not.

StatusUpdate

The StatusUpdate event fires at an interval of milliseconds specified by the UpdateInterval property. This allows the application to notify the user of updates to the MCI device's status, such as its current position.

Done

When a command issued to the MM control finishes, the Done event is fired. A single parameter, ***NotifyCode***, is passed to the event handler to indicate the status of the command. It assumes any of the following values:

NotifyCode	*Description*
1	Command completed successfully (`mciSuccessful`).
2	Command was superseded by another command (`mciSuperseded`).
4	Command was aborted by the user (`mciAborted`).
8	Command failed (`mciFailure`).

Example

```
Option Explicit

'For this example, create the following controls: _
  an MM control named mciMain and _
  a CommandButton named cmdTrack _
    with the Index property set to 0.

Dim WithEvents txtTrack As TextBox
Dim WithEvents txtTime As TextBox

Private Sub Form_Load()
  'Set up form and controls.
    Me.Caption = "No Disk"

  'Create TextBox controls.
    Set txtTrack = Me.Controls.Add("vb.textbox", _
                   "txtTrack", Me)
    txtTrack.Text = ""
    txtTrack.Visible = True
    txtTrack.Locked = True

    Set txtTime = Me.Controls.Add("vb.textbox", _
                  "txtTime", Me)
    txtTime.Text = ""
    txtTime.Visible = True
    txtTime.Locked = True

    Me.cmdTrack(0).Caption = ""
    Me.cmdTrack(0).Visible = False

  'Set MM control properties.
```

```
    Me.mciMain.DeviceType = "CDAudio"
    Me.mciMain.Wait = True
    Me.mciMain.Command = "Open"
    Me.mciMain.Wait = False
    Me.mciMain.AutoEnable = True
    Me.mciMain.BackVisible = False
    Me.mciMain.StepVisible = False
    Me.mciMain.RecordVisible = False
    Me.mciMain.TimeFormat = mciFormatTmsf
    Me.mciMain.UpdateInterval = 1000
    Me.mciMain.Shareable = False
End Sub

Private Sub Form_Resize()
  'Not much resizing going on in this form.
    txtTrack.Move 120, 120, 1095, 315
    txtTime.Move 1335, 120, 1095, 315
    Me.mciMain.Move 120, 555

    RedrawTracks
End Sub

Private Sub Form_Unload(Cancel As Integer)
  'Some clean-up here
    Me.mciMain.Command = "Close"
End Sub

Private Sub cmdTrack_Click(Index As Integer)
  'I've found that often the Seek doesn't work the _
  first time when the CD is already playing.
    Do While Me.mciMain.Position <> Index + 1
        Me.mciMain.To = Index + 1
        Me.mciMain.Command = "Seek"
        DoEvents
    Loop
End Sub

Private Sub mciMain_StatusUpdate()
    Static lPos As Long

  'If the old position was 0 and the new position _
  isn't, a CD has been loaded into the drive.
    If lPos = 0 And Me.mciMain.Position > 0 Then
        GetTracks
        RedrawTracks
  'If the new position is 0 and the old _
  position wasn't, the CD has been ejected.
    ElseIf Me.mciMain.Position = 0 And lPos > 0 Then
        ClearTracks
        RedrawTracks
    End If

    lPos = Me.mciMain.Position
```

```
   GetCurrentTrack
End Sub

Private Sub GetCurrentTrack()
   Dim iTrack As Integer
   Dim iMinute As Integer
   Dim iSecond As Integer
   Dim iFrame As Integer
   Dim lTime As Long

   If Me.mciMain.Position = 1 Then
      iMinute = Me.mciMain.Length And 255
      iSecond = (Me.mciMain.Length And 65280) \ 256
      Me.Caption = "CD Info: " & _
        Format$(Me.mciMain.Tracks, "##0") & _
        " Tracks - " & Format$(iMinute, "##0") & _
        ":" & Format$(iSecond, "00")
   End If

   If Me.mciMain.Position < 256 Then
   'Since the Position is 255 or less, we know _
   there is only a track and no minutes or _
   seconds. That means we're at the very beginning _
   of the track. Therefore we'll display the time _
   for the whole track in txtTime.
      iTrack = Me.mciMain.Position
      Me.mciMain.Track = iTrack
      lTime = Me.mciMain.TrackLength
      iMinute = lTime And 255
      iSecond = (lTime And 65280) \ 256
   Else
   'We're not at the beginning of a track so we'll _
   show the current positon in txtTime.
      lTime = Me.mciMain.Position
      iTrack = lTime And 255
      iMinute = (lTime And 65280) \ 256
      iSecond = (lTime And 16711680) \ 65536
   End If


   txtTrack = Format$(iTrack, "#00")
   txtTime = Format$(iMinute, "##0") & ":" & _
            Format$(iSecond, "00")
End Sub

Private Sub GetTracks()
   Dim iCtr As Integer

  'Here we want to create one button for each track _
  on the CD.
   For iCtr = 0 To Me.mciMain.Tracks - 1
      If iCtr > 0 Then
         Load Me.cmdTrack(iCtr)
      End If
```

```
        Me.cmdTrack(iCtr).Caption = iCtr + 1
        Me.cmdTrack(iCtr).Visible = True
    Next iCtr
End Sub

Private Sub ClearTracks()
     Dim iCtr As Integer
     Dim cmdVar As CommandButton

  'Since there's no CD in the drive, we'll delete _
  all the track buttons.
    For Each cmdVar In Me.cmdTrack()
        If cmdVar.Index > 0 Then
            Unload Me.cmdTrack(cmdVar.Index)
        Else
            cmdVar.Visible = False
        End If
    Next cmdVar

    Me.Caption = "No Disk"
End Sub

Private Sub RedrawTracks()
    Dim cmdVar As CommandButton

    Const TRACKS_ACROSS = 6

  'We'll show the tracks in rows of buttons. The _
  number of buttons across is set by the _
  TRACKS_ACROSS constant.
    For Each cmdVar In Me.cmdTrack()
        cmdVar.Move _
             120 + ((Me.mciMain.Width \ TRACKS_ACROSS) * _
             (cmdVar.Index Mod TRACKS_ACROSS)), _
             Me.mciMain.Top + Me.mciMain.Height + 120 + _
             (375 * (cmdVar.Index \ TRACKS_ACROSS)), _
             Me.mciMain.Width \ TRACKS_ACROSS, 375
    Next cmdVar
End Sub

Private Sub mciMain_StopCompleted(Errorcode As Long)
  'When the user hits the Stop button, we want to _
  make sure the position is reset.
    Me.mciMain.To = 1
    Me.mciMain.Command = "Seek"
End Sub
```

Order of Events

Here is the sequence of events in response to a mouseclick on the Eject button on an MM control named mciMain:

1. mciMain_EjectGotFocus
2. mciMain_EjectClick

3. mciMain_EjectLostFocus
4. mciMain_EjectCompleted

Other buttons fire the appropriate events in the same order.

VB6 *MonthView Control*

The MonthView control provides a calendar that can be placed on a form. This calendar can show one or more months, allows the user to navigate from month to month, and supports multiple date selection. The control maintains two internal arrays, one of dates displayed by the control and the other of dates marked in bold, which can be used to designate individual dates. The MonthView control is shown in Figure 5-35.

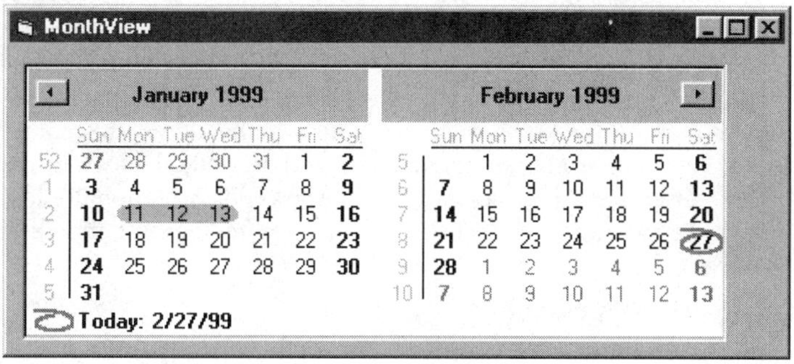

Figure 5-35: The MonthView control

The MonthView control is included with Version 6.0 or later of Microsoft Windows Common Controls-2 (*MSCOMCT2.OCX*).

MonthView Control Tasks

The following categories reflect the tasks that are executed when creating and using a MonthView control.

Set Properties

1. Set calendar appearance.

   Font

   The only way to change the size of a MonthView control (independently of changing the number of months displayed) is by changing the Font property. Setting the Font property to a smaller font makes the MonthView control smaller.

Be careful about readability when making the font of any control smaller.

StartOfWeek

Controls which day of the week is leftmost in the calendar display. It can be set to 1–mvwSunday, 2–mvwMonday, 3–mvwTuesday, 4–mvw-Wednesday, 5–mvwThursday, 6–mvwFriday, or 7–mvwSaturday.

ShowToday

When the ShowToday property is set to `True`, the bottom-left corner of the MonthView control (regardless of how many months or which months are displayed) shows today's date based on the computer's current date and time setting.

ShowWeekNumbers

When set to `True`, a vertical bar appears before the first day of each week. To the left of this bar is the number of the week relative to the beginning of the year, and the width of the calendar is increased accordingly.

MonthColumns, MonthRows

The MonthView control can display multiple months on one control. The number of months to be displayed is derived by multiplying the Month-Columns property (the number of months across the control) by the MonthRows (the number of rows of months down the control). For example, setting MonthColumns to 3 and MonthRows to 4 displays one full year in 4 rows of 3 months each. The product of MonthColumns and MonthRows cannot exceed 12 (i.e., no more than 12 months can be shown).

2. Set visible date information.

VisibleDays (property array)

Contains one element for each date visible on the MonthView control. Each element contains a Date value for the date displayed. The base of the property array is 1, not 0. If only one month is displayed, the array contains 48 elements.

DayBold (property array)

Contains one element for each date visible on the MonthView control. The elements of the DayBold property array correspond directly to the elements of the VisibleDays property array. Each element can be set to `True` to display that date in bold on the MonthView control.

3. Set calendar constraints.

MinDate, MaxDate

These properties set the earliest and latest date that the MonthView control can display. In setting the property, you can either assign a complete date or you can assign only a month and a year number. If you assign a complete date, its day component is ignored. If the calendar is currently displaying a month earlier than ***`MinDate`*** or later than ***`MaxDate`***, the calendar will be updated to display the month indicated by ***`MinDate`*** or ***`MaxDate`***, respectively. MinDate cannot be earlier than 1/1753, and MaxDate cannot be later than 12/9999.

4. Set multiple selection.

   MultiSelect, MaxSelCount

   When the MultiSelect property is set to `True`, multiple contiguous dates can be selected on the MonthView control using the mouse. The MaxSelCount property controls the number of days that can be selected when MultiSelect is `True`; its default value is 7. Date ranges can be selected across visible months only. Therefore, if only one month is visible, only dates in that month can be selected. In addition, when MultiSelect is `True`, the value of the Month property or the Year property cannot be modified programmatically.

5. Set date information

   Value

   Contains the currently selected date on the MonthView control. If MultiSelect is `True`, it represents the earliest date in the selected date range.

   SelStart, SelEnd

   When the MultiSelect property is set to `True`, the SelStart and SelEnd properties contain the lower and upper values of the selected date range. (Otherwise, both SelStart and SelEnd are equal to Value.) A date range can also be selected programmatically by assigning values to the SelStart and SelEnd properties. However, SelStart must be earlier than SelEnd, or only a single date, SelEnd, will be selected.

   Month, Year

   The Month and Year properties return the month number or year for the currently selected date. Assigning a value to the Month or Year property causes the MonthView control to display that month or the current month of that year, respectively, provided that the MultiSelect property is `False`. If MultiSelect is `True`, the date cannot be changed programmatically by modifying the Month or Year properties.

   Week

   Returns the week number based on the currently selected date. Assigning a value to the Week property causes the MonthView control to display the month containing that week, provided that the MultiSelect property is `False`. If MultiSelect is `True`, the week displayed cannot be changed programmatically by modifying the Week property.

   DayOfWeek

   Returns the number of the weekday for the currently selected date. The value returned will be 1–mvwSunday, 2–mvwMonday, 3–mvwTuesday, 4–mvwWednesday, 5–mvwThursday, 6–mvwFriday, or 7–mvwSaturday. You can also select a particular date programmatically by assigning a value to the DayOfWeek property when the value of the MultiSelect property is `False`.

Useful Methods

HitTest

Determines what portion of the control is located at specific coordinates. Its syntax is:

```
HitTest(X As Long, Y As Long, Date As Date)
```

where *X* and *Y* are longs containing the x and y coordinates and ***Date*** is a date argument that's passed to the method by reference. When the method returns, ***Date*** contains the date at that location, if there is one. In addition, the method returns a constant of the **MonthViewHitTestAreas** enumeration that indicates what portion of the control is located at these coordinates. Valid values are:

0–mvwCalendarBack
: The background of the calendar.

1–mvwCalendarDate
: The calendar date area; the particular date is returned as the ***Date*** argument.

2–mvwCalendarDateNext and 3–mvwCalendarDatePrev
: The date area of the next and previous months, respectively; the particular date is returned as the ***Date*** argument.

4–mvwCalendarDay
: The area where the days of the week are shown.

5–mvwCalendarWeekNum
: The area where week numbers are displayed, if they are visible.

6–mvwNoWhere
: The area below the calendar.

7–mvwTitleBack
: The background of the title area.

8–mvwTitleBtnNext and 9–mvwTitleBtnPrev
: The next and previous month buttons, respectively.

10–mvwTitleMonth
: The month name in the control's title area.

11–mvwTitleYear
: The year in the control's title area.

12–mvwTodayLink
: The area where today's date appears.

ComputeControlSize

Determines the size of the MonthView control based on the number of months shown. Its syntax is:

```
ComputeControlSize(Rows, Columns, Width, Height)
```

Rows and ***Columns*** are long integers containing the number of months down and across, respectively. The ***Width*** and ***Height*** arguments are Singles that are passed by reference; when the method returns, they contain the control's width and height, respectively. Their unit of measure is determined by the containing form's ScaleMode property.

If the *Rows* and *Columns* parameters of the ComputeControlSize method multiply to a number over 12, an error occurs.

Write Event Handlers

DateClick, DateDblClick

These events are both fired when the user clicks or double-clicks on a date in the MonthView control. The date clicked or double-clicked is passed as a parameter to the event.

GetDayBold

When the current set of dates displayed on the MonthView control is changed either through code or by the user, the GetDayBold event is fired so that the application can populate the DateBold property array. Three parameters are passed to the event:

StartDate

The first date to be populated in the control.

Count

The number of dates that need to be populated.

State()

A Boolean property array for *Count* dates beginning at *StartDate*.

MouseDown, MouseMove, DragOver

While these events are fired for most controls in Visual Basic, the HitTest method makes them particularly useful for the MonthView control. These events all supply *X* and *Y* parameters that can then be used as parameters for the HitTest method to determine the exact location of the mouse.

Example

The following example uses many of the elements described earlier for the MonthView control to update the contents of a label based on the location of the mouse pointer over the control:

```
Option Explicit

'For this example, create a MonthView _
  control named mvwMain.

Dim lblMain As Label

Private Sub Form_Load()
   Me.Caption = "MonthView"
```

```
    Me.mvwMain.ShowToday = True
    Me.mvwMain.ShowWeekNumbers = True

  'Create and set up lblMain.
    Set lblMain = Me.Controls.Add("vb.label", _
                  "lblMain", Me)
    lblMain.Caption = ""
    lblMain.Visible = True
End Sub

Private Sub Form_MouseMove(Button As Integer, _
        Shift As Integer, X As Single, Y As Single)
  'Here we just want to clear the label if the user _
  moves the mouse pointer out of the MonthView control.
    lblMain.Caption = ""
End Sub

Private Sub Form_Resize()
    Dim sngWidth As Single
    Dim sngHeight As Single

  'We want the label over the MonthView control.
    lblMain.Move 120, 120, Me.ScaleWidth - 240, 255
    Me.mvwMain.Move 120, 495

  'Now that the controls are positioned, we need to _
  check if the form is too small for the number _
  of months displayed or big enough to allow more _
  months to be displayed.
    Do While Me.ScaleHeight < Me.mvwMain.Height + 615
       If Me.mvwMain.MonthRows = 1 Then _
          Exit Do
       Me.mvwMain.MonthRows = Me.mvwMain.MonthRows - 1
    Loop

    Do While Me.ScaleWidth < Me.mvwMain.Width + 240
       If Me.mvwMain.MonthColumns = 1 Then _
          Exit Do
       Me.mvwMain.MonthColumns = _
                  Me.mvwMain.MonthColumns - 1
    Loop

    Do While Me.ScaleHeight > Me.mvwMain.Height + 615
    'We need to make sure we don't allow the total _
    months to exceed 12 or we'll generate an error.
       If Me.mvwMain.MonthColumns * _
          (Me.mvwMain.MonthRows + 1) <= 12 Then
             Me.mvwMain.ComputeControlSize _
                 Me.mvwMain.MonthRows + 1, _
                 Me.mvwMain.MonthColumns, _
                 sngWidth, sngHeight
       Else
          Exit Do
```

```
        End If
        If Me.ScaleHeight > sngHeight + 615 Then
           Me.mvwMain.MonthRows = Me.mvwMain.MonthRows + 1
        Else
           Exit Do
        End If
     Loop

     Do While Me.ScaleWidth > Me.mvwMain.Width + 240
        If (Me.mvwMain.MonthColumns + 1) * _
              Me.mvwMain.MonthRows <= 12 Then
              Me.mvwMain.ComputeControlSize _
                 Me.mvwMain.MonthRows, _
                 Me.mvwMain.MonthColumns + 1, _
                 sngWidth, sngHeight
        Else
           Exit Do
        End If
        If Me.ScaleWidth > sngWidth + 240 Then
           Me.mvwMain.MonthColumns = _
                       Me.mvwMain.MonthColumns + 1
        Else
           Exit Do
        End If
     Loop

  End Sub

  Private Sub mvwMain_GetDayBold( _
          ByVal StartDate As Date, _
          ByVal Count As Integer, State() As Boolean)

     Dim iCtr As Integer
```

'Here we'll make the weekends bold. The DateAdd _
function allows us to calculate the date through _
the range of displayed dates.

```
     For iCtr = 0 To Count - 1
        If Weekday(DateAdd("d", iCtr, StartDate)) = _
                 vbSaturday _
           Or Weekday(DateAdd("d", iCtr, StartDate)) = _
                 vbSunday Then _
           State(iCtr) = True
     Next iCtr
  End Sub

  Private Sub mvwMain_MouseMove(Button As Integer, _
              Shift As Integer, X As Single, Y As Single)

     Dim dtVar As Date
```

'This code would never exist in a final _
application. It's here to help explain the various _
values returned by HitTest.

Controls M–N

```
    Select Case mvwMain.HitTest(X, Y, dtVar)
       Case mvwCalendarBack
          lblMain.Caption = "mvwCalendarBack"
       Case mvwCalendarDate
          lblMain.Caption = "mvwCalendarDate: " & _
                            Format$(dtVar, "Short Date")
       Case mvwCalendarDateNext
          lblMain.Caption = "mvwCalendarDateNext"
       Case mvwCalendarDatePrev
          lblMain.Caption = "mvwCalendarDatePrev"
       Case mvwCalendarDay
          lblMain.Caption = "mvwCalendarDay"
       Case mvwCalendarWeekNum
          lblMain.Caption = "mvwWeekNum"
       Case mvwNoWhere
          lblMain.Caption = "mvwNoWhere"
       Case mvwTitleBack
          lblMain.Caption = "mvwTitleBack"
       Case mvwTitleBtnNext
          lblMain.Caption = "mvwTitleBtnNext"
       Case mvwTitleBtnNext
          lblMain.Caption = "mvwTitleBtnNext"
       Case mvwTitleBtnPrev
          lblMain.Caption = "mvwTitleBtnPrev"
       Case mvwTitleMonth
          lblMain.Caption = "mvwTitleMonth"
       Case mvwTitleYear
          lblMain.Caption = "mvwTitleYear"
       Case mvwTodayLink
          lblMain.Caption = "mvwTodayLink"
    End Select
End Sub
```

MSChart Control

The MSChart control provides the developer with a means of displaying various graphs to the user. Both two-dimensional and three-dimensional graphs are available in a variety of styles. Data can be entered into the MSChart control either by setting values one at a time, by using an array to set many values at once, or by populating a virtual DataGrid, which contains rows and columns of data for the chart. All three methods of defining a chart's data are covered in this section.

The MSChart control uses many objects, some of which are used by more than one chart element. Therefore, if something seems confusing, please refer to Figure 5-36, the MSChart object model.

The MSChart control is contained in the Microsoft Chart control (*MSCHRT20.OCX*) that comes with Visual Basic Professional and Enterprise editions.

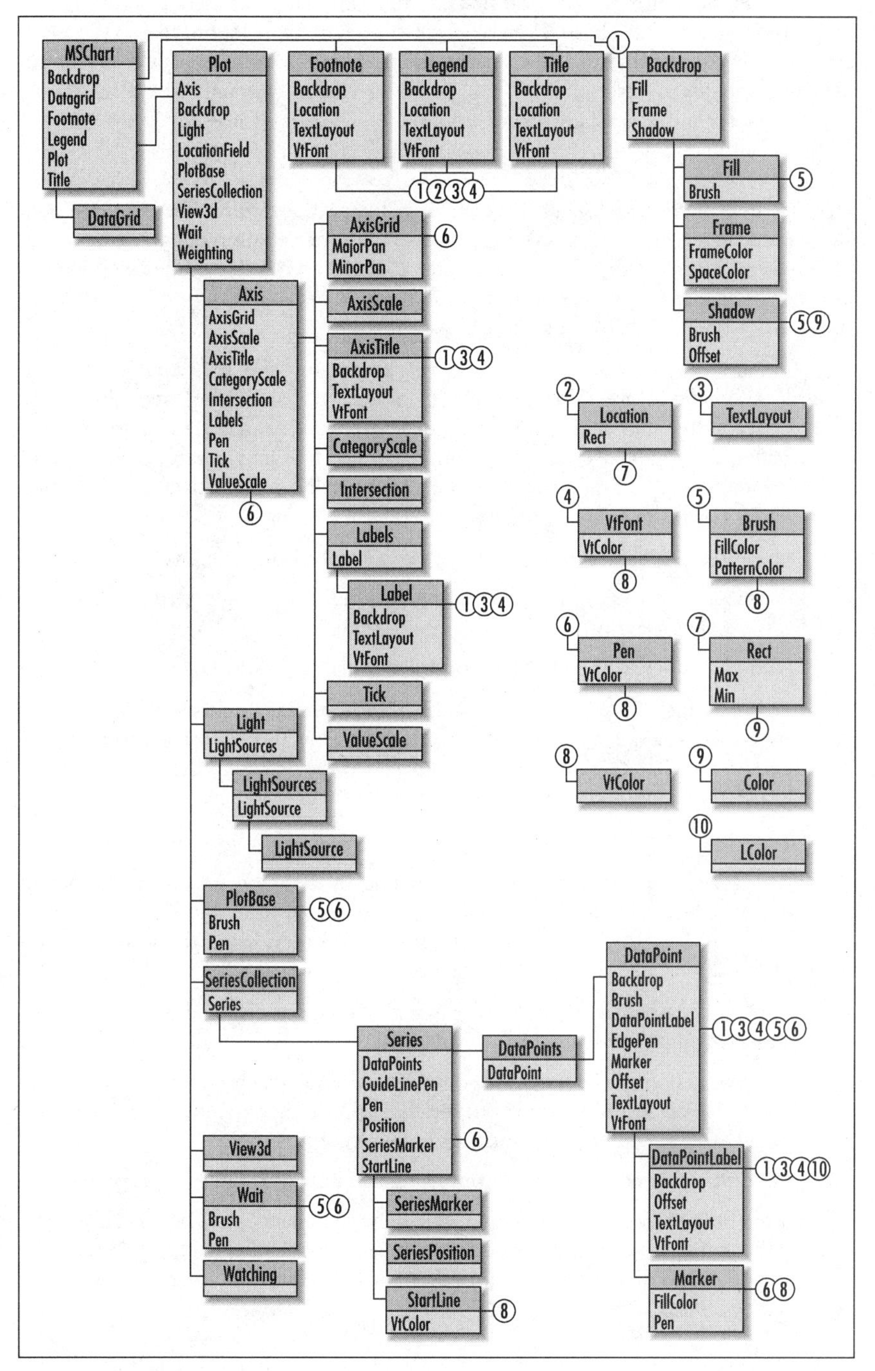

Figure 5-36: The MSChart object model

Typically, in using the control, you first examine the data that the chart is to reflect and import it into the chart. Then you set the chart type, define the basic chart elements, and determine how the chart will interact with the user. For finer control over the appearance of the chart, you can also manipulate any of the numerous objects that form the MSChart object model.

Defining the Chart's Data

The first step in creating a chart is necessarily to create or define the data that is to be charted. Some kinds of charts are inappropriate for certain types of data. For an excellent treatment of the considerations in using charts to depict the relationships between data elements, see Edward Tufte's *The Visual Display of Quantitative Information*, published by Graphics Press.

The MSChart control offers three ways of generating the data needed for the control. All of them are done at runtime either by "hardcoding" data in source code or by retrieving data from some external data source (like a text file, a spreadsheet, or a database) and assigning it to the MSChart control using one of the three methods. The control itself then graphically depicts data that is stored internally in the control. These three methods are:

1. Setting values one at a time by using the control's Data property
2. Assigning values to an array and applying them in a single step by using the control's ChartData property
3. Assigning values to the MSChart control's virtual DataGrid object

Regardless of which method is used, each value in a chart is derived from a set of data points within a series. These map to the columns and rows used to populate the chart or the DataGrid object. Multiple series can be shown in many ways, including side by side, stacked, and along the Z axis in a 3-D chart.

Assigning Values One at a Time

You add data to a chart one element at a time by defining a grid (a number of rows and columns) to hold data, assigning values to the Row and Column properties to indicate which cell of the grid is current, and then using the Data property to assign a value to the current cell. The steps are as follows:

1. Define the maximum number of rows and columns using the ColumnCount and RowCount properties.

   Each row represents a series of columns, each of which contains values. The ColumnCount and RowCount properties set how many values per series and how many series the chart contains, respectively.

2. Define the current row and column using the Row and Column properties.

   These properties define the next cell to which data is to be assigned. The value of the Row property must be between 1 and the value of RowCount, and the value of the Column property must be between 1 and the value of ColumnCount.

3. Assign a value to the current cell.

   Once the Row and Column properties are set, assigning a value to the Data property changes that value in the grid (as well as that point in the chart). The following code shows how to use the Data property to populate a data point:

```
Me.chtMain.Row = 1
Me.chtMain.Column = 1
Me.chtMain.Data = lngValues(1,1)
```

Assigning Multiple Values in a Single Step

You can provide the chart with all of its data in a single statement by creating an array containing the chart's data and then assigning it to the chart's ChartData property, as the following very simple code fragment (in which the starting element of an array has been set to 1 using the `Option Base 1` statement) illustrates:

```
Dim varArray(4, 5) As Variant

varArray(1, 1) = "Q1"
varArray(1, 2) = 10361
varArray(1, 3) = 11216
varArray(1, 4) = 11989
varArray(1, 5) = 13974

varArray(2, 1) = "Q2"
varArray(2, 2) = 9857
varArray(2, 3) = 10760
varArray(2, 4) = 11861
varArray(2, 5) = 13968

varArray(3, 1) = "Q3"
varArray(3, 2) = 9216
varArray(3, 3) = 10154
varArray(3, 4) = 12203
varArray(3, 5) = 14502

varArray(4, 1) = "Q4"
varArray(4, 2) = 11430
varArray(4, 3) = 13682
varArray(4, 4) = 14509
varArray(4, 5) = 15983

MSChart1.ChartData = varArray
MSChart1.chartType = VtChChartType2dBar
```

Each element of the first dimension corresponds to a row (or series), while each element of the second dimension corresponds to a value in the series. If the first element of each subarray contains strings, they'll be used for the series labels, as Figure 5-37, which shows the results of running this code fragment, illustrates. Note that assigning an array to the ChartData property causes the RowCount and ColumnCount properties to be updated automatically based on the size of the array.

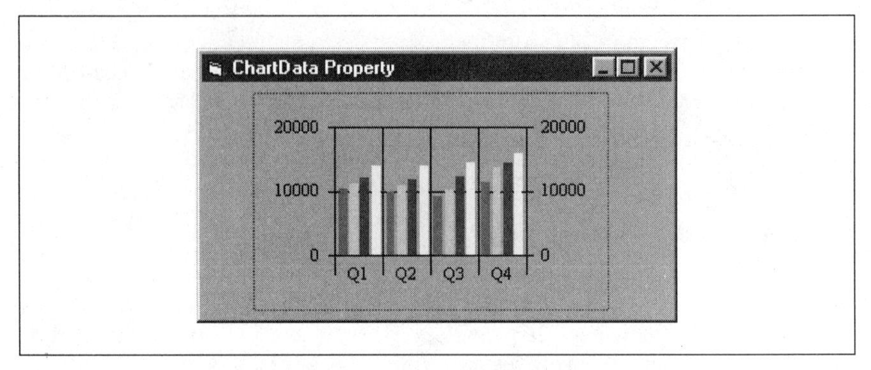

Figure 5-37: Chart created using the ChartData property

Using the MSChart Control's Data Grid Directly

The MSChart control contains a virtual data grid that is represented by a DataGrid object. The DataGrid object is organized into rows and columns that hold the chart's data. By retrieving a reference to this object and manipulating its properties and methods at runtime, you can populate the MSChart control with data as well as manipulate data entered using either of the other two methods. You do this as follows:

1. Retrieve a reference to the chart control's DataGrid object. A reference to the DataGrid object is returned by the MSChart control's DataGrid property. For example:

   ```
   Dim objDataGrid As DataGrid
   Set objDataGrid = Me.MSChart1.DataGrid
   ```

2. Manipulate the DataGrid object's properties and methods to configure the virtual grid, add data, modify the structure of the grid, or change data. Its most commonly accessed properties and methods include the following:

   GetData, SetData methods

   Allow you to retrieve and assign data to a DataGrid object cell, respectively. The syntax of GetData is:

   ```
   GetData Row, Column, DataPoint, nullFlag
   ```

   where *Row* and *Column* are integers representing the row and column number, respectively. *DataPoint* is a double that, when the method returns, contains the data value. *nullFlag* is an integer that indicates whether *DataPoint* is null.

   The syntax of SetData is identical to that of GetData:

   ```
   GetData Row, Column, DataPoint, nullFlag
   ```

   The difference, of course, is that *DataPoint* and *nullFlag* must be assigned values *before* calling the method.

RandomDataFill method

Provides random values to the data grid's cells. This is particularly useful for testing. The method takes no arguments.

ColumnCount, RowCount properties

Contain the number of columns and rows, respectively, in the DataGrid object. Changing either of these properties changes the number of columns or rows. Labels are *not* included in the count of rows or columns. The default MSChart control contains five rows and four columns.

SetSize method

Defines the size of the DataGrid object. Its syntax is:

```
SetSize(RowLabelCount, ColumnLabelCount, _
        RowCount, ColumnCount)
```

where each parameter corresponds to the property of the same name. Although properties can also be used to define the chart's size, the advantage of the SetSize method is that it allows you to define a chart's size with a single statement.

ColumnLabelCount, RowLabelCount properties

In the case of 3-D charts, a column or a row can include multiple levels of labels. For example, in a grid containing sales data, the rows might represent years, while the columns represent sales by region for particular products. These properties contain the number of column or row label levels, respectively, in the DataGrid object. Changing either of these properties changes the number of label levels for the column or row. The default MSChart control contains one level each of column labels and row labels.

For example, the following code fragment (the result of which is shown in Figure 5-38) defines two levels of column labels, the first (innermost) level for the region (East Coast, Midwest, and West Coast) and the second (outer) level for the product (widgets, cogs):

```
Dim objGrid As DataGrid

Set objGrid = Me.MSChart1.DataGrid

Me.MSChart1.chartType = VtChChartType3dBar

objGrid.rowCount = 2
objGrid.columnCount = 6
objGrid.columnLabelCount = 2
objGrid.rowLabelCount = 1
objGrid.RandomDataFill
objGrid.RowLabel(1, 1) = "1996"
objGrid.RowLabel(2, 1) = "1997"

objGrid.ColumnLabel(1, 1) = "East Coast"
objGrid.ColumnLabel(4, 1) = "East Coast"
objGrid.ColumnLabel(2, 1) = "Midwest"
objGrid.ColumnLabel(5, 1) = "Midwest"
```

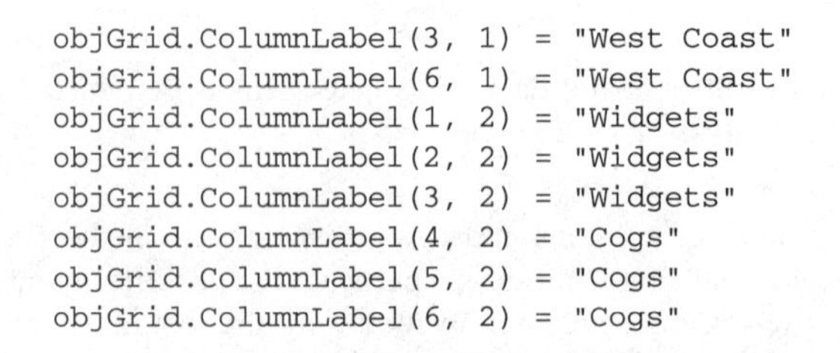

```
objGrid.ColumnLabel(3, 1) = "West Coast"
objGrid.ColumnLabel(6, 1) = "West Coast"
objGrid.ColumnLabel(1, 2) = "Widgets"
objGrid.ColumnLabel(2, 2) = "Widgets"
objGrid.ColumnLabel(3, 2) = "Widgets"
objGrid.ColumnLabel(4, 2) = "Cogs"
objGrid.ColumnLabel(5, 2) = "Cogs"
objGrid.ColumnLabel(6, 2) = "Cogs"
```

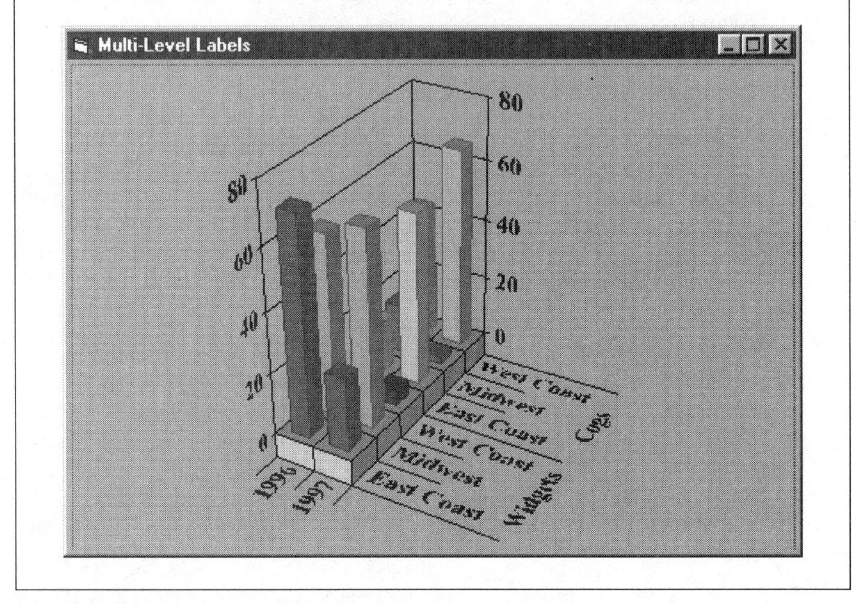

Figure 5-38: Table with two levels of column labels

ColumnLabel, RowLabel property arrays

Contain the text of a label. The syntax of ColumnLabel is:

```
ColumnLabel(column, labelIndex)
```

where *`column`* represents the number of the column containing the label and *`labelIndex`* represents the level of that column label. The syntax of RowLabel is:

```
RowLabel(row, labelIndex)
```

where *`row`* represents the number of the row containing the label and *`labelIndex`* represents the level of that column label.

CompositeColumnLabel, CompositeRowLabel property arrays

Return a string containing concatenated labels from all levels of a column or row. The syntax of the two properties is:

```
CompositeColumnLabel(column)
```

and

```
CompositeRowLabel(row)
```

where *column* and *row* represent the column or the row number whose composite label is to be returned. For example, in Figure 5-38, the statement:

```
MsChart1.DataGrid.CompositeColumnLabel(5)
```

returns the string "Cogs Midwest."

Determining the Chart Type

ChartType property

Sets the kind of graph or chart to display. Possible values are 0–VtChChartType3DBar for a 3-D bar chart, 1–VtChChartType2dBar, 2–VtChChartType3DLine, 3–VtChChartType2dDLine, 4–VtChChartType3dDArea, 5–VtChChartType2dDArea, 6–VtChChartType3dDStep, 7–VtChChartType2dDStep, 8–VtChChartType3dDCombination, 9–VtChChartType2dDCombination, 14–VtChChartType2dDPie, and 16–VtChChartType2dXY. Each of these chart types is shown in Figure 5-39.

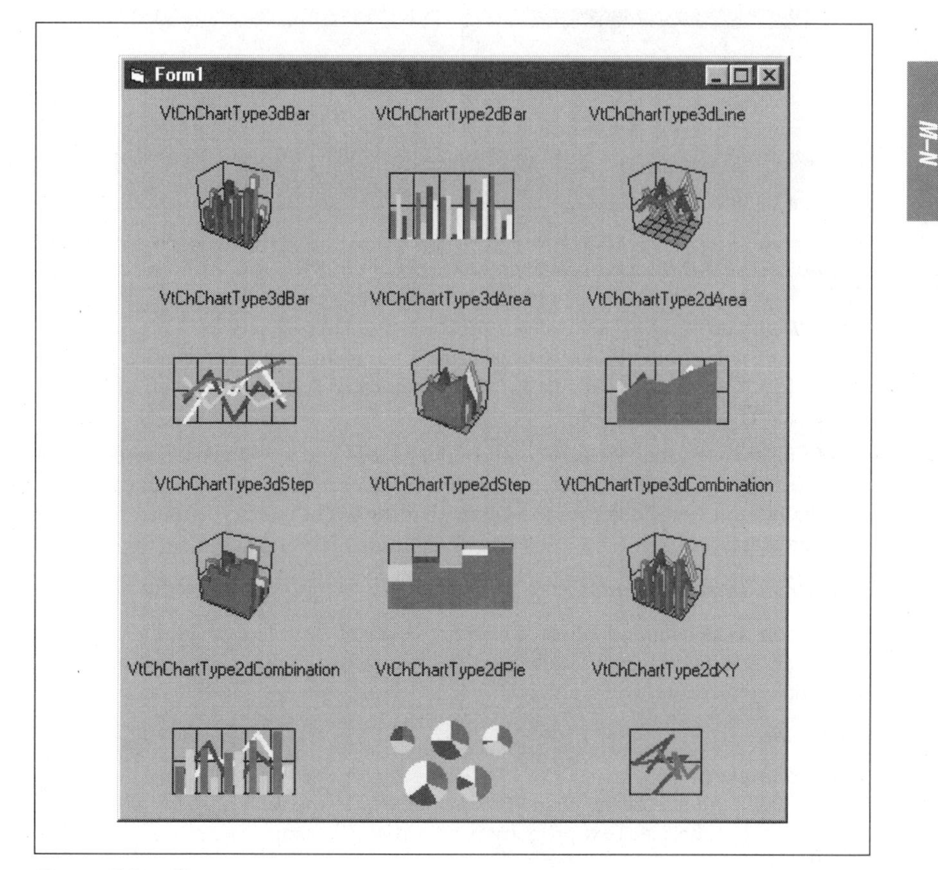

Figure 5-39: Chart types

Stacking property

When the set to **True**, values in the same column in different series (i.e., in different rows) are stacked one on top of the other. When set to **False** (its default value), the values are arranged side by side. Interestingly, Stacking is a write-only property.

Stacking changes the way in which data points are compared across series. Whereas nonstacked charts emphasize the differences among the data points of different series, stacked charts emphasize the degree to which each data element has contributed to the total. This is evident in Figure 5-40. which shows a 2-D bar chart on the left and its equivalent stacked 2-D bar chart on the right.

All chart types except 2-D pie and 2-D XY change to reflect the state of the Stacked property.

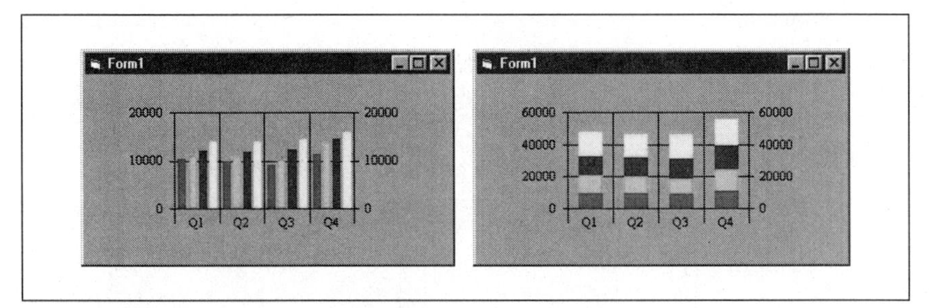

Figure 5-40: A 2-D bar chart and stacked 2-D bar chart

Chart3D property

A read-only property that returns **True** if the chart being displayed is 3-D and **False** if the chart is 2-D. Its value is completely dependent on the ChartType property's value.

In most cases, the MSChart control offers a 2-D and a 3-D version of the same chart. If you want to create a bar chart, for example, you can choose either **VtChChartType2DBar** for a 2-D bar chart or **VtChChartType3DBar** for a 3-D bar chart.

Defining Chart Elements

In addition to its data and labels, which are easily accessible through the DataGrid object, an effective chart typically includes a number of other standard elements, like a title, a footnote, and a legend.

Chart Title

TitleText property

Contains the title of the chart. This is identical to the Text property of the Title object, but the TitleText property is provided as a simpler means of setting the title.

Title object

Though the Title object's main function, like that of the TitleText property, is to define the chart's title, the Title object also allows you to control other attributes of the chart title, such as its location and font attributes. A reference to the Title object is returned by the chart control's Tab property.

The Title object includes the following properties:

Backdrop property
: Returns a reference to a Backdrop object, which contains information about the area behind the title area. The Backdrop object is described in "Common Objects," later in this section.

Font, VtFont properties
: The Font property returns a reference to a standard Visual Basic Font object; the VtFont property returns a reference to a VtFont object. Each is then used to set the font of the Title object's text. The VtFont object is covered in "Common Objects."

Location property
: Returns a reference to a Location object, which contains information about the location of the title area in the chart. The Location object is discussed in "Common Objects."

Text property
: Contains the text shown in the chart title.

TextLayout property
: Returns a reference to a TextLayout object, which contains information about the alignment and orientation of the text in the chart title. The TextLayout object is discussed in "Common Objects."

TextLength property
: Returns the number of characters in the chart title.

Controls M–N

Chart Legend

The chart's legend serves as a key to relate chart symbols and colors to the data that they represent. The legend can be controlled using the following properties and objects:

ShowLegend property
: When set to `True`, the ShowLegend property causes the chart's legend to be displayed. The default value of the ShowLegend property is `False`; the chart's legend is not displayed.

Legend object
: All aspects of the legend's appearance, including its location, font attributes, and backdrop, are controlled by the Legend object, which is referenced through the Legend property. The Legend object includes the following properties:

  Backdrop property
  : Returns a reference to a Backdrop object, which contains information about the area behind the chart's legend. The Backdrop object is described in "Common Objects."

  Font, VtFont properties
  : The Font property returns a reference to a standard Visual Basic Font object; the VtFont property returns a reference to a VtFont object. Each is

then used to set the font of the text in the legend. The VtFont object is covered in "Common Objects."

Location property

Returns a reference to a Location object, which contains information about the location of the legend in the chart. The Location object is discussed in "Common Objects."

TextLayout property

The TextLayout property contains a reference to a TextLayout object. The TextLayout object referenced contains information about the alignment and orientation of the text in the chart's legend.

Chart Footnote

A footnote provides additional text that appears at the bottom of the chart and that typically is used to indicate the source of the chart's data or to clarify the character of the data.

FootnoteText property

Contains the text of the footnote. There is also a Text property of the Footnote object that contains the same information, but the FootnoteText property provides a simpler method of setting the footnote text.

Footnote object

The Footnote object allows you to control not only the footnote text but other properties of the footnote, such as its location, backdrop, and font attributes, as well. A reference to the Footnote object is returned by the chart control's Footnote property. The following are its major properties and child objects:

Backdrop property

Returns a reference to a Backdrop object, which contains information about the area behind the footnote text. The Backdrop object is described in "Common Objects."

Font, VtFont properties

The Font property returns a reference to a standard Visual Basic Font object and the VtFont property returns a reference to a VtFont object, each of which is then used to set the font of the text in the Footnote object. The VtFont object is covered in "Common Objects."

Location property

Returns a reference to a Location object, which contains information about the location of the footnote area in the chart. The Location object is discussed elsewhere in this section.

Text property

Contains the text of the chart's footnote.

TextLayout property

Returns a reference to a TextLayout object, which contains information about the alignment and orientation of the text in the chart's footnote. The TextLayout property is discussed in "Common Objects."

TextLength property

Indicates the number of characters in the footnote.

Chart Background

The appearance of the background area of the chart is controlled by a single property:

Backdrop property

The Backdrop property returns a reference to a Backdrop object, which can be used to define the background fill, frame, and shadow. The Backdrop object is described in "Common Objects," later in this section.

Set Chart Behavior

AllowSelections property

When AllowSelections is set to `True`, chart elements can be selected by the user when they are clicked with the mouse. Selecting chart elements causes events to be fired depending on which element was selected.

You can also select some chart elements programmatically by invoking that element's Select method. The method's syntax is simply:

```
objElement.Select()
```

where *`objElement`* is a reference to the object that represents the chart element to be selected. Chart elements that support the Select method include the DataPoint, DataPointLabel, Footnote, Legend, Series, and Title objects.

AllowSeriesSelection property

Normally, when AllowSeriesSelection is set to `False`, the user's clicking on a chart point selects that point. When AllowSeriesSelection is set to `True`, the entire series containing the clicked point is selected, a useful behavior if you want to allow the user to customize such elements as the data series' points or colors.

AllowDynamicRotation property

When set to `True`, the user can rotate a chart whose Chart3D property is `True` by holding the CTRL key and dragging the mouse around the chart's plot area. When the Chart3D property is `False`, this property has no effect.

Write Event Handlers

The MSChart control supports a substantial number of events, though most are fired when a chart element is activated (i.e., double-clicked), selected (clicked), or updated. These sets of events, however, are fired only if the AllowSelections property is set to `True`. If it is set to `True`, the AllowSeriesSelection property determines whether clicks and double-clicks on a data point fire the PointSelected and PointActivated events (if its value is `False`) or the SeriesSelected and Series activated events (if its value is `True`, the default).

The sets of events commonly coded for the MSChart control are:

AxisActivated, AxisLabelActivated, AxisTitleActivated, ChartActivated, FootnoteActivated, LegendActivated, PlotActivated, PointActivated, PointLabelActivated, SeriesActivated, TitleActivated

Each is fired when the user double-clicks on the named chart element. Parameters are provided to aid in determining which specific chart element was double-clicked; for details, see their respective entries in Chapter 8, *Events*.

AxisSelected, AxisLabelSelected, AxisTitleSelected, ChartSelected, FootnoteSelected, LegendSelected, PlotSelected, PointSelected, PointLabelSelected, SeriesSelected, TitleSelected

Each of these events is fired when the user clicks on the named chart element. Parameters are provided to aid in determining which specific chart element was clicked; for details, see their respective entries in Chapter 8.

AxisUpdated, AxisLabelUpdated, AxisTitleUpdated, ChartUpdated, FootnoteUpdated, LegendUpdated, PlotUpdated, PointUpdated, PointLabelUpdated, SeriesUpdated, TitleUpdated

Each of these events is fired when the named chart element has been changed. Parameters are provided to aid in determining which specific chart element was changed; for details, see their entries in Chapter 8.

DonePainting

The DonePainting event is fired when the chart has finished drawing itself.

Useful Methods

Both the MSChart control itself and the DataGrid object have a number of useful methods that you can call.

MSChart Control

EditCopy, EditPaste methods

The EditCopy method (which has no parameters) copies the chart to the Windows Clipboard. Both the graphical chart and the chart's data are copied.

The EditPaste method (which has no parameters) alters the chart based on what type of data is in the Clipboard and what is currently selected. If the chart is selected and chart data (tab-delimited text) is in the Clipboard, the chart is recalculated and redrawn with the new data. If a chart element is selected and a graphic is in the Clipboard, that graphic is applied to the element or the element's backdrop.

GetSelectedPart, SelectPart, TwipsToChartPart methods

The GetSelectedPart method returns a set of parameters to determine what chart element is currently selected. Its syntax is:

```
GetSelectedPart Part, Index1, Index2, Index3, Index4
```

The SelectPart method takes the same parameters as GetSelectedPart to select a chart element. Its syntax is:

```
SelectPart Part, Index1, Index2, Index3, Index4
```

The TwipsToChartPart method accepts x- (*xVal*) and y- (*yVal*) coordinates to pinpoint a location on the chart control and then returns several parameters. Its syntax is:

```
TwipsToChartPart xVal (Long Integer), yVal (Long Integer), Part,
Index1, Index2, Index3, Index4
```

The common parameters of these three methods are as follows:

`Part` (`VtChPartType` *enumeration*)

Identifies the chart element. Possible values are 0–VtChPartTypeChart for the chart itself, 1–VtChPartTypeTitle for the chart title, 2–VtChPartType-

Footnote for the chart footnote, 3–VtChPartTypeLegend for the chart legend, 4–VtChPartTypePlot for the plot area, 5–VtChPartTypeSeries for a data series, 7–VtChPartTypePoint for a data point, 8–VtChPartTypePoint-Label, 9–VtChPartTypeAxis for an axis, 10–VtChPartTypeAxisLabel for an axis label, or 11–VtChPartTypeAxisTitle for an axis title.

Index1 (integer)
Helps to identify a particular element of type *Part* when there is more than one on the chart. If the value of *Part* is `VtChPartTypeSeries`, `VtChPartTypePoint`, or `VtChPartTypePointLabel`, *Index1* represents the series number. If the value of *Part* is `VtChPartTypeAxis`, `VtCh-PartTypeAxisLabel`, or `VtChPartTypeAxisTitle`, *Index1* is the axis number, where 0–VtChAxisIdX is the x-axis, 1–VtChAxisIdY is the y-axis, 2–VtChAxisIdY2 is a second y-axis (if one is present), and 3–VtChAx-isIdZ is the z-axis (in the case of a 3-D chart).

Index2 (integer)
Helps to identify a particular element of type *Part* when there is more than one on the chart. If *Part* is `VtChPartTypePoint` or `VtCh-PartTypePointLabel`, *Index2* is the point number within the series specified by *Index1*.

Index3 (integer)
Identifies a particular axis label. If *Part* is `VtChPartTypeAxisLabel`, *Index2* should always be 1, and *Index3* indicates the level of the axis label.

Index4 (integer)
Unused.

Layout method
The Layout method (which has no parameters) forces a recalculate and redraw based on any properties that have been changed. This should be done after all properties have been updated. Before you call the Layout method, properties can have values inconsistent with the chart.

ToDefaults method
Resets the chart to its default properties. The method has no parameters.

DataGrid Object

DeleteColumnLabels, DeleteRowLabels, InsertColumnLabels, InsertRowLabels
These methods delete or insert levels of labels in the DataGrid object. The syntax of each method is identical:

```
DeleteColumnLabels LabelIndex, Count
DeleteRowLabels LabelIndex, Count
InsertColumnLabels LabelIndex, Count
InsertRowLabels LabelIndex, Count
```

where the parameters are as follows:

LabelIndex (integer)
The first level of labels to delete or insert

Count (integer)
The number of levels to delete or insert

Controls M–N

In the case of DeleteColumnLabels and InsertColumnLabels, column labels are numbered starting from the bottom, which is 1. In the case of DeleteRowLabels and InsertRowLabels, row labels are numbered starting from the right, which is 1.

DeleteColumns, DeleteRows, InsertColumns, InsertRows

These methods delete or insert data in the DataGrid object. The syntax of DeleteColumns and InsertColumns is:

```
DeleteColumns Column, Count
InsertColumns Column, Count
```

where the parameters are as follows:

`Column` *(integer)*

The first column of data to delete or insert. Columns are numbered from left to right starting at 1.

`Count` *(integer)*

The number of columns to delete or insert.

The syntax of DeleteRows and InsertRows is similar:

```
DeleteRows Row, Count
InsertRows Row, Count
```

where the parameters are as follows:

`Row` *(integer)*

The first row of data to delete or insert. Rows are numbered from top to bottom starting at 1.

`Count` *(integer)*

The number of rows to delete or insert.

GetData, SetData

These methods retrieve data from and store data to a particular cell of the data grid. Their syntax is:

```
GetData Row, Column, DataPoint, NullFlag
SetData Row, Column, DataPoint, NullFlag
```

where the parameters are:

`Row` *(integer)*, `Column` *(integer)*

The row and column coordinate whose value is to be read or written.

`DataPoint` *(double)*

The value of the data at that location. It should be provided with a call to the GetData method, and it is returned by a call to the SetData method.

`NullFlag` *(Boolean)*

Flag indicating whether the cell contains a null value. To set a null value, set its value to `True` before calling SetData. If you retrieve a null, the value of this parameter is `True` when the GetData method returns.

InitializeLabels

Creates unique labels (which are assigned the default names of R1, R2, etc.) for data in the DataGrid object. The method has no parameters.

MoveData

Moves a block of data in the DataGrid object. Its syntax is:

```
MoveData Top, Left, Bottom, Right, OverOffset, DownOffset
```

with the following parameters:

`Top` *(integer)*, `Left` *(integer)*
The top row and the first column to move.

`Bottom` *(integer)*, `Right` *(integer)*
The last row and the last column to move. With `Top` and `Left`, they define the rectangular range that is to be moved.

`OverOffset` *(integer)*
The number of columns to move the data left or right. A negative value moves the data to the left; a positive value, to the right.

`DownOffset` *(integer)*
The number of rows to move the data up or down. A negative value moves the data up; a positive value, down.

RandomDataFill, RandomFillColumns, RandomFillRows

These methods fill areas of the DataGrid object with random data. The RandomDataFill populates the entire DataGrid with random data; its syntax is:

```
RandomDataFill
```

The RandomFillColumns method fills a number of columns with random data, while the RandomFillRows method fills a number of rows with random data. Their syntax is:

```
RandomFillColumns Column, Count
RandomFillRows Row, Count
```

where the parameters are:

`Column` *(integer) or* `Row` *(integer)*
The first column or first row to fill

`Count` *(integer)*
The number of columns or rows to populate with random data

SetSize

Sets the size of the entire DataGrid object. Its syntax is:

```
SetSize RowLabelCount, ColumnLabelCount, _
        DataRowCount, DataColumnCount
```

with the following parameters:

`RowLabelCount` *(integer)*
The number of levels of row labels

`ColumnLabelCount` *(integer)*
The number of levels of column labels

`DataRowCount` *(integer)*
The number of data rows

`DataColumnCount` *(integer)*
The number of data columns

Controlling the Chart with Chart Objects

Although the previous sections have covered the basic functionality of the MSChart control, virtually every aspect of a chart's appearance can be controlled programmatically by accessing the properties or calling the methods of an object in the MSChart object model. This section lists those additional objects alphabetically and presents their major associated properties and methods.

Axis Object

The Axis object represents a chart axis. The Plot object's Axis property array returns Axis objects representing the x-, y-, y2-, and z-axes. The properties of an Axis object are:

AxisGrid property
: Returns a reference to an AxisGrid object, which contains information about the gridlines extending from the axis. The AxisGrid object is described later in this section.

AxisScale property
: Returns a reference to an AxisScale object, which determines how values are scaled along an axis. The AxisScale object is described later in this section.

AxisTitle property
: Returns a reference to an AxisTitle object, which controls how an axis title is displayed. The AxisTitle object is described later in this section.

CategoryScale property
: Returns a reference to a CategoryScale object, which defines how values are scaled along a category axis. The CategoryScale object is described later in this section.

Intersection property
: Returns a reference to an Intersection object, which determines how the area of intersection of axes should appear. The Intersection object is described later in this section.

LabelLevelCount property
: Returns the number of labels for the axis.

Labels property
: Returns a reference to a Labels collection, which contains information about the labels displayed along the axis. Each member of the collection is a Label object. The Labels collection is described later in this section.

Pen
: Returns a reference to a Pen object, which determines how the axis itself should appear. The Pen object is described in "Common Objects."

Tick
: Returns a reference to a Tick object, which controls the appearance of tick markers along the axis. The Tick object is described later in this section.

ValueScale property
: Returns a reference to a ValueScale object, which controls how values are scaled along a value axis. The ValueScale object is described later in this section.

AxisGrid Object

Defines the gridlines extending from an axis. The AxisGrid object is returned by the Axis object's AxisGrid property. It has the following two properties:

MajorPen, MinorPen properties
: These properties each return a reference to a Pen object, which determines information about how the major and minor gridlines should appear, respectively. The Pen object is described in "Common Objects."

AxisScale Object

Controls how values are scaled along an axis. The AxisScale object is returned by the Axis object's AxisScale property. It has the following properties:

Hide property
: If set to `True`, all elements for that axis are hidden. When set to `False`, the elements are displayed.

LogBase property
: Sets the logarithm base to use for the axis if the Type property is set to `VtChScaleTypeLogarithmic`. Its value can range from 2 to 100; it defaults to 10.

PercentBasis property
: Specifies how 100% is calculated when the Type property is set to `VtChScaleTypePercent`. Possible values are 0–VtChPercentAxisBasisMaxChart, where the largest value becomes the 100%; 1–VChPercent-AxisBasisMaxRow, where the largest value in the row becomes the 100% for that row; 2–VtChPercentAxisBasisMaxColumn, where the largest value in the column becomes the 100% for that column; 3–VtChPercentAxisBasisSumChart, where the sum of all values in the chart becomes the 100%; 4–VtChPercentAxisBasisSumRow, where the sum of all values in the row becomes the 100% for that row; and 5–VtChPercentAxisBasisSumColumn, where the sum of all values in the column becomes the 100% for that column.

Type property
: Sets the type of scale to use for an axis. Possible values are 0–VtChScaleTypeLinear for a linear axis, 1–VtChScaleTypeLogarithmic for a log-based axis, or 2–VtChScaleTypePercent for a percent-based axis.

AxisTitle Object

Controls the appearance of an axis title. The AxisTitle object is returned by the Axis object's AxisTitle property. Its properties are:

Backdrop property
: Returns a reference to a Backdrop object, which contains information about the area behind the axis' title area. The Backdrop object is described later in "Common Objects."

Font, VtFont property
: Returns a reference to a standard Visual Basic Font object and the VtFont property returns a reference to a VtFont object, each of which is then used to set the font of the text in the Title object. The VtFont object is described in "Common Objects."

Text property

Contains the text to be shown in the title area of the axis.

TextLayout property

Returns a reference to a TextLayout object, which controls the alignment and orientation of the text in the axis title. The TextLayout object is described in "Common Objects."

TextLength property

Indicates the number of characters in the axis title.

Visible property

If set to `False`, the axis title does not appear. If set to `True`, the title is displayed as defined by its properties.

CategoryScale Object

Controls the scale for a category axis, which is an x-axis in the chart. The CategoryScale object is returned by the Axis object's CategoryScale property. Its properties are:

Auto property

When set to `True`, the object's other properties are set automatically by the MSChart control. When set to `False`, the properties can be set as desired.

DivisionsPerLabel property

Sets the number of divisions to skip between labels on the axis.

DivisionsPerTick property

Sets the number of divisions between major tick marks.

LabelTick property

When set to `True`, labels are centered on tick marks. When set to `False`, labels appear between tick marks.

DataPointLabel Object

Controls the label for a data point in a chart. A reference to the DataPointLabel object is returned by the DataPoint object's DataPointLabel property. Its members include:

Backdrop property

Returns a reference to a Backdrop object, which contains information about the area behind the label. The Backdrop object is described in the "Common Objects" section.

Component property

Sets the type of information to show in a data point's label. Possible values are 1–VtChLabelComponentValue to show the actual value of the point, 2–VtChLabelComponentPercent to show the value as a percent compared to the total of all values in the series, 4–VtChLabelComponentSeriesName to use the series name as a label, or 8–VtChLabelComponentPointName to use the data point name as the label. These values can be combined by using the `Or` operator to use more than one label component.

Custom property

When set to `True`, the DataPoint object's Text property is used in the label. When set to `False`, the label's contents are based on the Component property.

Font, VtFont properties

The Font property returns a reference to a standard Visual Basic Font object, and the VtFont property returns a reference to a VtFont object. Each is used to set the font of the label's text. The VtFont object is covered in the "Common Objects" section.

LineStyle property

Controls the type of line used to join the data point to the label. Possible values are 0–VtChLabelLineStyleNone for no line, 1–VtChLabelLine-StyleStraight for a straight line, or 2–VtChLabelLineStyleBent for a bent line.

LocationType property

Sets the default location for a data point label. Possible values are 0–VtChLocationTypeTopLeft for the upper-left corner, 1–VtChLocationTypeTop for the top, 2–VtChLocationTypeTopRight for the upper-right corner, 3–VtChLocation-TypeLeft for the left side, 4–VtChLocationTypeRight for the right side, 5–VtChLocationTypeBottomLeft for the lower-left corner, 6–VtChLocation-TypeBottom for the bottom, 7–VtChLocationTypeBottomRight for the lower-right corner, and 8–VtChLocationTypeCustom for a custom location.

Offset property

Returns a reference to an LCoor object, which defines the distance from the default label location set by the LocationType property. The LCoor object is described later in this section.

PercentFormat, ValueFormat properties

These properties each contain a format string that controls how either percentages or values are formatted in the label. The format string uses the same codes as the Visual Basic *Format* function.

ResetCustomLabel method

Resets any custom values assigned to a data point label to the series default.

Text property

When the Custom property is set to `True`, the Text property contains the text for the label.

TextLayout property

Returns a reference to a TextLayout object, which contains information about the alignment and orientation of the text in the label.

TextLength property

The number of characters in the label.

DataPoints Collection, DataPoint Object

The DataPoints collection contains DataPoint objects, each of which stores information about a value in the chart. The DataPoints collection is returned by the Series object's DataPoints property.

The DataPoints collection supports only two properties: Count, which returns the number of DataPoint objects in the collection, and Item, which allows you to retrieve a particular DataPoint object by its ordinal position (or index) in the collection. However, in this version of the MSChart control, only one DataPoint object is contained in the collection, and that object's index is -1.

The DataPoint object includes the following members:

Brush property
: Returns a reference to a Brush object, which contains information about the fill of the data point on the chart. The Brush object is described in the "Common Objects" section.

DataPointLabel property
: Returns a reference to a DataPointLabel object, which contains information about any visible label for the point shown in the chart.

EdgePen property
: Returns a reference to a Pen object, which contains information about the pen used to stroke the graphical edge of the point on the chart. The Pen object is described in the "Common Objects" section.

Marker property
: Returns a reference to a Marker object, which controls the graphic used to denote a point on the chart. The Marker object is described later in this section.

Offset property
: Sets the distance that the marker is offset from the standard label position. Values are specified in inches or centimeters, based on the measurement system in Windows settings.

ResetCustom method
: Resets any custom values assigned to a DataPoint object to the series default. Its syntax is:

```
ResetCustom()
```

Intersection Object

Controls the appearance of the area where two or more axes intersect. The Intersection object is returned by the Axis object's Intersection property. Physically, the Intersection object contains information about how the area where two or more axes meet should appear. Its major properties are:

Auto property
: When set to `True`, the axis appears at its default location. When set to `False`, the axis appears in a position dictated by the Point property.

AxisId property
: Returns a value identifying the axis that intersects with the current axis. Possible values are 0–VtChAxisIdX for the x-axis, 1–VtChAxisIdY for the y-axis, 2–VtChAxisIdY2 for a second y-axis (if one is used), 3–VtChAxisIdZ for the z-axis (only when a 3-D chart is referenced), and 4–VtChAxisIdNone.

LabelsInsidePlot property

When set to `True`, labels do not move when the axis is moved. When set to `False`, the labels move along with the axis.

Point property

A double that indicates the location on the axis where another axis intersects.

Labels Collection, Label Object

The Labels collection contains Label objects, which represent the labels that appear on an axis. The Labels collection is returned by the Axis object's Labels property.

The Labels collection supports only two standard collection members: the Count property and the Item property. The Item property can be used to retrieve Label objects from the collection by index number only.

The Label object has the following properties:

Auto

When set to `True`, axis labels may be rotated in alignment and/or orientation to allow for easier viewing of long labels. When set to `False`, the label appears as defined by the TextLayout property.

Backdrop

Returns a reference to a Backdrop object, which contains information about the area behind the axis label. The Backdrop object is described in the "Common Objects" section.

Font, VtFont

The Font property returns a reference to a standard Visual Basic Font object, and the VtFont property returns a reference to a VtFont object, each of which is then used to set the font of the text in the axis label. The VtFont object is discussed in the "Common Objects" section.

Format

Contains a format string that controls how values are formatted in the axis label. The format string uses the same codes as the Visual Basic *Format* function.

FormatLength

Returns the length, in characters, of the Format property string.

Standing

When set to `True`, axis labels appear on the Y plane (the back wall). When set to `False`, axis labels appear on the X or Z plane.

TextLayout

Returns a reference to a TextLayout object, which determines the alignment and orientation of text in the axis label. The TextLayout property is discussed under "Common Objects."

LCoor Object

Represents a coordinate. The LCoor object is returned by the DataPointLabel object's Offset property. Its members are:

Set method

Allows the LCoor object's coordinates to be set in a single method call rather than separate assignments to the X and Y properties. Its syntax is:

```
Set(X, Y)
```

where *X* and *Y* represent the values to be assigned to the X and Y properties, respectively.

X, Y properties

The X and Y properties together represent a coordinate. The values for these properties are long integers.

Light Object

Controls the visual lighting effect of a 3-D chart. The Light object is returned by the Plot object's Light property. Its properties are:

AmbientDensity property

Represents the percentage of ambient light on the chart. A value of 0 represents no ambient light. A value of 1 represents complete illumination. Values between 0 and 1 represent varying degrees of ambient light.

Ambient light is the light that appears where no light is directed. For example, if a light is shined on a ball, the area where that light does not fall is usually still visible; it is lit by ambient light.

EdgeIntensity property

Controls the amount of light used to highlight edges in the chart. A value of 0 represents no light (black edges), while a value of 1 represents fill light (the edges are the same color as the faces that the edges join). Values between 0 and 1 represent varying degrees of edge light.

EdgeVisible property

When set to `False`, edges are not visible on the chart. When set to `True`, edges appear and are shaded as defined by the EdgeIntensity property.

LightSources property

Returns a reference to a LightSources collection of LightSource objects that contain information about directed light on a 3-D chart.

LightSources Collection, LightSource Object

The LightSources collection is a container for LightSource objects, each of which represents a virtual light pointing at a 3-D chart. The LightSources collection is returned by the Light object's LightSources property.

The LightSources collection supports the standard collection properties and methods: Count, Item, Add, and Delete. You can retrieve and delete LightSource objects by their ordinal position in the collection only and not by key. To add a LightSource object, you use the following syntax:

```
Add(X, Y, Z, Intensity) As LightSource
```

where *X*, *Y*, *Z*, and *Intensity* correspond to properties of the LightSource object.

The properties and methods of the LightSource object are:

Intensity property
: Controls the strength of the light coming from a LightSource object. Values range from 0, representing no light at all, to 1, representing full illumination.

Set method
: Allows the properties of the LightSource object to be set with a single method call rather than separately. Its syntax is:

```
Set(X, Y, Z, Intensity)
```

where each parameter is a single that corresponds to the property of the same name.

X, Y, Z properties
: These properties represent a coordinate in three-dimensional space at which a virtual light pointing at the chart will be placed.

Marker Object

Contains information about the graphic used to mark a point on a chart. A reference to a Marker object is returned by the DataPoint object's Marker property. Its properties are:

FillColor property
: Returns a reference to a VtColor object, which contains information about the color of the Marker object. The VTColor object is described in the "Common Objects" section.

Pen property
: Returns a reference to a Pen object that contains information about the line drawn around the marker. The Pen object is described in the "Common Objects" section.

Size property
: Defines the size in points of the marker.

Style property
: Controls the appearance of the Marker object. Possible values are 0–VtMarkerStyleDash for a dash, 1–VtMarkerStylePlus for a plus sign, 2–VtMarkerStyleX for an X mark, 3–VtMarkerStyleStar for a star symbol, 4–VtMarkerStyleCircle for a round marker, 5–VtMarkerStyleSquare for a square marker, 6–VtMarkerStyleDiamond for a diamond shape, 7–VtMarkerStyleUpTriangle for a triangle with the point facing up, 8–VtMarkerStyleDownTriangle for a triangle with the point facing down, 9–VtMarkerStyleFilledCircle for a filled circle, 10–VtMarkerStyleFilledSquare for a filled square, 11–VtMarkerStyleFilledDiamond for a filled diamond, 12–VtMarkerStyleFilledUpTriangle for a filled triangle with the

point facing up, 13–VtMarkerStyleFilledDownTriangle for a filled triangle with the point facing down, 14–VtMarkerStyle3dBall for a three-dimensional ball, and 15–VtMarkerStyleNull for no marker. Markers with various values of the Style property are shown in Figure 5-41.

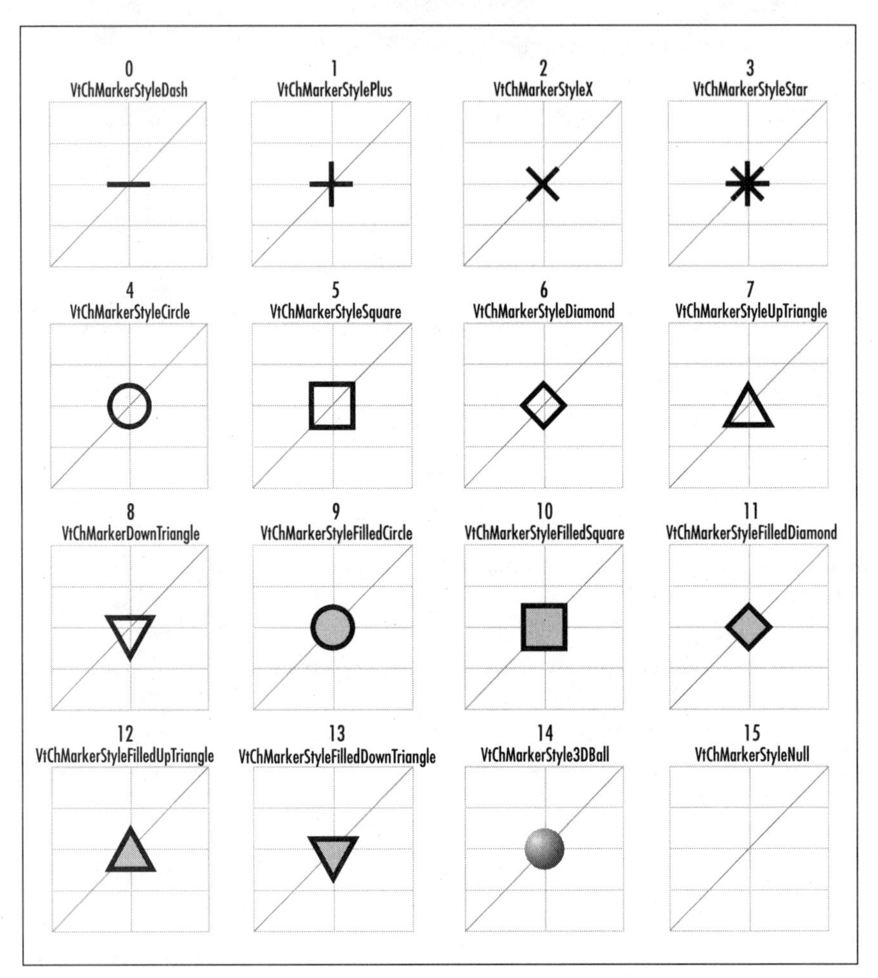

Figure 5-41: Markers

Visible property

When set to `False`, the marker does not appear on the chart. When set to `True`, the marker appears as normal.

Plot Object

Represents the area of the MSChart control on which the data is charted. The Plot object is contained by the MSChart control and is referenced by using the MSChart's Plot property. The Plot object itself is the parent of a number of objects, including the Axis object, the Backdrop object, the Light object, the LocationRect object, the SeriesCollection collection, the View3D object, and the Wall object, all shown in the MSChart object model in Figure 5-36.

The following are the major properties of the Plot object:

AutoLayout property
: When set to `True` (its default value), the Plot object's size and location are automatically set based on the size of elements in the plot area and the size and location of other elements on the control, such as the Legend object. When set to `False`, the positioning of the Plot object is determined by the value of the LocationRect property.

Axis property array
: Contains an array of Axis objects representing the axes in the chart. A specific Axis object can be retrieved with the syntax:

```
Plot.Axis(axisID)
```

where ***axisID*** can be 0–VtChAxisIdX for the x-axis, 1–VtChAxisIdY for the y-axis, 2–VtChAxisIdY2 for a second y-axis (if one is being used), and 3–VtChAxisIdZ for the z-axis (only when a 3-D chart is being referenced. The Axis object is described earlier in this section.

Backdrop property
: Returns a reference to a Backdrop object, which contains information about the area behind the plot area. The Backdrop object is described in the "Common Objects" section.

BarGap, XGap, ZGap properties
: These properties represent the percentage of the value indicator's width to specify the gap between multiple values. The BarGap property specifies the gap between values from different series in the same category. The XGap property specifies the gap between categories. The ZGap property specifies the gap between values in a three-dimensional chart along the z-axis.

DataSeriesInRow property
: Specifies how series values are read from the chart control's data grid. When set to `True`, data in a series is read from a row in the DataGrid. When set to `False`, its default value, data in a series is read from a column in the DataGrid.

DefaultPercentBasis property
: In charts using percentage axes, the DefaultPercentBasis specifies how 100% is calculated. Possible values are 0–VtChPercentAxisBasisMaxChart, where the largest value becomes the 100%; 1–VtChPercentAxisBasisMaxRow, where the largest value in the row becomes the 100% for that row; 2–VtChPercentAxisBasisMaxColumn, where the largest value in the column becomes the 100% for that column; 3–VtChPercentAxisBasisSumChart, where the sum of all values in the chart becomes the 100%; 4–VtChPercentAxisBasisSumRow, where the sum of all values in the row becomes the 100% for that row; and 5–VtChPercentAxisBasisSumColumn, where the sum of all values in the column becomes the 100% for that column.

DepthToHeightRatio, WidthToHeightRatio properties

These properties are used only in 3-D charts and aid in sizing each axis in relation to the other axes. The DepthToHeightRatio specifies the depth of the chart in relation to its height. The WidthToHeightRatio specifies the width of the chart in relation to its height.

Light property

Returns a reference to a Light object, which defines the lighting applied to a 3-D chart. The Light object is described earlier in this section.

LocationRect property

Returns a reference to a Rect object that contains information about the positioning of the Plot object on the chart. The Rect object is described in the "Common Objects" section later in this section.

PlotBase property

Returns a reference to a PlotBase object, which contains information about the area beneath the plot area of the chart. The PlotBase object is described later in this section.

Projection property

Controls the three-dimensional appearance of the chart when viewing a 3-D chart. Possible values are 0–VtProjectionTypePerspective, where charts are shown in true 3-D; 1–VtProjectionTypeOblique, where the vertical alignment remains constant; 2–VtProjectionTypeOrthogonal, where vertical lines always appear vertical; 3–VtProjectionTypeFrontal, where the chart appears two-dimensional but can be viewed from different sides; and 4–VtProjectionTypeOverhead, where the user sees the chart from the top.

SeriesCollection property

Returns a reference to a SeriesCollection collection, which contains information about the series in the chart. The SeriesCollection collection is described later in this section.

View3D property

Returns a reference to a View3D object, which contains information about the current three-dimensional orientation of the chart. The View3D object is described later in this section.

Wall property

Returns a reference to a Wall object, which contains information about the back wall of the current 3-D chart. The Wall object is described later in this section.

Pie Chart-Specific Properties

A number of the Plot object's properties apply only to pie charts. These include the following:

AngleUnit property

Specifies the units used to specify angles. Possible values are 0–VtAngleUnitsDegrees for degrees, 1–VtAngleUnitsRadians for radians, and 2–VtAngleUnitsGrads for grads.

Clockwise property

When set to `True`, values in the pie chart are drawn clockwise around the chart. When set to `False`, they are drawn counterclockwise instead.

Sort property

Values in a pie chart are sorted based on the Sort property. Possible values are 0–VtSortTypeNone, where the values are not sorted; 1–VtSortType-Ascending, where the values are sorted from the lowest to the highest value; and 2–VtSortTypeDescending, where the values are sorted from the highest to the lowest. In all cases, the Clockwise property defines the direction of the values, whether they are sorted or not.

StartingAngle property

Specifies the location of the first value. A value of 0 specifies that the first value will appear directly to the right (three o'clock). Other values are specified in units based on the AngleUnit property and appear in a direction based on the Clockwise property.

SubPlotLabelPosition property

Specifies the location of labels for the values in a pie chart. Possible values are 0–VtChSubPlotLabelLocationTypeNone, where no labels are displayed; 1–VtChSubPlotLabelLocationTypeAbove, where the labels appear above the values; 2–VtChSubPlotLabelLocationType, where the labels appear below the values; and 3–VtChSubPlotLabelLocationTypeCenter, where the labels are centered over the values.

UniformAxis property

When set to `True`, all axes are scaled uniformly. When set to `False`, each axis is scaled as defined by its size, location, and the value of its AutoLayout property.

Weighting property

Returns a reference to a Weighting object, which contains information about the size of a pie chart in relation to other pie charts being displayed. The Weighting object is described later in this section.

PlotBase Object

Represents the area of the Plot above which the data is charted. The PlotBase object is returned by the Plot object's PlotBase property. Its properties are:

BaseHeight property

Specifies the height in points of the PlotBase object.

Brush property

Returns a reference to a Brush object, which contains information about the graphical fill of the PlotBase. The Brush object is described in the "Common Objects" section.

Pen property

Returns a reference to a Pen object, which contains information about stroked lines in the PlotBase. The Pen object is described under "Common Objects."

SeriesCollection Collection, Series Object

The SeriesCollection collection is a container for Series objects and is referenced by the Plot object's SeriesCollection property. The Series object contains all the information about a data series, including the values of each point in the series.

The SeriesCollection collection has only two members: the Count method, which returns the number of Series objects in the collection, and the Item property, which returns a particular Series object based on its ordinal position in the Series-Collection collection.

The Series object supports the following properties:

DataPoints property
: Returns a reference to a DataPoints collection, which contains DataPoint objects that provide information about the data within the series being referenced. The DataPoints collection and DataPoint object are described earlier in this section.

LegendText property
: The description for the series that appears in the chart's legend, if one is displayed.

Pen, GuidelinePen properties
: Each of these properties returns a reference to a Pen object, which contains information about any lines displayed between values in the series. The Pen object referenced by the GuidelinePen property contains information about the guidelines drawn. The Pen object is described later, under "Common Objects."

Position property
: Returns a reference to a SeriesPosition object, which contains information about where the series will be located with the other series in the chart. The SeriesPosition object is described later in this section.

SecondaryAxis property
: If a secondary y-axis is displayed, the SecondaryAxis property controls whether the series will be displayed on that axis. When set to `True`, the series is displayed on the secondary axis. When set to `False`, the series is displayed on the primary axis.

SeriesMarker property
: Returns a reference to a SeriesMarker object, which contains information about the marker used to represent the points in the series. The SeriesMarker object is described later in the next section.

SeriesType property
: Specifies the type of chart to use when displaying the series. Generally, this value corresponds to the MSChart control's ChartType property, but when the ChartType property is set to `VtChChartType2DCombination` or `VtChChartType3dCombination`, different series can use different types on one chart. Possible values are 0–VtChSeriesType3dBar, 1–VtChSeriesType2dBar, 5–VtChSeriesType3dLine, 6–VtChSeriesType2dLine, 7–VtChSeriesType3dArea,

8–VtChSeriesType2dArea, 9–VtChSeriesType3dStep, 10–VtChSeriesType2dStep, 11–VtChSeriesType2dXY, and 24–VtChSeriesType2dPie. Each of these values appears similar to its ChartType counterpart; see Figure 5-39 for reference.

ShowGuideline property array

When an element in the ShowGuideline property array is set to `True`, guidelines appear on the appropriate axis for the series. When set to `False`, guidelines do not appear on the appropriate axis. The guidelines shown appear based on the Pen object referenced by the Series object's GuidelinePen property. The index of the array can be 0–VtChAxisIdX for the x-axis, 1–VtChAxisIdY for the y-axis, 2–VtChAxisIdY2 for a second y-axis (if one is used), 3–VtChAxisIdZ for the z-axis (only when a 3-D chart is used), and 4–VtChAxisIdNone.

ShowLine property

When set to `True`, lines appear between points in the series. When set to `False`, lines do not appear between the points. The lines shown appear based on the Pen object referenced by the Series object's Pen property.

StatLine property

The StatLine property returns a reference to a StatLine object, which contains information about how statistical information lines appear for the series. The StatLine object is described later in this section.

SeriesMarker Object

Controls the appearance of the markers used to show points in a series. A reference to the SeriesMarker object is returned by the Series object's SeriesMarker property. Its properties are:

Auto property

When set to `True`, the appearance of each series marker is handled automatically by the MSChart control. When set to `False`, the appearance of each series marker is controlled by the Marker object returned by the DataPoint object's Marker property.

Show property

When set to `True`, markers appear for all values in the series. When set to `False`, no markers appear for the series.

SeriesPosition Object

Controls the appearance of the series in relation to other series on the chart. The SeriesPosition object is returned by the Series object's Position property. Its properties are as follows:

Excluded property

When set to `True`, the series containing the SeriesPosition object is not included in the chart. When set to `False`, the series is included.

Hidden property

When set to `True`, the series containing the SeriesPosition object is not drawn on the chart. When set to `False`, the series is drawn.

Both the Excluded and Hidden properties cause a Series object not to be displayed. However, the Hidden property leaves an empty space for the hidden object, while the Excluded property does not.

Order property

Defines the position of the series in the chart. The Order property can be set to any integer. The Series object with the lowest value appears first in the chart. Multiple series with Order properties of the same value appear to be stacked.

StackOrder property

When multiple series are stacked because the value of their Order property is the same, the StackOrder property controls which series appears first in the stack. The StackOrder property can be set to any integer. The Series object with the lowest value in its StackOrder appears at the bottom of the stack.

StatLine Object

Controls how statistic indicator lines are shown on a chart. The StatLine object is returned by the Series object's StatLine property. Its properties are:

Flag property

Specifies what type of statistic is highlighted by a line. Possible values are defined by the `VtChStats` enumeration, as follows: 1–VtChStatsMinimum for the minimum value, 2–VtChStatsMaximum for the maximum value, 4–VtChStatsMean for the mean value, 8–VtChStatsStddev for the standard deviation, and 16–VtChStatsRegression for a linear regression. These values can be combined by using the `Or` operator to show more than one statistic line for a series.

Style property array

Controls the line type of each statistic line. Its syntax is:

```
object.Style(type ) [ = style]
```

where ***`type`*** is a constant of the **`VtChStats`** enumeration that defines the statistic type and ***`style`*** is one of the following **`VtPenStyle`** constants: 0–VtPenStyleNull for no line, 1–VtPenStyleSolid for a solid line, 2–VtPenStyleDashed for a dashed line, 3–VtPenStyleDotted for a dotted line, 4–VtPenStyleDashDot for a line composed of alternating dashes and dots, 5–VtPenStyleDashDotDot for a line composed of a repeating pattern of one dash followed by two dots, 6–VtPenStyleDitted for a ditted line, 7–VtPenStyleDashDit for a line composed of alternating dashes and dits, and 8–VtPenStyleDashDitDit for a line composed of a repeating pattern of one dash followed by two dits. This allows each statistic line to have its own Style property.

VtColor property

Returns a reference to a VtColor object, which contains information about the color of the statistic line. The VtColor object is described in the "Common Objects" section.

Width property

Sets the width in points of the statistic line.

Tick Object

Contains information about the division markers along an axis line. A reference to the Tick object is returned by the Axis object's Tick property. Its properties are:

Length property

Indicates the actual size of the tick marker in points.

Style property

Controls the location of the tick marks in relation to the axis. Possible values are 0–VtChAxisTickStyleNone for no tick marks, 1–VtChAxisTickStyleCenter for tick marks centered on the axis, 2–VtChAxisTickStyleInside for tick marks inside the axis, and 3–VtChAxisTickStyleOutside for tick marks outside the axis.

ValueScale Object

Controls the scale of the Axis object to which it applies. A reference to the ValueScale object is returned by the Axis object's ValueScale property. Its properties are:

Auto property

When set to `True`, the ValueScale object's other properties are set automatically based on the data. When set to `False`, the properties must be set manually.

MajorDivision, MinorDivision properties

Each of these properties controls the number of the appropriate division marks that will appear on the axis. The MajorDivision property sets the number of major divisions, while the MinorDivision property sets the number of minor divisions. The Tick object contained by the Axis object controls the appearance of the divisions.

Maximum, Minimum property

The Minimum and Maximum properties control the lowest and highest values on the axis, respectively.

View3D Object

Controls the 3-D angle used to display a 3-D chart. The View3D object is returned by the Plot object's View3D property. Its properties and methods are:

Elevation property

Sets the angle at which the chart is viewed vertically. Values are specified in units based on the Plot object's AngleUnit property. In degrees, values can range from 0 (straight ahead) to 90 (directly above, looking down).

Rotation property

Sets the angle at which the chart is viewed horizontally. Values are specified in units based on the Plot object's AngleUnit property. In degrees, values can range from 0 (straight ahead) to 360 (also straight ahead, but after having rotated completely around).

Set method

Allows the Elevation and Rotation properties to be set in a single method call. Its syntax is:

```
Set(Rotation, Elevation)
```

where *`Rotation`* and *`Elevation`* are parameters of type single that represent the value to be assigned to the property of the same name.

Wall Object

Contains information about how to display the back wall (y-axis) in a 3-D chart. The Wall object is returned by the Plot object's Wall property. Its properties are:

Brush property

Returns a reference to a Brush object, which controls the fill of the Wall object. The Brush object is described in the "Common Objects" section.

Pen property

Returns a reference to a Pen object, which controls the line around the Wall object. The Pen object is described in the "Common Objects" section.

Width property

Sets the width in points of the Wall object.

Weighting Object

Controls the size of a pie chart in relation to the chart's other pie charts. The Weighting object is returned by the Plot object's Weighting property. Its members are:

Basis property

Controls how each pie chart is compared to set its size. Possible values are 0–VtChPieWeightBasisNone to size all pies the same, 1–VtChPieWeightBasis-Total to size all pies by comparing the sum of their slices, or 2–VtChPieWeightBasisSeries to cause the first column of data for each series to be used to size the pie for that series.

Set method

Sets the Basis and Style properties in a single method call. Its syntax is:

```
Set(Basis, Style)
```

where *`Basis`* is a member of the **`VtChPieWeightBasis`** enumeration and *`Style`* is a member of the `VtChPieWeightStyle` enumeration. The parameters set the properties of the same name.

Style property

When the Style property is set to 0–VtChPieWeightStyleArea, the pies' areas are used comparatively to size the charts. When the Style property is set to 1–VtChPieWeightStyleDiameter, the diameters are used instead.

Common Objects

In numerous instances, the "Control Tasks" section refers to a property that returns an object—like the Backdrop object—that is common to the MSChart control and one or more objects. This section surveys these common objects and their properties and methods.

Backdrop Object

The Backdrop object, which controls the visible area behind a chart element, is returned by numerous other objects, including the Plot object, the Title object, the Footnote object, and the Legend object, typically by their Backdrop property. (For a complete list, see the MSChart object model in Figure 5-36.) It supports the following properties:

Fill property
: Returns a reference to a Fill object, which contains information about the fill of the Backdrop object. The Fill object is described later in this section.

Frame property
: Returns a reference to a Frame object, which contains information about the frame around the Backdrop object. The Frame object is described later in this section.

Shadow property
: Returns a reference to a Shadow object, which contains information about any graphical shadow cast by the Backdrop object. The Shadow object is described later in this section.

Brush Object

Defines the inside (fill) of its parent. The Brush object is a child of the DataPoint, Fill, PlotBase, Shadow, and Wall objects and is usually returned by its parent's Brush property. Its properties include:

FillColor, PatternColor properties
: Return a reference to a VtColor object that defines a color to use for the Brush object. The two colors returned by these two properties are combined according to the Style and Index properties. The VtColor object is covered later in this section.

Style property
: Controls how the FillColor and PatternColor properties are combined to form a fill. Possible values are 0–VtBrushStyleNull to ignore the values of the Brush object, 1–VtBrushStyleSolid to use only the solid fill color, 2–VtBrushStylePattern to define a color and pattern using a constant of the `VtBrushPatterns` enumeration, and 3–VtBrushStyleHatched to define a color and pattern using a constant of the `VtBrushHatches` enumeration.

Index property
: Defines the color and pattern to be used when the Brush object's Style property is set to `VtBrushPattern` or `VtBrushHatch`.

  When the Style property is set to `VtBrushPattern`, possible values are 0–VtBrushPattern94Percent for 94% color (that is, the color used is defined by 94% of the PatternColor property's color and by 6% of the FillColor property's color), 1–VtBrushPattern88Percent for 88% color, 2–VtBrushPattern75Percent for 75% color, 3–VtBrushPattern50Percent for 50% color, 4–VtBrushPattern25Percent for 25% color, 5–VtBrushPatternBoldHorizontal for bold horizontal lines, 6–VtBrushPatternBoldVertical for bold vertical lines, 7–VtBrushPatternBoldDownDiagonal for bold diagonal lines from upper-left to lower-right, 8–VtBrushPatternBoldUpDiagonal for bold diagonal lines from lower-left to upper-right, 9–VtBrushPatternChecks for a checked pattern, 10–VtBrushPatternWeave for a woven pattern, 11–VtBrushPatternHorizontal for horizontal lines, 12–VtBrushPatternVertical for vertical lines, 13–VtBrushPatternDownDiagonal for diagonal lines from upper-left to lower-right, 14–VtBrush-Pattern-UpDiagonal for diagonal lines from lower-left to upper-right, 15–VtBrushPatternGrid for both horizontal and vertical lines, 16–VtBrushPatternTrellis for a trellis pattern, and 17–VtBrushPatternInvertedTrellis for an inverted trellis pattern. These patterns are shown in Figure 5-42.

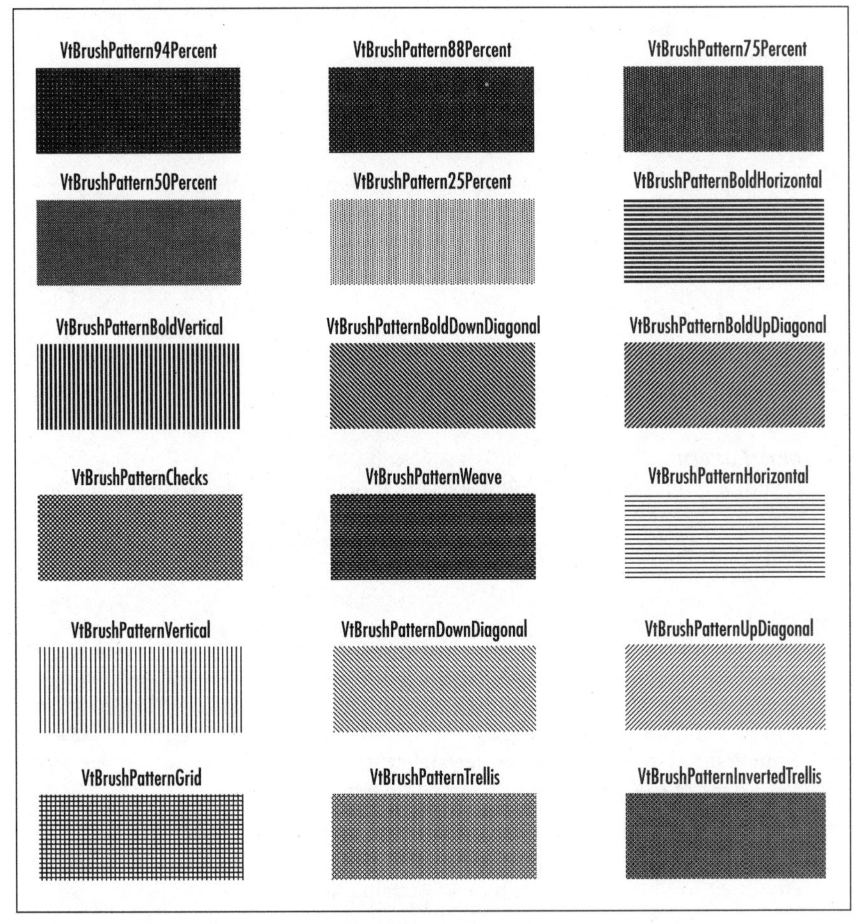

Figure 5-42: The effect of VtBrushPattern constants

When the Style property is set to `VtBrushHatch`, possible values are 0–VtBrushHatchHorizontal for horizontal hatch lines, 1–VtBrushHatchVertical for vertical hatch lines, 2–VtBrushHatchDownDiagonal for diagonal hatch lines from upper-left to lower-right, 3–VtBrushHatchUpDiagonal for diagonal hatch lines from lower-left to upper-right, 4–VtBrushHatchCross for both horizontal and vertical hatch lines, and 5–VtBrushHatchDiagonalCross for both types of diagonal hatch lines. These patterns are shown in Figure 5-43. Note that in this case, if the Style property is set to `VtBrushHatch`, the largest possible value of Style is 5; attempting to assign a larger value to Style generates a runtime error 380, "Invalid property value."

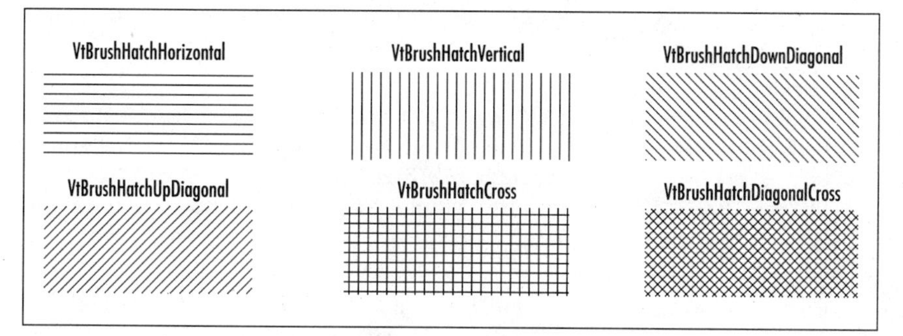

Figure 5-43: The effect of VtBrushHatch constants

Coor Object

Represents a coordinate. A Coor object is returned by a number of properties, including the Offset property of the DataPoint, DataPointLabel, and Shadow objects, as well as the Min and Max properties of the Rect object.

Set method

Allows you to set the `X` and `Y` values in a single step. Its syntax is:

```
Set(X, Y)
```

where *X* and *Y* represent the same values as the X and Y properties.

X, Y properties

The X and Y properties together represent a coordinate; X represents its horizontal value, and Y represents its vertical value. The values for these properties are of type single. You can use these properties both to retrieve and to set the property value.

Fill Object

Contains information about how to fill a chart element. The Fill object is referenced by using the Backdrop object's Fill property. It supports the following properties:

Style property

When the Style property is set to 0–VtFillStyleNull, the chart element is not filled. When it is set to 1–VtFillStyleBrush, the Brush property is used to set the fill.

Brush property

Returns a reference to a Brush object, which contains information about the graphical fill of the chart element. The Brush object is described earlier in this section.

Frame Object

Controls the appearance of the area around a Backdrop object. The Frame object is referenced by the Backdrop object's Frame property. It has the following properties:

FrameColor property
: Returns a reference to a VtColor object that controls the color of the frame around the object. The VtColor object is described later in this section.

SpaceColor property
: Returns a reference to a VtColor object that defines the color of the area between the two lines of a double frame around the object if the Style property is set to `VtFrameStyleDoubleLine`, `VtFrameStyleThickInner`, or `VtFrameStyleThickOuter`. The VtColor object is described later in this section.

Style property
: Controls how the frame around an object appears. Possible values are 0–VtFrameStyleNull for no frame, 1–VtFrameStyleSingleLine for a single line around the frame, 2–VtFrameStyleDoubleLine for a double line around the frame, 3–VtFrameStyleThickInner for a double line with the inner line appearing thicker than the outer line, or 4–VtFrameStyleThickOuter for a double line with the outer line appearing thicker than the inner line.

Width property
: Controls the width of the frame around an object. The value is specified in points.

Location Object

Contains information about a rectangular object on a chart. The Location object is the child of a number of parent objects and is usually returned by their Location property. Its properties are:

LocationType property
: Sets the default location for the parent object of the Location object. Possible values are 0–VtChLocationTypeTopLeft for the upper-left corner, 1–VtChLocationTypeTop for the top, 2–VtChLocationTypeTopRight for the upper-right corner, 3–VtChLocationTypeLeft for the left side, 4–VtChLocationTypeRight for the right side, 5–VtChLocationTypeBottomLeft for the lower-left corner, 6–VtChLocationTypeBottom for the bottom, 7–VtChLocationTypeBottomRight for the lower-right corner, and 8–VtChLocationTypeCustom for a custom location.

Rect property
: Returns a reference to a Rect object that determines where to locate the Location object when the LocationType is set to `VtChLocationTypeCustom`. The Rect object is discussed later in this section.

Visible property
: When set to `False`, the parent object of the Location object is not displayed. When set to `True`, the object is displayed as normal.

Pen Object

Defines the graphical line drawn around its parent object. The Pen object is returned by the Pen property of the Axis, Marker, PlotBase, Series, and Wall objects. Its properties are:

Cap property
: Controls how the end of a line appears. Possible values, which are shown in Figure 5-44, are 0–VtPenCapButt, where the line ends flat at the endpoint; 1–VtPenCapRound, where the line ends with a semicircle with the endpoint of the line as the center; and 2–VtPenCapSquare where the line ends as a square with the line's endpoint as its center.

Join property
: Controls the appearance of the area where two line segments meet. Possible values, which are illustrated in Figure 5-44, are 0–VtPenJoinMiter, where the segments extend until there is a solid joint; 1–VtPenJoinRound, where a circle is drawn where the lines meet, with the meeting point of the segment as the center of the circle and the width of the circle equaling the width of the line; and 2–VtPenJoinBevel, where each line ends at the endpoint and the area left is filled.

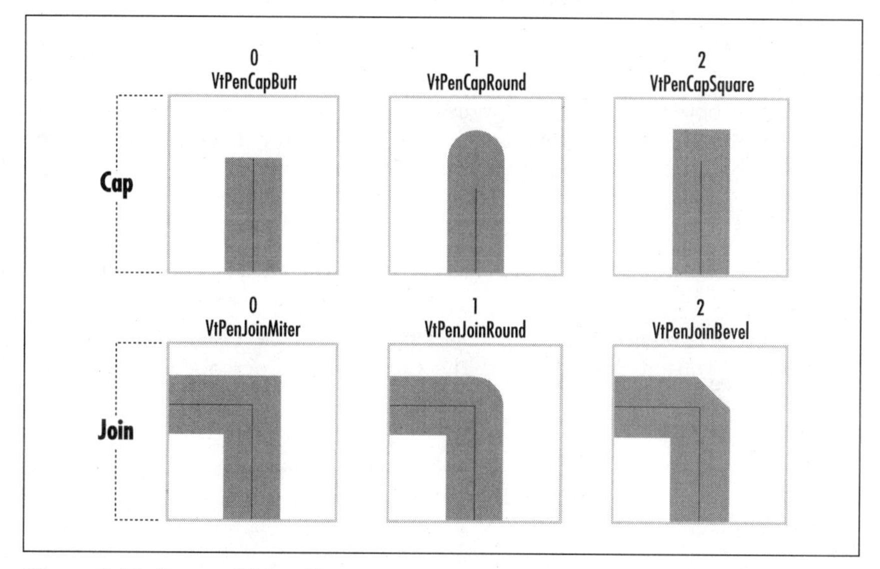

Figure 5-44: Cap and Join effects

Limit property
: Sets the maximum distance that lines can be extended when the Join property is set to `VtPenJoinMiter`.

Style property
: Controls how the line is drawn. Possible values are 0–VtPenStyleNull for no line, 1–VtPenStyleSolid for a solid line, 2–VtPenStyleDashed for a dashed line, 3–VtPenStyleDotted for a dotted line, 4–VtPenStyleDashDot for a line

composed of alternating dashes and dots, 5–VtPenStyleDashDotDot for a line composed of a repeating pattern of one dash followed by two dots, 6–VtPenStyleDitted for a ditted line, 7–VtPenStyleDashDit for a line composed of alternating dashes and dits, and 8–VtPenStyleDashDitDit for a line composed of a repeating pattern of one dash followed by two dits.

VtColor property
Returns a reference to a VtColor object, which contains information about the color of the Pen object. The VtColor object is described later in this section.

Width property
Sets the width of the pen. The value is specified in points.

Rect Object

The Rect object is returned by the Location object's Rect property and is used to define the location of its parent object. The Rect object has only two properties:

Min, Max properties
The Min and Max properties each contain a reference to a Coor object. The Coor object referenced by the Min property represents the lower-left corner of the Rect object, and the Coor object referenced by the Max property represents the upper-right corner of the Rect object. The Coor object is described earlier in this section.

Shadow Object

The Shadow object is referenced by using the Backdrop object's Shadow property. The Shadow object controls the type of shadow that appears on the Backdrop object's parent chart element. Its properties include:

Brush property
Returns a reference to a Brush object, which contains information about the Shadow object's fill. The Brush object is described earlier in this section.

Offset property
Returns a reference to a Coor object that defines the distance to offset the shadow from the parent object. The Coor object is described earlier in this section.

Style property
When the Style property is set to 1–VtShadowStyleDrop, a drop shadow whose attributes are defined by the other Shadow object properties appears on the parent object. When set to 0–VtShadowStyleNull, no shadow appears.

TextLayout Object

Defines the appearance, alignment, and orientation of text. The TextLayout object is returned by the TextLayout property of the AxisTitle, DataPointLabel, Footnote, Label, Legend, and Title objects. Its properties are:

HorzAlignment, VertAlignment properties
Control the alignment of the text in the parent object. HorzAlignment controls the horizontal positioning of text, while VertAlignment controls the vertical positioning of text. Possible values for the HorzAlignment property are 0–VtHorizontalAlignmentRight for right-aligned text, 1–VtHorizontalAlign-

mentLeft for left-aligned text, 2–VtHorizontalAlignmentCenter for centered text, 3–VtHorizontalAlignmentFill for fully justified text (both left and right), and 4–VtHorizontalAlignmentFlush for flush-aligned text. Possible values for the VertAlignment property are 0–VtVerticalAlignmentTop for top-aligned text, 1–VtVerticalAlignmentBottom for bottom-aligned text, and 2–VtVerticalAlignmentCenter for centered text.

Orientation property

Controls the orientation of the parent object's text. Possible values are 0–VtOrientationHorizontal for text that reads left to right, 1–VtOrientationVertical for vertical text that reads top to bottom, 2–VtOrientationUp for text that is rotated so that it is read from the bottom, and 3–VtOrientationDown for text that is rotated so that it is read from the top.

WordWrap property

When set to `True`, the parent object's text wraps to multiple lines. When set to `False`, the text does not wrap.

VtColor Object

Controls the color of a chart element. The VtColor object is contained by numerous other objects and is usually referenced by its parent object's VtColor property. It has the following properties and methods:

Automatic property

When set to `True`, the color for the chart element to which the VtColor object applies is set automatically by the control. When set to `False`, the Red, Green, and Blue properties are used to set the color.

Red, Green, Blue properties

These properties each range in value from 0 to 255 and when used together can form a single color for the VtColor object. In each property, the value 0 represents black and the value 255 represents the solid named color. If all three properties are set to 255, the color displayed will be white.

Set method

Allows the color to be set in a single step, rather than by assigning color values to the Red, Green, and Blue properties separately. Its syntax is:

```
Set(Red, Green, Blue)
```

where *Red*, *Green*, and *Blue* are integers representing the Red, Green, and Blue color values, respectively.

VtFont Object

Controls the font used by a chart element. The VtFont object is returned by numerous other objects, typically by their VtFont property. Although a VtFont object cannot be set equal to a Font object, the properties of a Font object can be used to set similar properties in a VtFont object to duplicate a given font. It includes the following properties:

Name property

The name of the font used for the chart element that's the parent of the VtFont object.

Size property

The size, in points, for the font referred to by the VtFont object.

Effect property

Controls font effects displayed by the VtFont object. Possible values are 256–VtFontEffectStrikeThrough and 512–VtFontEffectUnderline. These values can be combined by using the `Or` operator.

Style property

Controls the font style used by the VtFont object. Possible values are 1–VtFontStyleBold, 2–VtFontStyleItalic, and 4–VtFontStyleOutline. These values can be combined by using the `Or` operator.

VtColor property

Returns a reference to a VtColor object, which contains information about the color of the font represented by the VtFont object.

Example

The example, whose form appears in Figure 5-45, shows how to assign values to an MSChart control using the "assigning values one at a time" method described earlier. It also shows various chart types, as well as the difference between values in rows and values in columns:

```
Option Explicit

'For this example, create the following controls: _
   an MSChart control named chtMain and _
   a Menu named mnuPopupTop with a child menu called _
   mnuPopup with the Index property set to 0.

Dim WithEvents cmdMain1 As CommandButton
Dim WithEvents cmdMain2 As CommandButton
Dim WithEvents cmdMain3 As CommandButton
Dim WithEvents cmdReset As CommandButton
Dim WithEvents optColumns As OptionButton
Dim WithEvents optRows As OptionButton

Private Sub Form_Activate()
   UpdateChart
End Sub

Private Sub Form_Load()
   Dim iCtr As Integer

  'Create/Set up controls.
   Set cmdMain1 = Me.Controls.Add("vb.commandbutton", _
                  "cmdMain1", Me)
   cmdMain1.Visible = True
   cmdMain1.Caption = "&1"
   Set cmdMain2 = Me.Controls.Add("vb.commandbutton", _
                  "cmdMain2", Me)
   cmdMain2.Visible = True
   cmdMain2.Caption = "&2"
   Set cmdMain3 = Me.Controls.Add("vb.commandbutton", _
```

```
                  "cmdMain3", Me)
    cmdMain3.Visible = True
    cmdMain3.Caption = "&3"
    Set cmdReset = Me.Controls.Add("vb.commandbutton", _
                  "cmdReset", Me)
    cmdReset.Visible = True
    cmdReset.Caption = "&Reset"

    Set optColumns = Me.Controls.Add("vb.optionbutton", _
                    "optColumns", Me)
    optColumns.Visible = True
    optColumns.Caption = "Values in &Columns"
    optColumns.Value = True
    Set optRows = Me.Controls.Add("vb.optionbutton", _
                 "optRows", Me)
    optRows.Visible = True
    optRows.Caption = "Values in Ro&ws"

    Me.mnuPopupTop.Visible = False
    Me.mnuPopupTop.Caption = "&Chart Types"
    Me.mnuPopup(0).Caption = "3D"
    Load Me.mnuPopup(1)
    Me.mnuPopup(1).Caption = "-"
    Load Me.mnuPopup(2)
    Me.mnuPopup(2).Caption = "Pie"
    Load Me.mnuPopup(3)
    Me.mnuPopup(3).Caption = "Area"
    Load Me.mnuPopup(4)
    Me.mnuPopup(4).Caption = "Bar"
    Me.mnuPopup(4).Checked = True
    Load Me.mnuPopup(5)
    Me.mnuPopup(5).Caption = "Line"
    Me.mnuPopuptop.Visible = True

    cmdReset.Value = True
End Sub

Private Sub Form_Resize()
   If Me.ScaleHeight < 3140 Or Me.ScaleWidth < 2550 Then
      Exit Sub
   End If

   cmdMain1.Move 120, 120, 1095, 375
   cmdMain2.Move 120, 605, 1095, 375
   cmdMain3.Move 120, 1120, 1095, 375
   cmdReset.Move 120, 1635, 1095, 375
   optColumns.Move 120, 2150, 1095, 495
   optRows.Move 120, 2645, 1095, 495
   Me.chtMain.Move 1335, 120, Me.ScaleWidth - 1455, _
                  Me.ScaleHeight - 240
End Sub

Private Sub chtMain_MouseDown _
      (Button As Integer, Shift As Integer, _
```

```
        X As Single, Y As Single)
   If (Button And vbRightButton) > 0 Then _
        PopupMenu Me.mnuPopupTop
End Sub

Private Sub cmdMain1_Click()
    cmdMain1.Tag = cmdMain1.Tag + 1

    UpdateChart
End Sub

Private Sub cmdMain2_Click()
    cmdMain2.Tag = cmdMain2.Tag + 1

    UpdateChart
End Sub

Private Sub cmdMain3_Click()
    cmdMain3.Tag = cmdMain3.Tag + 1

    UpdateChart
End Sub

Private Sub cmdReset_Click()
    cmdMain1.Tag = 0
    cmdMain2.Tag = 0
    cmdMain3.Tag = 0

    UpdateChart
End Sub

Private Sub mnuPopup_Click(Index As Integer)
   Dim iCtr As Integer

  'Update the menu.
   Select Case Index
      Case 0 '3D
         If Me.mnuPopup(0).Checked Then
            Me.mnuPopup(0).Checked = False
         Else
            Me.mnuPopup(0).Checked = True
         End If
      Case 1 'Separator—no effect
      Case Else
         For iCtr = 2 To 5
            If iCtr = Index Then
               Me.mnuPopup(iCtr).Checked = True
            Else
               Me.mnuPopup(iCtr).Checked = False
            End If
         Next iCtr
   End Select
```

```
   UpdateChart
End Sub

Private Sub optColumns_Click()
    UpdateChart
End Sub

Private Sub optRows_Click()
    UpdateChart
End Sub

Private Sub UpdateChart()
   If Not Me.Visible Then _
      Exit Sub

   If optColumns Then
      Me.chtMain.RowCount = 1
      Me.chtMain.Row = 1
      Me.chtMain.ColumnCount = 3
      Me.chtMain.Column = 1
      Me.chtMain.Data = cmdMain1.Tag
      Me.chtMain.Column = 2
      Me.chtMain.Data = cmdMain2.Tag
      Me.chtMain.Column = 3
      Me.chtMain.Data = cmdMain3.Tag
   Else
      Me.chtMain.ColumnCount = 1
      Me.chtMain.Column = 1
      Me.chtMain.RowCount = 3
      Me.chtMain.Row = 1
      Me.chtMain.Data = cmdMain1.Tag
      Me.chtMain.Row = 2
      Me.chtMain.Data = cmdMain2.Tag
      Me.chtMain.Row = 3
      Me.chtMain.Data = cmdMain3.Tag
   End If

   Select Case True
      Case Me.mnuPopup(2).Checked
         Me.chtMain.chartType = VtChChartType2dPie
      Case Me.mnuPopup(3).Checked
         If Me.mnuPopup(0).Checked Then
            Me.chtMain.chartType = VtChChartType3dArea
         Else
            Me.chtMain.chartType = VtChChartType2dArea
         End If
      Case Me.mnuPopup(4).Checked
         If Me.mnuPopup(0).Checked Then
            Me.chtMain.chartType = VtChChartType3dBar
         Else
            Me.chtMain.chartType = VtChChartType2dBar
         End If
```

```
        Case Me.mnuPopup(5).Checked
           If Me.mnuPopup(0).Checked Then
              Me.chtMain.chartType = VtChChartType3dLine
           Else
              Me.chtMain.chartType = VtChChartType2dLine
           End If
     End Select
  End Sub
```

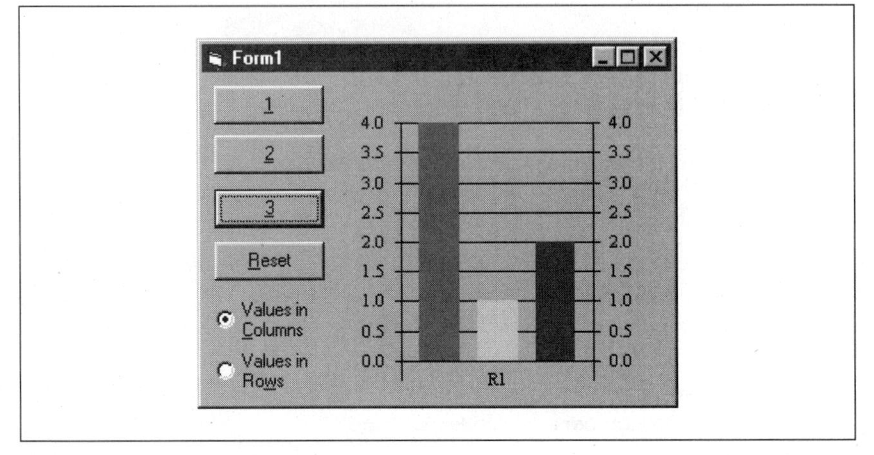

Figure 5-45: The MSChart code example

MSFlexGrid Control

Like both the DataGrid control and the Microsoft Horizontal FlexGrid control, the MSFlexGrid control is designed to display tabular data—that is, data stored in rows or columns. In contrast to other data controls, the MSFlexGrid control has some limitations and a number of strengths. Its two major weaknesses are:

- When the MSFlexGrid control is bound to a data source using the DataSource property, the resulting recordset is read-only. Although various machinations can be used to "extend" the control by adding editing capability programmatically, this is probably more trouble than it's worth.
- The control cannot bind to an ADO data source.

Its strengths are equally notable:

- The availability of several methods to get data into the control. Your application doesn't necessarily have to rely on a bound data source.
- An ability to easily sort records based on their values in particular columns.
- Support for cell merging and pivoting.
- The ability to designate portions of the grid that remain fixed while the others can be scrolled by the user.
- The capability of displaying images as part of the grid's data.

The Microsoft FlexGrid control is shipped with the Professional and Enterprise editions of Visual Basic; its filename is *MSFLXGRD.OCX*.

Defining the Data Source

The starting point—and, depending on the role that the MSFlexGrid will play in your application, sometimes the only step involved—in using the control is to select one of the available methods to place data into it. (Note that all but the first of these methods apply as well to modifying existing values in some or all of the grid.) These methods are:

Binding to a data source
: By using the DataSource property, you can link the MSFlexGrid with a Data control on the same Form object. Note, however, that this must be done at design time; it cannot be done at runtime. This means that the statement:

```
Set flxMain.DataSource = datMain     'WRONG
```

generates a syntax error. In addition, when the DataSource property is set, the MSFlexGrid's recordset becomes read-only. See Chapter 2 for details.

The MSFlexGrid control can be bound only to the intrinsic Data control, not the ADO Data Control. Conversely, the MSHFlexGrid (Hierarchical) can be bound only to an ADO Data Control.

Adding rows to the MSFlexGrid programmatically
: The MSFlexGrid control supports an AddItem method that allows you to add data to the grid one row at a time. Individual columns within the row should be separated by tab characters. The syntax of the AddItem method is:

```
objFlexGrid.AddItem Item, [Index]
```

where `Item` is a delimited string containing text for each column in the row separated by `vbTab` characters and `Index` is the row at which the data is to be inserted. If `Index` is 0, the row is inserted before any existing rows; if `Index` is absent, the row is appended after all existing rows.

Adding a range of data programmatically
: It is possible to extract a range of data from a data source and to import it into the MSDataGrid without binding to the data source. For this purpose, the Clip property, which sets or returns the cells in a selected region of the MSFlexGrid, is used.

To populate some portion of the grid, the steps are as follows:

a. Select the region of the MSFlexGrid to which you'd like to import the data.

b. Call a property or method of the data source that's compatible with the Clip property. (The Clip property expects the text content of the selected fields to be in a delimited string in which columns are delimited by the vbTab character and rows are delimited by the vbCr character.) RDO, for example, supports a GetClipString method that provides text that the MSFlexGrid control can successfully import. You can also clip data from one region of the MSFlexGrid and place it in another.

c. Assign the result to the MSFlexGrid's Clip property. If more cells are provided than are selected in the control, the extra values are ignored.

Adding data cell by cell

Finally, you can select a particular cell and programmatically place a value in it. There are a number of ways to do this:

By working with the current cell

You can set the current cell and then assign the value you'd like to place in the cell to the Text property. The Text property contains the text contents of the current cell. (Note that you can both assign and retrieve the cell's contents using the Text property.) The following code fragment shows how you might populate a range:

```
For iRow = 0 To 9
   flxMain.Row = iRow
   For iCol = 0 to 9
      flxMain.Col = iCol
      flxMain.Text = strArray(iRow, iCol) ' string _
                          array populated from a file
   Next
Next
```

Note, though, that this can have unintended consequences. When you set the Text property, if the FillStyle property is set to flexFillRepeat, multiple cells will be affected by this property.

Adding data to a one-dimensional array

Rather than setting the current cell and assigning data to it, you can leave the current cell unchanged and still selected by assigning values to the TextArray property array, which contains an element for each cell in the MSFlexGrid control. A cell can be located by using the following formula:

```
Me.flxMain.TextArray( lDesiredRow * Me.flxMain.Cols _
                     + lDesiredCol) = sNewValue
```

Setting an element of the TextArray property array updates the corresponding cell's contents.

Adding data to a two-dimensional array

Since the grid is two-dimensional, you may find it easiest to use a two-dimensional array for populating the MSFlexGrid control. The TextMatrix property array is a two-dimensional array, each element of which corresponds to a cell in the MSFlexGrid control and contains the text contents of that cell. The first index of the array corresponds to the desired row, while the second index corresponds to the desired column.

Setting the Control's Appearance

A number of properties allow you to configure the appearance of the MSFlexGrid and the way in which it interfaces with users. Changes to most of these properties are reflected in the appearance of the control as soon as the property value is changed. The values of all color properties are either RGB colors or system color constants.

CellAlignment, CellPictureAlignment properties, ColAlignment property array

The CellAlignment property controls how the contents of the current cell are aligned both vertically and horizontally. The CellPictureAlignment controls how an image within the current cell or a range of cells is aligned. If the FillStyle property is set to `flexFillSingle`, it affects the current cell; if `flexFillRepeat`, it affects the selected range. Each element of the ColAlignment property array contains the alignment for all cells in the corresponding column. The following table lists the `AlignmentSettings` constants for these three properties:

Constant	*Value*	*Description*
`flexAlignLeftTop`	0	The contents of the cell are aligned to the upper-left corner of the cell.
`flexAlignLeftCenter`	1	The contents of the cell are aligned to the left edge of the cell—centered from top to bottom. This is the default for string data.
`flexAlignLeftBottom`	2	The contents of the cell are aligned to the lower-left corner of the cell.
`flexAlignCenterTop`	3	The contents of the cell are centered at the top of the cell.
`flexAlignCenterCenter`	4	The contents of the cell are centered within the cell.
`flexAlignCenterBottom`	5	The contents of the cell are centered at the bottom of the cell.
`flexAlignRightTop`	6	The contents of the cell are aligned to the upper-right corner of the cell.
`flexAlignRightCenter`	7	The contents of the cell are aligned to the right edge of the cell—centered from top to bottom. This is the default for numeric data.
`flexAlignRightBottom`	8	The contents of the cell are aligned to the lower-right corner of the cell.
`flexAlignGeneral`	9	Strings are aligned `flexAlignLeftCenter`, and numbers are aligned `flexAlignRightCenter`. This value is not available for the CellPictureAlignment property.

CellBackColor, CellForeColor property

These properties set the foreground color (CellForeColor) and background color (CellBackColor) of the current cell. Note that these values return 0 unless the cell's foreground and background colors have been explicitly set.

CellFontName, CellFontSize, CellFontBold, CellFontItalic, CellFontStrikeThrough, CellFontUnderline, CellFontWidth properties

Each of these properties controls an aspect of the font used for the current cell. CellFontName contains the name of the font. CellFontSize contains the size (height) of the font in points, while CellFontWidth contains the width of the font in points. CellFontBold, CellFontItalic, CellFontStrikeThrough, and CellFontUnderline each contain `True` for the named text style or `False` for normal text.

CellTextStyle, TextStyle, TextStyleFixed properties

Set the appearance of text in the current cell, the entire control, and fixed rows and columns, respectively. Note that setting the CellTextStyle value applies to the cell that is the current cell at the time the property value is changed and not to whatever cell happens to be current at any particular time. Possible values for these properties are the members of the `TextStyleSetting` enumeration: 0–flexTextFlat for no 3-D effect, 1–flexTextRaised for a raised effect, 2–flexTextInset for an inset effect, 3–flexTextRaisedLight for raised text with a lesser 3-D effect, and finally, 4–flexTextInsetLight for inset text with a lesser 3-D effect.

ColIsVisible property array, RowIsVisible property array

Indicate whether the row or column in a particular ordinal position is visible (`True`) or hidden (`False`). Although the documentation mentions this is a read/write property, it is read-only. To hide a visible row, set its height to 0:

```
if flxMain.RowIsVisible(lPos) Then _
   flxMain.RowHeight(lPos) = 0
```

To hide a visible column, set its width to 0:

```
if flxMain.ColIsVisible(lPos) Then _
   flxMain.ColWidth(lPos) = 0
```

ColPosition property array, RowPosition property array

These property arrays are used to determine or adjust the location of a column or row in the MSFlexGrid control. Setting the element of the ColPosition array that corresponds to a column to a valid new column position moves that column, along with any data, to that new location. Setting the element of the RowPosition array that corresponds to a row to a valid new row position moves that row, along with any data, to that new location.

FixedCols, FixedRows properties

An MSFlexGrid control can contain any number of "fixed" columns and "fixed" rows that do not scroll when the rest of the columns or rows are scrolled. The FixedCols property contains the number of columns to lock in position in this manner. The FixedRows property contains the number of rows to lock.

FocusRect property

Indicates how to highlight the current cell in the MSFlexGrid control. Possible values include one of the `FocusRectSettings` constants: 0–flexFocusNone for no highlighting; 1–flexFocusLight, the default, for a rectangle around the current cell; or 2–flexFocusHeavy for a bold rectangle around the current cell.

FontWidth property

Sets the width of the font (as opposed to its height, the normal measurement of font size) in points to be used throughout the MSFlexGrid control.

ForeColorFixed, ForeColorSel properties

These properties set the foreground color for the fixed columns and rows (ForeColorFixed) and any selected cells (ForeColorSel). If these are not set, the control's ForeColor property is used.

FormatString property

The FormatString property can be set to a preformatted string in order to completely format an MSFlexGrid control. The string can contain information about the widths, alignment, and header text of each column and the height and header text of each row. The FormatString contains two sections separated by a semicolon (;). The first section contains information about columns; the second contains information about rows. The column section contains the header text of each column, preceded by a character to denote alignment, separated by pipe characters (|). The character used for alignment is a left angle bracket (<) for left alignment, a caret (^) for center alignment, or a right angle bracket (>) for right alignment. The row section contains the header text of each row separated by pipe characters (|).

GridColor, GridColorFixed properties

These properties set the color of the gridlines for the entire control (GridColor) or just the gridlines within the fixed rows and columns (GridColorFixed).

GridLines, GridLinesFixed properties

These properties control whether the control (GridLines) and/or the fixed columns and rows (GridLinesFixed) have gridlines drawn. When either of these properties is set to `True`, the default, gridlines will appear in the appropriate areas. When either is set to `False`, no gridlines will appear.

GridLineWidth property

Sets the width (in number of pixels) of gridlines in the MSFlexGrid control.

HighLight property

The Highlight property determines the appearance of a *range* of selected cells (that is, a multicell selection) within the MSFlexGrid control. Possible values include one of the `HighLightSettings` constants: 0–flexHightlightNever to never highlight the selection, 1–flexHighlightAlways to always highlight the selection (the default value), or 2–flexHighlightWithFocus to highlight the selection only when the MSFlexGrid control has the focus.

ColWidth property array

The ColWidth property array has one element for each column in the grid, plus an element at -1. Each element contains the width in twips of its corresponding column. Changing this value resizes the column. Setting an element of the ColWidth property array to -1 resets the width of the column according to its font. Setting an element of the ColWidth property array to 0 makes that column invisible. Setting the -1 element to a new value resizes all columns in the control, a behavior not noted in the documentation.

RowHeight property array
The RowHeight property array has one element for each row of the grid, plus an element at -1. Each element contains the height in twips of its corresponding row. Changing this value resizes the row. Setting an element of the RowHeight property array to -1 resets the height of the row according to its font and the RowHeightMin property. Setting the -1 element to a new value resizes all rows in the control.

RowHeightMin property
Defines the minimum height to which any row in the MSFlexGrid control can be resized.

ScrollBars property
Controls whether the MSFlexGrid displays scrollbars. Possible values include 0–flexScrollNone for no scrollbars, 1–flexScrollHorizontal for a horizontal scrollbar only, 2–flexScrollVertical for a vertical scrollbar only, or 3–flexScrollBoth (the default value) for both a horizontal and vertical scrollbar.

WordWrap property
When the WordWrap property is set to `False`, text that does not fit in a cell extends past the right edge of the cell on the same line. When it is set to `True`, the contents of the cell are broken into multiple lines if they do not fit. Note, however, that rows are not resized to accommodate the changed formatting of the text.

Defining the Grid's Interface

A number of properties allow you to determine or to control how the user interacts with the MSFlexGrid control. You can, for example, allow the user to resize rows and columns or determine what is selected when the user attempts to select a cell. The properties that either indicate the state of the grid's interface or can be used to control how the control interacts with the user are:

AllowBigSelection property
Determines the response to clicking on a column header. When set to `True`, its default value, the entire column is selected. When set to `False`, the header itself is selected.

AllowUserResizing property
Determines whether columns and rows can be resized by the user. When set to 0–flexResizeNone, its default value, the user cannot resize columns. When set to 1–flexResizeColumns, 2–flexResizeRows, or 3–flexResizeBoth, the user can resize the appropriate object by positioning the mouse between two headers (row or column as appropriate) and dragging to a new location.

ScrollTrack property
Determines whether the MSFlexGrid control should scroll its contents when the user drags the scroll box on a scrollbar. When set to `True`, the grid's contents are updated as the scroll box is dragged. When set to `False`, the contents of the control are updated only when the scroll box is dropped.

SelectionMode property

Controls how the user can select cells in the MSFlexGrid control. Possible values include 0–flexSelectionFree to allow the user to select cells as desired, 1–flexSelectionByRow to select entire rows only, or 2–flexSelectionByColumn to select entire columns only.

Determining Control Information

Virtually every event-driven program needs to track the actions of the user in some way. From knowing what the user has selected as the current cell or range to knowing whether the user has resized rows and columns to determining which cell the user is leaving and which he or she is entering, the MSFlexGrid control provides a number of properties, property arrays, and events that you can use to help you determine the state of the control.

CellTop, CellHeight, CellLeft, CellWidth properties

These properties provide the location (relative to the upper-left corner of the control) and size of the current cell in twips.

Col, Row properties

Together, these properties define the coordinates of the current cell of an MSFlexGrid control. The Col property refers to the column containing the current cell (the first column is column 1), and the Row property refers to the row containing the current cell (the first row is row 1). When used with the ColSel and RowSel properties, a range of cells can be selected.

ColPos property array, RowPos property array

These property arrays are useful in determining the physical location of a particular column, row, or both, thereby giving the location of a cell. An element of the ColPos property array gives the location of the corresponding column relative to the left edge of the MSFlexGrid control. An element of the RowPos property array gives the location of the corresponding row relative to the top of the MSFlexGrid control. All values returned are specified in twips.

Cols, Rows properties

The Cols property indicates the number of columns in the MSFlexGrid control; the Rows property indicates the number of rows. You'd expect this property to be read-only, but it's not: setting either property to a new value adjusts the size of the MSFlexGrid control accordingly. For example, you can delete the rows of a grid with the simple statement:

```
flxMain.Rows = 0
```

ColSel, RowSel properties

When used with the Col and Row properties, these properties form a range of cells that are selected (if their value is retrieved) or will be selected (if their value is being assigned). The range of cells selected will have the cell referenced by Col and Row at one corner and the cell referenced by ColSel and RowSel at the other.

EnterCell, LeaveCell, RowColChange events

These events are fired when the focus is about to leave a cell (LeaveCell), when the focus is about to enter another cell (EnterCell), and when the focus has entered the new cell (RowColChange). This gives the opportunity to validate data entered into the cell being left or to prepare data in the cell being entered. See "Order of Events" later in this section for a detailed description of when the events fire in relation to one another.

LeftCol, TopRow properties
These properties contain the leftmost (LeftCol) and topmost (TopRow) cell visible in the control. Setting these properties to valid values scrolls the MSFlexGrid to place that cell in the appropriate location.

MouseCol, MouseRow properties
These properties return the index of the current column (MouseCol) and row (MouseRow) that the mouse is over.

Scroll event
Fired whenever the MSFlexGrid control is scrolled. The firing of this event is affected by the value of the ScrollTrack property. If ScrollTrack is `False`, only one Scroll event is fired when the scroll box is dropped; if ScrollTrack is `True`, the event is fired repeatedly while the scroll box is being dragged.

SelChange event
Fired whenever the selected cell or selected range of cells is changed. See "Order of Events" later in this section for a detailed description of when the SelChange event fires in relation to EnterCell, LeaveCell, and RowColChange.

Performing Operations with the Data

Once your application places data in the MSFlexGrid control, you can handle it in a variety of ways: you can, for example, add images, sort the data, and merge rows or columns containing common values. The following properties, methods, and events can be used to perform assorted operations on the control's data:

CellPicture property
A picture can be placed in a cell of an MSFlexGrid control by setting the CellPicture property. The picture can be assigned at runtime in many ways, including the *LoadPicture* function, assignment from the Picture property of some other control, and by an ImageList control.

Clear method
Clears all nonformatting data from the MSFlexGrid control.

ColData property array, RowData property array
These properties contain one element for each column (ColData) or row (RowData) and can be assigned any long value. They are very much like the Tag property: it can be used to store application-defined information about the column or row. One such use is to indicate whether a row or a column includes a calculated formula or a sum.

Compare event
Fired when control's data needs to be sorted and the Sort property is set to `flexSortCustom`. The parameters passed to the event handler are:

`Row1`
Index of the first row to be sorted.

`Row2`
Index of the second row to be sorted.

Cmp

Integer passed by reference that, when the procedure returns, determines how *Row1* and *Row2* should be sorted. Possible values are -1 to sort *Row1* before *Row2*, 0 to treat the rows as equal, or 1 to sort *Row2* before *Row1*.

Sorting by using the Compare event and setting the Sort property to `flexSortCustom` is generally slower than any other sorting method. However, it's indispensable when data cannot be sorted using normal means.

FillStyle property

FillStyle is a rather unusual property that determines whether particular operations (such as assigning data to the Text property) apply to only the current cell or to a range of cells. When the FillStyle property is set to 0–flexFillSingle, changes made to the current cell apply to only that cell. When it is set to 1–flexFillRepeat, changes made to the current cell apply to the selected range of cells. Properties whose behavior is affected by the FillStyle property include:

CellBackColor
CellForeColor
CellFontBold
CellFontItalic
CellFontName
CellFontSize
CellFontStrikeThrough
CellFontUnderline
CellFontWidth
CellPicture
CellPictureAlignment
CellTextStyle
Text

MergeCells property

Controls how adjacent rows or columns with identical data can be combined into one cell. The MergeCol and MergeRow property arrays control whether each column or row is merged in the manner defined by the MergeCells property. The value of MergeCells is a member of the `MergeCellsSettings` enum. When set to 0–flexMergeNever, the default value, no merging occurs. When set to 1–flexMergeFree, all columns and rows merge identical data based on the value of the corresponding element of the MergeCol or MergeRow property array. When set to 2–flexMergeRestrictRows, 3–flexMergeRestrictColumns, or 4–flexMergeRestrictBoth, adjacent cells are merged (provided that the MergeCol and MergeRow property arrays allow it) only if previous rows, columns, or both are also merged.

MergeCol property array, MergeRow property array

When the MergeCells property is not set to `flexMergeNever`, the MergeCol and MergeRow property arrays control whether a given column or row is affected by the MergeCells property. Each array has one element for each row or each column of the grid. When an element of the MergeCol property array is set to `True`, the corresponding column is affected by the MergeCells property. When an element of the MergeCol property array is set to `False`, the column is not affected by the MergeCells property. When an element of the MergeRow property array is set to `True`, the corresponding row is affected by the MergeCells property. When an element of the MergeRow property array is set to `False`, the row is not affected by the MergeCells property.

Picture, PictureType properties

The Picture property returns a Picture object containing an image of the entire MSFlexGrid control. The PictureType property determines whether the Picture returned by the Picture property will be color (0–flexPictureColor) or black and white (1–flexPictureMonochrome).

RemoveItem method

Removes a row from the MSFlexGrid control. Its syntax is:

```
objFlexGrid.RemoveItem  Index
```

where *`Index`* is a long indicating the position of the row to be removed.

Sort property

Defines the order in which a range of rows is displayed. The rows to be sorted are determined by the Row and RowSel properties; only entire rows can be sorted. If these properties are different, they represent the upper and lower boundary of the rows to be sorted. If the values are the same, the entire MSFlexGrid is sorted. The columns used by the sort are determined by the Col and ColSel properties. All columns between those represented by the Col and ColSel properties, inclusive, make up the sorting order—that is, the set of key fields—to be used. The Sort property then determines how the rows are sorted. Possible values for the Sort property are:

SortSettings Constant	*Value*	*Description*
`flexSortNone`	0	Not sorted.
`flexSortGenericAscending`	1	Ascending sort; the control determines whether to use strings or numbers for each column in the sort.
`flexSortGenericDescending`	2	Descending sort; the control determines whether to use strings or numbers for each column in the sort.
`flexSortNumericAscending`	3	Ascending order using a numeric sort.
`flexSortNumericDescending`	4	Descending order using a numeric sort.
`flexSortStringNoCaseAscending`	5	Ascending order using a case-insensitive string sort.

SortSettings Constant	*Value*	*Description*
`flexSortNoCaseDescending`	6	Descending order using a case-insensitive string sort.
`flexSortStringAscending`	7	Ascending order using a case-sensitive string sort.
`flexSortStringDescending`	8	Descending order using a case-sensitive string sort.
`flexSortCustom`	9	The Compare event is fired repeatedly to sort the rows.

Order of Events

When the user leaves the current cell to move to a new current cell, the following is the order of events:

1. LeaveCell event.

   The Row and Col properties together give the coordinate of the cell being left.

2. SelChange event

   The Row and Col properties together give the coordinate of the cell being entered.

3. EnterCell event

   The Row and Col properties together give the coordinate of the cell being entered.

4. RowColChange event

   The Row and Col properties together give the coordinate of the cell that was entered.

The order of events when the user selects a row or a column and then changes the selection is somewhat different:

1. LeaveCell event
2. EnterCell event
3. RowColChange event
4. SelChange event

If the user selects a range, the following is the order of events:

1. LeaveCell event
2. SelChange event
3. EnterCell event
4. RowColChange event
5. SelChange event fired repeatedly, a total of `NCol + NRows - 1` times, once for every new row or column selected.

OLE Control

The OLE control, which is also known as the OLE Container control, serves as a container for insertable OLE objects. *Insertable OLE objects* are data or data files that can be created or managed by an application capable of functioning as an OLE server. The OLE control offers two options for handling data:

Linking
: The data resides in a data file that exists apart from the control and the Visual Basic application. This means that other applications can access and modify the data file. When the data file linked to the OLE control is activated from the Visual Basic application, typically by the user double-clicking on the OLE control, an instance of the OLE server application is launched to work with the data file. Linking is useful in two cases: when a data file must be accessible to multiple applications and maintaining multiple copies of the data file is undesirable; and (because embedding, the alternative to linking, tends to create bloated files) when keeping file sizes small is an important consideration.

Embedding
: The data is embedded as an OLE object within the application. This means that, although the data may have been based on an external data file, this copy is now accessible only to the Visual Basic application in which it's embedded. Typically in response to a user double-click, the OLE data object is activated *in place*; that is, some portion of the OLE server application is run within the OLE control container, and the menus of the OLE server application appear in the menu bar of the Visual Basic application. Embedding is useful when performance is important (it typically performs better than linking) and when having local copies of a data file is desirable.

For example, when an OLE control in a VB application is linked to an Excel spreadsheet, the information saved by the VB application indicates where to find the Excel spreadsheet on the system. When an Excel spreadsheet is embedded in an OLE control, all data about the OLE object is saved through the OLE control.

The OLE control/OLE data object can present two interfaces to the user:

- An icon. The default icon is that of the OLE server application, although the icon displayed is customizable. Usually, when the user double-clicks on it, the OLE server application is activated either in place or in a separate instance.
- The OLE object itself. For linked objects, the OLE control saves an image of the data along with a reference to the file containing the data. For embedded objects, the OLE control saves an image of the data along with the data file itself. Typically, the OLE control is a display-only medium until the user double clicks, when the OLE server application is activated either in place or in a separate instance.

The OLE data object can be defined either at design time or at runtime.

Defining the OLE Object

This section first lists the ways to define an OLE object at design time, then catalogs the ways to do it at runtime.

Design-Time Definition

When you know in advance either the specific OLE object (like, for example, a range of an Excel spreadsheet) that a particular application will display or the type of data file (like a Word document) that the OLE control will handle, you can provide its definition to the OLE control at design time.

The Insert Object dialog. When it is first positioned on a form at design time, the OLE control opens the Insert Object dialog, shown in Figure 5-46, and uses it to set a number of the control's basic properties. (The dialog is also available at design time by selecting the control, right-clicking, and selecting Insert Object from its context menu.)

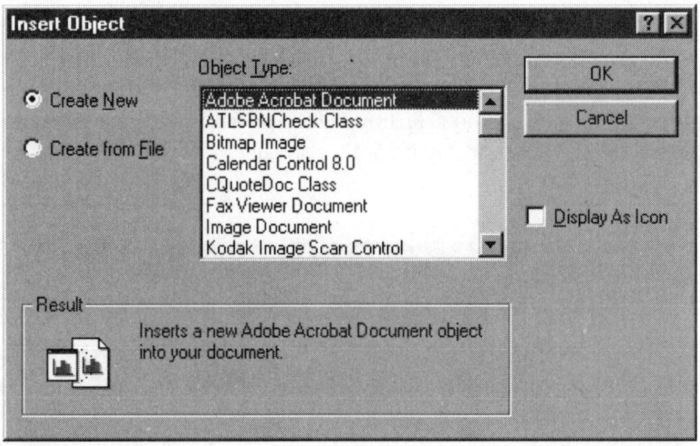

Figure 5-46: The Insert Object dialog

Using the dialog, you can create the following kinds of OLE documents:

New embedded document with data displayed
: Select the Object Type, check Create New.

New embedded document displayed as an icon
: Select the Object Type, check Create New, check Display As Icon.

Embedded document with data displayed
: Select the Object Type, check Create from File, select the filename.

Embedded document displayed as an icon
: Select the Object Type, check Create from File, select the filename, check Display As Icon.

Linked document with data displayed

Select the Object Type, check Create from File, select the filename, check Display As Icon, check Link (a checkbox that appears when Create from File is selected).

Linked document displayed as an icon

Select the Object Type, check Create from File, select the filename, check Display As Icon, check Link (a checkbox that appears when Create from File is selected).

Insert Object Dialog and OLE Control Settings

The selections made in the Insert Object dialog automatically set the OLE control's Class, DisplayType, OLEType, SourceDoc, and SourceItem properties. For details on these properties, see Chapter 6, *Properties.*

Pasting from the Clipboard. If the Clipboard contains data capable of being handled as an insertable object, it can be defined as an OLE object by selecting the OLE control, right-clicking, and selecting Paste Special from the context menu. The Paste Special dialog, shown in Figure 5-47, appears.

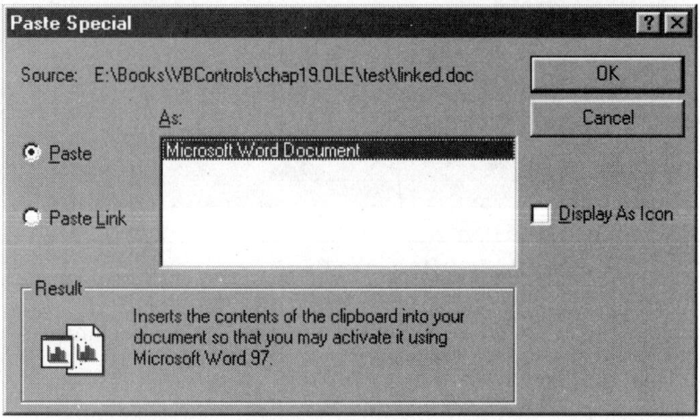

Figure 5-47: The Paste Special dialog

Using the dialog, you can create the following kinds of OLE documents:

Embedded document with data displayed

Select the data format if multiple formats are displayed, check Paste.

Embedded document displayed as an icon

Select the data format if multiple formats are displayed, check Paste, check Display As Icon.

Linked document with data displayed

Select the data format if multiple formats are displayed, check Paste Link.

Linked document displayed as an icon

Select the data format if multiple formats are displayed, check Paste Link, check Display As Icon.

Typically, the Paste Link option is unavailable if the entire contents of a document have been placed on the Clipboard; it is available if only a range or some portion of a document has been placed on the Clipboard, and the resulting link will be to only that portion of the document that was copied to the Clipboard.

Using the Context Menu to create an embedded or linked document. If the OLE control's SourceDoc property (which defines the document to be embedded in the control or to which the control is to link) has been set to an existing document, that document can be embedded in or linked to the OLE control by selecting the control and right-clicking. On the context menu, selecting Create Link creates a linked OLE object; selecting Create Embedded Object creates an embedded OLE object.

Runtime Definition

Just as the design-time environment offers numerous ways of defining the OLE data object to the OLE control, so too does the runtime environment.

The Insert Object dialog. At runtime, the Insert Object dialog, shown in Figure 5-46, can be opened by calling the OLE control's InsertObjDlg method; the method takes no parameters. Unfortunately, though, the dialog will not reflect the state of the control's current properties when it is displayed. Its use, therefore, requires a fair level of sophistication from the user.

Pasting from the Clipboard. At runtime, the Paste Special dialog, shown in Figure 5-47, can be opened by calling the OLE control's PasteSpecialDlg method; the method takes no parameters. The options selected in the dialog cannot be controlled programmatically. In addition, if the Clipboard does not contain an appropriate data format, runtime error 31035, "Incorrect Clipboard format," is generated. This can be prevented by checking the value of the PasteOK property before displaying the dialog; for details, see "Using the Clipboard," later in this section.

Drag and drop. If you implement support for Drag and Drop, the user can open an OLE object by dragging it and dropping it onto the OLE control. The following are the steps involved:

1. Set the OLEDropAllowed property to `True` to allow the OLE control to serve as a drop target. The default value is `False`.
2. Set the OLETypeAllowed property to define the kind of OLE object (linked, embedded, or either) that can be dropped onto the control. The OLETypeAllowed property is described in "Defining the Interface," later in this section.

The OLE container control itself handles the process of embedding or linking to dropped objects. Note, however, that when the OLEDropAllowed property is set to `True`, the OLE container control does not receive any DragDrop events, which makes it difficult both to control the objects that can be dropped on the control and to determine when and what kind of object has been dropped.

Using properties and methods in code. Defining an OLE object programmatically at runtime requires calls to either of the following methods, depending on the object to be inserted and the relationship of the object to its container:

CreateEmbed

Creates an embedded OLE object. Its syntax is:

```
objOLE.CreateEmbed(SourceDoc, [Class])
```

where *SourceDoc* and *Class* are the filename and the ProgID of the OLE object; these values are assigned to the *SourceDoc* and *Class* properties, respectively; for details, see the discussion of each property later in this section.

To embed an existing OLE document, *SourceDoc* must be a valid filename, and *Class* is optional; the OLE control can determine the class from the contents of the file. To embed a new document, *SourceDoc* must be a null string, and *Class* must be the programmatic identifier of the OLE data type. In order to successfully embed an OLE object, the OLETypeAllowed property must be set to either `vbOLEEmbedded` or `vbOLEEither`.

CreateLink

Creates a link to an existing OLE object. Its syntax is:

```
objOLE.CreateLink SourceDoc, [SourceItem]
```

where *SourceDoc* is the filename of the OLE document and *SourceItem* is an optional unit of data (such as a Word bookmark or an Excel range) within *SourceDoc*. These two parameters are assigned to the properties of the same name; for details, see the discussion of each property later in this section. For the method call to succeed, the OLETypeAllowed property must be set to either `vbOLEEmbedded` or `vbOLEEither`.

Calls to the CreateLink or CreateEmbed methods will ignore any property values that have already been assigned. Because of this, a code fragment like:

```
objOLE.SourceItem = "Bookmark1"
objOLE.CreateLink "LinkedDoc.Doc"
```

will not produce the intended result.

Among the properties set when either method is called are the following, whose values you can then retrieve to determine the attributes of the current OLE object:

Class

Contains the class name (also known as the programmatic identifier, or ProgID) of the embedded object contained by the OLE control. ProgIDs take the form *application.objecttype.version* (the version-dependent ProgID) or *application.objecttype* (the version-independent ProgID).

Table 5-1 shows some common programmatic identifiers; their presence or absence on a particular system depends on the presence of the software that assigns that ProgID. ProgIDs are defined in the system registry as direct subkeys of `HKEY_CLASSES_ROOT`.*

Note that you can find the ProgIDs of OLE data objects that are available on the development system by clicking the button beside the Class property value in the Properties window; this opens the Choose Class dialog, like the one shown in Figure 5-48, which displays the actual programmatic identifiers that are available. (In contrast, the Insert Object dialog, shown in Figure 5-46, displays the descriptive names of insertable OLE objects rather than their ProgIDs.)

There is some advantage to assigning the Class property at runtime rather than design time. In cases where both version-independent and version-dependent ProgIDs are available for the same object, assigning the value at runtime allows you to use the version-independent ProgID. The Insert Object and Choose Class dialogs include only the version-dependent ProgID if both are available.

Table 5-1: Some Common Version-Independent ProgIDs

ProgID	*Description*
Excel.Sheet	Microsoft Excel sheet
mplayer	Media clip
Paint.Picture	Bitmap image
PowerPoint.Show	PowerPoint presentation
soundrec	Wave sound
Word.Document	Microsoft Word document

Controls O–R

OLEType

Read-only property that indicates the type of OLE object contained in the OLE control. Possible values are 0–vbOLELinked for a linked object, 1–vbOLEEmbedded for an embedded object, or 3–vbOLENone if no OLE object is contained.

SourceDoc

Specifies the filename that contains an insertable OLE object. In the case of a linked object, this is the object to which the control will link. In the case of an embedded object, this is the template file that will be copied and embedded in the control.

* Specifically, the Class property can be assigned any ProgID that is marked as Insertable (i.e., the ProgID key has a subkey named Insertable in the system registry. This means that the object is capable of being embedded in a container application.

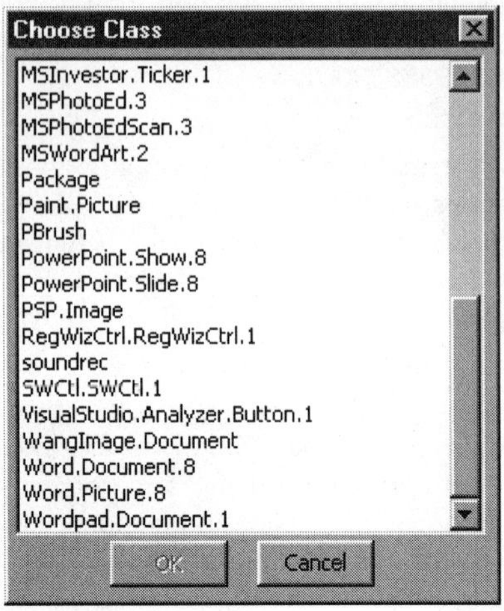

Choose Class

MSInvestor.Ticker.1
MSPhotoEd.3
MSPhotoEdScan.3
MSWordArt.2
Package
Paint.Picture
PBrush
PowerPoint.Show.8
PowerPoint.Slide.8
PSP.Image
RegWizCtrl.RegWizCtrl.1
soundrec
SWCtl.SWCtl.1
VisualStudio.Analyzer.Button.1
WangImage.Document
Word.Document.8
Word.Picture.8
Wordpad.Document.1

OK Cancel

Figure 5-48: The Choose Class dialog

Is an Object Present?

In many cases, attempting to retrieve a property value when an object is not present in the OLE control container results in a syntax error (in this case, runtime error 31004, "No object"). To prevent this, you can check the state of the control with a line of code like the following:

```
If Not objOLE.OLEType = vbOLENone Then
```

SourceItem

Defines the specific data that's to be sent or retrieved from the linked OLE object named *SourceDoc*. Each application that supports insertable OLE objects has its own syntax for designating an insertable OLE object's data unit. For example, a named bookmark can be used to designate a particular data set in Microsoft Word, while a range or a named range can be used to designate a particular data set in Microsoft Excel.

Defining the Interface

You can define both the appearance of the OLE object and the way it interacts with the user by setting the following properties either explicitly or, in the case of the DisplayType property, through the Insert Object and Paste Special dialogs:

AutoActivate property

Controls the way the OLE object is activated by the user. Possible values are 0–vbOLEActivateManual, where the object is activated only through code; 1–vbOLEActivateGetFocus, where the object is activated if it gets the focus;

2–vbOLEActivateDoubleClick (the default value), where the object is activated when it is double-clicked; or 3–vbOLEActivateAuto, where the OLE object controls the way it is activated.

If you select `vbOLEActivateManual`, or otherwise activate the application that handles the OLE object, you can call the OLE control's DoVerb method.

When AutoActivate is set to `vbOLEActivateGetFocus`, only objects that activate normally on a single click are activated when the object gets the focus.

AutoVerbMenu property

When set to `True` (its default value), the user can right-click the OLE object to pop up a menu of verbs (see "Using Verbs to Control an Object," later in this section) supported by the object. When set to `False`, the menu does not pop up automatically.

If AutoVerbMenu is set to `True` and the user selects a pop-up menu option, the action indicated by that verb is carried out automatically, without the need to supply additional code.

DisplayType property

An OLE object can be displayed in the OLE control as an icon, or the contents of the OLE object can be displayed. When the DisplayType property is set to 0–vbOLEDisplayContent (its default value), the contents are displayed. When set to 1–vbOLEDisplayIcon, an icon is displayed.

The property must be set before an OLE object is assigned to the control; otherwise, attempting to modify the property will have no effect.

HostName property

When available, contains the name of the host application as it appears in its window titlebar. Some applications will not return a HostName property value. It is most useful to update the containing form's Caption property when an embedded document is being edited in an OLE control.

OLEDropAllowed property

When set to `False` (its default value), OLE objects that are being dragged cannot be dropped onto the OLE control. When set to `True`, insertable OLE objects can be dropped onto the control. Whether they are embedded or linked depends on the value of the OLETypeAllowed property.

OLETypeAllowed property

The OLETypeAllowed property controls the type(s) of OLE objects that the OLE control can contain. Possible values are 0–vbOLELinked for linked objects, 1–vbOLEEmbedded for embedded objects, or 2–vbOLEEither (the default value) where the object itself determines its type.

SizeMode property

Controls the size and positioning of the OLE object in its container. Its setting is particularly important for embedded objects because of in-place activation, where the size of the container defines the total editing or browsing area. Possible values are 0–vbOLESizeClip (the default), where the OLE object is sized normally and portions that extend outside the OLE control are clipped; 1–vbOLESizeStretch, where the object is stretched both vertically and horizontally to fit inside the OLE control when it is larger than the control; 2–vbOLESizeAutoSize, where the OLE control resizes to fit the entire OLE object; or 3–vbOLESizeZoom, where the OLE object is resized proportionally to fit inside the OLE control. When the OLE control is resized due to its SizeMode property being set to `vbOLESizeAutoSize`, the Resize event is fired to allow other elements on the form, as well as the form itself, to adjust to the new size.

UpdateOptions property

Unlike an embedded OLE object, which is contained by the OLE control and is accessible only to it, a linked object can be accessed concurrently by other applications. The UpdateOptions property controls how often such linked data shown by the OLE control is updated to reflect possible changes made by other applications. Possible values are 0–vbOLEAutomatic, where changes are reflected immediately when they are made; 1–vbOLEFrozen, where data is updated only when it is saved in the host application; and 2–vbOLEManual, where data is not updated at all. Even when the UpdateOptions property is set to `vbOLEManual`, data can be updated by using the Update method.

Object Communication

Once the OLE object is bound (linked or embedded) to the OLE control, the following properties help to get information from and provide information to the OLE object.

Is the OLE Server Running?

AppIsRunning property

When the AppIsRunning property returns `True`, the application associated with the contained OLE object is currently running. If the application is not running, setting the AppIsRunning property to `True` launches that application. Although setting the AppIsRunning property to `False` does not terminate the application if the OLE object has the focus, the application will close when the object loses the focus if AppIsRunning is set to `False`.

Using the Clipboard

The Clipboard plays a dual role as a general medium for exchanging data between applications:

- It can define the data to be handled by the OLE control, thereby defining as well the OLE server that handles that data. This was discussed in the earlier section, "Defining the OLE Object."
- It can contain data to be embedded into the data stream of an existing object. For instance, the Clipboard might be used to hold an image that is pasted into a Microsoft Word document.

This section surveys the properties and methods that are related to Clipboard operations. Note that some methods in particular, like InsertObjDlg and PasteSpecialDlg, are covered in "Defining the OLE Object," earlier in this section.

Copy method

Copies the OLE object to the Clipboard. Its syntax is simply:

```
objOLE.Copy
```

where `objOLE` is a reference to the OLE control.

Paste method

The Paste method copies an OLE object from the Windows Clipboard into the OLE container control. Its syntax is simply:

```
objOLE.Paste
```

where `objOLE` is a reference to the OLE control. Before using the Paste method, set the OLETypeAllowed property to the data types and check that the PasteOK property is set to `True`. If the OLE object could not be successfully pasted, any existing OLE object in the control is deleted.

PasteOK property

Returns `True` if the contents of the Windows Clipboard are valid to be pasted into the OLE control; otherwise, it returns `False`. Whether an object can be pasted is based on a variety of factors, including the value of the OLETypeAllowed property.

Using Verbs to Control an Object

Every automation object supports a set of *verbs*, which are labels that describe some action the OLE server is capable of performing. (These are the items that appear on the context menu when the user right-clicks on the OLE control container when the AutoVerbMenu property is set to `True`.) You need only "send" it that verb in order to cause it to perform that action. The following properties and methods are used when working with the contained OLE object's verbs:

DoVerb method

Initiates the action indicated by a verb. Its syntax is:

```
objOLE.DoVerb(index)
```

where *`index`* is either the index of the verb in the ObjectVerbs property array or one of the following values:

Constant	*Value*	*Description*
`vbOLEPrimary`	0	Initiate the object's default verb.
`vbOLEShow`	-1	Edit the object.
`vbOLEOpen`	-2	Open the object in its own window.
`vbOLEHide`	-3	Hide the host application if it is visible.
`vbOLEUIActivate`	-4	Activate an object that supports in-place activation.

Controls O–R

Constant	Value	Description
vbOLEInPlaceActivate	-5	Activate an object when the OLE control gets the focus.
vbOLEDiscardUndoState	-6	Cause the application to lose any undo information.

If *index* is not supplied, the object's default verb—the verb found at objOLE.ObjectVerbs(0)—will be executed.

FetchVerbs method

Updates the ObjectVerbs and the ObjectVerbFlags property arrays and the ObjectVerbsCount property.

ObjectVerbs property array

A zero-based string array containing the verbs supported by the object in the OLE container control. The verb at element zero is the default verb that will be executed if no verb is explicitly specified. Typically, it is a duplicate member of the property array; the default verb also appears as another element of the array. Note that the verb strings usually contain ampersand characters to indicate which letter serves as the item's accelerator key in a context menu.

ObjectVerbsCount property

The total number of elements in the ObjectVerb and ObjectVerbFlags property arrays.

ObjectVerbFlags property array

A zero-based array, each element of which indicates the state of the corresponding member of the ObjectVerbs property array. The following flags are used:

Constant	Value	Description
vbOLEFlagEnabled	0	The verb is enabled.
vbOLEFlagGrayed	1	The verb is grayed.
vbOLEFlagDisabled	2	The verb is disabled.
vbOLEFlagSeparator	8	The item is a menu separator bar.

You can determine whether a particular flag is set by using a code fragment like the following:

```
If (Me.oleMain.ObjectVerbFlags(1) And _
    vbOLEFLagDisabled) Then
  'The Verb is disabled.
Else
  'The Verb is not disabled.
End If
```

The values in the ObjectVerbs array are available for use with the DoVerb method.

Handling Data Formats

When sending data to or retrieving data from an OLE object, it is necessary to know what type of data the OLE object can accept and/or is expecting. The following properties help to determine whether it is possible to use automation to exchange data with an OLE object.

Note that to retrieve values from the ObjectAcceptFormatsCount, ObjectGetFormatsCount, ObjectAcceptFormats, or ObjectGetFormats properties, the OLE server application must be running (i.e., the control's IsAppRunning property must return `True` or be set to `True`).

Data, DataText properties

The Data and DataText properties are used to send or retrieve data from the OLE object's parent application. The Data property should contain a handle to a valid object. The DataText property should contain a valid string. The format of the data being passed is set by the Format property.

Format property

The Format property contains the format of the data to be sent or retrieved from the OLE object's parent application using the Data or DataText property. Valid values for the Format property should be derived using the ObjectAcceptsFormats and ObjectGetFormats properties.

ObjectAcceptFormats property array

A zero-based string array containing one element for each format the OLE object's host application can accept; see the following list for some common format types. The values in the ObjectAcceptFormats array can be used to set the Format property to transfer data to the OLE object's host application. You can enumerate the array using the ObjectAcceptFormatsCount property, as shown in the following code fragment:

```
If oleMain.ObjectAcceptFormatsCount > 0 Then
   For iCtr = 0 To oleMain.ObjectAcceptFormatsCount-1
      Debug.Print oleMain.ObjectAcceptsFormats(iCtr)
   Next iCtr
End If
```

Some common format types are:

CF_BTIMAP
CF_DIB
CF_DIF
CF_PICTMETAFILE
CF_SYLK
CFTEXT
Rich Text Format

ObjectAcceptFormatsCount property

Indicates the number of elements in the ObjectGetFormats property array.

ObjectGetFormats property array

A zero-based string array containing one element for each format the OLE object's host application can provide; the preceding list shows some common format types. The values in the ObjectGetFormats array can be used to set the Format property to transfer data from the OLE object's host application. You can enumerate the array using the ObjectGetFormatsCount property, as shown in the following code fragment:

```
If oleMain.ObjectGetFormatsCount > 0 Then
   For iCtr = 0 To oleMain.ObjectGetFormatsCount - 1
      Debug.Print Me.oleMain.ObjectGetFormats(iCtr)
   Next iCtr
End If
```

ObjectGetFormatsCount property
Indicates the number of elements in the ObjectGetFormats property array.

Using Automation

By using the OLE control's Object property, you can retrieve a reference to some portion of the OLE server application's object model. You can then use that reference to access the object's properties and methods, thereby controlling the object programmatically through a process called *automation*.

For example, if the OLE control contains a Word document, you can retrieve the document name with the following code:

```
strName = Me.OLE1.Object.Name
```

This is equivalent to the following line of code, which requires that a reference to the Word object model be added to the Visual Basic project:

```
strName = Word.Application.Documents(1).Name
```

However, using the OLE control's object property is usually not recommended for two reasons:

- The object returned by the OLE control's object property is late bound; that is, because the OLE control can serve as a container for any object that supports embedding, Visual Basic is unable to resolve references to that object's properties and methods at compile time and instead must resolve them at runtime. In general, late binding offers extremely poor performance.
- Not all of the OLE server application's object model is necessarily exposed through the OLE control's object property. In the case of our Word example, for instance, the top-level object to which you can retrieve a reference is the Document object; the Application object and the Documents collection, which are the parents of the Document object, are not programmatically accessible.

Unless you don't know in advance the type of object that the OLE control will hold, it's far better to add a reference to that object type to your project and control it more directly using early binding.

Persisting the Data

Ordinarily, when you use the OLE control, its data is not loaded from or saved to disk. The control features three methods to provide for data persistence:

ReadFromFile, SaveToFile, SaveToOle1File methods

These methods allow OLE objects to be loaded from and saved to disk. All three methods have the same syntax:

```
objOLE.ReadFromFile Filenumber
objOLE.SaveToFile Filenumber
objOLE.SaveToOle1File Filenumber
```

where ***Filenumber*** is the number of a file that has been opened as a binary file. SaveToOle1File saves the file in OLE Version 1.0 format. The following syntax can be used to save the data from an open OLE object:

```
Open "c:\myfile.dat" For Binary Access Write As #1
oleMain.SaveToFile 1
Close #1
```

The following syntax can be used to load saved data into an open OLE object:

```
Open "c:\myfile.dat" For Binary Access Read As #1
oleMain.ReadFromFile 1
Close #1
```

Closing Communication

When you've finished manipulating the data, call the OLE control's Close method to terminate the connection between the OLE object and its server application:

Close method

Terminates the connection between the OLE control and the contained OLE object.

Writing Event Handlers

ObjectMove

Anytime the user resizes or moves an active OLE object, the ObjectMove event is fired. The ObjectMove event provides parameters for object location and size (***Left, Top, Width, Height***). If the ObjectMove event finishes without the OLE control actually resizing, the OLE object will revert back to its original size from before the move/resize.

When AutoActivate is set to `vbOLEActivateDoubleClick`, the DoubleClick event is not fired when the user double-clicks the OLE object. The object is activated instead.

Updated

Whenever the OLE object contained by the OLE control has been modified, the Updated event is fired. The type of change is passed as a parameter (***Code***). Possible values are 0–vbOLEChanged if the data has been changed, 1–vbOLESaved when the data has been saved, 2–vbOLEClosed when the OLE object is closed, and 3–vbOLERenamed if the contents were saved under a new name.

Option Button Control

Option button controls provide the user with an easy way to choose one option from a list of available options. Each option button consists of a caption and a graphic (typically a circle, with a dot in the center to indicate the selected button). Two or more option buttons form a set, with each button representing one of a series of mutually exclusive choices. When these option buttons are placed in a container, such as a frame, only one of these options can be selected.

A lightweight version of the Option Button control is also available; see the entry for Windowless Controls later in this chapter.

Control Tasks

The following categories reflect the tasks that are executed when creating option buttons.

Set Properties

1. Specify index (optional).

   Index

   While the use of an index is completely optional, you'll find it much easier to work with option button groups if you use their Index property to group option buttons into one or more control arrays. Give each option group its own name and set of indexes.

2. Specify graphical label (optional).

   Style

   Set to the default, 0 or `vbButtonStandard`, to display the standard, circular graphic. When set to 1 or `vbButtonGraphical`, alternate graphics display for the button. The graphic used for all but the selected option button is the image assigned to the control's Picture property. For the selected option button, the image assigned to the control's DownPicture property is used instead.

   Picture

   Pictures can be set at design time to a graphic file on the disk or at runtime to any picture object. The picture will be invisible unless the Style property is set to 1–Graphical.

   DisabledPicture

   The image to be used when the Enabled property is `False`. If this is omitted, Visual Basic will do its best to "gray" out the normal picture for use here.

   DownPicture

   The image to be used when the button is pressed. If no image file is supplied, the image will be the one specified in the Picture property.

Although the selected option will appear different from unselected options, using a specific picture for this is usually desirable.

Write Event Handlers

Click

Fires when the user clicks an option button with the mouse or presses a keyboard alternative to select the button. At times you will need to perform actions immediately based on a selected option button. The example illustrates this type of action; the application form is shown in Figure 5-49.

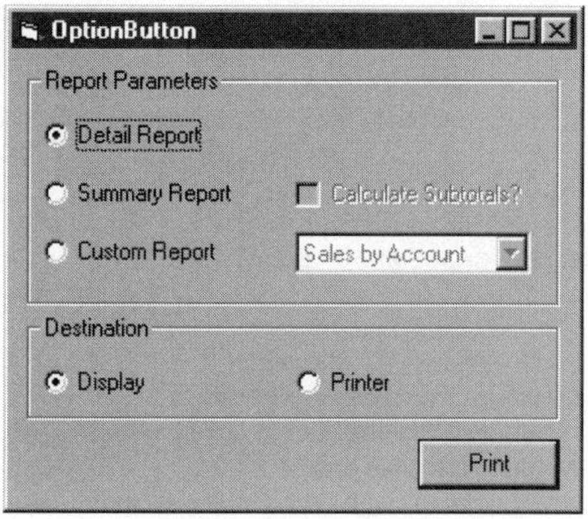

Figure 5-49: Responding to option button click events

Example

You can turn a `Select` statement upside down by putting the literal in the `Select` and the variables on each `Case`. This works particularly well with option buttons, as the following example illustrates:

```
Option Explicit

'For this example, create the following controls: _
  a ComboBox named cboCustomReports with the Style _
    property set to 2–Dropdown List, and_
  an OptionButton named optReportType with the _
    Index property set to 0.

Dim fraReportParameters As Frame
Dim fraDestination As Frame
Dim chkSubTotals As CheckBox
Dim WithEvents cmdPrint As CommandButton
Dim optDisplay As OptionButton
Dim optPrinter As OptionButton

'This enumeration makes the later code more readable.
Private Enum ReportType
```

```
   rptDetail = 0
   rptSummary = 1
   rptCustom = 2
End Enum

Private Sub Form_Load()
   Dim iCtr As Integer

  'Create controls and set properties.
   Set fraReportParameters = Me.Controls.Add("vb.frame", _
                            fraReportParameters", Me)
   fraReportParameters.Visible = True
   fraReportParameters.TabIndex = 0
   fraReportParameters.Caption = "Report Parameters"

   Set fraDestination = Me.Controls.Add("vb.frame", _
                        "fraDestination", Me)
   fraDestination.Visible = True
   fraDestination.TabIndex = 1
   fraDestination.Caption = "Destination"

   For iCtr = 0 To 2
      If iCtr > 0 Then _
         Load Me.optReportType(iCtr)
      Set Me.optReportType(iCtr).Container = _
          fraReportParameters
      Me.optReportType(iCtr).Visible = True
      Me.optReportType(iCtr).TabIndex = 1 + iCtr
   Next iCtr

   Me.optReportType(rptDetail).Caption = "Detail Report"
   Me.optReportType(rptSummary).Caption = "Summary Report"
   Me.optReportType(rptCustom).Caption = "Custom Report"

   Set chkSubTotals = Me.Controls.Add( _
      "vb.checkbox", "chkSubTotals", fraReportParameters)
   chkSubTotals.Visible = True
   chkSubTotals.Caption = "Calculate Subtotals?"
   chkSubTotals.TabIndex = _
             Me.optReportType(rptSummary).TabIndex + 1

   Set Me.cboCustomReports.Container = fraReportParameters
   Me.cboCustomReports.AddItem "Sales by Account"
   Me.cboCustomReports.AddItem "Sales by Month"
   Me.cboCustomReports.ListIndex = 0
   Me.cboCustomReports.TabIndex = _
             Me.optReportType(rptCustom).TabIndex + 1
   UpdateForm

   Set optDisplay = Me.Controls.Add( _
      "vb.optionbutton", "optDisplay", fraDestination)
   optDisplay.Visible = True
```

```
    optDisplay.Caption = "Display"
    optDisplay.TabIndex = fraDestination.TabIndex + 1
    Set optPrinter = Me.Controls.Add( _
       "vb.optionbutton", "optPrinter", fraDestination)
    optPrinter.Visible = True
    optPrinter.Caption = "Printer"
    optPrinter.TabIndex = optDisplay.TabIndex + 1

    Set cmdPrint = Me.Controls.Add("vb.commandbutton", _
                                   "cmdPrint", Me)
    cmdPrint.Visible = True
    cmdPrint.Caption = "Print"
    cmdPrint.Default = True

    Me.Caption = "OptionButton"
    Me.Move Me.Left, Me.Top, 4450, 3800

  'Make the Detail Report the default report.
    Me.optReportType(rptDetail).Value = True
  'Make the Display Button the default destination.
    optDisplay.Value = True
End Sub

Private Sub Form_Resize()
    Dim iCtr As Integer

    If Me.ScaleWidth < 4300 Or Me.ScaleHeight < 3350 Then _
       Exit Sub

    fraReportParameters.Move 120, 120, _
             Me.ScaleWidth - 240, Me.ScaleHeight - 1605
    For iCtr = 0 To Me.optReportType.UBound
       Me.optReportType(iCtr).Move 120, _
          240 + 120 * (iCtr + 1) + 315 * iCtr, 1815, 315
       If iCtr = 1 Then
          chkSubTotals.Move 2055, _
             240 + 120 * (iCtr + 1) + 315 * iCtr, 1815, 315
       ElseIf iCtr = 2 Then
          Me.cboCustomReports.Move _
             2055, 240 + 120 * (iCtr + 1) + 315 * iCtr, 1815
       End If
    Next iCtr
    fraDestination.Move _
       120, Me.ScaleHeight - 1425, Me.ScaleWidth - 240, 795
    optDisplay.Move 120, 360, 1815, 315
    optPrinter.Move 2055, 360, 1815, 315
    cmdPrint.Move Me.ScaleWidth - 1215, _
                  Me.ScaleHeight - 495, 1095, 375
End Sub
```

```
Private Sub optReportType_Click(Index As Integer)
  'Any time the user changes the option, we need to _
     enable/disable other controls on the form.
   UpdateForm
End Sub

Private Sub cmdPrint_Click()
   Dim sMessage As String

  'Just to make sure it all worked
   sMessage = "Send a "
   Select Case True
      Case Me.optReportType(rptDetail).Value
         sMessage = sMessage & "Detail Report"
      Case Me.optReportType(rptSummary).Value
         sMessage = sMessage & "Summary Report, With"
         If chkSubTotals.Value <> vbChecked Then _
            sMessage = sMessage & "out"
         sMessage = sMessage & "Subtotals"
      Case Me.optReportType(rptCustom).Value
         sMessage = sMessage & Me.cboCustomReports.Text
         sMessage = sMessage & "Custom Report"
   End Select
   If optDisplay.Value = True Then
      sMessage = sMessage & "to the Display."
   Else
      sMessage = sMessage & "to the Printer."
   End If

   MsgBox sMessage
End Sub

Private Sub UpdateForm()
   Select Case True
      Case optReportType(rptDetail).Value
     'If the Detail Report was selected, disable the other _
        form elements.
         chkSubTotals.Enabled = False
         cboCustomReports.Enabled = False
      Case optReportType(rptSummary).Value
     'If the Summary Report was selected, enable only _
        the Subtotals checkbox.
         chkSubTotals.Enabled = True
         cboCustomReports.Enabled = False
      Case optReportType(rptCustom).Value
     'If the Custom Report was selected, enable only _
          the custom report selector combo.
         chkSubTotals.Enabled = False
         cboCustomReports.Enabled = True
   End Select
End SubInteractions
```

Interactions

Action	*Result*
Set the option button's Value property to `True` or `False`.	Fires the option button's Click event.
`Form_Load`, if no option button in a group has been designated as the default by having its Value property set to `True` at design time.	Fires the Click event for the first option button in the group and sets its Value property to `True`.
The user presses any key other than the Tab key, the arrow keys, or the accelerator keys when an option button has the focus.	The KeyPress event fires. Note that the exceptions make the KeyPress event an unreliable method of trapping a pressed key.

PictureBox Control

The PictureBox control can be used to display an image, to display graphics created through graphic methods, to contain other controls, or for all of these reasons. A Picture property is provided to display a Picture object. Many graphic methods are provided for custom graphic creation. Each of these is described in this section. As a container, the PictureBox has an added benefit: it has an Align property that allows it to be placed directly on an MDI form along with any contained controls. This is useful when creating custom toolbars or other dockable elements.

Control Tasks

The following categories reflect the tasks that are executed when creating a PictureBox.

Set Properties

1. Set picture.

Picture

The picture shown in a PictureBox control is set by the Picture property. This property can be assigned in many ways, including at design time by selecting a graphics file from the Load Picture file dialog and at runtime by calling the *LoadPicture* function or by using an ImageList control. If the control is smaller than the image, the image shown is clipped to the size of the control.

AutoSize

When set to `True`, the AutoSize property causes the size of the PictureBox control to match the size of the contained image.

AutoRedraw

When the contents of a PictureBox need to be redrawn, the AutoRedraw property determines whether the output from graphics methods will automatically be redrawn from memory. When set to `True`, all changes to the PictureBox are saved in memory and redrawn when needed. When set to `False`, only the image loaded by the Picture property before any subsequent calls to graphics methods is redrawn. When AutoRedraw is set to `True`, more memory is generally used to store a second copy of the image.

2. Set graphics method parameters.

CurrentX, CurrentY

These properties are used to set or determine where the next graphics method will start drawing. Measurements are in twips.

FontTransparent

When set to `True`, the FontTransparent property causes text output to the PictureBox using the Print method to have a transparent background. When set to `False`, the BackColor property is used around the text.

DrawMode, DrawStyle, DrawWidth, FillColor, FillStyle

When graphic methods are used to draw on a PictureBox control, these properties control the relationship of these methods to the contents of the PictureBox.

The DrawMode property controls how the method is drawn. It can be set to 1–vbBlackness, 2–vbNotMergePen, 3–vbMaskNotPen, 4–vbNotCopyPen, 5–vbMaskPenNot, 6–vbInvert, 7–vbXorPen, 8–vbNotMaskPen, 9–vbMaskPen, 10–vbNotXorPen, 11–vbNop, 12–vbMergeNotPen, 13–vbCopyPen, 14–vbMergePenNot, 15–vbMergePen, or 16–vbWhiteness.

The DrawStyle property controls how the line or stroke appears and can be set to 0–vbSolid, 1–vbDash, 2–vbDot, 3–vbDashDot, 4–vbDasDotDot, 5–vbInvisible, or 6–vbInsideSolid. The DrawWidth property controls how wide a line or outline is drawn in pixels.

The FillColor property sets the color with which filled objects will be filled. The FillStyle sets how the object will be filled and can be set to 0–vbFSSolid, 1–vbFSTransparent, 2–vbHorizontalLine, 3–vbVerticalLine, 4–vbUpwardDiagonal, 5–vbDownwardDiagonal, 6–vbCross, or 7–vbDiagonalCross.

The example program shows how each of these properties affect the contents of the PictureBox control.

Useful Methods

Circle, Cls, Line, PaintPicture, Print, PSet

These methods create simple graphics on a PictureBox.

The Circle method draws a circle, ellipse, or arc. Its syntax is:

```
Circle [Step] (x, y), radius, [color, start, end, aspect]
```

The required parameters are `x` and `y`, which represent the center of the circle (the `Step` keyword makes this coordinate relative to the current position), and the radius. There are also optional parameters for *`color`* (a long integer representing the RGB color of the circle's outline), *`start`* and *`end`* to draw an arc, and *`Aspect`*, which allows ellipses to be drawn.

The Cls method clears all drawing methods used on the PictureBox while leaving the image set by the Picture property alone.

The Line method draws lines and boxes on the PictureBox. Its syntax is:

```
Line [Step] (x1, y1) [Step] (x2, y2), [color], [B][F]
```

Parameters are required for start (*x1*, *y1*) and end (*x2*, *y2*) points (the `Step` keyword, indicating that these coordinates are relative to the current position, is available on each). ***color*** is an optional parameter, a long integer indicating the RGB color of the line. There is also a parameter that can be set to `B` for a box with the endpoints at opposite corners filled according to the FillColor and FillStyle or to `BF` for a box filled with the same attributes as the border.

The PaintPicture method draws an image from a graphics file to a specific location in the PictureBox. Its syntax is:

```
PaintPicture picture, x1, y1, width1, height1, x2, y2, width2,
height2, opcode
```

The required parameters are ***picture***, the optional path and filename of the image to be drawn, and (*x1*, *y1*), the upper-left corner for the image (the `Step` keyword is available). Optional parameters are ***width1*** and ***height1***, the width and height of the image. If these differ from the image's size, the image is stretched to fit in this area. Parameters are also available for a clipping area. These are (*x2*, *y2*), the upper-left corner of the clipped area within the image, and ***width2*** and ***height2***, the width and height of the clipped area.

The Print method uses the PictureBox control's font-related properties to draw text on the control. The only parameter used with the Print method is ***OutputList***, which contains any number of expressions separated by semicolons or commas.

The PSet method draws one point to the PictureBox. Its syntax is:

```
PSet [Step] (x, y), [color]
```

The location of the point, (*x*, *y*) is required (the `Step` keyword is available), and ***color***, which is the RGB color of the point, is optional.

Point

The Point method returns a long integer containing the RGB color of the point at the current position within the PictureBox. Its syntax is:

```
Point X, Y
```

Write Event Handlers

Paint

Anytime the contents of a PictureBox need to be repainted for any reason, the Paint event is fired. This does not occur if the PictureBox control's AutoRedraw property is set to `True`.

Example

```
Option Explicit

'For this example, create the following controls: _
  a ComboBox named cboValues with the Index property _
    set to 0 and the Style set to 2-Dropdown List, and_
```

Controls O–R

```
  two CommonDialog controls named cdlFillColor and _
    cdlForeColor. _
  You'll also need an image file named TEST.BMP in the _
  current directory (or alter the LoadPicture statement).

Private lFillColor As Long

Private WithEvents picMain As PictureBox
Private WithEvents lblDrawMode As Label
Private WithEvents lblDrawStyle As Label
Private WithEvents lblDrawWidth As Label
Private WithEvents lblFillStyle As Label
Private WithEvents txtWidth As TextBox
Private WithEvents cmdFillColor As CommandButton
Private WithEvents cmdForeColor As CommandButton
Private WithEvents cmdDraw As CommandButton
Private WithEvents cmdReset As CommandButton

Private Sub cmdFillColor_Click()
  'We'll just use the CommonDialog's Color property _
  when we need it, so there's no reason to store it _
  to a variable
   Me.cdlFillColor.ShowColor
End Sub

Private Sub cmdForeColor_Click()
  'We'll just use the CommonDialog's Color property _
  when we need it, so there's no reason to store _
  it to a variable.
   Me.cdlForeColor.ShowColor
End Sub

Private Sub cmdDraw_Click()
  'Set all properties according to the user's _
  selections.
   picMain.DrawMode = _
     Me.cboValues(0).ItemData(Me.cboValues(0).ListIndex)
   picMain.DrawStyle = _
     Me.cboValues(1).ItemData(Me.cboValues(1).ListIndex)
   picMain.DrawWidth = txtWidth.Text
   picMain.FillColor = Me.cdlFillColor.Color
   picMain.FillStyle = _
     Me.cboValues(2).ItemData(Me.cboValues(2).ListIndex)
   picMain.ForeColor = Me.cdlForeColor.Color

  'Upper-left corner, draw a circle. We need to make _
  sure the circle will fit into the quadrant, so we _
  compare the width to the height in the IIF function.
   picMain.Circle _
        (picMain.ScaleWidth/4, picMain.ScaleHeight/4), _
        IIf(picMain.ScaleHeight > picMain.ScaleWidth, _
            picMain.ScaleWidth / 4, _
            picMain.ScaleHeight / 4)
```

```
 'Upper-right corner, draw a horizontal line and a _
  vertical line.
   picMain.Line _
        (picMain.ScaleWidth/2, picMain.ScaleHeight/4)- _
        (picMain.ScaleWidth, picMain.ScaleHeight / 4)
   picMain.Line _
     (picMain.ScaleWidth/2 + picMain.ScaleWidth/4, 0)- _
     (picMain.ScaleWidth/2 + picMain.ScaleWidth/4, _
     Me.ScaleHeight / 2)
  'Upper-left corner, draw a box (B parameter set)
   picMain.Line _
       (0, picMain.ScaleHeight / 2)- _
       (picMain.ScaleWidth / 2, picMain.ScaleHeight), _
        , B
  'Upper-left corner, draw a box (BF parameter set)
    picMain.Line _
        (picMain.ScaleWidth/2, picMain.ScaleHeight/2)- _
        (picMain.ScaleWidth, picMain.ScaleHeight), _
        , BF

  'This message box is just a reminder. Feel free to _
   comment this line out. I did :)
    MsgBox "Upper Left - Circle" & vbCrLf & _
        "Upper Right - Horizontal Line and " & _
         "Vertical Line" & vbCrLf & _
        "Lower Left - Box with 'B' only" & vbCrLf & _
        "Lower Right - Box with 'BF'"
End Sub

Private Sub cmdReset_Click()
  'This gets rid of all the drawing we've done.
   picMain.Cls
End Sub

Private Sub Form_Load()
   Dim lCtr As Long

  'Create more ComboBox controls and set properties.
   For lCtr = 0 To 2
      If lCtr > 0 Then _
         Load Me.cboValues(lCtr)
      Me.cboValues(lCtr).TabIndex = lCtr
      Me.cboValues(lCtr).Visible = True
   Next lCtr

  'Create all other controls and set properties.
   Set picMain = Me.Controls.Add("vb.picturebox", _
                 "picMain", Me)
   picMain.Visible = True
  'Change this next line if necessary to a valid image.
   picMain.Picture = LoadPicture("TEST.BMP")

   Set lblDrawMode = Me.Controls.Add("vb.label", _
                     "lblDrawMode", Me)
```

```
lblDrawMode.TabIndex = 0
lblDrawMode.Visible = True
lblDrawMode.Caption = "DrawMode:"

Set lblDrawStyle = Me.Controls.Add("vb.label", _
                   "lblDrawStyle", Me)
lblDrawStyle.TabIndex = 2
lblDrawStyle.Visible = True
lblDrawStyle.Caption = "DrawStyle:"

Set lblDrawWidth = Me.Controls.Add("vb.label", _
                    "lblDrawWidth", Me)
lblDrawWidth.TabIndex = 4
lblDrawWidth.Visible = True
lblDrawWidth.Caption = "DrawWidth:"

Set txtWidth = Me.Controls.Add("vb.textbox", _
               "txtWidth", Me)
txtWidth.TabIndex = 5
txtWidth.Visible = True
txtWidth.Text = 1

Set cmdFillColor = _
               Me.Controls.Add("vb.commandbutton", _
               "cmdFillColor", Me)
cmdFillColor.TabIndex = 6
cmdFillColor.Visible = True
cmdFillColor.Caption = "FillColor"

Set lblFillStyle = Me.Controls.Add("vb.label", _
                   "lblFillStyle", Me)
lblFillStyle.TabIndex = 7
lblFillStyle.Visible = True
lblFillStyle.Caption = "FillStyle:"

Set cmdForeColor = _
     Me.Controls.Add("vb.commandbutton", _
     "cmdForeColor", Me)
cmdForeColor.TabIndex = 9
cmdForeColor.Visible = True
cmdForeColor.Caption = "ForeColor"

Set cmdDraw = Me.Controls.Add("vb.commandbutton", _
              "cmdDraw", Me)
cmdDraw.TabIndex = 10
cmdDraw.Visible = True
cmdDraw.Caption = "Draw"

Set cmdReset = Me.Controls.Add("vb.commandbutton", _
               "cmdReset", Me)
cmdReset.TabIndex = 11
cmdReset.Visible = True
cmdReset.Caption = "Reset"
```

```
'Set up the CommonDialog controls so they remember _
the color last used and initialize to black.
    Me.cdlFillColor.Flags = cdlCCRGBInit
    Me.cdlFillColor.Color = vbBlack

    Me.cdlForeColor.Flags = cdlCCRGBInit
    Me.cdlForeColor.Color = vbBlack

    LoadCombos

    Me.Caption = "PictureBox Example"
    Me.Height = 5235
    Me.Width = 7530
End Sub

Private Sub Form_Resize()
'Without going into too much detail, this arranges _
 the form for the picture box taking the upper-left _
 and doing all the resizing, the user entry _
 controls down the right side, and the commands _
 centered at the bottom.
    If Me.Width < 3645 Or Me.Height < 5235 Then _
        Exit Sub

    picMain.Move 120, 120, Me.ScaleWidth - 2550, _
                 Me.ScaleHeight - 735
    lblDrawMode.Move Me.ScaleWidth - 2310, 180, _
                     2190, 255
    Me.cboValues(0).Move Me.ScaleWidth - 2310, 495, 2190
    lblDrawStyle.Move Me.ScaleWidth - 2310, 990, _
                      2190, 255
    Me.cboValues(1).Move Me.ScaleWidth - 2310, 1305, _
                          2190
    lblDrawWidth.Move Me.ScaleWidth - 2310, 1740, _
                      2190, 255
    txtWidth.Move Me.ScaleWidth - 2310, 2115, 2190, 315
    cmdFillColor.Move Me.ScaleWidth - 2310, 2550, _
                      2190, 375
    lblFillStyle.Move Me.ScaleWidth - 2310, 3045, _
                      2190, 255
   Me.cboValues(2).Move Me.ScaleWidth - 2310, 3420, 2190
    cmdForeColor.Move Me.ScaleWidth - 2310, 3855, _
                      2190, 375
    cmdDraw.Move _
        Me.ScaleWidth / 2 - 1155, _
        Me.ScaleHeight - 495, 1095, 375
    cmdReset.Move Me.ScaleWidth / 2 + 60, _
        Me.ScaleHeight - 495, 1095, 375
End Sub

Private Sub LoadCombos()
'Load the DrawMode values into cblValues(0).
```

Controls O–R

```
Me.cboValues(0).AddItem "1 - vbBlackness"
Me.cboValues(0).ItemData(Me.cboValues(0).NewIndex) = 1
Me.cboValues(0).AddItem "2 - vbNotMergePen"
Me.cboValues(0).ItemData(Me.cboValues(0).NewIndex) = 2
Me.cboValues(0).AddItem "3 - vbMaskNotPen"
Me.cboValues(0).ItemData(Me.cboValues(0).NewIndex) = 3
Me.cboValues(0).AddItem "4 - vbNotCopyPen"
Me.cboValues(0).ItemData(Me.cboValues(0).NewIndex) = 4
Me.cboValues(0).AddItem "5 - vbMaskPenNot"
Me.cboValues(0).ItemData(Me.cboValues(0).NewIndex) = 5
Me.cboValues(0).AddItem "6 - vbInvert"
Me.cboValues(0).ItemData(Me.cboValues(0).NewIndex) = 6
Me.cboValues(0).AddItem "7 - vbXorPen"
Me.cboValues(0).ItemData(Me.cboValues(0).NewIndex) = 7
Me.cboValues(0).AddItem "8 - vbNotMaskPen"
Me.cboValues(0).ItemData(Me.cboValues(0).NewIndex) = 8
Me.cboValues(0).AddItem "9 - vbMaskPen"
Me.cboValues(0).ItemData(Me.cboValues(0).NewIndex) = 9
Me.cboValues(0).AddItem "10 - vbNotXorPen"
Me.cboValues(0).ItemData(Me.cboValues(0).NewIndex) = 10
Me.cboValues(0).AddItem "11 - vbNop"
Me.cboValues(0).ItemData(Me.cboValues(0).NewIndex) = 11
Me.cboValues(0).AddItem "12 - vbMergeNotPen"
Me.cboValues(0).ItemData(Me.cboValues(0).NewIndex) = 12
Me.cboValues(0).AddItem "13 - vbCopyPen"
Me.cboValues(0).ItemData(Me.cboValues(0).NewIndex) = 13
Me.cboValues(0).AddItem "14 - vbMergePenNot"
Me.cboValues(0).ItemData(Me.cboValues(0).NewIndex) = 14
Me.cboValues(0).AddItem "15 - vbMergePen"
Me.cboValues(0).ItemData(Me.cboValues(0).NewIndex) = 15
Me.cboValues(0).AddItem "16 - vbWhiteness"
Me.cboValues(0).ItemData(Me.cboValues(0).NewIndex) = 16

'Load the DrawStyle values into cblValues(1).
  Me.cboValues(1).AddItem "0 - vbSolid"
  Me.cboValues(1).ItemData(Me.cboValues(1).NewIndex) = 0
  Me.cboValues(1).AddItem "1 - vbDash"
  Me.cboValues(1).ItemData(Me.cboValues(1).NewIndex) = 1
  Me.cboValues(1).AddItem "2 - vbDot"
  Me.cboValues(1).ItemData(Me.cboValues(1).NewIndex) = 2
  Me.cboValues(1).AddItem "3 - vbDashDot"
  Me.cboValues(1).ItemData(Me.cboValues(1).NewIndex) = 3
  Me.cboValues(1).AddItem "4 - vbDashDotDot"
  Me.cboValues(1).ItemData(Me.cboValues(1).NewIndex) = 4
  Me.cboValues(1).AddItem "5 - vbInvisible"
  Me.cboValues(1).ItemData(Me.cboValues(1).NewIndex) = 5
  Me.cboValues(1).AddItem "6 - vbInsideSolid"
  Me.cboValues(1).ItemData(Me.cboValues(1).NewIndex) = 6

'Load the FillStyle values into cblValues(2).
  Me.cboValues(2).AddItem "0 - vbFSSolid"
  Me.cboValues(2).ItemData(Me.cboValues(2).NewIndex) = 0
  Me.cboValues(2).AddItem "1 - vbFSTransparent"
  Me.cboValues(2).ItemData(Me.cboValues(2).NewIndex) = 1
```

```
    Me.cboValues(2).AddItem "2 - vbFSHorizontalLine"
    Me.cboValues(2).ItemData(Me.cboValues(2).NewIndex) = 2
    Me.cboValues(2).AddItem "3 - vbFSVerticalLine"
    Me.cboValues(2).ItemData(Me.cboValues(2).NewIndex) = 3
    Me.cboValues(2).AddItem "4 - vbFSUpwardDiagonal"
    Me.cboValues(2).ItemData(Me.cboValues(2).NewIndex) = 4
    Me.cboValues(2).AddItem "5 - vbFSDownwardDiagonal"
    Me.cboValues(2).ItemData(Me.cboValues(2).NewIndex) = 5
    Me.cboValues(2).AddItem "6 - vbFSCross"
    Me.cboValues(2).ItemData(Me.cboValues(2).NewIndex) = 6
    Me.cboValues(2).AddItem "7 - vbFSDiagonalCross"
    Me.cboValues(2).ItemData(Me.cboValues(2).NewIndex) = 7

    Me.cboValues(0).ListIndex = 0
    Me.cboValues(1).ListIndex = 0
    Me.cboValues(2).ListIndex = 0
End Sub

Private Sub txtWidth_Change()
  'If the user causes an invalid value to be placed _
   into DrawWidth, beep and set it to 1.
    If Not IsNumeric(txtWidth.Text) Or _
          Val(txtWidth.Text) < 0 Then
        Beep
        txtWidth.Text = 1
    End If
End Sub

Private Sub txtWidth_GotFocus()
  'Select on entry
    txtWidth.SelStart = 0
    txtWidth.SelLength = Len(txtWidth.Text)
End Sub
```

ProgressBar Control

The progress bar, shown in Figure 5-50, indicates a value that cannot be altered by the user. A bar that is partially filled shows the current value of the ProgressBar control. Usually, progress bars are used to represent a percentage completion of an action.

The ProgressBar control is included with the Windows Common Controls (*COMCTL32.OCX*) that come with Visual Basic Professional and Enterprise editions.

Control Tasks

The following categories reflect the tasks that are executed when creating a progress bar.

1. Set appearance (optional).

   Appearance

   As with most controls, the progress bar's Appearance property can be set to its default of 1–cc3D or 0–ccFlat. However, with the progress bar, the flat appearance seems to be more in line with the standard Windows appearance.

2. Set constraints.

   Min and Max

   Sets the minimum and maximum values that the progress bar can represent. For example, when the progress bar is used to represent the progress of a loop, these are set to the minimum and maximum values in the loop.

3. Set value.

   Value

   This property represents the current size of the progress portion of the progress bar relative to its Min and Max properties. When displaying the progress of an action, be sure there is a *DoEvents* command that punctuates the code responsible for changing the Value property multiple times. Otherwise, the value may not appear to change on the screen.

Figure 5-50: A form with a ProgressBar control

Example

In the following example, a progress bar is used to track the status of an update:

```
Option Explicit

'For this example, create a ProgressBar named pbrUpdate.

Dim lblUpdate As Label
Dim txtFont As TextBox
Dim WithEvents cmdUpdate As CommandButton

'Set up an enumeration to track the status.
Private Enum UPD_STAT
    updBefore
    updDuring
    updAfter
    updAbort
End Enum
```

```
Private miStatus As UPD_STAT
'Variable to track status—will be maintainted _
                 through a property.

Private Property Get UpdateStatus() As UPD_STAT
    UpdateStatus = miStatus
End Property

Private Property Let UpdateStatus(iStatus As UPD_STAT)
    miStatus = iStatus
End Property

Private Sub Form_Load()
  'Create and/or set up controls.
    Set lblUpdate = Me.Controls.Add("vb.label", _
                    "lblUpdate", Me)
    lblUpdate.Visible = True
    lblUpdate.Caption = ""
    lblUpdate.Alignment = 2 'Center

    Set txtFont = Me.Controls.Add("vb.textbox", _
                  "txtFont", Me)
    txtFont.Visible = True
    txtFont.Text = "Font Sample"

    Set cmdUpdate = Me.Controls.Add("vb.commandbutton", _
                    "cmdUpdate", Me)
    cmdUpdate.Visible = True
    cmdUpdate.Caption = "Start"

    Me.Caption = "ProgressBar"
    Me.Move Me.Left, Me.Top, 4800, 1700

    UpdateStatus = updBefore
End Sub

Private Sub Form_Resize()
    If Me.ScaleHeight < 1290 Or Me.ScaleWidth < 2550 Then _
        Exit Sub

    lblUpdate.Move 120, 120, Me.ScaleWidth - 240, 255
    pbrUpdate.Move 120, 375, Me.ScaleWidth - 240, 315
    txtFont.Move 120, Me.ScaleHeight - 435, _
                 Me.ScaleWidth - 1455, 315
    cmdUpdate.Move Me.ScaleWidth - 1215, _
                   Me.ScaleHeight - 495, 1095, 375
End Sub

Private Sub cmdUpdate_Click()
  'Based on the current status, the command button can _
      do different things.
   Select Case UpdateStatus
      Case updBefore
         DoUpdate
```

Controls O–R

```
      Case updDuring
         If MsgBox("Stop Processing?", vbQuestion + vbYesNo) _
                  = vbYes Then _
            UpdateStatus = updAbort
      Case updAfter
          Unload Me
   End Select
End Sub

Private Sub DoUpdate()
   Dim iCtr As Integer

   UpdateStatus = updDuring

   pbrUpdate.Min = 0
   pbrUpdate.Max = Screen.FontCount

   cmdUpdate.Caption = "&Abort"

   For iCtr = 0 To Screen.FontCount - 1
      If UpdateStatus = updAbort Then _
         Exit For
      txtFont.Font = Screen.Fonts(iCtr)
      txtFont.FontBold = False
      txtFont.FontItalic = False

      lblUpdate.Caption = "Displaying" & iCtr & _
            "of" & Screen.FontCount
      pbrUpdate.Value = iCtr
      DoEvents
   Next iCtr

   If UpdateStatus = updAbort Then
      lblUpdate.Caption = "Aborted"
   Else
      lblUpdate.Caption = "Finished"
   End If

   pbrUpdate.Value = 0

   UpdateStatus = updAfter
   cmdUpdate.Caption = "&Exit"
End Sub
```

RichTextBox Control

The RichTextBox control provides an enhanced text box that allows programmatic control over the formatted text contained by the control. For example, blocks of text can appear in bold or italic, different blocks of text can have different font sizes or different colors, and blocks of text can be indented differently. In addition, the RichTextBox control supports OLE Drag and Drop and allows you to embed OLE objects within the control. Properties are also provided for loading and saving the control's contents.

The RichTextBox control is contained in the Microsoft RichTextBox control (*RICHTX32.OCX*) that comes with Visual Basic Professional and Enterprise editions.

Control Tasks

The following categories reflect the tasks that are executed when creating a RichTextBox control.

Set Properties

1. Set general appearance and behavior.

   MultiLine

   Generally set to `True`, the MultiLine property can be set to `False` to restrict the user from entering multiple lines in a RichTextBox control. The property defaults to `True` and is read-only at runtime.

   Note that if you set the MultiLine property to `False`, you should also set the ScrollBars property to either `rtfHorizontal` or `rtfBoth` to provide the user with an effective means of navigating to text that is not currently shown in the control's displayable area. If you set MultiLine to `True`, you should also set ScrollBars to `rtfVertical` or `rtfBoth`, since text automatically wraps to the next line if it becomes longer than the current line.

   ScrollBars

   The ScrollBars property can be set to 0–rtfNone to show no scrollbars at all, 1–rtfHorizontal to show horizontal scrollbars, 2–rtfVertical to show vertical scrollbars, or 3–rtfBoth to show both horizontal and vertical scrollbars. The property defaults to `rtfNone` and is read-only at runtime.

   DisableNoScroll

   If the ScrollBars property is set to a value other than `rtfNone`, setting DisableNoScroll to `True` causes disabled scrollbars to be displayed when none of the control's contents is hidden from view. When set to its default value of `False`, scrollbars appear only when the control is not able to display all content. The property is read-only at runtime.

   AutoVerbMenu

   Determines whether a pop-up menu (which offers Clipboard support as well as an Undo option) appears automatically in response to the user pressing the right mouse button when the mouse is over the control. By default, its value is `False`. If the mouse is right-clicked on an embedded OLE object, its context menu is displayed. However, contrary to the documentation, the RichTextBox control does continue to receive MouseDown and Click events if AutoVerbMenu is set to `True` and the user right-clicks the mouse on an embedded OLE object.

Locked

Determines whether the control's content can be edited. If set to `True`, it is read-only. The property's default value is `False`.

HideSelection

Determines whether or not the control's selected content remains highlighted when the control loses the focus. Its default value is `True`.

2. Selected text style properties.

The selected text style properties each provide information about the currently selected text. If the currently selected text contains more than one possible value for the property, the property will return the constant `vbNull`. (Contrary to the documentation, that's true of all the selected text style properties, including SelIndent, SelRightIndent, and SelHangingIndent.) Setting the property to a valid value affects all of the selected text. No selected text style properties are available at design-time.

SelFontName, SelFontSize

These properties contain the font's name and size. Setting the SelFontName property to the name of a valid, installed font causes the selected text to change to that font. Changing the SelFontSize to a different integer value changes the selected text to that point size.

SelBold, SelItalic, SelStrikeThru, SelUnderline

These properties return whether the selected text is bolded, italicized, struck through, or underlined, respectively. Setting any of these properties to `True` or `False` causes that text to conform to the appropriate style.

SelColor

Returns the RGB color of the selected text. Setting SelColor to a valid RGB color value or VB color constant causes the selected text to change to that color.

SelCharOffset

Returns the vertical position of the selected text relative to the baseline. The value returned is in twips: positive for superscripted text (i.e., text above the baseline), negative for subscripted text (i.e., text below the baseline), or 0 for text on the baseline. Setting this property to an integer causes the selected text's vertical position to be updated.

SelAlignment

Returns 0–rtfLeft, 1–rtfRight, or 2–rtfCenter, based on the alignment of the selected text. Setting the property to one of these values aligns all selected text in that fashion.

SelIndent, SelRightIndent

These properties return the amount of space between the edge of the text and the left or right edge of the control, respectively. The value is specified in units based on the parent Form object's ScaleMode property. Setting this property causes paragraphs that contain the selected text to adhere to these indents.

SelHangingIndent

Returns the amount of space between the left margin of the first line of the paragraph containing the selected text and the left margin of the remaining lines of the paragraph. The value is specified in units based on the parent Form object's ScaleMode property. Setting this property causes all but the first line of any paragraphs containing selected text to be indented by that value.

SelBullet

Indicates whether the selected text is bulleted or not. Bulleted text is indented based on the BulletIndent property. Setting the SelBullet property to `True` causes paragraphs containing selected text to be bulleted; setting it to `False` removes existing bullets.

SelProtected

Determines whether the selected text is protected (read-only). Setting this property to `True` causes the selected text to become protected. Note that once you protect the text, you cannot unprotect it by setting the SelProtected property to `False`; attempting to do so generates runtime error 32011, "Operation cannot be performed on protected text."

3. Set tab stops.

SelTabCount

Sets or returns the number of tab stops in paragraphs containing the selected text. The locations of those tabs are set by using the SelTabs property. If you are setting tabs, the SelTabCount property must be set before the position of individual tab stops is set, as follows:

```
me.rtbMain.SelTabCount = 1
me.rtbMain.SelTabs(0) = 1200
```

SelTabs

A zero-based property array containing a number of elements equal to the SelTabCount property. Each element of the SelTabs array contains the distance from the left margin to the tab stop. These values are in units based on the parent Form object's ScaleMode property.

Because the RichTextBox control is part of the parent form's tab order, pressing the Tab key while in a RichTextBox causes the next control in the tab order to get the focus. Holding the CTRL key while pressing Tab adds a tab into the RichTextBox control. In addition, if no controls on the parent form have their TabStop properties set to `True`, the Tab key will add a tab into the RichTextBox control.

4. Create the text.

Text, TextRTF

The contents of the RichTextBox control can be returned through either of these properties. Because rich text contains formatting information, the

TextRTF property shows these formatting elements as additional text. The Text property strips all of these elements and provides only the actual text. Similarly, text can be stored in the control by assigning it to the control's Text or TextRTF property. Note that if formatted (rich) text is assigned to the Text property, all formatting is lost; to preserve formatting, formatted text must be assigned to the TextRTF property.

SelText, SelRTF

These properties act in much the same way as the Text and TextRTF properties just shown, but only return or set the selected text.

SelStart, SelLength

If you want to know the relationship of the selected text to the total contents of the text box, or if you want to modify the selection, you can retrieve or set the SelStart and SelLength properties. SelStart returns the starting character position of the selection; the control's first character position is 0. SelLength returns the length of the selection. If SelLength is 0, no characters are selected, and the selection is simply the insertion point.

5. Access contained OLE objects.

OLEObjects Collection, OLEObject Object

A RichTextBox control can contain a number of OLE objects in the OLEObjects collection. For information on OLE objects, see the entry for the OLE control.

Useful Methods

LoadFile

Loads a text or rich text file from disk into the RichTextBox control. Its syntax is as follows:

```
object.LoadFile PathName, FileType
```

where `PathName` contains the path and filename of the file to be loaded, and `FileType` indicates the type of file and can be set to 0–rtfRTF or 1–rtfText. You can also load a file into the control by assigning the file's path and filename to the control's Filename property.

You can also load the contents of a text or *.RTF* file into the control at design time by using the control's Filename property.

SaveFile

Saves the contents of the RichTextBox control to disk. Its syntax is:

```
object.SaveFile(PathName, FileType)
```

where `PathName` contains the path and filename of the file to be saved, and `FileType` indicates the type of file and can be set to 0–rtfRTF or 1–rtfText.

SelPrint

Sends the currently selected text to an hDC. If no text is currently selected, the contents of the RichTextBox are sent in their entirety. Its syntax is:

```
object.SelPrint(hdc)
```

where *hdc* represents the handle to the device context of the device to which the rich text is to be sent.

Find

Searches for a string within the contents of the RichTextBox control. This search can include the entire contents or just a portion. Its syntax is:

```
object.Find(String, Start, End, Options)
```

where *String* is the string to search for, *Start* and *End* represent the character position (starting from 0) at which to begin and end the search, and *Options* defines the character of the search. *Options* can be set to any combination of 2–rtfWholeWord, which searches for only entire words; 4–rtfMatchCase, which searches based on case; and 8–rtfNoHighlight, which causes the found text to not be highlighted. If the specified string is not found in the range, a negative one (-1) will be returned. Otherwise, the position at which the string was found is returned.

GetLineFromChar

GetLineFromChar returns the line on which a given character position is found in a RichTextBox control. Its syntax is:

```
object.GetLineFromChar(CharPos)
```

where *CharPos* is the position for which you require the line number. For example, the following code returns the total number of lines in the RichTextBox control:

```
iTotalLines = _
   Me.rtbMain.GetLineFromChar(Len(Me.rtbMain.Text))
```

Span, UpTo

The Span method extends the selected text based on a set of characters. Its syntax is:

```
object.Span CharacterSet, Forward, Negate
```

where *CharacterSet* is a string that contains the characters on which to base the new selection, *Forward* can be set to `True` to extend the selection from the end of the selection forward (to the end of the text) or `False` to extend the selection from the beginning of the selection backward (to the beginning of the text), and *Negate* can be set to `True` to cause all characters except for those in *CharacterSet* to be used to extend the selection and to `False` to cause the characters in the *CharacterSet* to be used to extend the selection.

The following code causes all text between the start of the current selection and the next carriage return to be selected:

```
Me.rtbMain.Span vbCR, True, True
```

The UpTo method acts in the same way, except that it moves the insertion point instead of extending the selection. Its parameters are identical to those of the Span method.

Write Event Handlers

SelChange

Whenever the selection changes in the RichTextBox control, the SelChange event is fired. This allows you to update any controls whose appearance is based on the currently selected text, as in this code fragment:

```
Private Sub chkBold_Click()
    If Me.chkBold.Value = vbChecked Then
        Me.rtbMain.SelBold = True
    Else
        Me.rtbMain.SelBold = False
    End If
End Sub

Private Sub rtbMain_SelChange()
    If IsNull(Me.rtbMain.SelBold) Then
        Me.chkBold.Value = vbGrayed
    Else
        Select Case Me.rtbMain.SelBold
            Case True
                Me.chkBold.Value = vbChecked
            Case False
                Me.chkBold.Value = vbUnchecked
        End Select
    End If
End Sub
```

Example

The following example, which is illustrated in Figure 5-51, uses many of the properties, methods, and events mentioned earlier in this section:

```
Option Explicit

'For this example, create the following controls: _
  a RichTextBox control named rtbMain, _
  a CommonDialog control named cdlMain, _
  a Menu named mnuFileTop with a child menu named _
     mnuFile with an Index of 0, and _
  a Menu named mnuFormatTop with a child Menu named _
     mnuFormat with an Index of 0.

Private Enum eFormat
    fmtFont
    fmtBold
    fmtItalic
    fmtUnderline
    fmtColor
End Enum

Private Enum eFile
    filNew
```

```
    filOpen
    filSave
    filSaveAs
    filSeparator
    filExit
End Enum

Private Sub Form_Load()
    'Set up menus and controls.
    mnuFileTop.Caption = "&File"
    mnuFile(0).Caption = "&New"
    Load mnuFile(1)
    mnuFile(1).Caption = "&Open ..."
    Load mnuFile(2)
    mnuFile(2).Caption = "&Save ..."
    Load mnuFile(3)
    mnuFile(3).Caption = "Save &As ..."
    Load mnuFile(4)
    mnuFile(4).Caption = "-"
    Load mnuFile(5)
    mnuFile(5).Caption = "E&xit"

    mnuFormatTop.Caption = "F&ormat"
    mnuFormat(0).Caption = "&Font ..."
    Load mnuFormat(1)
    mnuFormat(1).Caption = "&Bold"
    Load mnuFormat(2)
    mnuFormat(2).Caption = "&Italic"
    Load mnuFormat(3)
    mnuFormat(3).Caption = "&Underline"
    Load mnuFormat(4)
    mnuFormat(4).Caption = "&Color ..."

    Me.rtbMain.Text = ""

    Me.Caption = "RichTextBox Example"
End Sub

Private Sub Form_Resize()
    If Me.ScaleHeight < 600 Or Me.ScaleWidth < 600 Then
        Exit Sub
    End If

    Me.rtbMain.Move 120, 120, Me.ScaleWidth - 240, _
                    Me.ScaleHeight - 240
End Sub

Private Sub mnuFormatTop_Click()
    Dim iCtr As Integer
    Dim sProp As String
```

Controls O–R

```
    'If these were visible more often, I'd move this _
    logic to the SelChange event for rtbMain
    For iCtr = 1 To 3
        Select Case iCtr
            Case fmtBold
                sProp = "SelBold"
            Case fmtItalic
                sProp = "SelItalic"
            Case fmtUnderline
                sProp = "SelUnderline"
        End Select

        If CallByName(Me.rtbMain, sProp, VbGet) Or _
                IsNull(CallByName(Me.rtbMain, sProp, _
                                  VbGet)) Then
            mnuFormat(iCtr).Checked = True
        Else
            mnuFormat(iCtr).Checked = False
        End If
    Next iCtr
End Sub

Private Sub mnuFormat_Click(Index As Integer)
    Dim sProp As String

    On Error Resume Next

    Select Case Index
        Case fmtBold, fmtItalic, fmtUnderline
            Select Case Index
                Case fmtBold
                    sProp = "SelBold"
                Case fmtItalic
                    sProp = "SelItalic"
                Case fmtUnderline
                    sProp = "SelUnderline"
            End Select

            If mnuFormat(Index).Checked Then
                CallByName Me.rtbMain, sProp, VbLet, _
                           False
            Else
                CallByName Me.rtbMain, sProp, VbLet, _
                           True
            End If
        Case fmtFont
            'Although if/then is slightly faster than _
            the IIF function, this is more legible here
            Me.cdlMain.Flags = cdlCFBoth + cdlCFEffects
            Me.cdlMain.FontBold = _
                IIf(IsNull(Me.rtbMain.SelBold), _
                False, Me.rtbMain.SelBold)
```

```
            Me.cdlMain.FontItalic = _
                IIf(IsNull(Me.rtbMain.SelItalic), _
                False, Me.rtbMain.SelItalic)
            Me.cdlMain.FontName = _
                IIf(IsNull(Me.rtbMain.SelFontName), _
                "", Me.rtbMain.SelFontName)
            Me.cdlMain.FontSize = _
                IIf(IsNull(Me.rtbMain.SelFontSize), _
                0, Me.rtbMain.SelFontSize)
            Me.cdlMain.Color = _
                IIf(IsNull(Me.rtbMain.SelColor), _
                0, Me.rtbMain.SelColor)
            Me.cdlMain.FontStrikethru = _
                IIf(IsNull(Me.rtbMain.SelStrikeThru), _
                False, Me.rtbMain.SelStrikeThru)
            Me.cdlMain.FontUnderline = _
                IIf(IsNull(Me.rtbMain.SelUnderline), _
                False, Me.rtbMain.SelUnderline)
            Me.cdlMain.ShowFont
            If Not Err.Number Then
                Me.rtbMain.SelBold = Me.cdlMain.FontBold
                Me.rtbMain.SelItalic = _
                           Me.cdlMain.FontItalic
                Me.rtbMain.SelFontName = _
                           Me.cdlMain.FontName
                Me.rtbMain.SelFontSize = _
                           Me.cdlMain.FontSize
                Me.rtbMain.SelColor = Me.cdlMain.Color
                Me.rtbMain.SelStrikeThru = _
                           Me.cdlMain.FontStrikethru
                Me.rtbMain.SelUnderline = _
                           Me.cdlMain.FontUnderline
            End If
        Case fmtColor
            Me.cdlMain.Flags = cdlCCRGBInit
            Me.cdlMain.Color = _
                IIf(IsNull(Me.rtbMain.SelColor), 0, _
                    Me.rtbMain.SelColor)
            Me.cdlMain.ShowColor
            Me.rtbMain.SelColor = Me.cdlMain.Color
    End Select
End Sub

Private Sub mnuFile_Click(Index As Integer)
   On Error Resume Next

   Select Case Index

   Case filNew
      Me.rtbMain.Text = ""
   Case filOpen
      Me.cdlMain.Filter = _
```

Controls O–R

```
                "Rich Text (*.rtf)|*.rtf" _
                & "|Text (*.txt)|*.txt"
         Me.cdlMain.Flags = cdlOFNFileMustExist + _
                            cdlOFNHideReadOnly
         Me.cdlMain.ShowOpen
         If Not Err.Number Then
            Me.rtbMain.LoadFile Me.cdlMain.FileName, _
                IIf(LCase$(Right$( _
                Me.cdlMain.FileName, 4)) = ".txt", _
                rtfText, rtfRTF)
            Me.rtbMain.Tag = Me.cdlMain.FileName
         End If
      Case filSave, filSaveAs
         Me.cdlMain.FileName = Me.rtbMain.Tag
         If Me.rtbMain.Tag = "" Or _
            Index = filSaveAs Then
            Me.cdlMain.Filter = _
                   "Rich Text (*.rtf)|*.rtf" _
                   & "|Text (*.txt)|*.txt"
            Me.cdlMain.Flags = cdlOFNOverwritePrompt + _
                               cdlOFNPathMustExist + _
                               cdlOFNHideReadOnly
            Me.cdlMain.ShowSave
         End If
         If Not Err.Number Then
            If LCase$(Right$(Me.cdlMain.FileName, 4)) = _
             ".txt" Then _
             If MsgBox( _
             "Saving as text will lose all formatting." _
             & "Save anyway?" , vbYesNo) = vbNo Then _
             Exit Sub
             Me.rtbMain.SaveFile Me.cdlMain.FileName, _
                IIf(LCase$(Right$( _
                Me.cdlMain.FileName, 4)) = ".txt", _
                rtfText, rtfRTF)
             Me.rtbMain.Tag = Me.cdlMain.FileName
         End If
      Case filExit
         Unload Me
      End Select
   End Sub
```

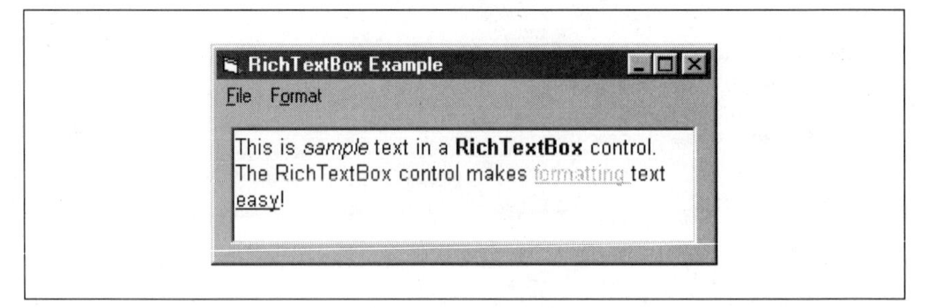

Figure 5-51: The RichTextBox control example

Interactions

Action	Result
Call LoadFile method.	If text is selected, it fires the SelChange event twice, followed by the Change event, then changes the Filename property. If no text is selected (the selection is the insertion point only), it fires the Change event, then changes the Filename property.

Scrollbar Controls

The HScrollBar, VScrollBar, and FlatScrollBar controls are provided to allow programmers to write scrolling logic into their applications. The controls themselves do not scroll other controls in any way. They merely supply properties and fire events that facilitate the creation of scrollable controls. For example, horizontal and vertical scrollbars can be used with a picture box that is too small to display its entire contents. Then the value of the scrollbar can be used to move the picture box, thereby changing the part of the picture being viewed. This is useful, of course, for only those controls that provide their own means of navigating their data; some controls, such as the ListBox, have their own scrollbars to scroll through contained data.

The FlatScrollBar control is contained in the Windows Common Controls 2 library (*COMCT232.OCX*) that comes with the Visual Basic Professional and Enterprise editions. The HScrollBar and VScrollBar controls are Visual Basic intrinsic controls. Lightweight versions of the horizontal and vertical scrollbar controls are also available; see the entry for Windowless Controls later in this chapter.

Controls S

Control Tasks

The following categories reflect the tasks that are executed when creating a scrollbar.

Set Properties

1. Set appearance.

Appearance (FlatScrollBar only) **VB6**
The look of the FlatScrollBar (see Figure 5-52) is controlled by the Appearance property. This property can be set to 0–fsb3D, which mimics the appearance of the other scrollbar controls; 1–fsbFlat, which eliminates the control's 3-D appearance; or 2–fsbTrack3D, which gives the same flat appearance as `fsbFlat`, except that the scrollbar's arrows and value indicator become 3-D when the mouse moves over them.

Orientation (FlatScrollBar only) **VB6**
The FlatScrollBar can appear as either a horizontal or vertical scrollbar (see Figure 5-52) by setting its Orientation property to either 0–cc2OrientationHorizontal or 1–cc2OrientationVertical, respectively.

Because the Orientation property allows the FlatScrollBar to appear as either a horizontal or vertical scrollbar, it can replace both the HScrollBar and VScrollBar controls in an application. However, since the HScrollBar and VScrollBar are Visual Basic intrinsic controls, they generally have a smaller memory footprint. Therefore, the FlatScrollBar should be used when its other capabilities are needed.

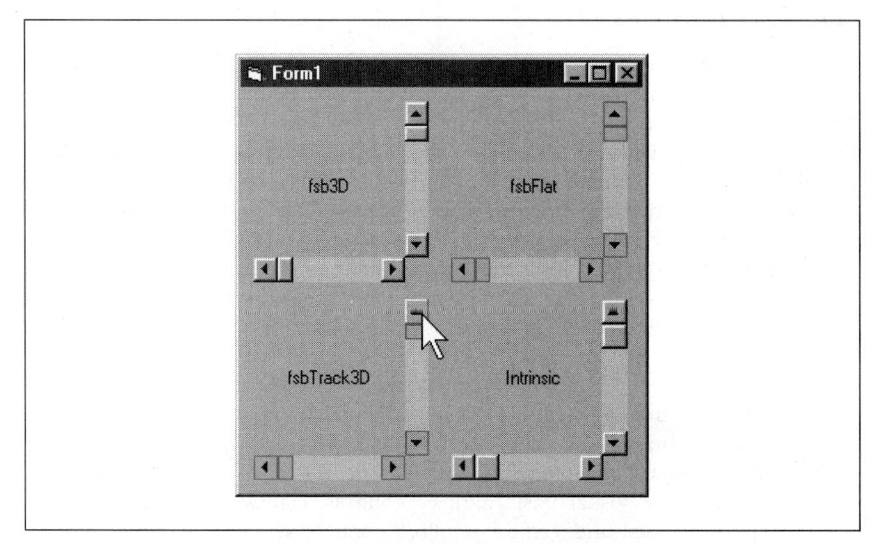

Figure 5-52: FlatScrollBar control styles and orientations

Arrows (FlatScrollBar only) VB6

The Arrows property determines which buttons on the FlatScrollBar are enabled at any time. By setting the Arrows property to 0–cc2Both, both buttons are enabled. Setting the Arrows property to 1–cc2LeftUp or 2–cc2RightDown enables the button named in the value (for example, for `cc2LeftUp`, the left button in a horizontal scrollbar or the upper button in a vertical scrollbar). The other button is disabled.

2. Set constraints.

Min and Max

Sets the minimum and maximum values that the scrollbar can contain.

3. Set change amounts.

SmallChange

Sets the amount that the scrollbar increases or decreases when the user clicks on the arrow icons at each end of the scrollbar.

LargeChange

Sets the amount that the scrollbar increases or decreases when the user clicks between the sliding scroll box and the arrow icon at each end of the scrollbar.

4. Set or retrieve scroll value.

   Value

   This property represents the current position of the scrollbar relative to the Min and Max properties.

Write Event Handlers

Change

The change event is fired whenever the scrollbar's value has been changed, whether by code or by the user. When the value indicator is dragged, this event is fired only after it is dropped.

Scroll

When the user drags the scroll box, the Scroll event is fired repeatedly. When you need to update information based on a scrollbar's value, both the Change and Scroll events are useful. This is particularly true when scrolling through data that doesn't fit on a form, as in the following example.

Example

The following code example dynamically creates a horizontal and a vertical scrollbar (the resulting form is shown in Figure 5-53):

```
'For this example, create the following controls: _
 Label named lblMain with the Index property set to 0, and _
 TextBox named txtMain with the Index property set to 0.

Dim picOutside As PictureBox
Dim picInside As PictureBox
Dim WithEvents hsbMain As HScrollBar
Dim WithEvents vsbMain As VScrollBar

Private Sub Form_Load()
   Dim iCtr As Integer

   'Create and/or setup controls.
   Set hsbMain = Me.Controls.Add("vb.hscrollbar", _
                              "hsbMain", Me)
   Set vsbMain = Me.Controls.Add("vb.vscrollbar", _
                              "vsbMain", Me)

   Set picOutside = Me.Controls.Add("vb.picturebox", _
                              "picOutside", Me)
   picOutside.Visible = True
   picOutside.BorderStyle = vbBSNone

   Set picInside = Me.Controls.Add("vb.picturebox", _
                              "picInside", Me)
   'Note that picOutside contains picInside, but not the scrollbars.
   Set picInside.Container = picOutside
   picInside.Visible = True
   picInside.BorderStyle = vbBSNone
```

Controls S

```
    For iCtr = 0 To 19
       If iCtr <> 0 Then
          Load lblMain(iCtr)
          Load txtMain(iCtr)
       End If
       lblMain(iCtr).Visible = True
       Set lblMain(iCtr).Container = picInside
       lblMain(iCtr).Caption = "Field " & _
                             Format$(iCtr, "00") & ":"
       txtMain(iCtr).Visible = True
       Set txtMain(iCtr).Container = picInside
       txtMain(iCtr).Text = ""
    Next iCtr

    Me.Caption = "Data Entry Form"
End Sub

Private Sub Form_Resize()
    Dim iCtr1 As Integer
    Dim iCtr2 As Integer
    Dim lSbH As Long
    Dim lSbW As Long

    Static bAlreadyDone As Boolean

    'Need to move controls in picInside only once.
    If Not bAlreadyDone Then
       For iCtr1 = 0 To 1
          For iCtr2 = 0 To 9
             lblMain(iCtr2 + (10 * iCtr1)).Move _
                   120 + (2430 * iCtr1), _
                   (180 * iCtr2) + (255 * iCtr2) + 180, _
                   1095, 255
             txtMain(iCtr2 + (10 * iCtr1)).Move _
                   1135 + (2430 * iCtr1), _
                   (120 * iCtr2) + (315 * iCtr2) + 120, _
                   1095, 315
          Next iCtr2
       Next iCtr1
       picInside.Move 0, 0, 4980, (10 * 120) + _
                   (10 * 315) + 120
       bAlreadyDone = True
    End If

    Const SB_SMCHG = 0.05  'The % change for small change
    Const SB_LGCHG = 0.25  'The % change for a large change
    Const SB_SIZE = 195    'Width of vertical scrollbar _
                            and height of the horizontal _
                            scrollbar

    If Me.ScaleWidth < 395 Or Me.ScaleHeight < 395 Then
        Exit Sub
    End If
```

```
   If Me.ScaleWidth > picInside.Width + SB_SIZE Then
      'If the form is wide enough, don't show the _
        HScrollBar.
      hsbMain.Visible = False
      lSbH = 0
   Else
      hsbMain.Visible = True
      lSbH = SB_SIZE
   End If

   If Me.ScaleHeight > picInside.Height + SB_SIZE Then
      'If the form is high enough, don't show the
      'VScrollBar.
      vsbMain.Visible = False
      lSbW = 0
   Else
      vsbMain.Visible = True
      lSbW = SB_SIZE
   End If

   hsbMain.Move 0, Me.ScaleHeight - lSbH, _
             Me.ScaleWidth - lSbW, SB_SIZE
   vsbMain.Move Me.ScaleWidth - lSbW, 0, _
             SB_SIZE, Me.ScaleHeight - lSbH
   picOutside.Move 0, 0, Me.ScaleWidth - lSbW, _
                Me.ScaleHeight - lSbH

   If hsbMain.Visible Then
      'Set the HScrollBar properties based on form size.
      hsbMain.Min = 0
      hsbMain.Max = picInside.Width - picOutside.Width
      hsbMain.SmallChange = IIf(hsbMain.Max * _
          SB_SMCHG < 1, 1, hsbMain.Max * SB_SMCHG)
      hsbMain.LargeChange = IIf(hsbMain.Max * _
          SB_LGCHG < 1, 1, hsbMain.Max * SB_LGCHG)
   Else
      hsbMain.Value = 0
   End If

   If vsbMain.Visible Then
      'Set the VScrollBar properties based on form size.
      vsbMain.Min = 0
      vsbMain.Max = picInside.Height - picOutside.Height
      vsbMain.SmallChange = IIf(vsbMain.Max * _
          SB_SMCHG < 1, 1, vsbMain.Max * SB_SMCHG)
      vsbMain.LargeChange = IIf(vsbMain.Max * _
          SB_LGCHG < 1, 1, vsbMain.Max * SB_LGCHG)
   Else
      vsbMain.Value = 0
   End If
End Sub

Private Sub hsbMain_Change()
    ScrollPic
```

Controls S

```
End Sub

Private Sub hsbMain_Scroll()
    ScrollPic
End Sub

Private Sub vsbMain_Change()
    ScrollPic
End Sub

Private Sub vsbMain_Scroll()
    ScrollPic
End Sub

Private Sub ScrollPic()
  'This procedure scrolls the picture box to wherever
  'the values of the scrollbars say.
   picInside.Move 0 - hsbMain.Value, 0 - vsbMain.Value
End Sub
```

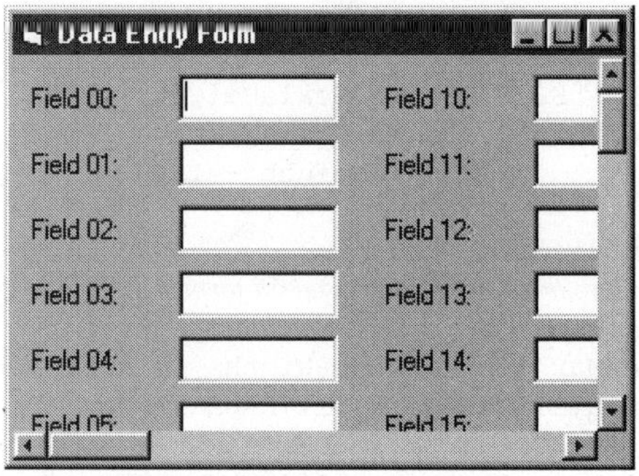

Figure 5-53: The scrollbar example

Interactions

Action	Result
Change the Value property through code.	Change event fires; scrollbar visibly changes.

Shape Control

The Shape control is graphically represented as a geometric shape. This control can be useful to respond to mouse events but is of limited use in most applications.

Set Properties

1. Set shape.

   Shape

   The actual shape displayed by a Shape control is controlled by the Shape property. The Shape property can be set to 0–Rectangle, 1–Square, 2–Oval, 3–Circle, 4–Rounded Rectangle, or 5–Rounded Square.

2. Set appearance.

   BorderColor, BorderStyle, BorderWidth, DrawMode, FillColor, FillStyle

   These properties control the appearance of the shape drawn by the Shape control. BorderColor sets the color of the stroked border around the shape. BorderStyle can be set to 0–vbTransparent, 1–vbBSSolid, 2–vbBSDash, 3–vbBSDot, 4–vbBSDashDot, 5–vbBSDashDotDot, or 6–vbBSInsideSolid and appears the same as the PictureBox control's DrawStyle property. The BorderWidth, FillColor, and FillStyle properties act the same as the PictureBox control's DrawWidth, FillColor, and FillStyle properties.

Slider Control

Similar to the scrollbars (see Scrollbar Controls earlier in this chapter), the Slider control graphically represents a numeric value to the user. However, where as a scrollbar is used primarily to scroll other controls, the slider is used to actually represent a value. Optionally, the slider can be made to represent a range of values.

The Slider control is included with the Windows Common Controls (*COMCTL32.OCX*) that come with Visual Basic Professional and Enterprise editions.

Control Tasks

The following categories reflect the tasks that are executed when creating and using a slider.

Set Properties

1. Set appearance (optional).

   Orientation

   Controls whether the slider appears horizontally with the minimum value to the left (0–sldHorizontal) or vertically with the minimum value on top (1–sldVertical). It can be set either at design time or at runtime.

   TickStyle

   When set to 0–sldBottomRight, tick marks on the slider appear at the bottom of vertical sliders (Orientation = 0) or on the right side of horizontal sliders (Orientation = 1). When set to 1–sldTopLeft, the tick marks appear on the opposite side of the slider. When set to 2–sldBoth, tick marks appear on both sides of the slider, and the value indicator changes from pointing to the ticks to not pointing at all. When set to 3–sldNoTicks, the value indicator appears as it does when set to 0, but there are no tick marks.

TickFrequency
: Determines the incremental value of each successive tick mark. For example, the default value of 1 indicates that each tick mark represents one unit greater than the preceding tick mark.

TextPosition **VB6**
: Can be set to 0–sldAboveLeft to display the contents of the Text property above the value indicator when the Orientation property is set to `sldHorizontal` or to the left when the Orientation property is set to `sldVertical`, or it can be set to 1–sldBelowRight for the opposite effect.

Text **VB6**
: Text associated with the Slider control's value can be shown by setting the Text property. The text then appears in a location based on the TextPosition property.

2. Set constraints.

Min and Max
: Set the minimum and maximum values that the slider can contain.

3. Set change values.

SmallChange
: Sets the amount that the slider's value changes when the slider has the focus and the user presses the Left or Right Arrow keys.

LargeChange
: Set the amount that the slider's value changes when the user clicks to the side of the value indicator.

4. Set slider value.

Value
: Represents the current position of the slider relative to the Min and Max properties. Sometimes, it may be desirable to have the value represent something other than a smooth scale. Although the slider will always have sequential integer values, the example shows how to do this. (You can inspect the different interval values by moving the slider bar and then right-clicking on it once it's positioned at a new value.)

5. Adjust range settings.

SelectRange
: When set to the default, `False`, the slider can represent only one value at a time. This value is represented by the Value property. When set to `True`, the slider can be placed under program control to represent a range of values, which are indicated by the SelStart and SelLength prop-

erties. The following code fragment shows how to use the slider to indicate a range of values rather than a single value:

```
Dim blnSliderSelection As Boolean

Private Sub Slider1_MouseDown(Button As Integer, _
    Shift As Integer, x As Single, y As Single)

If Button = vbLeftButton Then
  'Clear selection if MouseDown is on slider.
   If blnSliderSelection Then
      Slider1.ClearSel
      blnSliderSelection = False
   End If

  'If Shift, begin selection
If Not blnSliderSelection And (Button = vbLeftButton) _
    And (Shift = 1) Then
      blnSliderSelection = True
      Slider1.SelStart = Slider1.Value
   End If
End If

End Sub

Private Sub Slider1_MouseUp(Button As Integer, _
    Shift As Integer, x As Single, y As Single)

'Make sure MouseUp is part of selection process.
If blnSliderSelection And (Button = vbLeftButton) _
    And (Shift = 1) Then
  'Current pos. must be greater than starting pos.
   If Slider1.Value > Slider1.SelStart Then _
      Slider1.SelLength = _
              Slider1.Value - Slider1.SelStart
End If

End Sub
```

SelStart

This property represents the lower end of a range of values shown on a slider when SelectRange is `True`.

SelLength

When a range of values needs to be shown on a slider, this property represents the number of values shown by the range. SelLength cannot be negative; that is, the range must begin with a lower value and extend to a higher value.

Useful Methods

ClearSel

Clears any selection shown on a slider. It does this by setting both the SelStart and SelLength properties to 0.

GetNumTicks

Returns the number of tick marks shown on the slider. This value can be easily calculated without this method as follows:

```
iNumTicks = Int(sldMain.Max - sldMain.Min) / _
            sldMain.TickFrequency
```

Write Event Handlers

Change

Fired whenever the value indicator of the slider is moved, whether by code or by the user.

Scroll

When the user drags the value indicator of the slider, the Scroll event is fired repeatedly, once for each unit that it has been dragged. This helps to provide real-time information to the user based on the current value of the slider.

Example

The result of running this example code is shown in Figure 5-54:

```
Option Explicit

'For this example, create a Slider control _
  (part of MSCOMCTL.OCX) named sldInterval.

Private WithEvents cmdExit As CommandButton

Private maSlider(10, 1) As Variant

Public Property Get Interval() As Integer
  'This would allow another form or module to retrieve_
   the interval.
    Interval = maSlider(sldInterval.Value, 1)
End Property

Private Sub cmdExit_Click()
  'Once again, by hiding the form instead of closing it, _
    another form or module can retrieve the interval.
    Me.Hide
End Sub

Private Sub Form_Load()
  'Create and/or set up controls.
    Set cmdExit = Me.Controls.Add("vb.commandbutton", _
                 "cmdExit", Me)
    cmdExit.Visible = True
    cmdExit.Caption = "E&xit"

    Me.sldInterval.TickStyle = sldTopLeft
    Me.sldInterval.Min = 0
    Me.sldInterval.Max = 10
    Me.sldInterval.SmallChange = 1
    Me.sldInterval.LargeChange = 2
    Me.sldInterval.TickFrequency = 1
```

```
    Me.sldInterval.TextPosition = sldAboveLeft

    Me.Caption = "Slider Example"
    Me.Move Me.Left, Me.Top, 4770, 1755

'Initialize Interval Array.
    maSlider(0, 0) = 0
    maSlider(0, 1) = "Constant"
    maSlider(1, 0) = 1
    maSlider(1, 1) = "Every Second"
    maSlider(2, 0) = 2
    maSlider(2, 1) = "Every Two Seconds"
    maSlider(3, 0) = 5
    maSlider(3, 1) = "Every Five Seconds"
    maSlider(4, 0) = 10
    maSlider(4, 1) = "Every Ten Seconds"
    maSlider(5, 0) = 15
    maSlider(5, 1) = "Every Fifteen Seconds"
    maSlider(6, 0) = 30
    maSlider(6, 1) = "Every Thirty Seconds"
    maSlider(7, 0) = 60
    maSlider(7, 1) = "Every Minute"
    maSlider(8, 0) = 300
    maSlider(8, 1) = "Every Five Minutes"
    maSlider(9, 0) = 900
    maSlider(9, 1) = "Every Fifteen Minutes"
    maSlider(9, 0) = 3600
    maSlider(9, 1) = "Every Hour"
    maSlider(10, 0) = 7200
    maSlider(10, 1) = "Every Two Hours"

    UpdateSlider
End Sub

Private Sub Form_Resize()
    If Me.ScaleWidth < 1335 Or Me.ScaleHeight < 1250 Then _
        Exit Sub

    Me.sldInterval.Move 120, 120, Me.ScaleWidth - 240
    cmdExit.Move Me.ScaleWidth - 1215, _
                Me.ScaleHeight - 495, 1095, 375
End Sub

Private Sub sldInterval_Change()
    UpdateSlider
End Sub

Private Sub sldInterval_Scroll()
    UpdateSlider
End Sub

Private Sub UpdateSlider()
    Me.sldInterval.Text = maSlider(sldInterval.Value, 1)
End Sub
```

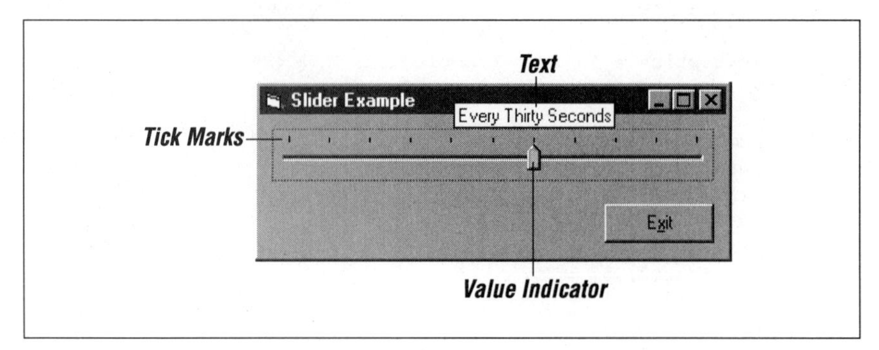

Figure 5-54: The Slider control

Interactions

Action	*Result*
Value changes if SelectRange is `False`.	SelectStart changes to equal Value.
Change Value property in code.	Fires Change event.

StatusBar Control

The StatusBar is a dockable control usually located at the bottom of a form that provides status information to the user. It can display a simple text message or a series of messages in multiple panels.

The StatusBar control is included with the Windows Common Controls (*COMCTL32.OCX*) that come with Visual Basic Professional and Enterprise editions.

Control Tasks

The following categories reflect the tasks that are executed when creating a status bar.

Set StatusBar Properties

1. Set appearance (optional).

   Style

   When set to the default, 0–sbrNormal, the status bar can display multiple panels, each with its own properties. When Style is set to 1–sbrSimple, the status bar contains only one panel, which displays the contents of the SimpleText property. The Style property can be set either at design time or at runtime.

2. Create panels.

Panels (collection)

When the Style property is set to 0, all of the panels are contained in the Panels collection. As with all collections, the Panels collection has a Count property and an Item property, as well as an Add method, a Remove method, and a Clear method.

Panel (object)

Each panel in a status bar is represented in code by a Panel object. The properties of the Panel object control its contents as well as how the panel appears and behaves relative to other panels.

3. Set panel properties.

Style

Aside from the default, 0–sbrText, the values in the following table can be assigned to the Panel object's Style property:

Constant	*Value*	*Description*
`sbrCaps`	1	Shows the current state of the Caps Lock key
`sbrNum`	2	Shows the current state of the Num Lock key
`sbrIns`	3	Shows whether Windows is in Insert mode
`sbrScrl`	4	Shows the current state of the Scroll Lock key
`sbrTime`	5	Shows the current time
`sbrDate`	6	Shows the current date
`sbrKana`	7	Shows the state of the `KANA` key on Japanese versions of Windows

Text

When the Style of the panel is set to 0–sbrText, the contents of the Text property are displayed in the panel. Most users are familiar with a left-most text panel that contains information about their current action. This can be done as shown in the example.

Bevel

Panels are distinguished from adjacent panels and from their container form based on the Bevel property. They can be displayed as 1–sbrInset (the default), 0–sbrNoBevel, or 2–sbrRaised.

Alignment

The contents of a panel are aligned within the panel based on this property. The possible values are the default, 0–sbrLeft, 1–sbrCenter, and 2–sbrRight.

AutoSize

When a status bar is resized, the contained panels resize based on their AutoSize properties. When set to its default, 0–sbrNoAutoSize, the panel remains sized according to its Width property, regardless of the size of the status bar. When set to 1–sbrSpring, the panel resizes proportionally along with the status bar, never allowing its width to fall below its MinWidth property. When set to 2–sbrContents, the panel maintains a size large enough to display its contents, once again never allowing its width to fall below its MinWidth property. Generally, `sbrSpring` and `sbrContents` are preferable to the default value of `sbrNoAutoSize`, since Panel objects set to `sbrNoAutoSize` can easily have their contents obscured.

MinWidth

When a Panel object's AutoSize property is set to `sbrSpring` or `sbrContents`, it will never resize smaller than the value set by the MinWidth property.

Write Event Handlers

PanelClick and PanelDblClick

Aside from the standard Click and DblClick events, the status bar has these two additional events to provide the application with the actual panel that was clicked on. This Panel object is passed to the method as a parameter.

Example

The result of running this code is shown in Figure 5-55:

```
Option Explicit

'For this exampe, create the following controls: _
   a StatusBar named sbrMain, a TextBox named _
   txtMain with the Index property set to 0, and _
   a Label named lblMain with the Index property _
      set to 0.

Private Sub Form_Load()
    Dim iCtr As Integer
    Dim pnlAdd As Panel

   'Create and/or set up controls.
    For iCtr = 0 To 9
        If iCtr > 0 Then
            Load Me.lblMain(iCtr)
            Load Me.txtMain(iCtr)
        End If
        Me.lblMain(iCtr).Visible = True
        Me.lblMain(iCtr).Caption = "Field " & _
                                  Format$(iCtr + 1, "0")
        Me.lblMain(iCtr).TabIndex = iCtr * 2
        Me.txtMain(iCtr).Visible = True
        Me.txtMain(iCtr).Text = ""
        Me.txtMain(iCtr).TabIndex = iCtr * 2 + 1
    Next iCtr

   'Create panels and set panel properties.
    sbrMain.Panels(1).AutoSize = sbrSpring
```

```
    Set pnlAdd = sbrMain.Panels.Add(Index:=2, _
                 Style:=sbrCaps)
    pnlAdd.Alignment = sbrCenter
    pnlAdd.AutoSize = sbrContents
    pnlAdd.Width = 1

    Set pnlAdd = sbrMain.Panels.Add(Index:=3, _
                 Style:=sbrNum)
    pnlAdd.Alignment = sbrCenter
    pnlAdd.AutoSize = sbrContents
    pnlAdd.Width = 1

    Set pnlAdd = sbrMain.Panels.Add(Index:=4, _
                 Style:=sbrIns)
    pnlAdd.Alignment = sbrCenter
    pnlAdd.AutoSize = sbrContents
    pnlAdd.Width = 1

    Set pnlAdd = sbrMain.Panels.Add(Index:=5, _
                 Style:=sbrScrl)
    pnlAdd.Alignment = sbrCenter
    pnlAdd.AutoSize = sbrContents
    pnlAdd.Width = 1

    Set pnlAdd = sbrMain.Panels.Add(Index:=6, _
                 Style:=sbrDate)
    pnlAdd.Alignment = sbrCenter
    pnlAdd.AutoSize = sbrContents
    pnlAdd.Bevel = sbrNoBevel
    pnlAdd.Width = 1

    Set pnlAdd = sbrMain.Panels.Add(Index:=7, _
                 Style:=sbrTime)
    pnlAdd.Alignment = sbrCenter
    pnlAdd.AutoSize = sbrContents
    pnlAdd.Bevel = sbrNoBevel
    pnlAdd.Width = 1

    Me.Caption = "StatusBar"
    Me.Move Me.Left, Me.Top, 6500, 5250
End Sub

Private Sub Form_Resize()
   Dim iCtr As Integer

   If Me.ScaleHeight < 500 Or Me.ScaleWidth < 2550 Then _
      Exit Sub

   For iCtr = 0 To 9
      Me.lblMain(iCtr).Move _
         120, (120 * iCtr) + (315 * iCtr) + 180, 1095, 255
      Me.txtMain(iCtr).Move _
       1335, (120 * iCtr) + (315 * iCtr) + 120, _
            Me.ScaleWidth - 1455, 315
```

Controls S

```
    Next iCtr
End Sub

Private Sub txtMain_GotFocus(Index As Integer)
   'Update the contents of Panel 1 based on the current TextBox.
   sbrMain.Panels(1).Text = _
        "Enter value for " & lblMain(Index).Caption
End Sub
```

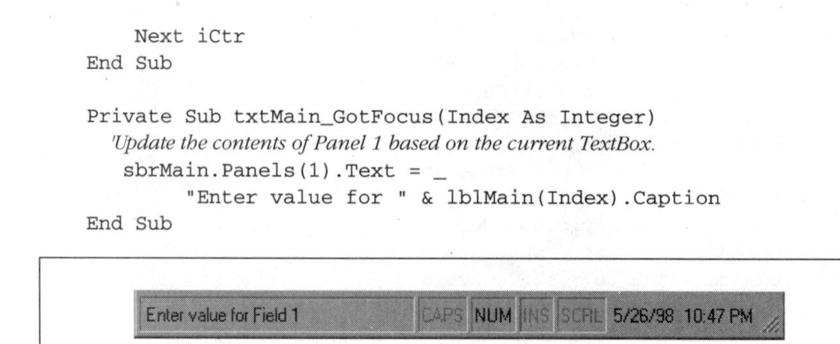

Figure 5-55: The StatusBar control

SysInfo Control

The SysInfo control provides some information about the environment in which your application is running. Even more valuable perhaps, the SysInfo control fires events when the environment changes, which allows you to use Visual Basic to respond to Plug-and-Play event notifications. While many of the events raised and properties provided by the SysInfo control pertain to notebook computers and battery power, many others are useful on any type of system. The control does not have a user interface.

The SysInfo control is contained in the Microsoft SysInfo control (*SYSINFO.OCX*) that comes with Visual Basic Professional and Enterprise editions.

Control Tasks

The following categories reflect the tasks that are executed when creating a SysInfo control.

Retrieve Properties

1. Determine operating system.

   OSPlatform

   Depending on the operating system that the application is running, the OSPlatform property will return either 0–Win32s, 1–Windows 9x, or 2–Windows NT. This is useful for determining the capabilities of the system and various API issues.

   OSVersion

   You can determine the version of the operating system your application is running on by retrieving the OSVersion property. This can be important in a wide variety of situations. For instance, if your application is running under WinNT, you may need to know whether the 32-bit shell is present (in WinNT 4.x and greater) or not (in WinNT 3.x).

2. Determine usable screen size.

   WorkAreaHeight, WorkAreaLeft, WorkAreaTop, WorkAreaWidth
   Because the usable area of the screen can be affected by elements such as the Windows Start menu, these properties return the area of the screen that your application can safely use. Values are always expressed in twips, regardless of the setting of the containing form's ScaleMode property.

3. Determine power status.

   ACStatus
   When accessed on a desktop system, the ACStatus property will usually return 255–Unknown. However, many notebook computers will return either 0–Battery or 1–AC. This also depends on the BIOS installed.

   BatteryStatus, BatteryLifePercent, BatteryLifeTime, BatteryFullTime
   Each of these properties returns information about the battery being used in a notebook computer. BatteryStatus returns 1–High, 2–Low, 4–Critical, 8–Charging, 128–No Battery, or 255–Unknown, depending on the current status of the battery. BatteryFullTime and BatteryLifeTime return the life, in seconds, of a full battery and the current battery, respectively. Each of these properties will return &HFFFFFFFF (-1) if the battery life information is unknown. BatteryLifePercent returns the current percentage of the battery charge on the system. This is useful for an indicator, such as a progress bar, that shows the amount of charge left. If the amount is unknown, the BatteryLifePercent property returns 255.

Write Event Handlers

DisplayChanged
Indicates that the screen resolution has changed. You can get information about the new screen resolution by retrieving the Screen object's Height and Width properties, as well as by reading the SysInfo control's WorkArea-Height, WorkAreaLeft, WorkAreaTop, and WorkAreaWidth properties. This allows you to reposition your application windows and other interface objects in response to the change in screen resolution.

SysColorsChanged
Indicates that a change has been made to Windows system colors. Since no information about the change is provided as a parameter to the event handler, you'll have to call the Win32 *GetSysColor* function to determine what the new colors are.

TimeChanged
The event is fired when the time of the system clock is changed. The *Now* function can be used to retrieve the new date and time.

SettingChanged
When a system setting is changed, the SettingChanged event is fired. Version 5.0 of the SysInfo control passed two parameters to the event handler. In contrast, Version 6.0 of the control passes only one: `Item`, an integer that reflects the item changed; possible values for `Item` are shown in Table 5-2.

SettingChanged reflects the Windows `WM_SETTINGCHANGED` message. The message itself can be sent directly by an application using the *SendMessage* or *PostMessage* functions in the Win32 API, or it can be sent by Windows when an application calls the Win32 *SystemParametersInfo* function to change a system setting. In the former case, the value of the `Item` parameter may be 0, and the event may not indicate what system setting has changed.

Table 5-2: The Item Parameter of the SettingChanged Event

Item	*Description*
2	The warning beeper has been turned on or off.
4	Mouse acceleration or mouse threshold values have changed.
6	The width of a window's sizing border has changed.
11	The keyboard repeat speed has changed.
13	The icon cell width has changed.
15	The screensaver time-out interval has changed.
17	The screensaver has been activated or deactivated.
19	The granularity of the desktop sizing grad has changed.
20	The desktop wallpaper has changed.
21	The current desktop pattern has changed.
23	The keyboard repeat delay setting has changed.
24	The icon cell height has changed.
26	Icon title wrap has been turned on or off.
28	Pop-up menus have changed from right-aligned to left or vice versa.
29	The width of the double-click rectangle has changed.
30	The height of the double-click rectangle has changed.
32	Mouse double-click time has changed.
33	The function of the left and right mouse buttons has been swapped or restored.
34	The font used for icon titles has changed.
37	Full dragging of windows has been turned on or off.
42	The metrics of the nonclient area of nonminimized windows have changed.
44	The metrics of minimized windows have changed.
46	The metrics of icons have changed.
47	The size of the work area has changed.
51	The parameters of the FilterKeys accessibility feature have changed.
53	The parameters of the ToggleKeys accessibility feature have changed.
55	The parameters of the MouseKeys accessibility feature have changed.
57	The ShowSounds accessibility feature has been turned on or off.
59	The parameters of the StickyKeys accessibility feature have changed.
61	The time-out period of the accessibility features has changed.
63	The parameters of the SerialKeys accessibility feature have changed.
64	The parameters of the SoundSentry accessibility feature have changed.

Table 5-2: The Item Parameter of the SettingChanged Event (continued)

Item	Description
67	The parameters of the high-contrast accessibility feature have changed.
69	Keyboard preference has been enabled or disabled.
71	A screen review utility is now running or has stopped running.
73	Animation effects have changed.
75	Font smoothing has been enabled or disabled.
76	The width in pixels used to detect a drag operation has changed.
77	The height in pixels used to detect a drag operation has changed.
81	The time-out value for the low-power phase of screen saving has changed.
82	The time-out value for the power-off phrase of screen saving has changed.
85	The low-power phase of screen saving has been activated or deactivated.
86	The power-off phase of screen saving has been activated or deactivated.
87	The system cursors have been reloaded.
88	The system icons have been reloaded.
90	The default input language for the system shell and applications has changed.
91	The hot key for switching between input languages has changed.
93	Mouse trails have been enabled or disabled.
99	The mouse hover width has changed.
101	The mouse hover height has changed.
103	The mouse hover time has changed.
105	The number of lines to scroll when the mouse wheel is rolled has changed.
111	The display of the Input Method Editor user interface has been turned on or off (Far Eastern version only).
113	The mouse speed has changed.
4,097	Active window tracking has been turned on or off.
4,099	Menu animation has been turned on or off.
4,102	The slide-open effect of combo boxes has been enabled or disabled.
4,103	The smooth-scrolling effect of list boxes has been enabled or disabled.
4,105	The gradient effect of titlebars has been enabled or disabled.
4,107	Menu underlines have been enabled or disabled.
4,109	The use of active window tracking to bring active windows to the front has been turned on or off.
4,111	Hot tracking (the display of tooltips for nonclient-area buttons and menu bar items) has been turned on or off.
8,193	The foreground lock time-out value has changed.
8,195	The active-window-tracking delay has changed.
8,197	The number of times a taskbar button will flash when a foreground switch request is rejected has changed.

ConfigChanged, ConfigChangeCancelled, QueryChangeConfig

These events are fired in response to the change in the hardware configuration (typically a docking or undocking from a docking station) and therefore a change in the registry key from which configuration information is retrieved. The QueryChangeConfig event allows the application to stop a change from occurring by setting the `Cancel` parameter to `True`. The ConfigChanged event provides information about the registry key that was linked to the top-level registry key `HKEY_CURRENT_CONFIG` and the registry key that now is linked to it. In both cases, these are long integers whose string versions, when padded with zeros to become four characters in length, indicate a particular subkey of `HKEY_LOCAL_MACHINE\Config`. To actually retrieve configuration settings from the registry, though, you'll need to use the registry retrieval functions in the Win32 API.

DeviceArrival, DeviceOtherEvent, DeviceQueryRemove, DeviceQueryRemoveFailed, DeviceRemoveComplete, DeviceRemovePending

These events are fired when a device is added or removed from the system or when information about a device is changed. Four standard parameters identify the device by providing its type, ID, name, and a pointer to device-specific data. In addition, the DeviceQueryRemove event includes a `Cancel` parameter; if set to `True` by the event handler, the event handler can deny permission to remove the device.

PowerStatusChanged, PowerResume, PowerQuerySuspend, PowerSuspend

These events fire in response to the Power Suspend feature found in many notebook computers. The PowerQuerySuspend event supplies a parameter called `Cancel` that can be set to `True` to cancel the suspend operation. This is useful if the program should not be suspended at its current point.

TabStrip Control

The TabStrip allows the user to flip between virtual pages in one area of the form. The control appears as a set of tabs that can be clicked to move from one to another. While the tabs change automatically, the TabStrip is not a container, and any other actions (like the appearance of particular controls on particular tabs) must be controlled by the program. For example, controls that appear to be contained in the TabStrip are generally placed in another control, such as a Frame, which then is set to behave according to properties and events of the TabStrip.

The TabStrip control is included with the Windows Common Controls (*COMCTL32.OCX*) that come with Visual Basic Professional and Enterprise editions.

Control Tasks

The following categories reflect the tasks that are executed when creating a TabStrip.

Set Properties

1. Set general appearance.

Changing many of these properties (like Placement and TabStyle) at runtime can affect the size and location of the client area of the TabStrip.

Style

The TabStrip can display either a set of notebook divider-type tabs or a set of buttons. When set to the default, 0–tabTabs, the tabs have the appearance of notebook tabs. These tabs have a border that appears to contain the entire tab. When set to 1–tabButtons, the TabStrip has a set of buttons that act in every way like the notebook tabs. When set to 2–tabFlatButtons (in VB6 only), the buttons appear flat until pressed. When pressed, they appear recessed. There is no visible border when Style is set to `tabButtons` or `tabFlatButtons`. The three different styles for the TabStrip control are shown in Figure 5-56.

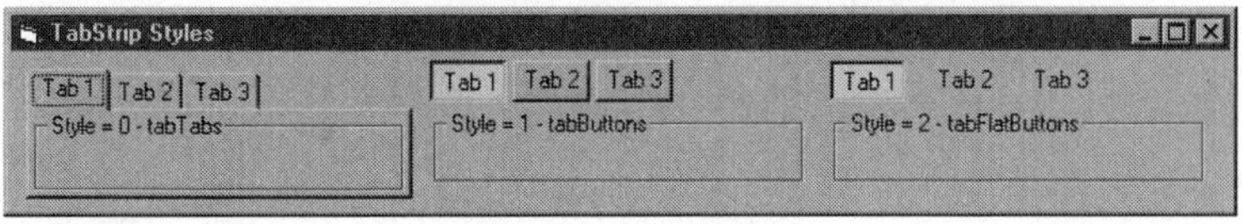

Figure 5-56: The different styles for a TabStrip control

Placement **VB6**

When the Placement property is set to the default value of 0–tabPlacementTop, the tabs or buttons appear at the top of the control. Setting the Placement property to 1–tabPlacementBottom, 2–tabPlacementLeft, or 3–tabPlacementRight causes the tabs or buttons to appear on that side of the TabStrip control. Note, though, that with Placement set to either `tabPlacementLeft` or `tabPlacementRight`, problems have been reported with the sizes of the tabs and the legibility of their captions.

ImageList

Rather than using only a caption to identify each button or notebook tab, you can use an image or an image along with a caption. In the latter cases, the ImageList property contains the name of an ImageList control on the same form as the TabStrip. Each Tab object placed in the TabStrip can choose which image to use from this ImageList.

TabWidthStyle

Can be set to 0–tabJustified, its default value, where the tabs are extended to fill an entire row if the MultiRow property is set to `True`; if the MultiRow property is `False`, it is identical to the `tabNonJustified` setting. When set to 1–tabNonJustified, the tabs are sized only wide enough to display their contents regardless of the MultiRow property. When set to 2–tabFixed, all tabs are as wide as the TabStrip's TabFixedWidth property.

TabMinWidth **VB6**

When TabWidthStyle is set to `tabJustified` or `tabNonJustified`, tabs will not resize smaller than the value of TabMinWidth.

TabFixedHeight, TabFixedWidth

Controls the height of the tab portion of the TabStrip control. When an image is shown on any tab, the image's height becomes the default for TabFixedHeight. Otherwise, if TabFixedHeight is set to 0, the font's height is used instead. The TabFixedWidth property is used only when the TabWidthStyle property is set to `tabFixed`. In this case, all tabs on the control are sized to that width.

Separators **VB6**

When Style is set to `tabFlatButtons`, setting the Separators property to `True` displays a vertical line between the buttons. Since these buttons appear only when pressed, this allows the user to easily see the options on the TabStrip.

2. Set TabStrip behavior.

MultiRow

When set to `True`, tabs that do not fit in a single row are placed in additional rows of tabs. These additional rows are placed according to the TabStyle property. When MultiRow is set to `False`, all tabs are placed in a single row, and tabs that are not visible are accessible by using arrow icons that appear when not all tabs are visible. Adding and subtracting tabs that might create or remove rows and resizing the TabStrip to create or remove rows can cause the client area to change.

TabStyle **VB6**

When MultiRow is set to `True` and Style is set to `tabTabs`, setting TabStyle to `tabTabStandard` causes any additional rows of tabs to appear on the same side of the TabStrip but visually behind the selected row. When TabStyle is set to `tabTabOpposite`, the additional rows appear on the other side of the TabStrip. For example, if the Placement were set to `tabPlacementTop`, additional rows of tabs would appear at the bottom of the TabStrip. Note that the property must be set at design time; modifying it at runtime, although it does not produce a runtime error, has no effect.

HotTracking **VB6**

When HotTracking is set to `True`, moving the mouse over a tab highlights that tab for the user. When set to `False`, this does not occur. The Tab object provides a HighLighted property to determine which tab is highlighted.

MultiSelect **VB6**

When the Style property is set to `tabButtons`, setting the MultiSelect property to `True` allows the user to select multiple tabs by holding the

CTRL key and selecting an additional tab. The selected tabs can then be determined by using the Tab objects' Selected property.

3. Create tabs.

Tabs (collection), Tab (object)

Each tab in a TabStrip is a Tab object that is part of the Tabs collection. Tab objects can be created at design time by using the TabStrip's custom property page, or at runtime by using the Add method of the Tabs collection. This method also allows the program to set some of the tab's properties by passing their values as parameters to it. Its syntax is:

```
object.Add(index, key, caption, image)
```

where ***object*** is a reference to a Tabs collection object, ***index*** is an optional integer indicating the position at which the tabbed page is to be inserted, ***key*** is a unique string that identifies the tabbed page, ***caption*** is the string that appears in the tab itself, and ***image*** is the index of the tab's image in the ImageList control. All parameters other than ***object*** are optional. If the ***index*** parameter is absent, the new tabbed page is inserted at the end of the Tabs collection.

4. Set tab properties.

Individual tabs on a TabStrip cannot be made invisible or disabled through properties.

Caption, Image

The caption and the index of the image to use for the tab in the ListImage control can be set either as parameters of the Tabs collection's Add method or by using these properties.

Images placed on tabs do not have any mask color support. Therefore, no areas of the image will appear transparent. For this reason, only images that extend to their extents should be used on a tab.

5. Determine the highlighted or selected tab(s).

SelectedItem (TabStrip control), Selected (Tab object)

The SelectedItem property of the TabStrip returns the currently selected Tab object. The Selected property of a Tab object returns a Boolean value indicating whether that tab is currently selected. By retrieving the SelectedItem property or iterating the Tabs collection and examining each Tab object's Selected property, you can determine which tabbed page is selected. By assigning a new Tab object to the SelectedItem property or by assigning `True` to a Tab object's Selected property, you can change the selected tab programmatically.

Note that you need to determine which tab is selected in order to make the controls that are supposed to appear on it visible; the example program illustrates how to do this.

HighLighted VB6

Setting the HighLighted property to `True` for a Tab object highlights that tab to the user. If the TabStrip control's HotTracking property is set to `True`, any highlighted tab will have its HighLighted property set to `True`.

6. Determine tab size and location.

ClientLeft, ClientTop, ClientHeight, ClientWidth

These properties provide the exact location and size of the client (usable) area of the Tab objects in a TabStrip control. Another control's placement is generally determined by these properties as follows:

```
fraMain.Move _
    Me.tbsMain.ClientLeft, _
    Me.tbsMain.ClientTop, _
    Me.tbsMain.ClientWidth, _
    Me.tbsMain.ClientHeight
```

Useful Methods

DeselectAll VB6

Causes any selected tabs to no longer be selected. This is particularly useful when the MultiSelect property is set to `True`.

Write Event Handlers

BeforeClick, Click

When the mouse button is clicked on a tab, the BeforeClick event is fired. This event has a *`Cancel`* parameter, which when set to `False`, will cause the tab not to change. If the *`Cancel`* parameter is left set to `True`, or no code is placed in the BeforeClick event, the Click event will fire. From the Click event, the SelectedItem property can be used to determine the clicked tab.

Example

```
Option Explicit

'For this example, create the following controls: _
  a TabStrip named tbsMain, _
  a CommandButton named cmdMain with the Index _
     property set to 0, _
  a Frame named fraMain with the Index property _
     set to 0 _
  a Label named lblMain with the Index property _
     set to 0, and _
  a TextBox named txtMain with the Index property _
     set to 0.

Private Sub Form_Load()
    Dim iCtr As Integer

  'Set up form.
    Me.Caption = "TabStrip Sample"
```

```
'Set up TabStrip.
  Me.tbsMain.TabIndex = 0
  Me.tbsMain.Tabs(1).Caption = "Tab &One"
  Me.tbsMain.Tabs.Add , , "Tab &Two"
  Me.tbsMain.Tabs.Add , , "Tab Thr&ee"

'Set up Frame(s).
  Me.fraMain(0).BorderStyle = vbBSNone
  Load Me.fraMain(1)
  Load Me.fraMain(2)

'Set up Label(s).
  For iCtr = 0 To 8
      If iCtr > 0 Then
          Load Me.lblMain(iCtr)
      End If
      Me.lblMain(iCtr).TabIndex = iCtr + 1
      Me.lblMain(iCtr).Caption = "Label &" & _
                                 Format(iCtr, "0")
      Set Me.lblMain(iCtr).Container = _
          Me.fraMain(Int(iCtr / 3))
      Me.lblMain(iCtr).Move 120, 180 + _
                     (315 * (iCtr Mod 3)), 1215, 255
      Me.lblMain(iCtr).Visible = True
  Next iCtr

'Set up TextBox(s).
  For iCtr = 0 To 8
      If iCtr > 0 Then
          Load Me.txtMain(iCtr)
      End If
      Me.txtMain(iCtr).Text = ""
      Set Me.txtMain(iCtr).Container = _
          Me.fraMain(Int(iCtr / 3))
      Me.txtMain(iCtr).Move 1335, 120 + (315 * _
                            (iCtr Mod 3)), 1215, 315
      Me.txtMain(iCtr).Visible = True
  Next iCtr

'Set up CommandButton(s).
  Me.cmdMain(0).Caption = "Cancel"
  Me.cmdMain(0).Cancel = True
  Load Me.cmdMain(1)
  Me.cmdMain(1).Caption = "Ok"
  Me.cmdMain(1).Default = True
  Me.cmdMain(1).Visible = True
End Sub

Private Sub Form_Resize()
  Dim ctlVar As Control

'We want the TabStrip to occupy the entire form _
except for some space at the bottom for the _
```

Controls T

*buttons. As always, we'll put a 120-twip _
border around and between all controls.*

```
    Me.tbsMain.Move 120, 120, Me.ScaleWidth - 240, _
                    Me.ScaleHeight - 735
    For Each ctlVar In Me.fraMain
        ctlVar.Move _
            Me.tbsMain.ClientLeft, _
            Me.tbsMain.ClientTop, _
            Me.tbsMain.ClientWidth, _
            Me.tbsMain.ClientHeight
    Next ctlVar

    For Each ctlVar In Me.cmdMain
        ctlVar.Move _
           Me.ScaleWidth -(1215 * (ctlVar.Index + 1)), _
           Me.ScaleHeight - 495, _
           1095, _
           375
    Next ctlVar
End Sub

Private Sub tbsMain_Click()
    Dim ctlVar As Control

    For Each ctlVar In Me.fraMain
        If ctlVar.Index = _
            Me.tbsMain.SelectedItem.Index - 1 Then
      'Show the corresponding frame and send _
      it to the front.
            ctlVar.Visible = True
            ctlVar.ZOrder 0
        Else
      'Hide the corresponding frame.
            ctlVar.Visible = False
        End If
    Next ctlVar
End Sub

Private Sub cmdMain_Click(Index As Integer)
   'Normally we'd take some sort of action here, but _
   that would have little to do with the TabStrip.
    Unload Me
End Sub
```

Interactions

Action	*Result*
The user clicks on a tab.	The BeforeClick Event is fired. If the `Cancel` parameter is not changed to `False`, the SelectedItem and Selected properties are updated and the Click event is fired.

TextBox Control

TextBox is Visual Basic's text entry control. It allows the user to enter single or multiple lines of text and accepts any characters that are supported by Windows. Windows automatically provides a pop-up menu with standard editing commands when a text box is right-clicked.

A lightweight version of the TextBox control is also available; see Windowless Controls later in this chapter.

Control Tasks

The following categories reflect the tasks executed when creating a text box.

Set Properties

1. Specify text alignment (optional).

   Alignment

   Can be set to 0 or `vbLeftJustify`, 1 or `vbRightJustify`, or 2 or `vbCenter` to align the text in the text box.

   MultiLine

   With MultiLine set to `False`, all text is aligned to the left, regardless of the Alignment property. With MultiLine set to `True`, pressing Enter while in a text box yields another line, and any single line of text longer than the width of the text box wraps onto a new line.

2. Set password character (optional).

   When a character such as an asterisk (*) is assigned to the PasswordChar property, each character typed is represented on the screen as that character. Using this property causes the Windows Copy and Cut commands not to work on this text box. If the MultiLine property is set to `True`, setting PasswordChar has no effect.

3. Set maximum text length (optional).

   When a number other than 0 is used in the MaxLength property, the text box will beep and stop accepting characters after that number of charaters has been entered.

4. Specify text (optional).

   The text that appears in a text box can be set or retrieved using the Text property, which is the TextBox control's default member.

Write Event Handlers

Change

Anytime the contents of a text box are changed, the Change event is triggered. While pasting text into a text box lets invalid data past a KeyDown or KeyPress event, the Change event captures these as well.

KeyDown and KeyPress

When a key is depressed on the keyboard, the KeyDown event is triggered with the key code of the specific key pressed. If that key corresponds to an ANSI character, the KeyPress event is triggered with the key's ASCII value. Therefore, when trapping keys or key combinations with no ANSI equivalent (such as ALT and ALT-key combinations and the function keys) or ambiguous ANSI equivalents (such as the two Enter keys), use the KeyDown event. For all others, use the KeyPress event.

GotFocus

This event fires whenever the text box receives the focus. While its usefulness is limited, the following example shows how GotFocus can be used to select text.

Example

In the example, Change, KeyPress, KeyDown, and GotFocus are used in a numeric text box. The text in the text box is selected automatically when the text box receives focus or an invalid number is entered or pasted. If a character other than a number or numeric symbol is entered, it is rejected by the KeyPress event. If the characters pressed result in an invalid number, the Change event "undoes" the edit. If the user presses ALT-Down Arrow, the KeyDown event starts the Windows Calculator program.

```
Option Explicit

'No controls are needed on the form for this example.

Dim WithEvents txtNumber As TextBox

Private Sub Form_Load()
   'Create and/or set up controls.
    Set txtNumber = Me.Controls.Add("vb.textbox", _
                    "txtNumber", Me)
    txtNumber.Visible = True

    Me.Caption = "TextBox Example"
End Sub

Private Sub Form_Resize()
   If Me.ScaleWidth < 1335 Or Me.ScaleHeight < 555 Then _
      Exit Sub

   txtNumber.Move 120, 120, Me.ScaleWidth - 240, 315
End Sub

Private Sub txtNumber_Change()
   Static vOldValue As Variant
  'Hold the last valid value.

   If txtNumber.Text = "" Or IsNumeric(txtNumber.Text) Then
   'When selected text is replaced, two change _
    events are fired. The first one makes the _
    selected text disappear.
```

```
      vOldValue = txtNumber.Text
   Else
      Beep
      txtNumber.Text = vOldValue
      SelectIt txtNumber
   End If
End Sub

Private Sub txtNumber_GotFocus()
    SelectIt txtNumber
End Sub

Private Sub txtNumber_KeyDown(KeyCode As Integer, _
            Shift As Integer)
   If KeyCode = vbKeyDown Then
  'Remember, get the user out of this ASAP if we know _
  we don't want the key combo. If we checked the _
  Shift each time, we would slow down the program.
      If (Shift And vbAltMask) > 0 Then
         Shell "c:\windows\calc.exe", vbNormalFocus
      End If
   End If
End Sub

Private Sub txtNumber_KeyPress(KeyAscii As Integer)
    Dim sValidChars As String

    sValidChars = "1234567890.,-"
   'Other characters could also be used

    If KeyAscii >= 32 And _
       InStr(sValidChars, Chr(KeyAscii)) = 0 Then
   'ASCII values below 32 include Backspace, CTRL key
    combos, and others.
        KeyAscii = 0
        Beep
    ElseIf KeyAscii = 13 Then
   'The user pressed Enter.
        KeyAscii = 0
        SendKeys "{Tab}"
    End If
End Sub

Private Sub SelectIt(txtVar As TextBox)
    txtVar.SelStart = 0
    txtVar.SelLength = Len(txtVar.Text)
End Sub
```

Order of Events

Here is the sequence of events in response to a CTRL-V (paste) pressed in a text box:

1. Text1_GotFocus
2. Text1_KeyDown: KeyCode = 17 (CTRL key), Shift = 2 (control)
3. Text1_KeyDown: KeyCode = 86 (V key), Shift = 2 (control)
4. Text1_KeyPress: KeyAscii = 22 (CTRL-V)
5. Text1_Change

Interactions

Action	*Result*
Change text (the value of the Text property) through code or user entry.	Fires TextBox's Change event
Execute SendKeys when a TextBox has the focus.	Fires KeyDown, KeyPress, and Change events

Timer Control

The timer is an invisible control that fires a Timer event at a regular interval of time that you can define. If you attach an event handler to its Timer event, your program's foreground process can be interrupted to perform some regularly scheduled operation or to execute some background process.

The 16-bit versions of Visual Basic imposed a limit on the number of Timer controls that could be placed on a single form. As of VB5, there is no practical limit.

Control Tasks

The following categories reflect the tasks that are executed when creating a timer.

Set Interval

Interval

Specifies the interval, in milliseconds, at which the timer will fire the Timer event. To set the timer to fire every second, you would set the Interval property to 1,000. Its value can range from 0 to 65,536 (about 65 seconds).

On occasion, you may want to set the Timer control's interval to more than one minute. The following example shows how this can be done with a minute counter:

```
Option Explicit

Dim iMinutes As Integer
Dim WithEvents tmrMain As Timer
```

```
Private Sub Form_Load()
    Set tmrMain = Me.Controls.Add("vb.timer", "tmrMain", Me)
    'Set the actual Timer control to 60 seconds
    tmrMain.Interval = 60000
End Sub

Private Sub tmrMain_Timer()
    'Increase the Minute counter by 1
    iMinutes = iMinutes + 1
    'Check to see if 5 minutes have elapsed
    If iMinutes = 5 Then
      'Stop the timer since it will stop during the message _
          box anyway
       tmrMain.Enabled = False
       MsgBox "5 Minutes!"
      'Reset the Minute counter back to 0
       iMinutes = 0
       'Turn the Timer back on
       tmrMain.Enabled = True
    End If
End Sub
```

Enabled

When the Timer control is disabled (Enabled = `False`), it no longer generates Timer events. When Enabled is `True`, the control generates events at a frequency governed by the Interval property.

You should disable all timers on a form that is hidden or is otherwise not being used. This will ensure that your application is not using processor time to track the timer and to fire events that are invisible to the user.

When you open a modal dialog, such as the dialog that appears when you call the *MsgBox* or *InputBox* functions, the Timer event is suspended until the dialog is closed. This is also the case if you run a processor-intensive loop that doesn't check the message queue regularly by calling the *DoEvents* function. This makes the use of the Timer control for real-time background processing very problematic.

Write Event Handlers

Timer

When the interval set by the Interval property has been reached, the Timer event fires.

Interactions

Action	*Result*
Disable a timer	Resets the Timer's internal interval counter

Toolbar Control

The Toolbar control is a strip of elements (usually buttons) that can be aligned to its container. It is used to provide one-click access to some frequently accessed feature of an application, and the particular buttons or interface elements that it holds can be customized by the user.

The Toolbar control can be placed on either a form or an MDI form as well as in a container control (such as a PictureBox control, for example). In addition, the Toolbar control is frequently used along with the CoolBar control, which provides a series of Band objects that serve as its containers, with one Toolbar control in each band; this provides the appearance of the Toolbar area of both Visual Basic and Microsoft Office. Both of these controls are usable within an MDI form.

The Toolbar control is contained in the Microsoft Windows Common Controls (*MSCOMCTL.OCX*) that come with Visual Basic 6.0 Professional and Enterprise editions. In Visual Basic 5.0, the filename of the Microsoft Windows Common Control library is *COMCTL32.OCX*.

The following are the tasks that you execute when creating and using a toolbar.

Set Properties

1. Set graphical properties.

   BorderStyle
   Defines the appearance of any border around the Toolbar control. Possible values are 0–ccNone for no border (which, surprisingly, is the default value) and 1–ccFixedSingle for a border around the Toolbar control. Ordinarily, you should set its value to `ccFixedSingle`. But when the Toolbar is contained by a CoolBar, you should set the Toolbar control's BorderStyle property to `ccNone`.

   ImageList, HotImageList **VB6**, *DisabledImageList* **VB6**
   Each of these properties contains a reference to an ImageList control on the same form as the Toolbar control. This ImageList control contains images that are normally shown on the Toolbar control's buttons. Images contained by the HotImageList property's ImageList control are shown when the mouse moves over a Button object only if the Toolbar control's Style property is set to `tbrFlat`. Disabled Button objects display images from the DisabledImageList property's ImageList control.

   Note that separate ImageList controls should be used, since each set of images assigned to a particular button must have the same key name or index value. In addition, the set of ImageList controls must contain images of the same size.

Style

Determines the Toolbar control's general appearance. Possible values are 0–tbrStandard, the default, where the Button objects contained by the Toolbar control always appear raised and their appearance is not affected by mouse movement, and 1–tbrFlat, where the Button objects appear flat but become raised when the mouse pointer moves over them. Button objects that are contained by a Toolbar control with its HotImageList property set display the image from the HotImageList property's ImageList control when the mouse pointer moves over them.

tbrTransparent and tbrRight

According to the documentation, the Toolbar control's Style property can take on any of three values in the `ToolbarStyleConstants` enumeration: `tbrStandard`, `tbrTransparent`, or `tbrRight`. `tbrTransparent` and `tbrRight`, however, are not defined in the control's type library. `tbrFlat` corresponds to `tbrTransparent`; they both have the same value, and the type library describes `tbrFlat` as "transparent." `tbrRight` is simply not implemented in VB6.

TextAlignment

Controls how the Caption property for a Button object, if one has been assigned, is aligned to the Button object itself. Possible values are the default, 0–tbrTextAlignBottom, which aligns the text at the bottom of the Button, or 1–tbrTextAlignRight, which aligns the text on the right side of the Button object.

Wrappable

When a Toolbar control is placed on a form, setting the Wrappable property to `True` (its default value) allows the Button objects to occupy more than one row if there are too many buttons to fit on one row. Setting the Wrappable property to `False` keeps the Button objects on one row; buttons that do not fit on the toolbar are wholly or partly hidden from view. When the Toolbar control is contained by a CoolBar control, this property has no effect.

2. Set general properties.

AllowCustomize

When the AllowCustomize property is set to its default value of `True`, the user can initiate the Customize Toolbar dialog by double-clicking on a Button object. When set to `False`, the toolbar cannot be customized. For details on customizing the toolbar, see "SaveToolbar, RestoreToolbar," later in this section.

ShowTips

When the ShowTips property is set to its default value of `True`, tooltips are shown when the mouse pointer pauses over a toolbar button that has a value in its ToolTipText property. When set to `False`, no tooltips are displayed for Button objects contained by the Toolbar control.

3. Create buttons.

Buttons (collection), Button (object)

The graphical buttons on the Toolbar control are the visual representation of Button objects. At design time, Button objects can be created through the Toolbar's custom properties. However, at runtime they must be created using the Add method of the Toolbar control's Buttons collection. Its syntax is:

```
objButtons.Add(index, key, caption, style, image)
```

where ***index*** is an optional integer indicating where the button is to be inserted in the Buttons collection, ***key*** is an optional string that uniquely identifies the button in the Buttons collection, ***caption*** is the optional text to be displayed on the button face, ***style*** is an optional constant indicating the button type, as shown in Table 5-3, and ***image*** is the optional index or key of an image in the ListImage control.

Table 5-3: Values of the style Parameter

Constant	*Value*	*Description*
`tbrDefault`	0	A standard push button; this is the default value.
`tbrCheck`	1	A check button; it remains depressed until pressed again.
`tbrButtonGroup`	2	A group button; when pressed, it remains depressed until another button in the group is pressed.
`tbrSeparator`	3	The button is a separator with a fixed width of eight pixels.
`tbrPlaceholder`	4	The button is a separator but has a definable width.
`tbrDropDown`	5	The button is a drop-down that displays menu button objects (VB6 only).

4. Set button properties.

Caption, Style, Image

Any caption associated with the Button object, the type or style of button, and the index or key of the image within the ImageList controls referenced by the Toolbar control's ImageList, HotImageList, and DisabledImageList properties should be set when creating the Button object. Possible values for the Style property are shown in Table 5-3. When using the Buttons.Add method, these are all parameters to the Add method, as discussed earlier. However, every Button object also has corresponding properties (Caption, Style, and Image, respectively) that can be set at design time and can also be set directly in code.

Description

The contents of the Description property are displayed in the Customize Toolbar dialog when the user is customizing the Toolbar control.

Height, Left, Top, Width

These properties give the location and width of a Button object within the Toolbar control. When they are used with a Button object of type **tbrPlaceholder**, this allows the application to easily display another contained control in the correct location, as in this example, which would generally be found in a Form object's Resize event:

```
txtMain.Move btnVar.Left, btnVar.Top, btnVar.Width, _
             btnVar.Height
```

Value

When a Button object with its Style property set to **tbrCheck** or **tbrButtonGroup** is currently depressed, its Value property is set to **True**. When the button is not depressed or another button in a button group is depressed, its Value property is set to **False**.

MixedState

If you wish to portray a Button object as not being **True** or **False**, you can set its MixedState property to **True**. This makes the button appear grayed but not disabled. You might do this in the case of a Bold button, for example, if the user's selection includes both bold and normal text.

5. Create ButtonMenus. **VB6**

ButtonMenus (collection), ButtonMenu (object)

In VB6, when a Button object has its Style property set to **tbrDropdown**, the user can click on the drop-down icon next to the Button to display ButtonMenu objects. ButtonMenu objects can be created at design time, or they can be created at runtime using the Add method of the Button object's ButtonMenus collection. Its syntax is:

```
objButtonMenus.Add(index, key, text)
```

For a description of these parameters, see "Set ButtonMenu Properties," the next section.

6. Set ButtonMenu properties. **VB6**

Text

Contains the caption to be displayed for the ButtonMenu object when the list of ButtonMenu objects has been dropped down. When you are using the ButtonMenus.Add method, this is a parameter to the Add method. However, every ButtonMenu object also has a corresponding Text property that can be set directly in code.

When using Toolbar controls with a CoolBar control, you should set all size-related properties of the Toolbar first, issue a *DoEvents* command, and then link the Toolbar to the Band object. Otherwise, the Band object's size can be set based on incorrect size parameters.

Useful Methods

Customize

Calling the Customize method displays the Customize Toolbar dialog to the user, regardless of the setting of the AllowCustomize property. The dialog is shown in Figure 5-57. Note that the Customize Toolbar dialog can also be opened if the AllowCustomize property is set to `True` and the user double-clicks on an empty area of the toolbar. Since this is just one of the standard ways of opening the Customize dialog in applications such as the members of the Microsoft Office suite, it's best to implement the others—a Customize menu option and a Customize option on a context menu—by calling the Customize method.

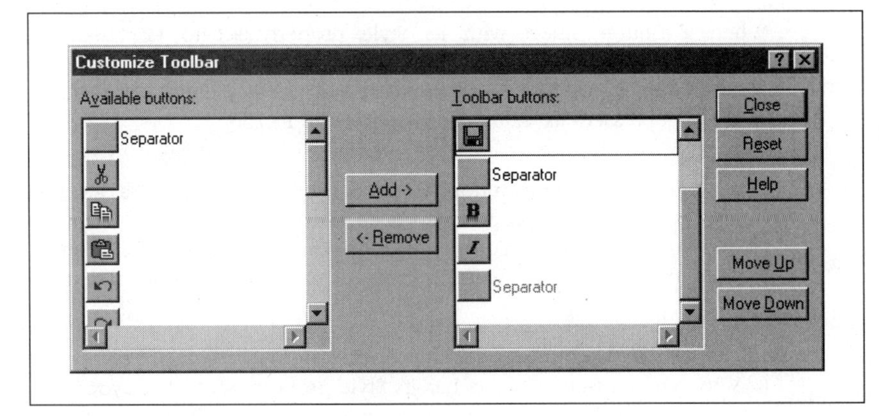

Figure 5-57: The Customize Toolbar dialog

SaveToolbar, RestoreToolbar

These poorly documented methods are used to save and to retrieve toolbar settings from the `HKEY_CURRENT_USER` branch of the registry in cases in which a customizable toolbar is supported (i.e., the AllowCustomize property is `True`, or the program makes calls to the Customize method). Both take identical parameters; their syntax is:

```
SaveToolbar(Key, Subkey, Value)
RestoreToolbar(Key, Subkey, Value)
```

In VB5, ***Key*** must not be `Null` or an error occurs. Otherwise, the parameter is ignored. VB6 corrects this problem: ***Key*** must be the first subkey of `HKEY_CURRENT_USER` in the complete path to the key where the toolbar settings will eventually be stored.

In VB5, ***Subkey*** must be the complete registry path from `HKEY_CURRENT_USER` (but excluding `HKEY_CURRENT_USER` itself) to the key where the toolbar settings are stored. In VB6, it is the remainder of the path from the key designated by the ***Key*** parameter to the key in which the toolbar settings are stored. Finally, ***Value*** is the name of the value entry that contains the toolbar's configuration information.

For example, the following displays a call to the SaveToolbar method in VB6, to save toolbar settings in the `EditingToolbar` value entry of `HKEY_CURRENT_USER\Software\MyCompany\MyApp`:

```
Toolbar1.SaveToolbar "Software", "MyCompany\MyApp", _
                     "EditingToolbar"
```

Notice that the `HKEY_CURRENT_USER` key itself is not specified in the method call. Also note that the methods don't specify the data to be saved; that's handled automatically by the control, which only needs to know the key and named value where it should either write or retrieve the toolbar data.

Defining a Customizable Toolbar

Under VB5, setting up a customizable toolbar is a two-step process:

1. Define all available buttons that can appear on the toolbar and that will be represented by Button objects in the Buttons collection. You can do this either by adding the buttons to the control at design-time or by calling the Buttons collection's Add method at runtime.
2. Call the RestoreToolbar method to define which buttons in the Buttons collection are to appear on the toolbar. Buttons currently on the toolbar that are not found in the registry appear in the "Available buttons" list box.

But in this case, the call to the RestoreToolbar method assumes that toolbar settings are already contained in the registry. In addition, the registry itself saves data only about the buttons that are actually displayed on the toolbar.

This means that to populate the "Available buttons" list box for a user running your application for the first time, when toolbar information cannot be found in the registry, you should build the application's toolbar as follows:

1. Define the buttons that are to appear on the toolbar itself. You can do this either at design time or by calling the Buttons collection's Add method at runtime.
2. Call the SaveToolbar method to save the default toolbar.
3. Call the Buttons collection's Add method to add the buttons that are to appear in the "Available buttons" list box of the Customize Toolbar dialog.
4. Call the RestoreToolbar method to define which buttons are to appear on the toolbar.

VB6 and Customizable Toolbars

Unfortunately, the customizable toolbar feature in Version 6.0 of the Microsoft Windows Common Controls, the set of controls that is included with VB6, is completely broken. If a customizable toolbar is an important feature in your application, you must continue to use the version of Microsoft Windows Common Controls that ships with VB5. Fortunately, the installation of VB6 does not overwrite the VB5 version of the file, which has a different filename and programmatic identifier than its VB6 counterpart.

Write Event Handlers

ButtonClick, ButtonDropDown

The ButtonClick event is fired when the user clicks on a Button object. The ButtonDropDown event is fired when a Button object with its `Style` parameter set to `tbrDropdown` has its drop-down arrow clicked by the user. Each of these events handlers receives the Button object as a parameter.

ButtonMenuClick VB6

The ButtonMenuClick event is fired when a ButtonMenu object is clicked. The ButtonMenu object that was clicked is passed to the event handler as a parameter.

Change

The Change event is fired after the user has made a change to the Toolbar control using the Customize Toolbar dialog.

TreeView Control

The TreeView control is a hierarchical list of related Node objects. The user can expand and collapse these node families easily while navigating through the control; depicting the trees and expanding and contracting the nodes are handled automatically by the TreeView control itself. An example of a TreeView control used in an application is the Windows Explorer program, where the TreeView occupies the left side of the form.

The TreeView control is contained in the Windows Common Controls (*COMCTL32.OCX*) that come with Visual Basic Professional and Enterprise editions.

Control Tasks

The following categories reflect the tasks that are executed when creating a TreeView.

Set Properties

1. Set general appearance.

   Style

   There are eight variations to the appearance of the TreeView. Basically, they control whether there are pictures, plus and minus symbols, and lines. The following table, as well as Figure 5-58, show how each value for the Style property affects the look of the TreeView:

Constant	*Value*	*Description*
`tvwTextOnly`	0	Only the text is displayed.
`tvwPictureText`	1	The text and images are displayed.
`tvwPlusMinusText`	2	The text and a plus or minus symbol are displayed.

Constant	*Value*	*Description*
`tvwPlusPictureText`	3	The text, image, and a plus or minus symbol are displayed.
`tvwTreelinesText`	4	The text and lines are displayed.
`tvwTreelines-PictureText`	5	The text, image, and lines are displayed.
`tvwTreelines-PlusMinusText`	6	The text, plus or minus symbols, and lines are displayed.
`tvwTreelinesPlus-MinusPictureText`	7	The text, image, plus or minus symbols, and lines are displayed. This is the default value.

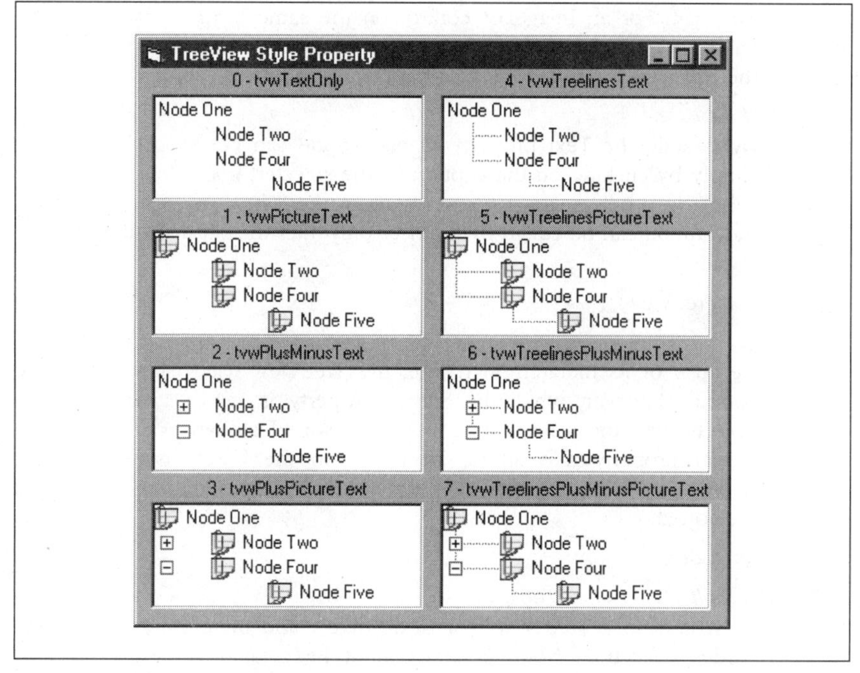

Figure 5-58: The Style property of the TreeView control

LineStyle

When the Style selected includes lines, the LineStyle property controls whether the lines start at the top-level nodes (0–tvwTreeLines) or at the root above the top-level nodes (1–tvwRootLines). Figure 5-59 shows how the value of the LineStyle property affects the appearance of the TreeView control.

Indentation

The width by which each new child node is indented from its parent node.

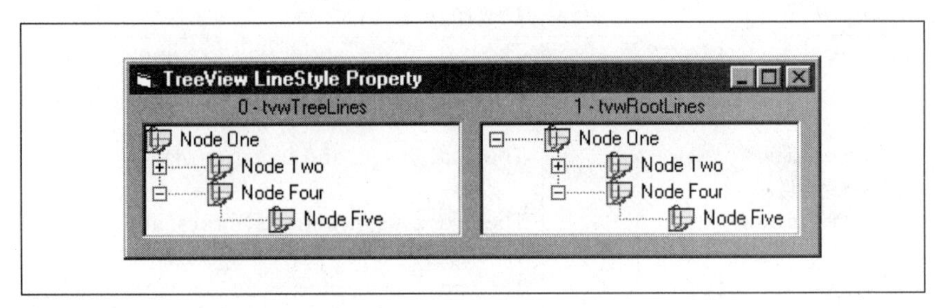

Figure 5-59: The LineStyle property of the TreeView control

ImageList
: The name of an ImageList control on the same form as the TreeView. Each node placed in the ListView can choose which image to use from the ImageList.

LabelEdit
: By default, the Text property of each node can be edited by the user simply by clicking on the caption of the selected node. In this case, the LabelEdit property is set to 0–tvwAutomatic. When set to 1–tvwManual, the caption can be edited by the user only after the StartLabelEdit method is called.

2. Sort the TreeView.

Sorted
: Because of its hierarchical nature, the TreeView itself cannot really be sorted. However, when the Sorted property is set to `True`, all Node objects with the same parent node are sorted alphabetically. This is a global property that affects all nodes in the TreeView; each node, however, also has a Sorted property that controls whether its child nodes are sorted.

3. Create Nodes.

Nodes (collection), Node (object)
: Each item in a TreeView is a Node object and therefore is part of the Nodes collection. Node objects cannot be created at design time. At runtime, they can be created by using the Add method of the Nodes collection. This also allows the program to set some of the node's properties. Its syntax is:

```
objNodes.Add(relative, relationship, key, text, _
             image, selectedimage)
```

All of these arguments except *key* are discussed in the following section, "Set node properties." *key* represents a unique string by which a reference to the node can be retrieved from the Nodes collection's Item property.

4. Set node properties.

   Text, Image, SelectedImage

   The caption of the node and the index or key of the ListImage to use for both unselected and selected nodes can be set either as parameters of the Nodes collection's Add method or by assigning values to these properties.

   Relative, Relationship

   These are not actually properties. However, as parameters of the Nodes collection's Add method, they are used to position the new node in the TreeView and therefore to set properties. When you are adding a node, ***`Relative`*** represents another node that is somehow related to the node being added. ***`Relationship`*** denotes how the two nodes are related. When the ***`Relationship`*** parameter is set to 0–tvwFirst, 1–tvwLast, 2–tvwNext, or 3–tvwPrevious, the new node is placed at the same level as the ***`Relative`*** node (i.e., both have the same parent), but either as the first or last node at that level or just after or just before the ***`Relative`*** node, respectively. When set to 4–tvwChild, the new node becomes a child node of the ***`Relative`*** node. Note that when adding a child node, you can choose between defining it in relationship to its parent or to the other child nodes.

   Expanded

   When the Expanded property is set to `True`, any child nodes are revealed. When set to `False`, they are hidden.

   ExpandedImage

   Optionally, a node can display a different image when it is expanded than when it is collapsed. The Index or Key of the desired ListImage in the related ImageList can be used in the ExpandedImage property.

5. Determine the selected node.

   SelectedItem (TreeView control), Selected (Node object)

   The SelectedItem property of the TreeView returns the currently selected Node object. The Selected property of a Node object returns a Boolean value indicating whether that node is currently selected. By retrieving the SelectedItem property or iterating the Nodes collection and examining each Node object's Selected property, you can determine which node is selected. By assigning a new Node object to the SelectedItem property or by assigning `True` to a Node object's Selected property, you can change the selected node programmatically.

6. Navigate the TreeView's trees.

   Typically, in response to a user action such as a click, it is necessary for your application to navigate to or from the current node. This can be done with the following properties:

   Parent

   The Node object's Parent property returns the node that is above the current node in the hierarchy. When you are changing this property to a new node, all child nodes of the node being changed remain connected.

Any change that would result in a node becoming its own descendant will rip a hole in the time-space continuum (or cause an error).

Root

The Node object's Root property returns the node that is the topmost in the node's hierarchy.

FullPath

Provides the full path from the top-level node to the referenced node. The path separator used to delimit individual nodes is defined by the TreeView control's PathSeparator property; its default value is a backslash (\).

Children, Child

The Children property of a node returns its number of child nodes. The Child property returns the first child node. If the Child property is referenced for a node with no child nodes, an error will occur. Therefore, you should always check the Children property first.

FirstSibling, LastSibling, Next, Previous

Each of these properties returns a node at the same level as the node being referenced. The node returned is denoted by the property name. These properties are useful for "walking" through nodes at the same level, as in this example:

```
Private Sub tvwMain_DblClick()
    Dim nodItem As Node

    If Me.tvwMain.SelectedItem.Children > 0 Then
    'Check for children nodes.
        Set nodItem = Me.tvwMain.SelectedItem.Child
    'Get first child node.
        Do
            Debug.Print nodItem.Text
            If nodItem = nodItem.LastSibling Then
        'This is the last node.
                Exit Do
            Else
        'Get the next node.
                Set nodItem = nodItem.Next
            End If
        Loop
    End If
End Sub
```

Figure 5-60 displays a TreeView control with six node objects. Some of the relationships between the nodes include the following:

- Node1.Child = Node2
- Node2.FirstSibling = Node2
- Node2.Next = Node3
- Node2.LastSibling = Node6
- Node6.Previous = Node3

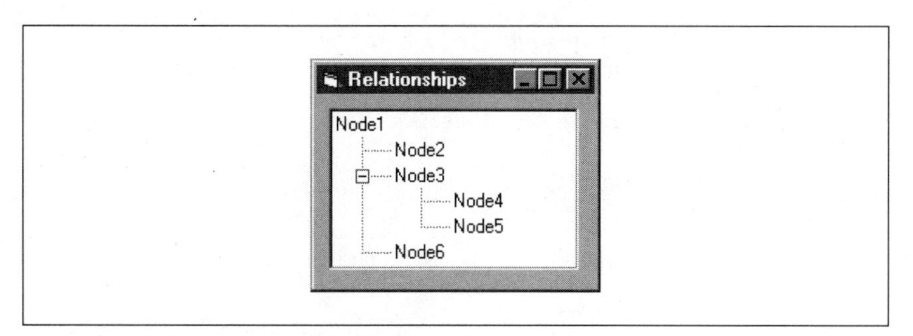

Figure 5-60: Node relationships

Useful Methods

HitTest

When provided with x and y coordinates, the HitTest method will return a Node object if there is one at those coordinates. Otherwise, `Nothing` will be returned. The syntax of HitTest is:

```
Function HitTest(X As Single, Y As Single) As Node
```

StartLabelEdit

When the StartLabelEdit method is called, the caption of the node becomes both editable by the user and selected. This is unnecessary when the LabelEdit property is set to `tvwAutomatic`.

Write Event Handlers

Expand, Collapse

When a node is expanded or collapsed, whether through code or by the user, the Expand or Collapse event is fired. This is fired *after* the node has been visibly expanded or collapsed. However, the Expanded property can be used to reverse this action, as in this example:

```
Private Sub tvwMain_Expand(ByVal Node As ComctlLib.Node)
    If Node.Tag = "Do Not Expand" Then
    'The Tag property would have been set earlier.
        Node.Expanded = False
    End If
End Sub
```

ItemClick

When a node is clicked by the user, the NodeClick event is fired. This event also passes the clicked node as a parameter to the event handler.

Example

The following example uses many of the conventions mentioned in this section (see Figure 5-61 for the resulting form):

```
Option Explicit

'For this example, create the following controls: _
  a TextBox named txtTotal with the MultiLine _
    property set to True and the Alignment _
```

Controls T

```
    property set to vbRightJustify, _
  an ImageList named imlIcons, and _
  a TreeView named tvwMain.

Dim WithEvents lstMain As ListBox

Private Sub Form_Load()
    Dim imgVar As ListImage

    'We don't want the user to edit the total in _
    the TextBox
    Me.txtTotal.Locked = True

    Set lstMain = Me.Controls.Add("vb.listbox", _
                  "lstMain", Me)
    lstMain.Visible = True

    'Set up ImageList for Icons
    Me.imlIcons.ImageHeight = 32
    Me.imlIcons.ImageWidth = 32
    Set imgVar = Me.imlIcons.ListImages.Add _
        (1, "food", LoadPicture("Food.ico"))
    Set imgVar = Me.imlIcons.ListImages.Add _
        (2, "burger", LoadPicture("Burger.ico"))
    Set imgVar = Me.imlIcons.ListImages.Add _
        (3, "pizza", LoadPicture("Pizza.ico"))
    Set imgVar = Me.imlIcons.ListImages.Add _
        (4, "sides", LoadPicture("Sides.ico"))
    Set imgVar = Me.imlIcons.ListImages.Add _
        (5, "drinks", LoadPicture("Drinks.ico"))
    Set imgVar = Me.imlIcons.ListImages.Add _
        (6, "dessert", LoadPicture("Dessert.ico"))

    'Set up TreeView
    Me.tvwMain.Style = tvwTreelinesPlusMinusPictureText
    'This is actually the default
    Me.tvwMain.ImageList = imlIcons

    GetFoodRecords

    Me.Caption = "Restaurant"
    Me.Height = 3600
    Me.Width = 5175
End Sub

Private Sub Form_Resize()
   If Me.ScaleHeight < 1000 Or Me.ScaleWidth < 1000 Then
      Exit Sub
   End If
```

```
    Me.tvwMain.Move _
        120, _
        120, _
        Me.ScaleWidth * 0.6 - 180, _
        Me.ScaleHeight - 240
    lstMain.Move _
        Me.ScaleWidth * 0.6 + 60, _
        120, _
        Me.ScaleWidth * 0.4 - 180, _
        Me.ScaleHeight - 655
    Me.txtTotal.Move _
        Me.ScaleWidth * 0.6 + 60, _
        Me.ScaleHeight - 435, _
        Me.ScaleWidth * 0.4 - 180, _
        315
End Sub

Private Sub tvwMain_DblClick()
    Dim sItem As String

   'Since the dbl-click can occur when the user wants _
   to expand a node, we have to distinguish _
   between that and double-clicking a product.
   If Me.tvwMain.SelectedItem.Children > 0 Then
      'This node has children, so we ignore the _
      dbl-click
      Exit Sub
   Else
      'This node doesn't have children, so we process _
      it as a sale
      sItem = Me.tvwMain.SelectedItem.Text & _
          vbTab & Format$(Me.tvwMain.SelectedItem.Tag, _
          "##0.00")
      lstMain.AddItem sItem
      Me.txtTotal.Text = Val(Me.txtTotal.Text) + _
                  Val(Me.tvwMain.SelectedItem.Tag)
   End If
End Sub

Private Sub GetFoodRecords()
   Dim nodItem As Node

   'Normally we'd get this information from a _
   database, but for this example we'll create the _
   data by hand. I'm using the Tag property of a node _
   to store the price.
   Set nodItem = Me.tvwMain.Nodes.Add _
        (, , "Top", "Select Item", "food")
   Set nodItem = Me.tvwMain.Nodes.Add _
```

Controls
T

```
        ("Top", tvwChild, "BurgerTop", "Burgers", _
        "burger")
    Set nodItem = Me.tvwMain.Nodes.Add _
        ("BurgerTop", tvwChild, , "Hamburger", "burger")
    nodItem.Tag = 1.99
    Set nodItem = Me.tvwMain.Nodes.Add _
        ("BurgerTop", tvwChild, , "Double Burger", _
        "burger")
    nodItem.Tag = 2.49
    Set nodItem = Me.tvwMain.Nodes.Add _
        ("BurgerTop", tvwChild, "TEST", _
        "Burger Deluxe", "burger")
    nodItem.Tag = 2.99

    Set nodItem = Me.tvwMain.Nodes.Add _
        ("Top", tvwChild, "PizzaTop", "Pizza", "pizza")
    Set nodItem = Me.tvwMain.Nodes.Add _
        ("PizzaTop", tvwChild, , "Personal Pizza", _
        "pizza")
    nodItem.Tag = 2.49
    Set nodItem = Me.tvwMain.Nodes.Add _
        ("PizzaTop", tvwChild, , "10 Inch Pizza", _
        "pizza")
    nodItem.Tag = 5.49
    Set nodItem = Me.tvwMain.Nodes.Add _
        ("PizzaTop", tvwChild, , "12 Inch Pizza", _
        "pizza")
    nodItem.Tag = 7.49
    Set nodItem = Me.tvwMain.Nodes.Add _
        ("PizzaTop", tvwChild, , "Super Family Pizza", _
        "pizza")
    nodItem.Tag = 9.99

    Set nodItem = Me.tvwMain.Nodes.Add _
        ("Top", tvwChild, "SidesTop", "Sides", "sides")
    Set nodItem = Me.tvwMain.Nodes.Add _
        ("SidesTop", tvwChild, , "Small Fries", "sides")
    nodItem.Tag = 0.99
    Set nodItem = Me.tvwMain.Nodes.Add _
        ("SidesTop", tvwChild, , "Large Fries", "sides")
    nodItem.Tag = 1.39
    Set nodItem = Me.tvwMain.Nodes.Add _
       ("SidesTop", tvwChild, , "Garlic Bread", "sides")
    nodItem.Tag = 0.99
    Set nodItem = Me.tvwMain.Nodes.Add _
        ("SidesTop", tvwChild, , "Side Salad", "sides")
    nodItem.Tag = 0.99

    Set nodItem = Me.tvwMain.Nodes.Add _
        ("Top", tvwChild, "DrinksTop", "Drinks", _
        "drinks")
```

```
    Set nodItem = Me.tvwMain.Nodes.Add _
         ("DrinksTop", tvwChild, , "Cola Soda", "drinks")
    nodItem.Tag = 1.09
    Set nodItem = Me.tvwMain.Nodes.Add _
         ("DrinksTop", tvwChild, , "Diet Cola Soda", _
         "drinks")
    nodItem.Tag = 1.09
    Set nodItem = Me.tvwMain.Nodes.Add _
         ("DrinksTop", tvwChild, , "Lemon/Lime Soda", _
         "drinks")
    nodItem.Tag = 1.09
    Set nodItem = Me.tvwMain.Nodes.Add _
         ("DrinksTop", tvwChild, , "Domestic Beer", _
         "drinks")
    nodItem.Tag = 2.49
    Set nodItem = Me.tvwMain.Nodes.Add _
         ("DrinksTop", tvwChild, , "Red/White Wine", _
         "drinks")
    nodItem.Tag = 2.99

    Set nodItem = Me.tvwMain.Nodes.Add _
         ("Top", tvwChild, "DessertTop", "Dessert", _
         "dessert")
    Set nodItem = Me.tvwMain.Nodes.Add _
         ("DessertTop", tvwChild, , "Apple Pie Slice", _
         "dessert")
    nodItem.Tag = 2.49
    Set nodItem = Me.tvwMain.Nodes.Add _
         ("DessertTop", tvwChild, , "Cheesecake Slice", _
         "dessert")
    nodItem.Tag = 2.49
    Set nodItem = Me.tvwMain.Nodes.Add _
         ("DessertTop", tvwChild, , "Ice Cream Cone", _
         "dessert")
    nodItem.Tag = 1.49
    Set nodItem = Me.tvwMain.Nodes.Add _
         ("DessertTop", tvwChild, , "Hot Fudge Sundae", _
         "dessert")
    nodItem.Tag = 2.99
    Set nodItem = Me.tvwMain.Nodes.Add _
         ("DessertTop", tvwChild, , "Asst Fruit Cup", _
         "dessert")
    nodItem.Tag = 0.99

    'Expand the top level node
    Me.tvwMain.Nodes("Top").Expanded = True
End Sub
```

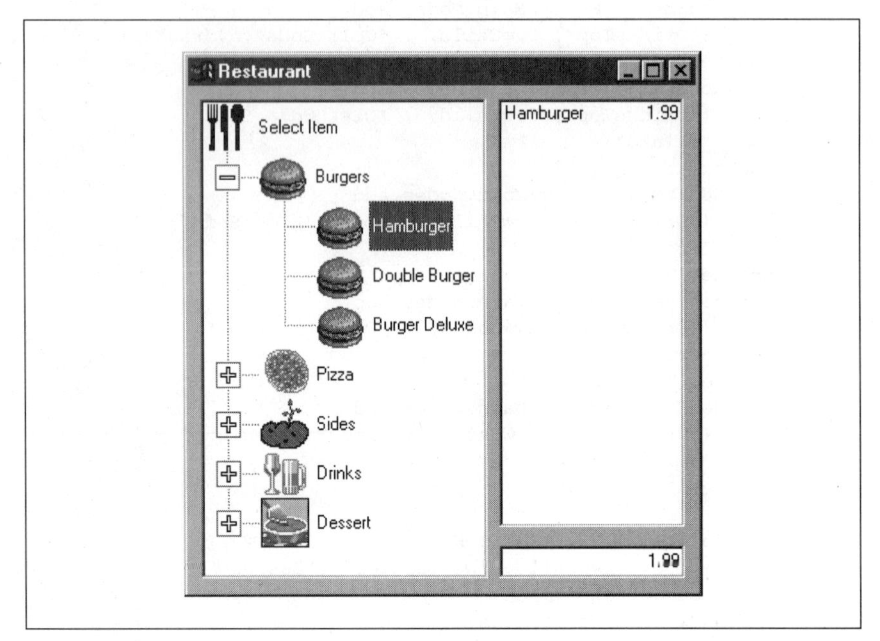

Figure 5-61: TreeView example

Interactions

Action	*Result*
A node is expanded or collapsed either through code (by settings its Expand property) or by the user.	The Expand or Collapse event is fired.
User clicks on the caption of the selected node. LabelEdit property is set to `tvwAutomatic`.	BeforeLabelEdit event is fired.
User finishes editing the caption.	AfterLabelEdit event is fired.

UpDown Control

The UpDown control (previously called the Spinner control) provides the user with buttons pointing up and down that can be pressed to increase or decrease a value. The UpDown control is a *buddy* control, which means it can be linked to another control on the same form. Once bound in this manner, the UpDown control moves and resizes along with its buddy, and changes in the value of the UpDown control can be reflected automatically in its buddy control.

The UpDown control is included with the Windows Common Controls 2 (*COMCT232.OCX*) that come with Visual Basic Professional and Enterprise editions.

Control Tasks

The following categories reflect the tasks that are executed when creating an UpDown control.

Set Properties

1. Set buddy.

   BuddyControl, BuddyProperty

   These properties allow the UpDown control to be bound to another buddy control. The BuddyControl property is set to the buddy control, and the BuddyProperty property is set to the name of the property of the buddy control to be changed when the value of the UpDown control is changed. The UpDown control cannot be bound to any of the lightweight controls included with Visual Basic 6.0 or to other controls that do not have an hWnd property, such as the Label control. The following example shows how an UpDown control can be bound to the Text property of a TextBox control at runtime:

   ```
   Me.updMain.BuddyControl = Me.txtMain
   Me.updMain.BuddyProperty = "Text"
   ```

   Figure 5-62 shows the UpDown control with a buddy control.

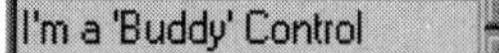

Figure 5-62: The UpDown control with a buddy control

   SyncBuddy

   When the BuddyControl and BuddyProperty properties are set, the SyncBuddy property automatically changes to `True`, which indicates that the property specified in the buddy control is automatically synchronized with the Value property of the UpDown control. When the SyncBuddy property is set to `True`, the Value property is also synchronized with the contents of the property specified by the BuddyProperty property.

2. Set appearance.

   Alignment

   The UpDown control can be positioned to the left or to the right of its buddy control by setting the UpDown control's Appearance property to 0–cc2AlignmentLeft or 1–cc2AlignmentRight, respectively.

3. Set constraints.

   Min and Max

   Sets the minimum and maximum values that the UpDown control can contain.

Alignment and Orientation

Although the UpDown control can be aligned to the left or to the right of its buddy control, it cannot be placed above or below it. Besides alignment, which determines the positioning of the UpDown control in relationship to its buddy control, there is an Orientation property that positions the UpDown control's up and down buttons horizontally or vertically. We recommend that you always leave the control set to its default, which is 0–cc2OrientationVertical. In our experience, the control always has a good deal of difficulty redrawing its arrows in the correct position when the Orientation property is set to 1–ccOrientationHorizontal.

The UpDown control can be positioned to the left or to the right of its buddy control by setting the UpDown control's Appearance property to 0–cc2AlignmentLeft or 1–cc2AlignmentRight, respectively.

4. Set change amounts.

   Increment

   Sets the amount that the UpDown control's value increases or decreases when the user clicks on the up and down arrow icons.

5. Set value.

   Value

   Represents the current value of the UpDown control relative to the Min and Max properties.

Write Event Handlers

Change

The Change event is fired whenever the Value property of the UpDown control is changed, whether by the user, through the buddy control, or through code.

DownClick, UpClick

These events are fired when their respective buttons are pressed. These events do not occur until after the Change event has already fired. Note that you ordinarily do not need to modify the value of the UpDown control's Value property in response to clicks; this is handled automatically by the control.

Order of Events

Here is the sequence of events in response to a mouse click on either the up or down button of an UpDown control named UpDown1:

1. UpDown1_MouseDown
2. UpDown1_Change
3. UpDown1_MouseUp
4. UpDown1_UpClick or UpDown1_DownClick

Interactions

Action	*Result*
Change the value of the property referred to in the BuddyProperty property of the buddy control.	The Change event is fired and the Value property changes.
Change the value of the UpDown control's Value property.	The Change event is fired and the value of the buddy control's buddy property changes.
Set BuddyProperty to the name of a property on the control indicated by the BuddyControl property.	Value of SyncBuddy property changes to `True`.
Change SyncBuddy property from `False` to `True`.	Value of BuddyProperty changes to "_Default."

VScrollBar Control

See: ScrollBar Controls

VB6 *Windowless Controls*

As of Version 6.0, Visual Basic ships with a set of lightweight, windowless controls. The CheckBox, ComboBox, CommandButton, Frame, ListBox, Option Button, TextBox, and Vertical and Horizontal ScrollBar controls each have a windowless version available.

The windowless controls are contained in the Microsoft Windowless Controls (*MSWLESS.OCX*) that come with Visual Basic Professional and Enterprise editions.

These windowless controls act in every way like their intrinsic counterparts with a few exceptions:

- Most important, these controls do not have an hWnd property. Therefore, API calls and other functions that require a handle to the control's window will not work with these controls. When this is necessary, use the intrinsic version of the control instead.
- Windowless controls cannot be containers. This is important only with the WLFrame (Windowless Frame) control, which cannot contain other controls. However, other controls can be placed over the WLFrame control to appear as if they were contained.
- Many properties that are normally read-only at runtime with the intrinsic controls are read/write at runtime with the windowless version. This makes the windowless controls particularly useful with dynamic control creation (see Chapter 2 for more information).

Because of their small memory and resource footprint, windowless controls are particularly useful for applications that are experiencing memory problems. Also, windowless controls are beneficial when creating custom controls that contain other controls. In these cases, windowless controls can make a large difference in the memory used by complex forms or controls.

The following is a list of windowless controls and their intrinsic counterparts:

Windowless Control	*Intrinsic Control*
`WLCheck`	CheckBox
`WLCombo`	ComboBox
`WLCommand`	CommandButton
`WLFrame`	Frame
`WLHScroll`	HScrollBar
`WLList`	ListBox
`WLOption`	OptionButton
`WLText`	TextBox
`WLVScroll`	VScrollBar

Winsock Control

The Winsock control is a relatively low-level control that serves as a wrapper around the Windows Sockets API, the API designed to implement the TCP and UDP protocols at the packet level. Unlike the Internet Transfer control, which is suitable for building client applications only, the Winsock control can be used for building either client or server applications using the TCP protocol and for building peer-to-peer applications using the UDP protocol. The Winsock control can be used for virtually any Internet application, depending, of course, on how much coding you'd like to do and on the kind of performance your application can tolerate. It is most suitable, however, for those applications that require the low-level Internet protocols but not its higher-level services. Examples of fairly high-performance applications that can be built using the Winsock control include:

- Applications that require that a client and a server establish a connection and then "talk" to each another without using a higher-level protocol. A chat program is an example of this type of application.
- Notification programs that inform other Internet computers of some event. For example, a series of systems used for order entry might be notified by a server that batch processing is in progress and no orders should be transmitted until the next notification.
- Query programs that request finite amounts of information from a computer. For example, a Ping program simply sends a UDP packet to a remote system and awaits a response, thereby allowing the application to determine whether the remote system is online.

This section is meant to explain the use of the Internet controls. It is not meant to explain the Internet, Internet protocols, or any other concepts relating to the Internet itself. If you require this type of information, see *Internet in a Nutshell*, *Webmaster in a Nutshell, Second Edition*, and *The World Wide Web Journal*, vol. 1, issue 2: "Key Specifications of the World Wide Web," all published by O'Reilly & Associates.

The steps involved in using the control follow.

Selecting a Protocol

The Winsock control can communicate over the Internet using either the TCP or the UDP protocols. The former is a stateful protocol; it requires that a connection be established between two machines, one of which is a server (that is, it waits for incoming requests and responds to them as they arrive), while the second is a client (that is, its role is to send a request to a server and await a response). The latter is a stateless protocol; it does not require a connection and implies that two peers are communicating with each another.

The first step in using the control—and one typically performed at design time—is to select the protocol by setting the Protocol property to either 0–sckTCPProtocol, or 1–sckUDPProtocol.

Beginning Communication

The protocol you select and, if you are using the TCP protocol, whether you are implementing a client or a server define your subsequent steps in using the control. In all cases, though, communication occurs over a defined TCP or UDP port.

Implementing a TCP Server

A server in its inactivate state is simply a piece of software that polls a TCP port waiting for an incoming request. The sequence of steps involved in creating a TCP server mirrors this precisely:

1. Determine whether the application will handle one connection or multiple connections at a time. The latter requires that the Winsock control be defined as a control array (i.e., at least one control whose Index property is set to 0 should be placed on the form) and a new instance created to handle each incoming connection request.
2. Define the port on which the server will listen by assigning the port's number to the LocalPort property. Assigning a value of 0 indicates that the port will be

assigned randomly. RFC 1060 defines port assignments for ports in the range 0 to 1000. The following table lists some common port assignments for both the TCP and UDP protocols:

Port	*TCP*	*UDP*	*Name*
7	✓	✓	echo
20	✓	✓	ftp default data port
21	✓	✓	ftp control port
23	✓	✓	telnet
25	✓	✓	SMTP
42	✓	✓	nameserver
43	✓	✓	Who Is
49	✓	✓	Login Host Protocol
53	✓	✓	Domain Name Server
70	✓	✓	Gopher
79	✓	✓	Finger
80	✓	✓	HTTP/World Wide Web
110	✓	✓	POP3
119	✓	✓	nntp
123	✓	✓	Network Time Protocol (ntp)
161	✓	✓	snmp
194	✓	✓	Internet Relay Chat
531	✓		Chat

3. Wait for an incoming connection request by invoking the Listen method.
4. Handle an incoming request by calling the Accept method in the Winsock control's ConnectionRequest event handler. The event handler's syntax is:

   ```
   sckMain.ConnectionRequest(ByVal requestID As Long)
   ```

   where *requestID* is a unique value generated by the control to identify the request. This value can be provided as an argument to the Accept method, whose syntax is:

   ```
   sckMain.Accept(requestID As Long)
   ```

   Before calling the Accept method, it's important to ensure that the control's socket is closed by calling the Close method, as in the following code fragment:

   ```
   If sckMain.State <> sckClosed Then sckMain.Close
   ```

Implementing a TCP Client

In client/server architecture, a client is simply the system initiating a request. Consequently, to submit a request to a server, a TCP client needs to know the server's IP address or domain name as well as the port on which it is listening. Once again, the steps required to implement a TCP client mirror this fairly closely:

1. (Optional) Assign a port number to the LocalPort property. However, in the absence of an assigned port, the Winsock control will assign one arbitrarily and pass its value to the server when it requests a connection.
2. (Optional) Assign the IP address or domain name of the remote server to the RemoteHost property.
3. (Optional) Assign the port number on which the server is listening to the RemotePort property. Note that Visual Basic appears to be unable to coerce data other than long integers into the RemotePort property. If necessary, you should use the *CLng* function to explicitly convert data to type long before assigning it to the property.
4. Call the Connect method. Its syntax is:

   ```
   sckMain.Connect [remoteHost], [remotePort]
   ```

   where `remoteHost` is the remote host's IP address or domain name and `remotePort` is the port number. The parameters are optional, although if either has been omitted, a value must previously have been explicitly assigned to its respective property.
5. Wait for the Connect event to fire to signal that the connection is complete. Its syntax quite simply is:

   ```
   sckMain.Connect()
   ```

Implementing a UDP Peer

Although the UDP protocol offers a peer-to-peer model for communications, one peer must nevertheless initiate the conversation as the client, while the other must respond as the server. UDP is a connectionless protocol; unlike TCP, no explicit connection is required for two systems to begin exchanging data. The most important consideration is that the two applications attempt to communicate using the same logical port on the server system.

Since either system can begin communication with a system or respond to communications with that system, applications typically are prepared to assume either role. All of the steps required to exchange information using the UDP protocol are:

1. Indicate the port to be used for incoming data by calling the Bind method, which allows the program to reserve a UDP port for use with the Winsock control. Once the port is bound, no other process can use that port. The Bind method's syntax is:

   ```
   object.Bind LocalPort, LocalIP
   ```

   where `LocalPort` is the UDP port to bind, and `LocalIP` is the IP address of the local machine; the latter should be used only in the case of systems with multiple IP addresses.

2. Assign the remote system's domain name or IP address to the RemoteHost property, and assign the remote system's UDP port number to the Remote-Port property.
3. Transmit the data using the SendData method, which is discussed in the next section, "Transmitting Data."
4. Receive data by calling the GetData method within the DataArrival event handler. The DataArrival event handler is fired whenever data arrives on a socket, and it indicates the number of bytes that have arrived; it is described in greater detail in "Receiving Data," later in this section. The GetData method, which is used to read data sent by another system, is also discussed in "The GetData Method," later in this section.

Transmitting Data

To send data to a remote computer, use the Winsock control's SendData method. Its syntax is:

```
winsock.SendData data
```

where *data* is the data to be sent. If *data* is text or string data, a string variable should be used; if data is a Unicode string, it is converted to an ANSI string before being transmitted to the remote system. Finally, if *data* is binary, a byte array should be used.

Receiving Data

Typically, incoming data transmitted from a remote computer is read within the DataArrival event handler. The DataArrival event is fired whenever new data arrives on a socket. Its syntax is:

```
winsock.DataArrival (bytesTotal As Long)
```

where *bytesTotal* is the total number of bytes that have arrived.

Either of two methods (GetData and PeekData) is used within the DataArrival event handler to retrieve the data.

The GetData Method

The GetData method is typically used in the DataArrival event handler to retrieve data from the Winsock control's input buffer and at the same time remove it from the input buffer. Its syntax is:

```
winsock.GetData data, [type,] [maxLen]
```

where the parameters are as follows:

data
: A buffer variable to which the data will be stored when the function returns. If *data* is not sufficiently large to hold data of type *type*, `Empty` is returned. Typically, the datatype of *data* should correspond to that of *type*, except that binary data is best stored in a byte array of *maxLen* characters.

type

An optional parameter indicating the type of data to be retrieved. Possible values are shown in the following table:

Constant	*Value*	*Description*
vbInteger	2	Integer
vbLong	3	Long integer
vbSingle	4	Single floating point
vbDouble	5	Double floating point
vbCurrency	6	Currency
vbDate	7	Date
vbString	8	String
vbError	10	Error object
vbBoolean	11	Boolean
vbByte	17	Byte
vbArray or vbByte	8,209	Byte array

maxLen

Indicates the desired amount of data to retrieve to a string or byte array; in the case of other datatypes, the parameter is ignored. Usually, the value of *maxLen* is provided by the *bytesTotal* parameter that's passed to the DataArrival event handler. If GetData is called from within the DataArrival event handler and *maxLen* is less than *bytesTotal*, sckMsgTooBig is passed to the Error event.

The PeekData Method

The PeekData method is less commonly used but nevertheless can be indispensable in some situations. Like GetData, it reads data from a socket's buffer, but unlike GetData, it does not remove that data from the control's input buffer. Its syntax is:

```
sckMain.GetData data, [type,] [maxLen]
```

where the parameters are the same as those for the GetData method described earlier. It's particularly useful for cases in which the incoming data consists of structured data, and data headers provide some key to the size and datatypes of the data itself.

Closing the Connection

Since the Winsock control is able to handle only a single connection at a time, it is particularly important to close the connection as soon as it is no longer needed or in use. The Close method is used for this purpose. Its syntax is:

```
sckMain.Close
```

The Close method should be used only with the TCP protocol to close a TCP connection; it should not be used to close a UDP socket, since sending and receiving data using the UDP protocol does not entail creating a connection.

Note that the connection can be closed in response to a number of events that are fired by the Winsock control:

The Close event

Indicates that the remote computer has terminated its connection. In response, the local computer should call the Close event, as the following event handler illustrates:

```
sckMainTCP_Close()
   sckMainTCP.Close
  'Perform any other connection-related cleanup.
End Sub
```

The SendComplete event

Fired when the transmission of data sent using the SendData method has been completed. Note that the event is fired on the system calling the SendData method. If the connection was established primarily to transmit the data for which the event has been fired, the Close method can then be called:

```
sckMainTCP_SendComplete()
   sckMainTCP.Close
  'Perform any other connection-related cleanup.
End Sub
```

Handling Errors

Any communications program (and any communications protocol) has to be built under the assumption that errors are normal and will occur more or less frequently. To allow your application to handle TCP or UDP errors, the Winsock control provides the Error event. Its syntax is:

```
sckMain_Error(Number, Description, Scode, Source, _
              HelpFile, HelpContext, CancelDisplay)
```

where the parameters are as follows:

Number

The error code, as reflected in the following table:

Constant	*Value*	*Description*
sckOutOfMemory	7	Out of memory.
sckInvalidPropertyValue	380	The property value is invalid.
sckGetNotSupported	394	The property can't be read.
sckSetNotSupported	383	The property is read-only.
sckBadState	40006	Wrong protocol or connection state for the transaction or request.
sckInvalidArg	40014	The argument passed to a function was not in the correct format or in the specified range.
sckSuccess	40017	Successful.
sckUnsupported	40018	Unsupported variant type.
sckInvalidOp	40020	Invalid operation at current state.
sckOutOfRange	40021	Argument is out of range.

Constant	*Value*	*Description*
sckWrongProtocol	40026	Wrong protocol for the transaction or request.
sckOpCanceled	1004	The operation was cancelled.
sckInvalidArgument	10014	The requested address is a broadcast address, but flag is not set.
sckWouldBlock	10035	Socket is nonblocking and the specified operation will block.
sckInProgress	10036	A blocking Winsock operation in progress.
sckAlreadyComplete	10037	The operation is completed. No blocking operation in progress.
sckNotSocket	10038	The descriptor is not a socket.
sckMsgTooBig	10040	The datagram is too large to fit into the buffer and is truncated.
sckPortNotSupported	10043	The specified port is not supported.
sckAddressInUse	10048	Address in use.
sckAddressNotAvailable	10049	Local address not available.
sckNetworkSubsystemFailed	10050	Network subsystem failed.
sckNetworkUnreachable	10051	The network is not reachable from this host now.
sckNetReset	10052	Connection has timed out when SO_KEEPALIVE is set.
sckConnectAborted	11053	Connection is aborted due to timeout or other failure.
sckConnectionReset	10054	Connection reset by remote system.
sckNoBufferSpace	10055	No buffer space is available.
sckAlreadyConnected	10056	Socket is already connected.
sckNotConnected	10057	Socket is not connected.
sckSocketShutdown	10058	Socket has been shut down.
sckTimedout	10060	Connection has timed out.
sckConnectionRefused	10061	Connection is refused.
sckNotInitialized	10093	Socket not initialized.
sckHostNotFound	11001	Authoritative answer: host not found.
sckHostNotFoundTryAgain	11002	Nonauthoritative answer: host not found.
sckNonRecoverableError	11003	Nonrecoverable errors.
sckNoData	11004	Valid name, no data record of requested type.

Description
A textual description of *Number*.

SCode
A COM error code of type `vbError`. SCodes are used internally by COM to report errors.

Source
A string describing the source of the error.

HelpFile
The name of the file providing help on *Number*.

HelpContext
The help context ID of the error.

CancelDisplay
A flag passed by reference that indicates whether the display of the error message should be cancelled. Its default value is `False`.

Note that the error display can be suppressed by assigning *CancelDisplay* a value of `True` before the event handler terminates.

Other Operations

The Winsock control allows you to perform several operations in addition to the ones listed previously. By retrieving the value of its State property, you can determine its state. And by retrieving several properties, you can determine the local system's Internet configuration.

Determining State

The Winsock control supports *blocking operations* only; that is, calls to the Windows Sockets API do not return until the operation they support has been completed. As a result, attempts to perform some operation on a socket will produce an error if the previous operation has not yet completed. To prevent this, it is important to determine the state of the control before calling a Winsock method.

You can determine the state of the socket by retrieving the control's read-only State property. The constants indicating the control's state are 0–sckClosed, 1–sckOpen, 2–sckListening, 3–sckConnectionPending, 4–sckResolvingHost, 5–sck-HostResolved, 6–sckConnecting, 7–sckConnected, 8–sckClosing, or 9–sckError.

Getting Local Information

As more and more systems rely on dynamically assigned IP addresses, knowing the IP address of the local system in particular is sometimes difficult. However, the Winsock control provides access to some basic information about the configuration of the local system through three properties:

LocalHostName
A read-only property that indicates the name of the local computer

LocalIP
A read-only property that provides the IP address of the local computer

LocalPort

A read/write property that determines the port to be used for incoming and outgoing communication

Example

The following sample uses the SendData Method as well as many of the other elements described for the Winsock control:

```
Option Explicit

'For this example, create the following controls: _
  a TextBox control named txtResponse with the _
    MultiLine property set to True and the _
    ScrollBars property set to Both, _
  a ComboBox control named cboPorts with the Style _
    property set to 2—Dropdown List, and _
  a Winsock control named sckMain.

'Also, the form's BorderStyle should be set to _
3-Fixed Dialog, and txtResponse's Font set to a _
fixed width font such as Courier New.

Dim WithEvents lblIP As Label
Dim WithEvents lblPort As Label
Dim WithEvents lblSend As Label
Dim WithEvents lblResponse As Label
Dim WithEvents lblPorts As Label
Dim WithEvents txtIP As TextBox
Dim WithEvents txtPort As TextBox
Dim WithEvents txtSend As TextBox
Dim WithEvents cmdConnect As CommandButton
Dim WithEvents cmdSend As CommandButton
Dim WithEvents cmdInfo As CommandButton

Private Sub Form_Load()
   Me.Caption = "Winsock Example"

  'Create and/or set up controls.
   Set lblIP = Me.Controls.Add("vb.Label", "lblIP", Me)
   lblIP.Caption = "&IP Address:"
   lblIP.TabIndex = 0
   lblIP.Visible = True

   Set txtIP = Me.Controls.Add("vb.TextBox", "txtIP", _
               Me)
   txtIP.Text = ""
   txtIP.TabIndex = 1
   txtIP.Visible = True

   Set lblPort = Me.Controls.Add("vb.Label", _
                 "lblPort", Me)
   lblPort.Caption = "&Port:"
   lblPort.TabIndex = 2
```

Controls U–Z

```
  lblPort.Visible = True

  Set txtPort = Me.Controls.Add("vb.TextBox", _
              "txtPort", Me)
  txtPort.Text = ""
  txtPort.TabIndex = 3
  txtPort.Visible = True

  Set lblPorts = Me.Controls.Add("vb.Label", _
               "lblPorts", Me)
  lblPorts.Caption = "Sample Por&ts:"
  lblPorts.TabIndex = 4
  lblPorts.Visible = True

'Set up cboPorts.
  Me.cboPorts.AddItem "Echo"
  Me.cboPorts.ItemData(Me.cboPorts.NewIndex) = 7
  Me.cboPorts.AddItem "Day/Time"
  Me.cboPorts.ItemData(Me.cboPorts.NewIndex) = 13
  Me.cboPorts.AddItem "Quote of the Day"
  Me.cboPorts.ItemData(Me.cboPorts.NewIndex) = 17
  Me.cboPorts.AddItem "FTP"
  Me.cboPorts.ItemData(Me.cboPorts.NewIndex) = 21
  Me.cboPorts.AddItem "Finger"
  Me.cboPorts.ItemData(Me.cboPorts.NewIndex) = 79
'Not all of these work on every server.
  Me.cboPorts.TabIndex = 5

  Set lblSend = Me.Controls.Add("vb.Label", _
              "lblSend", Me)
  lblSend.Caption = "&Data to Send:"
  lblSend.TabIndex = 6
  lblSend.Visible = True

  Set txtSend = Me.Controls.Add("vb.TextBox", _
              "txtSend", Me)
  txtSend.Text = ""
  txtSend.TabIndex = 7
  txtSend.Visible = True

  Set lblResponse = Me.Controls.Add("vb.Label", _
                  "lblResponse", Me)
  lblResponse.Caption = "Server &Response:"
  lblResponse.TabIndex = 8
  lblResponse.Visible = True

  Me.txtResponse.Text = ""
  Me.txtResponse.TabIndex = 9

  Set cmdConnect = Me.Controls.Add( _
        "vb.CommandButton", "cmdConnect", Me)
  cmdConnect.Caption = "&Connect"
  cmdConnect.TabIndex = 10
  cmdConnect.Visible = True
```

```
    Set cmdSend = Me.Controls.Add("vb.CommandButton", _
                  "cmdSend", Me)
    cmdSend.Caption = "&Send"
    cmdSend.TabIndex = 11
    cmdSend.Visible = True

    Set cmdInfo = Me.Controls.Add("vb.CommandButton", _
                  "cmdInfo", Me)
    cmdInfo.Caption = "Inf&o"
    cmdInfo.TabIndex = 12
    cmdInfo.Visible = True

    Me.Width = 5000
    Me.Height = 4000
End Sub

Private Sub Form_Resize()
  'Because this form is not resizable, we can just _
  position the controls as desired.
    lblIP.Move 120, 180, 2190, 255
    txtIP.Move 1430, 120, 3285, 315
    lblPort.Move 120, 575, 2190, 255
    txtPort.Move 1430, 515, 3285, 315
    lblPorts.Move 120, 970, 2190, 255
    cboPorts.Move 1430, 910, 3285
    lblSend.Move 120, 1360, 2190, 255
    txtSend.Move 1430, 1300, 3285, 315
    lblResponse.Move 120, 1755, 2190, 255
    txtResponse.Move 1430, 1695, 3285, 1260
    cmdConnect.Move 620, 3135, 1095, 375
    cmdSend.Move 1835, 3135, 1095, 375
    cmdInfo.Move 3050, 3135, 1095, 375
End Sub

Private Sub cboPorts_Click()
  'The Port number is stored in the ItemData.
    txtPort.Text = _
            Me.cboPorts.ItemData(Me.cboPorts.ListIndex)
End Sub

Private Sub sckMain_Connect()
  'Provide the user with some visual feedback.
    Me.Caption = "Winsock Example" & " - Connected"
End Sub

Private Sub sckMain_DataArrival(ByVal bytesTotal As _
                                Long)
    Dim sResponse As String

  'We take the string and append it to whatever is _
  already in txtResponse.
    If bytesTotal > 0 Then
```

Controls U–Z

```
        Me.sckMain.GetData sResponse, vbString
        Me.txtResponse.Text = Me.txtResponse.Text & _
                              sResponse
    End If
End Sub

Private Sub sckMain_Error(ByVal Number As Integer, _
     Description As String, _
     ByVal Scode As Long, _
     ByVal Source As String, _
     ByVal HelpFile As String, _
     ByVal HelpContext As Long, _
     CancelDisplay As Boolean)

   'We need to inform the user of the error. Because _
    many servers don't necessarilly support all of _
    the messages we can send, we'll get lots of errors.
    MsgBox "Error " & Number & vbCrLf & Description
    Me.sckMain.Close
    Me.Caption = "Winsock Example"
End Sub

Private Sub cmdConnect_Click()
    If Me.sckMain.State <> sckClosed Then
    'You may want to inform the user instead of just _
     closing the port here.
        Me.sckMain.Close
    End If

    Me.txtResponse.Text = ""
    Me.Caption = "Winsock Example" & " - Connecting"
    Me.sckMain.Connect txtIP.Text, txtPort.Text
End Sub

Private Sub cmdSend_Click()
    If Me.sckMain.State <> sckConnected Then
        MsgBox "You must connect first"
        Exit Sub
    End If

    Me.txtResponse.Text = ""
    Me.sckMain.SendData txtSend.Text & vbCrLf
End Sub

Private Sub cmdInfo_Click()
    Dim sInfo As String

    sInfo = "Your Machine Name: " & _
            Me.sckMain.LocalHostName & vbCrLf & _
            "Your IP Address: " & Me.sckMain.LocalIP
    MsgBox sInfo, vbInformation
End Sub
```

CHAPTER 6

Properties

This chapter documents the properties of each of the controls discussed in Chapter 5, *Controls*. Each entry includes the following information:

- Whether the property is available at design time and runtime (indicated by a DT) or at runtime only (indicated by a RT) and whether it is read-only (indicated by a RO) or read/write (indicated by a RW) in the runtime environment. A few properties are neither read-only nor read/write; in these cases, an explanation can be found in the property's description.
- The controls to which the property applies. Where the property's availability and status differ depending on the control to which it applies, we've used the same icons to note that here.
- The property's datatype.
- A description of the property.

AbsolutePage, PageCount, PageSize RT RW

Applies to: Recordset object of ADO DC

Type: Long integer (or `PositionEnum` enumeration, AbsolutePage only)

These properties allow the application to work with groups of records, or pages of data, instead of just individual records. The PageCount property contains the number of pages in the recordset. PageSize contains the number of records in each page. Changing either of these properties changes the other property accordingly. The AbsolutePage property contains the current page being accessed, or -1–adPosUnknown if the current page is unknown, -2–adPosBOF if the recordset is at the beginning-of-file marker, or -3–adPosEOF if the recordset is at the end-of-file marker.

AbsolutePosition

RT RW

Applies to: Recordset object of Data and ADO DC controls

Type: Long integer (or `PositionEnum` enumeration, ADO DC recordset only)

Indicates the position of the record pointer within the recordset. For an ADO recordset, AbsolutePosition can also return: -1–adPosUnknown, if the current page is unknown; -2–adPosBOF, if the recordset is at the beginning-of-file marker; and -3–adPosEOF, if the Recordset is at the end-of-file marker.

AccessType

DT RW

Applies to: Inet control

Type: Enumeration (AccessConstants)

Determines whether the control accesses the Internet using the system's default method of access (0–icUseDefault), a direct connection (1–icDirect), or a proxy server (2–icNamedProxy). The Proxy property contains the name of the proxy to use if AccessType is set to `icNamedProxy`.

ACStatus

RT RO

Applies to: SysInfo

Type: Integer

Returns 0 if the system is not using A/C power, 1 if the system is using A/C power, or 255 if the system cannot determine if A/C power is being used.

Action

RT RW

Applies to: CommonDialog, OLE Container

Type: Integer

The Action property remains in Visual Basic for backward compatibility with previous versions. Its functionality has been replaced by various methods that control the operation of their respective control. For example, the following statement opens the File Save common dialog:

```
cdlSave.Action = 2
```

The following, however, is much more readable:

```
cdlSave.ShowSave()
```

ActiveCommand, ActiveConnection

RT RO
RT RW

Applies to: Recordset object of ADO DC

Type: Variant

Contain the string used to create the current command (ActiveCommand) and the string used for the current connection (ActiveConnection). Each can contain `vbNull` if it has not yet been set. The ActiveConnection property can be set to a valid connection string to connect to a data source.

ActiveControl

RT RO

Applies to: Form object and MDIForm object

Type: Control object

Returns the control on the parent object that currently has the focus. The Active-Control property is useful when checking whether validation logic has prevented the focus from getting to a selected control. This is done by the following code:

```
Private Sub cmdOk_Click()
    cmdOk.SetFocus

    DoEvents

    If Me.ActiveControl <> cmdOk Then
    'cmdOk does not have the focus!
        Exit Sub
    End If

  'Perform actions for cmdOk.
End Sub
```

Note that the object returned by the ActiveControl property is late bound. A similar but more complete example can be found in the "Order of Events" section under the CommandButton Control entry in Chapter 5.

ActiveForm

RT RO

Applies to: MDIForm object

Type: Form object

Returns a reference to the active MDI child form of an MDIForm object. When your code responds to an MDIForm event with multiple child forms open, the ActiveForm property indicates to which child form the event applies. For example, when the Print command is chosen from an MDI form's menu, the following code can be used to initiate a Print method of the current active child form:

```
Private Sub mnuFilePrint_Click()
    Me.ActiveForm.Print
End Sub
```

ActiveSeriesCount RT RO

Applies to: MSChart

Type: Integer

Contains the number of series in the displayed chart.

AddNewMode RT RO

Applies to: DataGrid

Type: `AddNewModeConstants` enumeration

When a DataGrid is edited and its AllowAddNew property is set to `True`, the AddNewMode property indicates whether the new record is being added. This property also provides information about the current selected row in relation to the last AddNew row. The property returns one of the following values:

Constant	*Value*	*Description*
`dbgNoAddNew`	0	No new record is being added, and the current selected row is not the last row.
`dbgAddNewCurrent`	1	No new record is being added, and the current selected row is the last row.
`dbgAddNewPending`	2	A new record is being added, and the current selected row is the row above the last row.

If AllowAddNew is `False`, the value of the AddNewMode property is always `dbgNoAddNew`.

Align DT RW

Applies to: ADO DC, Data, DataGrid, PictureBox, ProgressBar, StatusBar, Toolbar, and CoolBar controls

Type: `AlignConstants` enumeration

When the Align property is set to a value other than 0–vbAlignNone, the control is aligned to the parent object as indicated by its value. Once created, an aligned control resizes along with the parent control. Only controls that have an Align property can be placed directly on an MDI form:

Constant	*Value*	*Description*
`vbAlignNone`	0	The control is not aligned to the parent object. This value is unavailable when the parent is an MDI form. It is the default when the parent is not an MDI form.
`vbAlignTop`	1	The control is aligned to the top of its parent. When the parent object is resized, the control is

Constant	Value	Description
		also resized, with its width always remaining equal to its parent's ScaleWidth property. This is the default when the parent is an MDI form.
vbAlignBottom	2	The control is aligned to the bottom of its parent. When the parent object is resized, the control is also resized, with its width always remaining equal to its parent's ScaleWidth property.
vbAlignLeft	3	The control is aligned to the left side of its parent. When the parent object is resized, the control is also resized with its Height always remaining equal to its parent's ScaleHeight property.
vbAlignRight	4	The control is aligned to the right side of its parent. When the parent object is resized, the control is also resized, with its height always remaining equal to its parent's ScaleHeight property.

Alignment

DT RW

Applies to: Column, Panel, and ColumnHeader objects; Checkbox, Label, Option Button, TextBox, and UpDown controls

Type: Enumeration

Indicates or sets the alignment of the text in the control or object, as specified by the following values.

When Used with a CheckBox Control

AlignmentConstants	Value	Description
vbLeftJustify	0	The text is left-justified, with the CheckBox graphic to the left. This is the default value.
vbRightJustify	1	The text is right-justified, with the CheckBox graphic to the right.

When Used with a Column Object (DataGrid Control)

AlignmentConstants	Value	Description
dbgLeft	0	Text and numbers in the column are left-justified.
dbgRight	1	Text and numbers in the column are right-justified.
dbgCenter	2	Text and numbers in the column are centered.
dbgGeneral	3	Text in the column is left-justified and numbers in the column are right-justified. This is the default value.

When Used with a ColumnHeader Object (ListView Control)

ListColumn-AlignmentConstants	*Value*	*Description*
`lvwColumnLeft`	0	Text is left-justified. This is the default value.
`lvwColumnRight`	1	Text is right-justified.
`lvwColumnCenter`	2	Text is centered.

When Used with a Label Control

AlignmentConstants	*Value*	*Description*
`vbLeftJustify`	0	Text is left-justified. This is the default value.
`vbRightJustify`	1	Text is right-justified.
`vbCenter`	2	Text is centered.

When Used with an Option Button Control

AlignmentConstants	*Value*	*Description*
`vbLeftJustify`	0	The text is left-justified with the Option Button graphic to the left. This is the default value.
`vbRightJustify`	1	The text is right-justified with the Option Button graphic to the right.

When Used with a Panel Object (StatusBar Control)

PanelAlignment-Constants	*Value*	*Description*
`SbrLeft`	0	Text is left-justified in the panel. If there is a picture, it is positioned to the left of the text. This is the default value.
`SbrCenter`	1	Text is centered in the panel. If there is a picture, it is positioned to the left of the text.
`SbrRight`	2	Text is right-justified in the panel. If there is a picture, it is positioned to the right of the text.

When Used with a Label Control

AlignmentConstants	*Value*	*Description*
`vbLeftJustify`	0	Text is left-justified. This is the default value.
`vbRightJustify`	1	Text is right-justified.
`vbCenter`	2	Text is centered.

When Used with an UpDown Control

AlignmentConstant	*Value*	*Description*
`cc2AlignmentLeft`	0	The UpDown control appears to the left of the buddy control.
`cc2Alignment-Right`	1	The UpDown control appears to the right of the buddy control. This is the default value

AllowAddNew

DT RW

Applies to: DataGrid

Type: Boolean

When set to the default value of `False`, new records cannot be added by using the DataGrid. When set to `True`, an extra blank row is added to the bottom of the DataGrid for the user to add new records.

AllowArrows

DT RW

Applies to: DataGrid

Type: Boolean

When set to the default value of `True`, the arrow keys move from cell to cell in the DataGrid. When set to `False`, the arrow keys move to other controls on the form based on the form's tab order.

AllowBigSelection

DT RW

Applies to: MSFlexGrid, MSHFlexGrid

Type: Boolean

When set to its default value of `True`, clicking a column or row header selects the entire column or row. When set to `False`, the header itself is selected.

AllowColumnReorder

DT RW

Applies to: ListView

Type: Boolean

When set to its default value of `False`, the user cannot reorder columns automatically. When set to `True`, the user can drag a column to a new position. This property only applies when the View property is set to `lvwReport`.

AllowCustomize DT RW

Applies to: Toolbar

Type: Boolean

When set to the default value of `True`, the user can display the toolbar's Customize dialog by double-clicking on the toolbar. When set to `False`, double-clicking the toolbar does not have this effect. Regardless of this property setting, you can still open the Customize dialog by calling the Toolbar control's Customize method.

AllowDelete DT RW

Applies to: DataGrid

Type: Boolean

When set to the default value of `False`, records cannot be deleted by using the DataGrid. When set to `True`, a record can be deleted by selecting the entire row and pressing the Delete key.

AllowDithering DT RW

Applies to: MSChart

Type: Boolean

When set to its default value of `False`, the MSChart control uses available colors to draw the chart. When set to `True`, colors can be dithered to display unavailable colors on the chart.

AllowDynamicRotation DT RW

Applies to: MSChart

Type: Boolean

When set to its default value of `True`, the user can rotate the chart in all three dimensions by using the CTRL key along with the mouse. When set to `False`, the chart cannot be rotated automatically by the user.

AllowFocus

Applies to: Split object of DataGrid

Type: Boolean

When set to the default value of `True`, the split can receive the focus as normal. When set to `False`, the split cannot receive the focus, and whatever control or split had the focus will keep the focus.

AllowPrompt DT RW

Applies to: MaskedEditBox

Type: Boolean

When set to its default value of `False`, the character denoted by the PromptChar property is not considered a valid character to be entered by the user. When set to `True`, that character is valid. This is useful if the control is meant to contain a numeric value and the prompt character is nonnumeric (such as "#").

AllowRowSizing DT RW

Applies to: Split object of DataGrid; DataGrid control

Type: Boolean

When set to the default value of `True`, rows in the control or object can be resized with the mouse. When set to `False`, these rows cannot be resized in this manner.

AllowSelections, AllowSeriesSelections DT RW

Applies to: MSChart

Type: Boolean

When one of these properties is set to its default value of `True`, the user can select chart elements (AllowSelections) or entire series (AllowSeriesSelections) with the mouse. When set to `False`, the user cannot select chart elements (AllowSelections) and can select only individual data points (AllowSeriesSelections).

AllowSizing DT RW

Applies to: Column and Split object of DataGrid

Type: Boolean

When set to the default value of `True`, the control or object's width can be resized with the mouse. When set to `False`, the control or objects cannot be resized in this manner.

AllowUpdate DT RW

Applies to: DataGrid

Type: Boolean

When set to the default value of `True`, the user can modify records in the DataGrid by typing over existing values. When set to `False`, data cannot be modified in this manner.

AllowUserResizing

DT RW

Applies to: MSFlexGrid, MSHFlexGrid

Type: `AllowUserResizeSettings` enumeration

Controls whether a user can resize rows or columns with the mouse. When set to the default value of 0–flexResizeNone, the user cannot resize rows or columns. The setting of 1–flexResizeColumns allows the user to resize columns only. Setting the property to 2–flexResizeRows allows the user to resize rows only. Setting it to 3–flexResizeBoth gives the user the ability to resize both rows and columns.

AllowVertical

DT RW

Applies to: Band object of CoolBar

Type: Boolean

When set to the default value of `True`, the Band object is visible when the CoolBar control's Orientation property is set to `cc3OrientationVertical`. When set to `False`, the Band object is not displayed in a vertical CoolBar.

AmbientIntensity

RT RW

Applies to: Light object of MSChart

Type: Single

Controls the intensity of ambient light illuminating the chart. A value of 0 represents no ambient light (only elements lit by active lights are visible), and a value of 1 represents complete ambient light (full illumination). Values in between represent varying degrees of ambient light.

AngleUnit

RT RW

Applies to: Plot object of MSChart

Type: `VtAngleUnits` enumeration

Controls whether angles in the chart are measured in default degrees (0–VtAngleUnitsDegrees), radians (1–VtAngleUnitsRadians), or grads (2–VtAngleUnitsGrads).

Appearance

DT RO

Applies to: All controls with a visual interface

Type: Integer

When the Appearance property is set to its default value of 1, the control is drawn with a standard 32-bit Windows three-dimensional effect. This effect may make the control appear raised or inset or may have some other visual effect. When the property is set to 0, the control appears flat or two-dimensional. In the case of the ProgressBar, setting the Appearance property to 0 or `ccFlat` produces a 3-D effect, while the control has an even more deeply beveled effect with the Appearance set to 1.

Since a 3-D appearance is central to the 32-bit Windows interface, you should consider leaving the Appearance property set to its default of 0 unless you have a compelling reason to change it.

AppIsRunning

RT RW

Applies to: OLE

Type: Boolean

Controls whether the OLE object's application is currently running. If the value is `False` and is set to `True`, the application is run. Conversely, if AppIsRunning is `True` and is set to `False`, the application is closed.

ApproxCount

RT RW

Applies to: DataGrid

Type: Long integer

When a DataGrid is being used unbound, ApproxCount can be set to the approximate number of rows in the DataGrid. This keeps the vertical scrollbar on the DataGrid from inaccurately depicting how many rows are in the DataGrid. For cases in which the rows in the DataGrid are loaded as they are needed, setting this property helps to not confuse the user.

Arrange

DT RW

Applies to: ListView

Type: Enumeration

When a ListView's View property is set to `lvwIcon` or `lvwSmallIcon`, the Arrange property controls how these Icons are arranged in the ListView. When the View property is set to any other setting, the Arrange property has no effect. The Arrange property can be set as follows:

ListArrangeConstants	*Value*	*Description*
`lvwNone`	0	Icons are not arranged at all. This is the default value.
`lvwAutoLeft`	1	The icons are aligned along the left side of the ListView.
`lvwAutoTop`	2	Icons are aligned along the top of the ListView.

Arrows [DT] [RW]

Applies to: FlatScrollBar

Type: `ArrowsConstants` enumeration

Controls whether both arrows are enabled (0–cc2Both, the default value), only the left or up arrow is enabled (1–cc2LeftUp), or only the right or down arrow is enabled (2–cc2RightDown).

Auto

Applies to: Intersection, Label, and SeriesMarker objects of MSChart [RT] [RW]

Applies to: CategoryScale and ValueScale objects of MSChart [DT] [RW]

Type: Boolean

When set to the default value of `True`, the appropriate object is automatically configured. When set to `False`, other properties override the object's behavior.

AutoActivate [DT] [RW]

Applies to: OLE

Type: Enumeration

Controls how the OLE object is activated by the user. It can be set as follows:

vbOLEContainerConstants	*Value*	*Description*
`vbOLEActivateManual`	0	The object can be activated only by the DoVerb method.
`vbOLEActivateGotFocus`	1	Whenever the object receives the focus, it is activated.
`vbOLEActivateDoubleclick`	2	The object is activated when the user double-clicks on it. The OLE control does not receive the DblClick event. This is the default value.
`vbOLEActivateAuto`	3	The object controls its own activation. Generally, this is either when it gets the focus or is double-clicked.

AutoBuddy [DT] [RW]

Applies to: UpDown

Type: Boolean

When set to `True`, the control prior to the UpDown control in the tab order becomes the UpDown control's buddy control. When set to its default of `False`, the buddy control must be set manually.

AutoEnable

DT RW

Applies to: MM

Type: Boolean

When set to its default of `True`, the buttons on the MM control are automatically enabled based on which actions are currently available for the multimedia device. When set to `False`, each button can be enabled individually.

AutoIncrement

DT RW

Applies to: MSChart

Type: Boolean

When set to `True`, the Row property is increased by 1 each time the Data property is set. When the Data property is set for the last available row, the Column property is increased by 1 and the Row property is set to 1. When set to its default of `False`, setting the Data property has no effect on the Row or Column properties.

AutoLayout

RT RW

Applies to: Plot object of MSChart

Type: Boolean

When set to its default of `True`, the size and location of the Plot area are automatically determined by the size and location of the other chart elements (such as the Legend and Title). When set to `False`, the size and location of the Plot area must be set by the user or in code (through the Plot object's LocationRect object).

Automatic

RT RW

Applies to: VtColor object of MSChart

Type: Boolean

When set to `True`, the color is automatically chosen based on other colors in the chart element. When set to its default of `False`, the color is based on the VtColor object's other properties.

AutoPlay

DT RW

Applies to: Animation

Type: Boolean

When set to `True`, any *.AVI* file loaded into the Animation control begins playing immediately. When set to its default of `False`, the animation begins playing only when the Play method is called.

AutoRedraw

DT RW

Applies to: Form object, PictureBox

Type: Boolean

Controls whether the object will receive the Paint event to redraw the object or Visual Basic will automatically redraw the object itself. When set to the default value of `False`, the Paint event fires when the object needs to be repainted, and the application is responsible for handling redrawing the object. When set to `True`, all visual changes to the object are also stored to a copy of the control's image in memory, and the object is automatically redrawn from that copy. Because of this reliance on persistent graphics (i.e., the additional copy of the image in memory), setting AutoRedraw to `True` can make the application perform slower.

AutoShowChildren

DT RW

Applies to: MDIForm object

Type: Boolean

When the AutoShowChildren property is set to its default value of `True`, as soon as a child form is loaded, it is immediately shown. When it is set to `False`, loaded child forms are kept hidden until displayed with the Show method.

AutoSize

DT RW

Applies to: Label, PictureBox, MaskEditBox

Type: Boolean

When set to the default value of `False`, the control's size is not affected by its contents. When set to `True`, the control resizes itself based on the size of the text (Label, MaskEdBox) or picture (PictureBox) contained.

Applies to: Panel object

Type: `PanelAutoSizeConstants` enumeration

Panel objects on a status bar are resized in relation to one another based on the AutoSize property (see the example under StatusBar Control in Chapter 5 for more information):

Constant	*Value*	*Description*
`sbrNoAutoSize`	0	The panel is sized to the Width property and is not resized along with the status bar. This is the default value.
`sbrSpring`	1	The panel is never sized smaller than its MinWidth property but can grow larger if space is available.
`sbrContents`	2	The panel is sized to the width of its contents. When resizing, the panel is never sized smaller than its MinWidth property.

AutoTab

DT RW

Applies to: MaskEdBox

Type: Boolean

When set to `True`, and the number of characters defined by the length of the MaskEdBox control's Mask property has been entered, the focus advances through the tab order. When set to the default, `False`, this interaction does not occur.

AutoVerbMenu

DT RW

Applies to: OLE, RichTextBox

Type: Boolean

When an OLE control or OLE object in a RichTextBox control is right-clicked, the AutoVerbMenu property determines whether the OLE object's pop-up menu will display. When set to the default value of `True`, the pop-up menu displays and the control does not receive the Click or MouseDown event. When set to `False`, the menu does not display, but the Click and MouseDown events are fired as normal.

Axis

RT RO

Applies to: Plot object of MSChart

Type: Array of Axis objects

Each element of the Axis property array returns a reference to an Axis object, which contains information about the applicable axis in the chart. Elements of the Axis array include 0–VtChAxisIdX for the x-axis, 1–VtChAxisIdY for the primary y-axis, 2–VtChAxisIdY2 for a secondary y-axis, or 3–VtChAxisIdZ for the z-axis (in a 3-D chart only).

AxisGrid

RT RO

Applies to: Axis object of MSChart

Type: AxisGrid object

Returns a reference to an AxisGrid object, which defines the appearance of tick marks on the axis.

AxisId

RT RO

Applies to: Axis object

Type: `VtChAxisId` enumeration

Returns a pointer to the element of the Plot object's Axis property array, which contains the Axis object that intersects with the current Axis object. Possible values include 0–VtChAxisIdX for the x-axis, 1–VtChAxisIdY for the primary y-axis,

2–VtChAxisIdY2 for a secondary y-axis, 3–VtChAxisIdZ for the z-axis (in a 3-D chart only), or 4–vtChAxisIdNone for no axis.

AxisScale RT RO

Applies to: Axis object

Type: AxisScale object

Returns a reference to an AxisScale object, which defines the axis' display.

AxisTitle RT RO

Applies to: Axis object

Type: AxisTitle object

Contains a reference to an AxisTitle object, which controls the axis' title.

BackColor, ForeColor DT RW

Applies to: All controls with a visual interface

Type: Long integer

The ForeColor property controls the color of text on a control or object. The BackColor property controls the background color. These properties can be set to a value by using a function such as *QBColor* or *RGB,* or by using one of Visual Basic's color constants. See Appendix A, *Visual Basic Colors*, for details.

BackColorBand, BackColorBkg, BackColorFixed, BackColorHeader,BackColorIndent, BackColorSel, BackColorUnpopulated, ForeColorBand, ForeColorFixed, ForeColorHeader, ForeColorSel DT RW

Applies to: MSFlexGrid, MSHFlexGrid

Type: Long integer

The ForeColor... properties listed here control the color of text on the applicable object. The BackColor... properties control the background color of the objects. These properties can be set to a value by using a function such as *QBColor* or *RGB* or by using one of Visual Basic's color constants.

BackDrop

Applies to: AxisTitle, DataPointLabel, Label, Legend, Plot, and Title objects of MSChart; MSChart control

Type: BackDrop object

Returns a reference to a BackDrop object, which contains information about the visible area behind the object.

BackEnabled, EjectEnabled, NextEnabled, PauseEnabled, PlayEnabled, PrevEnabled, RecordEnabled, StepEnabled, StopEnabled DT RW

Applies to: MM

Type: Boolean

When the AutoEnabled property is set to `False` and any of these properties is set to `True`, the corresponding button is enabled; when any is set to the default value of `False`, the button appears disabled. When the AutoEnabled property is set to `True`, the buttons are enabled and disabled automatically.

BackStyle DT RW

Applies to: Animation, Label, OLE, Shape

Type: Integer

When set to its default value of 1, the background of the control becomes transparent. When set to 0, the background color is defined by the BackColor property.

BackVisible, EjectVisible, NextVisible, PauseVisible, PlayVisible, PrevVisible, RecordVisible, StepVisible, StopVisible DT RW

Applies to: MM

Type: Boolean

When any of these properties is set to the default value of `True`, the corresponding button is visible. When set to `False`, the button is not visible.

BandBorders DT RW

Applies to: CoolBar

Type: Boolean

When set to its default value of `True`, visible lines separate the bands in the CoolBar control. When set to `False`, the bands are not visibly separated.

BandData, ColData, RowData RT RW

Applies to: MSFlexGrid, MSHFlexGrid (BandData only)

Type: Array of long integer

These property arrays supply each band (BandData), column (ColData), or row (RowData) with a long integer value that can be used to associate the band, column, or row with related data.

BandDisplay

DT RW

Applies to: MSHFlexGrid

Type: `BandDisplaySettings` enumeration

Controls how bands are displayed in the MSHFlexGrid control. When set to the default value of 0–flexBandDisplayHorizontal, bands are displayed horizontally. When set to 1–flexBandDisplayVertical, bands are displayed vertically.

BandExpandable

RT RO

Applies to: MSHFlexGrid

Type: Array of Boolean

Contains one element for each band and returns `True` if that band can be expanded. If the band cannot be expanded, the property returns `False`.

BandIndent

DT RW

Applies to: MSHFlexGrid

Type: Long integer

Defines the number of columns by which bands are indented.

BandLevel

RT RO

Applies to: MSHFlexGrid

Type: Integer

Returns the number of the band that contains the current cell.

Bands

RT RO

Applies to: CoolBar

Type: Collection

Returns a reference to the Bands collection in the CoolBar control.

Bands RT RO

Applies to: MSHFlexGrid

Type: Integer

Returns the number of Band objects in the MSHFlexGrid control.

BarGap RT RW

Applies to: Plot object of MSChart

Type: Single

Controls how much space appears between the bars in a chart relative to the bars themselves. For example, setting the BarGap property to 50 causes the space between the bars to be half (50%) the size of the bars.

BaseHeight RT RW

Applies to: PlotBase object of MSChart

Type: Single

Contains the height of the base on which a chart appears when displayed three-dimensionally.

Basis RT RW

Applies to: Weighting object of MSChart

Type: `VtChPieWeightBasis` enumeration

Controls how pies are sized relative to one another when multiple pie charts are displayed. When set to 0–VtChPieWeightBasisNone, the pies are not sized relative to one another. When set to 1–VtChPieWeightBasisTotal, the pies are sized according to all other pies in the chart. When set to 2–VtChPieWeightBasisSeries, the pies are sized according to other pies in the same series.

BatteryFullTime, BatteryLifePercent, BatteryLifeTime, BatteryStatus RT RO

Applies to: SysInfo

Type: Long integer (BatteryFullTime, BatteryLifeTime), integer (BatteryLifePercent, BatteryStatus)

The BatteryFullTime property returns the number of seconds the battery will store when it is fully charged. The BatteryLifeTime property returns the number of seconds of power remaining in the current battery. The BatteryLifePercent property returns the percentage of power remaining in the current battery. The BatteryStatus property returns 1 if there is plenty of power in the battery, 2 if there is little power remaining, 4 if there is very little power, 8 if the battery is currently charging, 128 if there is no battery, or 255 if the status is unknown.

Bevel DT RW

Applies to: Panel object

Type: Enumeration

Controls the 3-D appearance of the Panel object according to the following settings:

Constant	*Value*	*Description*
`sbrNoBevel`	0	The panel appears to be part of the status bar with no visible 3-D effect.
`sbrInset`	1	The panel appears to be inset into the status bar. This is the default value.
`sbrRaised`	2	The panel appears to be raised from the status bar.

Blue, Green, Red RT RW

Applies to: VtColor object of MSChart

Type: Integer

These properties contain a value from 0 to 255 that controls the amount of that color from which the resulting VtColor object is formed. Although it is available at runtime, its availability at design time depends on its parent object.

BOF, EOF RT RO

Applies to: Recordset object of ADO DC and Data controls

Type: Boolean

Returns `True` if the recordset is at the beginning of file (BOF) or end of file (EOF). Otherwise, returns `False`.

BOFAction DT RW

Applies to: ADO DC, Data control

Design Time: Read/write

Runtime: Read/write

Type: `DataBOFConstants` enumeration

When the record pointer of a Data control is moved before the first record of the recordset, the control reacts based on the following settings:

Constant	*Value*	*Description*
`vbMoveFirst`	0	The record pointer remains at the first record. This is the default value.
`vbBOF`	1	The Validate event fires on the first record, the record pointer is positioned to the BOF (nonexistent) record, and the Reposition event fires on the BOF record. The left arrow icon on the Data control is also disabled.

Instead of `vbMoveFirst` and `vbBOF`, the Visual Basic documentation refers to the constants `vbBOFActionMoveFirst` and `vbBOFActionBOF`. However, neither of these constants is defined in Visual Basic's type library. This means that if you use them in code, you'll need to define them using the `Const` statement.

Bold

RT RW

Applies to: ListItem and ListSubItem objects of ListView; Node object of TreeView

Type: Boolean

When set to `True`, the text associated with the object appears bold. When set to `False`, its default value, the text does not appear bold.

Bookmark

RT RW

Applies to: Recordset object of ADO DC and Data controls; DataGrid control

Type: Variant

Stores a value that permits navigation back to the original record. For example, setting a variable equal to the Bookmark property of a recordset, then moving to a new record, then setting the Bookmark property to the value of that variable returns the record pointer to the original record.

Bookmarkable

RT RO

Applies to: Recordset object of Data control

Type: Boolean

Returns `True` if bookmarks can be used with the current recordset. Otherwise, returns `False`.

BorderColor

RT RW

Applies to: Line, Shape

Type: Variant

The BorderColor property controls the color of the outline of a Shape control or the color of the line in a Line control. It can be set to a value by using *QBColor* or *RGB*, or by using one of Visual Basic's color constants. See Appendix A.

BorderStyle

DT RW

Applies to: All controls with a border

Type: `FormBorderStyleConstants` enumeration

The BorderStyle property controls the appearance of the border around the control according to the following settings.

With a DataGrid, Frame, Image, Label, OLE, PictureBox, MSFlexGrid, or MSHFlexGrid control

Constant	*Value*	*Description*
`vbBSNone`	0	No border appears around the control. This is the default value for Image controls and Label controls.
`vbFixedSingle`	1	A flat or 3-D border appears around the control, depending on the value of the Appearance property. This is the default for DataGrid, Frame, OLE and PictureBox controls.

With a Line or Shape Control

BorderStyle-Constants	*Value*	*Description*
`vbTransparent`	0	No border appears around the shape. A Line control would be invisible.
`vbBSSolid`	1	A solid line border appears around the shape or as the line. The border is centered on the outside edge of the shape. This is the default value.
`vbBSDash`	2	A dashed border appears around the shape or as the line.
`vbBSDot`	3	A dotted border appears around the shape or as the line.
`vbBSDashDot`	4	An alternating dash and dot border appears around the shape or as the line.
`vbBSDashDot-Dot`	5	A pattern consisting of one dash followed by two dots appears around the shape or as the line.
`vbBSInside-Solid`	6	Like `vbBSSolid`, except that the border appears inside the outer edge.

With a ListView, ProgressBar, Slider, Toolbar, or TreeView Control

BorderStyleConstants	*Value*	*Description*
`ccNone`	0	No border appears around the control. This is the default value for the ProgressBar, Slider, Toolbar, and TreeView controls.
`ccFixedSingle` (default)	1	A border as defined by the Appearance property appears around the control.

With a RichTextBox Control

BorderStyleConstants	*Value*	*Description*
`rtfNoBorder`	0	No border appears around the control.
`rtfFixedSingle` (default)	1	A border as defined by the Appearance property appears around the control.

With a MaskEdBox Control

BorderStyleConstants	*Value*	*Description*
`mskNone`	0	No border appears around the control.
`mskFixedSingle` (default)	1	A border as defined by the Appearance property appears around the control.

With an MM Control

BorderStyleConstants	*Value*	*Description*
`mciNone`	0	No border appears around the control.
`mciFixedSingle` (default)	1	A border as defined by the Appearance property appears around the control.

With a MonthView Control

BorderStyleConstants	*Value*	*Description*
`cc2NoBorder`	0	No border appears around the control.
`cc2FixedSingle` (default)	1	A border as defined by the Appearance property appears around the control.

With an MSChart Control

BorderStyleConstants	*Value*	*Description*
`vtBorderStyleNone`	0	No border appears around the control.
`vtBorderStyleFixedSingle` (default)	1	A border as defined by the Appearance property appears around the control.

With a Form Object

FormBorderStyle-Constants	*Value*	*Description*
`vbBSNone`	0	The form has no border at all. With this setting, the form can't have a titlebar or any other border elements.
`vbFixedSingle`	1	The form has a border but cannot be resized. The titlebar and other border elements can be shown on the form.
`vbSizable`	2	The form has a border that can be used to resize the form. The titlebar and other border elements can be shown on the form. This is the default value.
`vbFixedDialog`	3	The form has a border but cannot be resized. The titlebar is shown along with only the control box.
`vbFixedTool-Window`	4	The form has a border but cannot be resized. The titlebar is shown but is reduced in size. There is a Close button shown. This type of window does not appear in the task list.
`vbSizableTool-Window`	5	The form has a border that can be used to resize the form. The titlebar is shown but is reduced in size. There is a Close button shown. This type of window does not appear in the task list.

In the case of the Form object and the TextBox control, the Border-Style property is read only at runtime.

With a TextBox Control

Constant	*Value*	*Description*
`vbBSNone`	0	No border appears around the control.
`vbFixedSingle`	1	A border appears around the control as defined by the Appearance property. This is the default value.

BorderWidth

DT RW

Applies to: Line, Shape

Type: Integer (1–8,192)

Controls the width of the stroked line around the outer edge of a shape or along a line. The BorderWidth applies only when the BorderStyle is set to 1–vbBSSolid or 6–vbBSInsideSolid.

BoundColumn, BoundText DT RW

Applies to: DataCombo, DataList, DBCombo, and DBList

Type: String

These controls each display a list of values from a data source (RowSource). These values are displayed to the user, but a different field can be used to determine the control's value. The BoundColumn property refers to this column of the control's RowSource from which the control's value will be determined. This value is then passed to the control's DataField and DataSource. The BoundText property contains the value derived from the control's BoundColumn property. For example, a DBList control can display employee names in the list portion, but the employee ID (which is not displayed) can be the BoundColumn that determines the record to ultimately be saved.

Brush DT RW

Applies to: DataPoint, PlotBase, Shadow, and Wall objects of MSChart

Type: Brush object

Returns a reference to a Brush object, which contains information about the graphical fill of a chart element.

BuddyControl DT RW

Applies to: UpDown

Type: Control

Returns a reference to the UpDown control's buddy control.

BuddyProperty DT RW

Applies to: UpDown

Type: String

Contains the name of the property in the buddy control (specified through the BuddyControl property) that is controlled by the UpDown control.

BulletIndent DT RW

Applies to: RichTextBox

Type: Long

When the SelBullet property is set to `True`, the BulletIndent property determines the amount to indent the bulleted text. The units of measurement are defined by the containing form's ScaleMode property. Note that this determines how much the text is indented from the bullet; how much the bullet is indented from the left margin is determined by the value of the SelIndent property.

Button DT RW

Applies to: Column object of DataGrid

Type: Boolean

When `True`, a selected cell in the column appears with a drop-down button. If pressed, this button generates a ButtonClick event for the control. When set to the default value of `False`, the button does not appear.

ButtonHeight, ButtonWidth DT RW

Applies to: Toolbar

Type: Double

The ButtonHeight and ButtonWidth properties determine the height and width of all buttons on a Toolbar control.

ButtonMenus DT RO

Applies to: Button object of Toolbar

Type: Collection

Returns a reference to the Button object's collection of ButtonMenu objects, which allow a button to appear as a drop-down list.

Buttons RT RO

Applies to: Toolbar

Type: Collection

Returns a reference to the Buttons collection. The Buttons collection object in turn supports the following members:

Name	*Description*
Count property	Returns the number of Button objects in the collection.
Item property	Returns a reference to a Button object based on its index (its position in the collection) or its key (a unique string assigned when the object was created). This is the collection's default property.

Name	Description
Add method	Adds a Button object to the collection.
Clear method	Removes all Button objects from the collection.
Remove method	Removes a single Button object from the collection.

BytesReceived RT RO

Applies to: Winsock

Type: Long integer

Returns the number of bytes waiting in the buffer. These bytes can be viewed by using the PeekData method or retrieved by using the GetData method.

CacheSize

Applies to: ADO DC DT RW

Applies to: Recordset objects of ADO DC and Data controls RT RW

Type: Long integer

Controls the number of records retrieved into memory in one read operation. Setting CacheSize to 0 disables record caching.

CacheStart

Applies to: Recordset object of Data control

Type: Variant (Bookmark)

Returns the bookmark for the first record in the cache.

CalendarBackColor, CalendarForeColor, CalendarTitleBackColor, CalendarTitleForeColor, CalendarTrailingForeColor DT RW

Applies to: DTPicker

Type: Long integer

The ...ForeColor properties listed control the color of text on the calendar (CalendarForeColor), text on the calendar title (CalendarTitleForeColor), and text for dates in months other than the month being viewed (CalendarTrailingForeColor). The ...BackColor properties listed control the background color of the calendar (CalendarBackColor) and the calendar title (CalendarTitleBackColor). These properties can be set to a value by using a function such as *QBColor* or *RGB* or by using one of Visual Basic's color constants.

Cancel

DT RW

Applies to: CommandButton

Type: Boolean

When set to `True`, the Cancel property causes the CommandButton to become clicked when the Escape key is pressed on the form. When this occurs, the Click event of the CommandButton is fired with no other events.

CancelError

DT RW

Applies to: CommonDialog

Type: Boolean

When set to `True`, raises an error when the dialog's Cancel button is pressed. When set to its default value, `False`, no error is generated.

CanEject, CanPlay, CanRecord, CanStep

RT RO

Applies to: MM

Type: Boolean

Returns `True` if the current media device can eject (CanEject), play (CanPlay), record (CanRecord), or step frame by frame (CanStep). Otherwise, returns `False`.

Cap

RT RW

Applies to: Pen object of MSChart

Type: `VtPenCap` enumeration

Controls the appearance of line caps (the area at the end of a line). Possible values include 0–vtPenCapButt for a line that ends sharply at the end, 1–vtPenCapRound for a line that is rounded with the endpoint at the center and the width of the line being the diameter of a 180° arc, or 2–vtPenCapSquare for a squared-off end with the endpoint at the center. See Figure 5-44 in Chapter 5 for more information.

Caption

DT RW

Applies to: Band object of CoolBar, Button object of Toolbar, Column object of DataGrid, Form object, MDIForm object, Tab object of TabStrip; ADO DC, Checkbox, CommandButton, Data, DataGrid, Frame, Label, Menu, and Option Button controls

Type: String

The caption appears as an uneditable, visible text heading displayed on the control.

When you place an ampersand (&) in the caption of all controls except the Data and DataGrid controls and the Form, MDIForm, and Column objects, the character following the ampersand appears underlined on the control. In the case of the CheckBox, CommandButton, Label, and OptionButton controls and the Tab object, the underlined character serves as an access key for the control. When the user presses the ALT key and the access key, the focus moves to the control, the Click event is generally fired, and any action that ordinarily results from clicking the control with the mouse occurs. For a Label control, the UseMnemonic property must be set to `True` for the control to have an access key.

CategoryScale DT RO

Applies to: Axis object of MSChart

Type: CategoryScale object

Contains a reference to a CategoryScale object, which contains information about the scale used for the category axis.

CausesValidation DT RW

Applies to: All controls with a visual interface

Type: Boolean

When set to the default value of `True`, the control will fire its Validate event before allowing the focus to pass to another control. When set to `False`, the Validate event is not fired.

CellAlignment, CellPictureAlignment, ColAlignment, ColAlignmentBand, ColAlignmentFixed, ColAlignmentHeader, FixedAlignment DT RW

Applies to: MSFlexGrid, MSHFlexGrid (except FixedAlignment)

Type: `AlignmentSettings` enumeration

Aligns the picture (CellPictureAlignment) or text in the current cell (CellAlignment), all cells in the column (ColAlignment), all cells in a fixed column (FixedAlignment), band cells in the columns (ColAlignmentBand), fixed cells in the column (ColAlignmentFixed), or header cells in the column (ColAlignment-Header), as shown in the following chart:

Constant	*Value*	*Description*
`flexAlignLeftTop`	0	The cell contents are aligned to the upper-left corner.
`flexAlignLeftCenter`	1	The cell contents are aligned to the left edge of the cell and centered from top to bottom.

Constant	*Value*	*Description*
`flexAlignLeftBottom`	2	The cell contents are aligned to the lower-left corner.
`flexAlignCenterTop`	3	The cell contents are centered at the top of the cell.
`flexAlignCenterCenter`	4	The cell contents are centered.
`flexAlignCenterBottom`	5	The cell contents are centered at the bottom of the cell.
`flexAlignRightTop`	6	The cell contents are aligned to the upper-right corner.
`flexAlignRightCenter`	7	The cell contents are aligned to the right edge of the cell—centered from top to bottom.
`flexAlignRightBottom`	8	The cell contents are aligned to the cell's lower-right corner.
`flexAlignGeneral`	9	The alignment of strings is flexAlignLeft-Center; the alignment of numbers is flex-AlignRightCenter. (Not available for the CellPictureAlignment property.)

CellBackColor, CellForeColor DT RW

Applies to: MSFlexGrid, MSHFlexGrid

Type: Long integer

The CellForeColor property controls the color of text in the current cell. The Cell-BackColor property controls the background color. These properties can be set by using a function such as *QBColor* or *RGB*, or by using one of Visual Basic's color constants.

CellFontBold, CellFontItalic, CellFontName, CellFontSize, CellFontStrikeThrough, CellFontUnderline, CellFontWidth DT RW

Applies to: MSFlexGrid, MSHFlexGrid

Type: Boolean (CellFontBold, CellFontItalic, CellFontStrikeThrough CellFontUnderline), string (CellFontName), single (CellFontSize, CellFontWidth)

These properties control all aspects of the font displayed in the current cell. The CellFontName property contains the name of the font. CellFontSize contains the point size, while CellFontWidth contains the width (in points) of the font. Other properties indicate whether the font is bold (CellFontBold), italicized (CellFontI-talic), struck through (CellFontStrikeThrough), or underlined (CellFontUnder-line).

CellForeColor DT RW

Applies to: MSFlexGrid, MSHFlexGrid

See: CellBackColor

CellHeight, CellLeft, CellTop, CellWidth DT RW

Applies to: MSFlexGrid, MSHFlexGrid

Type: Long integer

These properties return, in twips (always), the location and size of the current cell.

CellPicture DT RW

Applies to: MSFlexGrid, MSHFlexGrid

Type: Picture object

Contains a reference to the Picture object to be displayed in the current cell.

CellPictureAlignment DT RW

Applies to: MSFlexGrid, MSHFlexGrid

See: Cell Alignment

CellTextStyle DT RW

Applies to: MSFlexGrid, MSHFlexGrid

Type: `TextStyleSettings` enumeration

Controls the 3-D appearance of the text in the current cell. Possible values are 0–flexTextFlat for flat text, 1–flexTextRaised for raised text, 2–flexTextInset for inset text, 3–flexTextRaisedLight for lightly raised text, or 4–flexTextInsetLight for lightly inset text.

CellTop DT RW

Applies to: MSFlexGrid, MSHFlexGrid

See: Cell Height

CellType RT RO

Applies to: MSHFlexGrid

Type: `CellTypeSettings` enumeration

Returns the current cell's type. Possible values include 0–flexCellTypeStandard for a normal cell, 1–flexCellTypeFixed for a cell in a fixed row or column, 2–flexCellTypeHeader for a cell in a band header, 3–flexCellTypeIndent for an indent cell (used to indent other data), or 4–flexCellTypeUnpopulated for an unpopulated cell.

CellWidth DT RW

Applies to: MSFlexGrid, MSHFlexGrid

See: CellHeight

Center DT RW

Applies to: Animation

Type: Boolean

When set to `True`, the animation clip appears centered in the control. When set to its default of `False`, the animation is not centered.

Chart3D DT RW

Applies to: MSChart

Type: Boolean

When set to its default value of `False`, the displayed chart is two-dimensional. When set to `True`, the chart will appear three-dimensional.

ChartType, SeriesType DT RW

Applies to: Series object of MSChart (SeriesType only); MSChart control

Type: `VtChChartType` enumeration

Defines the type of chart to display for the chart as a whole (ChartType) or the individual series (SeriesType). Possible values are:

Constant	*Value*	*Description*
VtChChartType3dBar	0	3-D bar chart
VtChChartType2dBar	1	2-D bar chart
VtChChartType3dLine	2	3-D line chart
VtChChartType2dLine	3	2-D line chart
VtChChartType3dArea	4	3-D area chart
VtChChartType2dArea	5	2-D area chart
VtChChartType3dStep	6	3-D step chart

Constant	Value	Description
VtChChartType2dStep	7	2-D step chart
VtChChartType3dCombination	8	3-D combination chart (one or more combined charts)
VtChChartType2dCombination	9	2-D combination chart (one or more combined charts)
VtChChartType2dPie	14	Pie chart
VtChChartType2dXY	16	X/Y chart

CheckBox

DT RW

Applies to: DTPicker

Type: Boolean

When set to `True`, a checkbox is displayed next to the date. When set to its default value of `False`, the checkbox is not displayed.

CheckBoxes

DT RW

Applies to: ListView, TreeView

Type: Boolean

When set to `True`, a checkbox appears next to each item (ListItem or Node) displayed in the control. When set to its default value of `False`, the checkboxes do not appear. Checkboxes allow for multiple items to be selected in these controls. Whether the item is checked is indicated by the ListItem's or Node object's Checked property.

Checked

RT RW

Applies to: ListItem object of ListView, Node object of TreeView; Menu control

Type: Boolean

Returns `True` when the object is checked; otherwise, returns `False`. Objects can be checked only when the ListView or TreeView control's CheckBoxes property is set to `True`.

Child

DT RW

Applies to: Band object of CoolBar

Type: Control

Returns a reference to the control contained by the CoolBar control that is a child of the Band object.

Child

RT RO

Applies to: Node object of TreeView

Type: Node object

In a TreeView control, each Node object can contain one or more child Node objects. The Child property returns a reference to the first child Node object. Before using the Child property, you should ensure that there is at least one child by checking that the Children property (which returns the number of children of a Node object) is nonzero.

Children

RT RO

Applies to: Node object of TreeView

Type: Long integer

In a TreeView control, each Node object can contain one or more child Node objects. The Children property returns the number of child Node objects.

Class

DT RW

Applies to: OLEObject object of OLE; OLE control

Type: String

Returns or sets the *programmatic identifier* of an embedded object. The programmatic identifier, or class name, is a string stored in the system registry that serves to identify the OLE server component capable of handling a particular embedded object. Programmatic identifiers can come in either of two forms: version-dependent programmatic identifiers, which usually take the form `Vendor.Component.Version`, and version-independent programmatic identifiers, in the form `Vendor.Component`. An example of the former is `PowerPoint.Application.8` (for Microsoft PowerPoint 8.0); of the latter, `Paint.Picture` (for Microsoft Paintbrush).

Although it is possible to assign a new programmatic identifier to the Class property, doing so deletes the currently embedded object. There is a warning when this is done at design time, but there is no warning at runtime.

ClientHeight, ClientLeft, ClientTop, ClientWidth

RT RO

Applies to: TabStrip

Type: Long integer

These properties define the usable area of a TabStrip control. When you place a control, such as a Frame control, into a TabStrip, these properties are used to position and size the Frame control. This can be done as follows:

```
Private Sub tbsMain_Click()

With tbsMain
  'Check that Tab 1 was clicked if multiple tabs.
   If .SelectedItem = .Tabs(1) Then
  'Move the frame to match the Tab Client area.
      fraMain.Move .ClientLeft, .ClientTop, _
                   .ClientWidth, .ClientHeight
  'Make the Tab visible and put it on top.
      fraMain.Visible = True
      fraMain.ZOrder 0
   End If
End With

End Sub
```


Clip RT RW

Applies to: MSFlexGrid, MSHFlexGrid

Type: String

Contains the text content of the selected fields in a delimited string. Setting the Clip property populates the selected cells. If content is provided for more cells than are selected in the control, the extra values are ignored. The property's string value consists of columns delimited by the `vbTab` character and rows delimited by the `vbCr` character.

ClipControls DT RW

Applies to: Form object; Frame and PictureBox controls

Type: Boolean

When set to the default value of `True`, when any part of the object that was obscured is revealed, the object is completely repainted. When set to `False`, only the portion of the object that was obscured is repainted. In cases of objects containing a large number of graphics derived from graphical methods, ClipControls should be set to `True`. However, when fewer graphics are present, setting ClipControls to `False` generally increases application performance.

ClipMode DT RW

Applies to: MaskEdBox

Type: `ClipModeConstants` enumeration

When set to the default value of 0–mskIncludeLiterals, all literals in the input mask are included when copying the contents of the MaskEdBox control to the Clipboard. When set to 1–mskExcludeLiterals, the literals are not included.

ClipText RT RO

Applies to: MaskEdBox

Type: String

Returns the contents of the MaskEdBox, excluding any literal characters in the input mask.

Clockwise RT RW

Applies to: Plot object of MSChart

Type: Boolean

When set to the default value of `True`, pie charts are drawn in a clockwise direction. When set to `False`, pie charts are drawn in a counterclockwise direction.

Col, Row RT RW

Applies to: DataGrid, MSChart, MSFlexGrid, MSHFlexGrid

Type: Long integer

The Col and Row properties can be used together to determine or set the currently selected cell in the control.

ColAlignment, ColAlignmentBand, ColAlignmentFixed, ColAlignmentHeader DT RW

Applies to: MSFlexGrid, MSHFlexGrid

See: CellAlignment

ColData DT RW

Applies to: MSFlexGrid, MSHFlexGrid

See: BandData

ColHeader RT RW

Applies to: MSHFlexGrid

Type: `ColHeaderSettings` enumeration

Contains 0–flexColHeaderOn for headers to appear on each band or 1–flexColHeaderOff for headers not to appear.

ColHeaderCaption RT RW

Applies to: MSHFlexGrid

Type: Array of string

Contains the text of the header for a particular column in a band. Its syntax is:

```
MSHFlexGrid.ColHeaderCaption(number, index)
```

where *number* is the number of the band, and *index* is the number of the column.

ColIndex RT RO

Applies to: Column object of DataGrid

Type: Long integer

Returns the Column object's position within the Columns collection.

ColIsVisible, RowIsVisible RT RW

Applies to: MSFlexGrid, MSHFlexGrid

Type: Array of Boolean

Contains one element for each row (RowIsVisible) or column (ColIsVisible) of the grid. The element returns `True` if its corresponding row or column is visible or `False` if it is not. Setting the element to `True` forces that row or column to become visible.

Color DT RW

Applies to: CommonDialog

Type: Long

Contains the color selected by the user when the a call to the CommonDialog's ShowColor or ShowFont methods returns. To set this property prior to calling the ShowColor method, the Flags property must contain the `cdlCCRGBInit` constant. For the Color property to return the font color when you are using the ShowFont method, the Flags property must contain the `cdlCFEffects` constant. These constants can be added (or `Ored`) to other constants to assign multiple flags to the Flags property.

ColPos, RowPos RT RO

Applies to: MSFlexGrid, MSHFlexGrid

Type: Array of long integer

Contains one element for each column (ColPos) or row (RowPos). Each element indicates the distance in twips from the column's left (ColPos) or top (RowPos) border to the left of the column (ColPos) or top of the Row (RowPos).

ColPosition, RowPosition

DT RW

Applies to: MSFlexGrid, MSHFlexGrid

Type: Array of integer

Moves columns (ColPosition) and rows (RowPosition) to new positions. Each element of the array represents a particular row or column, and the value assigned to it represents its new position. For the ColPosition property of the MSHFlexGrid control, the property array is two-dimensional:

```
MSHFlexGrid.ColPosition index, number
```

where *index* is the position of the column to be moved, and *number* is the band containing the column in the *index* position.

Cols, FixedCols, FixedRows, Rows

DT RW

Applies to: MSFlexGrid, MSHFlexGrid

Type: Long integer

Contains the number of columns (Cols), fixed columns (FixedCols), fixed rows (FixedRows), and rows (Rows) in the control. The documentation indicates that for MSHFlexGrid, Rows is a property array, where each element indicates the number of rows in a particular band. This, however, is not the case; it is the MSHFlex-Grid's Cols property that is a property array of long integers indicating the number of columns in a band. If the index is omitted, the first band is assumed.

ColSel, RowSel

RT RW

Applies to: MSFlexGrid, MSHFlexGrid

Type: Long integer

These properties, along with the Row and Col properties, define the selected area within the control. The cell referenced by the Row and Col properties defines one corner of the selection, and the cell referenced by the RowSel and ColSel properties defines the other corner.

Column, Row

DT RW

Applies to: MSChart

Type: Integer

These properties define the current cell in the MSChart data grid and are usually used to add or modify a data value. For example, setting the Column property to

5, the Row property to 2, and the Data property to 10 causes the data point at row 5, column 2 to be set to the value 10.

ColumnCount, RowCount

DT RW

Applies to: DataGrid object of MSChart; MSChart control

Type: Integer

These properties define the size of the MSChart control's DataGrid object.

ColumnHeaderIcons, Icons, SmallIcons

DT RW

Applies to: ListView

Type: String

These properties contain the name of the ImageList controls that store the icons used for column headers (ColumnHeaderIcons) or for data items when the ListView control's View property is set to `lvwIcon` (Icons) or any other value (SmallIcons).

ColumnHeaders

RT RO

Applies to: DataGrid

Type: Boolean

When set to `True`, headings appear at the top of each column in the data grid. When set to `False`, these headings do not appear.

ColumnHeaders

DT RW

Applies to: ListView

Type: Collection

Contains a reference to a collection of ColumnHeader objects, each of which contains information about a column in the ListView control. (The column is visible when the View property is set to `lvwReport`.) The ColumnHeaders collection itself has the following members:

Add method

Adds a column header to the collection. Its syntax is:

```
Add([Index], [Key], [Text], [Width], [Alignment], [Icon])
```

The method returns a ColumnHeader object.

Clear method

Removes all members from the ColumnHeaders collection.

Count property

Returns the number of ColumnHeader objects in the collection.

Item property

Retrieves a particular member from the collection based on its index or key.

Remove method

Removes a particular member from the collection based on its index or key.

ColumnLabel, ColumnLabelCount, ColumnLabelIndex, RowLabel, RowLabelCount, RowLabelIndex [DT] [RW]

Applies to: DataGrid object of MSChart; MSChart control

Type: String (ColumnLabel, RowLabel), integer (all others)

These properties contain the row and column labels for the chart (RowLabel and ColumnLabel) as well as the number of row and column labels in the chart (RowLabelCount and ColumnLabelCount). To set an individual label, first set the ColumnLabelIndex or RowLabelIndex to determine which label will be changed.

Columns [RT] [RO]

Applies to: Split object of DataGrid; DataGrid control

Type: Collection

Returns a reference to the Columns collection. The Columns collection itself supports the following members:

Add property

Adds a new column. Its syntax is simply:

```
Add index
```

where *index* is an integer indicating the position at which to add the column. It returns a Column object representing the added column.

Count property

Returns the number of Column objects in the collection.

Item property

Returns a reference to a Column object based on its index (i.e., on its position in the collection only). This is the collection's default property.

Remove method

Removes a single Column object from the collection based on its index.

The following code could be used to perform an action (change a property, access a method) on all columns in a DataGrid control:

```
Dim colX As Column

For Each colX In dbgMain.Columns
'Perform action on Column object
Next colX
```

ColWidth, RowHeight RT RW

Applies to: MSFlexGrid, MSHFlexGrid

Type: Array of long integer

Each element of these arrays contains the width of the column (ColWidth) or height of the row (RowHeight) specified by the array element. When an index value of -1 is used, all columns or rows are affected.

The ColHeight property of the MSHFlexGrid control is a two-dimensional array; its syntax is:

```
MSHFlexGrid.RowHeight(index, [number])
```

where *number* is the ordinal number of a band, and *index* is the ordinal position of a column in that band; if *number* is omitted, it defaults to the first band.

ColWordWrapOption, DT RW *ColWordWrapOptionBand, ColWord-WrapOptionFixed, ColWordWrapOptionHeader* RT RW

Applies to: MSHFlexGrid

Type: Array of Boolean

When set to `True`, word wrap is in effect for the column specified (ColWordWrap-Option), the column and (optionally) the band specified (ColWordWrap-OptionBand), the fixed column specified (ColWordWrapOptionFixed), or the header column of (optionally) the band specified (ColWordWrapOptionHeader). When set to the default value of `False`, word wrap is not in effect.

ComboItems RT RO

Applies to: ImageCombo

Type: Collection

Returns a reference to a collection of ComboItem objects, each of which contains information about an item in the ImageCombo control. The ComboItems collection in turn supports the following members:

Add method

Adds a ComboItem object to the collection. Its syntax is:

```
Add([Index], [Key], [Text], [Image], [SelImage], [Indentation])
```

The method returns the ComboItem object added to the collection.

Clear method

Removes all members from the ComboItems collection.

Count property

Returns the number of ComboItem objects in the collection.

Item property

Retrieves a particular member from the collection based on its index or key.

Remove method

Removes a particular member from the collection based on its index or key.

Command

RT RW

Applies to: MM

Type: String

Contains a command string for the multimedia device loaded into the MM control. See the MM (Multimedia MCI) Control entry in Chapter 5 for a complete list of command strings.

CommandTimeout, ConnectionTimeout

DT RW

Applies to: ADO DC

Type: Long integer

Contains a number of seconds to wait before generating an error after a command is issued but no data is returned (CommandTimeout) or a connection attempt is made (ConnectionTimeout). Setting the property to 0 causes the control to wait indefinitely for a response.

CommandType

DT RW

Applies to: ADO DC

Type: `CommandTypeEnum` enumeration

Indicates the type of command that the Command object represents. This can be determined automatically, but for improved performance it can also be set directly. The following table lists valid values of the CommandType property:

Constant	*Value*	*Description*
`adCmdText`	1	An SQL statement.
`adCmdTable`	2	A table name.
`adCmdStoredProc`	4	A stored procedure.
`adCmdUnknown`	8	Unknown; the ADO engine determines the type of Command object to use.
`adExecuteNoRecords`	128	An SQL statement or stored procedure that doesn't return rows. It must be added or `Or`ed with either `adCmdText` or `adCmdStoredProc`.
`adCmdFile`	256	The name of a persisted recordset.
`adCmdTableDirect`	512	A table name whose columns are all returned.

Component RT RW

Applies to: DataPointLabel object of MSChart

Type: `VtChLabelComponent` enumeration

Contains the type of label used for the data point. Possible values are 1–VtChLabelComponentValue for the actual value, 2–VtChLabelComponentPercent for the percent of the value compared to all other values, 4–VtChLabelComponentSeriesName to use the series name as the label, or 8–VtChLabelComponentPointName to use the data point name for the label.

Properties C

CompositeColumnLabel, CompositeRowLabel RT RO

Applies to: DataGrid object of MSChart

Type: Array of string

These properties return the label for the specified column (CompositeColumnLabel) or specified row (CompositeRowLabel). They return a string that concatenates all labels for the column or row.

Connect, ConnectionString DT RW

Applies to: Database object of Data control (Connect); ADO DC (ConnectionString) and Data controls (Connect)

Type: String

Contains the connection string used to establish a connection to the data source. The connection string contains various semicolon-delimited parameters about the data source. See the entries for the Data Control and the ADO Data Control in Chapter 5 for more information.

ConnectionTimeout DT RW

Applies to: ADO DC

See: CommandTimeout

Container RT RW

Applies to: All controls

Type: Control/object

Returns a reference to the control or form/MDI form on which the control is located. For example, if a TextBox control is placed into a Frame control, the TextBox control's Container property provides a reference to the Frame object. If the same text box is placed directly on a form, its Container property provides a reference to the Form object. The value of the Container property can also be changed at runtime to change the control's container in the application.

ControlBox, MaxButton, MinButton, WhatsThisButton DT RW

Applies to: Form object

Type: Boolean

These properties control the display of the control box on the left side of the titlebar and the context-sensitive help, Minimize, and Maximize buttons on the left side of the titlebar of a Form object. Whether these border elements can be displayed is based on the value of the BorderStyle Property. The following table shows the relationship of these four interface objects to the BorderStyle property. Yes indicates that, if the button's respective property is set to `True`, the button *can* be displayed, while No indicates that the button is not displayed, regardless of its property value:

BorderStyle	*CtrlBox*	*Min*	*Max*	*What*
None	No	No	No	No
Fixed single	Yes	Yes	Yes	Yes
Sizable	Yes	Yes	Yes	Yes
Fixed dialog	Yes	No	No	Yes
Fixed tool	No	No	No	No
Sizable tool	No	No	No	No

For the `vbFixedSingle` and `vbSizable` border styles, if ControlBox is set to `False`, it overrides the other three settings; that is, the Maximize, Minimize, and "What's This" buttons are not displayed, regardless of their property values.

For the `vbFixedSingle` and `vbSizable` border styles, if both MinButton and MaxButton are `True`, the WhatsThisButton button will not be displayed, regardless of its setting. If only one of MinButton and MaxButton is set to `False`, both buttons will be displayed, but the button set to `False` will be disabled; once again, the WhatsThisButton setting is ignored. If both MinButton and MaxButton are `False` and WhatsThisButton is `True`, the context-sensitive help button will be displayed.

Controls RT RO

Applies to: Form and MDIForm objects; Toolbar control

Type: Collection

Returns a reference to the Controls collection, which contains one element for each control on the form, MDI form, or Toolbar control. In the case of the Toolbar control, Button objects are not part of this collection but are accessible through the Buttons collection; only standard and custom controls for which the Toolbar serves as a container are members of the collection.

The Controls collection has the following members:

Add method VB6

Dynamically adds a control to the collection at runtime. Its syntax is:

```
Add(ProgID, name, container)
```

where *ProgID* is the control's programmatic identifier, as defined in the registry, *name* is the string to be a assigned to the control's Name property, and *container* is a reference to the container in which the control will be placed.

Count property

Indicates the number of Control objects in the collection.

Item property

Returns a reference to a Control object based on its index (i.e., its ordinal position in the collection) or its name (i.e., the value of its Name property).

If a Toolbar control is contained by a form or MDI form, the members of the Toolbar object's Controls collection are also members of the Form or MDIForm object's Controls collection. This relationship applies only to Toolbar controls and their containers. The controls on a child form, for example, are members of that Form object's Controls collection, not of the containing MDIForm object's Controls collection.

Note that the Controls collection is late-bound, which typically results in poorer performance when compared with the use of early-bound objects. This also means that Auto List Members and Auto Quick Info are not available for the Controls collection at design time.

Copies

DT RW

Applies to: CommonDialog

Type: Integer

When set prior to activating the Print dialog with the ShowPrint method, it sets the value for the "Number of Copies" text box. After the dialog box is closed, the Copies property contains the number of copies to be printed after user editing.

Count

RT RO

Applies to: All collections

Type: Long

Returns the number of items in a collection.

CurrentCellModified [RT] [RW]

Applies to: DataGrid

Type: Boolean

When the user modifies the contents of a cell, the value of CurrentCellModified is set to `True`. To cancel a pending edit of a cell, set the CurrentCellModified property to `False`. This will restore any changes the user has made.

CurrentCellVisible [RT] [RW]

Applies to: Split object of DataGrid; DataGrid control

Type: Long

Returns `False` if the currently selected cell is not visible in the DataGrid control or Split object; returns `True` if the cell is visible. To automatically scroll a Split or DataGrid to the current cell, set the CurrentCellVisible property to `True`.

CurrentX, CurrentY [RT] [RW]

Applies to: Form object; PictureBox control

Type: Long

When using the graphics methods to draw on a form or PictureBox, the CurrentX and CurrentY properties return the location from which the next method will originate. To change this location, these properties can be set as follows:

```
Private Sub Form_MouseDown(Button As Integer, _
            Shift As Integer, X As Single, Y As Single)
    If (Button And vbLeftButton) Then
    'If left button pressed, draw line to point.
        Me.Line -(X, Y)
    ElseIf (Button And vbRightButton) Then
    'If right button pressed, set new point.
       CurrentX = X
        CurrentY = Y
    End If
End Sub
```

Custom [RT] [RW]

Applies to: DataPointLabel object of MSChart

Type: Boolean

When set to `True`, the DataPointLabel object's Text property is shown on the data point label. When set to the default value of `False`, the data point label's caption is set automatically based on its other properties.

CustomFormat

DT RW

Applies to: DTPicker

Type: String

Can contain a format string similar to those used with VBA's *Format* function. When the Format property is set to `dtpCustom`, this string is used to control the input and display of the control's value. In addition, one or more groups of one or more capital Xs can be used in the format string as placeholders for callback fields. These callback fields are then passed by reference to the Format event and by value to the FormatSize event so that they can be replaced with values.

Data

DT RW

Applies to: MSChart

Type: Integer

Returns or sets the value for the data point at the coordinates specified by the Row and Column properties.

Database

RT RO

Applies to: Data control

Type: Database object

Returns the DAO database object used by the control. This allows the use of DAO functions on this database.

DatabaseName

Applies to: Data control

Type: String

Contains the name of the database to which the control is bound. To open a database, set the DatabaseName property to a valid database and initiate the Refresh method to connect the database. However, until the RecordSource property is set, no data will actually be available. The following example shows how the DatabaseName and RecordSource properties can be set to access a database:

```
Me.datMain.DatabaseName = "MyDatabase.mdb"
Me.datMain.RecordSource = "MyTable"
Me.datMain.Refresh
```

When setting the DatabaseName property in Design mode, be sure to write error-handling code in the Data control's Error event. Better still, leave the DatabaseName property blank in Design mode and set it in code after verifying the existence of the physical database.

DataBindings

DT RW

Applies to: All nonintrinsic controls

Type: Collection

Contains a reference to a collection of DataBinding objects, each of which contains information about the bindable properties of the control.

DataChanged

RT RW

Applies to: All controls that can be bound to a Data control

Type: Boolean

When the contents of a bound control are changed through code or by the user, the DataChanged property is set to `True`. This property is reset each time the data is changed by the Data control itself, and any actions performed through the Data control—such as changing records—do not cause the DataChanged property to be set to `True`. If the DataChanged property is directly changed to `False` through code in the Data control's Validate event handler, its new contents are not saved. For example, the following event handler gives the user the choice of saving or discarding changes to a field:

```
Private Sub Data1_Validate(Action As Integer, _
                           Save As Integer)
If Text1.DataChanged Then
   If vbNo = MsgBox("Data has been changed!" & _
             "Save changes?", _
             vbYesNo Or vbQuestion, _
             "Data Changed") Then
      Text1.DataChanged = False
   End If
End If

End Sub
```

DataField

DT RW

Applies to: All controls that can be bound to a Data control except DataGrid

Type: String

Contains the name of a field within the recordset provided by the Data control to which the control is bound. See the entry for the Data Control in Chapter 5 for more information.

DataFormat

DT RW

Applies to: All controls that support multiple data formats

Type: StdDataFormat object

Contains a reference to a StdDataFormat object, which contains information about how to format the data from the data source.

DataGrid

DT RO

Applies to: MSChart

Type: DataGrid object

Returns a reference to a DataGrid object, which contains information about the values and labels used in the chart.

DataMember

DT RW

Applies to: All bindable controls

Type: String

Indicates which data member to use when the data source contains multiple members.

DataPointLabel

RT RW

Applies to: DataPoint object of MSChart

Type: DataPointLabel object

Contains a reference to a DataPointLabel object, which contains information about the label for the data point.

DataPoints

RT RW

Applies to: Series object of MSChart

Type: Collection

Contains a reference to a collection of DataPoint objects, each of which contains information about a specific point on the chart.

DataSeriesInRow

RT RW

Applies to: Plot object of MSChart

Type: Boolean

When set to the default value of `False`, data series points are read from column data in the DataGrid object. When set to `True`, data series points are read from row data in the data grid.

DataSource

DT RO

Applies to: All controls that can be bound to a Data control

Type: Data

Defines the Data control to which the control is bound. See the Data Control entry in Chapter 5 for more information.

DataText

RT RW

Applies to: OLE

Type: String

Used to send text to and receive text from an OLE object. However, if there is an alternative, it is preferable to use automation for interprocess control and communication.

DateCreated, LastUpdated

RT RO

Applies to: Recordset object of Data control

Type: Date

Returns the date that the recordset was created (DateCreated) or last modified (LastUpdated).

Day, Month, Year, Hour, Minute, Second, Week

RT RW

Applies to: DTPicker, MonthView (Day, Month, Year, and Week only)

Type: Integer

These properties contain the year (Year), month number (Month), day number (Day), week number (Week), hour (Hour), minute (Minute), and second (Second) currently set in the control.

DayBold

RT RW

Applies to: MonthView

Type: Array of Boolean

Contains one element for each date visible on the control. Each element directly corresponds to an element of the VisibleDays property array. Each element can be set to `True` to display that date in bold on the MonthView control.

DayOfWeek

RT RO

Applies to: DTPicker, MonthView

Type: `DayConstants` enumeration

Contains a value that represents the day of the week currently selected in the control. Possible values are 1–mvwSunday, 2–mvwMonday, 3–mvwTuesday, 4–mvwWednesday, 5–mvwThursday, 6–mvwFriday, or 7–mvwSaturday.

Default

DT RW

Applies to: CommandButton

Type: Boolean

When set to `True`, causes the CommandButton to become clicked when the Enter key is pressed on the form. When this occurs, the Click event of the CommandButton is fired with no other events. See the CommandButton Control entry in Chapter 5 for more information.

DefaultCursorType

DT RW

Applies to: Data control

Type: `DefaultCursorTypeConstants` enumeration

When the Data control's DefaultType is set to `dbUseODBC`, the DefaultCursorType property controls what type of cursor the Data control should use, as follows:

Constant	*Value*	*Description*
`vbUseDefaultCursor`	0	Allows the current ODBC driver to determine the type of cursor to create. This is the default value.
`vbUseODBCCursor`	1	Uses the ODBC cursor library for cursors.
`vbUseServerSideCursor`	2	Uses a server-side cursor.

The type of cursor you should use largely depends on the size of the cursor, your database engine, and the speed of the server computer and network. (It is beyond the scope of this book to discuss cursor selection with ODBC drivers.) The property is ignored when DefaultType is set to `dbUseJet`.

DefaultExt DT RW

Applies to: CommonDialog

Type: String

The CommonDialog control uses the DefaultExt property when it is activated using the ShowOpen or ShowSave methods. If no explicit file extension is entered in the "File name" text box, the DefaultExt property is used to control which filenames are displayed in the files list for the ShowOpen method and what extension is used when saving a file for the ShowSave method.

DefaultPercentBasis, PercentBasis RT RW

Applies to: Plot object of MSChart (DefaultPercentBasis), AxisScale object of MSChart (PercentBasis)

Type: `VtChPercentAxisBasis` enumeration

Controls the display of a percent axis. Possible values are 0–vtChPercentAxisBasisMaxChart, where all values are compared to the largest value in the chart; 1–vtChPercentAxisBasisMaxRow, where all values are compared to the largest value in the row; 2–vtChPercentAxisBasisMaxColumn, where all values are compared to the largest value in the column; 3–vtChPercentAxisBasisSumChart, where all values are compared to the sum of all values in the chart; 4–vtChPercentAxisBasisSumRow, where all values are compared to the sum of all values in the row; or 5–vtChPercentAxisBasisSumColumn, where all values are compared to the sum of all values in the column.

DefaultType DT RW

Applies to: Data control

Type: Enumeration

The DefaultType property determines the type of connection used by the Data control as follows:

Constant	*Value*	*Description*
`dbUseJet`	1	Uses the Jet database engine. This is appropriate for most file-based databases. This is the default value.
`dbUseODBC`	2	Uses ODBC. This is appropriate for most database servers.

DefColWidth

DT RW

Applies to: DataGrid

Type: Integer

When the DefColWidth property is set to its default value of 0, new columns are sized using either the width of the text in their ColumnHeader or their Size property, whichever is larger. When set to any other value, the new column is sized to that value using the ScaleMode of the parent Form object.

DepthToHeightRatio

RT RW

Applies to: Plot object of MSChart

Type: Single

Contains the percentage of the chart's height to be used as the chart's depth on a three-dimensional chart.

Description

DT RW

Applies to: Button object of Toolbar

Type: String

In the Toolbar control's Customize dialog, each button appears alongside the value of its Description property. This should be a phrase that adequately describes the function of the button. If the toolbar cannot be customized (that is, if the AllowCustomize property is set to `False` and the application does not make calls to the Customize method), this property does not need to be set.

DeviceID

RT RO

Applies to: MM

Type: Integer

Returns the ID of the multimedia device currently opened by the MM control.

DeviceType

DT RW

Applies to: MM

Type: String

Contains the string naming the type of multimedia device that the MM control is set for or currently contains. See the MM (Multimedia MCI) Control entry in Chapter 5 for a complete list of device type names.

DialogTitle DT RW

Applies to: CommonDialog

Type: String

Defines the text that appears in the titlebar of the appropriate dialog box when the CommonDialog control is activated using the ShowOpen and ShowSave methods. When other methods are used to activate the CommonDialog control, the DialogTitle is not used. If left blank, the titlebar is populated as follows:

Method Used	*Default Caption*
ShowOpen	Open
ShowSave	Save As

DisabledImageList, HotImageList, ImageList DT RW

Applies to: Toolbar

Type: String

These properties contain the name of the ImageList controls that store the icons to use for buttons (ImageList), disabled buttons (DisabledImageList), or "hot" buttons (HotImageList).

DisabledPicture DT RW

Applies to: CheckBox, CommandButton, Option Button

Type: Picture object

Defines the Picture object to be displayed when the control's Style property is set to `vbButtonGraphical` and its Enabled property is set to `False`. If this property is not set, a grayed version of the Picture property is used.

DisableNoScroll DT RW

Applies to: RichTextBox

Type: Boolean

Ordinarily, when the ScrollBars property of the RichTextBox control is set to `rtfHorizontal`, `rtfVertical`, or `rtfBoth`, horizontal and/or vertical scrollbars appear when there is too much text to display in full either horizontally or vertically; this occurs because the DisableNoScroll property is set to its default of `False`. Rather than have scrollbars appear suddenly and mysteriously, though, you can elect to display disabled scrollbars until there is too much text to display either horizontally or vertically by setting the DisableNoScroll property to `True`.

DisplayType

DT RW

Applies to: OLEObject object of OLE; OLE control

Type: Enumeration

Controls how an OLE object is displayed once it is created, as follows:

Constant	*Value*	*Description*
`vbOLEDisplayContent`	0	The OLE object's content is displayed. This is the default value.
`vbOLEDisplayIcon`	1	An icon representing the OLE object is diplayed.

Once the OLE object is created, the DisplayType property becomes read-only.

Properties D–F

DividerStyle

DT RW

Applies to: Column object of DataGrid

Type: `DividerStyleConstants` enumeration

Controls the appearance of the line on the right edge of the column, as follows:

Constant	*Value*	*Description*
`dbgNoDividers`	0	The line is invisible.
`dbgBlackLine`	1	The line is black.
`dbgDarkGrayLine`	2	The line is dark gray. This is the default value.
`dbgRaised`	3	The line appears to be raised using the Windows colors for 3-D objects.
`dbgInset`	4	The line appears to be inset using the Windows colors for 3-D objects.
`dbgUseForeColor`	5	The line is the color of the ForeColor property of the DataGrid control.
`dbgLightGrayLine`	6	The line is light gray.

DivisionsPerLabel, DivisionsPerTick

DT RW

Applies to: CategoryScale object of MSChart

Type: Integer

Contains the number of units to skip between ticks (DivisionsPerTick) and labels (DivisionsPerLabel) on the category axis.

Document

DT RW

Applies to: Inet control

Type: String

Contains the name of the document to use with subsequent Execute method calls.

DoSetCursor

Applies to: MSChart

Type: Boolean

When set to the default value of `True`, the chart can change the mouse cursor while the mouse is over the chart. When set to `False`, the control does not affect the mouse cursor directly.

DownPicture

DT RW

Applies to: CheckBox, CommandButton, Option Button

Type: Picture object

Defines the Picture object to be displayed when the control's Style property is set to `vbButtonGraphical` and its Enabled property is set to `False`. If this property is not set, the Picture property is used.

DragIcon

DT RW

Applies to: All controls

Type: Icon object

Controls the appearance of the cursor when a drag action is taking place. When the DragIcon is left blank, the icon appears as an arrow inside a rectangle the size of the control. When set to a valid icon, that icon will appear during drag actions.

DragMode

DT RW

Applies to: All controls

Type: `DragModeConstants` enumeration

Controls how dragging in drag-and-drop operations is initiated, as follows:

Constant	*Value*	*Description*
`vbManual`	0	The Drag method is used to initiate dragging the control. This is the default value.
`vbAutomatic`	1	The control is dragged automatically by clicking on the control and dragging with the button down.

DrawMode

DT RW

Applies to: Form object; Line, PictureBox, and Shape controls

Type: `DrawModeConstants` enumeration

Controls the appearance of the Line and Shape controls and the output of drawing methods. It can be set to 1–vbBlackness, 2–vbNotMergePen, 3–vbMaskNotPen, 4–vbNotCopyPen, 5–vbMaskPenNot, 6–vbInvert, 7–vbXorPen, 8–vbNotMaskPen, 9–vbMaskPen, 10–vbNotXorPen, 11–vbNop, 12–vbMergeNotPen, 13–vbCopyPen (the default), 14–vbMergePenNot, 15–vbMergePen, or 16–vb-Whiteness.

DrawMode

DT RO

Applies to: MSChart

Type: `VtChDrawMode` enumeration

Controls how the contents of the chart are drawn to the screen. Possible values are 0–vtChDrawModeDraw to draw the chart or 1–vtChDrawModeBlit to draw the chart to an offscreen area and then quickly move it to the screen.

DrawStyle

DT RW

Applies to: Form object; PictureBox control

Type: `DrawStyleConstants` enumeration

Defines the line style used by graphic methods performed on the object or control, as follows:

Constant	*Value*	*Description*
`vbSolid`	0	A solid line border appears around the shape or as the line. The line is centered on the outside edge of the shape. This is the default value.
`vbDash`	1	A dashed border appears around the shape or as the line.
`vbDot`	2	A dotted border appears around the shape or as the line.
`vbDashDot`	3	An alternating dash and dot border appears around the shape or as the line.
`vbDashDotDot`	4	A pattern consisting of one dash followed by two dots appears around the shape or as the line.
`vbInvisible`	5	No line appears.
`vbInsideSolid`	6	As in `vbSolid`, except that the border appears inside the outer edge.

The exact appearance of lines drawn with a particular style, however, is determined by the value of the DrawWidth property.

DrawWidth

DT RW

Applies to: Form object; PictureBox control

Type: Integer

Controls the width of lines drawn by using graphic methods on the object or control. If set to a value higher than 1, the DrawStyles `vbDash`, `vbDot`, `vbDashDot`, and `vbDashDotDot` all appear as `vbSolid`.

DropHighlight

RT RW

Applies to: ListView, TreeView

Type: ListItem or Node object

When set to a child object (ListItem object for ListView control, Node object for TreeView control), highlights that object using the Windows system highlight color. This is generally done in conjunction with a MouseMove or DragOver event. Once set, the DropHighlight property contains a reference to that object until it is set to another object or to `Nothing`.

EdgeIntensity, EdgeVisible

RT RW

Applies to: Light object of MSChart

Type: Single (EdgeIntensity), Boolean (EdgeVisible)

These properties control whether edges are visible (EdgeVisible) on the chart and how bright they appear (EdgeIntensity).

EdgePen

DT RO

Applies to: DataPoint object of MSChart

Type: Pen object

Returns a reference to a Pen object, which contains information about how edges are drawn for the data point.

EdgeVisible

RT RW

Applies to: Light object of MSChart

Type: Boolean

See: *EdgeIntensity*

EditActive

RT RW

Applies to: DataGrid

Type: Boolean

When a cell in a DataGrid is currently being edited, the EditActive property returns `True`. When `False`, the property can be set to `True` to initiate an edit. If `True` and set to `False`, the edit will be terminated and any validation events will take place.

EditMode

RT RO

Applies to: Recordset object of Data control; Data control

Type: `EditModeEnum` enumeration

Returns the current action status of a Data control as follows:

EditModeEnum	*Value*	*Description*
`dbEditNone`	0	There is no edit taking place.
`dbEditInProgress`	1	There is an edit taking place.
`dbEditAdd`	2	A new record is being added.

EditMode

RT RO

Applies to: ADO DC

Type: `EditModeEnum` enumeration

Returns the current action status of the control as follows:

EditModeEnum	*Value*	*Description*
`adEditNone`	0	There is no edit taking place.
`adEditInProgress`	1	There is an edit taking place.
`adEditAdd`	2	A new record is being added.
`adEditDelete`	3	A record is being deleted.

Effect

DT RW

Applies to: VtFont object of MSChart

Design Time: Read/write

Runtime: Read/write

Type: `VtFontEffect` enumeration

Indicates whether the font is struck through (256–VtFontEffectStrikeThrough) or underlined (512–VtFontEffectUnderline).

EjectEnabled

DT RW

Applies to: MM

See: BackEnabled

EjectVisible

DT RW

Applies to: MM

See: BackVisible

Elevation, Rotation

RT RW

Applies to: View3D object of MSChart

Type: Single

Contains the angle (in units defined by the Plot object's AngleUnit property) of rotation (Rotation) and elevation (Elevation) from which the 3-D viewpoint of the chart originates.

EmbossHighlight, EmbossPicture, EmbossShadow

DT RW

Applies to: Band object of CoolBar; CoolBar control

Type: Long integer (EmbossHighlight, EmbossShadow),
Boolean (EmbossPicture)

When set to the default value of `False`, the picture set in the Picture property appears as normal. When set to `True`, the picture is embossed in the colors defined by the EmbossHighlight and EmbossShadow properties. This usually makes the controls contained by the CoolBar control easier to see.

Enabled

DT RW

Applies to: Form, MDIForm, and Panel objects; all controls with a visual interface

Type: Boolean

When set to its default value of `True`, the object or control appears and functions normally. When set to `False`, the object or control appears grayed and does not respond to mouse or keyboard events. If the object or control contains other objects or controls, they too do not respond to events. However, objects and controls in a disabled container are not grayed.

EOF

RT RO

Applies to: Recordset object of ADO DC and Data controls

See: BOF

EOFAction

DT RW

Applies to: Data control

Type: `DataEOFConstants` enumeration

When the record pointer of a Data control is moved after the last record of the recordset, the control reacts based on the following settings:

Constant	*Value*	*Description*
`vbMoveLast`	0	The record pointer remains at the last record. This is the default value.
`vbEOF`	1	The record pointer is positioned to the EOF record. The right arrow icon on the Data control is also disabled.
`vbAddNew`	2	The Data control is placed in New mode, ready to enter a new record.

The online documentation for VB5 incorrectly identifies the DataEOF constants as `vbEOFActionMoveLast`, `vbEOFActionEOF`, and `vbEOFActionAddNew`. None, however, are defined in the VB runtime type library.

EOFAction

DT RW

Applies to: ADO DC

Type: `EOFActionEnum` enumeration

When the record pointer of an ADO DC is moved after the last record of the recordset, the control reacts based on the following settings:

Constant	*Value*	*Description*
`adDoMoveLast`	0	The record pointer remains at the last record. This is the default value.
`adStayEOF`	1	The record pointer is positioned to the EOF record. The right arrow icon on the Data control is also disabled.
`adDoAddNew`	2	The Data control is placed in Add mode, ready to enter a new record.

Error, ErrorMessage RT RO

Applies to: MM

Type: Integer (Error), string (ErrorMessage)

Returns the number (Error) and description (ErrorMessage) of the error (if any) returned from the last command.

ErrorText RT RO

Applies to: DataGrid

Type: String

When an error occurs in a Data control to which a DataGrid control is bound, that error message is returned in the DataGrid control's ErrorText property.

Excluded, Hidden RT RW

Applies to: SeriesPosition object of MSChart

Type: Boolean

When set to `True`, the series is excluded (Excluded property) or hidden (Hidden property) in the chart. When set to the default value of `False`, the series is included (Excluded) or displayed (Hidden) in the chart.

Exclusive DT RW

Applies to: Data control

Type: Boolean

Returns `True` if the bound database is opened exclusively by the control. Databases opened exclusively cannot be opened by any other processes or users. When you are opening a database, if the Exclusive property is set to `True`, the Data control will attempt to open the database exclusively. If another process is using the database, runtime error 3045 will result. Changing the Exclusive property for a database that is already open has no effect unless the Refresh method is called. However, the next database to be bound to that Data control will be opened exclusively.

Expanded RT RW

Applies to: Node object of TreeView

Type: Boolean

Returns `True` if the node is expanded, showing any child nodes. If the node is collapsed, the Expanded property returns `False`. When you set the Expanded property to `True` or `False`, the node will be expanded or collapsed, respectively.

ExpandedImage

RT RW

Applies to: Node object

Type: Long integer

The ExpandedImage property can be set to the index of a ListImage object in the bound ImageList control that you wish to appear when the Node object is expanded.

Fields

RT RO

Applies to: Recordset object of ADO DC and Data controls

Type: Collection

Contains a reference to a collection of Field objects, each of which contains information about the attributes and contents of a field returned from the data source.

FileName

DT RW

Applies to: CommonDialog

Type: String

When set to the name of a valid file prior to calling the ShowOpen or ShowSave methods, the FileName property causes the appropriate dialog box to default to the file specified. When the dialog is exited after selecting a file, regardless of whether the FileName property was set before calling the method, the FileName property contains the fully qualified path and filename of the selected file.

If the `cdlOFNAllowMultiselect` flag is used in the Flags property, a call to the ShowOpen or ShowSave method will open a 16-bit file dialog, the user can select multiple filenames, and when the method returns, multiple filenames will be separated by a space. The first space-delimited item stored to the FileName property, though, will be the directory in which the selected files are located, followed by each filename.

If the `cdlOFNExplorer` flag is used along with `cdlOFNAllowMultiselect`, the standard 32-bit file dialog is opened by the calls to the ShowOpen and ShowSave methods. When the method returns, individual items stored to the FileName property are delimited by a null character (i.e., by `Chr(0)`). First is the folder common to all selected files, followed by the names of selected files themselves.

FileName

DT RW

Applies to: MM

Type: String

Contains the name of the file to be affected by the next command. Generally, this is the name of a file to be opened or saved.

FileName

DT RW

Applies to: RichTextBox

Type: String

The name of a file you wish to open in the RichTextBox control.

FileNumber

RT RW

Applies to: OLE

Type: Integer (1–511)

The FileNumber property is supported only for backward compatibility with previous versions. Its functionality is no longer required.

FileTitle

RT RO

Applies to: CommonDialog

Type: String

After a CommonDialog control is displayed using the ShowOpen or ShowSave methods and the dialog is exited after the user selects a file, the FileTitle property contains the filename of the selected file without any path information. The filename along with the path is available through the FileName property.

Fill

DT RW

Applies to: Backdrop object of MSChart

Type: Fill object

Returns a reference to a Fill object, which defines how to fill the chart's backdrop.

FillColor

RT RO

Applies to: Brush and Marker objects of MSChart

Type: VtColor object

Returns a reference to a VtColor object, which contains information about the color to use with the object.

FillColor

DT RW

Applies to: Form object; PictureBox and Shape controls

Type: Long integer

When the FillStyle property is not set to `vbFSTransparent`, the FillColor property controls the color with which a graphics method like Circle executed on a Form object or PictureBox control will be filled. In addition, in combination with the FillStyle property, the FillColor property controls the color with which the shape in a Shape control is filled. This property can be set to a value by using a function such as *QBColor* or *RGB,* or by using one of Visual Basic's color constants.

Properties D–F

FillStyle

DT RW

Applies to: Form object; PictureBox and Shape controls

Type: `FillStyleConstants` enumeration

Controls the manner in which a graphics method executed on a Form object or picture box is filled, as follows:

Constant	*Value*	*Description*
`vbFSSolid`	0	The object is filled with the solid FillColor.
`vbFSTransparent`	1	The object is not filled. This is the default value.
`vbHorizontalLine`	2	The object is filled with horizontal lines in the FillColor.
`vbVerticalLine`	3	The object is filled with vertical lines in the FillColor.
`vbUpwardDiagonal`	4	The object is filled with diagonal lines that start at the upper left and go toward the lower right in the FillColor.
`vbDownwardDiagonal`	5	The object is filled with diagonal lines that start at the lower left and go toward the upper right in the FillColor.
`vbCross`	6	The object is filled with both horizontal and vertical lines in the FillColor.
`vbDiagonalCross`	7	The object is filled with both types of diagonal lines in the FillColor.

Except in the case of `vbFSSolid`, the areas that are not filled with the FillColor are filled with the BackColor, except when the BackStyle is set to 0, which makes the background transparent to the underlying object or control.

FillStyle

DT RW

Applies to: MSFlexGrid, MSHFlexGrid

Type: `FillStyleSettings` enumeration

When set to the default value of 0–flexFillSingle, setting the formatting or contents of a range of cells affects only the current cell. When set to 1–flexFillRepeat, the action affects all selected cells.

Filter

DT RW

Applies to: CommonDialog

Type: String

A formatted string containing the types of files to display when a dialog is activated using the ShowOpen and ShowSave methods. The string should contain a description followed by a pipe character (|) followed by a file mask (i.e. **.txt*). Multiple file masks can be separated by a semicolon (;). Multiple filters can be placed in one string separated by pipe characters and appear in the File Type selector at the bottom of the dialog box. For example, a filter that allows the user to select web graphics files could be set as follows:

```
Me.cdlMain.Filter = "GIF Files (*.gif)|*.gif" & _
    "|JPEG Files (*.jpg)|*.jpg" & _
    "|All web graphics formats " & _
    "(*.gif;*.jpg)|*.gif;*.jpg"
```

Filter

RT RW

Applies to: Recordset object of ADO DC and Data controls

Type: String (or array of variant or `FilterGroupEnum` enumeration, ADO DC only)

Contains a criteria string (`WHERE <field> = <value>` or a similar statement) by which the recordset will be restricted beyond its source. With an ADO recordset, the Filter property can also contain an array of bookmarks to restrict the data, or one of the constants listed here:

Constant	*Value*	*Description*
`adFilterNone`	0	Resets the filter. All records are available.
`adFilterPendingRecords`	1	Only records that have been updated but not yet written are available.
`adFilterAffectedRecords`	2	Only records that were affected by the last update are available.

Constant	*Value*	*Description*
adFilterFetchedRecords	3	Only records last fetched are available.
adFilterConflictingRecords	5	Only records that failed the last batch action are available.

FilterIndex DT RW

Applies to: CommonDialog

Type: Integer

When multiple filters are present in the Filter property of a CommonDialog control, the FilterIndex sets the default filter. Once a ShowOpen or ShowSave method returns, the FilterIndex property contains the last filter selected from the dialog.

Properties D–F

FirstRow RT RW

Applies to: Split object of DataGrid; DataGrid control

Type: Bookmark Object

The FirstRow property contains a bookmark for the top row currently visible in a DataGrid control or Split object. Setting FirstRow to a valid bookmark scrolls the data grid or split to that row.

FirstSibling, LastSibling, Next, Previous RT RO

Applies to: Node object of TreeView

Type: Node object

In a TreeView control, each Node object can contain one or more child Node objects. The FirstSibling property returns a reference to the first Node object with the same parent Node object. The Next, Previous, and LastSibling properties can then be used to step through Node objects at the same level.

FixedAlignment RT RW

Applies to: MSFlexGrid

See: CellAlignment

FixedBackground DT RW

Applies to: Band object of CoolBar

Type: Boolean

When set to the default value of `True`, the picture referenced by the CoolBar control's Picture property is tiled across the entire CoolBar control. When set to `False`, the picture is tiled across each band individually.

FixedCols DT RW

Applies to: MSFlexGrid, MSHFlexGrid

See: Cols

FixedOrder DT RW

Applies to: CoolBar

Type: Boolean

When set to the default value of `False`, Band objects in the CoolBar control can be arranged by the user. When set to `True`, they cannot be arranged.

FixedRows DT RW

Applies to: MSFlexGrid, MSHFlexGrid

See: *Cols*

Flag RT RW

Applies to: StatLine object of MSChart

Type: `VtChStats` enumeration

Defines the type of statistical lines that should be displayed on the chart. Possible values include 1–VtChStatsMinimum to display a line for the minimum value, 2–VtChStatsMaximum to display a line for the maximum, 4–VtChStatsMean to display a line for the mean value, 8–VtChStatsStddev to display a line for the standard deviation, and 16–VtChStatsRegression to display a trend line. Values can be added for multiple statistical lines.

Flags DT RW

Applies to: CommonDialog

Type: Long

Contains one or more values added or logically `Or`ed together that control various aspects of the dialog boxes displayed by the CommonDialog control. The values are explained in the following tables.

For Use with the ShowColor Method

Constant	Value	Description
cdlCCRGBInit	1	Uses the Color property as the default color.
cdlCCFullOpen	2	Opens the Custom Colors section when displaying the Color dialog box.
cdlCCIPreventFull-Open	4	Disables the Define Custom Colors button.
cdlCCIHelpButton	8	Displays a Help button in the Color dialog box.

For Use with the ShowFont Method

Constant	Value	Description
cdlCFScreenFonts	1	Displays only screen fonts.
cdlCFPrinterFonts	2	Displays only printer fonts.
cdlCFBoth	3	Displays both screen and printer fonts.
cdlCFHelpButton	4	Displays a Help button.
cdlCFEffects	256	Displays options for strikethrough, underline, and colored font effects.
cdlCFApply	512	Supposedly enables an Apply button on the dialog (according to the Visual Basic documentation); however, this flag actually has no effect.
cdlCFANSIOnly	1,024	Displays fonts that have only ANSI characters. No symbol fonts will be displayed.
cdlCFNoVectorFonts	2,048	Displays only vector fonts.
cdlCFNoSimulations	4,096	Hides font simulations which would allow normal device fonts to simulate italic, bold, underlined, or struck-out text.
cdlCFLimitSize	8,192	Allows sizes only between the Min and Max properties in the Font dialog box's Font Size selector.
cdlCFFixedPitch-Only	16,384	Displays only fixed-width fonts (such as Courier).
cdlCFWYSIWYG	32,768	Shows fonts that are both screen and printer fonts only.
cdlCFForceFont-Exist	65,536	Generates an error if the font selected from the Font dialog box does not exist.
cdlCFScalableOnly	131,072	Displays only scalable fonts.
cdlCFTTOnly	262,144	Displays only True Type fonts.
cdlCFNoFaceSel	524,288	Prevents the display of a selected font when the Font dialog opens.

Constant	Value	Description
cdlCFNoStyleSel	1,048,576	Prevents the display of a selected style when the Font dialog opens.
cdlCFNoSizeSel	2,097,152	Prevents the display of a selected font size when the Font dialog opens.

For Use with the ShowOpen and ShowSave Methods

Constant	Value	Description
cdlOFNReadOnly	1	Displays the Open dialog box with the read-only checkbox checked. Once the dialog box is exited, this flag can be re-checked to see the status of the read-only checkbox.
cdlOFNOverwrite-Prompt	2	Displays a message in the Save As dialog box if the file chosen already exists.
cdlOFNHideReadOnly	4	Prevents the Open dialog box from displaying the read-only checkbox.
cdlOFNNoChangeDir	8	Supposedly prevents the dialog's current directory from changing to the directory to which the user has navigated; however, it has no effect.
cdlOFNHelpButton	16	Displays a Help button.
cdlOFNNoValidate	256	Allows invalid characters in the filename.
cdlOFNAllowMulti-select	512	Allows the user to select more than one file. Also, sets the cdlOFNLongNames flag, though the latter has no effect. See the FileName property for more information.
cdlOFNExtension-Different	1,024	Check this flag after the dialog box is closed. If set, the extension chosen by the user is different from the default extension.
cdlOFNPathMust-Exist	2,048	Displays a message if the path chosen by the user does not exist.
cdlOFNFileMust-Exist	4,096	Displays a message if the file chosen by the user does not exist.
cdlOFNCreatePrompt	8,192	Creates the file if the user chooses a file that doesn't exist; also sets the cdlOFNPathMustExist and cdlOFNFileMustExist flags.
cdlOFNShareAware	16,384	Ignores sharing violation errors.
cdlOFNNoReadOnly-Return	32,768	Prevents the user from choosing a read-only file.
cdlOFNNoLongNames	262,144	Supposedly allows the use of long filenames; however, this flag appears to have no effect.

Constant	Value	Description
cdlOFNExplorer	524,288	Forces the use of the 32-bit rather than the default 16-bit Open/Save dialog; useful only when used with cdlOFNAllowMultiselect.
cdlOFNNoDereferenceLinks	1,048,576	Returns shortcuts as the shortcut filename (*.lnk). Without this flag set, selecting a shortcut returns the file to which the shortcut points.
cdlOFNLongNames	2,097,152	For use with cdlOFNAllowMultiselect; however, it has no effect.

For Use with the ShowPrint Method

Constant	Value	Description
cdlPDAllPages	0	Selects All (to print all pages). Once the dialog box is exited, this flag can be rechecked to see the status of the All option.
cdlPDSelection	1	Disables the Selection option.
cdlPDPageNums	2	Selects the Page option (to print a range). Once the dialog box is exited, this flag can be rechecked to see the status of the Page option.
cdlPDNoSelection	4	Disables the Selection option.
cdlPDNoPageNums	8	Disables the Page option.
cdlPDCollate	16	Checks the Collate option. Once the dialog box is exited, this flag can be rechecked to see the status of the Collate option.
cdlPDPrintToFile	32	Displays and checks the Print dialog box's "Print to File"checkbox. When the dialog box is exited, this flag can be rechecked to see the status of the "Print to File" checkbox option.
cdlPDPrintSetup	64	Displays the Print Setup dialog box instead of the Print dialog box.
cdlPDNoWarning	128	Does not display a warning message if there is not a default Windows printer.
cdlPDReturnDC	256	Sets the hDC property of the CommonDialog control to the device context of the selected printer.
cdlPDReturnIC	512	Sets the hDC property of the CommonDialog control to the information context of the selected printer.

Constant	Value	Description
cdlPDReturnDefault	1,024	Returns the default printer name without showing the dialog box. However, the call to the ShowPrint method does not behave reliably when this flag is set.
cdlPDHelpButton	2,048	Displays a Help button in the dialog box.
cdlPDUseDevMode-Copies	262,144	Displays the Copies text box if the selected printer supports copies.
cdlPDDisablePrint-ToFile	524,288	Disables the "Print to File" option.
cdlPDHidePrintTo-File	1,048,576	Displays the Print dialog box without the "Print to File" option.

FlatScrollBar DT RW

Applies to: ListView

Type: Boolean

When set to `True`, any scrollbar displayed on the ListView control appears flat. When set to the default value of `False`, scrollbars appear normal.

Although this is the way that the FlatScrollBar property is supposed to work, it currently has no effect.

FocusRect DT RW

Applies to: MSFlexGrid, MSHFlexGrid

Type: `FocusRectSettings` enumeration

Controls the appearance of the focus rectangle around the current cell. Possible values are 0–flexFocusNone for no focus rectangle, 1–flexFocusLight for a light focus rectangle, or 2–flexFocusHeavy for a heavy focus rectangle.

Font DT RW

Applies to: All controls with a text caption

Type: Font object

Contains all information about the font used to display a control's caption or text. After the CommonDialog control's Font dialog has been activated using the ShowFont method, its Font property can be used to set the Font property of other controls.

FontBand, FontFixed, FontHeader DT RW

Applies to: MSHFlexGrid

Type: Font object

Sets the font to use in bands (FontBand), fixed rows and columns (FontFixed), and headers (FontHeader) in the MSHFlexGrid control.

FontBold, FontItalic, FontStrikeThrough, FontUnderline DT RW

Applies to: All controls with a text caption except Windows Common controls

Type: Boolean

When set to the default value of `False`, the font of the Caption or Text property appears normal. When set to `True`, the desired effect (bold, italics, strikethrough, underlining) is shown.

FontFixed, FontHeader DT RW

Applies to: MSHFlexGrid

See: FontBand

FontName DT RW

Applies to: All controls with a text caption except Windows Common controls

Type: String

Contains the name of the current font used for the Caption or Text property.

FontSize DT RW

Applies to: All controls with a text caption except Windows Common controls

Type: Integer (1–2,160)

Defines the size in points of the current font used for the Caption or Text property.

FontTransparent DT RW

Applies to: Form object; PictureBox control

Type: Boolean

When set to the default value of `True`, text drawn on the object or control appears to have a transparent background; that is, any colors remain visible underneath the

Properties D–F

text when text is drawn. When set to `False`, the background of the text is defined by the BackColor property. Of course, if the color of the image or control consists only of the background color, the setting of the FontTransparent property will have no visual effect on the background color used with text.

FontWidth [RT] [RW]

Applies to: MSFlexGrid, MSHFlexGrid

Type: Single

Controls the width of the font (in points) used throughout the control, except when overridden.

FontWidthBand, FontWidthFixed, FontWidthHeader [RT] [RW]

Applies to: MSHFlexGrid

Type: Single

Defines the width of the font (in points) used in bands (FontWidthBand), fixed rows and columns (FontWidthFixed), and headers (FontWidthHeader).

Footnote [RT] [RO]

Applies to: MSChart

Type: Footnote object

Returns a reference to a Footnote object, which contains information about the footnote on the chart.

FootnoteText, LegendText, TitleText [DT] [RW]

Applies to: MSChart

Type: String

Contains the text to show in the footnote portion (FootnoteText), legend (LegendText), and title (TitleText) of the chart.

ForeColor [DT] [RW]

Applies to: All controls with a visual interface

See: BackColor

ForeColorBand, ForeColorFixed, ForeColorHeader, ForeColorSel [DT] [RW]

Applies to: MSFlexGrid, MSHFlexGrid

See: BackColorBand

Format [DT] [RW]

Applies to: DTPicker

Type: `FormatConstants` enumeration

Defines the formatting method used by the DTPicker control. Possible values are 0–dtpLongDate to use the Windows default long date format, 1–dtpShortDate to use the Windows default short date format, 2–dtpTime to use the Windows default time format, or 3–dtpCustom to use custom formatting (defined by the CustomFormat property).

Format [RT] [RW]

Applies to: Label object of MSChart

Type: String

Contains a format string similar to those used with VBA's *Format* function to format labels on the chart axis.

Format [DT] [RW]

Applies to: MaskEdBox

Type: String

When populated with a format string similar to those used in VBA's *Format* function, used both to display the contents of the control and to return its contents by an assignment from the FormattedText Property.

Format [RT] [RW]

Applies to: OLE

Type: String

Defines the format used when sending data to or getting data from an OLE server application.

FormatLength RT RO

Applies to: Label object of MSChart

Type: Integer

Returns the length of the format string contained by the Format property.

FormatString RT RW

Applies to: MSFlexGrid, MSHFlexGrid

Type: String

Can be set to a preformatted string in order to completely format the control. The string can contain information about the width, alignment, and header text of each column and the height and header text of each row. The FormatString contains two sections separated by a semicolon (;). The first section contains information about columns; the second, about rows. The column section contains the header text of each column, preceded by a character to denote alignment, each separated by a pipe character (|). The character used for alignment is a left angle bracket (<) for left alignment, a carat (^) for center alignment, or a right angle bracket (>) for right alignment. The row section contains the header text of each row separated by a pipe character (|).

FormattedText DT RW

Applies to: MaskEdBox

Type: String

Returns the contents of the MaskEdBox control formatted using the Format property.

Frame RT RO

Applies to: Backdrop object of MSChart

Type: Frame object

Returns a reference to a Frame object, which determines how to frame a chart element.

FrameColor RT RO

Applies to: Frame object of MSChart

Type: VtColor object

Returns a reference to a VtColor object, which contains information about the color of the frame.

Frames

DT RW

Applies to: MM

Type: Long integer

Defines the number of frames used in step operations. For example, setting the Frames property to 5 causes the Step command to advance five frames and the Back command to "rewind" five frames.

From, To

RT RW

Applies to: MM

Type: Long integer

Set to the location to start a play or record operation from (`From`) and to (`To`). These locations should be specified using units defined by the current TimeFormat value. See the MM (Multimedia MCI) Control entry in Chapter 5 for more information.

FromPage, ToPage

DT RW

Applies to: CommonDialog

Type: Integer

When set prior to activating the CommonDialog with the ShowPrint method, the FromPage and ToPage properties set the default values for the appropriate text boxes in the Print dialog box. After the dialog box is closed, the properties contain the value after user editing.

FullPath

RT RO

Applies to: Node object of TreeView

Type: String

The FullPath property of a Node object returns the Text properties of each of its ancestors starting with the root node, separated by the character specified in the TreeView control's PathSeparator property.

FullRowSelect

DT RW

Applies to: ListView, TreeView

Type: Boolean

When set to `True`, full rows are selected when you access the control. When set to the default value of `False`, the entire row is not selected. For the ListView control, the View property must be set to `lvwReport` to select rows.

GetNumTicks RT RO

Applies to: Slider

Type: Long integer

Indicates the number of tick marks visible on the Slider control.

Ghosted RT RW

Applies to: ListItem object of ListView

Type: Boolean

When set to `True`, the ListItem appears dimmed (or disabled) and cannot be selected. When set to the default value of `False`, the ListItem object acts as normal. Ghosted, in other words, is the ListItem object's equivalent of the Enabled property.

Green RT RW

Applies to: VtColor object of MSChart

See: Blue

GridColor, GridColorBand, GridColorFixed, GridColorHeader, GridColorIndent, GridColorUnpopulated DT RW

Applies to: MSFlexGrid, MSHFlexGrid

Type: Long integer

These properties control the color of text on the applicable object. They can be set by using a function such as *QBColor* or *RGB,* or by using one of Visual Basic's Color Constants.

GridLines DT RW

Applies to: ListView

Type: Boolean

When set to `True`, gridlines appear between columns and rows when the View property is set to `lvwReport`. When set to the default value of `False`, gridlines do not appear.

GridLines, GridLinesBand, GridLinesFixed, GridLinesHeader, GridLinesIndent, GridLinesUnpopulated [DT] [RW]

Applies to: MSFlexGrid, MSHFlexGrid

Type: `GridLineSettings` enumeration

Controls the type of gridlines present on the associated types of cells in the control. Possible values are 0–flexGridNone for no gridlines, 1–flexGridFlat for normal flat gridlines, 2–flexGridInset for inset gridlines, or 3–flexGridRaised for raised gridlines.

GridLineWidth, GridLineWidthBand, GridLineWidthFixed, GridLineWidthHeader, GridLineWidthIndent, GridLineWidthUnpopulated [DT] [RW]

Applies to: MSFlexGrid, MSHFlexGrid

Type: Integer

Contains the width (in pixels) of any gridlines displayed on the associated types of cells in the control.

Properties G–L

GuideLinePen [RT] [RO]

Applies to: Series object of MSChart

Type: Pen object

Returns a reference to a Pen object, which defines how to draw guidelines on the chart.

HasDC

Applies to: Form object; PictureBox control

Type: Boolean

When set to the default value of `True`, the control allocates and maintains an hDC. When set to `False`, the hDC is not maintained.

hDC [RT] [RO]

Applies to: CommonDialog

Type: Handle

After the ShowPrint method of a CommonDialog with the flags `cdlPDReturnDC` or `cdlPDReturnIC` set returns, the hDC property contains the handle to the device context of the selected printer for the cdlPDReturnDC flag or the handle to the information context of the selected printer for the cdlPDReturnIC flag.

hDC RT RO

Applies to: Form object; PictureBox control

Type: Handle

Returns a handle to the device context of the object or control. This can then be used with methods or API calls that require an hDC. hDCs can change unpredictably, so it is not recommended that the hDC be stored in a variable at any time. Instead, it should be used directly, as in this example:

```
'Draws the first ListImage object directly on the Form.
Me.imlMain.ListImages(1).Draw Me.hDC
```

HeadFont DT RW

Applies to: DataGrid

Type: Font object

Determines the Font object used for ColumnHeader objects. See the Font property for more information.

HeadLines DT RW

Applies to: DataGrid

Type: Single (0–10)

Defines the number of lines to display in the ColumnHeader object. When set to 0, column headers are not displayed at all.

Height, Left, Top, Width DT RW

Applies to: Form, MDIForm, Column, and Tab objects; all controls with a visual interface

Type: Long

These four properties set the size and location of the object or control. In general, at runtime it is faster to use the Move method of the object or control to change its location and/or size. In the case of a form or MDI form, the Top and Left properties are used only if the StartUpPosition is set to vbStartUpManual.

HelpCommand

DT RW

Applies to: CommonDialog

Type: Enumeration

Defines the interaction between the application and the help file as shown in the following table:

HelpConstants	*Value*	*Description*
`cdlHelpContext`	1	Displays help for the topic set in the HelpContext property.
`cdlHelpQuit`	2	Closes the active help window.
`cdlHelpContents`	3	Displays the contents of the help file. Not recommended with newer help files.
`cdlHelpIndex`	3	Displays the index of the help file. Not recommended with newer help files.
`cdlHelpHelpOnHelp`	4	Help for the help program is run.
`cdlHelpSetContents`	5	Sets a topic as the help contents topic.
`cdlHelpSetIndex`	5	Sets an index as the current index.
`cdlHelpContextPopup`	8	Displays a context help topic.
`cdlHelpForceFile`	9	Displays a single font version of the help file.
`cdlHelpKey`	257	Displays help for the keyword in the HelpKey property.
`cdlHelpCommandHelp`	258	Displays help for the command in the HelpKey property.
`cdlHelpPartialKey`	261	Starts the help search dialog.

HelpContext

DT RW

Applies to: CommonDialog

Type: Long integer

When the HelpCommand property's `cdlHelpContext` flag is set, the HelpContext contains the desired help context to display.

HelpContextID

DT RW

Applies to: Form and MDIForm oibjects, all controls with a visual interface except Image and Label

Type: Long integer

When set to a number other than 0, the HelpContextID of a control or object sets the context in the help file that will be accessed if the user presses the F1 key.

HelpFile DT RW

Applies to: CommonDialog

Type: String

The HelpFile property contains the name of the help file that will be used when the CommonDialog control's ShowHelp method is activated.

Applies to: Toolbar

Type: String

When populated, the HelpFile property displays a Help button on the Customize Toolbar dialog box. The HelpFile property contains the name of the help file that will be used if the user presses that Help button.

HelpKey DT RW

Applies to: CommonDialog

Type: String

When the HelpCommand property's `cdlHelpKey` flag is set, the HelpKey contains the desired keyword that help will display.

Hidden RT RW

Applies to: SeriesPosition object of MSChart

See: *Excluded*

Hide RT RW

Applies to: AxisScale object of MSChart

Type: Boolean

When set to `True`, all axis elements are hidden in the chart. When set to the default value of `False`, the axis elements are not hidden.

HideColumnHeaders

Applies to: ListView

Type: Boolean

When the ListView control's View property is set to `lvwReport`, the HideColumn-Headers property controls whether the column headers are displayed. When set to `True`, these headers are not displayed. When set to the default value of `False`, the headers display as normal.

HideSelection

DT RW

Applies to: ListView, RichTextBox, TextBox, TreeView

Type: Boolean

When set to the default value of `True`, the selected text or object(s) in the control do not appear highlighted when the control does not have the focus. When set to `False`, the selected text or object(s) remain highlighted.

HighLight

DT RW

Applies to: MSFlexGrid, MSHFlexGrid

Type: `HighLightSettings` enumeration

Determines when the control's selected cells are highlighted. Possible values are 0–flexHighLightNever to never highlight selected cells, 1–flexHighLightAlways to always highlight selected cells, or 2–flexHighLightWithFocus to only highlight selected cells when the control has the focus.

Properties G–L

Highlighted

RT RW

Applies to: Tab object of TabStrip

Type: Boolean

When set to `True`, the Tab object is highlighted. When set to the default value of `False`, the Tab object is not highlighted.

hImageList

RT RO

Applies to: ImageList

Design Time: Not available

Runtime: Read-only

Type: Handle

Returns a handle to the ImageList control. This can then be used with methods or API calls that require a handle to an ImageList. Handles can change unpredictably, so it is not recommended that the value be stored in a variable at any time.

hInternet

Applies to: Inet control

Design Time: Not available

Runtime: Not available

Type: Long integer

This property is currently not used with Visual Basic.

HorzAlignment, VertAlignment DT RW

Applies to: TextLayout object of MSChart

Type: `VtHorizontalAlignment` enumeration (HorzAlignment), `VtVerticalAlignment` enumeration (VertAlignment)

These properties control the horizontal (HorzAlignment) and vertical (VertAlignment) alignment of the text associated with the TextLayout object. Possible values for HorzAlignment are 0–VtHorizontalAlignmentLeft for left alignment, 1–VtHorizontalAlignmentRight for right alignment, 2–VtHorizontalAlignmentCenter for centered text, 3–VtHorizontalAlignmentFill to have the text fill the area, or 4–VtHorizontalAlignmentFlush for flush left and right (full) justification. Possible values for VertAlignment are 0–VtVerticalAlignmentTop for top alignment, 1–VtVerticalAlignmentBottom for bottom alignment, or 2–VtVerticalAlignmentCenter for center (vertical) alignment.

HostName DT RW

Applies to: OLE

Type: String

When some OLE objects are being edited by their native application, they will display the contents of the HostName property in their titlebar.

HotImageList DT RW

Applies to: Toolbar

See: *DisabledImageList*

HotTracking DT RW

Applies to: ListView, TabStrip, TreeView

Type: Boolean

When set to `True`, icons associated with child objects switch to "hot" icons when the mouse pauses over the object. When set to the default value of `False`, this does not occur.

Hour [RT] [RW]

Applies to: DTPicker, MonthView

See: Day

HoverSelection [DT] [RW]

Applies to: ListView

Type: Boolean

When set to `True`, ListItem objects are selected when the mouse pauses briefly over the object. When set to the default value of `False`, objects are not selected in this way.

hWnd [RT] [RO]

Applies to: Form and MDIForm objects, all controls with a visual interface except Image, Label, and OLE

Type: Handle

Returns the window handle of an object or control. This can then be used with methods or API calls that require a window handle. Handles can change unpredictably, so it is not recommended that the value be stored in a variable at any time.

hWndDisplay, UsesWindows [RT] [RW]

Applies to: MM

Type: Long integer (hWndDisplay), Boolean (UsesWindows)

Can contain a handle for the window to use for displaying multimedia objects (hWndDisplay) and indicate whether to then display the device on that window (UsesWindows).

hWndEditor [RT] [RO]

Applies to: DataGrid

Design Time: Not available

Runtime: Read-only

Type: Handle

While the contents of a cell in a DataGrid control are being edited, the hWndEditor property returns that cell's window handle. This can then be used with methods or API calls that require a window handle. Handles can change unpredictably, so it is not recommended that the value be stored in a variable at any time.

VB6

Icon

DT RW

Applies to: Form and MDIForm objects

Type: Icon object

The Icon property contains the Icon object to be displayed as the form's control menu button and when the object is minimized. An icon can be assigned at design time, in which case it is included with the compiled application. It can also be assigned at runtime in one of several ways:

- By using the *LoadPicture* function. For example:

  ```
  Form1.Icon = LoadPicture("C:\icons\myicon.ico")
  ```

  In this case, however, the icon (*.ico*) file has to be available to your application at runtime.

- By including a resource file containing one or more icons with your project. You can then use the *LoadResPicture* function to load the icon, as in the following code fragment:

  ```
  Private Const IDI_ICON1 = 101
  Form1.Icon = LoadResPicture(IDI_ICON1, vbResIcon)
  ```

  This method requires that you define the symbols (in this case, `IDI_ICON1`) by which the icons in the resource file are identified. Using this method, the icon is simply a resource within the compiled resource file, which in turn is included in the executable file.

- By storing the icon in an ImageList control included on the form. The icon can then be assigned to the form's Icon property by the following code:

  ```
  Set Form1.Icon = ImageList1.ListImages(1).Picture
  ```

  Images stored in an ImageList control are also included with compiled applications.

Icon

RT RW

Applies to: ColumnHeader object of ListView

Type: Long or string integer

Contains the index or key of the ListImage object in the ImageList control bound to the ColumnHeaderIcons property to display in the column header.

Icon, SmallIcon

DT RW

Applies to: ListItem object of ListView

Type: Long or string integer

The Icon and SmallIcon properties contain the index or key of the ListImage object in the bound ImageList control to be displayed when the ListView control's View property is set to `lvwIcon` or `lvwSmallIcon`, respectively

---

Icons

DT RW

Applies to: ListView

See: ColumnHeaderIcons

Image

DT RW

Applies to: Band object of CoolBar, Button object of Toolbar, ComboItem object of ImageCombo, Node object of TreeView, Tab object of TabStrip

Type: Long integer

Contains the index of the ListImage object in the ImageList control bound to the parent control to display on the object.

Applies to: Form Object, PictureBox RT RO

Type: Handle

Returns a handle to the graphics on an object or control. This can then be used with methods or API calls that require a handle to an image. Handles can change unpredictably, so it is not recommended that the value be stored in a variable at any time.

ImageHeight, ImageWidth

DT RW

Applies to: ImageList

Type: Long integer

All images in an ImageList are restricted in size to the dimensions contained in the ImageHeight and ImageWidth properties. If these are not set beforehand, they are automatically set to match the size of the first image added to the ImageList. Thereafter, as long as images continue to be stored in the ImageList control, they remain read-only.

ImageList

DT RW

Applies to: CoolBar, ImageCombo, TabStrip, Toolbar, TreeView

Type: String

Set to the name of the ImageList control to which the control is bound. Generally, the control then uses the Image property of child objects to select the index of a ListImage object to display.

For the Toolbar control's ImageList property, see the DisabledImageList, HotImage-List, ImageList entry.

Increment DT RW

Applies to: UpDown

Type: Long integer

Defines the amount by which to increase or decrease any values associated with the UpDown control.

Indentation DT RW

Applies to: TreeView

Type: Long integer

Sets the amount of space, in twips, to separate each level in a TreeView control.

Indentation DT RW

Applies to: ComboItem object of ImageCombo; ImageCombo control

Type: Long integer

Sets the amount of space, in multiples of 10 twips, to indent all ComboItems or an individual ComboItem.

Index DT RO

Applies to: All objects and controls except Form and MDIForm objects

Type: Integer

In a control array, the Index property denotes which element of the control array is being referred to. With objects, the Index property denotes which object in the object's collection is being referred to.

InitDir DT RW

Applies to: CommonDialog

Type: String

When a CommonDialog control is activated using the ShowOpen or ShowSave methods, the InitDir property can be set to the desired initial directory to show in the dialog box.

IntegralHeight

DT RO

Applies to: ComboBox, DataCombo, DataList, DBCombo, DBList, ListBox

Type: Boolean

When set to the default value of **`True`**, the IntegralHeight property causes the control to resize down to the last complete item in the list when its height is changed. When set to **`False`**, the control will resize to any desired height.

Intensity

RT RW

Applies to: LightSource object of MSChart

Type: Single

Controls the intensity of the light coming from the LightSource object in values ranging from 0 (no light) to 1 (full intensity).

Intersection

RT RO

Applies to: Axis object of MSChart

Type: Intersection object

Returns a reference to an Intersection object, which contains information about the intersection between axes on the chart.

Interval

DT RW

Applies to: Timer

Type: Long integer (0–65,535)

The Interval property specifies the interval, in milliseconds, at which the Timer control will fire its Timer event. To set the Timer event to fire every second, you would set the Interval property to 1,000.

Item

Applies to: All collections

Type: Object

The Item property of a collection returns the object with the specified index or key in that collection. For example, to return the first ListItem object from a ListView control, the following code could be used:

```
Dim lsiVar as ListItem
Set lsiVar = Me.lsvMain.ListItems.Item(1)
```

Item is the default member of a collection. Therefore, the following code fragment is identical to the previous line:

```
Set lsiVar = Me.lsvMain.ListItems(1)
```

ItemData

DT RW

Applies to: ComboBox, ListBox

Type: Array of long integers

For each item in the List property array of a ListBox or ComboBox control, there is an additional, hidden value associated with the item. This value is contained in the ItemData property array. Generally, this array is used to associate the descriptive, visible items in the list with additional data, such as a database key. See the ListBox Control entry in Chapter 5 for more information.

Join

RT RW

Applies to: Pen object of MSChart

Type: `VtPenJoin` enumeration

Controls the appearance of the area where two lines meet. Possible values include 0–VtPenJoinMiter, where the two lines continue until all ends meet; 1–VtPenJoinRound, where a filled arc is centered at the point where two lines meet with a radius to the edge of the line; or 2–VtPenJoinBevel, where both lines end and straight lines are drawn from the edges of one line to the edges of the other. See the entry for the MSChart Control in Chapter 5 for more information.

Key

RT RW

Applies to: All objects except Form and MDIForm objects

Type: String

The Key property of an object contains a unique identifier for that object within the object's collection. It can be set directly or can be supplied as a parameter when using the collection's Add method.

KeyPreview

DT RW

Applies to: Form object

Design Time: Read/write

Runtime: Read/write

Type: Boolean

When set to `True`, the KeyPreview property causes the Form object to receive KeyDown and KeyPress events before the controls on the Form object receive them. When set to `False`, the Form object does not receive these events.

LabelEdit

DT RW

Applies to: ListView, TreeView

Type: `ListLabelEditConstants` enumeration

Controls how the user can edit labels of list items and nodes, as shown in the following tables.

For Use with the ListView Control

Constant	*Value*	*Description*
`lvwAutomatic`	0	When the user clicks on the label, the label goes into Edit mode. This is the default value.
`lvwManual`	1	The label goes into Edit mode only when the Start-LabelEdit method is activated.

For Use with the TreeView Control

LabelEdit-Constants	*Value*	*Description*
`tvwAutomatic`	0	When the user clicks on the label, the label goes into Edit mode. This is the default value.
`tvwManual`	1	The label goes into Edit mode only when the Start-LabelEdit method is activated.

LabelLevelCount

RT RW

Applies to: Axis object of MSChart

Type: Integer

Contains the number of levels of labels for the axis.

Labels

RT RO

Applies to: Axis object of MSChart

Type: Collection

Returns a reference to a collection of Label objects, each of which contains information about an axis label.

Properties G–L

LabelsInsidePlot

RT RW

Applies to: Intersection object of MSChart

Type: Boolean

When set to `False`, axis labels are moved inside the plot area along with the intersection. When set to the default value of `True`, the axis labels are not moved.

LabelTick

RT RW

Applies to: CategoryScale object of MSChart

Type: Boolean

When set to the default value of `False`, labels appear between tick marks on the category axis. When set to `True`, the labels appear on the tick marks.

LabelWrap

DT RW

Applies to: ListView

Type: Boolean

When set to the default value of `True`, labels that are too long to display on one line are wrapped to additional lines. When set to `False`, the label appears on one line.

LargeChange, SmallChange

DT RW

Applies to: FlatScrollBar, HScrollBar, Slider, VScrollBar

Type: Long integer

The LargeChange property sets the amount that the control's Value property increases or decreases when the user clicks between the value indicator and the end of the control. The SmallChange property sets the amount that the control's Value property increases or decreases when the user clicks on the arrow box for a ScrollBar control, or presses the Left or Right Arrow keys while a Slider control has the focus.

LastModified

RT RO

Applies to: Recordset object of Data control

Type: Variant

Contains a bookmark pointing to the record that was changed by the last action performed on the recordset.

LastSibling

RT RO

Applies to: Node object of TreeView

See: FirstSibling

LastUpdated

RT RO

Applies to: Recordset object of Data control

See: DateCreated

LBound, UBound

RT RO

Applies to: Menu control array, all control arrays

Type: Integer

Returns the lowest (LBound) and highest (UBound) values of the Index property in a control array or menu control array.

Left

DT RW

Applies to: Form, MDIForm, Column, and Tab objects; all controls with a visual interface

See: Height

LeftCol, TopRow

RT RW

Applies to: Split object of DataGrid (LeftCol only); DataGrid (LeftCol only), MSFlexGrid and MSHFlexGrid controls

Type: Integer

Contains the index of the leftmost visible column (LeftCol) or topmost visible row (TopRow) in the control. Changing the value of the property scrolls the control to the new area.

Legend

RT RO

Applies to: MSChart

Type: Legend object

Returns a reference to a Legend object, which contains information about the chart's legend.

LegendText [DT] [RW]

Applies to: MSChart

See: *FootnoteText*

Length [RT] [RO]

Applies to: MM

Type: Long integer

Returns the length of the multimedia device currently opened. The value is returned using the current TimeFormat value.

Length [RT] [RO]

Applies to: Tick object of MSChart

Type: Integer

Contains the distance, in points, between tick marks on an axis.

Light [RT] [RO]

Applies to: Plot object of MSChart

Type: Light object

Returns a reference to a Light object, which contains information about the light that illuminates the chart.

LightSources [RT] [RO]

Applies to: Light object of MSChart

Type: Collection

Returns a reference to a collection of LightSource objects, each of which contains information about an individual light source that illuminates the chart.

Limit [RT] [RW]

Applies to: Pen object of MSChart

Type: Single

Controls how long, in points, an angle with the Join property set to `VtPenJoinMiter` can extend from the point of meeting.

LineStyle

DT RW

Applies to: DataPointLabel object of MSChart

Type: `VtChLabelLineStyle` enumeration

Controls the style of the line between a value and data point label on the chart. Possible values are 0–VtChLabelLineStyleNone for no line, 1–VtChLabelLineStyleStraight for a straight line, or 2–VtChLabelLineStyleBent for a bent line.

LineStyle

DT RW

Applies to: TreeView

Type: `TreeLineStyleConstants` enumeration

When the Style property of a TreeView control is set to 4 (`tvwTreelinesText`), 5 (`tvwTreelinesPictureText`), 6 (`tvwTreelinesPlusMinusText`), or 7 (`tvwTreelinesPlusMinusPictureText`), the LineStyle property controls the behavior of the lines on the control as follows:

Constant	*Value*	*Description*
`tvwTreeLines`	0	Lines are displayed between parent and sibling Node objects. This is the default value.
`tvwRootLines`	1	Lines are displayed between parent and sibling Node objects as well as from the parent Node object to the root.

Properties G–L

LinkItem

DT RW

Applies to: Label, PictureBox, TextBox

Type: String

Contains the message to be passed through a DDE conversation.

LinkMode

DT RW

Applies to: Form object

Type: `LinkModeConstants` enumeration

The LinkMode property controls the type of connection established in a DDE conversation as follows:

Constant	Value	Description
`vbLinkNone`	0	The Form object does not support any DDE conversations. This is the default value.
`vbLinkSource`	1	Allows other applications to initiate a DDE conversation with the Form object. If a DDE conversation is taking place and the contents of a Label control, PictureBox control, or TextBox control on the Form object are changed, the application on the other end of the DDE conversation is notified.

Applies to: MDIForm object; Label, PictureBox, and TextBox controls

Type: `LinkModeConstants` enumeration

The LinkMode property controls the type of connection established in a DDE conversation as follows:

Constant	Value	Description
`vbLinkNone`	0	The control or object does not support any DDE conversations. This is the default value.
`vbLinkAutomatic`	1	While a DDE conversation takes place with the control or object, changes are sent to the application on the other end of the DDE conversation.
`vbLinkManual`	2	While a DDE conversation takes place with the control or object, changes to the control or object can be sent to the application on the other end of the DDE conversation when the LinkRequest method is used.
`vbLinkNotify`	3	While a DDE conversation takes place with the control or object, the application on the other end of the DDE conversation is notified of changes to the control or object. The LinkRequest method can then be used to send the data.

LinkTimeout

DT RW

Applies to: Label, PictureBox, TextBox

Type: Long integer (0–65,536)

When a request is sent over a DDE conversation, the LinkTimeout property controls how long to wait for an answer before generating an error. The value of the LinkTimeout property specifies the number of tenths of a second to wait.

LinkTopic

DT RW

Applies to: Form and MDIForm objects; Label, PictureBox, and TextBox controls

Type: String

Contains the application topic to be used for a DDE conversation. In the case of a Form object, the LinkTopic property represents the topic to which the Form object will respond.

List

DT RW

Applies to: ComboBox, ListBox

Type: Array of strings

The List property array represents the contents of the control. Elements are added to the array through the AddItem method (and they can also be added manually at design time). The contents of the current selected element of the control can be represented with the following syntax:

```
lstMain.List(lstMain.ListIndex)
```

Properties G–L

ListCount

RT RO

Applies to: ComboBox, ListBox

Type: Long integer

Returns the total number of elements in the control's List property array.

ListField

DT RW

Applies to: DataCombo, DataList, DBCombo, DBList

Type: String

Contains the name of the field used to fill the control's list. It must be a field in the recordset contained in the Data control bound to the control's RowSource property.

ListImages

DT RW

Applies to: ImageList

Type: Collection

Returns a reference to the ListImages collection. The ListImages collection itself supports the following properties and methods:

Member	*Description*
Count	Returns the number of ListImage objects in the collection.
Item	Returns a reference to a ListImage object based on its index or its key. This is the collection's default property.
Add	Adds a new image to the collection.
Clear	Removes all images from the collection.
Remove	Removes a single image object from the collection based on its index or key.

ListIndex RT RW

Applies to: ComboBox, ListBox

Type: Long integer

Contains the index of the currently selected item in the control. If no item is selected, its value is -1.

ListItems RT RO

Applies to: ListView

Type: Collection

Returns a reference to the ListItems collection. The ListItems collection itself supports the following properties and methods:

Member	*Description*
Count	Returns the number of Column objects in the collection.
Item	Returns a reference to a Column object based on its index or its key. This is the collection's default property.
Add	Adds a new item to the ListItems collection.
Clear	Removes all items from the collection.
Remove	Removes a single ListItem object from the collection based on its index or key.

ListSubItems RT RO

Applies to: ListItem object of ListView

Type: Collection

Contains a reference to a collection of ListSubItem objects, each of which contains data for the columns in a ListView control with the View property set to `lvwReport`.

LocalHostName, LocalIP, RemoteHost, RemoteHostIP RT RO

Applies to: Winsock

Type: String

These properties return the local IP address (LocalIP) and machine name (LocalHostName), and the remote IP address (RemoteHostIP) and machine name (RemoteHost).

LocalPort, RemotePort DT RW

Applies to: Winsock

Type: Long integer

Contains the port to use on the local machine (LocalPort) or used on the remote machine (RemotePort) for a TCP/IP connection.

Location RT RO

Applies to: Legend object of MSChart, Title object of MSChart

Type: Location object

Returns a reference to a Location object, which contains information about the location of the parent object on the chart.

LocationRect RT RO

Applies to: Plot object of MSChart

Type: Rect object

Returns a reference to a Rect object, which contains information about the location of the plot area on the chart.

LocationType RT RW

Applies to: DataPointLabel object of MSChart, Location object of MSChart

Type: `VtChLocationType` enumeration

Controls the location of the parent object. Possible values are 0–VtChLocationTypeTopLeft for the upper-left corner, 1–VtChLocationTypeTop for the top, 2–VtChLocationTypeTopRight for the upper-right corner, 3–VtChLocationTypeLeft for the left side, 4–VtChLocationTypeRight for the right side, 5–VtChLocationTypeBottomLeft for the lower-left corner, 6–VtChLocationTypeBottom for the bottom, 7–VtChLocationTypeBottomRight for the lower-right corner, and 8–VtChLocationTypeCustom for a custom location defined by a Rect object contained by the parent object.

Locked

DT RW

Applies to: Column and Split objects; ComboBox, DBCombo, DBList, RichTextBox, and TextBox controls

Type: Boolean

When set to `True`, the control appears normally, except that its contents cannot be edited. When set to the default value of `False`, the control can be edited.

LockEdits

RT RW

Applies to: Recordset object of Data control

Type: Boolean

When set to the default value of `True`, pessimistic locking is in effect for the recordset object. When set to `False`, optimistic locking is in effect. In pessimistic locking, records are locked immediately when an edit begins. In optimistic locking, records are locked only when they need to be updated.

LockType

DT RW

Applies to: Recordset object of ADO DC; ADO DC control

Type: `LockTypeEnum` enumeration

Controls how records are locked in the Recordset object. Possible values are 1–adLockReadOnly for a read-only recordset, 2–adLockPessimistic for pessimistic locking, or 3–adLockOptimistic for optimistic locking.

LogBase

RT RW

Applies to: AxisScale object of MSChart

Type: Integer

Defines the logarithmic base to use for the axis when plotting values.

lpOleObject

RT RO

Applies to: OLE

Type: Address

Returns the address of the OLE object for use in API calls.

MajorDivision, MinorDivision

Applies to: ValueScale object of MSChart

Type: Integer

Contains the number of major divisions (MajorDivision) or minor divisions (MinorDivision) displayed on the axis.

MajorPen, MinorPen

DT RO

Applies to: AxisGrid object of MSChart

Type: Pen object

Returns a reference to a Pen object, which controls the pen used for the gridlines (MajorPen for major gridlines, MinorPen for minor gridlines).

Marker

RT RW

Applies to: DataPoint object of MSChart

Type: Marker object

Returns a reference to a Marker object, which controls the type of marker used for the data point.

MarqueeStyle

RT RW

Applies to: Split object of DataGrid; DataGrid control

Type: `MarqueeStyleConstants` enumeration

Controls the appearance of the currently selected cell as follows:

Constant	*Value*	*Description*
`dbgDottedCellBorder`	0	A dotted border appears around the current cell.
`dbgSolidCellBorder`	1	A solid, dark border appears around the current cell.
`dbgHighlightCell`	2	Colors in the current cell are reversed.
`dbgHighlightRow`	3	Colors in the row containing the current cell are reversed. This value is useful for highlighting a row but not for highlighting a cell within that row, since the current cell is indistinguishable from other cells in the row.

Constant	*Value*	*Description*
`dbgHighlightRowRaiseCell`	4	Colors in the row containing the current cell are reversed, and the current cell appears raised, with a 3-D effect.
`dbgNoMarquee`	5	There is nothing to distinguish the current cell from other cells.
`dbgFloatingEditor`	6	The text in the current cell is highlighted. This is the default value.

Mask

DT RW

Applies to: MaskEdBox

Type: String

Contains the character map used for entering data into the MaskEdBox control. The following characters can be used in the mask to obtain the listed effect:

Character	*Result*
#	Only digits (0–9) can be entered.
. (Period)	Decimal separator. Although a period is used to represent the symbol, the actual character used depends on the current international settings.
, (Comma)	Thousands separator. Although a comma is used to represent the symbol, the actual character used depends on the current international settings.
: (Colon)	Marks the time separator. Although a colon is used to represent the symbol, the actual character used depends on the current international settings.
/ (Slash)	Marks the date separator. Although a slash is used to represent the symbol, the actual character used depends on the current international settings.
\ (Backslash)	Indicates that the next character is to be treated as a literal, even if it is contained in this list.
& (Ampersand)	Allows any printable ANSI character to be entered.
> (Right angle bracket)	Uppercases subsequent characters.
< (Left angle bracket)	Lowercases subsequent characters.
A	Allows alphabetic characters (uppercase or lowercase) or digits (0–9) to be entered.
a	Allows, but does not require, alphabetic characters (uppercase or lowercase) or digits (0–9) to be entered.
9	Allows only, but does not require, digits (0–9) to be entered.
C	Produces same result as ampersand.

Character	Result
?	Allows alphabetic characters (uppercase or lowercase) to be entered.
Others	Are unchanged.

MaskColor

DT RW

Applies to: CheckBox, CommandButton, ImageList, Option Button

Type: Long

Defines a color that will appear transparent when the picture or ListImage object is displayed. When used with the ImageList control, this property is ignored if the UseMaskColor property is set to `False`.

MatchedWithList

RT RO

Applies to: DataCombo, DataList, DBCombo, DBList

Type: Boolean

Returns `True` if the current value of the BoundText property is found within the List property array, and returns `False` if the value is not found.

MatchEntry

DT RW

Applies to: DataCombo, DataList, DBCombo, DBList

Type: `MatchEntryConstants` enumeration

When characters are typed into a DBCombo or DBList control, the list is searched based on the following values of the MatchEntry property:

Constant	Value	Description
`dblBasicMatching`	0	The list is set to the first entry that begins with the last key pressed. This is the default value.
`dblExtendedMatching`	1	Each character typed extends the search until the Backspace key is pressed or the user waits a few seconds without typing.

Max, Min

DT RW

Applies to: CommonDialog

Type: Integer

When used with the ShowFont method, the Min and Max properties represent the range of font sizes that can be entered in the Font dialog. When used with the

Properties M–O

ShowPrint method, the Min and Max properties represent the range of pages that the user can enter in the From and To text boxes of the Print dialog.

Max, Min DT RW

Applies to: FlatScrollBar, HScrollBar, ProgressBar, Slider, UpDown, VScrollBar

Type: Integer

These properties control the lower and upper range that the controls represent.

Max, Min

Applies to: Rect object of MSChart

Type: Coor object

Returns a reference to a Coor object, which contains information about the upper-left corner (Min) and lower-right corner (Max) of the Rect object.

MaxButton DT RO

Applies to: Form object

See: *ControlBox*

MaxDate, MinDate DT RW

Applies to: DTPicker, MonthView

Type: Date

These properties control the largest (MaxDate) and smallest (MinDate) dates allowed by the controls.

MaxFileSize DT RW

Applies to: CommonDialog

Type: Integer

Determines the maximum number of characters returned in the FileName property after a ShowOpen or ShowSave method call. Its default value is 260, the value of the Win32 `MAXPATH` constant. There is little reason to modify it unless you call the ShowOpen method when setting the `cdlOFNAllowMultiselect` and `cdlOFNExplorer` flags.

Maximum, Minimum

RT RW

Applies to: ValueScale object of MSChart

Type: Double

These properties define the highest (Maximum) and lowest (Minimum) values shown on the value axis.

MaxLength

DT RW

Applies to: MaskEdBox, RichTextBox, TextBox

Type: Long integer

When the MaxLength property is set to the default value of 0, the amount of content the control can contain is unrestricted. Any other value becomes the maximum number of characters the control can contain.

MaxRecords

DT RW

Applies to: ADO DC, Recordset object of ADO DC

Type: Long integer

Sets the maximum number of records that can be returned by the recordset. Setting MaxRecords to 0 causes all records to be returned.

MaxSelCount

DT RW

Applies to: MonthView

Type: Integer

Contains the maximum number of dates simultaneously selectable in the control.

MDIChild

DT RO

Applies to: Form object

Type: Boolean

When set to `True`, the Form object becomes an MDI child form and can be shown only within an MDIForm object (its parent form). When set to the default value of `False`, the Form object can be displayed outside or without an MDIForm object.

MergeCells

RT RW

Applies to: MSFlexGrid, MSHFlexGrid

Type: `MergeCellsSettings` enumeration

Controls how and when cells should be merged within the control. Possible values are 0–flexMergeNever to not merge cells; 1–flexMergeFree to always merge adjacent, identical cells; 2–flexMergeRestrictRows to merge only identical cells in the same row; 3–flexMergeRestrictColumns to merge only identical cells in the same column; or 4–flexMergeRestrictBoth to merge cells in columns or rows.

MergeCol, MergeRow

RT RW

Applies to: MSFlexGrid, MSHFlexGrid

Type: Array of Boolean

Each element of the property array controls whether the corresponding column (MergeCol) or row (MergeRow) allows merging as defined by the MergeCells property.

Min

DT RW

Applies to: CommonDialog

See: Max

Applies to: HScrollBar, ProgressBar, Slider, VScrollBar

See: Max

MinButton

DT RO

Applies to: Form object

See: ControlBox

MinDate

DT RW

Applies to: DTPicker, MonthView

See: MaxDate

MinHeight

DT RW

Applies to: Band object of CoolBar

Type: Single

Contains the minumum height for the Band object.

Minimum

RT RW

Applies to: ValueScale object of MSChart

See: Maximum

MinorDivision

RT RW

Applies to: ValueScale object of MSChart

See: MajorDivision

MinorPen

DT RO

Applies to: AxisGrid object of MSChart

See: MajorPen

Minute

RT RW

Applies to: DTPicker

See: Day

MinWidth

DT RW

Applies to: Panel object of StatusBar

Type: Long integer

When the Panel object's AutoSize property is set to `sbrSpring` or `sbrContents`, the MinWidth property sets the smallest width to which the Panel object is able to be resized.

MiscFlags

DT RW

Applies to: OLE

Type: `OLEContainerConstants` enumeration

Can contain one or both values combined using the `Or` operator. These values control various aspects of the OLE object as follows:

OLEContainer-Constants	*Value*	*Description*
`vbOLEMiscFlagMemStorage`	1	The OLE object will load into memory, as opposed to loading into a temporary disk file. This sometimes causes problems with memory-intensive OLE objects.
`vbOLEMiscFlag-DisableInPlace`	2	When activated, the OLE object will activate in another window, regardless of whether the OLE object supports in-place activation.

MixedState DT RW

Applies to: Button object of Toolbar

Type: Boolean

When set to `True`, the Button object appears dimmed. This is used to represent cases in which the information represented by the Button object is neither `True` nor `False`. (For example, the button might be used to indicate whether selected text appears in boldface, and the selection spans text that is both bold and normal.) When set to the default value of `False`, the Button object appears normal.

Mode RT RO

Applies to: MM

Type: `ModeConstants` enumeration

Returns the current mode of operation for the multimedia device. Possible values are 524–mciModeNotOpen if the device is not open, 525–mciModeStop if the device is currently stopped, 526–mciModePlay if the device is playing, 527–mciModeRecord if the device is recording, 528–mciModeSeek if the device is currently in a seek operation, 529–mciModePause if the device is paused, or 530–mciModeReady if the device is ready.

Month RT RW

Applies to: DTPicker, MonthView

See: Day

MonthBackColor, TitleBackColor, TitleForeColor, TrailingForeColor DT RW

Applies to: MonthView

Type: Long integer

The ...ForeColor properties listed here control the color of text on the applicable sections of the MonthView calendar. The ...BackColor properties control the background color of the sections of the MonthView calendar. These properties can be set by using a function such as *QBColor* or *RGB,* or by using one of Visual Basic's Color Constants.

MonthColumns, MonthRows DT RW

Applies to: MonthView

Type: Integer

These properties contain the number of columns (MonthColumns) and rows (MonthRows) of months to display on the MonthView control.

MouseCol, MouseRow

RT RO

Applies to: MSFlexGrid, MSHFlexGrid

Type: Long integer

These properties return the current row (MouseRow) and column (MouseCol) that the mouse pointer is over.

MouseIcon

DT RW

Applies to: Form and MDIForm objects; all controls with a visual interface

Type: Icon object

When the MousePointer property is set to `ccCustom`, the Icon object contained in the MouseIcon property is displayed when the mouse cursor moves over the object or control.

MousePointer

DT RW

Applies to: Form and MDIForm objects; all controls with a visual interface

Type: `MousePointerConstants` enumeration

Controls the appearance of the mouse cursor when it moves over the object/control, as follows:

Constant	*Value*	*Description*
`vbDefault`	0	The object or control determines the shape of the mouse cursor. This is the default value.
`vbArrow`	1	The mouse cursor is shaped like an arrow.
`vbCrossHair`	2	The mouse cursor is shaped like a plus.
`vbIbeam`	3	The mouse cursor is shaped like an I-beam.
`vbIconPointer`	4	The mouse cursor is shaped like an arrow with a small rectangle.
`vbSizePointer`	5	The mouse cursor is shaped like arrows pointing up, down, left, and right.
`vbSizeNESW`	6	The mouse cursor is shaped like arrows pointing to the lower left and upper right.
`vbSizeNS`	7	The mouse cursor is shaped like arrows pointing up and down.
`vbSizeNWSE`	8	The mouse cursor is shaped like arrows pointing to the upper left and lower right.
`vbSizeWE`	9	The mouse cursor is shaped like arrows pointing to the left and right.

Constant	*Value*	*Description*
`vbUpArrow`	10	The mouse cursor is shaped like an arrow pointing up.
`vbHourglass`	11	The mouse cursor is shaped like an hourglass.
`vbNoDrop`	12	The mouse cursor is shaped like a circle with a slash through it.
`vbArrowHourglass`	13	The mouse cursor is shaped like an arrow with an hourglass.
`vbArrowQuestion`	14	The mouse cursor is shaped like an arrow with a question mark.
`vbSizeAll`	15	The mouse cursor is shaped like four arrows pointing up, down, left, and right.
`vbCustom`	99	The mouse cursor is defined by the MouseIcon property.

MouseRow

RT RO

Applies to: MSFlexGrid, MSHFlexGrid

See: MouseCol

Moveable

DT RW

Applies to: Form and MDIForm objects

Type: Boolean

When set to its default value of `True`, the form can be moved by dragging its titlebar. When set to `False`, the form cannot be moved.

MultiLine

DT RO

Applies to: RichTextBox, TextBox

Type: Boolean

When set to `True` (the default for the RichTextBox control), the control allows the user to enter multiple lines of text. Pressing the Enter key while in the control moves to the next line. When set to `False` (the default for the TextBox control), the control allows only one line of text. Pressing the Enter key advances to the next control or presses the default CommandButton control, if one is present.

MultiRow

DT RW

Applies to: TabStrip

Type: Boolean

When set to its default value of `False`, tabs that do not fit on the tab row are accessible by buttons that allow the user to scroll to the left and right. When set to `True`, tabs that do not fit on the tab row form additional tab rows.

MultiSelect DT RO

Applies to: ListBox

Type: Integer

When set to its default value of 0 (none), multiple items cannot be selected. When set to 1 (simple), multiple items can be selected by pressing the spacebar or clicking on each desired record. When set to 2 (extended), multiple items can be selected by holding the Shift key to select consecutive items and by holding the CTRL key to select other items.

Applies to: ListView DT RO

Type: Boolean

When the MultiSelect property is set to the default value of `False`, multiple ListItem objects cannot be selected in the ListView control. When set to `True`, multiple items can be selected by holding the Shift key to select consecutive items and by holding the CTRL key to select other items.

Name DT RO

Applies to: Form and MDIForm objects; all controls

Type: String

For Form objects, MDI objects, and controls that are not part of a control array, the Name property contains a unique string identifier for the control. When the control is part of a control array, the controls in the control array will have the same Name property but different Index properties. See Chapter 2, *Common Control Features*, for more information.

Negotiate DT RO

Applies to: PictureBox, ProgressBar

Type: Boolean

When the NegotiateToolbars property of a parent MDIForm object is set to `True`, and the Negotiate property is set to the default value of `False`, the control is hidden when an OLE object on a child form displays a toolbar on the MDIForm object. When set to `True`, the control remains visible at these times. When the control is not on an MDIForm object or the MDIForm object's NegotiateToolbars property is set to `False`, the Negotiate property has no effect.

NegotiateMenus

DT RO

Applies to: Form object

Type: Boolean

When set to its default value of `True`, menus created by OLE objects appear on the menu bar of the Form object. When set to `False`, the menus do not appear on the menu bar of the Form Object. If the form is an MDI child form that contains an OLE object, the NegotiateMenus property is ignored; the OLE object's menu always appears on the MDI form.

According to the documentation, if NegotiateMenus is set to `True`, the form must have a menu bar. This, however, is not the case; the OLE object's menu bar will appear on the form whether or not the Form object contains a menu bar.

NegotiateToolbars

DT RO

Applies to: MDIForm object

Type: Boolean

When the NegotiateToolbars property is set to the default value of `True`, toolbars created by OLE objects can appear docked on the MDIForm object. When set to `False`, the toolbars created do not dock on the MDIForm object.

NewIndex

RT RO

Applies to: ComboBox, ListBox

Type: Long integer

When a new item is added to a list box or combo box, the index of the new item is provided in the NewIndex property. See the entry for the ListBox Control in Chapter 5 for an example.

NewRow

DT RW

Applies to: Band object of CoolBar

Type: Boolean

When set to `True`, the Band object will start a new row of bands in the CoolBar control. When set to its default value of `False`, the band will start a new row only if it does not fit in the current row.

Next

RT RO

Applies to: Node object

See: FirstSibling

NextEnabled

DT RW

Applies to: MM

See: BackEnabled

NextVisible

DT RW

Applies to: MM

See: BackVisible

Nodes

RT RO

Applies to: TreeView

Type: Collection

Returns a reference to the Nodes collection. The Nodes collection in turn has the following members:

Member	*Description*
Add method	Adds a new item to the Nodes collection.
Clear method	Removes all items from the collection.
Count property	Returns the number of Node objects in the collection.
Item property	Returns a reference to a Node object based on its index or its key. This is the collection's default property.
Remove method	Removes a single Node object from the collection based on its index or key.

NoMatch

RT RO

Applies to: Recordset object of Data control

Type: Boolean

Returns `True` if the last Seek operation found any records; otherwise, returns `False`.

Notify

RT RW

Applies to: MM

Type: Boolean

When set to `True`, the Done event will fire when the next command has completed execution. When set to its default value of `False`, the Done event is not fired.

NotifyMessage, NotifyValue

RT RO

Applies to: MM

Type: String (NotifyMessage), `NotifyConstants` enumeration (NotifyValue)

These properties contain the notification number (NotifyValue) and description (NotifyMessage) returned by the last command. Possible values for the NotifyValue property are 1–mciNotifySuccessful for success, 2–mciNotifySuperceded for an interrupted command, 4–mciNotifyAborted for an aborted command, or 8–mciNotifyFailure if the command failed.

NumberFormat

DT RW

Applies to: Column object of DataGrid

Type: String

Formats information in the Column object. It contains a format string like that of the *Format* function, which is used to format the Value property, thereby creating the contents of the Text property.

Object

RT RO

Applies to: All objects and nonintrinsic controls

Type: Object

Visual Basic automatically supplies a set of properties, methods, and events for every ActiveX control and OLE object (see the following table). When the names of these objects conflict with "native" properties and methods implemented by the control, the Visual Basic properties and methods take precedence, and the control's properties and methods are ignored. Even more commonly, the names of Visual Basic-supplied properties and methods conflict with those of OLE objects like Excel spreadsheets or Word documents. In these cases, the Object property returns a reference to the control or OLE object that allows its own properties or methods to be accessed and those supplied by Visual Basic to be bypassed.

For instance, if an OLE control containing a Microsoft Word document is added to a form, the statement:

```
Debug.Print OLE1.Parent.Name
```

identifies the form as the parent of the OLE control. On the other hand, the statement:

```
Debug.Print OLE1.Object.Parent.Name
```

identifies Microsoft Word, the name of the Word Application object, as the parent of the OLE object.

Note that the Object property returns a generic object type. This has two implications. First, the object reference is resolved at runtime (i.e., it uses late binding), with all of the performance penalties this entails. Second, because late-bound objects cannot take advantage of type libraries, you can't use Visual Basic's Auto List Members feature to determine precisely what properties and methods are accessible through the Object property. The following table lists the standard properties, methods, and events available for every ActiveXcontrol and OLE object:

Properties		
Align	Height	Object
Binding	HelpContextID	Parent
Bindings	Index	TabIndex
Cancel	Left	TabStop
Container	LeftNoRun	TagParent
DataChanged	LinkItem	ToolTipText
DataField	LinkMode	Top
DataSource	LinkTimeout	TopNoRun
Default	LinkTopic	VisibleTabStop
DragIcon	Name	WhatsThisHelpID
DragMode	NegotiateLinkItem	Width
Methods		
Drag	LinkSend	ShowWhatsThis
LinkExecute	Move	ZOrder
LinkPoke	Refresh	
LinkRequest	SetFocus	
Events		
GotFocus	LinkError	LinkOpen
LinkClose	LinkNotify	LostFocus

Properties M–O

ObjectAcceptFormats RT RO

Applies to: OLE

Type: String array

Contains one element for each data format that the activated OLE object can accept. This array is zero-based and contains the number of elements indicated by the ObjectAcceptFormatsCount property.

ObjectAcceptFormatsCount RT RO

Applies to: OLE

Type: Integer

Indicates the number of formats that the activated OLE object can accept. This can be used with the ObjectAcceptFormats property to enumerate the formats.

ObjectGetFormats

RT RO

Applies to: OLE

Type: String array

Contains one element for each data format that the activated OLE object control can provide. This array is zero-based and contains the number of elements indicated by the ObjectGetFormatsCount property.

ObjectGetFormatsCount

RT RO

Applies to: OLE

Type: Integer

Indicates the number of formats that the activated OLE object in an OLE control can provide. This can then be used with the ObjectGetFormats property to enumerate the formats.

ObjectVerbFlags

RT RO

Applies to: OLEObject object of OLE; OLE control

Type: Enumeration array

Contains one element for each verb that the activated OLE object supports. This array is zero-based, and its number of elements is indicated by the ObjectVerbs-Count property. Its value is a flag that denotes the menu state of the verb in the parallel ObjectVerbs property array, as follows:

OLEContainerConstants	*Value*	*Description*
`vbOLEFlagEnabled`	0	The verb is enabled.
`vbOLEFlagGrayed`	1	The verb is dimmed.
`vbOLEFlagDisabled`	2	The verb is disabled.
`vbOLEFlagChecked`	8	The verb is checked.
`vbOLEFlagSeparator`	2,048	The verb represents a menu separator bar.

ObjectVerbs

RT RO

Applies to: OLEObject object of OLE; OLE control

Type: String array

The ObjectVerbs property array contains one element for each verb, or menu item, that the activated OLE object supports. This array is zero-based, and its number of elements is indicated by the ObjectGetVerbs property.

ObjectVerbsCount RT RO

Applies to: OLEObject object of OLE; OLE control

Type: Integer

Indicates the number of verbs that the activated OLE object supports. This can then be used with the ObjectVerbs property to enumerate the verbs.

Offset

Applies to: DataPoint object of MSChart

Type: Integer

Contains the distance (based on the current Windows settings) to offset the DataPoint from its point of origin.

Offset RT RO

Applies to: DataPointLabel and Shadow objects of MSChart

Type: Coor object

Returns a reference to a Coor object, which contains information about how far away to offset the current object from its point of origin.

OLEDragMode DT RW

Applies to: ComboBox, DataCombo, DataList, Image, ListBox, ListView, PictureBox, RichTextBox, TextBox, TreeView

Type: `OLEDragConstants` enumeration

The OLEDragMode property controls if and how the control can be dragged using OLE Drag and Drop, as follows:

Constant	*Value*	*Description*
`vbOLEDragManual`	0	The program initiates an OLE Drag operation by using the OLEDrag method.
`vbOLEDragAutomatic`	1	The user drags the control, initiating the OLE Drag, causing the OLEStartEvent to take place.

OLEDropAllowed DT RW

Applies to: OLE

Type: Boolean

When the OLEDropAllowed property is set to its default value of `False`, the OLE control will not accept an OLE object dropped into it. When set to `True`, a valid OLE object can be dropped onto the OLE control.

OLEDropMode

DT RW

Applies to: Form and MDIForm objects; all controls with a visual interface

Type: `OLEDropConstants` enumeration

The OLEDropMode property controls if and how an OLE object can be dropped onto the control using OLE Drag and Drop.

Constant	*Value*	*Description*
`vbOLEDropNone`	0	OLE objects cannot be dropped onto this object or control.
`vbOLEDropManual`	1	Dropping an OLE object onto the object or control fires the OLDEDragDrop event. The program must then handle the integration of the dropped OLE object with the object or control.
`vbOLEDropAutomatic`	2	The OLE control can contain either linked and embedded objects.

OLEType

RT RO

Applies to: OLE

Type: `OLEContainerConstants` enumeration

The OLEType property returns the type of OLE object contained in the OLE control, as follows:

Constant	*Value*	*Description*
`vbOLELinked`	0	The object is a linked OLE object.
`vbOLEEmbedded`	1	The object is an embedded OLE object.
`vbOLENone`	2	There is currently no object in the OLE control.

OLETypeAllowed

DT RW

Applies to: OLE

Type: `OLEContainerConstants` enumeration

The OLETypeAllowed property indicates the type of OLE object that can be contained in the OLE control. Valid `OLEContainerConstants` are listed in the previous entry, OLEType.

Options

DT RW

Applies to: Data control

Type: `RecordsetOptionEnum` enumeration

One or more flags that can be combined by adding them together or logically `Or`ing them. They control various aspects of the control's recordset, as follows:

Constant	*Value*	*Description*
`dbDenyWrite`	1	Other users of the data in the recordset cannot make changes to that data.
`dbDenyRead`	2	Other users cannot read the data in the recordset.
`dbReadOnly`	4	The Data control cannot add records or make changes to data in the recordset.
`dbAppendOnly`	8	The Data control can add to, but cannot change data in the recordset.
`dbInconsistent`	16	Changes to the recordset can violate a join condition. For example, for two tables joined on the field PersonID, the PersonID field in Table 2 could be changed so that it no longer matches the PersonID in Table 1.
`dbConsistent`	32	Changes in the recordset cannot violate a join condition (see `dbInconsistent`). This is the default value.
`dbSQLPassThrough`	64	The SQL statement used to create the recordset bypasses the Jet engine and must use the SQL syntax of the database engine.
`dbForwardOnly`	256	The MoveFirst, MoveLast, and MovePrevious methods will not function with this recordset. Only the MoveNext method can be used for record navigation.
`dbSeeChanges`	512	If another user saves data that is currently being edited by the Data control, an error is generated.

Order

RT RW

Applies to: SeriesPosition object of MSChart

Type: Integer

Contains the position of the series relative to other series in the chart.

Orientation

DT RW

Applies to: ADO DC, CoolBar, FlatScrollBar, MM, ProgressBar, Slider, UpDown

Type: `OrientationConstants` enumeration

Affects the control as follows:

OrientationConstants	*Value*	*Description*
`ccHorizontal, cc2Horizontal, adHorizontal, mciOrientHoriz`	0	The control is displayed horizontally.
`ccVertical, cc2Vertical, adVertical, mciOrientVert`	1	The control is displayed vertically.

OSBuild, OSPlatform, OSVersion

RT RO

Applies to: SysInfo

Type: Integer (OSBuild, OSPlatform), single (OSVersion)

These properties return information about the version and type of the operating system. The OSPlatform contains 0 for Win32s, 1 for Windows 9x, or 2 for Windows NT. The other properties contain the version number (OSVersion) and build number (OSBuild) for the operating system.

PageCount, PageSize

Applies to: Recordset object of ADO DC

See: AbsolutePage

Palette

DT RW

Applies to: Form object; PictureBox control

Type: Picture object

Palettes define the set of colors available to Windows and its applications for painting the Windows interface at any given time; the current palette is the one used by the foreground window. Visual Basic supports a 256-color palette (or, more precisely, 236 custom colors, along with 20 static colors that are defined by the system and cannot be changed) and allows you to define custom palettes for your application.

The PaletteMode property determines how an application derives its current palette. When it is set to `VbPaletteModeCustom`, an application extracts its palette from the image stored to the Palette property. To do this, you assign a Picture object to the Palette property using the *LoadPicture* function, a ListImage object, a PictureClip control, or any other property or function that returns a Picture object. The image containing the palette must be a Windows bitmap

(*.BMP*), device-independent bitmap (*.DIB*), or *.GIF* file. Palette (*.PAL*) files, the most common format for saving and importing palettes, however, are not supported by Visual Basic.

PaletteMode

DT RW

Applies to: Form object; PictureBox control

Type: `PaletteModeConstants` enumeration

Objects and controls with multicolored graphics interact with one another based on the PaletteMode property, as follows:

Constant	*Value*	*Description*
`vbPaletteModeHalfTone`	0	The standard Windows halftone palette is used for all graphics. This is the default value.
`vbPaletteModeUseZOrder`	1	The palette of the topmost control on the object or control is used for all graphics.
`VbPaletteModeCustom`	2	The Palette property is used as the palette for all graphics.
`vbPaletteModeContainer`	3	The palette of the custom control's container is used. This is for custom controls only.
`vbPaletteModeNone`	4	No palette is used. This is for custom controls only.
`vbPaletteModeObject`	5	The ActiveX designer's palette is used for all graphics.

Panels

RT RO

Applies to: StatusBar

Type: Collection

Returns a reference to the Panels collection. The collection object in turn supports the standard collection properties (Count and Item) and methods (Add, Clear, and Remove). Panel objects can be retrieved from the collection either by index or by key.

Parent

RT RO

Applies to: Form object; all controls

Type: Object

Returns a reference to the Form object on which the control is located. Controls within containers (like a command button stored in a PictureBox control) also return a reference to their parent Form object. Although the documentation indicates that the Parent property of Form objects that are MDI children returns their parent MDIForm objects, this is not the case; the Parent property is not supported in the case of both Form and MDIForm objects.

Applies to: Node object of TreeView

Type: Node object

In a TreeView control, each Node object can contain one or more child Node objects. The Parent property returns a reference to the parent node of a Node object.

Password, UserName DT RW

Applies to: ADO DC, Inet control

Type: String

Contains the username (UserName) and password (Password) for the data source or Internet site.

PasswordChar DT RW

Applies to: TextBox

Type: String (one character)

When the PasswordChar is set to any single character, all text in the TextBox control and entered into the TextBox control is represented visually by that character. However, the Text property still returns the actual text entered.

PasteOK RT RO

Applies to: OLE

Type: Boolean

The PasteOK property returns `True` if the current contents of the Windows Clipboard can be pasted into the OLE control. This is particularly useful when checked from an edit menu, as follows:

```
Private Sub mnuEditTop_Click()
  'mnuEdit(4).Caption = "Paste"
    If Me.ActiveControl.Name = "oleMain" Then
        If oleMain.PasteOK Then
            mnuEdit(4).Enabled = True
        Else
            mnuEdit(4).Enabled = False
        End If
    End If
End Sub
```

PathSeparator DT RW

Applies to: TreeView

Type: String (one character)

When a TreeView control returns the FullPath property, the Text properties of any other displayed Node objects are separated by the character assigned to the Path-Separator property. The default value of PathSeparator is the backslash (\).

PatternColor DT RO

Applies to: Brush object of MSChart

Type: VtColor object

Returns a reference to a VtColor object, which contains information about the color used to fill the object's parent.

PauseEnabled DT RW

Applies to: MM

See: BackEnabled

PauseVisible DT RW

Applies to: MM

See: BackVisible

Pen DT RO

Applies to: Axis, Marker, PlotBase, Series, and Wall objects of MSChart

Type: Pen object

Returns a reference to a Pen object, which controls the pen used to draw the outline around the object.

PercentBasis RT RW

Applies to: AxisScale object of MSChart

See: DefaultPercentBasis

PercentFormat

RT RW

Applies to: DataPointLabel object of MSChart

Type: String

Contains a format string similar to those used with VBA's *Format* function that is used to format labels for percent values.

PercentPosition

RT RW

Applies to: Recordset object of Data control

Type: Single

Indicates the position of the record pointer in the recordset relative to the total number of records.

Picture

DT RW

Applies to: Band Object of CoolBar, Form object, ListImage object, MDIForm object, Panel object; CheckBox, CommandButton, Image, ListView, MSFlexGrid, MSHFlexGrid, OLE, OptionButton, and PictureBox controls

Type: Picture object

Contains the Picture object to display when the control is displayed normally. This property can be set using any function or property that returns a Picture object.

PictureAlignment

DT RW

Applies to: ListView

Type: `ListPictureAlignmentConstants` enumeration

Controls the placement of the picture (referenced by the Picture property) within the ListView control. Possible values are 0–lvwTopLeft for upper-left alignment, 1–lvwTopRight for upper-right alignment, 2–lvwBottomLeft for lower-left alignment, 3–lvwBottomRight for lower-right alignment, 4–lvwCenter for centered alignment, and 5–lvwTile for a tiled image.

PictureType

DT RW

Applies to: MSFlexGrid, MSHFlexGrid

Type: `PictureTypeSettings` enumeration

Controls the type of picture displayed as either a full-color bitmap (0–flexPictureColor) or a monochrome bitmap (1–flexPictureMonochrome).

Placement

Applies to: TabStrip

Type: `PlacementConstants` enumeration

Controls the placement of tabs on the control. Possible values are 0–tabPlacementTop for tabs at the top, 1–tabPlacementBottom for tabs at the bottom, 2–tabPlacementLeft for tabs to the left, or 3–tabPlacementRight for tabs to the right.

PlayEnabled

DT RW

Applies to: MM

See: BackEnabled

PlayVisible

DT RW

Applies to: MM

See: BackVisible

Plot

RT RO

Applies to: MSChart

Type: Plot object

Returns a reference to a Plot object, which contains information about plotting the data on the chart.

PlotBase

RT RO

Applies to: Plot object of MSChart

Type: PlotBase object

Returns a reference to a PlotBase object, which controls the base (bottom) area of the plot.

Point

RT RW

Applies to: Intersection object of MSChart

Type: Double

Indicates the location at which the current axis intersects with another axis.

Position RT RW

Applies to: Band object of CoolBar, ColumnHeader object of ListView

Type: Integer

Contains the position of the object within all similar objects in the control. Changing the Position property moves the object.

Position RT RO

Applies to: MM

Type: Long integer

Returns the current location within the multimedia device. The value returned uses the current TimeFormat value.

Position RT RO

Applies to: Series object of MSChart

Type: SeriesPosition object

Contains a reference to a SeriesPosition object, which contains information about where the series is located relative to other series in the chart.

PrevEnabled DT RW

Applies to: MM

See: BackEnabled

Previous RT RO

Applies to: Node object of TreeView

See: FirstSibling

PrevVisible DT RW

Applies to: MM

See: BackVisible

PrinterDefault DT RW

Applies to: CommonDialog

Type: Boolean

When the PrinterDefault property is set to its default value of `True`, changes made in the Printer dialog box are applied to the Windows default printer as well. When set to `False`, the changes apply only to the current printer.

Projection

RT RW

Applies to: Plot object of MSChart

Type: `VtProjectionType` enumeration

Controls the appearance of a 3-D chart. Possible values are 0–VtProjectionType-Perspective for a normal 3-D appearance; 1–VtProjectionTypeOblique, where the vertical plane remains constant; 2–VtProjectionTypeOrthogonal, for a normal 3-D appearance without perspective adjustments; 3–VtProjectionTypeFrontal, where the view is from the front and no z- or y-axis rotation is allowed; or 4–VtProjectionTypeOverhead, where the view is from the top and no x- or y-axis rotation is allowed.

PromptChart

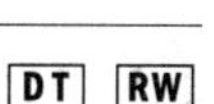

Applies to: MaskEdBox

Type: String

Contains the control's prompt character. The default value is an underscore (_).

PromptInclude

DT RW

Applies to: MaskEdBox

Type: Boolean

When set to its default value of `True`, any prompt characters in the control are included in the Text property. When set to `False`, the prompt characters are left out of the Text property.

Protocol

DT RW

Applies to: Inet control

Type: `ProtocolConstants` enumeration

Contains the protocol to be used for communication. Possible values are 0–icUnknown for an unknown protocol, 1–icDefault for the default protocol, 2–icFTP for File Transfer Protocol (FTP), 4–icHTTP for HyperText Transfer Protocol (HTTP), or 5–icHTTPS for secure HyperText Transfer Protocol.

Protocol

DT RW

Applies to: Winsock

Type: `ProtocolConstants` enumeration

When set to the default value of 0–sckTCPProtocol, TCP will be used for communication. When set to 1–sckUDPProtocol, UDP will be used.

Proxy

DT RW

Applies to: Inet control

Type: String

Contains the name of the proxy server to be used when the AccessType property is set to `icNamedProxy`.

RandomFill

DT RW

Applies to: MSChart

Type: Boolean

When set to its default value of `True`, random data populates the chart. When set to `False`, the chart is not populated with random data.

ReadOnly

DT RW

Applies to: Data control

Type: Boolean

Before you open a database with a Data control, the ReadOnly property determines whether the Data control will be able to edit any data in that database. When set to the default value of `False`, the data can be edited. When set to `True`, the data bound to the Data control cannot be edited. See the Data Control entry in Chapter 5 for more information.

RecordCount

RT RO

Applies to: Recordset object of ADO DC and of Data controls

Type: Long integer

Indicates the number of records in the recordset. However, this property is not accurate until the last record in the recordset has been accessed.

RecordEnabled

DT RW

Applies to: MM

See: BackEnabled

RecordMode

DT RW

Applies to: MM

Type: `RecordModeConstants` enumeration

When set to the default value of 1–mciRecordModeOverwrite, recording will overwrite current data in the multimedia device. When set to 0–mciRecordModeInsert, recording inserts the new data.

Some devices support only one of the record modes. Which mode is supported is unknown until recording is attempted.

RecordsAffected

RT RO

Applies to: Database object of Data control

Type: Long integer

Returns the number of records affected by the last database command.

RecordSelectors

DT RW

Applies to: Split object of DataGrid; DataGrid control

Type: Boolean

When the RecordSelectors property is set to its default value of `True`, a record selector appears on the left end of each row in the DataGrid control or Split object. When set to `True` for a DataGrid, all Split objects show a record selector. When set to `False`, the record selectors do not appear.

Recordset

RT RW

Applies to: ADO DC, Data, MSHFlexGrid

Type: Recordset object

A Recordset object is a DAO object (Data control) or ADO object (ADO DC or MSHFlexGrid control) that actually contains the data that the Data control provides. The Recordset property can be set to a Recordset object in any of three ways:

- By setting the DatabaseName and RecordSource properties at design time.
- By setting the DatabaseName and RecordSource Properties at runtime followed by calling the Refresh method
- By setting the Recordset property directly to a Recordset object, as in this DAO example:

```
Private Sub Form_Load()
    Dim sSQL As String
    Dim dbMain As Database
    Dim rsMain As Recordset

  'Open the database.
    Set dbMain = Workspaces(0).OpenDatabase( _
        Name:="c:\My Documents\AddressBook.MDB", _
        ReadOnly:=True)

    sSQL = "SELECT * FROM AddressList "

  'Create the Recordset object.
    Set rsMain = dbMain.OpenRecordset( _
        Name:=sSQL, Type:=dbOpenSnapshot)

    Set Me.dtcMain.Recordset = rsMain
End Sub
```

RecordsetType DT RW

Applies to: Data control

Type: `RecordsetTypeConstants` enumeration

When the Data control creates a Recordset object (as opposed to setting the Recordset property to a Recordset object directly), the type of Recordset object created depends on the RecordsetType property, as follows:

Constant	*Value*	*Description*
vbRSTypeTable	0	A table-type recordset.
vbRSTypeDynaset	1	A dynaset-type recordset. This is the default value.
vbRSTypeSnapshot	2	A snapshot-type recordset.

See the Data Control entry in Chapter 5 for more information.

RecordSource

DT RW

Applies to: ADO DC, Data control

Type: String

For the Data control, the RecordSource property can be set to a valid table in the database represented by the Database property that is used to create the Recordset object. When the RecordsetType property is set to `vbRSTypeDynaset` or `vbRSTypeSnapshot` in a Data control or ADO DC, the RecordSource property can be set to a valid SQL statement.

RecordVisible

DT RW

Applies to: MM

See: BackVisible

Rect

RT RO

Applies to: Location object of MSChart

Type: Rect object

Returns a reference to a Rect object, which defines a rectangular region on the control.

Red

RW

Applies to: VtColor object of MSChart

See: Blue

Redraw

DT RW

Applies to: MSFlexGrid, MSHFlexGrid

Type: Boolean

When set to the default value of `True`, the control is completely redrawn after each change. When set to `False`, the control is not redrawn automatically.

RemoteHost

DT RW

Applies to: Inet control

Type: String

Contains the remote machine's name in an Internet connection.

RemoteHost, RemoteHostIP DT RW

Applies to: Winsock

See: LocalHostName

RemotePort DT RW

Applies to: Inet control

Type: Long integer

Contains the port to use on the remote machine (RemotePort) for an Internet connection.

RemotePort DT RW

Applies to: Winsock

See: LocalPort

Repaint DT RW

Applies to: MSChart

Type: Boolean

When set to its default value of `True`, the control is completely redrawn after each change. When set to `False`, the control is not redrawn automatically.

ReportIcon RT RW

Applies to: ListSubItem object of ListView

Type: Long or string integer

Contains the index or key of the ListImage object in the bound ImageList control to be displayed for the ListSubItem object.

RequestTimeout DT RW

Applies to: Inet control

Type: Long integer

Defines the number of seconds to wait for a response after issuing a request before generating an error. Setting the RequestTimeout to 0 will cause a request to wait indefinitely for a response.

ResponseCode, ResponseInfo

RT RO

Applies to: Inet control

Type: Long integer (ResponseCode), string (ResponseInfo)

Returns the number (ResponseCode) and description (ResponseInfo) of the last error generated by the control.

Restartable

RT RO

Applies to: Recordset object of Data control

Type: Boolean

Returns `True` if the Recordset supports the Requery method; otherwise, returns `False`.

RightMargin

DT RW

Applies to: RichTextBox

Type: Long integer

When set to its default value of 0, text will not wrap until it reaches past the right edge of the control. When set to any other value, text will begin wrapping that many twips after the right edge of the control. When the MultiLine property is set to `False`, this property is ignored.

RightToLeft

DT RO

Applies to: All controls

Type: Boolean

Indicates the direction in which text is displayed. The RightToLeft property can be changed from its default value of `False` only when a version of Windows (like the Arabic or Hebrew version) that supports left-to-right text is running. When set to `True` on a system such as this, certain aspects of the control will change.

Root

RT RO

Applies to: Node object of TreeView

Type: Node object

In a TreeView control, each Node object can contain one or more child Node objects. The Root property returns a reference to the root node (the highest-level node) of a Node object.

Rotation RT RW

Applies to: View3D object of MSChart

See: Elevation

Row RT RW

Applies to: DataGrid, MSChart, MSFlexGrid, MSHFlexGrid

Type: Long integer

See: Col

RowCount DT RW

Applies to: CoolBar

Type: Long integer

Determines the number of rows of Band objects on the CoolBar control.

RowCount DT RW

Applies to: DataGrid object of MSChart, MSChart

See: ColumnCount

RowData RT RW

Applies to: MSFlexGrid, MSHFlexGrid (BandData only)

See: BandData

RowDividerStyle DT RW

Applies to: DataGrid

Type: Integer

Controls the appearance of the line drawn between rows in a DataGrid control. When set to 0, there is no border between the rows. When set to 1, a black line appears between the rows. When set to its default value of 2, a dark gray line separates the rows. When set to 3 or 4, the divider appears to be raised or inset, respectively. When the RowDividerStyle property is set to 5, the ForeColor property is used to determine the color of a solid line between the rows.

RowExpandable RT RW

Applies to: MSHFlexGrid

Type: Boolean

When set to `True`, the current row can be expanded. When set to `False`, the row cannot be expanded.

RowExpanded RT RW

Applies to: MSHFlexGrid

Type: Boolean

When set to `True`, the current row has been expanded. When set to `False`, the row is not expanded.

RowHeight DT RW

Applies to: DataGrid

Type: Single

Defines the height of all rows in the DataGrid control.

RowHeight DT RW

Applies to: MSFlexGrid, MSHFlexGrid

See: ColWidth

RowHeightMin DT RW

Applies to: MSFlexGrid, MSHFlexGrid

Type: Long integer

Defines the minimum height to which any row in the control can be set.

RowIsVisible RT RW

Applies to: MSFlexGrid, MSHFlexGrid

See: ColIsVisible

RowLabel, RowLabelCount, RowLabelIndex DT RW

Applies to: DataGrid object of MSChart; MSChart control

See: ColumnLabel

RowMember DT RW

Applies to: DataCombo, DataList

Type: String

Contains the name of the data member within the ADO DC from which the control's list is populated.

RowPos RT RO

Applies to: MSFlexGrid, MSHFlexGrid

See: ColPos

RowPosition DT RW

Applies to: MSFlexGrid, MSHFlexGrid

See: ColPosition

Rows DT RW

Applies to: MSFlexGrid, MSHFlexGrid

See: Cols

RowSel RT RW

Applies to: MSFlexGrid, MSHFlexGrid

See: ColSel

RowSizingMode DT RW

Applies to: MSHFlexGrid

Type: `RowSizingSettings` enumeration

When set to the default value of 0–flexRowSizeIndividual, rows in the control can be sized individually by the user. When set to 1–flexRowSizeAll, changing the height of one row affects all rows in the control.

RowSource DT RW

Applies to: DataCombo, DataList, DBCombo, DBList

Type: String

While the DataSource property contains the name of the Data control to which the control is bound, the RowSource property contains the name of the Data control from which the control's list is populated.

ScaleHeight, ScaleWidth DT RW

Applies to: Form and MDIForm objects; PictureBox control

Type: Long integer

These properties represent the height and width of the control within its unusable borders. Therefore, when positioning graphics or other controls within a form or picture box, do not base the coordinates on the Height and Width properties; instead, base the coordinates on these properties, as follows:

```
Private Sub Form_Resize()
  'cmdMain will remain 1,215x375. Otherwise, there _
   will be a 120-twip border around the controls.
  'txtMain will not resize its height under 1,215x375.

    If Me.ScaleWidth < 1215 + 240 _
        Or Me.ScaleHeight < 375 + 375 + 360 Then
    'The form is too small to resize the controls.
        Exit Sub
    End If

    Me.txtMain.Move 120, 120, Me.ScaleWidth - 240, _
                    Me.ScaleHeight - (375 + 360)

    Me.cmdMain.Move Me.ScaleWidth - (1215 + 120), _
                    Me.ScaleHeight - (375 + 120)
End Sub
```

For the MDIForm object, ScaleHeight and ScaleWidth are not available at design time and are read-only at runtime.

ScaleLeft, ScaleTop DT RW

Applies to: Form object; PictureBox control

Type: Long integer

When set to a value other than 0, these properties move the origin of the Form object or PictureBox control's coordinate system to the new location. This can be used to simplify drawing graphics that involve negative coordinates by moving the origin toward the middle of the object or control.

ScaleMode **DT** **RW**

Applies to: Form object; PictureBox control

Type: `ScaleModeConstants` enumeration

Defines the unit of measure in which the ScaleHeight, ScaleWidth, ScaleLeft, ScaleTop, Height, and Width properties are expressed. It can take the following values:

Constant	*Value*	*Description*
`vbUser`	0	Indicates a custom scale mode because one or more of the scale properties has been altered.
`vbTwips`	1	All scale property values are expressed in twips.
`vbPoints`	2	All scale property values are expressed in points.
`vbPixels`	3	All scale property values are expressed in pixels.
`vbCharacters`	4	All scale property values are expressed in a character measurement. This relates to 120×240 twips.
`vbInch`	5	All scale property values are expressed in inches.
`vbMillimeters`	6	All scale property values are expressed in millimeters.
`vbCentimeters`	7	All scale property values are expressed in centimeters.

ScaleTop **DT** **RW**

Applies to: Form object; PictureBox control

See: ScaleLeft

ScaleWidth **DT** **RW**

Applies to: Form and MDIForm objects; PictureBox control

See: ScaleHeight

Scroll **DT** **RW**

Applies to: TreeView

Type: Boolean

When set to its default value of `True`, scrollbars appear on the TreeView control. When set to `False`, no scrollbars appear.

ScrollBars

DT RO

Applies to: Split object of DataGrid; DataGrid and TextBox controls

Type: `ScrollBarConstants` enumeration

The presence of scrollbars on a control or Split object is based on the value of the ScrollBars property, as follows:

Constant	*Value*	*Description*
`vbSBNone`	0	No scrollbars appear on the object or control. This is the default value.
`vbHorizontal`	1	A horizontal scrollbar appears if the object or control's contents extend horizontally outside its client area.
`vbVertical`	2	A vertical scrollbar appears if the object or control's contents extend vertically outside its client area.
`vbBoth`	3	Each scrollbar is displayed based on the previous requirements.

The ScrollBars property of the TextBox control is read-only at runtime.

ScrollBars

DT RO

Applies to: MDIForm object

Type: Boolean

When the ScrollBars property is set to the default value of `True`, scrollbars appear on the MDIForm object when a child Form object (its MDIChild property is set to `True`) is positioned so that it extends outside the client area of the MDI form. When set to `False`, scrollbars do not display on the MDI form.

ScrollBars

DT RW

Applies to: MSFlexGrid, MSHFlexGrid

Type: `ScrollBarsSettings` enumeration

Defines when scrollbars are present on the control, as follows:

Constant	*Value*	*Description*
`flexScrollBarNone`	0	No scrollbars appear on the control.
`flexScrollHorizontal`	1	A horizontal scrollbar appears if the control's contents extend horizontally outside its client area.

Constant	Value	Description
flexScrollVertical	2	A vertical scrollbar appears if the control's contents extend vertically outside its client area.
flexScrollBoth	3	Each scrollbar is displayed based on the previous requirements. This is the default value.

ScrollBars

DT RO

Applies to: RichTextBox

Type: `ScrollBarsConstants` enumeration

When the MultiLine property of a RichTextBox control is set to `True`, the presence of scrollbars on the control is based on the value of the ScrollBars property, as follows:

Constant	Value	Description
rtfNone	0	No scrollbars appear on the control. This is the default value.
rtfHorizontal	1	A horizontal scrollbar appears on the control if its contents extend horizontally outside its client area.
rtfVertical	2	A vertical scrollbar appears on the control if its contents extend vertically outside its client area.
rtfBoth	3	Each scrollbar is displayed based on the previous requirements.

ScrollBarSize

RT RO

Applies to: SysInfo

Type: Single

Returns the size of normal scrollbars in Windows. The value is specified in twips.

ScrollGroup

DT RW

Applies to: Split object of DataGrid

Type: Integer

All Split objects in the same DataGrid control with the same value for ScrollGroup will automatically scroll together when one is scrolled.

Scrolling DT RW

Applies to: ProgressBar

Type: `ScrollingConstants` enumeration

When set to its default value of 0–ccScrollingStandard, values in the ProgressBar are always represented only by full, solid blocks within the control. When set to 1–ccScrollingSmooth, partial blocks are displayed when necessary, giving the appearance of smooth scrolling.

ScrollRate DT RW

Applies to: MonthView

Type: Integer

Defines the number of months scrolled when the control's arrow buttons are clicked.

ScrollTrack DT RW

Applies to: MSFlexGrid, MSHFlexGrid

Type: Boolean

When set to `True`, the contents of the control are updated as the user drags the scrollbar on the control. When set to the default value of `False`, the contents of the control are updated only when the user finishes scrolling.

Second RT RW

Applies to: DTPicker

See: Day

SecondaryAxis RT RW

Applies to: Series object of MSChart

Type: Boolean

When set to the default value of `False`, the series is plotted on the control's primary axis. When set to `True`, the series is plotted on the secondary axis.

SelAlignment RT RW

Applies to: RichTextBox

Type: `SelAlignmentConstants` enumeration

Indicates the alignment of the selected text or can force the alignment of the selected text, as follows:

Constant	*Value*	*Description*
	`Null`	The selected text is aligned in more than one way. The property cannot be set to this value.
`rtfLeft`	0	The selected text is left-aligned.
`rtfRight`	1	The selected text is right-aligned.
`rtfCenter`	2	The selected text is centered.

SelBold, SelBullet, SelItalic, SelProtected, SelStrikethru, SelUnderline

RT RW

Applies to: RichTextBox

Type: Boolean

When any of these properties is `True`, the selected text is formatted as indicated by the property. When `False`, the text is not formatted in the manner specified by the property. When `Null`, some but not all of the selected text is formatted as indicated by the property. Setting the property to `True` or `False` alters the formatting of the selected text as defined by the property. Protected text (SelProtected) appears as normal text but cannot be edited by the user.

SelBookmarks

RT RO

Applies to: DataGrid

Type: Collection

Returns a reference to the Bookmarks collection for the currently selected rows. See the entry for the DataGrid Control in Chapter 5 for more information.

SelBullet

RT RW

Applies to: RichTextBox

See: SelBold

SelCharOffset

RT RW

Applies to: RichTextBox

Type: Long integer

When the SelCharOffset property is set to 0, the selected text is vertically aligned with the baseline. When set to a positive number, the text is that many twips above the baseline. When set to a negative number, the text is that many twips below the baseline. A `Null` indicates that the selected text is aligned at various levels compared to the baseline. Setting the property alters the vertical alignment of the selected text as indicated by the property, except for the `Null`, which can only be assigned by the Visual Basic runtime engine.

SelColor

RT RW

Applies to: RichTextBox

Type: Long integer

When the SelColor property is set to any nonnull value, the selected text is colored as defined by the property. A `Null` indicates that the selected text is multicolored. Setting the property alters the color of the selected text to the color defined by the property. A `Null`, however, cannot be assigned in code; it can be set only by the Visual Basic runtime engine to indicate that the selected text consists of multiple colors.

SelCount

RT RO

Applies to: ListBox

Type: Long integer

Returns the number of elements in the list that are selected when a ListBox control's MultiSelect property is set to 1 or 2.

Selected

RT RW

Applies to: ListBox

Type: Boolean array

For each item in the control's list, the Selected property array returns `True` if the element is selected (or checked, in the case of a ListBox control whose Style property is set to `vbListBoxCheckbox`) and returns `False` if the current element is not selected. The following example shows how the Selected property array can be used to move selected elements from one list box to another:

```
Private Sub cmdMoveTo_Click()
    Dim lCtr As Long

  'Copy selected elements to lstTo.
    For lCtr = 0 To Me.lstFrom.ListCount - 1
        If Me.lstFrom.Selected(lCtr) Then
            Me.lstTo.AddItem Me.lstFrom.List(lCtr)
      'Don't forget the ItemData!
            Me.lstTo.ItemData(Me.lstTo.NewIndex) = _
                                Me.lstFrom.ItemData(lCtr)
        End If
    Next lCtr
```

Properties S

```
'Remove the selected elements from lstFrom in _
reverse order.
    For lCtr = Me.lstFrom.ListCount - 1 To 0 Step -1
        If Me.lstFrom.Selected(lCtr) Then
            Me.lstFrom.RemoveItem lCtr
        End If
    Next lCtr
End Sub
```

Selected RT RW

Applies to: ComboItem object of ImageCombo, ListItem object of ListView, Node object of TreeView, Tab object of TabStrip

Type: Boolean

If the object is currently selected in its parent control, the Selected property returns `True`. Otherwise, it is set to `False`. Objects can be selected from code by setting this property.

SelectedImage RT RW

Applies to: Node object of TreeView

Type: Picture object

Controls the image displayed when a Node object is selected. The Picture object can be obtained from the *LoadPicture* function, a ListImage object, or any other property or function that returns a Picture object.

SelectedItem RT RO

Applies to: DataCombo, DataList, DBCombo, DBList

Type: Variant

The SelectedItem property contains a reference to a DAO Bookmark object of the selected element of the list, which can be used to position a Recordset object to that record.

SelectedItem RT RO

Applies to: ImageCombo, ListView, TabStrip, TreeView

Type: Object

Returns a reference to the currently selected object in the control (i.e., to a ComboItem object for an ImageCombo control, a ListItem object for a ListView control, a Tab object for a TabStrip control, and a Node object for a TreeView control).

SelectionMode [DT] [RW]

Applies to: MSFlexGrid, MSHFlexGrid

Type: `SelectionModeSettings` enumeration

Controls the way that cells are selected in the control. Possible values are 0–flexSelectionFree to select any cells, 1–flexSelectionByRow to select complete rows only, or 2–flexSelectionByCol to select complete columns only.

SelectRange [DT] [RW]

Applies to: Slider

Type: Boolean

When set to the default value of `False`, the Slider control can represent only one value at a time, which is represented by the Value property. When set to `True`, in addition to the Value property, the slider can also represent a range of values, accessed through the SelStart and SelLength properties.

SelEnd, SelStart [RT] [RW]

Applies to: MonthView

Type: Date

These properties contain the first (SelStart) and the last (SelEnd) dates in the selected range of dates.

SelEndCol, SelStartCol [RT] [RW]

Applies to: Split object; DataGrid control

Type: Long integer

These properties define the boundary of the currently selected cells in a DataGrid control or its Split object. The cell to the left of the range is positioned at column SelStartCol. The cell to the right of the range is positioned at column SelEndCol.

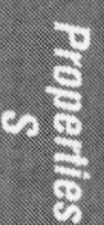

SelFontName [RT] [RW]

Applies to: RichTextBox

Type: String

When set to any nonnull value, the selected text is displayed in that font. When `Null`, the selected text is displayed using multiple fonts. Setting the property alters the font of the selected text. A `Null`, however, cannot be assigned in code; it is assigned by the runtime engine when the selected text is formatted using more than one font.

SelFontSize [RT] [RW]

Applies to: RichTextBox

Type: Integer (1–2,160)

When set to any nonnull value, the font size of the selected text is determined by the value of that property. When `Null`, the selected text is multiple sizes. A null value can be assigned only by the VB runtime engine, not through code; otherwise, setting the property alters the font size of the selected text.

SelHangingIndent, SelIndent, SelRightIndent [RT] [RW]

Applies to: RichTextBox

Type: Long integer

A nonnull value for any of these properties indicates how many twips the selected text is indented. A `Null` indicates that some but not all of the selected text is indented; a `Null` cannot be assigned by the application, but only by the runtime engine. Otherwise, setting the property to a value alters the indentation of the selected text.

SelImage [RT] [RW]

Applies to: ComboItem object of ImageCombo

Type: String or long integer

Contains the index or key to the ListImage object within the bound ImageList control for the ComboItem object.

SelIndent [RT] [RW]

Applies to: RichTextBox

See: SelHangingIndent

SelItalic [RT] [RW]

Applies to: RichTextBox

See: SelBold

SelLength, SelStart [RT] [RW]

Applies to: ComboBox, DataCombo, DataGrid, DBCombo, ImageCombo, MaskEdBox, RichTextBox, TextBox

Type: Long integer

The SelStart property represents the location of the first character that is selected in the text of the control, beginning with 0. The SelLength property returns the number of characters that are selected in the control. A value of 0 indicates that no text is selected. In the case of the ComboBox, DataCombo, DBCombo, and ImageCombo controls, the Style property must be set to `vbComboDropDown` or `vbComboSimple` for the SelStart and SelLength properties to return anything.

SelLength, SelStart

DT RW

Applies to: Slider

Type: Long integer

When a Slider's SelectRange property is set to `True`, SelStart and SelLength represent the lower end of that range and the size of the range. See the Slider Control entry in Chapter 5 for more information.

SelProtected

RT RW

Applies to: RichTextBox

See: SelBold

SelRightIndent

RT RW

Applies to: RichTextBox

See: SelHangingIndent

SelRTF

RT RW

Applies to: RichTextBox

Type: String

Returns or assigns the selected text in rich text format if it contains embedded formatting codes. Generally, if the property is used to retrieve the selected text, the string it returns is useful only with another RichTextBox control or an automation server (like Microsoft Word), because the formatting codes obscure the text when displayed in other controls. If rich text is assigned to the SelRTF property, it replaces the current selection.

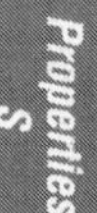

SelStart

RT RW

Applies to: Combo Box, DataCombo, DBCombo, DataGrid, ImageCombo, MaskEdBox, RichTextBox, Slider, TextBox

See: SelLength

SelStartCol RT RW

Applies to: Split object; DataGrid control

See: SelEndCol

SelStrikeThru RT RW

Applies to: RichTextBox

See: SelBold

SelTabCount RT RW

Applies to: RichTextBox

Type: Long integer

When the SelTabCount property is nonnull, it indicates the number of tab stops contained in the selected text. A value of 0 indicates that the selected text contains no tab stops, while a `Null` indicates that the selected text consists of multiple lines that have either a differing number of tab stops or tab stops in different positions.

Setting the property either increases or reduces the tab stops in the selected text to the number indicated by the property. If the number of tab stops is increased, any new tab stops are assigned a value of 0.0 until a position is explicitly assigned by setting the SelTabs property. If the number is decreased, the last elements of the SelTabs property array are removed.

SelTabs RT RW

Applies to: RichTextBox

Type: Single array

The SelTabs property array contains one value for each tab stop in the selected text. The tab stops are measured from the left margin in the Scale mode of the RichTextBox control's parent control. If the value of the SelTabCount property is `Null`, SelTabs is `Null` as well.

Tab stops can be set with the following code fragment, assuming that the tab stop positions have been stored in an array named `sngArray`:

```
Dim intCtr As Integer
For intCtr = 0 To RichTextBox1.SelTabCount - 1
   RichTextBox1.SelTabs(intCtr) = sngArray(intCtr)
Next
```

The positions of tab stops can be retrieved with the following code fragment:

```
If Not IsNull(RichTextBox1.SelTabCount) And _
       RichTextBox1.SelTabCount > 0 Then
```

```
    For intCtr = 0 To RichTextBox1.SelTabCount - 1
       sngTab(intCtr) = RichTextBox1.SelTabs(intCtr)
    Next
End If
```

SelText

Applies to: ComboBox, DataCombo, DBCombo, DataGrid, ImageCombo, RichTextBox, TextBox

Type: String

Contains the control's currently selected text. In the case of the RichTextBox control, the SelText property contains unformatted text.

SelUnderline

RT RW

Applies to: RichTextBox

See: SelBold

Separators

DT RW

Applies to: TabStrip

Type: Boolean

When set to `True`, separator lines are drawn between the buttons on a TabStrip with its Style property set to `tabButton` or `tabFlatButton`. When set to its default value of `False`, the separators do not appear.

SeriesCollection

RT RO

Applies to: Plot object of MSChart

Type: Collection

Returns a reference to a SeriesCollection collection, which contains information about all series displayed in the chart.

SeriesColumn

DT RW

Applies to: MSChart

Type: Integer

Contains the position of the column to use for the current series. If one column is referenced by more than one series, those series are stacked in that position.

SeriesMarker

RT RW

Applies to: Series object of MSChart

Type: SeriesMarker object

Contains a reference to a SeriesMarker object, which contains information about how to mark the current series on the chart.

SeriesType

DT RW

Applies to: Series object of MSChart; MSChart control

See: ChartType

Shadow

RT RO

Applies to: BackDrop object of MSChart

Type: Shadow object

Returns a reference to a Shadow object, which contains information about the appearance of any shadow for the BackDrop object's parent object.

Shape

DT RW

Applies to: Shape

Type: `ShapeConstants` enumeration

The Shape property represents the shape displayed in the Shape control, as follows:

Constant	*Value*	*Description*
`vbShapeRectangle`	0	The shape shown is a rectangle. This is the default value.
`vbShapeSquare`	1	The shape shown is a square.
`vbShapeOval`	2	The shape shown is an oval.
`vbShapeCircle`	3	The shape shown is a circle.
`vbShapeRoundedRectangle`	4	The shape shown is a rectangle with rounded corners.
`vbShapeRoundedSquare`	5	The shape shown is a square with rounded corners.

Shareable

DT RW

Applies to: MM

Type: Boolean

When set to `True`, the currently open multimedia device can be opened by other applications. When set to `False`, the device cannot be shared with other applications.

Show RT RW

Applies to: SeriesMarker object of MSChart

Type: Boolean

When set to `True`, the series markers will be displayed as normal. When set to its default value of `False`, the series markers are not displayed.

ShowGuideLine RT RW

Applies to: Series object of MSChart

Type: Boolean

When set to `True`, lines connect the data points in the series. When set to its default value of `False`, the lines are not displayed.

ShowInTaskbar DT RO

Applies to: Form object

Type: Boolean

When set to its default value of `True`, the form's caption and icon are shown in the taskbar (displayed by pressing ALT-Tab or ALT-Shift-Tab) and on the Windows Start menu bar. When set to `False`, the form is not represented in either of these places.

ShowLegend DT RW

Applies to: MSChart

Type: Boolean

When set to `True`, the legend appears on the chart. When set to its default value of `False`, the legend is not visible.

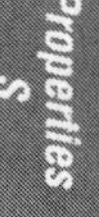

ShowLine RT RW

Applies to: Series object of MSChart

Type: Boolean

When set to its default value of `True`, lines connect the data points in the series. When set to `False`, the lines are not displayed.

ShowTips [DT] [RO]

Applies to: StatusBar, TabStrip, Toolbar

Type: Boolean

When set to its default value of `True`, objects contained by the control (in particular, Panel objects on the StatusBar control, Tab objects on the TabStrip control, and Button objects on the Toolbar control) display the contents of their ToolTipText property when the user places and leaves the cursor over the object. When set to `False`, the object will not show the text. Note that the ShowTips property does not affect the display of tooltip text belonging to any controls (such as a CommandButton control) contained by the StatusBar, TabStrip, or Toolbar controls.

ShowToday [DT] [RW]

Applies to: MonthView

Type: Boolean

When set to the default value of `True`, today's date appears on the MonthView control. When set to `False`, today's date does not appear on the control.

ShowWeekNumbers [DT] [RW]

Applies to: MonthView

Type: Boolean

When set to `True`, the week numbers appear to the left of each week on the calendar. When set to its default value of `False`, the week numbers do not appear.

Silent [DT] [RW]

Applies to: MM

Type: Boolean

When set to `True`, a playing device will generate no sound. When set to the default value of `False`, if the device includes sound, it will play.

SimpleText [DT] [RW]

Applies to: StatusBar

Type: String

When the StatusBar control's Style property is set to `sbrSimple`, the contents of the SimpleText property are displayed on the StatusBar control. If the StatusBar control's Style property is set to `sbrNormal`, an individual panel's text is defined by the Panel object's Text property if its Style property is set to `sbrText`.

SingleSel

DT RW

Applies to: TreeView

Type: Boolean

When set to `True`, items selected are automatically expanded. When set to its default value of `False`, items must be expanded manually.

Size

RT RW

Applies to: Marker and VtFont objects of MSChart

Type: Single

Defines the size, in points, of the chart element.

Size

DT RW

Applies to: Split object of DataGrid

Type: Long integer

Determines the size of the Split object in units based on its SizeMode property.

SizeMode

DT RW

Applies to: OLE

Type: `OLEContainerConstants` enumeration

The OLE object contained in an OLE control is sized according to the size of the OLE control as follows:

Constant	*Value*	*Description*
`vbOLESizeClip`	0	The OLE object is clipped to the size of the OLE control. This is the default value.
`vbOLESizeStretch`	1	The OLE object is stretched up or down to the size of the OLE control. In some cases, this will make the OLE object disproportional.
`vbOLESizeAutoSize`	2	The OLE control is resized to the size of the OLE object.
`vbOLESizeZoom`	3	The OLE object is stretched up or down to the size of the OLE control. However, the object is stretched proportionally.

Applies to: Split object of DataGrid

Type: `SplitSizeModeConstants` enumeration

The SizeMode property of the Split, along with the Size property, controls the actual size of the Split as follows:

Constant	*Value*	*Description*
`dbgScalable`	0	The Size property of each Split object is considered as a percentage of the sum of the Size properties of all the Splits.
`dbgExact`	1	The Size property of the Split is the exact size of the Split as defined by the ScaleMode of the DataGrid's parent.
`dbgNumberOfColumns`	2	The Size property represents the number of columns to display in the Split object. The columns currently displayed set the actual size of the Split object.

SmallChange DT RW

Applies to: FlatScrollBar, HScrollBar, Slider, VScrollBar

See: LargeChange

SmallIcon DT RW

Applies to: ListItem object

See: Icon

SmallIcons DT RW

Applies to: ListView

See: ColumnHeaderIcons

SocketHandle RT RO

Applies to: Winsock

Type: Long integer

Returns a handle to the TCP/IP communications socket for use with API calls.

Sort RT RW

Applies to: MSFlexGrid, MSHFlexGrid

Type: `SortSettings` enumeration

Controls how data in the control is sorted. Possible values are:

Constant	*Value*	*Description*
`flexSortNone`	0	The data is not sorted.
`flexSortGeneric-Ascending`	1	Ascending order based on whether the data appears to be string or numeric.
`flexSortGeneric-Descending`	2	Descending order based on whether the data appears to be string or numeric.
`flexSortNumeric-Ascending`	3	Ascending order based on numeric data.
`flexSortNumeric-Descending`	4	Descending order based on numeric data.
`flexSortString-NoCaseAscending`	5	Ascending order based on string data ignoring case.
`flexSortString-NoCaseDescending`	6	Descending order based on string data ignoring case.
`flexSortString-Ascending`	7	Ascending order based on string data.
`flexSortString-Descending`	8	Descending order based on string data.
`flexSortCustom`	9	The data is sorted using the Compare event.

Sort

RT RW

Applies to: Plot object of MSChart

Type: `VtSortType` enumeration

Controls how data in a pie chart is sorted. The following table explains the possible values for the Sort property:

Constant	*Value*	*Description*
`VtSortTypeNone`	0	The data is not sorted.
`VtSortTypeAscending`	1	Data is drawn from the smallest slice to the largest slice.
`VtSortTypeDescending`	2	Data is drawn from the largest slice to the smallest slice.

Sort

RT RW

Applies to: Recordset objects of ADO DC and Data controls

Type: String

Contains an `SQL ORDER BY` clause used to sort the data in the recordset. The clause should not include the string `ORDER BY`.

Sorted

DT RW

Applies to: Node object of TreeView; ComboBox, ListBox, ListView and TreeView controls

Type: Boolean

When the Sorted property is set to `True`, the contents of the control are sorted. In the case of the ComboBox and ListBox controls, the elements of the list are sorted alphabetically. In the case of the ListView control, the ListItem objects are sorted as defined by the ListView control's SortKey property. In the TreeView control, only Node objects at the same level are sorted. For Node items, child nodes are sorted.

SortKey

DT RW

Applies to: ListView

Type: Integer

When the SortKey property is set to its default value of 0, ListItem objects in the ListView control are sorted alphabetically by their Text properties. When set to a value other than 0, the objects are sorted by that numbered subitem. If the ListView control's Sorted property is set to `False`, the ListItem objects are not sorted at all.

SortOrder

Applies to: ListView

Type: `ListSortOrderConstants` enumeration

When the ListView object's Sorted property is `True` and the SortKey property is set to 0 or a valid SubItem index, the ListItems are sorted as follows:

Constant	*Value*	*Description*
`lvwAscending`	0	From lowest to highest
`lvwDescending`	1	From highest to lowest

Source

RT RW

Applies to: Recordset object of ADO DC

Type: Variant

Contains an SQL statement, a table name, a stored procedure name, or a Command object that defines the source of the recordset object.

SourceDoc, SourceItem DT RW

Applies to: OLE

Type: String

These properties are in VB6 for backward compatibility with previous versions only. Their functionality has been replaced by the CreateEmbed and CreateLink methods.

SpaceColor RT RO

Applies to: Frame object of MSChart

Type: VtColor object

Returns a reference to a VtColor object, which controls the color that appears between the two lines when double frames are used.

Split RT RW

Applies to: DataGrid

Type: Integer

Contains the index of the currently selected Split object.

Splits RT RO

Applies to: DataGrid

Type: Collection

Returns a reference to the Splits collection. The Splits collection object itself supports the Add, Count, and Item properties, as well as the Remove method.

Stacking DT RW

Applies to: MSChart

Type: Boolean

When set to `True`, all series in the chart are stacked. When set to its default value of `False`, all series are not stacked.

StackOrder RT RW

Applies to: SeriesPosition object of MSChart

Type: Integer

Controls the order in which stacked series appear. Lower values appear below higher values in the stack.

Standing RT RW

Applies to: Label object of MSChart

Type: Boolean

When set to `True`, axis labels are displayed vertically on the chart. When set to its default value of `False`, axis labels are displayed horizontally.

StartingAngle RT RW

Applies to: Plot object of MSChart

Type: Single

Contains the angle (in units defined by the Plot Object's AngleUnit property and a direction controlled by the Clockwise property) at which the first slice of a pie chart will be drawn. A value of 0 represents the three o'clock position.

StartOfWeek DT RW

Applies to: MonthView

Type: `DayConstants` enumeration

Indicates the day of the week that is considered to be the first day of the week for the displayed calendar. Possible values are 1–mvwSunday, 2–mvwMonday, 3–mvwTuesday, 4–mvwWednesday, 5–mvwThursday, 6–mvwFriday, or 7–mvwSaturday.

StartUpPosition DT RW

Applies to: Form and MDIForm objects

Type: `StartupPositionConstants` enumeration

When a form or MDI form is first displayed after it is loaded, the StartUpPosition property controls its initial placement as follows:

Constant	*Value*	*Description*
`vbStartUpManual`	0	The object is placed as defined by its Left and Top properties.
`vbStartUpOwner`	1	The object is centered on its parent object. This applies only to Form objects with the MDIChild property set to `True`.

Constant	*Value*	*Description*
vbStartUpScreen	2	The object is centered on the screen.
vbStartUpWindows-Default	3	The object is placed on the screen where the Windows system chooses to place it. This is the default.

State

RT RO

Applies to: Winsock

Type: StateConstants enumeration

Returns the state of the socket. Possible values are:

Constant	*Value*	*Description*
sckClosed	0	The socket is closed.
sckOpen	1	The socket is open.
sckListening	2	The socket is listening.
sckConnectionPending	3	A connection is pending for the socket.
sckResolvingHost	4	The hostname is being resolved.
sckHostResolved	5	The hostname has been resolved.
sckConnecting	6	The socket is connecting.
sckConnected	7	The socket is connected.
sckClosing	8	The socket is closing.
sckError	9	There has been an error.

StatLine

RT RO

Applies to: Series object of MSChart

Type: StatLine object

Returns a reference to a StatLine object, which contains information about the statistical lines drawn on the chart.

StayInSync

RT RW

Applies to: Recordset object of ADO DC

Type: Boolean

When set to `True`, parent records stay synchronized with child records when the record pointer is moved. When set to `False`, when the child is changed in a hierarchical recordset, the parent is not changed automatically.

StepEnabled [DT] [RW]

Applies to: MM

See: BackEnabled

StepVisible [DT] [RW]

Applies to: MM

See: BackVisible

StillExecuting [RT] [RO]

Applies to: Inet control

Type: Boolean

Returns `True` if the last command is still executing; otherwise, returns `False`.

StopEnabled [DT] [RW]

Applies to: MM

See: BackEnabled

StopVisible [DT] [RW]

Applies to: MM

See: BackVisible

Stretch [DT] [RW]

Applies to: Image

Type: Boolean

When set to its default value of `False`, the Image control resizes to the size of the contained Picture object. When set to `True`, the Picture object resizes to the size of the Image control.

Style [DT] [RW]

Applies to: Band object of CoolBar

Type: `BandStyleConstants` enumeration

When set to the default value of 0–cc3BandNormal, the band can be resized. When set to 1–cc3BandFixedSize, the band cannot be resized.

Style

RT RW

Applies to: Brush, Fill, Frame, Marker, Pen, Shadow, Tick, VtFont, and Weighting objects of MSChart

Type: Enumeration (assorted)

Each of these Style properties can contain one of the values in the following tables.

For the Brush Object

VtBrushStyle Constant	*Value*	*Description*
`VtBrushStyleNull`	0	No fill
`VtBrushStyleSolid`	1	A solid fill
`VtBrushStylePattern`	2	A patterned fill based on the Brush object's Index property
`VtBrushStyleHatched`	3	A hatched fill based on the Brush object's Index property

For the Fill Object

VtFillStyle Constant	*Value*	*Description*
`VtFillStyleNull`	0	No fill
`VtFillStyleBrush`	1	A solid fill

For the Frame Object

VtFrameStyle Constant	*Value*	*Description*
`VtFrameStyleNull`	0	No frame
`VtFrameStyleSingleLine`	1	A single frame
`VtFrameStyleDoubleLine`	2	A double frame with both lines equal
`VtFrameStyleThickInner`	3	A double frame with the inner line thicker
`VtFrameStyleThickOuter`	4	A double frame with the outer line thicker

For the Marker Object

VtMarkerStyle Constant	*Value*	*Description*
`VtMarkerStyleNull`	0	No marker
`VtMarkerStyleDash`	1	A dash
`VtMarkerStylePlus`	2	A plus sign
`VtMarkerStyleX`	3	An X
`VtMarkerStyleStar`	4	A star shape

VtMarkerStyle Constant	*Value*	*Description*
VtMarkerStyleCircle	5	A circle
VtMarkerStyleSquare	6	A square
VtMarkerStyleDiamond	7	A diamond shape
VtMarkerStyleUp-Triangle	8	A triangle with the point up
VtMarkerStyleDown-Triangle	9	A triangle with the point down
VtMarkerStyleFilled-Circle	10	A filled circle
VtMarkerStyleFilled-Square	11	A filled square
VtMarkerStyleFilled-Diamond	12	A filled diamond shape
VtMarkerStyleFilledUp-Triangle	13	A filled triangle with the point up
VtMarkerStyleFilled-DownTriangle	14	A filled triangle with the point down
VtMarkerStyle3dBall	15	A shaded, 3-D ball

For the Pen Object

VtPenStyle Constant	*Value*	*Description*
VtPenStyleNull	0	No line
VtPenStyleSolid	1	A solid line
VtPenStyleDashed	2	A dashed line
VtPenStyleDotted	3	A dotted line
VtPenStyleDashDot	4	A line composed of alternating dashes and dots
VtPenStyleDashDotDot	5	A line composed of a repeating pattern of one dash followed by two dots
VtPenStyleDitted	6	A ditted line
VtPenStyleDashDit	7	A line composed of alternating dashes and dits
VtPenStyleDashDitDit	8	A line composed of a repeating pattern of one dash followed by two dits

For the Shadow Object

VtShadowStyle Constant	*Value*	*Description*
VtShadowStyleNull	0	No shadow
VtShadowStyleDrop	1	A drop shadow

For the Tick Object

VtChAxisTickStyle Constant	Value	Description
VtChAxisTickStyleNone	0	No ticks
VtChAxisTickStyleCenter	1	Centered ticks
VtChAxisTickStyleInside	2	Tick marks inside the axis
VtChAxisTickStyleOutside	3	Tick marks outside the axis

For the VtFont Object (Can Be Combined)

VtFontStyle Constant	Value	Description
VtFontStyleBold	1	The text is bolded.
VtFontStyleItalic	2	The text is italicized.
VtFontStyleOutline	4	The text's outline is drawn unfilled.

For the Weighting Object

VtChPieWeightStyle Constant	Value	Description
VtChPieWeightStyleArea	0	The weighting affects the pie chart's area.
VtChPieWeightStyle-Diameter	1	The weighting affects the pie chart's diameter.

Style

Applies to: Button object of Toolbar, Panel object of StatusBar; StatusBar, TabStrip, Toolbar, and TreeView controls DT RW

Type: Enumeration

The Style property controls the basic look and functionality of the object or control as follows:

When Used with a Button Object

ButtonStyleConstants	Value	Description
tbrDefault	0	The button acts as a regular button. This is the default value.
tbrCheck	1	The button can be checked or unchecked.
tbrButtonGroup	2	All buttons between two separators or one separator and the end of the Toolbar control form a button group. Only one button in the button group can be pressed at any time. When one is pressed, any other that was pressed is released.

Properties S

ButtonStyleConstants	*Value*	*Description*
`tbrSeparator`	3	The button object is used only to separate button groups.
`tbrPlaceHolder`	4	The button object is similar to a separator, but its width is set by the Width property.

When Used with a Panel Object

PanelStyleConstants	*Value*	*Description*
`sbrText`	0	The Panel object shows the contents of the Text property. This is the default value.
`sbrCaps`	1	The Panel object shows the current state of the Caps Lock key.
`sbrNum`	2	The Panel object shows the current state of the Num Lock key.
`sbrIns`	3	The Panel object shows whether Windows is in Insert mode.
`sbrScrl`	4	The Panel object shows the current state of the Scroll Lock key.
`sbrTime`	5	The Panel object shows the current time.
`sbrDate`	6	The Panel object shows the current date.
`sbrKana`	7	The Panel object shows the word "KANA" if the Scroll Lock key is on.

When Used with a StatusBar Control

SbarStyleConstants	*Value*	*Description*
`sbrNormal`	0	The StatusBar control can display multiple panels. This is the default value.
`sbrSimple`	1	The StatusBar control shows only the contents of the SimpleText property. There are no Panel objects.

When Used with a TabStrip Control

TabStyleConstants	*Value*	*Description*
`tabTabs`	0	The tabs appear to be dividers as in a notebook. This is the default value.
`tabButtons`	1	The tabs appear to be command buttons.

When Used with a Toolbar Control

ToolbarStyleConstants	*Value*	*Description*
`tbrStandard`	0	The control displays standard, raised buttons.
`tbrFlat`	1	The control displays flat buttons.

When Used with a TreeView Control

TreeStyleConstants	*Value*	*Description*
`tvwTextOnly`	0	The TreeView displays the Node objects' Text properties only.
`tvwPictureText`	1	The TreeView displays the Node objects' Text and Image properties only.
`tvwPlusMinusText`	2	The TreeView displays the Node objects' Text properties and a plus or minus icon only.
`tvwPlusPicture-Text`	3	The TreeView displays the Node objects' Text and Image properties and a plus or minus icon only.
`tvwTreelinesText`	4	The TreeView displays the Node objects' Text properties connected by lines only.
`tvwTreelines-PictureText`	5	The TreeView displays the Node objects' Text and Image properties connected by lines only.
`tvwTreelines-PlusMinusText`	6	The TreeView displays the Node objects' Text properties and a plus or minus icon connected by lines only.
`tvwTreelinesPlus-MinusPictureText`	7	The TreeView displays the Node objects' Text and Image properties and a plus or minus icon connected by lines. This is the default value.

Applies to: CheckBox, ComboBox, CommandButton, DataCombo, DBCombo, ListBox, Option Button DT RO

Type: Enumeration

The Style property controls the basic look and functionality of the object or control as shown in the following tables.

When Used with a CheckBox, CommandButton, or Option Button Control

ButtonConstants	*Value*	*Description*
`vbButtonStandard`	0	Windows controls any graphics associated with the control. This is the default value.
`vbButtonGraphical`	1	The Picture property and other picture-related properties control the appearance of the control.

When Used with a ComboBox or DBCombo Object

ComboBoxConstants	*Value*	*Description*
`vbComboDropdown`	0	The control consists of a text box and a drop-down list. Items can be entered into the text box that are not present in the list. This is the default value.
`vbComboSimple`	1	The control consists of a text box and an already dropped-down list that cannot be closed. Items that are not present in the list can be entered into the text box.
`vbComboDropdown-List`	2	The control consists of a drop-down list from which a value must be chosen.

When Used with a ListBox Control

ListBoxConstants	*Value*	*Description*
`VbListBoxStandard`	0	A list of elements is displayed in the list box. This is the default value.
`VbListBoxCheckbox`	1	A list of checkboxes is displayed in the list box.

Style

RT RW

Applies to: StatLine object of MSChart

Type: Array of `VtPenStyle` enumeration

The Style array has the following elements:

VtChStats Constant	*Value*	*Description*
`VtChStatsMinimum`	1	The statistical line for the minimum value
`VtChStatsMaximum`	2	The statistical line for the maximum value
`VtChStatsMean`	4	The statistical line for the mean
`VtChStatsStdDev`	8	The statistical line for the standard deviation
`VtChStatsRegres-sion`	16	The statistical line for the regression trend

Each element contains one of the following values, which control the appearance of that statistical line:

VtPenStyle Constant	*Value*	*Description*
`VtPenStyleNull`	0	No line
`VtPenStyleSolid`	1	A solid line
`VtPenStyleDashed`	2	A dashed line
`VtPenStyleDotted`	3	A dotted line

VtPenStyle Constant	*Value*	*Description*
VtPenStyleDashDot	4	A line composed of alternating dashes and dots
VtPenStyleDash-DotDot	5	A line composed of a repeating pattern of one dash followed by two dots
VtPenStyleDitted	6	A ditted line
VtPenStyleDashDit	7	A line composed of alternating dashes and dits
VtPenStyleDash-DitDit	8	A line composed of a repeating pattern of one dash followed by two dits

SubItemIndex RT RW

Applies to: ColumnHeader object

Type: Integer

Represents the index of the SubItem to which that ColumnHeader belongs. The first ColumnHeader belongs to the Text property, and its SubItemIndex property returns 0.

SubItems RT RW

Applies to: ListItem object

Type: String array

When the ListView control's View property is set to `lvwReport`, multiple columns can appear on the control. Each of these columns represents a SubItem of the ListItem object. See the ListView Control entry in Chapter 5 for more information.

SubPlotLabelPosition RT RW

Applies to: Plot object of MSChart

Type: `VtChSubPlotLabelLocationType` enumeration

Controls the location of labels in a pie chart as follows:

VtChSubPlotLabelLocationType	*Value*	*Description*
VtChSubPlotLabelLocationTypeNone	0	No labels are displayed.
VtChSubPlotLabelLocationTypeAbove	1	Labels appear above the slices.
VtChSubPlotLabelLocationTypeBelow	2	Labels appear below the slices.
VtChSubPlotLabelLocationTypeCenter	3	Labels are centered over the slices.

SyncBuddy DT RW

Applies to: UpDown

Type: Boolean

When set to `True`, changing the Value property in the UpDown control also updates the value of the property bound to the BuddyProperty property, and changing the property in the bound control updates the Value property in the UpDown control. When set to its default value of `False`, the properties are not synchronized.

TabAcrossSplits DT RW

Applies to: DataGrid

Type: Boolean

When the TabAcrossSplits property is set to the default value of `False`, the effect of the user pressing the Tab key when on a split is determined by the TabAction property. When set to `True`, the tab key will move to the next split until the last split is reached, at which time it will act according to the TabAction property.

TabAction DT RW

Applies to: DataGrid

Type: Enumeration

Controls how the DataGrid control reacts when the user presses the Tab key, as follows:

TabActionConstants	*Value*	*Description*
`dbgControlNavigation`	0	The focus moves through the parent's tab order. This is the default value.
`dbgColumnNavigation`	1	The focus moves to the next or previous column in the DataGrid control. After the first or last column, the focus moves through the parent's tab order.
`dbgGridNavigation`	2	The focus moves to the next or previous column in the DataGrid control. After the first or last column, the focus moves as defined by the WrapCellPointer property.

TabFixedHeight, TabFixedWidth DT RW

Applies to: TabStrip

Type: Long integer

The size of the tab portion of all Tab objects contained in a TabStrip control is set by these properties. The TabFixedWidth property is used only if the TabStrip control's TabWidthStyle property is set to `tabFixed`.

TabIndex [DT] [RW]

Applies to: All controls with a visual interface

Type: Integer

Each control that is placed onto a form is automatically assigned the next available TabIndex. This controls the order in which the user moves through the controls on the form with the Tab key. When the TabIndex property of one control is changed either at design time or at runtime, the other TabIndex properties on the Form object are renumbered to accommodate the new TabIndex and to fill in the gap left by the old value. When a control that cannot receive the focus (like the Label control or the Frame control) is assigned a TabIndex, anytime that control is selected for the focus by use of an access key or by tabbing through the controls, the focus is passed to the next control in the tab order.

TabMinWidth [DT] [RW]

Applies to: TabStrip

Type: Single

Defines the minimum width of a Tab object contained by the TabStrip control. The value is specified in units based on the ScaleMode of the form or container.

Tabs [RT] [RO]

Applies to: TabStrip

Type: Collection

Returns a reference to the Tabs collection. The Tabs collection's members include the Count and Item properties and the Add, Clear, and Remove methods.

TabStop [DT] [RW]

Applies to: All controls that can receive the focus

Type: Boolean

When the TabStop property is set to `True`, the control takes its place in the tab order. When set to `False`, the control is skipped in the tab order and can be accessed only by access key or by mouse.

TabStyle

DT RW

Applies to: TabStrip

Type: `TabSelStyleConstants` enumeration

When set to 1–tabTabOpposite, unselected tabs appear on the opposite side of the TabStrip control. When set to the default value of 0–tabTabStandard, the unselected tabs remain on the same side.

TabWidthStyle

DT RW

Applies to: TabStrip

Type: `TabWidthStyleConstants` enumeration

The TabWidthStyle property controls how Tab objects on a TabStrip are arranged, as follows:

TabWidthStyleConstants	*Value*	*Description*
`tabJustified`	0	The Tab objects' widths are adjusted to accommodate the Text properties, if possible. If there is additional space, it is split between the Tab objects to fill in the entire row. This is the default value.
`tabNonJustified`	1	The Tab objects' widths are adjusted to accommodate the Text properties, if possible.
`tabFixed`	2	All tabs are sized based on the TabFixedWidth property of the TabStrip control.

Tag

DT RW

Applies to: All controls and objects

Type: String

The Tag property is not used by Visual Basic. It is present for programs to store any information beyond what the other properties can store.

The Tag property should not be overused, because of the performance hit when setting and retrieving data to and from it.

Text

DT RW

Applies to: Column, ColumnHeader, ListItem, and Node objects; ComboBox, DBCombo, DataGrid, DBList, ListBox, RichTextBox, and TextBox controls

Type: String

For the ComboBox, DBCombo, DBList, and ListBox controls, the Text property contains the text of the currently selected element of the list. For all other controls, the Text property contains the string contents of the control or object.

TextAlignment

DT RW

Applies to: Toolbar

Type: `TextAlignConstants` enumeration

When set to the default value of 0–tbrTextAlignBottom, text is aligned below the button. When set to 1–tbrTextAlignRight, the text appears to the right of the button.

TextArray

RT RW

Applies to: MSFlexGrid, MSHFlexGrid

Type: Array of string

The property array contains one element for every cell in the control. An individual cell's index is derived by multiplying the row times the column and then adding the column to that value. Each element contains the text for that cell.

TextBackground

DT RW

Applies to: ListView

Type: `ListTextBackgroundConstants` enumeration

When set to the default value of 0–lvwTransparent, the background of the ListView control shows through the areas around the letters of the text. When set to 1–lvwOpaque, the areas around the letters are colored based on the control's BackgroundColor property.

TextLayout

RT RO

Applies to: AxisTitle, DataPointLabel, Label, Legend, and Title objects of MSChart

Type: TextLayout object

Returns a reference to a TextLayout object, which contains information about the text's location, alignment, and orientation.

TextLength

RT RW

Applies to: AxisTitle, DataPointLabel, and Title objects of MSChart

Type: Integer

Returns or sets the number of characters in the text contained by the object.

TextLengthType

DT RW

Applies to: MSChart

Type: `VtTextLengthType` enumeration

When set to the default value of 0–VtTextLengthTypeVirtual, the text displayed on the MSChart control is optimized for printing. When set to 1–VtTextLengthType-Device, the text is optimized for viewing on the screen.

TextMatrix

RT RW

Applies to: MSFlexGrid, MSHFlexGrid

Type: Array of string

Each element of this two-dimensional property array contains the text for the specified row and column, which are the two dimensions.

TextPosition

DT RW

Applies to: Slider

Type: `TextPositionConstants` enumeration

When set to the default value of 0–sldAboveLeft, text is displayed above (when the slider is being viewed horizontally) or to the left (when the slider is being viewed vertically). When set to 1–sldBelowRight, the text appears below or to the right of the control.

TextRTF

RT RW

Applies to: RichTextBox

Type: String

Contains the entire contents of the control as a string, including all rich text formatting strings.

TextStyle, TextStyleBand, TextStyleFixed, TextStyleHeader DT RW

Applies to: MSFlexGrid, MSHFlexGrid

Type: `TextStyleSettings` enumeration

Controls the 3-D appearance of the text in the control (TextStyle), bands (TextStyleBand), fixed cells (TextStyleFixed), and header cells (TextStyleHeader). Possible values are 0–flexTextFlat for flat text, 1–flexTextRaised for raised text, 2–flexTextInset for inset text, 3–flexTextRaisedLight for lightly raised text, or 4–flexTextInsetLight for lightly inset text.

Tick RT RO

Applies to: Axis object of MSChart

Type: Tick object

Returns a reference to a Tick object, which defines how to display tick marks on the axis.

TickFrequency DT RW

Applies to: Slider

Type: Long integer

Tick marks appear on the Slider control based on the difference between the Min and Max properties along with the TickFrequency property. When set to the default value of 1, ticks appear for every value represented on the Slider control. As the value of the TickFrequency property increases, the number of tick marks decreases.

TickStyle DT RW

Applies to: Slider

Type: Enumeration

Tick marks appear on the Slider control as follows:

TickStyleConstants	*Value*	*Description*
`sldBottomRight` (default)	0	Tick marks appear along the bottom of the Slider control if its Style property is set to `sldHorizontal`. Otherwise, they appear along the right.
`sldTopLeft` (default)	1	Tick marks appear along the top of the Slider control if its Style property is set to `sldHorizontal`. Otherwise, they appear along the left.

TickStyleConstants	*Value*	*Description*
`sldBoth`	2	Tick marks appear along both sides of the Slider control.
`sldNoTicks`	3	There are no tick marks.

TimeFormat

RT **RW**

Applies to: MM

Type: `FormatConstants` enumeration

Specifies how time is represented by the control's other properties. It can be set to 0–mciFormatMilliseconds (milliseconds), 1–mciFormatHms (hours, minutes, and seconds), 2–mciFormatMsf (minutes, seconds, and frames), 3–mciFormatFrames (frames), 4–mciFormatSmpte24 (hours, minutes, seconds, and 24/second frames), 5–mciFormatSmpte25 (hours, minutes, seconds, and 25/second frames), 6–mciFormatSmpte30 (hours, minutes, seconds, and 30/second frames), 7–mciFormatSmpte30Drop (hours, minutes, seconds, and 30/second drop-frames), 8–mciFormatBytes (bytes), 9–mciFormatSamples (samples), 10–mciFormatTmsf (tracks, minutes, seconds, and frames). The TimeFormats that contain multiple items store them as 4-byte numbers ordered from least to most significant byte. If there are fewer than four elements, the most significant byte(s) are unused.

Title

RT **RO**

Applies to: MSChart

Type: Title object

Returns a reference to a Title object, which contains information about how to display the chart title.

TitleBackColor, TitleForeColor

DT **RW**

Applies to: MonthView

See: MonthBackColor

TitleText

DT **RW**

Applies to: MSChart

See: FootnoteText

To

RT **RW**

Applies to: MM

See: From

ToolTipText

DT RW

Applies to: All controls and objects with a visual interface except Form object and MDIForm object

Type: String

When the ToolTipText property is populated, objects and controls will display the contents of their ToolTipText property when the user places and leaves the cursor over the object.

Top

DT RW

Applies to: Form, MDIForm, Column, and Tab objects; all controls with a visual interface

See: Height

ToPage

DT RW

Applies to: CommonDialog

See: FromPage

TopIndex

RT RW

Applies to: ComboBox, ListBox

Type: Long integer

Represents the index of the top element currently displayed in the control. By setting the TopIndex property to a new value, you can scroll the list to that element.

TopRow

RT RW

Applies to: MSFlexGrid, MSHFlexGrid

See: LeftCol

Track, TrackLength, TrackPosition

RT RO

Applies to: MM

Type: Long integer

These properties return the current track (Track), the length of the current track (TrackLength), and the current position within that track (TrackPosition), all using the current TimeFormat value.

Tracks

RT RO

Applies to: MM

Type: Long integer

Returns the number of tracks on the currently opened multimedia device.

TrailingForeColor

DT RW

Applies to: MonthView

See: MonthBackColor

Type

RT RW

Applies to: AxisScale object of MSChart

Type: `VtChScaleType` enumeration

Controls the type of scale used for the axis. Possible values are 0–VtChScaleType-Linear for a standard, linear axis, 1–VtChScaleTypeLogarithmic for a logarithmic axis based on the AxisScale object's LogBase property, or 2–VtChScaleTypePercent for a percent axis.

Type

RT RO

Applies to: Recordset object of Data control

Type: `RecordsetTypeEnum` enumeration

Returns the type of an open recordset. Possible values are 1–dbOpenTable for a table-type recordset, 2–dbOpenDynaset for a dynaset-type recordset, 4–dbOpenSnapshot for an editable nondynamic recordset, 8–dbOpenForwardOnly for a recordset that can only process MoveNext methods for record pointer movement, or 16–dbOpenDynamic for a dynamic ODBC recordset.

TypeByChartType

RT RO

Applies to: Series object of MSChart

Type: Array of `VtChSeriesType` enumeration

Each element corresponds to one of the `VtChChartType` enumeration values and contains the series type for that chart type. Valid chart types are as follows:

Constant	*Value*	*Description*
`VtChChartType3dBar`	0	3-D bar chart
`VtChChartType2dBar`	1	2-D bar chart

Constant	Value	Description
`VtChChartType3dLine`	2	3-D line chart
`VtChChartType2dLine`	3	2-D line chart
`VtChChartType3dArea`	4	3-D area chart
`VtChChartType2dArea`	5	2-D area chart
`VtChChartType3dStep`	6	3-D step chart
`VtChChartType2dStep`	7	2-D step chart
`VtChChartType3dCombination`	8	3-D combination chart (one or more combined charts)
`VtChChartType2dCombination`	9	2-D combination chart (one or more combined charts)
`VtChChartType2dPie`	14	Pie chart
`VtChChartType2dXY`	16	X/Y chart

Values for the series type are as follows:

Constant	Value	Description
`VtChSeriesTypeDefault`	-1	The default series type
`VtChSeriesType3dBar`	0	3-D bar series
`VtChSeriesType2dBar`	1	2-D bar series
`VtChSeriesType3dLine`	5	3-D line series
`VtChSeriesType2dLine`	6	2-D line series
`VtChSeriesType3dArea`	7	3-D area series
`VtChSeriesType3dStep`	9	3-D step series
`VtChSeriesType2dStep`	10	2-D step series
`VtChSeriesType2dXY`	11	X/Y series
`VtChSeriesType2dPie`	24	Pie series

UBound

Applies to: Menu control array, all control arrays

See: LBound

UniformAxis

RT RW

Applies to: Plot object of MSChart

Type: Boolean

When set to `False`, the unit scale for all series is not uniform. When set to its default value of `True`, the unit scale for all series is uniform.

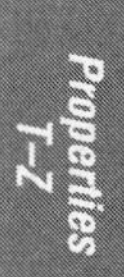

Updatable RT RO

Applies to: Database and Recordset objects of Data control

Type: Boolean

Returns `False` if the object can't be updated (is read-only); otherwise, returns `True`.

UpdateInterval DT RW

Applies to: MM

Type: Integer

Defines the frequency in milliseconds that the StatusUpdate event is fired. If the UpdateInterval is set to 0, the StatusUpdate event is not fired.

UpdateOptions DT RW

Applies to: OLE

Type: `OLEContainerConstants` enumeration

When data linked to the OLE object in an OLE control is changed, the object is updated as follows:

Constant	*Value*	*Description*
`vbOLEAutomatic`	0	The OLE object is changed when linked data is changed. This is the default value.
`vbOLEFrozen`	1	The OLE object is updated only when the linked data is actually saved by the host application.
`vbOLEManual`	2	The OLE object is updated only when the Update method is called.

UpDown DT RW

Applies to: DTPicker

Type: Boolean

When set to `True`, arrows appear on the "closed up" control to allow scrolling through data. When set to the default value, `False`, the arrows do not appear.

URL DT RW

Applies to: Inet control

Type: String

Contains the URL that will be used by the control with the Execute and OpenURL methods.

UseCoolbarColors, UseCoolbarPicture DT RW

Applies to: Band object of CoolBar

Type: Boolean

When set to its default value of `True`, the Band object uses the same picture (UseCoolbarPicture) or foreground and background colors (UseCoolbarColors) as its parent CoolBar control. When set to `False`, the Band object uses its own settings.

UseMaskColor DT RW

Applies to: CheckBox, CommandButton, ImageList, Option Button

Type: Boolean

When set to `True`, parts of the bound Picture object that match the color of the MaskColor property appear transparent. When set to the default value of `False`, the MaskColor property is ignored and none of the image is transparent.

UseMnemonic DT RW

Applies to: Label

Type: Boolean

When set to its default value of `True`, the first character in the Caption property that follows the first ampersand (&) appears underlined and becomes the access key for the control. When set to `False`, ampersands appear as any other character.

UserName DT RW

Applies to: ADO DC and Inet controls

See: Password

UsesWindows RT RO

Applies to: MM

See: hWndDisplay

Value DT RW

Applies to: Button object; CheckBox control

Type: Enumeration

Returns the current value of the control or object as shown in the following tables.

When Used with a Button Object

ValueConstants	*Value*	*Description*
`tbrUnPressed`	0	The button is not pressed.
`tbrPressed`	1	The button object is pressed.

When Used with a CheckBox Control

CheckBoxConstants	*Value*	*Description*
`vbUnchecked`	0	The check box is currently checked.
`vbChecked`	1	The check box is currently unchecked.
`vbGrayed`	2	The check box is currently neither checked nor unchecked. It appears gray.

Value DT RW

Applies to: CommandButton, Option Button

Type: Boolean

When an OptionButton is selected in its option group, its Value property is set to `True`. Otherwise, it is set to `False`. When the CommandButton control is clicked, its Value property changes from `False` to `True` and then back to `False` when the button is released. When you set the Value property of a Command button to `True` in code, the CommandButton is clicked and the Click event is fired.

Value DT RW

Applies to: FlatScrollBar, HScrollBar, ProgressBar, Slider, UpDown, VScrollBar

Type: Long integer

Represents the value of the control between its Min and Max properties.

Value DT RW

Applies to: Column object of DataGrid; DTPicker and MonthView controls

Type: Assorted

The Value property represents the contents of the control or object.

ValueFormat [RT] [RW]

Applies to: DataPointLabel object of MSChart

Type: String

Contains a format string similar to that used with VBA's *Format* function that is used to format data in the label.

ValueScale [RT] [RO]

Applies to: Axis object of MSChart

Type: ValueScale object

Returns a reference to a ValueScale object, which contains information about how to scale the value axis.

VariantHeight [DT] [RW]

Applies to: CoolBar

Type: Boolean

When set to `False`, all the CoolBar control's bands share the same height. When set to its default value of `True`, the bands can have different heights.

Verb [DT] [RW]

Applies to: OLE object

Type: Long integer

The Verb property is in Visual Basic for backward compatibility with previous versions only. Its functionality has been replaced by the DoVerb method.

Version [RT] [RO]

Applies to: MSFlexGrid, MSHFlexGrid

Type: Integer

Returns the version of the control.

VertAlignment

DT RW

Applies to: TextLayout object of MSChart

See: HorzAlignment

View

DT RW

Applies to: ListView

Type: `ListViewConstants` enumeration

The appearance of the ListView control is controlled by the View property, as follows:

Constant	*Value*	*Description*
`lvwIcon`	0	ListItem objects are represented by 32×32-pixel icons arranged in rows. No subitems are visible. This is the default value.
`lvwSmallIcon`	1	ListItem objects are represented by 16×16-pixel icons arranged in rows. No subitems are visible.
`lvwList`	2	ListItem objects are represented by 16×16-pixel icons arranged in columns. No subitems are visible.
`lvwReport`	3	ListItem objects are represented by 16×16-pixel icons along with all subitems. These subitems are placed in columns next to the Text property.

View3D

RT RO

Applies to: Plot object of MSChart

Type: View3D object

Returns a reference to a View3D object, which determines how the chart is viewed from 3-D space.

Visible

Applies to: Form and MDIForm objects DT RO

Type: Boolean

When the object is made visible by using the Show method, the object's Visible property is set to `True`, and the Visible properties of all objects that it contains are also set to `True` unless they have been explicitly set to `False`. When the object is made invisible by using the Hide method, the property is set to `False`. When the object's Visible property is set to `False`, the Visible properties of all objects that it contains are also set to `False`.

The Visible property of forms or controls loaded using the Load method and dynamically created controls is automatically set to `False`; they can be displayed by calling the Show method or by setting their Visible property to `True`.

Applies to: All controls with a visual interface DT RW

Type: Boolean

When the Visible property is set to its default value of `True`, the control is visible on its parent. When set to `False`, the control is no longer visible and no longer accessible. In addition, any controls contained on an invisible control are also invisible, and their Visible properties are set to `False`. Similarly, the Visible property of a contained control is set to True when its container's Visible property becomes `True` unless it's been explicitly set to `False`.

VisibleCols RT RO

Applies to: DataGrid

Type: Long integer

Returns the number of columns that are currently visible on the DataGrid control.

VisibleCount RT RO

Applies to: DataCombo, DataList, DBCombo, DBList

Type: Long integer

Returns the number of list elements currently visible on the control.

VisibleDays RT RO

Applies to: MonthView

Type: Array of Date

Contains one element for each date visible on the calendar. Each element contains the actual date that is visible.

VisibleItems RT RO

Applies to: DataCombo, DataList, DBCombo, DBList

Type: Bookmark object array

Contains a reference to a DAO Bookmark object for each visible element of the list. Each object can be used to position a Recordset object to that record.

VisibleRows RT RO

Applies to: DataGrid

Type: Long integer

Returns the number of rows currently visible in the DataGrid control.

VtColor DT RO

Applies to: Pen, Statline, and VtFont objects of MSChart

Type: VtColor object

Returns a reference to a VtColor object, which controls the color to apply to the object.

VtFont DT RO

Applies to: AxisTitle, DataPointLabel, Label, Legend, and Title objects of MSChart

Type: VtFont object

Returns a reference to a VtFont object, which contains information about the font to use for the object.

Wait RT RW

Applies to: MM

Type: Boolean

When set to `True`, control does not return to the application until after a multimedia device command has completed. When set to `False`, control returns to the application immediately.

Wall RT RO

Applies to: Plot object of MSChart

Type: Wall object

Returns a reference to a Wall object, which controls the appearance of the virtual wall behind a 3-D chart.

Week RT RW

Applies to: MonthView

See: Day

Weighting

RT RO

Applies to: Plot object

Type: Weighting object

Returns a reference to a Weighting object, which controls how pie charts are sized relative to one another.

WhatsThisButton

DT RO

Applies to: Form object

See: ControlBox

WhatsThisHelp

DT RO

Applies to: Form and MDIForm objects

Type: Boolean

When the WhatsThisHelp property is set to its default value, `False`, no "What's This Help" is available. When set to `True`, "What's This Help" can be accessed by the form's "What's This" button or the ShowWhatsThis method. The WhatsThis-HelpID property of the control or object must be set for it to function correctly.

WhatsThisHelpID

DT RW

Applies to: Form and MDIForm objects; all controls with a visual interface

Type: Long integer

When the WhatsThisHelpID property is set to 0 (its default value), no "What's This Help" is available for this control or object. When set to any other value, that value is treated as a Help context number, and Windows Help is started when the user requests context-sensitive help for the object or control.

Width

DT RW

Applies to: Form, MDIForm, Column, and Tab objects; all controls with a visual interface

See: Height

WidthToHeightRatio

RT RW

Applies to: Plot object of MSChart

Type: Single

Contains the height of the chart expressed as a percentage of the chart's width.

WindowList DT RO

Applies to: Menu

Type: Boolean

When set to `True`, the menu contains a list of all open MDI child forms belonging to the MDI form containing the menu. When set to its default value, `False`, the menu does not contain this list.

WindowState DT RW

Applies to: Form and MDIForm objects

Type: `FormWindowStateConstants` enumeration

The current state (normal, maximized, and minimized or iconized) of the Form object or MDIForm object is controlled by the WindowState property, as follows:

Constant	*Value*	*Description*
`vbNormal` (default)	0	The object is neither minimized nor maximized.
`vbMinimized`	1	The object is minimized.
`vbMaximized`	2	The object is maximized.

WordWrap DT RW

Applies to: Label

Type: Boolean

When set to its default value of `False`, the width of the caption of a Label control with its AutoSize property set to `True` is resized to accommodate the text; when set to `True`, the height of the Label control is resized to accommodate the text. When the AutoSize property is set to `False`, this property is ignored.

WordWrap DT RW

Applies to: MSFlexGrid, MSHFlexGrid

Type: Boolean

When set to `True`, enables word wrap for the control. When set to its default value of `False`, word wrap is disabled.

WordWrap RT RW

Applies to: TextLayout object of MSChart

Type: Boolean

When set to `True`, enables word wrap for the object containing the TextLayout object. When set to its default value of `False`, word wrap is disabled for that object.

WorkAreaHeight, WorkAreaLeft, WorkAreaTop, WorkAreaWidth [RT] [RO]

Applies to: SysInfo

Type: Single

Returns the left (WorkAreaLeft), top (WorkAreaTop), width (WorkAreaWidth), and height (WorkAreaHeight) of the screen, allowing for the size of the Windows taskbar.

Wrap [DT] [RW]

Applies to: UpDown

Type: Boolean

When set to `True`, when the upper or lower bound of the UpDown control has been reached, the value wraps around. When set to its default value of `False`, this does not occur.

WrapCellPointer [DT] [RW]

Applies to: DataGrid

Type: Boolean

If set to its default value of `False`, when the user uses the arrow keys to navigate to the first or last column in a row, the cursor stops there. When set to `True`, the cursor moves to the next or previous row automatically.

Wrappable [DT] [RW]

Applies to: Toolbar

Type: Boolean

If set to its default value of `True`, resizing the parent form or MDI form so that the toolbar buttons cannot fit on one row will cause the toolbar to grow in height and to wrap the buttons to another row. When set to `False`, some buttons can become unavailable if they do not all fit on one row.

WrapText

DT RW

Applies to: Column object

Type: Boolean

When the WrapText property is set to its default value of `False`, text that extends past the column boundaries is clipped. When set to `True`, the text is wrapped so that only complete words are present on each line. However, the RowHeight property remains the same. Therefore, you must either change your RowHeight property to allow for wrapped text or set the AllowRowSizing property to `True` to allow the user to resize the row height manually.

X, Y, Z

RT RW

Applies to: Coor (not Z) and LCoor (not Z) objects of MSChart; LightSource object of MSChart

Type: Single (Coor and LightSource objects), long integer (LCoor object)

Contain the x, y, and z (LightSource only) coordinates for the object.

X1, X2, Y1, Y2

DT RW

Applies to: Line

Type: Long integer

These properties represent the endpoints of the line in a Line control. While the X1 and Y1 properties set the location of the first endpoint, the X2 and Y2 properties position the other end of the line.

XGap

RT RW

Applies to: Plot object of MSChart

Type: Single

Defines the width of the gaps between values on the chart, expressed as a percentage of the width of the values.

Y

RT RW

Applies to: Coor, LCoor, and LightSource objects of MSChart

See: X

Y1, Y2

DT RW

Applies to: Line

See: X1

Year

RT RW

Applies to: DTPicker, MonthView

See: Day

Z

RT RW

Applies to: LightSource object of MSChart

See: X

ZGap

DT RW

Applies to: Plot object of MSChart

Type: Single

Defines the width of the gaps between values on the chart's z-axis, expressed as a percentage of the width of the values (on the x-axis).

CHAPTER 7

Methods

This chapter documents the methods of each of the controls discussed in Chapter 5, *Controls*. Each entry follows a standard format:

- The controls to which the method applies.
- The method's prototype.
- A description of the parameters that the method accepts. We've used brackets ([]) to denote optional parameters.
- The datatype returned by the method, if any.
- A description of the method.

Accept

Applies to: Winsock

Syntax: `sckMain.Accept RequestID`

Parameters:

`RequestID` *(long integer)*
A value that identifies the connection request

Returns: None

Used within a ConnectionRequest event handler to accept an incoming connection request. ***RequestID*** is an identifier that's passed as a parameter to the ConnectionRequest event.

AddItem

Applies to: ComboBox, ListBox, MSFlexGrid, MSHFlexGrid

Syntax: `cboMain.AddItem Item [, Index]`

Parameters:

`Item` *(string)*
    The data to be added to the new row

`Index` *(optional integer)*
    The position in which `Item` is to be added

`Number` *(integer – MSHFlexGrid only)*
    The band in which the new row is placed

Returns: None

Adds the appropriate type of row to the control. In the case of MSFlexGrid and MSHFlexGrid, the Tab character (`vbTab`) can be used to separate data that will form the individual columns in the row. The ***`Index`*** parameter controls where the new row will be placed within the control. The position is zero-based; that is, a value of 0 indicates that the new row is to be added before all existing rows. Attempting to add a row whose number exceeds the number of existing rows generates runtime error 5, "Invalid procedure call or argument." If ***`Index`*** is not supplied, the new row will appear at the end.

AddNew

Applies to: Recordset object of ADO DC and Data controls

Syntax:

```
rsObj.AddNew                            'Data Control
rsObj.AddNew [FieldList], Values]  'ADO Data Ctrl
```

Parameters:

`FieldList` *(optional variant string or variant string Array)*
    The name of a field or an array of strings, each containing the name of a field to be inserted. If this parameter is supplied, the data in the ***`Values`*** parameter is posted. If this parameter is not supplied, the recordset is set to AddNew mode, as described later in this section.

`Values` *(optional variant or variant Array)*
    A field value or an array of values for fields whose name(s) are supplied in the ***`FieldList`*** parameter. If ***`FieldList`*** contains one string, the ***`Values`*** parameter must contain one value. If ***`FieldList`*** contains a string array, the ***`Values`*** parameter must contain an array of values with the same number of elements.

Returns: None

Starts the process of adding a new record to the recordset. Once the AddNew method is called, fields within the record can be set and the Update method called to save the changes, as in the following example:

```
With rsVar
    .AddNew
    !FirstName = "Evan"
    !LastName = "Dictor"
    .Update
End With
```

Arrange

Applies to: MDIForm

Syntax: `frmMain.Arrange Arrangement`

Parameters:

`Arrangement` (`FormArrangeConstants` *enumeration)*
: Constant indicating how to arrange child objects. Possible values are 0–vbCascade to cascade all child forms, 1–vbTileHorizontal to tile the child forms horizontally, 2–vbTileVertical to tile the child forms vertically, or 3–vbArrangeIcons to arrange the icons at the bottom of the MDI form.

Returns: None

Reorganizes the child forms and icons contained by an MDI form.

BandColIndex

Applies to: MSHFlexGrid

Syntax: `mshMain.BandColIndex`

Parameters: None

Returns: Long integer

Returns the column number in the band containing the current cell.

Bind

Applies to: Winsock

Syntax: `sckMain.Bind LocalPort, LocalIP`

Parameters:

`LocalPort` *(long integer)*
: The UDP port to which to bind

`LocalIP` *(string)*
: The IP address to use

Returns: None

Reserves a UDP port for exclusive use with a Winsock control on a machine with more than one IP address.

Cancel

Applies to: Recordset object of Data and ADO DC, Data, and Inet controls

Syntax: `obj.Cancel`

Parameters: None

Returns: None

For the Internet control, cancels any pending asynchronous operations; for the Recordset object, stops any pending requests and closes the current connection.

CancelBatch

Applies to: Recordset object of ADO DC

Syntax: `adoMain.CancelBatch [AffectRecords]`

Parameters:

`AffectRecords` *(optional* `AffectEnum` *enumeration)*
: Defines the scope of the cancellation. Possible values are 1–adAffectCurrent to cancel batch updates for the current record only, 2–adAffectGroup to cancel batch updates for records valid for the current filter, or 3–adAffectAll (the default) to cancel batch updates for all records.

Returns: None

Cancels pending batch updates to the current recordset based on the parameters.

CancelUpdate

Applies to: Recordset object of ADO DC and Data controls

Syntax: `rsObj.CancelUpdate`

Parameters: None

Returns: None

Cancels a pending AddNew or Edit action for the recordset.

CaptureImage

Applies to: DataGrid

Syntax: `Set picVar = dtgMain.CaptureImage`

Parameters: None

Returns: Picture object

Returns whatever is currently displayed in the DataGrid control as a metafile image, typically for display in a PictureBox or Image control.

CellText, CellValue

Applies to: Column object of DataGrid

Syntax:

```
sVar = dtgMain.objCols(index).CellText(Bookmark)
sVar = dtgMain.objCols(index).CellValue(Bookmark)
```

Parameters:

Bookmark (variant)
A bookmark that represents a row

Returns: String

The CellValue method returns raw text, while the CellText method returns formatted text contained in a specific cell. This cell is defined by the Column object for which the method was called and the row referenced by the *Bookmark* parameter.

Circle

Applies to: Form object; PictureBox control

Syntax:

```
frmMain.Circle [Step] (X, Y), Radius _
          [, Color], Start], End], Aspect]
```

Parameters:

Step (optional keyword)
Indicates that the X and Y parameters are relative to the current coordinates as defined by the CurrentX and CurrentY properties; if not present, *X* and *Y* are absolute coordinates. If the Step keyword is present, it is not followed by a comma.

X (single), Y (single)
The x and y coordinates of the center of the graphic to be drawn. Depending on the presence or absence of the Step keyword, they are interpreted as either relative or absolute coordinates. Note that *X* and *Y* must be enclosed in parentheses. For example:

```
Circle (sngX, sngY), sngRad1
```

or

```
Circle Step(sngX, sngY), sngRad1
```

Radius (single)
Defines the graphic object's radius.

`Color` *(optional long integer)*

RGB color of the graphic's outline. If omitted, the control's ForeColor property is used. A valid value is generated by the *RGB* function; for example:

```
Circle (100,100),100,RGB(255,0,0)
```

draws a circle with a red border.

`Start` *(optional single)*

The beginning position of an arc or ellipse, in radians. Its default value is 0 radians, and its range is -2 * `pi` radians to 2 * `pi` radians.

`End` *(optional single)*

The ending position of an arc or ellipse, in radians. Its default value is 2 * `pi` radians, and its range is -2 * `pi` radians to 2 * `pi` radians.

`Aspect` *(optional single)*

The aspect ratio (that is, the ratio of the y- radius to the x-radius). The default value is 1.0, which produces a circle rather than an ellipse.

Returns: None

One of the graphic methods that draw a circle, arc, or ellipse on the control. The units in which *X*, *Y*, and ***Radius*** are expressed are determined by the value of the control's ScaleMode property.

Clear

Applies to: ComboBox, ListBox, MSFlexGrid, MSHFlexGrid

Syntax: `ctlMain.Clear`

Parameters: None

Returns: None

Removes all rows from the control.

ClearFields

Applies to: DataGrid

Syntax: `dtgMain.ClearFields`

Parameters: None

Returns: None

Removes all data and bindings from the DataGrid control, leaving the control with two columns and no data.

ClearSel

Applies to: Slider

Syntax: `sldMain.ClearSel`

Parameters: None

Returns: None

Clears any selection from the Slider control and sets the Slider's SelLength property to 0.

ClearSelCols

Applies to: Split object of DataGrid; DataGrid control

Syntax: `ObjMain.ClearSelCols`

Parameters: None

Returns: None

Unselects any selected columns in the DataGrid or Split.

ClearStructure

Applies to: MSHFlexGrid

Syntax: `mshMain.ClearStructure`

Parameters: None

Returns: None

Clears all band mapping information in the MSHFlexGrid control without clearing the actual data.

Clone

Applies to: Recordset object of ADO DC and Data controls

Syntax for Recordset object, Data Control:

```
Set rsVar = datMain.Recordset.Clone
```

Syntax for Recordset object, ADO DC:

```
Set rsVar = adoMain.Recordset.Clone([LockType])
```

Parameters:

LockType (LockTypeEnum *enumeration, ADO DC only)*

Specifies the type of locking to use on the new recordset. Values for the LockType parameter are -1–adLockUnspecified to use the same locking as the original recordset, or 1–adLockReadOnly to set the new recordset to read-only.

Returns: Recordset object (DAO and ADO, respectively)

Returns a recordset identical to the current Recordset object.

Close

Applies to: Recordset object of ADO DC and Data controls; Animation, Database, and Winsock controls

Syntax: `objMain.Close`

Parameters: None

Returns: None

Closes the *.AVI* file (Animation control), database (Database object), OLE object (OLE control), recordset (both types of recordsets), or TCP connection (Winsock control).

Cls

Applies to: Form object; PictureBox control

Syntax: `objMain.Cls`

Parameters: None

Returns: None

A graphic method that clears all graphics from the object. It also resets the CurrentX and CurrentY properties to 0 and resets the ScaleMode property to its default value of `vbTwips`.

ColContaining, RowContaining, SplitContaining

Applies to: DataGrid

Syntax:

```
iVar = dtgMain.ColContaining(X)
iVar = dtgMain.RowContaining(X)
iVar = dtgMain.SplitContaining(X, Y)
```

Parameters:

ColContaining: X (single)
: A horizontal coordinate based on the container's coordinate system

RowContaining: Y (single)
: A vertical coordinate based on the container's coordinate system

SplitContaining: X (single), Y (single)
: A horizontal and vertical coordinate based on the container's coordinate system

Returns: Integer

These methods accept a coordinate on the control as a parameter and return the number of the visible row, visible column, or split positioned at that point.

CollapseAll

Applies to: MSHFlexGrid

Syntax: `mshMain.CollapseAll([BandNumber])`

Parameters:

`BandNumber` *(long integer)*
Number of the band whose rows are to be collapsed.

Returns: None

Collapses all expanded rows in the band specified by the `BandNumber` parameter.

CompareBookmarks

Applies to: Recordset object of ADO DC

Syntax:

```
iVar = adoMain.Recordset.CompareBookmarks( _
        Bookmark1, Bookmark2)
```

Parameters:

`Bookmark1` *(variant)*
A bookmark that identifies a row in a recordset

`Bookmark2` *(variant)*
A second bookmark identifying a row in a recordset

Returns: `CompareEnum` enumeration

Compares the location of records within the recordset. `Bookmark1` and `Bookmark2` should contain the bookmarks to compare. (Bookmarks can be retrieved using a particular row object's Bookmark property.) The value returned will be 0–adCompareLessThan if `Bookmark1` comes before `Bookmark2`, 1–adCompareEqual if the bookmarks are the same, 2–adCompareGreaterThan if `Bookmark1` comes after `Bookmark2`, 3–adCompareNotEqual if the bookmarks are not equal but do not relate in an ordered way, or 4–adCompareNotComparable if the bookmarks do not relate to each other.

Note that the CompareBookmarks method assumes that `Bookmark1` and `Bookmark2` belong to the same recordset or to a recordset and its clone. In addition, the recordset's data provider must support the ability to compare rows using bookmarks.

ComputeControlSize

Applies to: MonthView

Syntax:

```
mvwMain.ComputeControlSize Rows, Columns, Width, Height
```

Parameters:

`Rows` *(integer)*
Number of rows in the control

`Columns` *(integer)*
Number of columns in the control

`Width` *(single)*
On return, contains the width of the control

`Height` *(single)*
On return, contains the height of the control

Returns: None

Accepts a number of rows and columns (months down and across) for the control and returns, by reference, the size of the control in twips. Once you know the control's size, you can position it on a form, or you can change its dimensions, as in this example, which sizes a form based on the size of the MonthView control:

```
Dim nWidth As Single
Dim nHeight As Single

mvwMain.ComputeControlSize 1, 2, nWidth, nHeight

Me.Move Me.Left, Me.Top, _
    nWidth + (Me.Width - Me.ScaleWidth), _
    nHeight + (Me.Height - Me.ScaleHeight)

mvwMain.MonthRows = 1
mvwMain.MonthColumns = 2

mvwMain.Move 0, 0
```

Connect

Applies to: Winsock

Syntax: *sckMain*.`Connect` *RemoteHost, RemotePort*

Parameters:

`RemoteHost` *(string)*
The IP address of the remote server

`RemotePort` *(long integer)*
The UDP port on which to establish the connection

Returns: None

Connects to another computer using the Winsock control.

Methods A–C

Copy

Applies to: OLE

Syntax: `oleMain.Copy`

Parameters: None

Returns: None

Sends a copy of the OLE object contained by the OLE control to the Clipboard.

CopyQueryDef

Applies to: Recordset object of Data control

Syntax: `Set qdVar = datMain.Recordset.CopyQueryDef`

Parameters: None

Returns: Queried object

Returns a QueryDef similar to the one used to create the recordset.

CreateDragImage

Applies to: ListItem (ListView), Node (TreeView)

Syntax: `Set picVar = objMain.CreateDragImage`

Parameters: None

Returns: Picture object

Returns a Picture object generated by dithering the image displayed for the object. This Picture object can then be used to set the DragIcon property for drag-and-drop operations.

CreateEmbed, CreateLink

Applies to: OLE

Syntax:

```
oleMain.CreateEmbed(SourceDoc [, Class])
oleMain.CreateLink(SourceDoc [, SourceItem])
```

Parameters:

SourceDoc (string)
The name of the file to be linked or embedded

`Class` *(optional string, CreateEmbed only)*
The class name, or programmatic identifier (ProgID), of the embedded object

`SourceItem` *(optional string, CreateLink only)*
The name of the item to be linked within *`SourceDoc`*

Returns: None

These methods are used to create an embedded (CreateEmbed) or linked (CreateLink) OLE object in the OLE control.

CreateQueryDef

Applies to: Database object of Data control

Syntax:

```
Set qdVar = datMain.Database.CreateQueryDef( _
    [Name] , SQLText])
```

Parameters:

`Name` *(optional string)*
The name of the new query

`SQLText` *(optional string)*
A valid SQL statement that defines the QueryDef

Returns:

QueryDef object

Creates a new query in the Database object. For example:

```
'qdMain already dimensioned as a QueryDef
'dbMain already dimensioned as a Database and Opened
Set qdMain = dbMain.CreateQueryDef("AllNames", _
    "Select LastName, FirstName " & _
    "From People Order By LastName, FirstName")
```

Once created, a recordset is populated with the results of the query as follows:

```
'qdMain already set as above
'rsMain already dimensioned as a Recordset
Set rsMain = qdMain.OpenRecordset(dbOpenDynaset)
```

CreateRelation

Applies to: Database object of Data control

Syntax:

```
Set relVar = datMain.Database.CreateRelation( _
    [Name], Table], ForeignTable], Attributes])
```

Parameters:

`Name` *(string)*
The name of the relation.

Table (string)

The name of the primary table in the relationship.

ForeignTable (string)

The name of the foreign table in the relationship.

Attributes (RelationAttributeEnum enumeration)

One or more of the constants shown in the following table that control the type of relationship and any restrictions (multiple constants can be added or Ored together):

Constant	Value	Description
dbRelationUnique	1	Only one record must exist in *Table* for each record in *ForeignTable*.
dbRelationDontEnforce	2	Referential integrity is not enforced.
dbRelationInherited	4	The relation is only for information purposes and generally refers to a relationship between tables that are linked to the current database.
dbRelationUpdateCascade	256	Updates performed on linked fields are applied to both tables.
dbRelationDeleteCascade	4,096	Records deleted are applied to both tables.
dbRelationLeft	16,777,216	Use a left outer join by default when the tables are joined.
dbRelationRight	33,554,432	Use a right outer join by default when the tables are joined.

Returns: Relation object

Creates a new relation in the Database object. A relation in an Access database tracks the relationships between tables and enforces referential integrity rules.

Once the relation has been created, one or more Field objects must be appended to the Relation object. Finally, the Relation object must be appended to the Database object's Relationship collection. The following example creates a one-to-many relationship from the People table to the Phones table on the PersonId field:

```
Dim dbMain As Database
Dim relMain As Relation
Dim fldMain As Field

Set dbMain = DBEngine.Workspaces(0).OpenDatabase( _
    "c:\My Documents\Book\Book.mdb")
'First, create the relation between the People and _
 Phones tables that will cascade updates and deletes
Set relMain = dbMain.CreateRelation("Relation1", _
    "People", "Phones", dbRelationUpdateCascade + _
    dbRelationDeleteCascade + dbRelationLeft)
```

```
'Now use the PersonId field for the relationship
Set fldMain = relMain.CreateField("PersonId")
fldMain.ForeignName = "PersonId"
relMain.Fields.Append fldMain

'With all the pieces in place, we can Append the _
 relationship to the Database
dbMain.Relations.Append relMain
```

CreateTableDef

Applies to: Database object of Data control

Syntax:

```
Set tblVar = datMain.Database.CreateTableDef( _
    [Name], Attributes], SourceTableName], Connect])
```

Parameters:

`Name` *(optional string)*
A unique name that identifies the TableDef object.

`Attributes` *(optional* `TableDefAttributeEnum` *enumeration)*
None or one or more of the constants shown in the following table that indicate the characteristics of the new TableDef object (multiple constants can be added or `Or`ed together):

Constant	*Value*	*Description*
`dbAttachExclusive`	&H20000000	The table is a local linked table opened for exclusive use (Jet only).
`dbAttachSavePWD`	&H20000	The user ID and password for the remotely linked table are saved with the connection information (Jet only).
`dbSystemObject`	&H80000002	The table is a system table (Jet only).
`dbHiddenObject`	1	The table is a hidden table (Jet only).
`dbAttachedTable`	&H40000000	The table is a read-only linked table from a non-ODBC data source such as a Microsoft Jet database.
`dbAttachedODBC`	&H20000000	The table is a read-only linked table from an ODBC data source, such as Microsoft SQL Server.

`SourceTableName` *(optional string)*
The name of a table in an external database that is the original source of the data.

`Connect` *(optional string)*
A valid connection string.

Returns: TableDef object

Creates a new table in the Database object. Once the table is created, fields must be appended before the TableDef can be appended to the database. The following example creates a Hobbies table in the Book database:

```
Dim dbMain As Database
Dim tdMain As TableDef
Dim fldMain As Field

Set dbMain = DBEngine.Workspaces(0).OpenDatabase( _
    "c:\My Documents\Book\Book.mdb")
'First, we create a TableDef object in the Database
Set tdMain = dbMain.CreateTableDef("Hobbies")

'Now we create the fields
Set fldMain = tdMain.CreateField("HobbyId")
fldMain.Type = dbLong
fldMain.Attributes = dbAutoIncrField
tdMain.Fields.Append fldMain

Set fldMain = tdMain.CreateField("HobbyDesc")
fldMain.Type = dbText
fldMain.Size = 50
tdMain.Fields.Append fldMain

'With all the fields created, we can Append the _
    table to the Database
dbMain.TableDefs.Append tdMain
```

Customize

Applies to: Toolbar

Syntax: `tbrMain.Customize`

Parameters: None

Returns: None

Displays the Customize Toolbar dialog, which allows the user to define which buttons are displayed on the toolbar.

Delete

Applies to: OLE

Syntax: `oleMain.Delete`

Parameters: None

Returns: None

Removes the association with an open OLE object. Once the association is removed, memory that was used by the OLE object is released.

Delete

Applies to: Recordset object of Data control

Syntax: `datMain.Recordset.Delete`

Parameters: None

Returns: None

Deletes the current record from a recordset.

DeleteColumnLabels, DeleteRowLabels

Applies to: DataGrid object of MSChart

Syntax:

```
chtMain.DataGrid.DeleteColumnLabels LabelIndex, Count
chtMain.DataGrid.DeleteRowLabels LabelIndex, Count
```

Parameters:

`LabelIndex` *(integer)*
: The index of the first level of column or row labels to be deleted

`Count` *(integer)*
: The number of levels to delete

Returns: None

These methods delete levels of labels in the DataGrid object. Column labels are numbered starting from the top, which is 1. Row labels are numbered starting from the left, which is 1.

DeleteColumns, DeleteRows

Applies to: DataGrid object of MSChart

Syntax:

```
dtgMain.DeleteColumns Column, Count
dtgMain.DeleteRows Row, Count
```

Parameters:

`Column` *(integer) or* `Row` *(integer)*
: The index of the first column (in the case of DeleteColumns) or row (in the case of DeleteRows) to be deleted. Columns are numbered starting from the top, which is 1. Rows are numbered starting from the left, which is 1.

`Count` *(integer)*
: The number of columns (in the case of DeleteColumns) or rows (DeleteRows) to delete.

Returns: None

These methods delete rows (DeleteRows) or columns (DeleteColumns) from the DataGrid object.

DeleteRowLabels

Applies to: DataGrid object of MSChart

See: DeleteColumnLabels

DeleteRows

Applies to: DataGrid object of MSChart

See: DeleteColumns

DeselectAll

Applies to: TabStrip

Syntax: `tbsMain.DeselectAll`

Parameters: None

Returns: None

Causes any selected tabs in the TabStrip to no longer be selected.

DoVerb

Applies to: OLEObject object of RichTextBox; OLE control

Syntax: `oleMain.DoVerb [Verb]`

Parameters: `Verb` (*optional enumeration*)

Returns: None

Causes the OLE object to initiate an action. Each object has its own set of verbs, which can be derived by retrieving the strings stored to the ObjectVerbs property array. The index of that verb in the ObjectVerbs property array can then be supplied as an argument to `Verb`. In addition to these verbs, OLE objects should support the following verbs:

Constant	*Value*	*Description*
`vbOLEPrimary`	0	Initiates the OLE object's default action.
`vbOLEShow`	-1	Opens the OLE object for editing.
`vbOLEOpen`	-2	Opens the OLE object in its own window.
`vbOLEHide`	-3	Hides the OLE object's host application if it is visible.

Constant	*Value*	*Description*
`vbOLEUIActivate`	-4	Activates an OLE object that supports in-place activation.
`vbOLEInPlaceActivate`	-5	Activates the OLE object when the control gets the focus.
`vbOLEDiscardUndoState`	-6	Causes the OLE object to lose any existing undo information.

Drag

Applies to: All controls except invisible controls; Menu, Shape, and Line controls

Syntax: `ctlVar.Drag [Action]`

Parameters:

`Action` (`DragConstants` *enumeration)*
The status of the drag-and-drop operation. `Action` can be one of the following constants:

Constant	*Value*	*Description*
`VbCancel`	0	Cancels a drag-and-drop operation.
`VbBeginDrag`	1	Begins a drag-and-drop operation.
`VbEndDrag`	2	Ends a drag-and-drop operation.

Returns: None

Begins, ends, or cancels a drag-and-drop operation. Drag and Drop is described in detail in Chapter 2, *Common Control Features.*

Edit

Applies to: Recordset object of Data control

Syntax: `datMain.Recordset.Edit`

Parameters: None

Returns: None

Prepares the current record in a recordset for editing. Once the Edit method is called, field changes are not saved until the Update method is called. The Cancel-Update method cancels a pending edit without saving.

EditCopy, EditPaste

Applies to: MSChart

Syntax:

```
chtMain.EditCopy
chtMain.EditPaste
```

Parameters: None

Returns: None

These methods transfer data between the MSChart and the Windows Clipboard. The EditCopy method copies the chart image and data to the Clipboard. The EditPaste method pastes data from the Clipboard into the MSChart control.

EnsureVisible

Applies to: ListItem object of ListView, Node object of TreeView

Syntax: `bVar = objMain.EnsureVisible`

Parameters: None

Returns: Boolean

Forces the specified object to become visible if it is currently scrolled off the visible control or, in the case of the TreeView control, hidden within an unexpanded section. The method returns `True` if the control is scrolled or nodes are expanded to make the object visible. Otherwise, it returns `False`. However, the object is made visible regardless.

Execute

Applies to: Database object of Data control

Syntax: `datMain.Database.Execute Source [, Options]`

Parameters:

`Source` *(string)*
: An SQL statement.

`Options` *(optional* `RecordsetOptionEnum` *enumeration)*
: None or one or more of the following constants that define the environment in which `Source` is executed (if no constants are specified, the default value is `dbConsistent`):

Constant	*Value*	*Description*
`dbDenyWrite`	1	Denies write permission to otherrs (Jet only).
`dbInconsistent`	16	Executes inconsistent updates (Jet only).
`dbConsistent`	32	Executes consistent updates (Jet only).
`dbSQLPassThrough`	64	Executes an SQL pass-through query (Jet only).
`dbFailOnError`	128	Rolls back updates if an error occurs (Jet only).
`dbSeeChanges`	512	Generates a runtime error if another user changes the data being modified (Jet only).

Returns: None

Runs an SQL statement that does not return data (such as an UPDATE or DELETE statement) on the database.

Execute

Applies to: Inet control

Syntax:

```
itcMain.Execute [Url], Operations], Data], RequestHeaders]
```

Parameters:

`Url` *(optional string)*
: The URL on which *`Operations`* is to be executed. If none is specified, the URL specified by the URL property is used instead.

`Operations` *(optional string)*
: The command to be executed. Valid commands depend on the protocol (HTTP or FTP) used and are shown in the following table.

`Data` *(optional string)*
: For HTTP `POST` requests, the form data accompanying the request; for HTTP `PUT` requests, writes the file indicated by *`Data`*.

`RequestHeaders` *(optional string)*
: One or more additional headers to be sent with an HTTP request. The format of an individual header is:

  `header_name``:` *`header_value`* `vbCrLf`

Returns: None

Executes the command indicated by *`Operations`* on the URL specified in the URL parameter. If no URL is specified, the URL property is used instead. The Execute method operates asynchronously, so the program will continue running after it is called. The StateChanged event then fires to give the status of the operation, and the GetChunk method is typically used to retrieve any data retrieved by the operation.

Valid HTTP operations for the Execute method are:

Operation	*Description*
`GET`	Retrieves the resource indicated by *`URL`*.
`HEAD`	Sends the client's request headers and retrieves the server's response headers.
`POST`	Sends the data from the *`Data`* parameter to the specified URL.
`PUT`	Sends the data from the *`Data`* parameter to the specified URL.

FTP requests do not use the *Data* and *RequestHeaders* parameters but instead include both the command and all necessary arguments in a single string supplied to *Operations*. Valid FTP operations for the Execute method are:

Operation	*Description*
CD *dir1*	The host computer makes *dir1* the current directory.
CDUP	The host computer changes to the parent directory.
CLOSE	Closes the connection to the host computer.
DELETE *file1*	Deletes the file specified by *file1*.
DIR [*file1*]	Returns the contents of the directory when issued without any arguments. If *file1* is present and indicates a file or directory (with or without wildcard characters), the host computer will return information on that file or directory.
GET *file1 file2*	Downloads *file1* from the host computer and stores it locally as *file2*.
LS *file1*	Same as DIR.
MKDIR *dir1*	Creates a directory named *dir1* on the host computer.
PUT *file1 file2*	Copies *file1* to *file2* on the remote host.
PWD	Returns the name of the current directory name.
QUIT	Closes the connection to the host computer.
RECV *file1 file2*	Same as GET.
RENAME *file1 file2*	Renames a file on the remote host from *file1* to *file2*.
RMDIR *dir1*	Deletes a directory from the host computer.
SEND *file1 file2*	Same as PUT.
SIZE *file1*	Returns the size of *file1*.

ExpandAll

Applies to: MSHFlexGrid

Syntax: `mshMain.ExpandAll [Number]`

Parameters:

Number (optional long integer)
Number of the band whose rows are to be expanded.

Returns: None

Expands all rows in the band specified by the *Number* parameter.

FetchVerbs

Applies to: OLEObject object of RichTextBox; OLE control

Syntax: `oleMain.FetchVerbs`

Parameters: None

Returns: None

Updates the verbs available for the OLE object. They can be retrieved using the ObjectVerbs property array.

FillCache

Applies to: Recordset object of Data control

Syntax: `datMain.Recordset.FillCache [Rows], StartBookmark]`

Parameters:

`Rows` *(optional integer)*
: Number of records to store in the cache

`StartBookmark` *(optional string)*
: Bookmark indicating the starting record

Returns: None

Reads records from the data source into the recordset. If the ***`Rows`*** and ***`StartBookmark`*** parameters are not supplied, the recordset's CacheSize and CacheStart properties are used instead.

Find

Applies to: RichTextBox

Syntax: `rtbMain.Find String [, Start], End], Options]`

Parameters:

`String` *(string)*
: The string to search for.

`Start` *(optional integer)*
: Character position (zero-based) from which the search is to begin.

`End` *(optional integer)*
: Character position (zero-based) at which the search is to end.

`Options` *(optional enumeration)*
: Any combination of the following constants, which define additional features: 2–rtfWholeWord, which searches for only entire words; 4–rtfMatchCase, which conducts a case-sensitive search; and 8–rtfNoHighlight, which causes the found text to not be highlighted.

Returns: Integer

Searches for a string within the contents of the RichTextBox control. This search can include the entire contents of the control or just a portion. If the specified string is not found in the range, a negative one (-1) is returned. Otherwise, the method returns the position at which the string was found.

FindFirst, FindLast, FindNext, FindPrevious

Applies to: Recordset object of Data control

Syntax:

```
datMain.Recordset.FindFirst Criteria
datMain.Recordset.FindLast Criteria
datMain.Recordset.FindNext Criteria
datMain.Recordset.FindPrevious Criteria
```

Parameters:

`Criteria` *(string)*
: Criteria that identifies the record. It is identical to the `WHERE` clause in an SQL statement, but without the `WHERE` keyword.

Returns: None

These respective methods find the first, last, next, and previous record in the recordset that matches the criteria defined in the *`Criteria`* parameter. The matching record is then made the current record. After calling any of these methods, check the value of the recordset's NoMatch property; if it is set to `True`, no match was found.

FindItem

Applies to: ListView

Syntax:

```
Set lsiVar = lvwMain.FindItem( _
    sString [, iValue], vIndex], iMatch])
```

Parameters:

`String` *(string)*
: The string to search for.

`Value` *(optional* `ListFindItemsWhere` *enumeration)*
: The ListItem property to be searched. Possible values are 0–lvwText to search the Text property of each ListItem, 1–lvwSubItem to search through all SubItems in each ListItem, or 2–lvwTag to search the Tag property of each ListItem. If *`Value`* is not specified, its default is `lvwText`.

`Index` *(optional integer or string)*
: The index or the key of the ListItem object at which the search is to begin. If *`Index`* is not specified, the search begins with the first ListItem object.

Match *(optional* `ListFindItemHowConstants` *enumeration)*

Determines what constitutes a match. When set to 0–lvwWholeWord, all of *String* must match all of the ListItem property value. When set to 1–lvwPartial, the match extends only to the length of the *String* parameter. Note that the default is `lvwWholeWord`.

Returns: ListItem object

Searches for a ListItem object whose Text, SubItems, or Tag property matches the *String* parameter and returns a reference to it. If there is no match, the FindItem method returns `Nothing`.

FindLast, FindNext, FindPrevious

Applies to: Recordset object of Data control

See: FindFirst

GetBookmark

Applies to: DataGrid

Syntax: `vVar = dtgMain.GetBookmark(RowNum)`

Parameters:

RowNum *(long integer)*

A row of the DataGrid relative to the current row. For rows before the current row, *RowNum* should be negative. For rows after the current row, *RowNum* should be positive. A value of 0 for *RowNum* indicates the current row.

Returns: Bookmark (variant)

Returns a bookmark for the row in the DataGrid designated by *RowNum*.

GetChunk

Applies to: Inet control

Syntax: `vVar = itcMain.GetChunk(Size [, DataType])`

Parameters:

Size *(long integer)*

The maximum size of the data chunk to be retrieved.

DataType *(optional* `DataTypeConstants` *enumeration)*

The data type of the retrieved chunk. Possible values are 0–icString, which is the default, and 1–icByteArray.

Returns: Variant

Reads data retrieved by the Internet control's Execute method. The method is generally called from the StateChanged event.

GetData

Applies to: DataObject object

Syntax:

```
vVar = objMain.GetData(Format)
```

Parameters:

Format (ClipBoardConstants *enumeration or integer*)
: The format in which the data is to be retrieved. This can be a custom format whose integer identifier is returned by the Win32 *RegisterClipboardFormat* function, or it can be one of the formats listed in the following table.

Returns: Variant

The DataObject object is a container for data transferred through OLE Drag and Drop; it is passed as a parameter to a number of the OLE Drag and Drop event procedures (OLEDragDrop, OLEDragOver, OLESetData, and OLEStartDrag) and exposes its own methods and a single property. The GetData method is used to retrieve data from an OLE object, generally when it is being dropped onto its target container in the OLEDragDrop event. Possible values for the *Format* parameter are:

Constant	*Value*	*Description*
VbCFText	1	Text
VbCFBitmap	2	Windows bitmap
VbCFMetafile	3	Windows metafile
VbCFDIB	8	Device-independent bitmap
VbCFPalette	9	Color palette
VbCFEMetafile	14	Enhanced metafile
VbCFFiles	15	A list of files
VbCFRTF	-16,639	Rich text

To determine whether a particular data format is supported by the OLE object, you can call the DataObject object's GetFormat method before calling GetData.

GetData, PeekData

Applies to: Winsock

Syntax:

```
sckMain.GetData(Data [, Type], MaxLen])
sckMain.PeekData(Data [, Type], MaxLen])
```

Parameters:

Data (variant)
: Buffer to contain data when methods return.

Type (optional `VbVarType` *enumeration)*

Type of data to be returned, as shown in the following table. Its default value is `vbArray + vbByte`.

MaxLen (optional long integer)

Maximum number of bytes to return. If it is not provided for `vbString` or `vbByte` data, all available data is retrieved. For other values of *Type*, the *MaxLen* parameter is ignored.

Returns: None

Retrieve data that is waiting at the socket, which is placed in the *Data* buffer that is passed to these methods by reference. Generally, these methods are called from the DataArrival event. GetData removes the data that it retrieves from the queue, whereas PeekData leaves the data in the queue. Values are as follows:

Constant	*Value*	*Description*
`vbInteger`	2	Integer
`vbLong`	3	Long integer
`vbSingle`	4	Single
`vbDouble`	5	Double
`vbCurrency`	6	Currency
`vbDate`	7	Date
`vbString`	8	String
`vbError`	10	SCODE
`vbBoolean`	11	Boolean
`vbByte`	17	Byte
`vbArray + vbByte`	8,209	Byte array

Note that if *Type* is `vbString`, *Data* will be returned as a Unicode string.

generally called from the StateChanged event.

GetData, SetData

Applies to: DataGrid object of MSChart

Syntax:

```
chtMain.DataGrid.GetData(Row, Column, DataPoint, NullFlag)
chtMain.DataGrid.SetData(Row, Column, DataPoint, NullFlag)
```

Parameters:

Row (integer)

The row in which the data is to be retrieved or set. Row numbers in the DataGrid object begin at 1.

Column (integer)

The column in which the data is to be retrieved or set. Column numbers in the DataGrid object begin at 1.

DataPoint (double)

In the case of the SetData method, ***DataPoint*** should contain the data value to be assigned to row ***Row*** and column ***Column***. For GetData, ***DataPoint*** contains the data value when the method call returns.

NullFlag (integer)

Indicates whether a particular data point has not been initialized or has missing data. To define a particular data point as missing, set ***NullFlag*** to **True** before calling the SetData method. For example:

```
SetData(lngRow, lngCol, 0, True)
```

To detect uninitialized or missing data, define an integer value that is passed to the ***NullFlag*** parameter of the GetData function. When the function returns, a value that evaluates to **True** indicates invalid data. For example:

```
GetData(lngRow, lngCol, dblData, intNullFlag)
If CBool(intNullFlag) Then
```

Returns: None

Returns (in the case of GetData) or sets (in the case of SetData) the data at a particular point in a chart's DataGrid object.

GetFirstVisible

Applies to: ImageCombo, ListView

Syntax: `Set objVar = ctlMain.GetFirstVisible`

Parameters: None

Returns: ComboItem (ImageCombo) or ListItem (ListView)

Returns a reference to the first object in the visible portion of the control.

GetFormat

Applies to: DataObject object

Syntax: `bVar = objVaroo.GetFormat(Format)`

Parameters:

Format (ClipBoardConstants enumeration)

The format whose availability is to be determined

Returns: Boolean

The DataObject object is a container for data transferred through OLE Drag and Drop; it is passed as a parameter to a number of the OLE Drag and Drop event procedures (OLEDragDrop, OLEDragOver, OLESetData, and OLEStartDrag) and exposes its own methods and a single property. The GetFormat method returns

`True` if the format passed in the *`Format`* parameter is available from the OLE object. Possible values for the *`Format`* parameter are as follows:

Constant	*Value*	*Description*
`VbCFText`	1	Text
`VbCFBitmap`	2	Windows bitmap
`VbCFMetafile`	3	Windows metafile
`VbCFDIB`	8	Device-independent bitmap
`VbCFPalette`	9	Color palette
`VbCFEMetafile`	14	Enhanced metafile
`VbCFFiles`	15	A list of files
`VbCFRTF`	-16,639	Rich text

GetHeader

Applies to: Inet control

Syntax: `sVar = itcMain.GetHeader([HdrName])`

Parameters:

`HdrName` (optional string)

The name of the HTTP header to be retrieved, with or without its closing colon (e.g., both "Server" and "Server:" are acceptable arguments to *`HdrName`*). *`HdrName`* is not case sensitive. The returned string contains the value of *`HdrName`*.

Returns: String

Returns a specified header from an HTTP response. If left blank, *`HdrName`* returns all of the header names along with their corresponding values, with each header name/value pair separated by a `vbCrLf` character combination. If a *`HdrName`* header was not sent in the HTTP response, the method returns an empty string. Some typical HTTP response headers are:

Header Name	*Description*
`Date`	The transmission date of the response.
`MIME-Version`	The MIME version.
`Server`	The name of the server software.
`Content-length`	The number of bytes in the response. This includes both the response header and response body.
`Content-type`	The MIME content type of the response.
`Last-modified`	The date that the file or resource transmitted in the HTTP response was last modified.

GetLineFromChar

Applies to: RichTextBox

Syntax: `lVar = rtbMain.GetLineFromChar(CharPos)`

Parameters:

CharPos (long integer)
Position of the character whose line is to be identified. The first character is at position 0.

Returns: Long integer

Determines the physical line that a certain character indicated by ***CharPos*** is on. The following example shows how a label can be updated with the number of the line being edited:

```
Private Sub rtbMain_SelChange()
    Me.lblCurrentLine.Caption = _
        Me.rtbMain.GetLineFromChar(Me.rtbMain.SelStart)
End Sub
```

GetRows

Applies to: Recordset object ADO DC and Data controls

Syntax: `vVar = ctlMain.Recordset.GetRows(NumRows)`

Parameters:

NumRows (long integer)
The number of rows to retrieve

Returns: Variant containing a two-dimensional array

An extremely useful method that retrieves ***NumRows*** rows from a recordset into an array, starting with the current row. The array will contain a row for each row retrieved and a column for each field from the recordset.

GetSelectedPart, SelectPart

Applies to: MSChart

Syntax:

```
chtMain.GetSelectedPart( _
    Part, Index1{, Index2}, Index3}, Index4})
```

Parameters:

Part (VtChPartType enumeration)
For the GetSelectedPart method, indicates the currently selected chart element when the function returns. For the SelectPart element, indicates the chart

element to be selected. The constants of the `VtChPartType` enumeration are listed in the following table.

Index1 (integer)

If *Part* is `VtChPartTypeSeries` or `VtChPartTypePoint`, *Index1* indicates which series. (Series correspond to data columns and are numbered from left to right starting with 1.) If *Part* is `VtChPartTypeAxis` or `VtChPartTypeAxisLabel`, *Index1* identifies the selected axis using a constant from the `VtChAxisId` enumeration, as follows:

Constant	*Value*	*Description*
`VtChAxisIdX`	0	x-axis
`VtChAxisIdY`	1	y-axis
`VtChAxisIdY2`	2	Secondary y-axis
`VtChAxisIdZ`	3	z-axis (3-D charts only)

Index2 (integer)

If *Part* is `VtChPartTypePoint`, identifies a particular point in the series indicated by *Index1*.

Index3 (integer)

If *Part* is `VtChPartTypeAxisLabel`, *Index3* indicates the level of the label.

Index4 (integer)

Unused.

Returns: None

The GetSelectedPart method returns information by reference that identifies the object selected in the MSChart control. All parameters passed to the GetSelectedPart method are returned by reference to indicate the selected element. The SelectPart method selects an object in the MSChart control. The constants representing chart objects are as follows:

Constant	*Value*	*Description*
`VtChPartTypeChart`	0	The chart control
`VtChPartTypeTitle`	1	The chart title
`VtChPartTypeFootnote`	2	The chart footnote
`VtChPartTypeLegend`	3	The chart legend
`VtChPartTypePlot`	4	The chart plot
`VtChPartTypeSeries`	5	A chart series
`VtChPartTypePoint`	7	An individual data point
`VtChPartTypePointLabel`	8	A data point label
`VtChPartTypeAxis`	9	An axis
`VtChPartTypeAxisLabel`	10	An axis label
`VtChPartTypeAxisTitle`	11	An axis title

GetVisibleCount

Applies to: TreeView

Syntax: `lVar = tvwMain.GetVisibleCount`

Parameters: None

Returns: Long integer

Returns the number of Node objects visible within the TreeView control.

Hide

Applies to: Form and MDIForm objects

Syntax: `ctlMain.Hide`

Parameters: None

Returns: None

Causes the form or MDI form to become invisible yet remain loaded. This is particularly useful when a calling process needs information from a form before it is unloaded, as in this example:

```
'Load and display the Form modally
Load frmMain
frmMain.Show vbModal
'The Form will be hidden with Me.Hide when it is done.
'Then information can be taken from the Form.
sValue = frmMain.txtMain.Text
'Now the Form can be unloaded normally
Unload frmMain
```

HitTest

Applies to: ListView, MonthView, TreeView

Syntax:

```
Set objVar = ctlMain.HitTest(X, Y)     ' ListView/TreeView
iVar = mvwMain.HitTest(X, Y, Date)     ' MonthView
```

Parameters:

X (single)
: The x-coordinate

Y (single)
: The y-coordinate

`Date` *(Date, MonthView only)*

Parameter passed by reference to hold the date located at the *X* and *Y*

Returns:

ListItem (ListView), `MonthViewHitTestAreas` enumeration (MonthView), Node (TreeView)

Determines what lies at a particular coordinate on the control. If the method call returns `Nothing` for the ListView or TreeView, no object is at those coordinates. Otherwise, the ListItem or Node object is returned. In the case of the MonthView control, if a date was clicked (that is, if the call to the HitTest method returns `mvwCalendarDate`, `mvwCalendarNext`, or `mvwCalendarPrev`), *Date* will contain the date clicked when the method returns. The value returned can be any of those listed in the following table:

Constant	*Value*	*Description*
`mvwCalendarBack`	0	The calendar background
`mvwCalendarDate`	1	A specific date indicated by the *Date* parameter
`mvwCalendarDateNext`	2	A day in the next month
`mvwCalendarDatePrev`	3	A day in the previous month
`mvwCalendarDay`	4	The day-of-the-week labels
`mvwCalendarWeekNum`	5	The week numbers
`mvwCalendarNoWhere`	6	The bottom edge of the calendar
`mvwCalendarTitleBack`	7	The background around the calendar
`mvwCalendarTitleBtnNext`	8	The next month button in the title area
`mvwCalendarTitleBtnPrev`	9	The previous month button in the title area
`mvwCalendarTitleMonth`	10	The month name in the title area
`mvwCalendarTitleYear`	11	The year number in the title area
`mvwCalendarTodayLink`	12	The "today" area of the calendar

If you're using the MonthView control's HitTest method to determine the date on which the user has clicked, note that this can be done in a much more straightforward fashion by writing an event handler for the DateClick event.

HoldFields

Applies to: DataGrid

Syntax: `dtgMain.HoldFields`

Parameters: None

Returns: None

Saves the current layout so that it is used anytime the control's Rebind method is called. The ClearFields method resets the layout.

InitializeLabels

Applies to: DataGrid object of MSChart

Syntax: `chtMain.DataGrid.InitializeLabels`

Parameters: None

Returns: None

Assigns unique keys (identifiers) to the labels in the DataGrid object's first level.

InsertColumnLabels, InsertRowLabels

Applies to: DataGrid object of MSChart

Syntax:

```
chtMain.DataGrid.InsertColumnLabels(LabelIndex, Count)
chtMain.DataGrid.InsertRowLabels(LabelIndex, Count)
```

Parameters:

`LabelIndex` *(integer)*
: The index of the first level of column or row labels to be inserted. Column labels are numbered starting from the top, which is 1; row labels are numbered starting from the left, which is 1.

`Count` *(integer)*
: The number of levels to insert.

Returns: None

These methods insert levels of labels in the DataGrid object.

InsertColumns, InsertRows

Applies to: DataGrid object of MSChart

Syntax:

```
chtMain.DataGrid.InsertColumns(Column, Count)
chtMain.DataGrid.InsertRows(Row, Count)
```

Parameters:

`Column` *(integer, InsertColumns only) or* `Row` *(integer, InsertRows only)*
: The position of the first column or row to be inserted. (Columns are numbered from the left starting at 1. Rows are numbered from the top starting at 1.)

`Count` *(integer)*
: The number of columns or rows to insert.

Returns: None

These methods insert one or more rows (in the case of InsertRows) or columns (in the case of InsertColumns) into the DataGrid object.

InsertObjDlg

Applies to: OLE

Syntax: `oleMain.InsertObjDlg`

Parameters: None

Returns: None

Displays the Insert Object dialog, which allows the user to create an OLE object at runtime.

InsertRowLabels

Applies to: DataGrid object of MSChart

See: InsertColumnLabels

InsertRows

Applies to: DataGrid object of MSChart

See: InsertColumns

Layout

Applies to: MSChart

Syntax: `chtMain.Layout`

Parameters: None

Returns: None

Forces the MSChart control to perform all calculations involved in displaying the chart. By calling this method, you ensure that all settings are accurate based on any changed data.

Line

Applies to: Form object; PictureBox control

Syntax:

```
ctlMain.Line [Step] [(X1, Y1)] - _
    [Step] (X2, Y2) [, Color], [B][F]
```

Parameters:

X1 (optional single), Y1 (optional single)
The line's starting x- and y-coordinates.

X2 (single), Y2 (single)
The line's ending x- and y-coordinates.

`Color` *(optional long integer)*
An RGB color representing the line's color. It can be generated by either the *RGB* function or the *QColor* function. If the parameter is omitted, the line's color is defined by the ForeColor property.

Returns: None

One of the graphic methods that draws a line on the control. When the first `Step` keyword is supplied, the *X1* and *Y1* parameters are relative to the current graphics coordinates defined by the CurrentX and CurrentY properties; otherwise, *X1* and *Y1* are interpreted as absolute coordinates. When the second `Step` keyword is supplied, the *X2* and *Y2* parameters are relative to the line's starting point; otherwise, they are absolute coordinates. The units of measure of *X1*, *Y1*, *X2*, and *Y2* are all defined by the value of the ScaleMode property. If the `F` keyword is supplied, the endpoints will become the opposite corners of a box. If the `BF` keyword is supplied, the endpoints will become the opposite corners of a filled box.

LinkExecute, LinkPoke, LinkRequest, LinkSend

Applies to: Label, PictureBox, TextBox

Syntax:

```
ctlMain.LinkExecute Command
ctlMain.LinkPoke
ctlMain.LinkRequest
ctlMain.LinkSend
```

Parameters:

`Command` *(string, LinkExecute only)*
The command for the receiving application to execute

Returns: None

These methods are used in a DDE conversation between applications. The LinkExecute method causes the source application to execute the command sent by the `Command` parameter. The LinkPoke method transfers the contents of the control (the Caption property, in the case of a Label; the Picture property, in the case of a PictureBox; and the Text property, in the case of a Textbox control) to the source application. The LinkRequest method causes the source application to update the contents of the control. Like the LinkPoke method, the LinkSend method transfers the contents of the control, in this case to the destination application.

Although you may occasionally have to maintain code that relies on DDE, this technology is almost never used in new development efforts. For a variety of reasons, DDE never caught on as a method of interprocess communication and is now extremely dated. It has largely been supplanted by automation using COM.

Listen

Applies to: Winsock

Syntax: `sckMain.Listen`

Parameters: None

Returns: None

Creates a socket that the Winsock control begins to monitor for data.

LoadFile, SaveFile

Applies to: RichTextBox

Syntax:

```
rtbMain.LoadFile PathName, FileType
rtbMain.SaveFile PathName, FileType
```

Parameters:

`Pathname` *(string)*
: The path and name of the file to load or save.

`FileType` (`LoadSaveConstants` *enumeration)*
: The type of file to load or save. Possible values are 0–rtfRTF for a rich text file or 1–rtfText for a text file.

Returns: None

The LoadFile method loads the contents of a file into the RichTextBox control. The SaveFile method saves the contents of the RichTextBox control.

MakeReplica

Applies to: Database object of Data control

Syntax:

```
datMain.Database.MakeReplica Replica, _
    Description [, Options]
```

Parameters:

`Replica` *(string)*
: The filename for the new database.

`Description` *(string)*
: Text describing the replica.

`Options` (`ReplicaTypeEnum` *enumeration)*
: Constants that define the characteristics of the replica. Possible values are 1–dbRepMakePartial to create a partial replica, 2–dbRepMakeReadOnly to make the replica read-only, or the two can be added to make a read-only, partial replica.

Returns: None

Creates a copy of the current database suitable for data replication.

Move

Applies to: All controls with a visible interface except Line and Shape

Syntax: `ctlMain.Move Left [, Top], Width], Height]`

Parameters:

`Left` *(single)*
: The x-coordinate to which to move the control

`Top` *(optional single)*
: The y-coordinate to which to move the control

`Width` *(optional single)*
: The control's new width

`Height` *(optional single)*
: The control's new height

Returns: None

Moves and resizes the object on its parent. All parameters are based on the current ScaleMode setting of the parent control. For example, a PictureBox control can be moved and resized to the size of the parent with a 120 twip border as follows:

```
picMain.Move 120, 120, Me.ScaleWidth - 240, _
             Me.ScaleHeight - 240
```

Move

Applies to: Recordset object of ADO DC

Syntax: `adoMain.Recordset.Move NumRecords, Start`

Parameters:

`NumRecords` *(long integer)*
: The number of records to move; it can be positive for records subsequent to ***`Start`*** or negative for records prior to ***`Start`***.

`Start` *(variant or* `BookmarkEnum` *enumeration)*
: The position from which the move should begin. ***`Start`*** can be either a bookmark or one of the following constants: 0–adBookmarkCurrent for the current record, 1–adBookmarkFirst for the first record or 2–adBookmarkLast for the last record.

Returns: None

Moves the record pointer within an ADO recordset.

MoveData

Applies to: DataGrid object of MSChart

Syntax:

```
chtMain.DataGrid.MoveData Top, Left, _
    Bottom, Right, OverOffset, DownOffset
```

Parameters:

`Top` *(integer)*
: The first row in the range to be moved.

`Left` *(integer)*
: The first column in the range to be moved.

`Bottom` *(integer)*
: The last row in the range to be moved.

`Right` *(integer)*
: The last column in the range to be moved.

`OverOffset` *(integer)*
: Controls how many cells to move the range horizontally. A positive value indicates cells should be moved to the right, a negative value to the left.

`DownOffset` *(integer)*
: Controls vertical movement. A positive value indicates cells should be moved down, a negative value up.

Returns: None

Moves a range of values to a different portion of the DataGrid. The `Top`, `Left`, `Bottom`, and `Right` parameters define the range to move.

MoveFirst, MoveLast, MoveNext, MovePrevious

Applies to: Recordset object of ADO DC and Data controls

Syntax:

```
ctlMain.Recordset.MoveFirst
ctlMain.Recordset.MoveLast
ctlMain.Recordset.MoveNext
ctlMain.Recordset.MovePrevious
```

Parameters: None

Returns: None

These methods are used to move the record pointer through a recordset. The MoveFirst method moves the record pointer to the first record, the MoveLast moves to the last, the MoveNext moves to the next record, and the MovePrevious moves to the prior record.

NewPassword

Applies to: Database object of Data control

Syntax: `datMain.Database.NewPassword(OldPassword, NewPassword)`

Parameters:

`OldPassword` *(string)*
The correct old password for the database

`NewPassword` *(string)*
The new password for the database

Returns: None

Changes the password for a Jet engine (Microsoft Access) database.

NextRecordset

Applies to: Recordset object of ADO DC and Data controls

Syntax: `Set rsVar = ctlMain.Recordset([RecordsAffected])`

Parameters:

`RecordsAffected` *(optional long integer, ADO Recordset Only)*
When the method returns, indicates the number of records affected.

Returns: Recordset

When the RecordSource for a DAO recordset contains multiple SQL statements, or when multiple Command objects exist for an ADO recordset, the NextRecordset method returns the recordset for the next SQL statement or Command object.

OLEDrag

Applies to: All controls with a visible interface except Line and Shape

Syntax: `oleMain.OLEDrag`

Parameters: None

Returns: None

Initiates an OLE Drag and Drop operation with the control's contents. See Chapter 2 for more information about OLE Drag and Drop.

Open

Applies to: Animation

Syntax: `aniMain.Open File`

Parameters:

`File` *(string)*

The *.AVI* file to be opened

Returns: None

Opens an *.AVI* file named in the `File` parameter. That *.AVI* file is played automatically if the AutoPlay property is set to `True`. Otherwise, it can be played by calling the Play method.

OpenRecordset

Applies to: Database object of Data control

Syntax:

```
Set rsVar = datMain.Database.OpenRecordset( _
    Source [, Type], Options], LockEdits])
```

Parameters:

`Source` *(string)*

A valid SQL statement or table name.

`Type` *(optional* `RecordsetTypeEnum` *enumeration)*

Should contain one of the following constants to indicate the type of recordset to open: 1–dbOpenTable for a direct table-type recordset, 2–dbOpenDynaset for a read/write dynamic recordset, 4–dbOpenSnapshot for a read-only recordset, or 8–dbOpenForwardOnly for a read-only recordset that will accept only MoveNext commands for pointer movement. The default value for `Type` depends on the value of the `Source` parameter. If `Source` contains a table name in the database, `dbOpenTable` is the default; if it contains an SQL statement or the name of a linked table, `dbOpenDynaset` is the default.

`Options` *(optional* `RecordsetTypeEnum` *enumeration)*

Sets various options for the recordset being opened. The following table lists the options, which can be combined:

Constant	*Value*	*Description*
`dbDenyWrite`	1	Locks the recordset's data from being edited by other users.
`dbDenyRead`	2	Prevents other users from reading data contained by the recordset.
`dbReadOnly`	4	Data in the recordset cannot be edited. This has been replaced by passing a value of `dbReadOnly` to the `LockEdits` parameter.
`dbAppendOnly`	8	Only new records can be added to the recordset.
`dbInconsistent`	16	Allows edits to the recordset to violate the integrity of joined tables.

Constant	Value	Description
`dbConsistent`	32	Does not allow edits to the recordset to violate the integrity of joined tables.
`dbSQLPassThrough`	64	The recordset bypasses the Jet engine and is sent directly to a connected ODBC data source. This can give much faster results when communicating to an ODBC data source.
`dbForwardOnly`	256	All methods that move the record pointer cause errors except for MoveNext. This has been replaced by passing a value of `dbOpenForwardOnly` to the *`Type`* parameter.
`dbSeeChanges`	512	An error is fired if two users attempt to change the same data in the recordset.
`dbRunAsync`	1,024	Allows an ODBC recordset to run asynchronously.
`dbExecDirect`	2,048	Creates a recordset for an ODBC data source, bypassing some preparatory internal steps.

`LockEdits` (optional enumeration)

Controls how data is protected in a multiuser environment. It can be set to 1–dbOptimisticValue to use optimistic record locking based on a comparison of old and new record values (ODBC Direct only), 2–dbPessimistic for pessimistic record locking, 3–dbOptimistic for optimistic record locking, 4–dbReadOnly for a recordset that cannot be updated, or 5–dbOptimisticBatch for optimistic batch updating of ODBC Direct recordsets.

Returns: Recordset

Creates a new recordset.

OpenURL

Applies to: Inet control

Syntax: `Set vVar = itcMain.OpenURL(Url [, DataType])`

Parameters:

`URL` (string)

The URL for the document or resource desired.

`DataType` (optional `DataTypeConstants` enumeration)

Format in which the data is to be returned. The value of this parameter must be either 0–icString to return a string or 1–icByteArray to return a byte array.

Returns: String or byte array, depending on *`DataType`*

Returns the contents of a URL; it is the equivalent of a call to the Execute method with a `GET` command string. When the method returns, the control's URL properties are updated to reflect the result of the call to the OpenURL method.

The following statement will return the contents of the O'Reilly Visual Basic web page in a string:

```
Me.txtHTML.Text = _
    Me.itcMain.OpenURL("http://vb.oreilly.com", icString)
```

Overlay

Applies to: ImageList

Syntax: `Set picVar = imlMain.Overlay(Index1, Index2)`

Parameters:

`Index1` *(integer)*
The index or key of the ListImage to be overlaid

`Index2` *(integer)*
The index or key of the ListImage to overlay

Returns: Picture

Applies the color defined in the MaskColor property to one ListImage from the ImageList control, combines it with another ListImage from the control, and returns the resulting image.

PaintPicture

Applies to: Form object; PictureBox control

Syntax:

```
ctlMain.PaintPicture picPicture, X1, Y1 [, Width1], _
    Height1], X2], Y2], Width2], Height2], OpCode]
```

Parameters:

`Picture` *(StdPicture Object)*
A picture object representing the image to be displayed. StdPicture objects can be returned by the *LoadPicture* function.

`X1` *(single)*, `Y1` *(single)*
The x- and y-coordinates of the top-right corner at which the image is to be positioned on the form or control.

`Width1` *(optional single)*
The width of the image on its destination. If `Width1` is less than or greater than the actual width of the image, it will be compressed or stretched horizontally. If omitted, the source width is used.

`Height1` *(optional single)*
The height of the image on its destination. If `Height1` is less than or greater than the actual size of the image, it will be compressed or stretched vertically. If omitted, the source height is used.

X2 (optional single), Y2 (optional single)

The coordinates of the image's clipping region (i.e., the x- and y-coordinates of the region of the image that is to be displayed). If omitted, the coordinates default to 0, 0.

`Width2` (optional single)

The width of the clipping region on the image. If omitted, the entire source width is used.

`Height2` (optional single)

The height of the clipping region on the image. If omitted, the entire source height is used.

`Opcode` (optional `RasterOpConstants` enumeration)

Constant indicating a bitwise operation to be performed on bitmaps *only*; using *`Opcode`* with nonbitmap images generates an error. In addition, if the image is an icon or metafile, the only valid constant for *`Opcode`* is `vbSrcCopy`. The members of the `RasterOpConstants` enumeration are:

Constant	*Value*	*Description*
`vbDstInvert`	&H00550009	Invert the destination bitmap.
`vbMergeCopy`	&H00C000CA	Combine the pattern defined by the Fill-Style property and the source.
`vbMergePaint`	&H00BB0226	Combine the inverted source with the destination by using `Or`.
`vbNotSrcCopy`	&H00330008	Copy the inverted source to the destination.
`vbNotSrcErase`	&H001100A6	Combine the source and destination by using `Or` and invert the result.
`vbPatCopy`	&H00F00021L	Copy the pattern defined by the FillStyle property to the destination.
`vbPatInvert`	&H005A0049L	Combine the destination with the pattern defined by the FillStyle property by using `XOR`.
`vbPatPaint`	&H00FB0A09L	Combine the inverted source with the pattern defined by the FillStyle property by using `Or`, then combine the result with the destination by using `Or`.
`vbSrcAnd`	&H008800C6	Combine the destination and source by using `AND`.
`vbSrcCopy`	&H00CC0020	Copy the source to the destination.
`vbSrcErase`	&H00440328	Invert the destination and combine the result with the source by using `AND`.
`vbSrcInvert`	&H00660046	Combine pixels of the destination and source by using `XOR`.
`vbSrcPaint`	&H00EE0086	Combine pixels of the destination and source by using `Or`.

Returns: None

One of the graphic methods that draws a bitmap on any form or PictureBox. The *`X1`*, *`Y1`*, *`Width1`*, and *`Height1`* parameters control the size of the picture to draw. This can extend outside the visible control and outside the desired boundaries. The *`X2`*, *`Y2`*, *`Width2`*, and *`Height2`* parameters control the clipping area. Only portions of the picture within these boundaries are actually drawn. The unit of measure of all eight of these parameters is controlled by the form or control's ScaleMode property.

Paste

Applies to: OLE

Syntax: `oleMain.Paste`

Parameters: None

Returns: None

Copies the contents of the Windows Clipboard into the OLE control.

PasteSpecialDlg

Applies to: OLE

Syntax: `oleMain.PasteSpecialDlg`

Parameters: None

Returns: None

Opens the Paste Special dialog, which allows the user to select data in one of the formats available on the Clipboard to paste into the OLE control. For example, rich text could be pasted as formatted or unformatted text.

PeekData

Applies to: Winsock

See: GetData, PeekData

Play

Applies to: Animation

Syntax: `aniMain.Play [Repeat], Start], End]`

Parameters:

`Repeat` *(optional integer)*
Number of times the *.AVI* file should repeat. A value of -1 means indefinitely.

`Start` *(optional integer)*
Starting frame number.

`End` *(optional integer)*
Ending frame number.

Returns: None

Begins playing the *.AVI* file loaded into the Animation control.

Point

Applies to: Form object; PictureBox control

Syntax: `ctlMain.Point X, Y`

Parameters:

`X` *(single)*, `Y` *(single)*
The coordinate whose color is to be returned.

Returns: Long integer

Returns the pixel's color at the coordinate represented by the `X` and `Y` parameters.

PopupMenu

Applies to: Form and MDIForm objects

Syntax:

```
ctlMain.PopupMenu MenuName [, Flags], X], Y], BoldCommand]
```

Parameters:

`MenuName` *(string)*
The name of the menu to pop up. According to the documentation, `MenuName` must contain at least one submenu, although this is inaccurate.

`Flags` *(optional* `MenuControlConstants` *enumeration)*
Constants that control the alignment and behavior of the pop-up menu. Possible values are 0–vbPopupMenuLeftButton to select menu items with the left mouse button, 2–vbPopupMenuRightButton to select menu items with either mouse button, 0–vbPopupMenuLeftAlign to left-align the menu on the `X` parameter, 4–vbPopupMenuCenterAlign to center the menu on the `X` parameter, and 6–vbPopupMenuRightAlign to right-align the menu on the `X` parameter. Flags can consist of one constant from the first group of two constants added or ORed with one constant from the second group of three constants. By default, pop-up menus are left-aligned, and menu items are selected using the left mouse button.

`X` *(optional single)*, `Y` *(optional single)*
The coordinates at which the pop up should appear. The units are defined by the form's ScaleMode property. The precise alignment of the menu at the

coordinates is controlled by the *Flags* parameter. If *X* and *Y* are omitted, the current mouse coordinates are used.

BoldCommand (optional Menu object)
The menu item to appear in bold. For example:

```
Me.PopupMenu mnuEdit, , , , mnuEdit_Paste
```

opens the mnuEdit context menu and displays the item named mnuEdit_Paste in bold. If omitted, no menu items appear in bold.

Returns: None

Displays a pop-up menu on the form or MDI form. Typically, the method is called in the MouseDown event procedure in response to the user's pressing the alternate mouse button, as the following code fragment shows:

```
Private Sub Form_MouseDown(Button As Integer, _
        Shift As Integer, X As Single, Y As Single)

If Button = vbRightButton Then
   Me.PopupMenu mnuContext
End If

End Sub
```

Once the menu has popped up, any actions taken by the user are handled by the menu item's Click event.

PrintForm

Applies to: Form object

Syntax: `frmMain.PrintForm`

Parameters: None

Returns: None

Sends the contents of the form to the current printer.

PSet

Applies to: Form object; PictureBox control

Syntax: `ctlMain.PSet [Step] (X, Y)[, Color]`

Parameters:

X (single), Y (single)
The coordinates at which to draw the point.

Color (optional long integer)
The RGB color in which to draw the point. If omitted, the ForeColor property defines the point's color. Use the *RGB* or *QBColor* functions to supply a color.

Returns: None

One of the graphic methods that draws a point on any form or picture box. When the `Step` keyword is supplied, the *X* and *Y* parameters are relative to the current graphics coordinates, which are defined by the values of the CurrentX and CurrentY properties. Otherwise, *X* and *Y* are absolute coordinates.

RandomDataFill, RandomFillColumns, RandomFillRows

Applies to: DataGrid object of MSChart

Syntax:

```
chtMain.DataGrid.RandomDataFill
chtMain.DataGrid.RandomFillColumns Column, Count
chtMain.DataGrid.RandomFillRows Row, Count
```

Parameters:

`Column` *(integer, RandomFillColumns only)*
: The first column to populate with data. (The leftmost column of the data grid is numbered 1.)

`Row` *(integer, RandomFillRows only)*
: The first row to populate with data. (The top row of the data grid is numbered 1.)

`Count` *(integer, RandomFillColumns and RandomFillRows)*
: The number of columns or rows to populate with random data.

Returns: None

These methods populate the DataGrid (RandomDataFill) or a section of the DataGrid (RandomFillColumns and RandomFillRows) with random data. This is useful for seeing how a chart will look with actual data.

ReadFromFile, SaveToFile, SaveToOle1File

Applies to: OLE

Syntax:

```
oleMain.ReadFromFile FileNumber
oleMain.SaveToFile FileNumber
oleMain.SaveToOle1File FileNumber
```

Parameters:

`FileNumber` *(integer)*
: The number of a file opened in Binary mode

Returns: None

The ReadFromFile method reads data from an open file into the OLE control. The SaveToFile method writes data from the OLE control to an open file. The SaveToOle1File method writes data from the OLE control to an open file in OLE Version 1.0 format. The SaveToFile and ReadFromFile methods are the standard way to save and restore information for an open OLE object.

Rebind

Applies to: DataGrid

Syntax: `dtgMain.Rebind`

Parameters: None

Returns: None

Refreshes all data in the DataGrid. The layout of the DataGrid is restored to whatever it was the last time the HoldFields method was called.

ReFill

Applies to: DataCombo, DataList

Syntax: `ctlMain.ReFill`

Parameters: None

Returns: None

Repopulates the contents of the list portion of the control and redraws the control. It differs from the Refresh method, which merely redraws the control.

Refresh

Applies to: All controls with a visible interface

Syntax: `ctlMain.Refresh`

Parameters: None

Returns: None

Causes a control to repaint and refresh. Use it when you wish to force the Paint event to fire in order to update the contents of a control such as a picture box.

RemoveItem

Applies to: ComboBox, ListBox, MSFlexGrid, MSHFlexGrid

Syntax:

```
ctlMain.RemoveItem Index                'ComboBox, ListBox, MSFlexGrid
mshMain.RemoveItem iIndex, iNumber       'MSHFlexGrid
```

Parameters:

`Index` *(integer)*
Number of the row to be removed. The first row is 0.

`Number` *(integer, MSHFlexGrid only)*
The band from which the row will be removed.

Returns: None

Removes a row from the control.

Requery

Applies to: Recordset object of ADO DC and Data controls

Syntax: `ctlMain.Recordset.Requery`

Parameters: None

Returns: None

Runs the SQL statement or Command object that created the recordset again and generates new results.

ResetCustom

Applies to: DataPoint object of MSChart

Syntax:

```
chtMain.Plot.SeriesCollection(Ctr). _
    DataPoints(-1).ResetCustom
```

Parameters: None

Returns: None

Resets any customization done to a DataPoint object by modifying its attributes.

ResetCustomLabel

Applies to: DataPointLabel object of MSChart

Syntax:

```
chtMain.Plot.SeriesCollection(Ctr). _
    DataPoints(-1).DataPointLabel.ResetCustomLabel
```

Parameters: None

Returns: None

Resets any customization done to a DataPointLabel object by modifying its attributes.

RestoreToolbar, SaveToolbar

Applies to: Toolbar

Syntax:

```
tbrMain.RestoreToolbar Key, SubKey, Value
tbrMain.SaveToolbar Key, SubKey, Value
```

Parameters:

Key (string)

Under VB5, *Key* can be either a string or a long integer. The parameter itself is unused, although the method call fails if *Key* is Null. Under VB6, *Key* can either be a null string or a portion of the path from a subkey of HKEY_CURRENT_USER to the key actually containing *Value*.

SubKey (string)

Under VB5, the complete path from HKEY_CURRENT_USER to the registry key containing *Value*. For example:

```
RestoreToolbar "", "Software\MyCompany\MyApp", _
               "CustToolbar"
```

Under VB6, the remaining portion of the path from *Key* (or, if key is a null string, from HKEY_CURRENT_USER) to the key containing *Value*. For example:

```
RestoreToolbar "Software", "MyCompany\MyApp", _
               "CustToolbar"
```

or

```
RestoreToolbar "", "Software\MyCompany\MyApp", _
               "CustToolbar"
```

Value (string)

The name of the value entry that contains toolbar data.

Returns: None

These methods are used to save and restore customized toolbar settings to and from the registry. Notice that the methods don't specify the data to be saved or allow you to handle the data that's been retrieved; that's handled automatically by the control, which needs to know only the key and named value where it should either write or retrieve the toolbar data.

RowBookmark

Applies to: DataGrid

Syntax: `vVar = dtgMain.RowBookmark(RowNum)`

Parameters:

RowNum (integer)

The zero-based number of the visible row for which the bookmark is desired

Returns: Variant

Returns a bookmark for one of the rows currently visible on the data grid. Note that the method bookmarks a visible record and bears no relationship to a recordset's current record, which may not necessarily be visible.

RowContaining

Applies to: DataGrid

See: ColContaining

RowTop

Applies to: DataGrid

Syntax: `Var = dtgMain.RowTop(RowNum)`

Parameters:

RowNum (integer)

The zero-based number of the visible row whose y-coordinate is desired

Returns: Single

Returns the vertical coordinate for the top of a given row.

SaveFile

Applies to: RichTextBox

See: LoadFile

SaveToFile

Applies to: OLE

See: ReadFromFile

SaveToolbar

Applies to: Toolbar

See: RestoreToolbar

SaveToOle1File

Applies to: OLE

See: ReadFromFile

Scale

Applies to: Form object; PictureBox control

Syntax: `ctlMain.Scale [(X1, Y1) - (X2, Y2)]`

Parameters:

X1 (optional single), Y1 (optional single)
: The coordinate that will be at the upper-left corner of the control. If ***X1*** and *Y1* are omitted, *X2* and *Y2* must also be omitted.

X2 (optional single), Y2 (optional single)
: The coordinate that will be at the lower-right corner of the control. If ***X2*** and *Y2* are omitted, *X1* and *Y1* must also be omitted.

Returns: None

Redefines the current scale used by the control. For example, the following code will set the scale for the PictureBox control to a 1×1 area; all values between 0 and 1 will be calculated automatically:

```
Me.picMain.Scale (0, 0)-(1, 1)
```

If both coordinates are omitted, the coordinate system is reset to its default of twips.

ScaleX, ScaleY

Applies to: Form object; PictureBox control

Syntax:

```
nVar = ctlMain.ScaleX Width [FromScale], ToScale]
nVar = ctlMain.ScaleY Height [FromScale], ToScale]
```

Parameters:

Width (single, ScaleX only)
: Horizontal units to be converted.

Height (single, ScaleY only)
: Vertical units to be converted.

FromScale (ScaleModeConstants *enumeration)*
: The coordinate system from which ***Width*** and ***Height*** are to be converted. If the parameter is omitted, **vbHiMetric** is assumed.

ToScale (ScaleModeConstants *enumeration)*
: The coordinate system into which ***Width*** and ***Height*** are to be converted. If the parameter is omitted, the form or picture box's ScaleMode property is assumed.

Returns: Single

These methods are used to convert from one scale to another; the ScaleX method converts the ***Width*** parameter, and the ScaleY method converts the ***Height*** parameter. The value passed as the ***Height*** or ***Width*** parameter is then converted to the scale specified in the ***FromScale*** parameter to the scale specified in the

ToScale parameter. The following table describes values for *FromScale* and *ToScale*:

Constant	*Value*	*Description*
vbUser	0	The scale has been changed by the user.
vbTwips	1	The scale is in twips.
vbPoints	2	The scale is in points.
vbPixels	3	The scale is in pixels.
vbCharacters	4	The scale is in characters.
vbInches	5	The scale is in inches.
vbMillimeters	6	The scale is in millimeters.
vbCentimeters	7	The scale is in centimeters.
vbHiMetric	8	The scale is HiMetric, which converts each logical unit to 0.01 millimeter.

Scroll

Applies to: DataGrid

Syntax: `dtgMain.Scroll Cols, Rows`

Parameters:

`Cols` *(long integer)*
Number of columns to scroll. A positive value scrolls to the right, a negative value to the left.

`Rows` *(long integer)*
Number of rows to scroll. A positive value scrolls down, a negative value up.

Returns: None

Scrolls the DataGrid horizontally and/or vertically. Note that you can also scroll the DataGrid control programmatically by setting the FirstRow and LeftCol properties, but this requires two separate operations that fire two separate Paint events.

Seek

Applies to: Recordset object of Data control

Syntax:

```
datMain.Seek Comparison, Key1 [, Key2], Key3], _
    Key4], Key5], Key6], Key7], Key8], Key9], _
    Key10], Key11], Key12], Key13]
```

Parameters:

`Comparison` *(string)*
A comparison operator, such as = (equal), < (less than), > (greater than), <= (less than or equal to), or >= (greater than or equal to).

Methods R–Z

Key1 (variant) through Key13 (variant)

One or more values to compare with the key fields defined by the Recordset object's Index property. Up to 13 values (for 13 key fields) are permitted. The datatype of *KeyX* must correspond to the datatype of the corresponding index field. There should be separate *KeyX* parameters for each field defined in the index; otherwise, *Comparison* should be set to >=.

Returns: None

Performs an index-based seek for data. The first record found that meets the search criteria becomes the current record, and the NoMatch property is set to `False`. If *Comparison* is =, >, or >=, the search starts at the beginning of the index and moves forward. If *Comparison* is < or <=, the search starts at the end of the index and moves backward. If no record meets the search criteria, the NoMatch property is set to `True`, and the current record is undefined.

Select

Applies to: DataPoint, DataPointLabel, Footnote, Legend, Series, and Title objects of MSChart

Syntax: `objVar.Select`

Parameters: None

Returns: None

Selects the object in the MSChart control.

SelPrint

Applies to: RichTextBox

Syntax: `rtbMain.SelPrint HDC`

Parameters:

HDC (long integer)

A handle to the device context of the output device, such as a printer.

Returns: None

Sends any selected data in the RichTextBox control to the device specified by the *HDC* parameter. If there is no selected data, the contents of the RichTextBox control are sent in their entirety.

SendData

Applies to: Winsock

Syntax: `sckMain.SendData Data`

Parameters:

`Data` *(variant)*
  Data to be sent

Returns: None

Sends data over the socket. If the data is binary, `Data` should be a byte array. If `Data` is a Unicode string, it will automatically be converted to ANSI before being transmitted.

Set

Applies to: Coor and LCoor objects of MSChart

Syntax:

```
crVar.Set X, Y              'Coor Object
lcVar.Set X, Y              'LCoor Object
```

Parameters:

`X` *(single for Coor, long for LCoor),* `Y` *(single for Coor, long for LCoor)*
  Horizontal and vertical coordinates

Returns:
  None

Populates the X and Y properties of its respective object in a single method call.

Set

Applies to: LightSource object of MSChart

Syntax: `lsVar.Set X, Y, Z, Intensity`

Parameters:

`X` *(integer),* `Y` *(integer),* `Z` *(integer)*
  The coordinates of the light source location

`Intensity` *(single)*
  The light source intensity

Returns: None

Populates multiple properties (the X, Y, Z, and Intensity properties) of the Light-Source object in a single method call.

Set

Applies to: View3D object of MSChart

Syntax: `v3Var.Set Rotation, Elevation`

Methods R–Z

Parameters:

`Rotation` *(single)*
: The chart's degree of rotation. If degrees are the unit of measure, valid values can range from 0 to 360.

`Elevation` *(single)*
: The chart's degree of elevation. If degrees are the unit of measure, valid values can range from 0 (a side view of the chart) to 90 (a top view of the chart).

Returns: None

Populates multiple properties of the View3D object (specifically, the Rotation and Elevation properties) in a single method call. Although the default unit of measure for both properties is degrees, the current unit of measure is defined by the AngleUnits property.

Set

Applies to: VtColor object of MSChart

Syntax: `vtcVar.Set` ***`Red, Green, Blue`***

Parameters:

`Red` *(integer)*
: The relative intensity of red in the new color. Valid values range from 0 to 255.

`Green` *(integer)*
: The relative intensity of green in the new color. Valid values range from 0 to 255.

`Blue` *(integer)*
: The relative intensity of blue in the new color. Valid values range from 0 to 255.

Returns: None

Sets multiple properties of the VtColor object (specifically its Red, Green, and Blue properties) in a single method call.

Set

Applies to: Weighting object of MSChart

Syntax: `wtvar.Set` ***`Basis, Style`***

Parameters:

`Basis` *(*`VtChPieWeightBasis` *enumeration)*

The Weighting object's weighting type, which defines the appearance of pies. Valid values are as follows:

Constant	*Value*	*Description*
`VtChPieWeightBasisNone`	0	All pies are drawn the same size.
`VtChPieWeightBasisTotal`	1	The size of each pie reflects the ratio of its size to that of the largest pie.
`VtChPieWeightBasisSeries`	2	The first column of data in the data grid indicates the size of the pie relative to the largest pie.

`Style` *(*`VtChPieWeightStyle` *enumeration)*

The Weighting object's weighting method, which determines how pies change to reflect their weighting. Valid values are:

Constant	*Value*	*Description*
`VtChPieWeightStyleArea`	0	The area of pies changes to reflect their weighting.
`VtChPieWeightStyleDiameter`	1	The diameter of pies changes to reflect their weighting.

Returns: None

Sets multiple properties of the Chart control's Weighting object (specifically, the Basis and Style properties) in a single method call. These properties control the meaning and appearance of pie charts.

SetData

Applies to: DataGrid object of MSChart

See: GetData

SetFocus

Applies to: All controls that can receive the application focus

Syntax: `ctlMain.SetFocus`

Parameters: None

Returns: None

Moves the focus to the control *`ctlMain`*. If the control is unable to receive the focus, an error occurs.

SetSize

Applies to: DataGrid object of MSChart

Syntax:

```
chtMain.DataGrid.SetSize RowLabelCount, _
    ColumnLabelCount, DataRowCount, DataColumnCount
```

Parameters:

`RowLabelCount` *(integer)*
: Number of row labels

`ColumnLabelCount` *(integer)*
: Number of column labels

`DataRowCount` *(integer)*
: Number of data rows

`DataColumnCount` *(integer)*
: Number of data columns

Returns: None

Resizes the DataGrid object by setting its RowCount, ColumnCount, RowLabelCount, and ColumnLabelCount properties in a single method call.

Show

Applies to: Form and MDIForm objects

Syntax: `frmMain.Show Modal [, OwnerForm]`

Parameters:

`Modal` *(optional* `FormShowConstants` *enumeration)*
: A constant that determines whether the form is *application* modal or modeless. If set to 0–vbModeless, its default value, the form or MDI form can interact with other forms. If set to 1–vbModal, no other form can receive the focus or process events or code until the modal form is hidden or unloaded. An MDI form cannot be modal.

`OwnerForm` *(optional Form or MDIForm Object)*
: The form or MDI form that owns the current form. Typically, its value is `Me` when a form is shown from within code belonging to the form that owns it. For example:

```
Private Sub cmdOpenDlg_Click()
   frmDlg.Show vbModal, Me
End Sub
```

Returns: None

Loads the form or MDI form if it has not yet loaded and makes it visible.

ShowColor, ShowFont, ShowHelp, ShowOpen, ShowPrinter, ShowSave

Applies to: CommonDialog

Syntax:

```
cdlMain.ShowColor
cdlMain.ShowFont
cdlMain.ShowHelp
cdlMain.ShowOpen
cdlMain.ShowPrinter
cdlMain.ShowSave
```

Parameters: None

Returns: None

Each of these methods shows the corresponding dialog box for the CommonDialog control. See the entry for the CommonDialog Control in Chapter 5 for more information.

Methods R–Z

ShowWhatsThis

Applies to: All controls with a visible interface except Line and Shape

Syntax: `ctlMain.ShowWhatsThis`

Parameters: None

Returns: None

Displays the help topic that corresponds to the control's WhatsThisHelpID property in the "What's This Help" pop up. It allows you to provide context-sensitive help for your user interfaces.

Span

Applies to: RichTextBox

Syntax: `rtbMain.Span CharacterSet [, Forward], Negate]`

Parameters:

`CharacterSet` *(string)*
: The set of characters to look for when extending the selection.

`Forward` *(optional Boolean)*
: Direction in which the selection should be extended. If `True`, it is extended forward; if `False`, it is extended backward.

`Negate` *(optional Boolean)*
: Determines whether the selection is extended based on the presence or absence of the characters in *`CharacterSet`*. If `True`, the selection will be

extended to the first occurrence of a character found in the *CharacterSet* parameter. If `False`, the selection will be extended to the first occurrence of a character *not* found in the *CharacterSet* parameter.

Returns: None

Selects text in the RichTextBox control from the current selection or insertion point to the first occurrence of a specified character or characters.

SplitContaining

Applies to: DataGrid

See: ColContaining

StartLabelEdit

Applies to: ListView, TreeView

Syntax: `ctlMain.StartLabelEdit`

Parameters: None

Returns: None

Puts a ListItem's label (for ListView) or a node (for TreeView) into Edit mode.

Stop

Applies to: Animation

Syntax: `aniMain.Stop`

Parameters: None

Returns: None

Stops playing any *.AVI* that the Animation control is currently playing.

TextHeight, TextWidth

Applies to: Form object; PictureBox control

Syntax:

```
nVar = ctlMain.TextHeight(Str)
nVar = ctlMain.TextWidth(Str)
```

Parameters:

Str (string)
The string whose height or width is to be calculated.

Returns: Single

These methods return the height (in the case of TextHeight) or width (in the case of TextWidth) of the string contained in the *Str* parameter if it were to be displayed in the control using the current Font and Scale settings.

ToDefaults

Applies to: MSChart

Syntax: `ChtMain.ToDefaults`

Parameters: None

Returns: None

Completely resets the MSChart control to its default settings.

TwipsToChartPart

Applies to: MSChart

Syntax:

```
chtMain.TwipsToChartPart XVal, YVal, Part, _
    Index1{, Index2}, Index3}, Index4}
```

Parameters:

XVal (long integer), YVal (long integer)
The coordinates at which a chart element is to be identified.

Part (VtChPartType enumeration)
Constant indicating the chart element when the method returns. The members of the `VtChPartType` enumeration are listed in the entry for the GetSelected-Part and SelectPart methods in this chapter.

Index1 (integer)
If *Part* is `VtChPartTypeSeries` or `VtChPartTypePoint`, *Index1* indicates which series. (Series correspond to data columns and are numbered from left to right starting with 1.) If *Part* is `VtChPartTypeAxis` or `VtChPart-TypeAxisLabel`, *Index1* identifies the selected axis using a constant from the `VtChAxisId` enumeration, as follows:

Constant	*Value*	*Description*
VtChAxisIdX	0	x-axis
VtChAxisIdY	1	y-axis
VtChAxisIdY2	2	Secondary y-axis
VtChAxisIdZ	3	z-axis (3-D charts only)

Index2 (integer)
If *Part* is `VtChPartTypePoint`, identifies a particular point in the series indicated by *Index1*.

Index3 (integer)
if `Part` is `VtChPartTypeAxisLabel`, *Index3* indicates the level of the label.

Index4 (integer)
Unused.

Returns: None

Returns information by reference about the chart element located at the `XVal`, `YVal` coordinates. The variables passed as the `Index1` through `Index4` parameters will return values to indicate which specific part was selected in a collection or array. See the entry for the MSChart Control in Chapter 5 for more information.

Update

Applies to: OLE

Syntax: `oleMain.Update`

Parameters: None

Returns: None

Updates the data from the server application to refresh the image shown in the OLE control.

Update

Applies to: Recordset object of Data control

Syntax: `datMain.Recordset.Update [UpdateType], Force]`

Parameters:

`UpdateType` *(optional* `UpdateTypeEnum` *enumeration)*
A constant indicating the type of update. The default is 0–dbUpdateRegular, which writes the changes to disk (bypassing the cache) immediately. The remaining values are 1–dbUpdateBatch to write all pending changes to disk and 2–dbUpdateCurrentRecord to write only changes from the current record to disk.

`Force` *(optional Boolean)*
If `True`, changes to the same data by any other users are simply overwritten. If `False`, the update fails for those changes that conflict with changes made by another user, and the BatchCollisionCount and BatchCollision properties are updated accordingly.

Returns: None

The Update method causes any pending Edit or Add New operations to be saved to the recordset's data source.

Update

Applies to: Recordset object of ADO DC

Syntax: `addMain.Recordset.Update [Fields], Values]`

Parameters:

`Fields` *(variant or variant Array)*
A single value or a variant array containing the names or the ordinal positions of fields to be modified

`Values` *(variant or variant Array)*
A single value or a variant array containing the values to be assigned to the fields specified in ***`Fields`***

Returns: None

The Update method causes any pending Edit or AddNew operations on the current record to be saved to the recordset's data source. The ***`Fields`*** and ***`Values`*** parameters can each be set to a variant value to update one field or to a variant array to update multiple fields.

WhatsThisMode

Applies to: Form and MDIForm objects

Syntax: `frmMain.WhatsThisMode`

Parameters: None

Returns: None

Places the form or MDI form "What's This Help" mode. The appearance of the mouse pointer changes, and the WhatsThisHelpID property of the object on which the user clicks is used to invoke context-sensitive help.

ZOrder

Applies to: All controls with a visible interface

Syntax: `ctlmain.ZOrder Position`

Parameters:

`Position(ZOrderConstants` *enumeration)*
A constant specifying the position of the object

Returns: None

Moves a control to the front or back of overlapping controls within a container. When Position is set to 0-vbBringToFront, the control is moved to the front. When Position is set to 1-vbSendToBack, the control is moved behind other controls.

CHAPTER 8

Events

This chapter documents all of the events raised by the controls covered in Chapter 5, *Controls*. Each entry follows a standard format, which includes:

- The controls to which the event applies
- A description of the parameters passed to the event, including mention of those passed by reference whose value you can change in your event handler
- A description of the event

All events can have an *Index* parameter if the control is part of a control array. The *Index* parameter uniquely identifies the control within the array, thereby allowing you to determine which control in the array fired the event and giving you access to that control's properties and methods. The *Index* parameter is not covered in the entries.

Activate, Deactivate

Applies to: Form and MDIForm objects

Parameters: None

Whenever a form or MDI form receives the focus in an application, the Activate event is fired. This can occur as a result of user interaction, by the user moving the focus from one application form to another. (Note that the Activate event is not fired when the user moves the focus from another application to the form or MDI form.) It can also occur programmatically in the following ways:

- When a form designated as a project's startup object loads
- As a result of a call to the form's Show method
- As a result of a call to the form's SetFocus method

The following table shows the order in which events are fired under these three circumstances:

Event	*Startup/Show*	*SetFocus*
Initialize	✓	
Load	✓	
Resize	✓	
Activate	✓	✓
GotFocus	✓	✓
Paint	✓	✓

When the focus shifts from the form or MDI form to another form belonging to the same application, the Deactivate event is fired after the LostFocus event. Note that the Deactivate event is not fired when the focus shifts to another application or when the form or MDI form is unloaded or closed.

AfterColEdit, BeforeColEdit

Applies to: DataGrid

Parameters:

`ColIndex` *(integer)*
: The index of the column being edited.

`KeyAscii` *(integer, BeforeColEdit only)*
: The ASCII value of the key that was pressed to initiate the edit.

`Cancel` *(integer, BeforeColEdit only)*
: Flag passed by reference that indicates whether the edit operation should be cancelled; its default value is `False`.

These events are triggered just before (BeforeColEdit) and just after (AfterColEdit) the user edits the contents of a cell. Setting the *`Cancel`* parameter in the BeforeColEdit event to `True` cancels the editing of the cell.

AfterColUpdate, BeforeColUpdate

Applies to: DataGrid

Parameters:

`ColIndex` *(integer)*
: The index of the column being edited.

`OldValue` *(variant, BeforeColUpdate only)*
: The value that the cell contained before being edited.

`Cancel` *(integer, BeforeColUpdate only)*
: Flag passed by reference that indicates whether the update operation should be cancelled; its default value is `False`.

These events are triggered after the user has edited the contents of a cell but just before (BeforeColUpdate) or after (AfterColUpdate) the data is sent to the data source. Setting the *Cancel* parameter in the BeforeColUpdate event to True cancels the updating of the data source.

AfterDelete, BeforeDelete

Applies to: DataGrid

Parameters:

Cancel (integer, BeforeDelete only)
Flag passed by reference that indicates whether the deletion should be cancelled; its default value is False.

These events are triggered just before (BeforeDelete) and just after (AfterDelete) a record is deleted through the DataGrid control. Setting the *Cancel* parameter in the BeforeDelete event to True cancels the deletion of the record.

AfterInsert, BeforeInsert

Applies to: DataGrid

Parameters:

Cancel (integer, BeforeInsert only)
Flag passed by reference that indicates whether the insertion should be cancelled; its default value is False.

These events are triggered just before (BeforeInsert) and just after (AfterInsert) a record is inserted through the DataGrid control. Setting the *Cancel* parameter in the BeforeInsert event to True cancels the insertion of the record.

AfterLabelEdit, BeforeLabelEdit

Applies to: ListView, TreeView

Parameters:

Cancel (integer)
Flag passed by reference that indicates whether the edit operation should be cancelled; its default value is False.

NewString (string, AfterLabelEdit only)
The new value of the label. If editing were cancelled, its value is vbNull.

These events are triggered when the user begins to edit (BeforeLabelEdit) and after the user finishes editing (AfterLabelEdit) the label of a Node or ListItem object. Setting the *Cancel* parameter to True cancels the editing of the label.

AfterUpdate, BeforeUpdate

Applies to: DataGrid

Parameters:

`Cancel` *(integer, BeforeUpdate only)*
: Flag passed by reference that indicates whether the pending update should be cancelled; its default value is **`False`**.

These events are triggered just before (BeforeUpdate) and just after (AfterUpdate) data is moved from the DataGrid to the data source. Setting the ***`Cancel`*** parameter in the BeforeUpdate event to **`True`** cancels the update.

AxisActivated, AxisSelected, AxisUpdated

Applies to: MSChart

Parameters:

`AxisID` (`VtChAxisID` *enumeration)*
: The axis affected, as follows:

Constant	*Value*	*Description*
`VtChAxisIdX`	0	The x-axis
`vtChAxisIdY`	1	The primary y-axis
`vtChAxisIdY2`	2	The secondary y-axis
`vtChAxisIdZ`	3	The z-axis

`AxisIndex` *(integer)*
: Reserved for future use; its value is always 1.

`MouseFlags` *(integer, AxisActivated and AxisSelected only)*
: An integer indicating which button was clicked and which key was depressed while the mouse button was clicked. Possible values for keys are 4–vtChMouseFlagShiftKeyDown for the Shift key, 8–vtChMouseFlagControlKeyDown for the CTRL key, or the two values added together (12) for both keys. That the value of the mouse button clicked is included in ***`MouseFlags`*** is not indicated in the documentation. If you're interested in detecting which key was depressed when either of these events was fired, use code like the following:

```
Select Case MouseFlags Xor vbLeftButton
   Case VtChMouseFlagControlKeyDown
      ' Handle Ctrl key
   Case VtChMouseFlagShiftKeyDown
      ' Handle Shift key
   Case VtChMouseFlagShiftKeyDown Or _
        VtChMouseFlagControlKeyDown
      ' Handle both keys
   Case Else
      ' Handle button click only
End Select
```

`UpdateFlags` (`VtChUpdateFlags` *enumeration, AxisUpdated only)*

Indicates the status of the update and can contain any combination of the values in the following chart:

Constant	*Value*	*Description*
`vtChNoDisplay`	0	The chart will not be updated.
`vtChDisplayPlot`	1	The chart will be repainted.
`vtChLayoutPlot`	2	Values for the chart will be recalculated.
`vtChDisplayLegend`	4	The legend will be repainted.
`vtChLayoutLegend`	8	Values for the legend will be recalculated.
`vtChLayoutSeries`	16	Values for the series will be recalculated.
`VtChPositionSection`	32	A chart section was moved or resized.

`Cancel` *(integer, AxisActivated and AxisSelected only)*

Unused.

These events are triggered when an axis in the MSChart control is clicked (AxisSelected), double-clicked (AxisActivated), or changed (AxisUpdated).

AxisLabelActivated, AxisLabelSelected, AxisLabelUpdated

Applies to: MSChart

Parameters:

`AxisID` (`VtChAxisID` *enumeration)*

The axis affected. The members of the **`VtChAxisID`** enumeration are listed in the entry for the AxisActivated, AxisSelected, and AxisUpdated events.

`AxisIndex` *(integer)*

Reserved for future use.

`LabelSetIndex` *(integer)*

The index of the level of labels involved in the event. Levels of labels are numbered from the axis out, beginning with 1.

`LabelIndex` *(integer)*

Unused.

`MouseFlags` *(integer, AxisLabelActivated and AxisLabelSelected only)*

An integer indicating which button was clicked and which key was depressed while the mouse button was clicked. Possible values for keys are 4–vtChMouseFlagShiftKeyDown for the Shift key, 8–vtChMouseFlagControlKeyDown for the CTRL key, or the two values added together (12) for both keys. That the value of the mouse button clicked is included in ***`MouseFlags`*** is not indicated in the documentation. If you're interested in detecting which key was depressed when either of these events was fired, use code like the following:

```
Select Case MouseFlags Xor vbLeftButton
   Case VtChMouseFlagControlKeyDown
      ' Handle CTRL key
```

```
        Case VtChMouseFlagShiftKeyDown
            ' Handle Shift key
        Case VtChMouseFlagShiftKeyDown Or _
             VtChMouseFlagControlKeyDown
            ' Handle both keys
        Case Else
            ' Handle button click only
    End Select
```

`UpdateFlags` (`VtChUpdateFlags` *enumeration, AxisLabelUpdated only)*
: Indicates the status of the update and can contain any combination of values in the `VtChUpdateFlags` enumeration. Its members are listed in the entry for the AxisActivated, AxisSelected, and AxisUpdated events.

`Cancel` *(integer, AxisLabelActivated and AxisLabelSelected only)*
: Unused.

These events are triggered when an axis label in the MSChart control is clicked (AxisLabelSelected), is double-clicked (AxisLabelActivated), or has changed (AxisLabelUpdated).

AxisTitleActivated, AxisTitleSelected, AxisTitleUpdated

Applies to: MSChart

Parameters:

`AxisID` (`VtChAxisID` *enumeration)*
: The axis affected. The members of the `VtChAxisID` enumeration are listed in the entry for the AxisActivated, AxisSelected, and AxisUpdated events.

`AxisIndex` *(integer)*
: Reserved for future use.

`MouseFlags` *(integer, AxisTitleActivated and AxisTitleSelected only)*
: An integer indicating which button was clicked and which key was depressed while the mouse button was clicked. Possible values for keys are 4–vtChMouseFlagShiftKeyDown for the Shift key, 8–vtChMouseFlagControlKeyDown for the CTRL key, or the two values added together (12) for both keys. That the value of the mouse button clicked is included in ***`MouseFlags`*** is not indicated in the documentation. For a code fragment that determines which key was pressed when the left mouse button was clicked, see the entry for the AxisActivated, AxisSelected, and AxisUpdated events.

`UpdateFlags` (`VtChUpdateFlags` *enumeration, AxisTitleUpdated only)*
: Indicates the status of the update and can contain any combination of values in the `VtChUpdateFlags` enumeration. Its members are listed in the entry for the AxisActivated, AxisSelected, and AxisUpdated events.

`Cancel` *(integer, AxisTitleActivated and AxisTitleSelected only)*
: Unused.

These events are triggered when an axis title in the MSChart control is clicked (AxisTitleSelected), is double-clicked (AxisTitleActivated), or has changed (AxisTitleUpdated).

Events A–C

BackClick, BackCompleted, BackGotFocus, BackLostFocus

Applies to: MM control

Parameters:

`Cancel` *(integer, BackClick only)*
: Flag passed by reference to indicate whether the Back command should be cancelled even though the user has clicked the button. Its default value is `False`.

`ErrorCode` *(long integer, BackCompleted only)*
: Contains 0 if the Back operation was successful; otherwise, it contains an error number.

These events are triggered when the user clicks on the Back button on the MM control (BackClick), when the Back button receives (BackGotFocus) or loses (BackLostFocus) the focus on its container, or when it has finished executing (BackCompleted). The BackGotFocus event is fired whenever the focus switches to the Back button, whether it comes from another button on the Multimedia control, another interface object in the application, or a window belonging to another application. Similarly, the BackLostFocus event is fired whenever the focus leaves the Back button, regardless of the object or application that receives the focus. The ***`Cancel`*** parameter of the BackClick event can be set to `True` to stop the control from executing the Back command. If the command executes, the ***`ErrorCode`*** parameter contains 0 if the back command were executed successfully or the error number if there were an error.

BeforeClick

Applies to: TabStrip

Parameters:

`Cancel` *(integer)*
: Flag passed by reference to indicate whether the Tab object that was clicked should be prevented from receiving the focus. Its default value is `False`. Strangely, although you can use the Tab object's SelectedItem property to determine the Tab object that had the focus before the BeforeClick event was fired, you cannot determine the tab on which the user clicked to fire the BeforeClick event. An additional peculiarity of this method is that setting the ***`Cancel`*** property to `True` to prevent the focus from moving to the clicked tab nevertheless does not prevent the Click event from firing.

Whenever a Tab object within a TabStrip control becomes selected, whether by code or the user and whether the focus moves from another tab, another object in the application, or another application, the BeforeClick event is fired. The `Cancel` parameter can be set to `True` to prevent the Tab object from being selected.

ButtonClick

Applies to: DataGrid

Parameters:

`ColIndex` *(integer)*
    The index of the Column containing the clicked button

When a column in the data grid has its Button property set to `True`, clicking on the visible button in a cell fires the ButtonClick event.

ButtonClick

Applies to: Toolbar

Parameters:

`Button` *(Button object)*
    A reference to the clicked Button object

Fired when the user clicks a Button object in a Toolbar control.

VB6 *ButtonDropDown*

Applies to: Toolbar

Parameters:

`Button` *(Button object)*
    A reference to the clicked Button object containing the drop-down arrow

Fired when the user clicks a drop-down arrow on a Button object in a Toolbar control. (Drop-down arrows are displayed with Button objects in the Toolbar control by setting its Style property to 5–tbrDropdown. Clicking the drop-down arrow displays the ButtonMenu objects associated with that Button object.) A reference to the Button object associated with the drop-down arrow is passed as the `Button` parameter.

VB6 *ButtonMenuClick*

Applies to: Toolbar

Parameters:

`ButtonMenu` *(ButtonMenu object)*
    A reference to the clicked ButtonMenu object

When ButtonMenu objects (which are the submenu items of a Button object that contains a drop-down area) are displayed in a Toolbar control, clicking a ButtonMenu object fires the ButtonMenuClick event.

VB6

CallbackKeyDown

Applies to: DTPicker

Parameters:

`KeyCode` *(*`KeyCodeConstants` *enumeration)*
: The standard key code constant (see Appendix B, *Key Codes*) for the key pressed.

`Shift` *(*`ShiftConstants` *enumeration)*
: Any combination of 1–vbShiftMask for the Shift key, 2–vbCtrlMask for the CTRL key, and 4–vbAltMask for the ALT key to test for key modifiers pressed.

`CallbackField` *(string)*
: The string of Xs for the callback field. (If there are multiple callback fields in a single date format, a different number of Xs can be used in each to distinguish one from any other callback fields in the format string.)

`CallbackDate` *(Date)*
: The current date value of the control, which is passed by reference to the event procedure and can be modified to change that date.

The DTPicker control allows you to define a custom date format by setting its Format property to `dtpCustom` and assigning a format string to its CustomFormat property. Within the format string, the letter X represents a callback field. The CallbackKeyDown event is fired whenever the user presses a key when the portion of the format string reserved for the callback field has the focus. The CallbackKeyDown event allows your code to modify the date display based on the key pressed.

Change

Applies to: ComboBox, DataCombo, DataGrid, DTPicker, FlatScrollBar, HScrollBar/VScrollBar, ImageCombo, Label, MaskedEditBox, PictureBox, RichTextBox, Slider, TextBox, Toolbar, UpDown

Parameters: None

Fired whenever the value contained by its control is changed, whether through code or by the user.

ChartActivated, ChartSelected, ChartUpdated

Applies to: MSChart

Parameters:

`MouseFlags` *(integer, ChartActivated and ChartSelected only)*
: An integer indicating which button was clicked and which key was depressed while the mouse button was clicked. Possible values for keys are 4–vtCh-

MouseFlagShiftKeyDown for the Shift key, 8–vtChMouseFlagControlKeyDown for the CTRL key, or the two values added together (12) for both keys. That the value of the mouse button clicked is included in ***MouseFlags*** is not indicated in the documentation. For a code fragment that determines which key was pressed when the left mouse button was clicked, see the entry for the AxisActivated, AxisSelected, and AxisUpdated events.

UpdateFlags (VtChUpdateFlags enumeration, ChartUpdated only)
Indicates the status of the update and can contain any combination of values in the `VtChUpdateFlags` enumeration. Its members are listed in the entry for the AxisActivated, AxisSelected, and AxisUpdated events.

Cancel (integer, CharActivated and ChartSelected only)
Unused.

These events are triggered when the MSChart control is clicked (ChartSelected), is double-clicked (ChartActivated), or has changed (ChartUpdated).

Click

Applies to: All controls with a visible interface except ADO DC, Data, FlatScrollbar, HScrollbar, Line, MaskedEditBox, Multimedia, Shape, UpDown, and VScrollbar

Parameters: None

The Click event is fired in a variety of circumstances:

- In response to the user clicking the control with the left mouse button. Of the standard VB controls, though, the ComboBox, ListBox, and Option Button controls necessarily don't respond to a click of the left mouse button.
- In response to the user clicking the control with the right mouse button. Of the standard VB controls, the CommandButton, ListBox, and Option Button controls do not fire the Click event when the right mouse button is pressed. In addition, the TextBox and ComboBox controls, rather than firing the Click event, display a pop-up menu.
- By selecting a *new* item in a list-based control (i.e., the ComboBox or ListBox) with the mouse or keyboard.
- By pressing the spacebar when a control that reacts to mouse clicks (the CheckBox, ComboBox, CommandButton, and Option Button controls) has the focus.
- By pressing the Enter key when a form that has a CommandButton control whose Default property is `True` has the focus.
- By pressing the Escape key when a form that has a CommandButton control whose Cancel property is `True` has the focus.
- By setting the ComandButton control's Value property to `True` or by changing the state of the Option Button and CheckBox controls by modifying their Value property.

Note that when the Enabled property of a control that supports a Click event is `False`, pressing either the left or the right mouse button on the control fires the Click event for the form.

Close

Applies to: Winsock

Parameters: None

Fired when the remote computer in a Winsock connection terminates the connection.

VB6 *CloseUp, DropDown*

Applies to: DTPicker

Parameters: None

The DropDown event is fired in response to the user pressing the drop-down button on the DTPicker control to display the calendar. The CloseUp event is fired when that calendar is closed by the user.

ColEdit

Applies to: DataGrid

Parameters:

`ColIndex` *(integer)*
    The index of the column containing the cell being edited

When the user begins to edit the data in a cell within a DataGrid control, the ColEdit event is fired.

Collapse, Expand

Applies to: MSHFlexGrid

Parameters:

`Cancel` *(Boolean)*
    Flag indicating whether the expansion or collapse should be cancelled. Its default value is `False`.

The Expand event is fired when the user expands a row in the MSHFlexGrid control. The Collapse event is fired when the user collapses an expanded row in the MSHFlexGrid control. Setting the *`Cancel`* parameter to `True` for either of these events cancels the action.

Collapse, Expand

Applies to: TreeView

Parameters:

`Node` *(Node Object)*

A reference to the Node object being expanded or collapsed

The Expand event is fired when the user expands a Node object in the TreeView control. The Collapse event is fired when the user collapses an expanded Node object in the TreeView control.

ColResize, RowResize

Applies to: DataGrid

Parameters:

`ColIndex` *(integer, ColResize only)*

The index of the column being resized.

`Cancel` *(integer)*

Flag passed by reference indicating whether the resize operation should be cancelled. Its default value is `False`.

When the user changes the size of a column in a DataGrid control, the ColResize event is fired. When the user changes the size of a row in a DataGrid control, the RowResize event is fired.

In both events, setting the *`Cancel`* parameter to `True` cancels the resizing.

ColumnClick

Applies to: ListView

Parameters:

`ColumnHeader` *(ColumnHeader object)*

A reference to the ColumnHeader object for the clicked column

When the user clicks the header at the top of a column in a ListView control with its View property set to 3–lvwReport, the ColumnClick event is fired. This is useful when sorting the ListView based on a clicked column, as in this example:

```
Private Sub lvwMain_ColumnClick(ByVal ColumnHeader _
            As MSComctlLib.ColumnHeader)
   If Me.lvwMain.Sorted = True Then
      'If the ListView is already sorted, we need
      to alter the sort
      If Me.lvwMain.SortKey = _
                   ColumnHeader.Index - 1 Then
```

```
        'If the ListView is sorted by this column,
        reverse the sort
        If Me.lvwMain.SortOrder = lvwAscending Then
           Me.lvwMain.SortOrder = lvwDescending
        Else
           Me.lvwMain.SortOrder = lvwAscending
        End If
     Else
        Me.lvwMain.SortKey = ColumnHeader.Index - 1
        Me.lvwMain.SortOrder = lvwAscending
     End If
  Else
     'If the ListView is not yet sorted we can just
     sort it here
     Me.lvwMain.Sorted = True
     Me.lvwMain.SortKey = ColumnHeader.Index - 1
     Me.lvwMain.SortOrder = lvwAscending
  End If
End Sub
```

Compare

Applies to: MSFlexGrid, MSHFlexGrid

Parameters:

Row1 (long integer)
: Number of the first row to be sorted

Row2 (long integer)
: Number of the second row to be sorted

Cmp (integer)
: Value passed by reference to indicate the sort order of *Row1* and *Row2*

Fired for each row in the control if the Sort property is set to 9–flexSortCustom. While this can be slow, it gives full control over the sorting process. The *Cmp* parameter should be set to -1 if the row represented by *Row1* should appear before the row represented by *Row2*, 1 if the row represented by *Row1* should appear after the row represented by *Row2*, or 0 if the rows should be considered equal.

ConfigChangeCancelled

Applies to: SysInfo

Parameters: None

Fired if a hardware change that was initiated is cancelled.

ConfigChanged, QueryChangeConfig

Applies to: SysInfo

Parameters:

`OldConfigNum` *(long integer, ConfigChanged only)*
Indicator of the old configuration's subkey in the registry.

`NewConfigNum` *(long integer, ConfigChanged only)*
Indicator of the new configuration's subkey in the registry.

`Cancel` *(Boolean, QueryChangeConfig only)*
Flag passed by reference indicating whether the configuration change should be cancelled; its default value is `False`.

The QueryChangeConfig event is fired when a system's hardware profile is about to be changed. The ***`Cancel`*** parameter for the QueryChangeConfig event can be set to `True` to not allow the configuration to change. The ConfigChanged event is fired once the hardware profile on the machine has been changed. The ***`OldConfigNum`*** parameter for the ConfigChanged event provides information about the registry key that was linked to the top-level registry key HKEY_CURRENT_CONFIG, and the ***`NewConfigNum`*** parameter contains information about the registry key that now is linked to it. In both cases, these are long integers whose string versions, when padded with zeros to become four characters in length, indicate a particular subkey of HKEY_LOCAL_MACHINE\Config.

Connect

Applies to: Winsock

Parameters:

`RemoteHost` *(string)*
The IP address of the remote machine

`RemotePort` *(string)*
The number of the port on which the connection was made

Fired when a connection is made between the local machine and the remote machine using the Winsock control.

ConnectionRequest

Applies to: Winsock

Parameters:

`RequestID` *(long integer)*
A unique identifier for the request

Fired when a remote machine attempts to connect to the local machine. The IP address and port number are contained in the RemoteHostIP and RemotePort properties, respectively. The *RequestID* parameter should be passed to the Accept method to connect to the remote machine.

DataArrival

Applies to: Winsock

Parameters:

BytesTotal (long integer)
Total number of bytes received into the buffer

Fired whenever data is received into the Winsock control's buffer. This data can then be read using the PeekData method or retrieved using the GetData method.

DataUpdated

Applies to: MSChart

Parameters:

Row (integer)
Row in the data grid that was changed.

Column (integer)
Column in the data grid that was changed.

LabelRow (integer)
Row label that was changed.

LabelColumn (integer)
Column label that was changed.

LabelSetIndex (integer)
Level of labels that was changed. Levels are numbered from the axis out, starting at 1.

UpdateFlags (VtChUpdateFlags enumeration)
Constant indicating how the control will be updated. It can contain any combination of the following values:

Constant	*Value*	*Description*
vtChNoDisplay	0	The chart will not be updated.
vtChDisplayPlot	1	The chart will be repainted.
vtChLayoutPlot	2	Values for the chart will be recalculated.
vtChDisplayLegend	4	The legend will be repainted.
vtChLayoutLegend	8	Values for the legend will be recalculated.
vtChLayoutSeries	16	Values for the series will be recalculated.

The DataUpdated event is fired whenever data in the MSChart control's DataGrid object is changed. The *Row*, *Column*, *LabelRow*, *LabelColumn*, and

LabelSetIndex parameters all identify the location of the data that was changed. Values of 0 indicate that that particular element has not changed. If all values are 0, the chart element that's changed cannot be identified.

VB6 *DateClick, DateDblClick*

Applies to: MonthView

Parameters:

DateClicked (Date, DateClick only)
    The date that was clicked by the user

DateDblClicked (Date, DateDblClick only)
    The date that was double-clicked by the user

These events are fired when a date on the MonthView control's calendar is clicked (DateClick) or double-clicked (DataDblClick).

DblClick

Applies to: All controls with a visible interface except Line and Shape

Parameters: None

Fired in response to the user double-clicking the control with the mouse.

Deactivate

Applies to: Form and MDIForm objects

See: Activate

DeviceArrival

Applies to: SysInfo

Parameters:

DeviceType (long integer)
    The type of the new device. Possible values are 0 for an OEM-defined device type, 1 for a Windows 9x device node, 2 for a logical disk drive (including a network drive), 3 for a serial or parallel port, and 4 for a network resource. The documentation lists a number of constants for these values, although these are not defined in the SysInfo control's type library.

DeviceID (long integer)
    Data that helps to identify the device. The precise type of data depends on *DeviceType*. For the most common device arrival, the addition of a new logical volume, *DeviceID* is a bit mask that identifies the drive added. Bit 0 represents drive A, bit 1 represents drive B, and so on.

`DeviceName` *(string)*

The name of the new device.

`DeviceData` *(long integer)*

Additional data that depends on ***`DeviceType`***. For the addition of a new logical volume, possible values are 1 for the arrival of new media and 2 for the addition of a new network drive.

Fired when a device is added to the system. The most common use of this function is to detect the addition of a new logical drive.

Events D–F

DeviceOtherEvent

Applies to: SysInfo

Parameters:

`DeviceType` *(long integer)*

The type of device that raised the event; for details, see the ***`DeviceType`*** parameter of the DeviceArrival event.

`EventName` *(string)*

The name of the custom event.

`DataPointer` *(long integer)*

A pointer to device-specific data.

Fired when an event not handled by the other device events occurs. Since this is a custom event, it should be documented in the manual accompanying the Plug-and-Play device that raises the event.

DeviceQueryRemove

Applies to: SysInfo

Parameters:

`DeviceType` *(long integer)*

The type of device whose removal is pending; for details, see the ***`DeviceType`*** parameter of the DeviceArrival event.

`DeviceID` *(long integer)*

Data that helps to identify the device. For details, see the ***`DeviceID`*** parameter of the DeviceArrival event.

`DeviceName` *(string)*

The name of the device whose removal is pending.

`DeviceData` *(long integer)*

Additional data that depends on ***`DeviceType`***. For details, see the ***`DeviceData`*** parameter of the DeviceArrival event.

`Cancel` *(Boolean)*

A flag passed by reference that indicates whether permission to remove the device should be denied; its default value is `False`.

Fired when a device is about to be removed from to the system. The Cancel event can be set to `True` to request that the device not be removed. Note, though, that if the device removal is dependent on the actions of the user, setting ***`Cancel`*** to `True` does not necessarily guarantee that the device will not be removed.

DeviceQueryRemoveFailed

Applies to: SysInfo

Parameters:

`DeviceType` *(long integer)*
: The type of device whose removal failed; for details, see the ***`DeviceType`*** parameter of the DeviceArrival event.

`DeviceID` *(long integer)*
: Data that helps to identify the device. For details, see the ***`DeviceID`*** parameter of the DeviceArrival event.

`DeviceName` *(string)*
: The name of the device.

`DeviceData` *(long integer)*
: Additional data that depends on ***`DeviceType`***. For details, see the ***`DeviceData`*** parameter of the DeviceArrival event.

Fired when the removal of a device was stopped by the DeviceQueryRemove event.

DeviceRemoveComplete

Applies to: SysInfo

Parameters:

`DeviceType` *(long integer)*
: The type of device that was removed; for details, see the ***`DeviceType`*** parameter of the DeviceArrival event.

`DeviceID` *(long integer)*
: Data that helps to identify the device. For details, see the ***`DeviceID`*** parameter of the DeviceArrival event.

`DeviceName` *(string)*
: The name of the removed device.

`DeviceData` *(long integer)*
: Additional data that depends on ***`DeviceType`***. For details, see the ***`DeviceData`*** parameter of the DeviceArrival event.

Fired when a device has been removed from the system.

DeviceRemovePending

Applies to: SysInfo

Parameters:

`DeviceType` *(long integer)*
: The type of device being removed; for details, see the `DeviceType` parameter of the DeviceArrival event.

`DeviceID` *(long integer)*
: Data that helps to identify the device. For details, see the `DeviceID` parameter of the DeviceArrival event.

`DeviceName` *(string)*
: The name of the device.

`DeviceData` *(long integer)*
: Additional data that depends on `DeviceType`. For details, see the `DeviceData` parameter of the DeviceArrival event.

Fired when a device is being removed from the system.

DevModeChanged

Applies to: SysInfo

Parameters: None

Fired when the system's Device mode settings are changed. Online help (but not the SysInfo type library) incorrectly names this method DevModeChange and also incorrectly describes it as passing by value a parameter named `devicename` to the event handler.

DisplayChanged

Applies to: SysInfo

Parameters: None

Fired when the Windows display settings (resolution or color depth) are changed. The new screen size can be derived from the Screen object's Width and Height properties, along with the SysInfo control's WorkAreaHeight, WorkAreaLeft, WorkAreaTop, and WorkAreaWidth properties.

Done

Applies to: MM control

Parameters:

`NotifyCode` (`NotifyConstants` *enumeration)*

A constant that indicates the result of the command. It can be one of the values in the following table:

Constant	*Value*	*Description*
`mciSuccessful`	1	Command completed successfully.
`mciSuperseded`	2	Command was superseded by another command.
`mciAborted`	4	Command was aborted by the user.
`mciFailure`	8	Command failed.

Triggered when an MM control's Notify property is set to `True` and an action completes.

DonePainting

Applies to: MSChart

Parameters: None

Fired when the MSChart control finishes redrawing.

DownClick, UpClick

Applies to: UpDown

Parameters: None

Fired in response to the user clicking on the Up button (UpClick) or Down button (DownClick).

DragDrop

Applies to: All controls with a visible interface except Line and Shape

Parameters:

`Source` *(control)*

A reference to the dropped control

`X` *(single)*, `Y` *(single)*

The coordinates at which the control was dropped

Fired when a control that was being dragged is dropped over the control whose DragDrop event fires.

DragOver

Applies to: All controls with a visible interface except Line and Shape

Parameters:

`Source` *(control)*
: A reference to the control being dragged.

`X` *(single)*, `Y` *(single)*
: The coordinates where the control is being dragged.

`State` *(integer)*
: The status of the drag operation. Possible values are 0–vbEnter when the control enters the area, 1–vbLeave when the control leaves the area, and 2–vbOver when the control is moving over the area.

Fired when a dragged control enters the area of the control whose event fires, when it is moved within that area, and when it leaves the area of the control. Note that the DragOver event is fired repeatedly while a control is over the potential target.

DropDown

Applies to: ComboBox, ImageCombo

Parameters: None

The DropDown event is triggered when the user presses the drop-down button on the control.

VB6 *DropDown*

Applies to: DTPicker

See: CloseUp

EjectClick, EjectCompleted, EjectGotFocus, EjectLostFocus

Applies to: MM control

Parameters:

`Cancel` *(integer, EjectClick only)*
: Flag passed by reference to indicate whether the Eject command should be cancelled even though the user has clicked the button. Its default value is `False`.

`ErrorCode` *(long integer, EjectCompleted only)*
: Contains 0 if the Eject operation was successful; otherwise, it contains an error number.

These events are triggered when the user clicks on the Eject button on the MM control (EjectClick), when the Eject button receives (EjectGotFocus) or loses (Eject-LostFocus) the focus on its container, or when it has finished executing (EjectCompleted). The EjectGotFocus event is fired whenever the focus switches to the Eject button, whether it comes from another button on the Multimedia control, another interface object in the application, or a window belonging to another application. Similarly, the EjectLostFocus event is fired whenever the focus leaves the Eject button, regardless of the object or application that receives the focus. The `Cancel` parameter of the EjectClick event can be used to stop the control from executing the Eject command.

EndOfRecordset

Applies to: ADO DC

Parameters:

`fMoreData` (Boolean)
: Indicator of whether more data is to be appended to the recordset that is passed by reference to the event handler. Its default value is `False`.

`adStatus` (`EventStatusEnum` enumeration)
: A constant passed by reference that indicates the status of the operation. These are defined in the Active Server Pages include file for VBScript, *adovbs.inc*, but not in the ADO control's type library. Consequently, before using them in your project, you must add them to a code module or class module with a code fragment like the following:

```
Public Enum EventStatusEnum
   adStatusOK = &H0000001
   adStatusErrorsOccurred = &H0000002
   adStatusCantDeny = &H0000003
   adStatusCancel = &H0000004
   adStatusUnwantedEvent = &H0000005
End Enum
```

`pRecordset` (Recordset object)
: A reference to the Recordset object for which this event was called.

Fired when an action attempts to move the record pointer past the last record in the recordset. It is possible for the error handler to respond to this condition by adding more records to the recordset. In that case, the *`fMoreData`* parameter should be set to `True` before the method returns. If subsequent notification of the EndOfRecordset event is not needed, the *`adStatus`* parameter can be set to `adStatusUnwantedEvent`.

EnterCell, LeaveCell

Applies to: MSFlexGrid, MSHFlexGrid

Parameters: None

These events are called as the user (or code) moves from cell to cell in the control. The LeaveCell event is always triggered before the EnterCell event. In the LeaveCell event, the control's Row and Cell properties contain information about the cell being left, and in the EnterCell event, those properties contain information about the cell being entered. The EnterCell event is *not* triggered in either of the following two circumstances:

- When the control first loads or receives the focus from another control
- When the mouse is dragged over a cell

Error

Applies to: ADO DC, Data, DataGrid, and Winsock controls

Parameters:

`ErrorNumber` *(long integer, ADO DC and Winsock only)*
: The number of the error.

`Description` *(string, ADO DC and Winsock only)*
: A textual description of the error.

`Scode` *(long integer, ADO DC and Winsock only)*
: The server's COM error number.

`Source` *(string, ADO DC and Winsock only)*
: The name of the control for which the error was generated.

`HelpFile` *(string, ADO DC and Winsock only)*
: Name of a file providing detailed help about `ErrorNumber`.

`HelpContext` *(long integer, ADO DC and Winsock only)*
: The context ID of the error's description in `HelpFile`.

`fCancelDisplay` *(Boolean, ADO DC and Winsock only)*
: A flag passed by reference to indicate whether the error display should be cancelled. Its default value is `True` to display the error. By setting it to `False`, your program can ignore the error and continue.

`DataErr` *(integer, Data and DataGrid only)*
: The error's numerical code.

`Response` *(*`DataErrorConstants` *enumeration, Data and DataGrid only)*
: Constant passed by reference that indicates how the error should be handled. Possible values are 0–vbDataErrContinue to ignore the error and continue or 1–vbDataErrDisplay to display the standard error dialog box.

Fires when a data error is triggered for the data source of the Data, ADO DC, DataGrid, or Winsock control. For the Winsock control, errors are an integral part of building a TCP/IP conversation. For the data-related controls, the error's data generally comes from the data source itself, so if the data source was an Oracle database, for instance, the error would be an Oracle error. The Error event allows you to respond to a non-Visual Basic error encountered in communication protocols such as TCP/IP, Jet, and ODBC.

Expand

Applies to: MSHFlexGrid

See: Collapse

Expand

Applies to: TreeView

See: Collapse

FieldChangeComplete, WillChangeField

Applies to: ADO DC

Parameters:

`cFields` *(long integer)*
: The number of fields changed.

`Fields` *(variant)*
: An array of affected Field objects.

`pError` *(Error object, FieldChangeComplete only)*
: A reference to an Error object if an error occurred (i.e., if the value of *`adStatus`* is `adStatusErrorsOccurred`); otherwise, it is undefined.

`adStatus` *(`EventStatusEnum` enumeration)*
: A flag passed by reference indicating the status of the event. For the members of the `EventStatusEnum` enumeration, see the description of the EndOf-Recordset event.

  For the WillChangeField event, if *`adStatus`* does not equal `adStatus-CantDeny` when the event handler is invoked, its value can be set to `adStatusCancel` to cancel the field change(s). If errors occurred during the attempt to change the field values, the value of the FieldChangeComplete event's *`adStatus`* parameter will be `adStatusErrorsOccurred`. To prevent the WillChangeField and FieldChangeComplete events from firing, set the FieldChangeComplete's *`adStatus`* parameter to `adStatusUnwantedEvent` before the event handler returns.

`pRecordset` *(Recordset object)*
: A reference to the Recordset object for which this event was fired.

These events are fired just before (WillChangeField) and just after (FieldChange-Complete) the value of one or more fields is changed.

FootnoteActivated, FootnoteSelected, FootnoteUpdated

Applies to: MSChart

Parameters:

`MouseFlags` *(integer, FootnoteActivated and FootnoteSelected only)*
An integer indicating which button was clicked and which key was depressed while the mouse button was clicked. Possible values for keys are 4–vtChMouseFlagShiftKeyDown for the Shift key, 8–vtChMouseFlagControlKeyDown for the CTRL key, or the two values added together (12) for both keys. That the value of the mouse button clicked is included in ***MouseFlags*** is not indicated in the documentation. For a code fragment that determines which key was pressed when the left mouse button was clicked, see the entry for the AxisActivated, AxisSelected, and AxisUpdated events.

`UpdateFlags` *(*`VtChUpdateFlags` *enumeration, FootnoteUpdated only)*
Indicates the status of the update and can contain any combination of values in the `VtChUpdateFlags` enumeration. Its members are listed in the entry for the AxisActivated, AxisSelected, and AxisUpdated events.

`Cancel` *(integer, FootnoteActivated and FootnoteSelected only)*
Unused.

These events are triggered when the footnote of the MSChart control is clicked (FootnoteSelected), is double-clicked (FootnoteActivated), or has changed (FootnoteUpdated).

VB6

Format

Applies to: DTPicker

Parameters:

`CallbackField` *(string)*
The string of Xs for the callback field to be populated. Multiple callback fields in a single custom format can be differentiated from one another by assigning them different numbers of Xs.

`FormattedString` *(string)*
A zero-length string passed by reference to the event handler. It should be set to the value to be placed into the callback field. The DTPicker control allows you to define a custom date format by setting its Format property to `dtpCustom` and assigning a format string to its CustomFormat property. Within the format string, the letter X represents a callback field. At runtime, if the Format property is set to `dtpCustom`, whenever the control's contents change, the Format event is fired.

VB6 *FormatSize*

Applies to: DTPicker

Parameters:

`CallbackField` *(string)*

The string of Xs for the callback field to be populated. Multiple callback fields in a single custom format can be differentiated from one another by assigning them different numbers of Xs. Note that because of the FormatSize event handler, the number of Xs in the callback field is totally unrelated to the callback.

`Size` *(integer)*

Integer passed by reference to the event handler. It should be set to the maximum size needed for the callback field.

The FormatSize event is fired whenever the string assigned to the CustomFormat property includes a callback and allows the length of a callback field to be defined. Because of this event handler, the number of Xs in the callback field is totally unrelated to the callback field's size. Instead, in custom dates with multiple callback fields, fields can be differentiated from one another by the use of different numbers of Xs.

VB6 *GetDayBold*

Applies to: MonthView

Parameters:

`StartDate` *(Date)*

The first date to be displayed by the control.

`Count` *(integer)*

The number of dates that the control's calendar will display.

`State()` *(Boolean)*

An array of `Count` elements, one for each date to be displayed, each of which is set to `False` by default. The first element is `State(0)`, which represents `StartDate`. To display a particular date in bold, set its `State` element to `True`.

Fired before the MonthView control displays a new month or series of months and allows you to indicate which dates are to be displayed in a bold font.

For example, the following event handler displays every even date displayed by the calendar control in bold:

```
Private Sub MonthView1_GetDayBold(ByVal StartDate As _
      Date, ByVal Count As Integer, State() As Boolean)

Dim datDate As Date
Dim intCtr As Integer
```

```
For intCtr = 0 To Count - 1
   datDate = StartDate + intCtr
   If Day(datDate) / 2 = Int(Day(datDate) / 2) Then
      State(intCtr) = True
   End If
Next

End Sub
```

GotFocus, LostFocus

Applies to: All controls which can receive the focus

Parameters: None

Whenever a control receives the focus from another control on the same form or from another form in the same application because of user action or when the SetFocus method is called to change the focus, the GotFocus event is fired. When a control loses the focus to another control in the same form or to another form in the application through user action or because of a call to another control's SetFocus method, the LostFocus event is fired.

Note that the Form object also has GotFocus and LostFocus events that are fired only when all controls on the form are disabled, and that the MDI form object lacks GotFocus and LostFocus events entirely.

HeadClick

Applies to: DataGrid

Parameters:

`ColIndex` *(integer)*
: The index of the column whose heading was clicked

Fired whenever the heading at the top of a column in the data grid is clicked by the user.

VB6 *HeightChanged*

Applies to: CoolBar

Parameters:

`NewHeight` *(single)*
: The new height for the CoolBar control

Fired whenever the height of the CoolBar control needs to be changed, whether from the user reorganizing the Band objects or the height being affected through code.

Initialize, Terminate

Applies to: Form and MDIForm objects

Parameters: None

These events are triggered when the form or MDI form is first instantiated (Initialize) or is destroyed (Terminate). The Initialize event is always fired before the Load event. The Terminate event is fired after the QueryUnload and Unload events. It is fired, however, either when an application terminates (that is, when its last form is unloaded) or when the form or MDI form is set to `Nothing`; if the application remains open, the event is not fired by the `Unload` statement.

ItemCheck

Applies to: ListBox, ListView

Parameters:

`Item` *(integer, Listbox; ListItem object, ListView)*
: For the ListBox control, the index of the clicked item in the List property array; for the ListView control, a reference to the clicked ListItem object

The ItemCheck event is fired under the following circumstances:

- An item in a ListBox control with its Style property set to 1 (Checkbox) is checked or unchecked, whether by the user or though code.
- The user checks or unchecks a ListItem object in a ListView control with its CheckBoxes property set to `True` and its View property set to 3–lvwReport.

ItemClick

Applies to: ListView

Parameters:

`Item` *(ListItem object)*
: A reference to the ListItem object that was clicked

Fired when a ListItem object is clicked in a ListView control. The ItemClick event differs from the Click event, since the latter is fired whenever a ListItem, ColumnHeader, or empty area of the control is clicked. In addition, if the Click event is fired because a ListItem object is clicked, the event handler is not passed a reference to that ListItem object. If a ListItem object is clicked, the ItemClick event precedes the Click event.

KeyDown, KeyPress, KeyUp

Applies to: All controls with a visible interface except Line and Shape

Parameters:

`KeyCode` (`KeyCodeConstants` *enumeration, KeyDown and KeyUp only)*
The standard keycode constant for the key pressed; see Appendix B.

`KeyAscii` *(integer, KeyPress only)*
The ASCII value of the key or key combination pressed.

`Shift` (`ShiftConstants` *enumeration, KeyDown and KeyUp only)*
Bitmask indicating the state of the CTRL, ALT, and Shift keys. It contains any combination of 1–vbShiftMask for the Shift key, 2–vbCtrlMask for the CTRL key, and 4–vbAltMask for the ALT key.

The KeyDown event is fired whenever any key on the keyboard is pressed. The KeyPress event is fired only when a key or combination of keys is pressed that results in an ASCII value. The KeyUp event is fired when any key that was pressed is released.

Events G–P

LeaveCell

Applies to: MSFlexGrid, MSHFlexGrid

See: EnterCell

LegendActivated, LegendSelected, LegendUpdated

Applies to: MSChart

Parameters:

`MouseFlags` *(integer, LegendActivated and LegendSelected only)*
An integer indicating which button was clicked and which key was depressed while the mouse button was clicked. Possible values for keys are 4–vtChMouseFlagShiftKeyDown for the Shift key, 8–vtChMouseFlagControlKeyDown for the CTRL key, or the two values added together (12) for both keys. That the value of the mouse button clicked is included in ***`MouseFlags`*** is not indicated in the documentation. For a code fragment that determines which key was pressed when the left mouse button was clicked, see the entry for the AxisActivated, AxisSelected, and AxisUpdated events.

`UpdateFlags` (`VtChUpdateFlags` *enumeration, LegendUpdated only)*
Indicates the status of the update and can contain any combination of values in the `VtChUpdateFlags` enumeration. Its members are listed in the entry for the AxisActivated, AxisSelected, and AxisUpdated events.

`Cancel` *(integer, LegendActivated and LegendSelected only)*
Unused.

These events are triggered when the legend of the MSChart control is clicked (LegendSelected), is double-clicked (LegendActivated), or has changed (LegendUpdated).

LinkClose

Applies to: Form object; Label, MDIForm, PictureBox, and TextBox controls

Parameters: None

Fired when an open DDE link is closed.

LinkError

Applies to: Form object; Label, MDIForm, PictureBox, and TextBox controls

Parameters:

`LinkErr` (integer)

Fired when an error occurs during a DDE connection. The ***`LinkErr`*** parameter contains one of the following errors:

Value	*Description*
1	Data was requested in an invalid format.
6	A further attempt was made to communicate to a closed connection.
7	The maximum number of source links (128) was exceeded.
8	Data that was sent failed to update the destination control.
11	Out of memory.

LinkExecute

Applies to: Form and MDIForm objects

Parameters:

`CmdStr` *(string)*
The command sent

`Cancel` *(integer)*
Flag passed by reference indicating if the command should be cancelled

Fired when a form or MDI form receives a DDE command. The ***`Cancel`*** parameter can be set to `True` to refuse the command.

LinkNotify

Applies to: Label, PictureBox, TextBox

Parameters: None

Fired when data is changed in a control with its LinkMode property set to 3–vbLinkNotify.

LinkOpen

Applies to: Form, Label, MDIForm, PictureBox, TextBox

Parameters: Cancel (integer)

Fired for the source control when a DDE conversation is initiated. Setting the *`Cancel`* parameter to `True` rejects the conversation.

Load

Applies to: Form and MDIForm objects

Parameters: None

Fired when a form or MDI form is first loaded. If the form is loaded using the Show method or loaded as the startup object, first the Initialize event is fired, then the Load event, and finally the Activate event. If the form is loaded using the `Load` statement, the Initialize event is fired, followed by the Load event.

LostFocus

Applies to: All controls that can receive the focus

See: GotFocus

MouseDown, MouseMove, MouseUp

Applies to: All controls with a visible interface except Line and Shape

Parameters:

`Button` (`MouseButtonConstants` *enumeration)*
: The mouse button or buttons pressed. It can contain any combination of 1–vbLeftButton for the left button, 2–vbRightButton for the right button, and 4–vbMiddleButton for the middle button.

`Shift` (`ShiftConstants` *enumeration)*
: The state of the Shift, CTRL, and ALT keys. It can contain any combination of 1–vbShiftMask for the Shift key, 2–vbCtrlMask for the CTRL key, and 4–vbAltMask for the ALT key

`X` *(single),* *`Y`* *(single)*
: The x- and y-coordinates of the mouse pointer when the event was fired.

The MouseMove event is fired whenever the mouse pointer is moved over the control. The MouseDown event is fired when a mouse button is depressed over the control, and the MouseUp event is fired if a mouse button is released over the control.

MoveComplete, WillMove

Applies to: ADO DC

Parameters:

`adReason` *(*`EventReasonEnum` *enumeration)*

A constant from the following table that gives the reason for the move operation. (Note that the enumeration is not defined in the ADO control's type library, so you'll have to add it to your project.)

Constant	*Value*	*Description*
`adRsnRequery`	7	The data source was requeried.
`adRsnMove`	10	A Move method was issued.
`adRsnFirstChange`	11	A new record was updated.
`adRsnMoveFirst`	12	A MoveFirst method was issued.
`adRsnMoveNext`	13	A MoveNext method was issued.
`adRsnMovePrevious`	14	A MovePrevious method was issued.
`adRsnMoveLast`	15	A MoveLast method was issued.

`pError` *(Error object, MoveComplete only)*

If `adStatus` is `adStatusErrorsOccurred`, a reference to the Error object.

`adStatus` *(enumeration)*

A flag passed by reference indicating the operation's status. These are defined in the Active Server Pages include file for VBScript, *adovbs.inc*. You must add them to your project before using them; see the EndOfRecordset event.

If the parameter does not equal 3–adStatusCantDeny to the WillMove event, you can cancel the move by setting `adStatus` to 4–adStatusCancel. If errors were encountered when moving the record pointer, the `adStatus` parameter for the MoveComplete event will be set to 2–adStatusErrorsOccurred. To cancel this event notification, set the `adStatus` parameter of the MoveComplete event to 5–adStatusUnwantedEvent before the event handler returns.

`pRecordset` *(Recordset object)*

A reference to the Recordset object for which this event was fired.

These events are fired just before (WillMove) and just after (MoveComplete) the record pointer is moved.

NextClick, NextCompleted, NextGotFocus, NextLostFocus

Applies to: MM control

Parameters:

`Cancel` *(integer, NextClick only)*

Flag passed by reference to indicate whether the Next command should be cancelled (though the user has clicked the button). Its default value is `False`.

ErrorCode (long integer, NextCompleted only)
: Contains 0 if the Next operation was successful; otherwise, it contains an error number.

These events are triggered when the user clicks on the Next button on the MM control (NextClick), when it receives (NextGotFocus) or loses (NextLostFocus) the focus on its container, or when it has finished executing (NextCompleted). The NextGotFocus event is fired whenever the focus switches to the Next button, whether it comes from another button on the Multimedia control, another interface object in the application, or a window belonging to another application. Similarly, the NextLostFocus event is fired whenever the focus leaves the Next button, regardless of the object or application that receives the focus. The *Cancel* parameter of the NextClick event can be used to stop the control from executing the Next command.

NodeCheck

Applies to: TreeView

Parameters:

Node (Node object)
: A reference to the Node object that was clicked

Fired when the user checks a Node object in a ListView control whose CheckBoxes property is set to `True`.

NodeClick

Applies to: TreeView

Parameters:

Node (Node object)
: A reference to the Node object that was clicked

Fired when a Node object is clicked in a TreeView control. This differs from the Click event, which is fired when either a node or an empty area of the control is clicked. The NodeClick event precedes the Click event when the user clicks on a Node object.

ObjectMove

Applies to: OLE

Parameters:

Left (single), Top (single), Width (single), Height (single)
: The new position and size of the OLE object

Fired when an OLE object contained by the OLE control is moved or resized.

OLECompleteDrag, OLEDragDrop, OLEDragOver, OLEGiveFeedback, OLESetData, OLEStartDrag

Applies to: All controls with a visible interface except Line and Shape

Parameters:

`Effect` *(enumeration, OLECompleteDrag, OLEDragDrop, OLEDragOver, and OLEGiveFeedback only),* `AllowedEffects` *(enumeration, OLEStartDrag only)*

Contains 0–vbDropEffectNone for no dropping allowed, 1–vbDropEffectCopy to allow copying the object, 2–vbDropEffectMove to allow moving the object, or 3 to combine `vbDropEffectCopy` and `vbDropEffectMove` to allow either moving or copying the object.

`Data` *(DataObject Object, OLEDragDrop, OLEDragOver, OLESetData and OLEStartDrag only)*

The DataObject object contains all necessary information about the object being dragged.

`Button` *(enumeration, OLEDragDrop and OLEDragOver only),* `Shift` *(enumeration, OLEDragDrop and OLEDragOver only),* `X` *(single, OLEDragDrop and OLEDragOver only),* `Y` *(single, OLEDragDrop and OLEDragOver only)*

These parameters contain information about the mouse buttons being pressed, keyboard modifiers being held down, and the position of the mouse.

`State` *(enumeration, OLEDragOver only)*

Contains 0 when the object is being dragged into the control's area, 1 when the object is being dragged out of the control's area, or 2 when the object is being dragged within the control's area.

`DefaultCursors` *(Boolean, OLEGiveFeedback only)*

Contains `True` to use the default Visual Basic cursor images for OLE Drag and Drop or `False` to use custom cursor images.

`DataFormat` *(integer, OLESetData only)*

Contains the type of data expected, as follows:

Constant	*Value*	*Description*
`vbCFText`	1	Text
`vbCFBitmap`	2	Windows bitmap
`vbCFMetafile`	3	Windows metafile
`vbCFDIB`	8	Device-independent bitmap
`vbCFPalette`	9	Color palette
`vbCFEMetafile`	14	Enhanced metafile
`vbCFFiles`	15	A list of files
`vbCFRTF`	-16,639	Rich text

The OLE Drag and Drop events work along with the OLE Drag and Drop methods to allow OLE objects to be moved by the user between controls and even applications in Windows. When the user drags from a control, the OLEStartDrag event is fired. When data is required, the OLESetData event is fired. When the object is dragged over a control, the OLEGiveFeedback event is called for the source control, and the OLEDragOver event is called for the control being dragged over. When the object is dropped, the OLEDragComplete event is fired for the source control, and the OLEDragDrop event is called for the destination control.

OnAddNew

Applies to: DataGrid

Parameters: None

Fired when a new record is added to a DataGrid control, whether by the user or through code.

Events G–P

Paint

Applies to: Form object; PictureBox control

Parameters: None

Fired when the contents of a form or PictureBox control need to be repainted by the application. Generally, this is when an obscured portion of the form or picture box is exposed. The Paint event is also fired by a call to the Refresh method.

Note that when the form or PictureBox control's AutoRedraw property is set to `False`, the Paint event is typically responsible for redrawing persistent graphics. If AutoRedraw is `True`, the Paint event does not fire, and repainting is handled automatically by Visual Basic.

In the following example, the circle will redraw only when a hidden part of the circle is uncovered. Resizing the form smaller will hide parts of the circle. Resizing the form larger will cause the circle to redraw:

```
Private Sub Form_Paint()
    Me.Cls
    Me.Circle (Me.ScaleWidth / 2, Me.ScaleHeight / 2), _
        IIf(Me.ScaleWidth < Me.ScaleHeight, _
        Me.ScaleWidth / 2, Me.ScaleHeight / 2)
End Sub
```

PanelClick, PanelDblClick

Applies to: StatusBar

Parameters:

`Panel` *(Panel object)*
A reference to the Panel object that was clicked or double-clicked

These events are fired when a Panel object on a StatusBar control is clicked (PanelClick) or double-clicked (PanelDblClick). The Click event is fired after the PanelClick event, and the PanelDblClick is fired after the DblClick event. Neither of these events, however, allows your code to determine the Panel object that was clicked or double-clicked.

PauseClick, PauseCompleted, PauseGotFocus, PauseLostFocus

Applies to: MM control

Parameters:

`Cancel` *(integer, PauseClick only)*
Flag passed by reference to indicate whether the Pause command should be cancelled even though the user has clicked the button. Its default value is `False`.

`ErrorCode` *(long integer, PauseCompleted only)*
Contains 0 if the Pause operation was successful; otherwise, it contains an error number.

These events are triggered when the user clicks on the Pause button on the MM control (PauseClick), when it receives (PauseGotFocus) or loses (PauseLostFocus) the focus on its container, or when it has finished executing (PauseCompleted). The PauseGotFocus event is fired whenever the focus switches to the Pause button, whether it comes from another button on the Multimedia control, another interface object in the application, or a window belonging to another application. Similarly, the PauseLostFocus event is fired whenever the focus leaves the Pause button, regardless of the object or application that receives the focus. The ***`Cancel`*** parameter of the PauseClick event can be used to stop the control from executing the Pause command.

PlayClick, PlayCompleted, PlayGotFocus, PlayLostFocus

Applies to: MM control

Parameters:

`Cancel` *(integer, PlayClick only)*
Flag passed by reference to indicate whether the Play command should be cancelled even though the user has clicked the button. Its default value is `False`.

`ErrorCode` *(long integer, PlayCompleted only)*
Contains 0 if the Play operation was successful; otherwise, it contains an error number.

These events are triggered when the user clicks on the Play button on the MM control (PlayClick), when it receives (PlayGotFocus) or loses (PlayLostFocus) the focus on its container, or when it has finished executing (PlayCompleted). The PlayGotFocus event is fired whenever the focus switches to the Play button, whether it comes from another button on the Multimedia control, another interface object in the application, or a window belonging to another application. Similarly, the PlayLostFocus event is fired whenever the focus leaves the Play button, regardless of the object or application that receives the focus. The `Cancel` parameter of the PlayClick event can be used to stop the control from executing the Play command.

PlotActivated, PlotSelected, PlotUpdated

Applies to: MSChart

Parameters:

`MouseFlags` *(integer, PlotActivated and PlotSelected only)*
: An integer indicating which button was clicked and which key was depressed while the mouse button was clicked. Possible values for keys are 4–vtChMouseFlagShiftKeyDown for the Shift key, 8–vtChMouseFlagControlKeyDown for the CTRL key, or the two values added together (12) for both keys. That the value of the mouse button clicked is included in ***MouseFlags*** is not indicated in the documentation. For a code fragment that determines which key was pressed when the left mouse button was clicked, see the entry for the AxisActivated, AxisSelected, and AxisUpdated events.

`UpdateFlags` *(`VtChUpdateflags` enumeration, PlotUpdated only)*
: Indicates the status of the update and can contain any combination of values in the `VtChUpdateFlags` enumeration. Its members are listed in the entry for the AxisActivated, AxisSelected, and AxisUpdated events.

`Cancel` *(integer, PlotActivated and PlotSelected only)*
: Unused.

These events are triggered when the plot area of the MSChart control is clicked (PlotSelected), is double-clicked (PlotActivated), or has changed (PlotUpdated).

PointActivated, PointSelected, PointUpdated

Applies to: MSChart

Parameters:

`Series` *(integer)*
: The index of the series containing the point that was affected. Series are numbered in column order starting at 1.

`DataPoint` *(integer)*
: The index of the affected point within its series. Points are numbered in row order starting at 1.

`MouseFlags` *(integer, PointActivated and PointSelected only)*
: An integer indicating which button was clicked and which key was depressed while the mouse button was clicked. Possible values for keys are 4–vtChMouseFlagShiftKeyDown for the Shift key, 8–vtChMouseFlagControlKeyDown for the CTRL key, or the two values added together (12) for both keys. That the value of the mouse button clicked is included in ***MouseFlags*** is not indicated in the documentation. For a code fragment that determines which key

was pressed when the left mouse button was clicked, see the entry for the AxisActivated, AxisSelected, and AxisUpdated events.

`UpdateFlags` (`VtChUpdateFlags` *enumeration, PointUpdated only)*
: Indicates the status of the update and can contain any combination of values in the `VtChUpdateFlags` enumeration. Its members are listed in the entry for the AxisActivated, AxisSelected, and AxisUpdated events.

`Cancel` *(integer, PointActivated and PointSelected only)*
: Unused.

These events are triggered when a point on the MSChart control is clicked (PointSelected), is double-clicked (PointActivated), or has changed (PointUpdated).

PointLabelActivated, PointLabelSelected, PointLabelUpdated

Applies to: MSChart

Parameters:

`Series` *(integer)*
: The index of the series containing the point whose label was affected. Series are numbered in column order starting at 1.

`DataPoint` *(integer)*
: The index of the point in its series whose label was affected. Points are numbered in row order starting at 1.

`MouseFlags` *(integer, PointLabelActivated and PointLabelSelected only)*
: An integer indicating which button was clicked and which key was depressed while the mouse button was clicked. Possible values for keys are 4–vtChMouseFlagShiftKeyDown for the Shift key, 8–vtChMouseFlagControlKeyDown for the CTRL key, or the two values added together (12) for both keys. That the value of the mouse button clicked is included in *`MouseFlags`* is not indicated in the documentation. For a code fragment that determines which key was pressed when the left mouse button was clicked, see the entry for the AxisActivated, AxisSelected, and AxisUpdated events.

`UpdateFlags` (`VtChUpdateFlags` *enumeration, PointLabelUpdated only)*
: Indicates the status of the update and can contain any combination of values in the `VtChUpdateFlags` enumeration. Its members are listed in the entry for the AxisActivated, AxisSelected, and AxisUpdated events.

`Cancel` *(integer, PointLabelActivated and PointLabelSelected only)*
: Unused.

These events are triggered when a label associated with a point on the MSChart control is clicked (PointLabelSelected), is double-clicked (PointLabelActivated), or has changed (PointLabelUpdated).

PowerQuerySuspend, PowerResume, PowerStatusChanged, PowerSuspend

Applies to: SysInfo

Parameters:

`Cancel` *(Boolean, PowerQuerySuspend only)*
: Flag passed by reference to the event handler to indicate whether the request to suspend the system should be granted; its default value is `False`.

These events relay information about the power status of the machine. The PowerQuerySuspend event is fired when the computer is about to be suspended. The PowerSuspend event is fired when the computer is suspended. The PowerResume event is fired when the computer is taken out of Suspended mode. The PowerStatusChanged event is fired in response to any power-related changes, such as a battery getting low on a notebook computer. The *`Cancel`* parameter for the PowerQuerySuspend can be set to `True` to attempt to not allow the computer to be suspended; this does not guarantee that it will not be suspended.

PrevClick, PrevCompleted, PrevGotFocus, PrevLostFocus

Applies to: MM control

Parameters:

`Cancel` *(integer, PrevClick only)*
: Flag passed by reference to indicate whether the Previous command should be cancelled even though the user has clicked the button. Its default value is `False`.

`ErrorCode` *(long integer, PrevCompleted only)*
: Contains 0 if the Previous command was successful; otherwise, it contains an error number.

These events are triggered when the user clicks on the Previous button on the MM control (PrevClick), when it receives (PrevGotFocus) or loses (PrevLostFocus) the focus on its container, or when it has finished executing (PrevCompleted). The PrevGotFocus event is fired whenever the focus switches to the Previous button, whether it comes from another button on the Multimedia control, another interface object in the application, or a window belonging to another application. Similarly, the PrevLostFocus event is fired whenever the focus leaves the Previous button, regardless of the object or application that receives the focus. The *`Cancel`* parameter of the PrevClick event can be used to stop the control from executing the Previous command.

QueryChangeConfig

Applies to: SysInfo

See: *ConfigChanged*

QueryUnload

Applies to: Form and MDIForm objects

Parameters:

`Cancel` *(integer)*
  Flag passed by reference that indicates whether unloading the form should be cancelled; its default value is `False`.

`UnloadMode` *(*`QueryUnloadConstants` *enumeration)*
  The action that is causing the form or MDI form to unload. Possible values are:

Constant	*Value*	*Description*
`VbFormControlMenu`	0	The Close option was selected from the form or MDI form's Control menu.
`VbFormCode`	1	The form or MDI form was unloaded through code.
`VbAppWindows`	2	Windows is shutting down.
`VbAppTaskManager`	3	The task was ended from the Task Manager.
`VbFormMDIForm`	4	The form is an MDI child form, and its parent MDI form is closing.
`VbFormOwner`	5	The form's owner is closing.

Fired when the form or MDI form is about to be closed. Setting the ***`Cancel`*** parameter to `True` cancels the unloading of the form or MDI form. The QueryUnload event is followed by the Unload and possibly the Terminate events; the latter events, however, do not provide a ***`Cancel`*** parameter that allows you to prevent the form or application from unloading. If an application is closed using the `End` statement, the QueryUnload event is *not* fired, nor are the Unload and Terminate events.

RecordChangeComplete, WillChangeRecord

Applies to: ADO DC

Parameters:

`adReason` *(*`EventReasonEnum` *enumeration)*
  The action that changed the record(s). The members of the `EventReasonEnum` enumeration, which are shown in the following table, are not defined in the ADO DC control's type library:

Constant	*Value*	*Description*
`adRsnAddNew`	1	A new record was added.
`adRsnDelete`	2	A record was deleted.
`adRsnUpdate`	3	A record was updated.

Constant	*Value*	*Description*
`adRsnUndoUpdate`	4	An update to a record was undone.
`adRsnUndoAddNew`	5	A new record was undone.
`adRsnUndoDelete`	6	A deleted record was undone.
`adRsnFirstChange`	11	A new record was updated.

`cRecords` (long integer)
The number of records affected.

`pError` (Error object, RecordChangeComplete only)
If ***`adStatus`*** is `adStatusErrorsOccurred`, ***`pError`*** contains the Error object for the error.

`adStatus` (enumeration)
For the WillChangeRecord event, if ***`adStatus`*** does not equal `adStatusCantDeny` when the event handler is invoked, its value can be set to `adStatusCancel` to cancel the record change(s). If errors occurred during the attempt to change the field values, the value of the RecordChangeComplete event's ***`adStatus`*** parameter will be `adStatusErrorsOccurred`. To prevent the WillChangeRecord and RecordChangeComplete events from firing, set the RecordChangeComplete's ***`adStatus`*** parameter to `adStatusUnwantedEvent` before the event handler returns.

`pRecordset` (Recordset object)
A reference to the Recordset object for which this event was fired.

These events are fired just before (WillChangeRecord) and just after (RecordChangeComplete) the values within one or more records are changed. Note that if the ADO control's LockType property is set to `adLockBatchOptimistic`, these events fire in response to the recordset's UpdateBatch method and not the recordset's Update method.

Events O–Z

RecordClick, RecordCompleted, RecordGotFocus, RecordLostFocus

Applies to: MM control

Parameters:

`Cancel` (integer, RecordClick only)
Flag passed by reference to indicate whether the Record command should be cancelled even though the user clicked the button. Its default value is `False`.

`ErrorCode` (long integer, RecordCompleted only)
Contains 0 if the Record command was successful; otherwise, it contains an error number.

These events are triggered when the user clicks on the Record button on the MM control (RecordClick), when it receives (RecordGotFocus) or loses (RecordLostFocus) the focus on its container, or when it has finished executing (RecordCompleted). The RecordGotFocus event is fired whenever the focus switches to the Record button, whether it comes from another button on the Multimedia control, another interface object in the application, or a window belonging to another application. Similarly, the RecordLostFocus event is fired whenever the focus leaves the Record button, regardless of the object or application that receives the focus. The `Cancel` parameter of the RecordClick event can be used to stop the control from executing the Record command.

RecordsetChangeComplete, WillChangeRecordset

Applies to: ADO DC

Parameters:

`adReason` *(*`EventReasonEnum` *enumeration)*

The action that changed the record(s). The members of the `EventReasonEnum` enumeration, which are shown in the following table, are not defined in the ADO DC control's type library and that one value listed in the documentation, `adRsnOpen`, does not actually exist:

Constant	*Value*	*Description*
`adRsnRequery`	7	The data source was requeried.
`adRsnResynch`	8	The ADO DC was resynchronized with the data source.
`adRsnClose`	9	The data source was closed.

`pError` *(Error object, RecordsetChangeComplete only)*

If `adStatus` is `adStatusErrorsOccurred`, `pError` contains the Error object for the error.

`adStatus` *(enumeration)*

For the WillChangeRecordset event, if `adStatus` does not equal `adStatusCantDeny` when the event handler is invoked, its value can be set to `adStatusCancel` to cancel the record change(s). If errors occurred during the attempt to change the field values, the value of the RecordsetChangeComplete event's `adStatus` parameter will be `adStatusErrorsOccurred`. To prevent the WillChangeRecordset and RecordsetChangeComplete events from firing, set the RecordsetChangeComplete's `adStatus` parameter to `adStatusUnwantedEvent` before the event handler returns.

`pRecordset` *(Recordset object)*

A reference to the Recordset object for which this event was fired.

These events are fired just before (WillChangeRecordset) and just after (RecordsetChangeComplete) the recordset is changed.

Reposition

Applies to: Data control

Parameters: None

Fired after the record pointer is updated in the Data control's Recordset object.

Resize

Applies to: Form and MDIForm objects; CoolBar, Data, OLE, and PictureBox controls

Parameters:

`HeightNew` *(single, OLE only)*, `WidthNew` *(single, OLE only)*
    The new size of the control

Fired whenever the size of the control is updated. For the OLE control, the `HeightNew` and `WidthNew` parameters contain the new size for the control; for the other controls, the Height and Width properties indicate the new size for the control.

RowColChange

Applies to: DataGrid, MSFlexGrid, MSHFlexGrid

Parameters:

`LastRow` *(integer, DataGrid only)*, `LastCol` *(integer, DataGrid only)*
    The coordinates of the previously selected cell

Fired when the current cell changes within a DataGrid, MSFlexGrid, or MSHFlexGrid control.

RowResize

Applies to: DataGrid

See: ColResize

Scroll

Applies to: ComboBox, DataGrid, FlatScrollBar, HScrollBar/VScrollBar, ListBox, MSFlexGrid, MSHFlexGrid

Parameters: None

Fired whenever the contents of the control are scrolled by the user or through code.

Scroll

Applies to: Slider

Parameters: None

Fired repeatedly when the user drags the indicator on the Slider.

VB6 *SelChange*

Applies to: DataGrid

Parameters:

`Cancel` *(integer)*
: Flag passed by reference indicating whether the selection should be cancelled; its default value is `False`.

Fired when there is a change to the cells selected in the DataGrid control. Setting the *`Cancel`* parameter to `True` cancels the new selection and reverts to the old selection.

SelChange

Applies to: MonthView

Parameters:

`StartDate` *(Date)*
: The first date selected in the control.

`EndDate` *(Date)*
: The last date selected in the control.

`Cancel` *(Boolean)*
: Flag passed by reference indicating whether the change of selection should be cancelled; its default value is `False`.

Fired when there is a change to the dates selected in the MonthView control. Setting the *`Cancel`* parameter to `True` cancels the new selection and reverts to the old selection.

SelChange

Applies to: MSFlexGrid, MSHFlexGrid, RichTextBox

Parameters: None

Fired whenever the selection changes in one of the applicable controls.

SendComplete

Applies to: Winsock

Parameters: None

Fired when data transmission using the Winsock control is complete.

SendProgress

Applies to: Winsock

Parameters:

`BytesSent` *(long integer)*
  Number of bytes sent since the last time the SendProgress event was fired

`BytesRemaining` *(long integer)*
  Number of bytes left to send

Fired repeatedly while data is being sent using the Winsock control.

SeriesActivated, SeriesSelected, SeriesUpdated

Applies to: MSChart

Parameters:

`Series` *(integer)*
  The index of the affected series. They are numbered in column order from 1.

`MouseFlags` *(integer, SeriesActivated and SeriesSelected only)*
  An integer indicating which button was clicked and which key was depressed while the mouse button was clicked. Possible values for keys are 4–vtChMouseFlagShiftKeyDown for the Shift key, 8–vtChMouseFlagControlKeyDown for the CTRL key, or the two values added together (12) for both keys. That the value of the mouse button clicked is included in ***`MouseFlags`*** is not indicated in the documentation. For a code fragment that determines which key was pressed when the left mouse button was clicked, see the entry for the AxisActivated, AxisSelected, and AxisUpdated events.

`UpdateFlags` (`VtChUpdateFlags` *enumeration, SeriesUpdated only)*
  Indicates the status of the update and can contain any combination of values in the `VtChUpdateFlags` enumeration. Its members are listed in the entry for the AxisActivated, AxisSelected, and AxisUpdated events

`Cancel` *(integer, SeriesActivated and SeriesSelected only)*
  Unused.

These events are triggered when a series on the MSChart control is clicked (SeriesSelected), is double-clicked (SeriesActivated), or has changed (SeriesUpdated).

SettingChanged

Applies to: SysInfo

Parameters:

`Item` *(integer)*
  Value indicating the setting changed; for a complete list of possible values, see the SysInfo Control in Chapter 5.

Fired when a system setting is changed. *Item* can assist in determining which change has been made. For example, if the *Item* parameter equals 47, a change was made to the Windows Start menu bar.

SplitChange

Applies to: DataGrid

Parameters: None

Fired when the user changes from a cell in one split to a cell in a different split.

StateChanged

Applies to: Inet control

Parameters:

`State` *(integer)*

Fired whenever the current state of a connection controlled by the Internet Transfer control is updated. The constants shown in the following table describe the new state:

Constant	*Value*	*Description*
`IcNone`	0	There is no current state.
`IcHostResolvingHost`	1	The IP address for the host URL is being derived.
`IcHostResolved`	2	The IP address for the host URL has been derived.
`IcConnecting`	3	The Inet control is connecting to the host computer.
`IcConnected`	4	The Inet control has connected to the host computer.
`IcRequesting`	5	Data is being requested from the host computer.
`IcRequestSent`	6	Data has been requested from the host computer.
`IcReceivingResponse`	7	Data is being received from the host computer.
`IcResponseReceived`	8	Data has been received from the host computer.
`IcDisconnecting`	9	The Inet control is disconnecting from the host computer.
`IcDisconnected`	10	The Inet control is disconnected from the host computer.
`IcError`	11	An error has occurred.
`IcResponseCompleted`	12	All pending data transmissions have completed.

StatusUpdate

Applies to: MM

Parameters: None

Fired repeatedly at intervals based on the UpdateInterval property's value. It can be used to display state information to the user by retrieving the values of such properties as Position, Length, and Mode.

StepClick, StepCompeted, StepGotFocus, StepLostFocus

Applies to: MM

Parameters:

`Cancel` *(integer, StepClick only)*
: Flag passed by reference to indicate whether the Step command should be cancelled even though the user clicked the button. Its default value is `False`.

`ErrorCode` *(long integer, StepCompleted only)*
: Contains 0 if the Step command was successful; otherwise, it contains an error number.

Events Q–Z

These events are triggered when the user clicks on the Step button on the MM control (StepClick), when it receives (StepGotFocus) or loses (StepLostFocus) the focus on its container, or when it has finished executing (StepCompleted). The StepGotFocus event is fired whenever the focus switches to the Step button, whether it comes from another button on the Multimedia control, another interface object in the application, or a window belonging to another application. Similarly, the StepLostFocus event is fired whenever the focus leaves the Step button, regardless of the object or application that receives the focus. The `Cancel` parameter of the StepClick event can be used to stop the control from executing the Step command.

StopClick, StopCompleted, StopGotFocus, StopLostFocus

Applies to: MM

Parameters:

`Cancel` *(integer, StopClick only)*
: Flag passed by reference to indicate whether the Stop command should be cancelled even though the user clicked the button. Its default value is `False`.

`ErrorCode` *(long integer, StopCompleted only)*
: Contains 0 if the Stop command was successful; otherwise, it contains an error number.

These events are triggered when the user clicks on the Stop button on the MM control (StopClick), when it receives (StopGotFocus) or loses (StopLostFocus) the focus on its container, or when it has finished executing (StopCompleted). The StopGotFocus event is fired whenever the focus switches to the Stop button, whether it comes from another button on the Multimedia control, another interface object in the application, or a window belonging to another application. Similarly, the StopLostFocus event is fired whenever the focus leaves the Stop button, regardless of the object or application that receives the focus. The `Cancel` parameter of the StopClick event can be used to stop the control from executing the Stop command.

SysColorsChanged

Applies to: SysInfo

Parameters: None

Fired when the user changes all or any of the Windows system colors.

Terminate

Applies to: Form and MDIForm objects

See: Initialize

TimeChanged

Applies to: SysInfo

Parameters: None

Fired when the Windows system time/date are changed. The new system date can be retrieved by calling the VBA *Date* function. The new system time can be retrieved by calling the VBA *Time* function. Finally, the VBA *Now* function can be used to retrieve both the new date and time.

Timer

Applies to: Timer

Parameters: None

Fired repeatedly at intervals based on the Interval property's value. The Timer control is typically used to add time-based interrupts to a program. The Interval property defines how often these interrupts occur. The Timer event handler then is responsible for performing whatever operations—and particularly for updating status information—the interrupt was designed to handle.

TitleActivated, TitleSelected, TitleUpdated

Applies to: MSChart

Parameters:

`MouseFlags` *(integer, TitleActivated and TitleSelected only)*

An integer indicating which button was clicked and which key was depressed while the mouse button was clicked. Possible values for keys are 4–vtChMouseFlagShiftKeyDown for the Shift key, 8–vtChMouseFlagControlKeyDown for the CTRL key, or the two values added together (12) for both keys. That the value of the mouse button clicked is included in ***`MouseFlags`*** is not indicated in the documentation. For a code fragment that determines which key was pressed when the left mouse button was clicked, see the entry for the AxisActivated, AxisSelected, and AxisUpdated events.

`UpdateFlags` *(*`VtChUpdateFlags` *enumeration, TitleUpdated only)*

Indicates the status of the update and can contain any combination of values in the `VtChUpdateFlags` enumeration. Its members are listed in the entry for the AxisActivated, AxisSelected, and AxisUpdated events

`Cancel` *(integer, TitleActivated and TitleSelected only)*

Unused.

These events are triggered when the title on the MSChart control is clicked (TitleSelected), is double-clicked (TitleActivated), or has changed (TitleUpdated).

Events O–Z

Unload

Applies to: Form and MDIForm objects

Parameters: None

Fired when the form or MDI form is unloading. Prior to this, the QueryUnload event is fired to allow the application to determine why the form or MDI form is closing and to prevent it from closing, if necessary. If the application is closing or the form or MDI form is set to `Nothing`, the Terminate event also fires. If the `End` statement is used to terminate program execution, the Unload event is not fired.

UpClick

Applies to: UpDown

See: DownClick

Updated

Applies to: OLE

Parameters:

`Code` *(*`OLEContainerConstants` *enumeration)*

Constant that indicates the state of the change. It can be one of the following values:

Constant	*Value*	*Description*
`VbOLEChanged`	0	The OLE object's data has changed.
`VbOLESaved`	1	The OLE object's data has been saved.
`VbOLEClosed`	2	The OLE object has been closed.
`VbOLERenamed`	3	The OLE object has been saved under a new name.

Fired when data in an OLE object contained by the OLE control is updated. Most commonly, the event is used to determine if data has been saved since it was last changed.

Validate

Applies to: All controls with a visible interface except Line and Shape

Parameters:

`KeepFocus` *(Boolean)*

Flag passed by reference indicating whether the current control should retain the focus. Its default value is `False`.

Fired whenever a control with its CausesValidation parameter set to `True` is about to lose focus. Setting the KeepFocus parameter to `True` causes the control not to lose focus. This is useful for validating data before moving the focus. However, the Validate event is not fired when the Enter key is pressed and the current form contains a CommandButton control with its Default property set to `True`.

ValidationError

Applies to: MaskedEditBox

Parameters:

`InvalidText` *(string)*

The full contents of the control

`StartPosition` *(integer)*

The character position within *`InvalidText`* where the invalid character was entered

Fired when the user attempts to enter invalid input into the MaskedEditBox control.

WillChangeField

Applies to: .

See: FieldChangeComplete

WillChangeRecord

Applies to: ADO DC

See: RecordChangeComplete

WillChangeRecordset

Applies to: ADO DC

See: RecordsetChangeComplete

WillMove

Applies to: ADO DC

See: MoveComplete

PART III

Appendixes

This section contains two appendixes that supplement the core reference material included in this book. These are:

- Appendix A, *Visual Basic Colors*, which discusses how VB color values work, shows the VBA functions that return color values, and lists the intrinsic VB color constants
- Appendix B, *Key Codes*, which lists the Visual Basic key code constants that are passed to the KeyUp and KeyDown events

APPENDIX A

Visual Basic Colors

Visual Basic forms, MDI forms, and controls that present a user interface typically have a number of properties that allow their color to be controlled programmatically. These include:

BackColor
: Defines the object's background color

BorderColor
: Sets the color of an object's border

FillColor
: Defines the color used to fill in shapes

ForeColor
: Defines the object's foreground color, which is used to display such things as text, the output of graphics methods, or data points

MaskColor
: For a UserControl object whose BackStyle property is set to 0, defines the color of the transparent region of a bitmap assigned to the MaskPicture property

In each case, the value of the property is a long (4-byte) integer that can be either a color value or an offset into the Windows system color palette. Colors are RGB color values, and, as Figure A-1 shows, are stored in reverse order in the lower three bytes of the long. That is, the low-order byte of the low-order word is the red color value, while the low-order byte of the high-order word is the blue color value. Values that are offsets into the Windows system palette are indicated by setting on the seventh bit of the high-order word, giving the byte a value of &H80, while the low-order byte of the low-order word indicates the color's offset in the system palette.

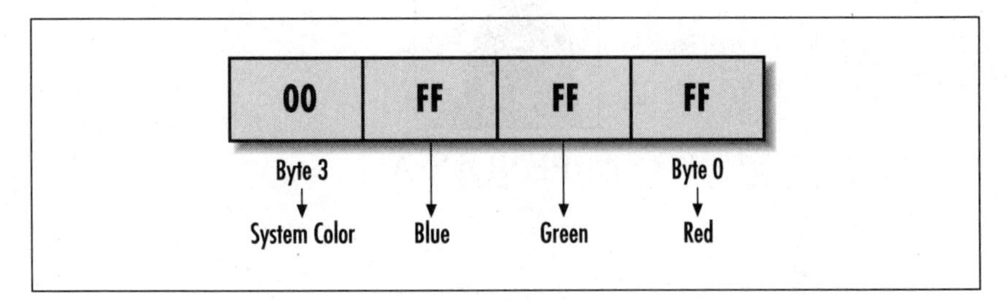

Figure A-1: How Visual Basic stores colors

While it is possible to assign a hexadecimal or decimal value directly to a color property, as in:

```
Me.ForeColor = 16711935
```

or

```
Me.ForeColor = -2147483630
```

this is not the most intuitive method, nor does it produce the most readable code. (Least readable of all is the apparently incongruous negative value that results from interpreting a system color—a value that is an unsigned long integer in C—as a Visual Basic signed long integer.) Instead, color values can be assigned to the color property using either functions or constants, while system color values can be assigned using constants. These are discussed in the following sections.

Color Values

Visual Basic provides two functions as well as a series of constants to define color values. These are:

QBColor function

This function, a remnant of QBasic, has the syntax:

```
RGBColor = QBColor(color)
```

where *color* is an integer whose value ranges from 0 to 15, according to the following table:

Value	*Color*
0	Black
1	Blue
2	Green
3	Cyan
4	Red
5	Magenta
6	Yellow
7	White
8	Gray
9	Light blue

Value	Color
10	Light green
11	Light cyan
12	Light red
13	Light magenta
14	Light yellow
15	Bright white

Note that the function returns an RGB color value and that the color integers do not have equivalent intrinsic color constants.

RGB function

Returns an RGB color from its component colors. Its syntax is:

```
RGBColor = RGB(red, green, blue)
```

where `red`, `green`, and `blue` are required parameters that represent the components of the color value and can range from 0 to 255. For example, *RGB(0, 0, 0)* returns the color black, while *RGB(255, 255, 255)* returns white.

`ColorConstants` *enumeration*

Rather than having to memorize the red, green, and blue values of eight of the major colors, you can just assign a constant of the `ColorConstants` enumeration to a color property. The constants are:

Constant	Value
`vbBlack`	0
`vbRed`	&HFF
`vbGreen`	&HFF00
`vbYellow`	&HFFFF
`vbBlue`	&HFF0000
`vbMagenta`	&HFF00FF
`vbCyan`	&HFFFF00
`vbWhite`	&HFFFFFF

System Colors

Internally, Windows maintains an array of 24 static colors that are used to paint assorted system objects and that can be defined by the user. If a color value is an index into this static color array, the high-order bit of its highest-order byte is set, and the low-order byte of its low-order word indicates the offset into the zero-based array of static values at which the color can be found.

In general, unless there is a compelling reason to define custom colors for controls (such as the need to adhere to a particular look and feel for custom corporate applications), applications should use system colors, rather than RGB color values, when defining their colors. This minimizes the probability that a particular interface object, which may look fine in a "hardcoded" application color scheme, will not look good (or may even be invisible) in a color scheme configured by the user.

To make accessing system colors easy, Visual Basic offers the `SystemColorConstants` enumeration, the members of which are shown in the following table:

Constant	*Value*	*Interface Element*
`vbScrollBars`	&H80000000	Scrollbars.
`vbDeskTop`	&H80000001	The Windows desktop (not including any pattern/ graphic).
`vbActiveTitleBar`	&H80000002	The titlebar of the application with the focus.
`vbInactiveTitleBar`	&H80000003	The titlebar of applications that don't have the focus.
`vbMenuBar`	&H80000004	The menu background.
`vbWindowBackground`	&H80000005	The window background.
`vbWindowFrame`	&H80000006	The window frame.
`vbMenuText`	&H80000007	Text in menus.
`vbWindowText`	&H80000008	Text in windows.
`vbTitleBarText` or `vbActiveTitleBarText`	&H80000009	Text on titlebars.
`vbActiveBorder`	&H8000000A	The border of the application with the focus.
`vbInactiveBorder`	&H8000000B	The 3-D border of applications without the focus.
`vbApplicationWorkspace`	&H8000000C	The background of an MDI form.
`vbHighlight`	&H8000000D	The background of selected text.
`vbHighlightText`	&H8000000E	Selected text.
`vbButtonFace` or `vb3DFace`	&H8000000F	Face of command buttons, other 3-D display elements. (This is the basic color constant used for the Office look in applications.)
`vbButtonShadow` `vb3DShadow`	&H80000010	Edge of command buttons, window shadows.
`vbGrayText`	&H80000011	Grayed (disabled) text.
`vbButtonText`	&H80000012	Text on command buttons.
`vbInactiveCaptionText` or `vbInactiveTitleBarText`	&H80000013	Caption of a window without the focus.
`vb3DHighlight`	&H80000014	Highlights on 3-D objects.
`vb3DDKShadow`	&H80000015	Dark shadows on 3-D objects.
`vb3DLight`	&H80000016	The second lightest highlight on 3-D objects.
`vbInfoText`	&H80000017	Text in tooltips.
`vbInfoBackground`	&H80000018	The background in tooltips.

The default values of each control's color properties are always set to one of these values, rather than to a "hardcoded" value. For example, the following table shows the default value of the ForeColor and BackColor properties for some intrinsic VB controls:

Control	*ForeColor*	*BackColor*
Combo	vbWindowText	vbWindowBackground
CommandButton		vb3DFace
Form	vbButtonText	vb3DFace
Frame	vbButtonText	vb3DFace
Label	vbButtonText	vb3DFace
Option Button	vbButtonText	vb3DFace
PictureBox	vbButtonText	vb3DFace
TextBox	vbWindowText	vbWindowBackground

APPENDIX B

Key Codes

The KeyUp and KeyDown events shared by most of Visual Basic's controls, along with the DTPicker control's CallBackKeyDown event, all have a *KeyCode* parameter to determine which key caused the event to fire. The following table lists each *KeyCode* value along with any available VB constant and the key on the keyboard to which it corresponds:

Constant	*Value*	*Description*
`VbKeyLButton`	1	Left mouse button
`VbKeyRButton`	2	Right mouse button
`VbKeyCancel`	3	
`VbKeyMButton`	4	Middle mouse button
`VbKeyBack`	8	Backspace
`VbKeyTab`	9	Tab
`VbKeyClear`	12	5 key (on numeric keypad) with Num Lock off
`VbKeyReturn`	13	Enter/Return
`VbKeyShift`	16	Shift key
`VbKeyControl`	17	CTRL key
`VbKeyMenu`	18	ALT key
`VbKeyPause`	19	Pause key
`VbKeyCapital`	20	Caps Lock key
`VbKeyEscape`	27	Escape key
`VbKeySpace`	32	Spacebar
`VbKeyPageUp`	33	Page Up key
`VbKeyPageDown`	34	Page Down key
`VbKeyEnd`	35	End key
`VbKeyHome`	36	Home key

Constant	*Value*	*Description*
VbKeyLeft	37	Left Arrow key
VbKeyUp	38	Up Arrow key
VbKeyRight	39	Right Arrow key
VbKeyDown	40	Down Arrow key
VbKeySelect	41	
VbKeyPrint	42	Print Screen key
VbKeyExecute	43	
VbKeySnapshot	44	
VbKeyInsert	45	Insert key
VbKeyDelete	46	Delete key
VbKeyHelp	47	
VbKey0	48	0 key (not keypad)
VbKey1	49	1 key (not keypad)
VbKey2	50	2 key (not keypad)
VbKey3	51	3 key (not keypad)
VbKey4	52	4 key (not keypad)
VbKey5	53	5 key (not keypad)
VbKey6	54	6 key (not keypad)
VbKey7	55	7 key (not keypad)
VbKey8	56	8 key (not keypad)
VbKey9	57	9 key (not keypad)
VbKeyA	65	A key
VbKeyB	66	B key
VbKeyC	67	C key
VbKeyD	68	D key
VbKeyE	69	E key
VbKeyF	70	F key
VbKeyG	71	G key
VbKeyH	72	H key
VbKeyI	73	I key
VbKeyJ	74	J key
VbKeyK	75	K key
VbKeyL	76	L key
VbKeyM	77	M key
VbKeyN	78	N key
VbKeyO	79	O key
VbKeyP	80	P key
VbKeyQ	81	Q key
VbKeyR	82	R key
VbKeyS	83	S key

Constant	*Value*	*Description*
`VbKeyT`	84	T key
`VbKeyU`	85	U key
`VbKeyV`	86	V key
`VbKeyW`	87	W key
`VbKeyX`	88	X key
`VbKeyY`	89	Y key
`VbKeyZ`	90	Z key
	91	"Windows key"
	93	"Windows Menu key"
`VbKeyNumpad0`	96	0 key (on numeric keypad)
`VbKeyNumpad1`	97	1 key (on numeric keypad)
`VbKeyNumpad2`	98	2 key (on numeric keypad)
`VbKeyNumpad3`	99	3 key (on numeric keypad)
`VbKeyNumpad4`	100	4 key (on numeric keypad)
`VbKeyNumpad5`	101	5 key (on numeric keypad) with Num Lock on
`VbKeyNumpad6`	102	6 key (on numeric keypad)
`VbKeyNumpad7`	103	7 key (on numeric keypad)
`VbKeyNumpad8`	104	8 key (on numeric keypad)
`VbKeyNumpad9`	105	9 key (on numeric keypad)
`VbKeyMultiply`	106	* key (on numeric keypad)
`VbKeyAdd`	107	+ key (on numeric keypad)
`VbKeySeparator`	108	
`VbKeySubtract`	109	- key (on numeric keypad)
`VbKeyDecimal`	110	. key (on numeric keypad)
`VbKeyDivide`	111	/ key (on numeric keypad)
`VbKeyF1`	112	F1 key
`VbKeyF2`	113	F2 key
`VbKeyF3`	114	F3 key
`VbKeyF4`	115	F4 key
`VbKeyF5`	116	F5 key
`VbKeyF6`	117	F6 key
`VbKeyF7`	118	F7 key
`VbKeyF8`	119	F8 key
`VbKeyF9`	120	F9 key
`VbKeyF10`	121	F10 key
`VbKeyF11`	122	F11 key
`VbKeyF12`	123	F12 key
`VbKeyF13`	124	F13 key
`VbKeyF14`	125	F14 key
`VbKeyF15`	126	F15 key

Constant	*Value*	*Description*
`VbKeyF16`	127	F16 key
`VbKeyNumlock`	144	Num Lock key
`VbKeyScrollLock`	145	Scroll Lock key
	186	;
	187	=
	188	,
	189	-
	190	.
	191	/
	192	`
	219	[
	220	\
	221	]
	222	'

Index

Numbers

A

B

C

D

E

F

H

I

M

N

O

P

Q

R

S

T

V

W

X

Y

Z

About the Author

Evan S. Dictor has developed software in a wide variety of languages on numerous platforms. He has used Visual Basic extensively for years, first as a prototyping tool and later as a full-time development tool. A Microsoft Certified Solutions Developer, today he develops and supports Visual Basic applications nationally as a contract programmer based out of southern Florida. In his spare time, Evan composes MIDI music and does woodworking.

Colophon

Our look is the result of reader comments, our own experimentation, and feedback from distribution channels. Distinctive covers complement our distinctive approach to technical topics, breathing personality and life into potentially dry subjects.

The animal featured on the cover of *Visual Basic Controls in a Nutshell: The Controls of the Professional and Enterprise Editions,* is an eared seal. There are 18 living species of seals, grouped into 13 genera. Of these, 14 species, in 6 genera, are eared seals, family *Otariidae.* Eared seals are widely distributed throughout the world, especially in the Southern Hemisphere. This marine mammal's diet consists mainly of fish. Some seals dive as deep as 600 feet in search of food.

Aside from the existence of external ears, eared seals differ from earless seals in that they can bring their rear flippers forward under their bodies. This makes them more mobile on land than earless seals. In the water, both eared and earless seals move with a rowing motion of the front flippers, not using their rear flippers at all.

Eared seals fall into one of two categories—fur seals or sea lions. Fur seals grow a thick undercoat of fur, used as insulation. In one species of fur seal, more than 50,000 hairs were counted in one square centimeter of skin. This thick undercoat of fur has made the fur seal very appealing to hunters.

Of the five species of sea lion, the California sea lion is best known. Because they are relatively small, and the most graceful on land of all the seals, California sea lions are the seals most likely to be used in circus acts or kept in zoos.

Sarah Jane Shangraw was the production editor for *Visual Basic Controls in a Nutshell: The Controls of the Professional and Enterprise Editions.* Debby English copyedited and Norma Emory proofread the book; Jane Ellin, Claire Cloutier LeBlanc, and Abigail Myers provided quality control; Sebastian Banker, Susan Reinbold, Anna Snow, and Melanie Wang provided production support; Mike Sierra provided FrameMaker technical support; Ellen Troutman Zaig, Seth Maislin, and Brenda Miller wrote the index.

Edie Freedman designed the cover of this book, using a 19th-century engraving from the Dover Pictorial Archive. The cover layout was produced by Kathleen Wilson, using Quark XPress 3.32 and the ITC Garamond font.

The inside layout was designed by Alicia Cech and implemented in FrameMaker 5.5.6 by Mike Sierra. The text and heading fonts are ITC Garamond Light and Garamond Book. The illustrations that appear in the book were produced by Robert Romano and Rhon Porter using Macromedia FreeHand 8 and Adobe Photoshop 5. This colophon was written by Clairemarie Fisher O'Leary.

Whenever possible, our books use RepKover™, a durable and flexible lay-flat binding. If the page count exceeds RepKover's limit, perfect binding is used.

More Titles from O'Reilly

In a Nutshell Quick References

VB & VBA in a Nutshell: The Languages

By Paul Lomax
1st Edition October 1998
656 pages, ISBN 1-56592-358-8

For Visual Basic and VBA programmers, this book boils down the essentials of the VB and VBA languages into a single volume, including undocumented and little documented areas essential to everyday programming. The convenient alphabetical reference to all functions, procedures, statements, and keywords allows VB and VBA programmers to use this book both as a standard reference guide to the language and as a tool for troubleshooting and identifying programming problems.

Windows 95 in a Nutshell

By Tim O'Reilly & Troy Mott
1st Edition June 1998
528 pages, ISBN 1-56592-316-2

A comprehensive, compact reference that systematically unveils what serious users of Windows 95 will find interesting and useful, capturing little known details of the operating system in a consistent reference format.

Windows NT in a Nutshell

By Eric Pearce
1st Edition June 1997
364 pages, ISBN 1-56592-251-4

Anyone who installs Windows NT, creates a user, or adds a printer is an NT system administrator (whether they realize it or not). This book features a new tagged call-out approach to documenting the 4.0 GUI as well as real-life examples of command usage and strategies for problem solving, with an emphasis on networking. *Windows NT in a Nutshell* will be as useful to the single-system home user as it will be to the administrator of a 1,000-node corporate network.

UML in a Nutshell

By Sinan Si Alhir
1st Edition September 1998
290 pages, ISBN 1-56592-448-7

The Unified Modeling Language (UML), for the first time in the history of systems engineering, gives practitioners a common language. This concise quick reference explains how to use each component of the language, including its extension mechanisms and the Object Constraint Language (OCL). A tutorial with realistic examples brings those new to the UML quickly up to speed.

Year 2000 in a Nutshell

By Norman Shakespeare
1st Edition September 1998
330 pages, ISBN 1-56592-421-5

This reference guide addresses the awareness, the managerial aspect, and the technical issues of the Year 2000 computer dilemma, providing a compact compendium of solutions and reference information useful for addressing the problem.

Windows 98 in a Nutshell

By Tim O'Reilly & Troy Mott
1st Edition July 1999 (est.)
600 pages (est.), ISBN 1-56592-486-X

From the authors of the bestselling Windows 95 in a Nutshell comes this easy-to-use quick reference for all serious users of Windows 98. It summarizes differences between Windows 95 and Windows 98, covers almost every Windows 98 comand and utility available, gives advice for using the Registry, includes short-hand instructions on many important Win98 tasks, and much more.

Windows Programming

Access Database Design & Programming

By Steven Roman
1st Edition June 1997
270 pages, ISBN 1-56592-297-2

This book provides experienced Access users who are novice programers with frequently overlooked concepts and techniques necessary to create effective database applications. It focuses on designing effective tables in a multi-table application; using the Access interface or Access SQL to construct queries; and programming using the Data Access Object (DAO) and Microsoft Access object models.

Learning VBScript

By Paul Lomax
1st Edition July 1997
616 pages, includes CD-ROM
ISBN 1-56592-247-6

This definitive guide shows web developers how to take full advantage of client-side scripting with the VBScript language. In addition to basic language features, it covers the Internet Explorer object model and discusses techniques for client-side scripting, like adding ActiveX controls to a web page or validating data before sending it to the server. Includes CD-ROM with over 170 code samples.

Learning Perl on Win32 Systems

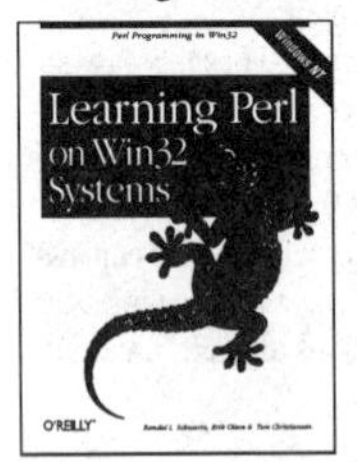

By Randal L. Schwartz, Erik Olson & Tom Christiansen
1st Edition August 1997
306 pages, ISBN 1-56592-324-3

In this carefully paced course, leading Perl trainers and a Windows NT practitioner teach you to program in the language that promises to emerge as the scripting language of choice on NT. Based on the "llama" book, this book features tips for PC users and new, NT-specific examples, along with a foreword by Larry Wall, the creator of Perl, and Dick Hardt, the creator of Perl for Win32.

Learning Word Programming

By Steven Roman
1st Edition October 1998
408 pages, ISBN 1-56592-524-6

This no-nonsense book delves into the core aspects of VBA programing, enabling users to increase their productivity and power over Microsoft Word. It takes the reader step-by-step through writing VBA macros and programs, illustrating how to generate tables of a particular format, manage shortcut keys, create FAX cover sheets, and reformat documents.

Developing Visual Basic Add-Ins

By Steven Roman
1st Edition December 1998
186 pages, ISBN 1-56592-527-0

A tutorial and reference guide in one, this book covers all the basics of creating useful VB add-ins to extend the IDE, allowing developers to work more productively with Visual Basic. Readers with even a modest acquaintance with VB will be developing add-ins in no time. Includes numerous simple code examples.

Windows NT File System Internals

By Rajeev Nagar
1st Edition September 1997
794 pages, includes diskette
ISBN 1-56592-249-2

Windows NT File System Internals presents the details of the NT I/O Manager, the Cache Manager, and the Memory Manager from the perspective of a software developer writing a file system driver or implementing a kernel-mode filter driver. The book provides numerous code examples included on diskette, as well as the source for a complete, usable filter driver.

Windows Programming

Inside the Windows 95 Registry

By Ron Petrusha
1st Edition August 1996
594 pages, includes diskette
ISBN 1-56592-170-4

An in-depth examination of remote registry access, differences between the Win95 and NT registries, registry backup, undocumented registry services, and the role the registry plays in OLE. Shows programmers how to access the Win95 registry from Win32, Win16, and DOS programs in C and Visual Basic. VxD sample code is also included. Includes diskette.

Inside the Windows 95 File System

By Stan Mitchell
1st Edition May 1997
378 pages, includes diskette
ISBN 1-56592-200-X

In this book, Stan Mitchell describes the Windows 95 File System, as well as the new opportunities and challenges it brings for developers. Its "hands-on" approach will help developers become better equipped to make design decisions using the new Win95 File System features. Includes a diskette containing MULTIMON, a general-purpose monitor for examining Windows internals.

Windows NT SNMP

By James D. Murray
1st Edition January 1998
464 pages, includes CD-ROM
ISBN 1-56592-338-3

This book describes the implementation of SNMP (the Simple Network Management Protocol) on Windows NT 3.51 and 4.0 (with a look ahead to NT 5.0) and Windows 95 systems. It covers SNMP and network basics and detailed information on developing SNMP management applications and extension agents. The book comes with a CD-ROM containing a wealth of additional information: standards documents, sample code from the book, and many third-party, SNMP-related software tools, libraries, and demos.

Win32 Multithreaded Programming

By Aaron Cohen & Mike Woodring
1st Edition December 1997
724 pages, includes CD-ROM
ISBN 1-56592-296-4

This book clearly explains the concepts of multithreaded programs and shows developers how to construct efficient and complex applications. An important book for any developer, it illustrates all aspects of Win32 multithreaded programming, including what has previously been undocumented or poorly explained.

Developing Windows Error Messages

By Ben Ezzell
1st Edition March 1998
254 pages, includes CD-ROM
ISBN 1-56592-356-1

This book teaches C, C++, and Visual Basic programmers how to write effective error messages that notify the user of an error, clearly explain the error, and most important, offer a solution. The book also discusses methods for preventing and trapping errors before they occur and tells how to create flexible input and response routines to keep unnecessary errors from happening.

How to stay in touch with O'Reilly

1. Visit Our Award-Winning Site

http://www.oreilly.com/

★ "Top 100 Sites on the Web" —*PC Magazine*
★ "Top 5% Web sites" —*Point Communications*
★ "3-Star site" —*The McKinley Group*

Our web site contains a library of comprehensive product information (including book excerpts and tables of contents), downloadable software, background articles, interviews with technology leaders, links to relevant sites, book cover art, and more. File us in your Bookmarks or Hotlist!

2. Join Our Email Mailing Lists

New Product Releases

To receive automatic email with brief descriptions of all new O'Reilly products as they are released, send email to:
listproc@online.oreilly.com
Put the following information in the first line of your message (*not* in the Subject field):
subscribe oreilly-news

O'Reilly Events

If you'd also like us to send information about trade show events, special promotions, and other O'Reilly events, send email to:
listproc@online.oreilly.com
Put the following information in the first line of your message (*not* in the Subject field):
subscribe oreilly-events

3. Get Examples from Our Books via FTP

There are two ways to access an archive of example files from our books:

Regular FTP

- ftp to:
  ftp.oreilly.com
  (login: anonymous
  password: your email address)
- Point your web browser to:
  ftp://ftp.oreilly.com/

FTPMAIL

- Send an email message to:
  ftpmail@online.oreilly.com
  (Write "help" in the message body)

4. Contact Us via Email

order@oreilly.com
To place a book or software order online. Good for North American and international customers.

subscriptions@oreilly.com
To place an order for any of our newsletters or periodicals.

books@oreilly.com
General questions about any of our books.

software@oreilly.com
For general questions and product information about our software. Check out O'Reilly Software Online at **http://software.oreilly.com/** for software and technical support information. Registered O'Reilly software users send your questions to:
website-support@oreilly.com

cs@oreilly.com
For answers to problems regarding your order or our products.

booktech@oreilly.com
For book content technical questions or corrections.

proposals@oreilly.com
To submit new book or software proposals to our editors and product managers.

international@oreilly.com
For information about our international distributors or translation queries. For a list of our distributors outside of North America check out:
http://www.oreilly.com/www/order/country.html

O'Reilly & Associates, Inc.
101 Morris Street, Sebastopol, CA 95472 USA
TEL 707-829-0515 or 800-998-9938
(6am to 5pm PST)
FAX 707-829-0104

International Distributors

UK, Europe, Middle East and Africa (except France, Germany, Austria, Switzerland, Luxembourg, Liechtenstein, and Eastern Europe)

INQUIRIES

O'Reilly UK Limited
4 Castle Street
Farnham
Surrey, GU9 7HS
United Kingdom
Telephone: 44-1252-711776
Fax: 44-1252-734211
Email: josette@oreilly.com

ORDERS

Wiley Distribution Services Ltd.
1 Oldlands Way
Bognor Regis
West Sussex PO22 9SA
United Kingdom
Telephone: 44-1243-779777
Fax: 44-1243-820250
Email: cs-books@wiley.co.uk

France

Orders

GEODIF
61, Bd Saint-Germain
75240 Paris Cedex 05, France
Tel: 33-1-44-41-46-16 (French books)
Tel: 33-1-44-41-11-87 (English books)
Fax: 33-1-44-41-11-44
Email: distribution@eyrolles.com

Inquiries

Éditions O'Reilly
18 rue Séguier
75006 Paris, France
Tel: 33-1-40-51-52-30
Fax: 33-1-40-51-52-31
Email: france@editions-oreilly.fr

Germany, Switzerland, Austria, Eastern Europe, Luxembourg, and Liechtenstein

INQUIRIES & ORDERS

O'Reilly Verlag
Balthasarstr. 81
D-50670 Köln
Germany
Telephone: 49-221-973160-91
Fax: 49-221-973160-8
Email: anfragen@oreilly.de (inquiries)
Email: order@oreilly.de (orders)

Canada (French language books)

Les Éditions Flammarion ltée
375, Avenue Laurier Ouest
Montréal (Québec) H2V 2K3
Tel: 00-1-514-277-8807
Fax: 00-1-514-278-2085
Email: info@flammarion.qc.ca

Hong Kong

City Discount Subscription Service, Ltd.
Unit D, 3rd Floor, Yan's Tower
27 Wong Chuk Hang Road
Aberdeen, Hong Kong
Tel: 852-2580-3539
Fax: 852-2580-6463
Email: citydis@ppn.com.hk

Korea

Hanbit Media, Inc.
Sonyoung Bldg. 202
Yeksam-dong 736-36
Kangnam-ku
Seoul, Korea
Tel: 822-554-9610
Fax: 822-556-0363
Email: hant93@chollian.dacom.co.kr

Philippines

Mutual Books, Inc.
429-D Shaw Boulevard
Mandaluyong City, Metro
Manila, Philippines
Tel: 632-725-7538
Fax: 632-721-3056
Email: mbikikog@mnl.sequel.net

Taiwan

O'Reilly Taiwan
No. 3, Lane 131
Hang-Chow South Road
Section 1, Taipei, Taiwan
Tel: 886-2-23968990
Fax: 886-2-23968916
Email: benh@oreilly.com

China

O'Reilly Beijing
Room 2410
160, FuXingMenNeiDaJie
XiCheng District
Beijing
China PR 100031
Tel: 86-10-86631006
Fax: 86-10-86631007
Email: frederic@oreilly.com

India

Computer Bookshop (India) Pvt. Ltd.
190 Dr. D.N. Road, Fort
Bombay 400 001 India
Tel: 91-22-207-0989
Fax: 91-22-262-3551
Email: cbsbom@giasbm01.vsnl.net.in

Japan

O'Reilly Japan, Inc.
Kiyoshige Building 2F
12-Bancho, Sanei-cho
Shinjuku-ku
Tokyo 160-0008 Japan
Tel: 81-3-3356-5227
Fax: 81-3-3356-5261
Email: japan@oreilly.com

All Other Asian Countries

O'Reilly & Associates, Inc.
101 Morris Street
Sebastopol, CA 95472 USA
Tel: 707-829-0515
Fax: 707-829-0104
Email: order@oreilly.com

Australia

WoodsLane Pty., Ltd.
7/5 Vuko Place
Warriewood NSW 2102
Australia
Tel: 61-2-9970-5111
Fax: 61-2-9970-5002
Email: info@woodslane.com.au

New Zealand

Woodslane New Zealand, Ltd.
21 Cooks Street (P.O. Box 575)
Waganui, New Zealand
Tel: 64-6-347-6543
Fax: 64-6-345-4840
Email: info@woodslane.com.au

Latin America

McGraw-Hill Interamericana
Editores, S.A. de C.V.
Cedro No. 512
Col. Atlampa
06450, Mexico, D.F.
Tel: 52-5-547-6777
Fax: 52-5-547-3336
Email: mcgraw-hill@infosel.net.mx

O'REILLY™

O'Reilly & Associates, Inc.
101 Morris Street
Sebastopol, CA 95472-9902
1-800-998-9938

Visit us online at:
http://www.ora.com/
orders@ora.com

O'REILLY WOULD LIKE TO HEAR FROM YOU

Which book did this card come from?

____

Where did you buy this book?

- ❑ Bookstore
- ❑ Computer Store
- ❑ Direct from O'Reilly
- ❑ Class/seminar
- ❑ Bundled with hardware/software
- ❑ Other ______________________

What operating system do you use?

- ❑ UNIX
- ❑ Macintosh
- ❑ Windows NT
- ❑ PC(Windows/DOS)
- ❑ Other ______________________

What is your job description?

- ❑ System Administrator
- ❑ Programmer
- ❑ Network Administrator
- ❑ Educator/Teacher
- ❑ Web Developer
- ❑ Other ______________________

❑ Please send me O'Reilly's catalog, containing a complete listing of O'Reilly books and software.

Name ______________________ Company/Organization ______________________

Address ______________________

City ____________ State ____________ Zip/Postal Code ____________ Country ____________

Telephone ______________________ Internet or other email address (specify network) ______________________

Nineteenth century wood engraving of a bear from the O'Reilly & Associates Nutshell Handbook®
Using & Managing UUCP.

NO POSTAGE NECESSARY IF MAILED IN THE UNITED STATES

BUSINESS REPLY MAIL

FIRST CLASS MAIL PERMIT NO. 80 SEBASTOPOL, CA

Postage will be paid by addressee

O'Reilly & Associates, Inc.
101 Morris Street
Sebastopol, CA 95472-9902